MODERN
EAST ASIA

AN INTEGRATED HISTORY

富國策

MODERN

EAST ASIA

AN INTEGRATED HISTORY

JONATHAN LIPMAN · BARBARA MOLONY · MICHAEL ROBINSON

Boston Columbus Indianapolis New York San Francisco Upper Saddle River
Amsterdam Cape Town Dubai London Madrid Milan Munich Paris Montréal Toronto
Delhi Mexico City São Paulo Sydney Hong Kong Seoul Singapore Taipei Tokyo

Editorial Director: Craig Campanella
Editor-in-Chief: Dickson Musselwhite
Executive Editor: Jeff Lasser
Editorial Assistant: Julia Feltus
Senior Marketing Manager: Maureen Prado Roberts
Marketing Assistant: Samantha Bennet

For related titles and support materials,
visit our online catalog at www.pearsonhighered.com

Library of Congress Cataloging-in-Publication Data

Lipman, Jonathan Neaman.
  Modern East Asia : an integrated history / Jonathan Lipman,
Barbara Molony, Michael Robinson.
    p. cm.
  Includes bibliographical references and index.
  ISBN-13: 978-0-321-23490-2 (pbk. : alk. paper)
  ISBN-10: 0-321-23490-1 (pbk. : alk. paper)
  1. East Asia--History. I. Molony, Barbara. II. Robinson,
Michael Edson. III. Title.

  DS511.L56 2012
  950'.3--dc22

                                2011010535

ISBN-13: 978-0-321-23490-2
ISBN 10: 0-321-23490-1

Printed in Hong Kong

10 9 8 7 6 5 4 3 2 1

Prentice Hall
is an imprint of

www.pearsonhighered.com

We dedicate this book
with love and gratitude
to
Ann
Tom and Katie
Matt, Jim, Sue, and Mary

LAURENCE KING

This book was designed and produced by
Laurence King Publishing Ltd
361–373 City Road
London EC1V 1LR
United Kingdom
www.laurenceking.com

Commissioning Editor: Kara Hattersley-Smith
Production: Simon Walsh
Design and Cover: Daniel Sturges
Picture Research: Julia Ruxton

Front cover: (from left to right) Jiang Jieshi and Mao Zedong
during negotiations at Chongqing, 1946; Kim Jong Il of North
Korea greets Kim Dae Jung of South Korea at the first North–
South Summit Meeting, June 13, 2000; The head of Japan's
socialist party Doi Takako meets South African leader Nelson
Mandela, 1990.

Inside front cover: (from left to right) detail of the Qianlong
Emperor dressed as a Chinese scholar, before 1767; detail of
Katsushika Hokusai. *Beyond the Kanaya Ford*, from the series
"Thirty-Six Views of Mt Fuji," 1821–31; detail of Sin Yunbok.
Women Bathing during the Tano Festival, late 18th century.

"Fukoku Kyōhei" calligraphy on front cover and frontispiece
by Tang Mengyun. "Fukoku Kyōhei" ("Rich Country, Strong
Army") is a Meiji-period (1868–1912) slogan that embodies
the goals not only of a modernizing Japan at the end of the
nineteenth century, but those of all East Asia—China, Korea,
and Japan—as these countries transformed from age-old
traditions of empire, kingdom and shogunate into those of
modern nation-states.

CONTENTS

THE EARLY MODERN TRANSITION IN TOKUGAWA JAPAN 125

CHAPTER FOUR

04 THE EIGHTEENTH CENTURY

WORLD CONTEXT 102

THE HIGH QING: TRIUMPH AND THE SOURCES OF DECLINE 104

CHOSŎN IN THE EIGHTEENTH CENTURY 117

CHAPTER FIVE

05 INTERNAL CONTRADICTIONS, EXTERNAL PRESSURES (1800–1860s)

WORLD CONTEXT 138

THE QING IN DECLINE 140

CHAPTER SIX

06 TRADITIONALIST REFORMS AND THE ORIGINS OF MODERNITY (1860s–1895)

WORLD CONTEXT 172

JAPAN'S MEIJI TRANSFORMATION 174

CHAPTER TEN

OCCUPATIONS, SETTLEMENTS, AND DIVISIONS (1945–1953)

10

CHAPTER NINE

THE FIFTEEN-YEAR WAR AND ANTI-JAPANESE WAR OF RESISTANCE (1931–1945)

09

PREFACE

We wrote this book to introduce the history of East Asia—the Chinese, Japanese, and Korean culture areas and the states that ruled them—from about 1600 to the present. We are professional historians with almost a century of teaching experience among us, and this textbook summarizes our classroom experience, narrating how East Asia arrived in the twenty-first century. This history differs from other English-language textbooks, for we have attempted to be integrative in our approach to the three (now five) "national" histories of modern East Asia and to place East Asia firmly in its global context. That is, this book stresses connections.

Even among specialists, an interconnected East Asian history has been the exception rather than the rule. In contrast to historians of Europe, who have to teach about the whole continent whether they specialize in Spain or Latvia, few graduate students are trained to teach all of "modern East Asian history," including China, Japan, and Korea. Most East Asia historians engage deeply with only one or two cultures, and they rarely learn all three East Asian languages. Many European and American universities teach East Asian history only as three disconnected national narratives, touching lightly, if at all, on the constant connections among Chinese, Japanese, and Korean states, cultures, and people. Despite the presence of East Asians everywhere in the modern world, few general courses deal with East Asian diasporas, the migrations which brought Japanese workers to Brazil, Korean merchants to Los Angeles, and Chinese to every inhabited continent.

WHY AN INTEGRATED HISTORY?

The importance of East Asia—China, Japan, and Korea—is usually demonstrated with very large numbers that describe enormous contemporary industrial economies: the foreign exchange in Taiwan's coffers, the population of China and the annual expansion of its GDP, the remarkable internet usage in South Korea, the dollars and euros that flow through Hong Kong, Japan's world-beating success in manufacturing automobiles,

to name only a few. For a modern historian, these measures of significance must be joined by recognition of the intellectual, religious, artistic, economic, environmental, and scientific contributions that East Asians have made to the human community's store within the past few centuries. Unlike the large numbers, these signs of East Asia's importance have not generally found their way into the historical consciousness of Europeans and North Americans.

In their formal education, many students encounter modern East Asia only in a high school survey, a general social studies or modern world history course covering all of humanity in a single term. In such courses, East Asian stories do not become crucial to their understanding of "the world as it is," the world in which they actually live. So when they come across China, Japan, or Korea in the news, that whole region seems exotic and strange. Despite thousands of scholarly books on university library shelves, for many Euro-Americans East Asia remains unnecessarily distant, unknowable, and inscrutable.

THE SHAPE OF OUR CHAPTERS

In writing this book, we have tried to remedy some of these deficiencies. Though we retain the "national narrative" form, we have integrated China, Japan, and Korea into each chapter, connecting them throughout the past four centuries. Each chapter begins with a "World Context" section, a brief synopsis of some crucial events of the period, chronologically linking the East Asian stories we tell to the rest of the world. After presenting each chapter's narrative of East Asia, we have added a "Diasporas" section, briefly introducing East Asians who left their own culture areas to go elsewhere in the region or even farther afield. We conclude each chapter with "Connections," our analysis of the importance of China, Japan, and Korea to one another during that period. The book does present separate "national" stories in each chapter—more than three after the late 1940s division of both China and Korea—but not in

CHAPTER	UNIFYING THEME
One: Lands and Languages of East Asia	Place, Time, and Language
Two: Ming China, Chosŏn Korea, and Warring States Japan in 1600	The Neo-Confucian Heritage
Three: The Seventeenth Century	Stabilizing States
Four: The Eighteenth Century	The Rise of Practical Learning
Five: Internal Contradictions, External Pressures (1800–1860S)	Declining States
Six: Traditionalist Reforms and the Origins of Modernity (1860S–1895)	Political Reform and Revolution
Seven: Meiji Japan Rises, Qing and Chosŏn Fall, 1895–1912	The Coming of Modernity
Eight: Triumphs, Revolutions, and Hard Times (1910–31)	Nationalism and Its Perils
Nine: The Fifteen-Year War and Anti-Japanese War of Resistance (1931–45)	Region-wide War
Ten: Occupations, Settlements, and Divisions (1945–53)	Creating the East Asia of Today
Eleven: Reconstruction and Divergent Development (1953–late 1970s)	State Engagement with Economy and Society
Twelve: Social Transformations and Economic Growth (mid-1970s–early 1990s)	The New Globalization
Thirteen: Globalization with East Asian Characteristics (early 1990s–2010)	Now and Future East Asia

isolation from one another or the rest of the world. This seems to us a more accurate and compelling method than disconnecting China, Japan, and Korea in separate chapters or even separate books.

Each chapter includes a wide variety of historical material: political, intellectual, economic, social, environmental, and cultural. But as readers, teachers, and students, you might also find it useful to consider unifying themes as well. As the chapter titles show, these are not our only themes, but you may consider them as suggestions for your analysis of "what was important" during each historical period (see table, left.)

GLOBALIZATION AND EAST ASIAN HISTORY

This book argues that "globalization"—the rapid, often overwhelming expansion of linkages among peoples and places in the past few decades—is neither new nor centered entirely on Europe and North America. The internet, container shipping, multinational corporations, and many other inventions have certainly accelerated the pace of globalization beyond what anyone could have imagined in the mid-twentieth century, not to mention earlier than that. But East Asian cultures, often imagined as "hermit" or "isolated" by outsiders, dealt regularly with one another and with many other places, even at the beginning of our account in the early seventeenth century. Had they not done so, they would have no chili peppers, tomatoes, or baked bread, and foreigners would have had to invent ketchup, paper, and paddy rice on their own. Without those connections, East Asians could not have shared a common heritage of texts and ideas. During our years of teaching, we have found textbooks to be missing the rich web of linkages among the East Asian cultures, compared to those discussing East Asia's relations with us (Europeans, North Americans, outsiders). This book is a first attempt to remedy that absence, and we hope you find it useful and stimulating.

ACKNOWLEDGMENTS

For institutional support and encouragement, we would like to extend our gratitude to Mount Holyoke College, Indiana University, and Santa Clara University, and in particular to Donal O'Shea, Dean of the Faculty at Mount Holyoke, for his generous financial aid and genuine interest.

Special thanks is due to André Schmid for his original contributions to the Korean sections of Chapters Two to Five. And for their collegial conversation and timely information we are indebted to Marnie Anderson, Patience Berkman, Dan Czitrom, Paul Dobosh, Graham Fuller, Daniel Gardner, Jeremy King, Jeff Knight, Yufeng Mao, Kathleen Woods Masalski, Fred McGinness, Tom Millette, Caro Pemberton, Mark Peterson, Robert Schwartz and Ying Wang. For help with making clear and transmissible images, we would like to thank James Gehrt and the Digitization Center (Mount Holyoke College). Thanks also to Eunjeong Shin, Librarian of the Korean Cultural Centre in London for her help with obtaining images from Korea.

We would also like to thank the following for their review of the manuscript: John Carroll, Saint Louis University; Jianyue Chen, Prairie View A&M University; Alan Christy, University of California–Santa Cruz; David B. Gordon, Shepherd College; Greg Guelcher, Morningside College; Thomas Hegarty, University of Tampa; David K. McQuilkin, Bridgewater College; Daniel Meissner, Marquette University; David G. Wittner, Utica College; Joyce Madancy, Union College; Tao Peng, Minnesota State University–Mankato; Ethan Segal, Michigan State University; Kristin Mulready-Stone, Kansas State University; James Carter, Saint Joseph's University; and Michael Shapiro, University of Michigan–Ann Arbor.

And finally we would like to thank our publishers. Many thanks to Jeff Lasser at Pearson Hall Higher Education, and our gratitude as well to all at Laurence King Publishing. Our thanks there goes first of all to Damian Thompson for having the idea for the book in the first place. Thanks also go to Lee Ripley, Laurence King and Kara Hattersley-Smith for standing behind the project over the many years it took to complete. Donald Dinwiddie was a remarkable (and collegial) editor, Julia Ruxton did stellar picture research, Daniel Sturges created a stunning design for text and pictures. And the specially-commissioned maps were the sterling work of Graham Malkin and his team at Advanced Illustration. Thanks also go to Nicola Hodgson for her copy-editing of the manuscript, Angela Koo for her final proofreading of it, and Vicki Robinson for the index.

Jonathan Lipman, South Hadley, MA
Barbara Molony, Santa Clara, CA
Michael Robinson, Bloomington, IN

January 2011

CHAPTER ONE

LANDS AND LANGUAGES OF EAST ASIA

LANDS

Everything in this book happened *somewhere*, not just in "China," "Korea," or "Japan." Those national names do not denote homogeneous spaces; all of them contain considerable regional differences of topography, climate, resources, and human adaptations. Any American knows the difference between Maine and Texas, and no Italian could confuse the Alps with Sicily. So, too, East Asians come from, live in, and grow deeply attached to diverse places within each of their countries. At the outset, we must understand the complex ground on which East Asia's modern history happened, for its impact on its human inhabitants has been inescapable.

East Asia lies in the western Pacific, its topography formed partially by the immense horseshoe of seismic activity surrounding that great water-filled basin. Volcanoes ring the Pacific, and the Korean peninsula and Japanese islands have been built to a great extent by their eruptions and erosion. Some of East Asia's most sacred and impressive mountains—including Mt. Fuji in Japan (12,388 ft [3,776 m]) and Mt. Paektu in Korea (9,003 ft [2,774 m])—are volcanic cones. The slow,

Ogata Gekkō. *Child on Ox before Mt. Fuji,* c. 1890–1910. Mt. Fuji is one of Japan's most iconic landmarks, located some sixty miles (100 km) to the southwest of Tokyo. An active volcano, it last erupted in 1707.

inexorable movement of the tectonic plates beneath the Pacific also pushed up non-volcanic mountain ranges, such as Taiwan's north–south spine.

Mainland East Asia, much of it occupied by the country we call China, gained its present shape less from volcanic activity and more from the shocks and mountain-building that accompanied the arrival of the Indian subcontinent, riding its tectonic plate. Pushing on the great Eurasian continent from the south, the

Indian plate gave birth to the Himalayan range, currently the earth's highest, and the deeply folded mountains and plateaus to its north, east, and west. Some scientists calculate that this process continues to this day—that Mt. Everest rises by ⅙ of an inch (4 mm) per year—but the claim remains controversial. The Tibetan plateau, high and studded with mountains, forms the western side of today's China and is the source of most of its rivers. All of eastern Eurasia tilts from that high plain eastward toward the sea.

Two weather patterns determine the macroclimate of the entire region. From the northwest, the continental winds—similar to those of North America—blow cold and dry from the center of Eurasia eastward, often carrying huge storms of dust and bringing substantial snow in the winter. From the southwest comes the monsoon, hot and wet, dropping predictable, substantial spring and summer rainfall on the southern parts of all three culture areas. These two weather systems interact across nearly 40 degrees of latitude and a mixed topography of plains and mountains, creating climates from arctic cold to tropical heat in which human beings have lived for tens of thousands of years. Like the western Atlantic with its hurricanes, East Asia can be hit in the fall by huge revolving oceanic storms—called typhoons—that can do great damage, especially to the Philippines, Taiwan, Ryūkyū Islands, and Japan. In addition to these regular patterns, East Asia can also be seriously affected by the oceanic currents called El Niño, which bring drought to the whole region on an irregular, unpredictable basis.

East Asia

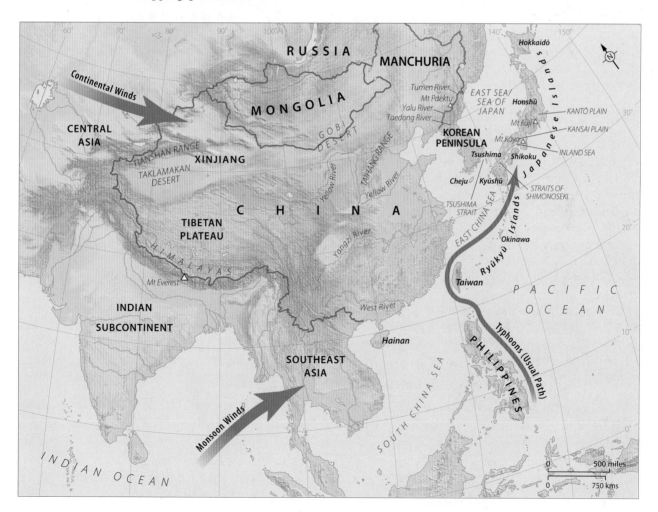

CHINA

In order to discuss the geography of China, we must define what we mean by the name. "China" can refer to two modern countries—the People's Republic of China and the Republic of China on the island of Taiwan—the former circled by an almost entirely delimited border (there are some small contested areas east and west of the Himalayas), the latter by the sea. It can also mean a *culture area*, the part of the world inhabited largely by people who are culturally Chinese. The term "China" is also used *historically*, to refer to kingdoms and empires inhabited by the assumed ancestors of the modern Chinese, states with their metropolitan centers in what is now the People's Republic of China. The ancient Zhou kingdom, for example, which flourished in the first half

of the first millennium BCE in modern North China, may thus be called "China." So, too, may the Qing empire (1636–1912), which expanded its frontiers far beyond *cultural* China and created (roughly) the borders of the modern state.

For geographical purposes, if we use modern China as our template, we must consider a number of separate zones. The *Chinese culture area* includes the eastern half to two-thirds of the People's Republic of China. The *frontier areas* conventionally include Manchuria (the northeast), Mongolia, Xinjiang (eastern Central Asia), Tibet, the Southeast Asian borderlands, Hainan island,

China

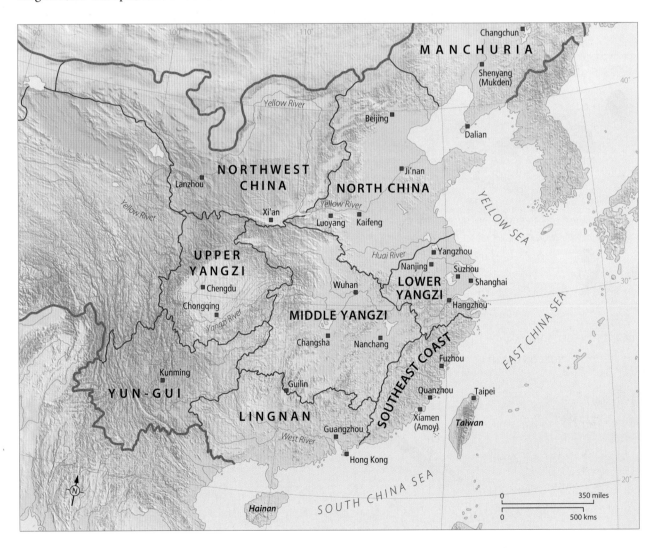

and Taiwan island, all different from the Chinese culture area and from one another.

The total area under consideration, around 3.7 million square miles (9.5 million sq km), is slightly smaller than the United States. From its eastern metropolis of Shanghai to its westernmost city, Kashgar, it stretches 2,600 miles (4,184 km). It crosses 38 degrees of latitude—nearly 2,500 miles (4,023 km)—from its northern border with Russia to southern Hainan, a far greater north–south distance than the contiguous United States. It contains some of the world's most densely populated regions and some of its least habitable deserts and mountains. It possesses rich mineral resources, including the world's third-largest coal reserves and considerable supplies of tin, iron, petroleum, natural gas, phosphorus, sulfur, and more. China's supply of rare earth metals, mostly in Inner Mongolia, exceeds the rest of the world combined and constitutes a major export.

The Chinese culture area has one overwhelming geographical and historical feature—it can be farmed. Living in environments from northern Manchuria, with its three-month growing season, to year-round cropping areas in the far south, until the late twentieth century the vast majority of its population grew plants and raised domestic animals in villages or (especially in Sichuan) on individual farmsteads. Some of

Zhang Deduan, *Qingming Shanghe Tu* (*Along the River at the Qingming Festival*), 12th century (detail). This painting illustrates the celebration of Qingming, the late spring "tomb-sweeping festival," at the then imperial capital of Bianliang (now Kaifeng), which straddled the Yellow River. A handscroll over 17 feet (5 m) long, it moves from quiet villages to the palace at the center of the bustling city, including thousands of people selling, buying, and amusing themselves on both sides of the river. The Yellow River unified northern China, serving as a major communications and transportation artery.

the most ancient Chinese texts argue that humankind's only natural, ideal environment is the agricultural community, surrounded by its fields and unsullied by commerce or urban culture. Chinese people looked upon peoples who did not farm—nomads, pastoralists, hunter-gatherers—as distasteful and hopelessly barbaric, to be converted to agriculture if possible or shunned and excluded.

Anthropologist G. William Skinner divided the Chinese culture area into nine *physiographic macroregions*, each centered on one or more river valleys and ringed by hills or mountains. He analyzed each macroregion as having a *regional core*, more urban and commercially active, and *peripheries*, usually less accessible, less populous, less developed, and less responsive to state control. With the exception of the northeast, the macroregions lie in three tiers, corresponding to the Yellow River valley in the north, the Yangzi River valley in the center, and the West River system in the south. All of those rivers follow the continent's downward tilt from Tibet to the sea, flowing from west to east. Though not corresponding precisely to administrative divisions or language/dialect differences, the macroregions do effectively map areas of relatively dense connections (cores) and the obstacles that separate them (peripheries).

The farms of central and southern China receive the copious, reliable rains of the monsoon and may thus grow rice. Requiring submersion in water for much of its life cycle—thus the name "wet-field" (or paddy) rice—the rice plant produces more food per acre than any other grain. The northern parts of the Chinese culture area, in contrast, have sufficient rainfall only for "dry-field" crops, which may be naturally or artificially irrigated but do not demand fields flooded with water. East Asians stereotypically eat rice as their daily grain, but in fact about one-third of the Chinese—those who live in the northern part of the country—do not. Northern Koreans and northern Japanese, also living north of the monsoon zone, are more likely to grow grains other than rice, unless rivers or irrigation canals enable them to flood their fields.

NORTH CHINA The northeast (Manchuria), the plateau of the upper Yellow River, and the North China plain lie outside the monsoon zone and thus depend on the less predictable rainfall of temperate Eurasia. Suitable for dry-field agriculture, they support grains such as wheat, sorghum, barley, millet, and, since the sixteenth and seventeenth centuries, corn (maize). The northeast has proved especially appropriate for the hardy, nutritious soybean, an important source of both proteins and fertilizers for the entire region. The Yellow River (see illustration on p. 17), named because it carries so much yellow silt, has both enriched its watershed and threatened it with flooding. Maintenance of its elaborate dikes has been a crucial task of northern Chinese states for more than 2,000 years.

CENTRAL CHINA The Yangzi River, called "long river" (*changjiang*) in Chinese, rises in eastern Tibet and carries the high country snowmelt through three macroregions, all with hot, humid climates and reliable

monsoon rains, enabling intensive rice agriculture. The Sichuan ("four rivers") basin in the west, surrounded by mountains, has a population greater than that of most countries—over 110,000,000—and rich, varied crops. Its western mountains are home to China's famous giant pandas. The Middle Yangzi, originally the river's natural flood-control zone of lakes and swamps, has been drained, diked, and farmed during the past 500 years. Its inhabitants receive good crops but live in annual danger of flooding. The Lower Yangzi is water country, China's "land of rice and fish," a highly commercialized region in which most goods and people move by boat. It has produced myriad famous scholars and holds many of China's urban centers, including its commercial capital, the great metropolis of Shanghai.

SOUTHERN CHINA The three southern macroregions differ in topography but all share hot summers and the reliable monsoon and thus the ability to grow wet-field rice. The Yun-Gui plateau, China's southwestern corner, has been incorporated into China-based states for only 700 years. Abutting southeast Asia (Myanmar, Laos, Vietnam), it contains many of China's culturally non-Chinese peoples and some of its most spectacular scenery. The Lingnan macroregion, centered on the West River delta and the great city of Guangzhou (Canton), can support three rice crops per year in its frost-free climate. Its dense population has a thousand-year tradition of emigration, and much of the Chinese diaspora claims Cantonese ancestry. The southeast coast, nearly coterminous with Fujian province, is cut off from the rest of the country by rough hills and thus very much oriented toward the sea. Its hillsides produce much of China's tea, and its people have both emigrated to and traded with the "southern ocean" (the South China Sea) and the offshore islands—the Ryūkyūs, Taiwan, and the Philippines.

The inhabitants of the cores of all nine macroregions are overwhelmingly Chinese in culture, as are some of the peripheries. But the northeast, upper Yellow River, Sichuan, and Yun-Gui macroregions, occupying the northern and western edges of the Chinese culture area, also include many culturally non-Chinese people. Their peripheries constitute the cultural transition zones, the "middle ground" in which cultures and peoples interact and change one another over time. Those inland zones of contact and danger have concerned China-based states more than the sea. Until the eighteenth century, Eurasian nomads and pastoral peoples constituted a greater military threat than any "ocean barbarians."

Outside the nine macroregions, which constitute China Proper, culturally non-Chinese people have historically inhabited the frontier zones. Their ecologies, many of them not conducive to agriculture, include vast grasslands, high mountain valleys, forests, desert oases, and dense jungles. With some exceptions, their productive lives have been organized around animals (goats, sheep, camels, cattle, yaks, horses), forests, or marginal agriculture. Despite centuries or even millennia of interaction with China Proper, their languages, written scripts, religions, folkways, and foods differed considerably from those of Chinese culture. Because this book focuses on East Asia as a region, they will remain peripheral to its narrative, but each could be the center of a history of its own (see Bibliography, p. 470).

NORTH OF CHINA Forest-dwelling pastoralists and nomadic herding people have long inhabited the mountains surrounding the northeastern macroregion and the great deserts (*gobi* in Mongolian) and grasslands to their west. Horse riders from infancy, Tungusic and Mongolian peoples had the reputation of fierce cavalry warriors who could trade with or raid the Chinese agricultural communities to their south. They spoke languages distantly related to Korean and Japanese, followed the advice of shamans who channeled the spirits of gods and ancestors, and occasionally gathered together in large-scale confederations led by warrior chieftains. When this happened, they threatened even distant states with their ruthless, fast-moving warfare—think of Attila the Hun, Chinggis (Genghis) Khan, and Tamerlane. Until the eighteenth century, China-based states fought, negotiated with, or walled out the northern peoples, always considering them a threat.

WEST OF CHINA Tibetan and Turkic people live in the forbidding territories west of China Proper, on the grasslands north of the Tianshan Mountains, in the oases surrounding the great Taklamakhan desert, and scattered across the high Tibetan plateau. Like the northern peoples, they sometimes organized effective armies and states, conquering both other Inner Asian peoples and the sedentary agriculturalists of China,

India, and Persia. Tibetan language and culture occupy the space between India and China, borrowing from both but belonging to neither. The Turkic peoples of what is now called Xinjiang—the "New Frontier" of the Qing empire—share both language (Turki) and religion (Islam) with peoples on the west side of the Pamir Mountains in Central Asia (Uzbeks, Kazakhs, etc.). Like the Tibetans, they live independently between two powerful culture zones.

SOUTH AND SOUTHEAST OF CHINA The hill-country peoples of China's southwest (Yun-Gui plateau) and Hainan island are close kin to Southeast Asians—Hmong (Miao), Thai, Lao, Burmese (Mon), Malay—and share their languages and cultures. Gradually moved into the mountains by the southern expansion of Chinese culture, they practice swidden (slash-and-burn) or sedentary agriculture. Some scholars now conceive of their territory as the eastern edge of "Zomia," a newly coined (2002) name for the vast swathe of mountains extending from northern Vietnam through southwestern China and the Himalayas to northern Pakistan. They argue that the diverse peoples of this enormous territory, beyond the control of centralized states, share a long history of maintaining their highland cultures, protected by rugged terrain and defended with independent spirit.

Until 400 years ago, the indigenous people of Taiwan—distantly related to the indigenes of the northern Philippines—similarly lived beyond the reach of centralized states. After brief Dutch and Spanish occupations and the Qing conquest (sixteenth–seventeenth centuries), a flood of migrants from Fujian claimed the island's plains for rice agriculture. The remnant indigenous populations—heavily intermarried with Chinese—now occupy small highland reservations.

Over more than two millennia, the dense population of China Proper has moved slowly but steadily outward, sometimes by conquest but often by migration. Once incorporated into China-based states, as we shall see, the frontier zones have become targets for considerable Chinese settlement, a process accelerated by the development of highways and railroads connecting the frontiers to China Proper. With the exception of Tibet, in 2010 all of them have populations more Chinese than indigenous. That change constitutes part of this book's story of China's modern history.

KOREA

The Korean peninsula juts southward from the coast of mainland East Asia, its base in dense, high mountains culminating in sacred Mt. Paektu, the mythical source of the Korean people. Its foot lies only 120 miles (193 km) from southwestern Japan. A common Korean saying, "Behind the mountains are more mountains," accurately describes its topography. About the size of Minnesota, surrounded by the sea and more than 3,500 islands, Korea presents many challenges to its human inhabitants. Only 15 percent of its land area can be used for agriculture, and north–south transportation routes—along which population must be concentrated—are very scarce. The east coast consists of a narrow, broken plain from which mountains rise precipitously, gradually tilting toward the low-lying, sometimes marshy west side.

The climate of the mountainous northern third of the peninsula is bitterly cold, contributing to the agricultural vulnerability of contemporary North Korea. Below Seoul, the capital of the last royal dynasty, the moderating influence of the ocean creates a fairly long growing season, and the monsoon rains, which cover the southern two-thirds of the peninsula, provide reliable water supplies for growing paddy rice. Extensive plains may be found only along the two major rivers (Han and Taedong), in the southwest (Chŏlla), and the southeast (Kyŏngsang).

Mountains impede transportation, as do the rapidly flowing, unnavigable rivers they spawn. Goods and people may be moved only in the lower reaches of the Han, which flows through Seoul (South Korea's capital); the Taedong, which runs past Pyongyang (North Korea's capital); and the Yalu, which marks the border between Korea and China. The rapid rise in elevation from the coast and inland valleys prevented canal construction. But Koreans learned early to use gravity to irrigate the valleys. Particularly in the southern provinces, skillful hydraulic engineering created the peninsula's grain bowl. The mountains, though forbidding, had strategic value, not only as defense but also as locations for a well-designed warning system of mountaintop beacon fires radiating out from Seoul in all directions.

The demographic gradient of the peninsula predictably follows the temperature and rainfall gradient from the densely populated south, with its higher temperatures, longer growing season, and more water, to the less arable, drier, more sparsely inhabited north. Though the south produces most of Korea's food, the peninsula's mineral resources are concentrated in the north. Through the past millennium and more, the peninsula has been ruled by a single state—the Koryŏ kingdom (918–1392), succeeded by the Chosŏn kingdom (1392–1910)—so the differences between north and south could be mitigated by public policy and planning. Since the division of the peninsula into two states in the wake of World War II, that balancing act can no longer be accomplished, with predictable effects for the economy of the north.

Topography also delineates regional identities in Korea. A relatively immobile population and mountainous divisions maintain regional differences in language, which correspond to different food cultures

Korea

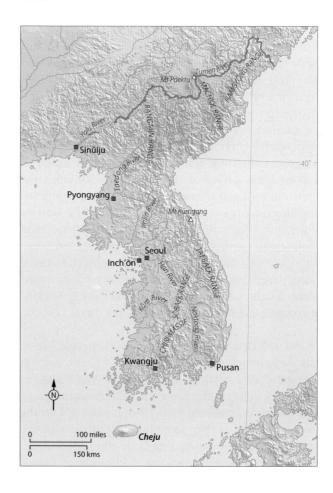

The Kŭmgang—Diamond—Mountains (ᴋ. *Kŭmgangsan*), run along North Korea's east coast. They are one of the great wonders of the peninsula, celebrated in poetry and painting since antiquity. Recently, North Korea opened this area to tourism as a means to earn foreign exchange.

and local religious customs. The relatively isolated northeast (Hamgyŏng) retains its strong, difficult dialect and remains rural and poor. In the northwest (P'yŏng'an), close to the main routes to China, the local population has a more commercial and cosmopolitan orientation but suffered discrimination by Seoul elites under Chosŏn.

The central region (Kyŏnggi) contains Seoul, the source of the now standard "national language" and most of the Chosŏn kingdom's elites and their sources of wealth. Mountains divide the lower peninsula into the Chŏlla and Kyŏngsang provinces. Chŏlla, Korea's rice bowl, consequently had high rates of tenancy and absentee landlordism—valuable land draws investment. Precisely because it was rural and its people were tenants, Chŏlla developed a reputation as a bucolic, low-class, impoverished backwater. Southeastern Korea (Kyŏngsang), though also predominantly rural, had the human and economic resources to produce the South Korea elite for most of the past half-century.

The omnipresent ocean provided Koreans with crucial food resources through fishing and, more recently, aquaculture. In premodern times, fisher folk occupied a low social stratum, not as prestigious as peasants working the land. Remarkably, despite being surrounded by water, Koreans did not develop a tradition of maritime commerce and transportation outside the coastal fisheries. For maritime defense, however, they did innovate in shipbuilding, creating some of the world's first iron-plated warships (sixteenth century). More recently, the Korean fishing industry has grown rapidly, harvesting fish and shellfish and raising many varieties of seaweed for both domestic consumption and export.

JAPAN

Like Korea, Japan is a mountainous country, its many short, fast rivers flowing down from a central "spine" of volcanic mountains. Made up of four major islands—Japanese rulers did not control the northernmost, Hokkaidō, until the late nineteenth century—and 1,700 small islands, Japan's long, narrow territory covers about 150,000 square miles (388,500 sq km), about the size of Montana. Superimposed on a map of the United States, the four main islands would stretch from Maine in the north to Florida in the south, and the climate resembles eastern America at similar latitudes. Hokkaidō, which hosted the 1972 Winter Olympics, has cold,

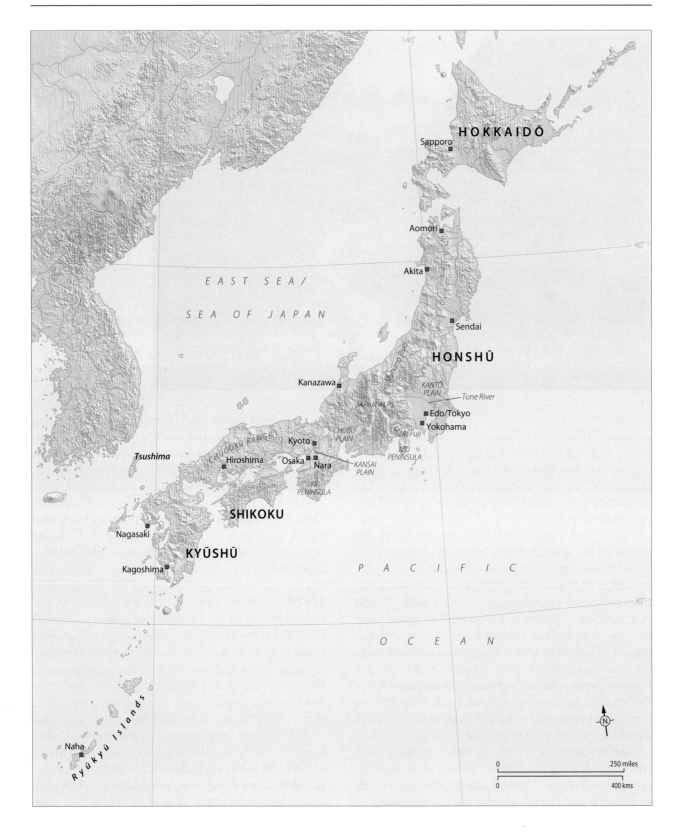

snowy winters, while the subtropical climate of Kyūshū, in the southwest, can support three harvests per year.

Most of Japan receives abundant rainfall in two rainy seasons: the monsoon season in June and early July irrigates spring crops (fruits, rice, vegetables), and the typhoon season in fall provides moisture for fall crops (wheat, millet, buckwheat). The mountains that cover 80 percent of the main island of Honshū trap frigid winter moisture—the continental winds—blowing in over the Sea of Japan from Siberia, depositing more than 10 feet (3 m) of snow on the island's western side.

Japan's geography played an important role in its prehistory. Before the end of the last Ice Age, Japan lay on the easternmost edge of Eurasia, with a land connection that permitted the easy movement of people throughout Northeast Asia. Linguistic similarities—Japanese grammar resembles that of the Korean, Manchu, and Mongolian languages—indicate that one strand of migration to Japan came from the northwest through Manchuria and Korea. Another likely came by sea from Southeast Asia and Micronesia.

By 10,000 BCE, rising sea levels at the end of the Ice Age covered the land bridge, making movement more difficult (but not impossible) between the newly formed islands and the continent. The nearest point on the main islands currently lies about 120 nautical miles from Korea and more than 500 from China, so cultural connections with the continent came mainly via Korea. In Japan, archaeologists have found large mounds of shells and animal bones, as well as the earliest pottery in East Asia (dating from the last Ice Age), indicating that the prehistoric Japanese lived along the coast, hunting and fishing.

In prehistoric Japan, tiny communities lay isolated by dense forests and hilly terrain that ran down to the sea. The abundant but non-navigable rivers flowed into the sea in deltas separated from one another by mountains. Each small community attached itself to its geographical region, worshipping regional deities specific to their places. Even after the importation of a monarchical model of governance from China and Korea in the seventh century, the various parts of the islands maintained an intense sense of localism. Not until the Tokugawa period did the notion of Japan as a

"realm" evolve, succeeded by the idea of a modern Japanese "nation" in the late nineteenth century.

Crop agriculture, animal domestication, and sericulture arrived from the continent with the immigration of a large number of people from the Korean peninsula around 300 BCE. Archaeological studies of gravesites from that time indicate that these new people lived mostly in western Japan—around the Inland Sea—rather than the east and north. Gradually they and their material and productive culture moved eastward, where two large plains could accommodate the new practice of agriculture.

The west-central plain, called Kansai, where Kyoto and Osaka are located, became the cradle of Japanese civilization. Its fertile lands produced wealth to support rulers and could be given to their supporters as rewards or fiefs. By the mid-500s CE, the Kansai plain, then known as Yamato, supported what evolved into the Japanese imperial household, a concentration of power, culture, religious belief, and wealth. Agriculturalists settled heavily on the east-central large plain, called Kantō from the late medieval period on, only around 1200 CE, and its great central city (now Tokyo) did not develop until the seventeenth century.

During the first millennium CE, the islands' population fluctuated around 5 million people. In the early modern period, new agricultural techniques overcame the limits of geography, allowing less fertile and more mountainous land to be farmed. As a result, Japan's population reached 30 million by the middle of the nineteenth century. In antiquity, urban folk in the islands considered the wilderness that surrounded them to be frightening. Only its connection to spirituality struck them as wonderful. In their folk religion, which continued even after the sixth-century introduction of Buddhism, they held mountains such as Kōya, Fuji, and others to be sacred spaces, the dwelling places of powerful spirits. Such deities also inhabited waterfalls and other sites of natural beauty.

LANGUAGES

SPEECH AND WRITING

When linguists use the word "language," they mean *speech*, the verbal communications that human beings have created over the millennia and that continue to evolve daily. *Written* forms, they argue, constitute the representation of language in two-dimensional space, not language itself. Until the twentieth century, however, speech could only be preserved beyond its immediate audience by writing it down or instantly memorizing it. So *written* language, because of its relative durability, has come to constitute an important component of cultural continuity in all cultures that use it. However we may define language, both speech and written forms have crucial functions in the study of modern East Asia.

Chinese, Japanese, and Korean are not mutually intelligible spoken languages in any of their varieties. As speech, they therefore divide this book's human subjects into no less than three large linguistic groups: "*We can understand one another when we talk; we cannot understand them.*" As we will see, the matter is actually far more complex than that, but *speech* stands as a fundamental unifier and divider. Because we depend so heavily on speech for our understanding of just about everything, it separates human beings from one another more definitively than almost any other characteristic. Lines of gender, race, class, culture, and many more have been and remain powerful and divisive, but two speakers of the same language may communicate across them. However much they may resemble one another, two people without a common speech can share information and ideas only with great difficulty and imprecision.

In contrast, for a very long time the three peoples at the center of this book have shared a single *written* form that unified them despite their differing speeches. Like Latin in Roman Catholicism, Arabic in Islam, and Hebrew in Judaism, *classical Chinese*—a written form that evolved away from spoken language more than 2,000 years ago—unified East Asia as a *truth language*. Literates in China, Korea, and Japan all learned to read fundamental texts in classical Chinese, though none of them spoke it. In all three cultures, elite children memorized the *Four Books* of the Confucian canon and selections from the vast literary heritage of ancient China. By virtue of their antiquity and the *correctness* of their content, these texts (like the Bible or the Qur'an) came to embody "universal" truths throughout East Asia.

Texts written with Chinese characters—called *hanzi* in Chinese, *hanja* in Korean, and *kanji* in Japanese—no

matter how any reader may have pronounced them, could be understood equally well by literates in China, Korea, and Japan.[1] Written Chinese performed this unifying function both because the East Asian cultures shared the classical Chinese curriculum and because written classical Chinese is predominantly *non-phonetic*. That is, Chinese characters have little or no inherent relationship to speech or sound. For example, the Korean word *yangban*—the upper class of Korean society—written 兩班 in Chinese characters, would be easily intelligible to a literate Chinese, who might pronounce it *liangban*,[2] or Japanese, who would read it *ryōhan*.

Like Latin in medieval Europe, this classical Chinese textual commonality enabled consistent communication throughout the region. Shipwrecked Korean elites or traveling ambassadors could "talk" with Chinese officials in writing, though not necessarily in speech. Japanese customs officers could read the bills of lading of incoming Chinese or Korean ships. In the first few chapters below, we shall see the importance of texts in producing a common cultural matrix made up of Confucian, Buddhist, Daoist, and other ideas expressed in Chinese characters, despite the very real differences among the three East Asian societies and the mutual unintelligibility of their spoken languages.

Although mutually unintelligible and very different in *sound*, Korean and Japanese strongly resemble one another in *grammar*, and historical linguists theorize that they derive from the same "root language," many millennia ago. Some linguists believe both belong to a larger group, the Altaic languages, which would include Mongolian and Manchu, perhaps even the Turkic languages, although recent scholarship has questioned that affiliation. They have the same sentence order—subject-object-verb (SOV)—and complex verb structures closely related to *levels of politeness*. Every Japanese or Korean sentence expresses the social relationship between the speaker and the audience through choice of verb ending, ranging from informal endings addressed to intimate friends all the way to endings reserved exclusively for addressing the king or emperor. The most important determinants of politeness level are age, gender, and social status. Younger people use humble verb endings in addressing older people; women use more humble verb endings than men; and low-status people use humble verb endings when addressing high-status people. Chinese, which has no verb endings of any kind, lacks this grammatical feature, relying instead on particular (sometimes highly specialized) vocabulary to express politeness, humility, or superiority.

Neither Japanese nor Korean bears any linguistic resemblance to Chinese, and both are *relatively* homogeneous. Strong differences in pronunciation and vocabulary exist between, for example, the Korean spoken in the northeastern mountains and that of Cheju island, off the south coast. Similarly, people from Kyūshū, in southern Japan, and people from the far north might have a hard time understanding one another, especially before the advent of modern media and "standardization" in the late nineteenth century. But Japanese and Korean are clearly single languages, with dialectal variations.

Geographically, the Chinese culture area is much larger than that of either Japan or Korea, and its long historical development has allowed for much more isolation of regional or even local languages and regionally different influences from other languages. Linguists count between seven and nine mutually unintelligible versions of Chinese speech, distinguished by geography. We must note here that Chinese people universally call these different speeches "dialects" (c. *fangyan*, "local speech") rather than separate "languages." This choice, political in nature, stems from the necessity for national unity, the imperative that everyone who is "Chinese" speak "Chinese," even if they cannot understand one another when they do.

So we are left with a problem: Is Chinese one language? Is it a language family, like the mutually unintelligible "Romance languages" derived from ancient Latin? How did the category "Chinese" come to include so many varieties of speech? Linguists cannot agree on answers to these questions, or on the specific historical mechanisms that caused such diversity. They do emphasize, however, the profound importance of the written Chinese characters—which are non-phonetic and thus mean the same thing no matter how they are pronounced—in unifying the Chinese culture area in the absence of universally comprehensible speech.

In the past century and more, as we shall see later in this book, each East Asian state tried to create a "standard national language," a crucial element in the formation of a unified nation-state, with its feeling of *nationalism* based on a sense of common identity. This process, fairly straightforward in Korea and Japan, remains unfinished, though far advanced, in China. The modernizing Chinese elites of the early twentieth century chose as the basis for standardization the generic northern speech (called *Mandarin* in English) that government officials from all over the empire had spoken to one another. Scholars estimate that a large majority of Chinese people can now at least understand Mandarin, if not speak it well, largely through the widespread influence of electronic media (film, radio, television, and other sound-transmission technology such as MP3). The rest of the population continues to use and cherish its local speech forms—Cantonese (around Guangzhou), Hokkien (in Fujian and Taiwan), Shanghainese, etc.—requiring an ongoing national effort to spread Mandarin, which has met with considerable local resistance.

VOCABULARY AND LOCAL WRITTEN FORMS

When Japanese and Koreans started using Chinese characters as their written form—in the third–sixth centuries CE—they borrowed vocabulary with them, words that had not existed in their own languages. They pronounced these new words as northern Chinese people did at that time—very different from today's Mandarin pronunciation—and those pronunciations have evolved within the Korean and Japanese spoken languages. Most of the borrowed vocabulary consisted of *nouns*, names for things or abstractions, and both Koreans and Japanese still use thousands of such words. That is why *yangban*, *liangban*, and *ryōhan* sound similar—they all derive from the same Chinese word of 1,500 years ago, and all have changed over the centuries.

Koreans and Japanese can clearly distinguish their "original" languages from their borrowed Chinese vocabulary; both Sino-Korean and Sino-Japanese loan words are easily recognizable by their pronunciations. In Chinese and Korean, each Chinese character has a single pronunciation in each spoken language/dialect. But Japanese people use Chinese characters to represent indigenous words as well, so a single character might have a dozen or more different pronunciations, depending on meaning and context. For example, the character 字, meaning "a Chinese character, a letter, a word, handwriting," would be pronounced *zi* in modern

Mandarin, *ja* in Sino-Korean, and *ji* in Sino-Japanese. But the same character, pronounced *aza*, may be used in Japan to mean "a section of a village," a meaning it does *not* have in Chinese or Korean.

Since Korean and Japanese do not share grammar with Chinese, Koreans and Japanese developed phonetic written forms to supplement and eventually replace (in Korea, at least) Chinese characters. Unlike Chinese, Japanese and Korean verbs have endings to indicate tense, conjugation, and level of politeness. Only the development of phonetic written forms enabled them to write their own languages as well as classical Chinese.

Early Japanese writers often used Chinese characters for their phonetic value to indicate Japanese sounds, and that awkward system—"Is this character here for its meaning or its sound value?"—evolved by the ninth century into a truly phonetic written form, *kana*. Each written *kana* sign represents one of the approximately 50 possible Japanese syllables, so we call the *kana* a "syllabary," not an alphabet. Modern Japanese uses a mixed writing system including Chinese characters (J. *kanji*) and two *kana* syllabaries, one for Japanese words and one for foreign words.

Since the fifteenth century, Koreans have been able to write their own language with a unique alphabet now called *han'gŭl*. Consciously created by a royal think-tank (K. *Chiphyŏnjŏn*, "Hall of Worthies") after a survey of all known writing forms, the alphabet was presented to the people by King Sejong (r. 1418–1450) in 1446. Very different from either Chinese characters or Japanese *kana*, *han'gŭl* contains signs for all possible consonants or vowels—like an alphabet—but combines them into a block for each syllable. For example, the symbols for *h* (ㅎ), *a* (ㅏ), and *k* (ㄱ) would be assembled thus 학 (*hak*, "learning"). *Han'gŭl* represents Korean sounds with great precision; Koreans now use it for almost all writing, reserving Chinese characters for names and academic prose.

Since the late nineteenth century, written Korean and Japanese (contrasted to classical Chinese) have both become important vehicles for *nationalist* ideas, separating them from—rather than uniting them with—Chinese culture and history for the first time in more than a millennium. Chinese, too, has had to cope with the demands of becoming a modern language. In the late nineteenth century, East Asians developed a new vocabulary of modernity to translate European and American concepts into their languages, *using Chinese characters*. These words rapidly became common coin throughout the region. We will deal with this subject more thoroughly in Chapters 5–7.

PRONUNCIATION, PHONETICS, AND ROMANIZATION

Since this is not a language textbook, you do not need to know Chinese, Korean, or Japanese in order to read or use it. But because we include East Asian words and names in our historical account, we must introduce some elements of phonetics and deal with the problem of "romanization"—how to represent East Asian words using our imprecise and limited 26-letter alphabet. Apart from personal and geographical names, these terms are marked c. (Chinese), k. (Korean), and j. (Japanese).

Some readers may want to learn to pronounce these words correctly. Rather than providing cumbersome charts or pronunciation guides, we recommend the many websites available for learning each of the three languages. They have romanization charts, with audio files for each possible syllable, and can guide you toward accurate pronunciation. Japanese romanization has been fairly standard for more than a century, but both Chinese and Korean have been represented with very different systems. English readers familiar with names like "Shantung" and "Mao Tse-tung"—both using the old British Wade-Giles system—will not find them here, for we have used the more recent *pinyin* romanization invented in China. For Korean, we have chosen the McCune-Reischauer system still commonly used in Britain and the United States rather than those used in either North or South Korea.

JAPANESE Of the three East Asian languages, Japanese has the least complex phonetic system—5 vowels and 15 consonants—and can be most effectively romanized. Japanese words, though long and repetitive-looking, actually sound more or less the way they look in the roman alphabet. The common surname *Yamamoto*, for example, written in Japanese with two Chinese characters, is pronounced "yah-mah-moh-toh." Japanese has no diphthongs, so each syllable, even if it consists only of a vowel, must be pronounced separately. *Aoi* ("blue-green") is thus "ah-oh-ee." All vowels can be lengthened with a macron, so *ō* is the same sound as *o*, but twice as long. Though *i* and *u* vowels occasionally disappear—*shikatsu* ("life and death") should be pronounced "sh-kah-ts"—you will find Japanese words generally easy to say, if not always easy to remember.

KOREAN Though grammatically close to Japanese, Korean has a very different phonetic system, with 10 vowels and 14–19 consonants (depending on who is counting), a number of them difficult for non-Koreans to pronounce. Unlike Japanese, Korean does have diphthongs, and its numerous vowels and vowel combinations cannot easily be represented with the roman alphabet. You will thus find *o* and *ŏ*, *u* and *ŭ*, in Korean words, as well as difficult *l* sounds, among others. Some of the Korean words in this book are not pronounced the way they look in the roman alphabet. For example, the name of a former president of South Korea, romanized as No T'aeu or Roh Tae Woo, is actually pronounced "No Tay Oo."

CHINESE With 21 consonants (plus one final consonant), 6 vowels, and a wide range of diphthongs, Mandarin Chinese (the Chinese language/dialect romanized in this book, with a few exceptions) is phonetically very complex. Like Korean, it does not lend itself easily to romanization. The name of the late General Zhu De, for example, should be pronounced something like "Joo Duh," which is not what the romanization looks like at all.

Not only does Chinese utilize a number of sounds difficult to represent with the roman alphabet, it also has *tones* (which Korean and Japanese do not). Unlike the rise and fall of pitch in an English sentence, a tone attaches to every individual Chinese syllable. Mandarin uses four tones—high, rising, low, and falling—while some southern versions of Chinese have as many as nine. The Mandarin syllable *bai*, for example, can mean "to break apart," "white," "a hundred," or "to defeat," depending on the tone. Because of this tonal quality, Chinese sounds like "sing-song" to speakers of other languages. We have not attempted to represent tones in any way in this book.

NAMES

Most of the Chinese, Korean, and Japanese words in this book are *names*, of places, people, institutions, policies, etc. East Asian people's names present English speakers with a consistent problem—all East Asians put their family names (*surnames*) *first*, followed by their personal names, a custom usually interpreted as emphasizing the importance of *family* (compared to the individual) in East Asia. In the countries we study, the authors of this book would be Lipman Jonathan, Molony Barbara, and Robinson Michael. We follow conventional East Asian usage throughout this book, requiring our readers to think backwards about names. When you meet Qiu Jin, Sin Ch'aeho, and Ichikawa Fusae, please remember that they are Ms. Qiu, Mr. Sin, and Ms. Ichikawa. You can remind yourself to do this by remembering that Mao Zedong was *Chairman Mao*, not Chairman Zedong, just as the United States' current leader is President Obama, not President Barack.

Because the English alphabet lacks the *visible* distinctions possible with Chinese characters, you will find some homophones—words that sound alike, and thus look alike when written with the English alphabet—in this book. For example, one word for "the Chinese people," *Han* 漢, is a homophone of a word meaning "Korea," *Han* 韓. Written with two obviously different Chinese characters and pronounced in Mandarin with two different tones, these two words nonetheless appear to be exactly the same in English. We can only apologize for the limitations of our 26-letter alphabet and note such problems as they arise.

CHAPTER TWO

MING CHINA, CHOSŎN KOREA, AND WARRING STATES JAPAN IN 1600

WORLD CONTEXT

In 1600, three great Muslim empires—the Ottomans with their capital in what is now Turkey, the Safavids in what is now Iran, and the Mughals in what is now India—dominated the center of the great Eurasian continent. In the north, the czars of the Russian or Muscovite empire had only recently defeated the Islamized Mongols who had surrounded or ruled them for centuries. The Russians had not yet begun their eastward expansion toward Siberia and the Pacific, though they had sent armies southward to obtain warm-water ports on the Black Sea.

Far to the east, the Ming dynasty held sway over the entire Chinese culture area, ruling over more people—between one-quarter and one-third of humankind—and more productive power than any other state on the globe. Although Eurasia had no single economic center at the turn of the seventeenth century, the vast population and dynamic, highly commercialized markets of Ming China made it a crucial source for goods of all kinds and a magnet for merchants from all over the continent. Scholars calculate that 50 percent of the silver that the Spanish and Portuguese took out of the New World found its way into the coffers of the Ming empire's merchants and officials.

By 1600, the complex, irreversible changes collectively known as the "scientific revolution" had begun. Many historians consider them to be as dramatic as the "Neolithic revolution," the ancient invention and spread of agriculture, metallurgy, cities, unequal social classes, and writing. Unlike the Neolithic revolution, however, which occurred independently in many places, the sixteenth to nineteenth-century development of mathematized science, technology, and economy—radically new ways to understand, control, and organize the natural and human worlds—happened only in geographically and historically fortunate Europe. These developments played a major role in several European states' ability to become the lords of the globe for several centuries. Using their evolving and powerful new tools, from ships that could sail against the wind to rifled cannon and locomotives, post-Renaissance Europeans transformed some of the world's peoples into slaves, colonized others, and gradually extended their political and economic power into even the most remote and inaccessible regions.

Since then, Europeans and their North American cousins have told humankind's story in light of their own victories—the winners write the histories—and judged all non-European societies as more or less backward on the basis of their technological levels and their willingness to become more European in their ways. The political and scientific patterns developed in Europe and its New World colonies carry indisputable power, though the people who use them may have no desire to become European or North American.

As Europe gained worldwide dominion, its story—diverse and complex and rich in contradictions and accidents—has been ironed out into a single Story of Civilization, a straight chronological line running from sites outside of Europe (Mesopotamia, Egypt, Phoenicia, and the "Bible lands") via Greece and Rome, to its most recent capitals in Western Europe and North America. In our history of writing history, that linear progression became the only path that civilization might take. As one American textbook of world history from the late

East Asia, c. 1600

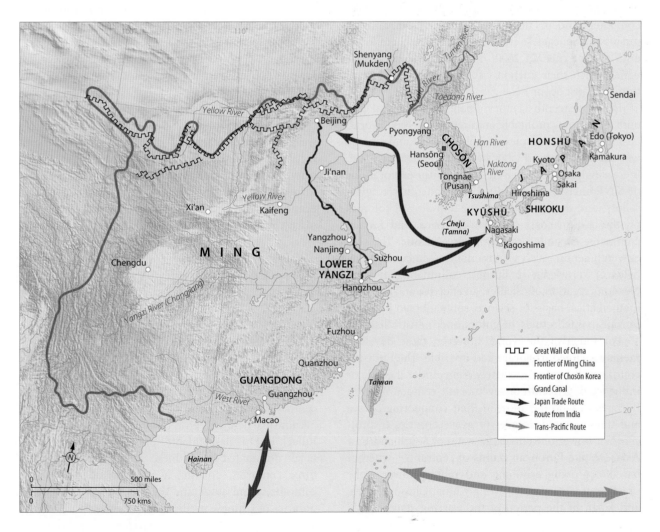

nineteenth century put it, "[T]he Caucasians form the only true *historical* race. Hence we may say that civilization is the product of the brain of this race."

This racialist arrogance, based on well-exercised military and scientific superiority, allowed Europeans to eliminate from historical memory the technological contributions of all other peoples—the Chinese invention of paper, for example, or Korean use of movable type centuries before Gutenberg, or the high achievements of Japanese metallurgy—and consign East Asia to "the haze of the world's horizon" from their own obvious position at the center.[1] Eurocentrism of this kind continues to be taught and defended at the beginning of the twenty-first century.

The heyday of European hegemony may now be over, or we may be in its final stages, and every land and people now has access to its tools. Indonesians make computers, Indians design software for them, and Samoans and Senegalese and Uruguayans use them to log onto the internet. In 1600, however, these processes, which reach their current culmination as "globalization," had just begun.

In the sixteenth century, Spain and Portugal had built enormous, profitable empires in the New World, basing their economies in plantations and mines worked by the forced labor of native populations and, increasingly, that of enslaved Africans. The explorations of Sir Francis Drake (1540–1596) and other English sailors were shortly to lead to the founding of colonies on the eastern coast of North America, and French commerce expanded rapidly in the Atlantic. The seventeenth century also saw dramatic advances in many fields of knowledge in Europe, culminating in Isaac Newton's creation of calculus, an effective and accurate mathematical basis for science, soon adopted by other European intellectuals, inventors, and industrialists.

For much of the world, however, these developments remained irrelevant and invisible. The Eurasian continent did not immediately come under the rule or influence of sixteenth or seventeenth-century Western Europeans, who did most of their conquering by sea and thus required decades or even centuries to project their power onto the large states of South and East Asia. Despite European claims of centrality—whether based on growing economic and military power or the practice of Christianity—Ming China, Chosŏn Korea, and Japan in the period of the warring states would

have had no reason to recognize themselves as inferior, or even equal, to the "barbarians from the sea" whose ships occasionally encountered their shores. Many scholars now argue that parts of East Asia in the sixteenth to eighteenth centuries shared many characteristics of "early modern" history with Europe at the time—especially commercial sophistication, proto-industrialization, and the emergence of the centralized state—but no one believes that Europeans *taught* these things to East Asians.

The Ming ruler did order Jesuits and their Portuguese allies to use their advanced technical skills in casting cannon to defend against frontier enemies. But musketry and artillery had long been part of the arsenals of the Eurasian states, often called "gunpowder empires," and the Ottomans, Safavids, Mughals, and Ming had not yet fallen far behind the Europeans in military hardware. When the Japanese laid hands on European muskets in the sixteenth century, they immediately set about improving them; within decades, Japanese smiths were making better firearms than their European models.

East Asians claimed the superiority of their own civilizations based on their high cultural heritage, wealth and technical skills, ritual decorum, and moral rectitude. In all three East Asian cultures, that superiority was seen to emanate at least in part from China, through its long history of political philosophy and economic power, so we can begin our modern history of East Asia there, in the largest of the regional states.

CHINESE SOCIETY AND CULTURE IN THE LATE MING

NEO-CONFUCIANISM AND THE IDEAL OF SELF-CULTIVATION

Zhu Yuanzhang, a successful general whose troops drove the Mongols northward in the mid-fourteenth century, founded the Ming dynasty (1368–1644) and became its first emperor (*Huangdi*, Supreme Divine Ruler). He, his descendants, and their government officials dominated the Chinese culture area for almost three centuries, creating a state considerably more centralized and autocratic than its European contemporaries or Chinese predecessors.

Historians usually call their style of government "Confucian," for Ming rulers, officials, and elites educated themselves and their families in a textual tradition they traced back to Confucius, a sagely teacher of ancient times. The textbooks, teachers, and families of literate Chinese encouraged them to live harmoniously by knowing and acting out their proper roles in society, by accepting the power of authorities—rulers, fathers, husbands, and older brothers—an attitude very useful to autocrats. According to Confucian ideals, a person who had properly absorbed the lessons of the ancient Classics would never disobey their parents, be unfaithful to spouse, siblings, or friends, and, perhaps most importantly, never rebel against a legitimate ruler.

Although the classical texts are indeed very ancient, Ming elites interpreted them using eleventh- and twelfth-century commentaries and educational methods called Neo-Confucian in English. Still emphasizing the ancient rituals, the Neo-Confucians advocated self-disciplined study as the Way (C. *Dao*) to activate the inner virtues dormant in all human beings. One of the ancient texts most often cited by Neo-Confucians, the *Daxue* or Greater Learning, put it this way:

> *Those of antiquity who wished that all men*
> *throughout the empire would keep their inborn*
> *luminous Virtue unobscured put governing their states*
> *well first. Wishing to govern their states well, they first*
> *established harmony in their households. Wishing*
> *to establish harmony in their households, they first*
> *cultivated themselves. Wishing to cultivate themselves,*
> *they first set their minds in the right. Wishing to set*
> *their minds in the right, they first made their thoughts*
> *true. Wishing to make their thoughts true, they first*
> *extended their knowledge to the utmost. The extension*
> *of knowledge lies in fully apprehending the principle*
> *in things.*[2]

Individuals differ in their capacity for letting their innate virtue shine into the world—depending on the clarity or murkiness of their natural physical and psychological endowment—so Neo-Confucians relied on both official (state) and unofficial (social) institutions to control those who could not control themselves.

Starting with texts like the *Daxue*, Neo-Confucians probed the fundamental nature of reality. They concluded that the entire cosmos, energized by the interaction of *yin* and *yang* (see p. 42), followed *principle* (C. *li*, K. *i*, J. *ri*)—the *patterns* (rather like Platonic *forms*) of nature and things and the core object of study in the *Daxue*. But *principle* had no substance in itself—only pure pattern—and had to be worked out in *material existence* (C. *qi*, K. *ki*, J. *ki*); what one scholar has called *psychophysical stuff*. East Asian scholars argued over that basic metaphysical conceptualization for centuries, debating whether *principle* or *material existence* should be considered primary, and how these abstract concepts could help us construct ideals for a good society and virtuous individuals. Their texts, written in classical Chinese, became crucial regional connections, as Chinese, Korean, and Japanese philosophers worked on the same problems and came to a wide variety of conclusions.

Society functioned through five hierarchical relationships that, properly performed by everyone, would guarantee a stable social order: father–son, king–minister, husband–wife, older brother–younger brother, and friend–friend. Every individual had the theoretical capacity to perfect the self through inner cultivation, and no one could escape from the network of roles and relationships that defined the places of that self in society.

The Ming rulers made the law apply even to the highest members of the elite, often vulnerable to charges of corruption or factionalism. But laws could never be enough, so the Ming government encouraged Neo-Confucianism's idealistic claims. The model of benevolent rulers, righteous officials, stern but loving fathers, and self-disciplined elites would trickle down to inspire every individual to copy them and thus create a good society. Knowing the limits of this idealistic vision in real political practice, Ming rulers also created a complex law code and enforced it through a large bureaucracy. Their government, riddled with the personal ambitions of powerful individuals and their families, floated lightly above a huge population whose interests only sometimes coincided with those of their rulers.

INDIVIDUALS AND FAMILIES, IDEALS AND REALITIES

Families constituted the building blocks of the society over which the Ming state ruled. The idealized family consisted of many generations, from wise elders to innocent infants, living in hierarchical harmony in a single compound, welded together by emotional bonds to one another, ritual devotion to their common ancestors, and mutual interests. The *patrilineage* (sometimes called a *clan*) formed the most basic human association, and it bore the common surname that gave individual males their fundamental social identity.

Whether through philosophical and religious texts or through proverbial knowledge reinforced by rituals and punishments, young men learned that obedience to authority was prized and that their personal successes and failures could determine the collective destinies of their families. They certainly became *individuals*, with all the quirks that their personalities and circumstances allowed, but their families did not encourage *individualism*, pressuring them rather to act for the benefit of all. Ming dynasty law provided for harsh punishment of the relatives of some convicted criminals, whether they had any knowledge of or role in the crime or not.

Love for parents and grandparents, and obedience to their wishes and instructions, came to be enshrined and praised as *filial piety* (C. *xiao*, K. *hyo*, J. *kō*), one of humankind's highest virtues.

In Ming times, some intellectuals did invest the individual with considerable autonomy, arguing that self-cultivation did not simply control or discipline people but could also lead to individual liberation. The school of Confucianism associated with the philosopher, soldier, and government official Wang Yangming (1472–1529) broke from conventional

---

Illustration from the *Classic of Filial Piety*, 12th century. In this scene, a young man and his wife and children offer their respects to his mother and father.

Neo-Confucianism in its understanding of the problem of "fully apprehending the principle in things," the core of self-cultivation as outlined in the *Daxue* text.

At the age of 36, Wang Yangming had experienced a sudden moment of enlightenment. Rather than search in the outer world for knowledge, extending his mind into the phenomena of external reality, he realized that we *inherently possess* the crucial knowledge for which we seek, namely the difference between good and evil. He therefore concluded that action in the world rises directly and inevitably from knowledge of the harmonious nature of reality generated within the innately moral individual mind.

Although his thought never became the Neo-Confucian mainstream in Ming China, it was influential not only there but also in Chosŏn Korea and Tokugawa Japan. Some of his more extreme followers went so far as to argue that human beings should follow all of their "natural instincts" in order to perfect themselves, even if they violated conventional Confucian moral norms. Wang Yangming's radical critique of conventional thought teaches us that tradition could lead in more than one direction, that Chinese culture was not homogeneous but rich in possibility, even regarding so basic an issue as human individuality and knowledge.

The family, as Chinese people thought about it, consisted of many more people than just those who actually lived together, for the kinsmen of the past, recently or long ago deceased, remained as necessary and vital members. They had to be honored regularly, at least once a year. Their memorial tablets, inscribed with their names, rested on a family altar, placed in the position of honor in the house's main room. There they received offerings of incense, food, and drink to keep them well disposed toward the living.

Social class determined how elaborate and frequent these rituals could be, ranging from a sparse New Year meal in an impoverished farmhouse to frequent, textually scripted, elaborately costumed performances for the ancestors in a high official's mansion. The divide between the living and the dead, obvious and recognized by all, did not prevent people from announcing important family events, such as the marriage of a son or daughter, to their late parents, grandparents, and more distant ancestors. These practices, called "ancestor veneration" in English, made up an essential part of the annual ritual cycle of Chinese families. Neglect of this fundamental responsibility created "hungry ghosts," unfed ancestors whose anger and envy could severely damage the living.

Only a small proportion of Chinese people, however, actually lived in extended families or multigenerational lineages. Economic realities and the rules of inheritance prevented most people from creating ideal "big families." With life expectancy very low (around 30 years in the late Ming), many people died before the births of their grandchildren. In addition, most Chinese did not possess the wealth necessary to sustain dozens of individuals under one roof or to perform elaborate rituals.

All Chinese had to divide their wealth equally among sons upon the death of the patriarch, who was by law the household head. This rule of *partible inheritance*, dating at least from the first millennium BCE, contrasts strongly with *primogeniture*, inheritance by the eldest son, which was preferred in Chosŏn Korea and among the elite of Tokugawa Japan. The division of family wealth in every generation caused both landholdings and commercial wealth to fragment, so some sons might have to leave home in search of land to farm or, if they stayed, become tenants of their better-off neighbors or relatives. Most Chinese families, therefore, consisted of parents and children, sometimes sharing the home with one or both of the husband's parents.

During the past thousand years, some families did manage to maintain elite status from generation to generation by *incorporating* their lineages. They assigned landed property or commercial investments to the surname itself rather than any individual, thus exempting some of their wealth from partible inheritance rules. Especially in the east and south, these *corporate lineages* endowed their ancestral halls—ritual spaces devoted to their ancestors—with agricultural land, usually farmed by kinsmen who became tenants of the lineage. They used the income to advance the family's interests.

Young kinsmen could be educated and prepared for success in lineage schools. As both a symbol and a tool of their long-term continuity, some families maintained written genealogies (C. *jiapu* or *zupu*, K. *chokpo*, J. *kafu*), which listed all their male (and some female) members, the living and the dead, and stipulated the conditions of collective property, common rituals, and ideological commitment to their patrilineage.

In Ming political theory, individuals and families could be classified by profession, according to an ancient hierarchy. At the top of the social system sat the emperor and his family, virtually out of reach of the law, governing "All Under Heaven" (C. *tianxia*, K. *chŏnha*, J. *tenka*) by their personal and collective virtue, by proper performance of the rites, and by ordering and acting out just rule over the people. Chosen to be the Son of Heaven and possessing Heaven's Mandate to rule and regulate the cosmos, the emperor, his ancestors, and his successors for "10,000 years" (C. *wansui*, K. *manse*, J. *banzai*) constituted a unique lineage in the Ming state.

The officials who governed in the emperor's name and all those who studied and cultivated themselves to serve in office made up the highest class of society, the scholar-officials. Military officers, who had to pass exams in the martial arts and strategy, composed a secondary hierarchy within the state. Next came the farmers who performed the basic work of producing food for all, and after them the artisans, who created useful materials and objects.

At the bottom of ordinary society—in theory at least—lay the merchants, a class judged as parasites by the ancient texts, and often called the "secondary occupation," as they created nothing of value but only made profit by buying and selling. The Classics contrasted "profit," a negative term in ancient Chinese, to "virtue" or "human heartedness."

But merchants often had more money than farmers or artisans. Indeed, the conventional hierarchy of statuses often conflicted with reality. Wealthy merchants might educate their sons for success in the official examinations, while many educated men could not take office and thus had to make a living some other way. Apart from holding office or teaching, the most respectable occupation for scholar-officials was landholding. By owning land, a family could contribute to society's welfare, take rent from tenants, and not sully its hands with commerce. Nonetheless, many members of scholar-official families did go into business, investing their profits in land, in educating their sons, and in temples and rituals to advance their families' prestige.

Below the merchants, at the very bottom of society, lay small groups of despised people whose occupations (leatherworking, for example) or way of life (such as dwelling permanently on boats) made them unfit for inclusion even in the lower ranks of respectable society. Although the state occasionally tried to abolish their hereditary status, they remained on the edges of ordinary communities with no possibility of becoming entirely human in the eyes of their neighbors. At times in Ming history, this lowest-status group included Buddhist monks, prostitutes, and actors, among others.

WOMEN'S LIVES

At least half of the Chinese population did not share in the lifelong belonging to a patrilineal surname, a lineage, a clan, a family, as described above. Obeying some of the most ancient traditions of their culture, Chinese families usually took in wives for their sons and married their daughters out into other families—a marriage system that anthropologists call *patrilocality*—thus rendering female children less important to their natal families than their brothers. Many exceptions to this "major form" of marriage existed, including adopting an infant girl, who would marry a son after both children passed puberty, or bringing a son-in-law into the family to marry a daughter.

But the normative weight of tradition generally kept girls from being permanent members of their natal families and alienated them to some extent from its wellbeing. Although Chinese girls technically kept their natal surnames when they were married out, most females were known not by surname or personal name but rather by their relationship to their husbands' families ("Third Sister-in-Law") or to their children ("Little Bao's Mother").

Certainly Chinese parents loved their daughters and wanted the best for them, but that usually consisted of finding them the best possible husbands and (even more important) mothers-in-law. To that end, from the twelfth century on, Chinese families began to express their quality and their self-discipline by causing their daughters excruciating pain. The binding of young girls' feet to make them attractively narrow, originally a practice of imperial court dancers, gradually spread to all classes of society. The original narrowing with cloth bands grew more restrictive, constricting the foot's length as well as its breadth during a young girl's years of rapid growth.

By the late Ming period, many Chinese girls of marriageable age were walking on the tops of their bent-under toes, balancing on their heels with only their big toes extended forward, their arches bowed high and their feet no more than a few inches long.

Young Chinese woman with bound feet, c. 1940. Prevalent by the end of the Ming period, the tradition of footbinding lasted well into the twentieth century.

This agonizing deformation served many purposes, not only making a woman more attractive and restricting her movement throughout her life but also marking her as part of a society that understood propriety and discipline. Her family could be proud because they had cared enough to express civilization through their daughter's pain. Although some social groups did not bind women's feet, the practice came to embody "Chineseness" for large segments of the population. Never known or endorsed by Confucius, who advocated complete preservation of the body received from parents, footbinding has become associated with "Confucianism," the practice of Our Chinese Tradition.

When a daughter married out of her father's lineage, ritual behavior indicated the termination of her association with her natal family—water was spilled and doors slammed behind her—though in some classes of society and some parts of China that relationship remained deep and emotionally engaging in practice. Even if they retained a close connection to their natal families, however, by the late Ming, married women and all their possessions belonged by law to their husbands' families (like women's property in nineteenth-century America). Given the wrenching detachment from all that was loving and familiar and entry into a family of potentially hostile strangers, a Chinese woman learned to be self-sufficient though appearing to lean on her father, her husband, and her son.

Once married, women's purpose in their husbands' families lay in producing male heirs, and in playing their appropriate roles in relationships and rituals. Young mothers found that their main allies were their sons, full members of their fathers' lineages from birth and thus able to protect their mothers. Confucian tradition defined devotion to parents (filial piety) as the highest virtue for all humankind, emphasizing in history and legend the importance of mothers, especially widowed mothers, to their sons' destinies. Widows who raised successful sons, cared for their late husbands' parents, and brought honor to their husbands' lineages by refusing to remarry received prestige, mention in local histories, and sometimes posthumous gifts from the emperor himself.

Chinese women in the Ming thus bore the triple burden of (1) patriarchy, the notion that men are inherently superior to women; (2) patriliny, the transmission of identity and property through the male line; and (3) patrilocality, the pattern of relocation into the husband's family upon marriage. Despite this heavy load, late Ming women of the elite classes still managed to find ways to express themselves and to find satisfaction in human relationships. Their education, in their natal parents' homes, made them literate in the classical tradition, able to read and write (especially poetry) as a vehicle for emotional communication, and to participate in the cultural lives of their husbands and children.

We know much less about the lives of women from the lower classes of society, for they rarely expressed themselves in writing, but some women received notice in official reports, local histories, or biographical literature. Usually they were praised for their tenacious resistance to remarriage, steadfast devotion to their sons or other members of their husbands' families, or their willingness to commit suicide rather than violate any social prohibitions.

NATIVE PLACE

Crucial though it was, the family did not encompass all of an individual's associations and identities in late Ming China. Because most people did not move very far from their birthplaces, *native place*—with its associated speech, local customs, foodways, scenery, temples, climate, and ecosystem—constituted a crucial facet of a person's individuality. When a person left the family's compound on official, commercial, or social business, s/he thus carried native place and its history, language, and foodways. Most people formed their crucial personal relationships within local society, so their hometowns provided them with a secure foundation when they traveled. As commercial enterprises spread in the wealthier and more urbanized regional cores of China—on the east and southeast coasts, up the major river valleys, and around the large cities of the north—merchants found it useful to create hometown societies in places where they stayed regularly. In such clubs or hostels they could find the spoken language of home and people they could trust more than the strangers of their target markets.

By the late Ming, some regional associations, such as the bankers of Shanxi province in the north or the money-shops run by natives of Ningbo, a seaport in eastern Zhejiang province, had begun to play transregional roles in transferring funds and/or offering credit to traveling merchants. After the Ming state ceased printing paper money in the fifteenth century, many of these institutions issued instruments of credit—private paper money—as a convenience to hometown merchants.

FOOD AND HOBBIES

The great twentieth-century Chinese scholar Lin Yutang claimed about his own culture, "If there is anything we are serious about, it is neither religion nor learning, but food."[3] Chinese elites had created and propagated a culture-wide theory of food, based on the hot/cold distinction between *yang* and *yin*, five flavors (salty, sour, sweet, bitter, spicy-peppery), and an elaborate array of criteria for excellence, such as "to taste deliciously of

fat without being oily." But within the Chinese culture area's wide variety of ecologies, each region developed its own cuisine based on local ingredients and tastes.

Few Chinese in the Ming period wrote or talked of "Chinese" food. Rather, each locale's special ingredients, unique methods of preparation, and famous dishes became reasons for hometown pride and spirited debate between people from different places when they met at the market. Shanxi merchants, for example, thought so highly of their local vinegar that they traveled with personal supplies of it rather than tolerate another place's inferior sourness.

A person might also have hobbies, such as practicing the martial arts with a boxing master or studying with a calligrapher, performer, or painter. A woman might affiliate herself with a poetry teacher, a master or employer (if she worked as a prostitute or domestic servant), or a religious group. In these social connections, people developed ties that resembled family—*fictive kinship*—and would adopt terms such as "sister," "brother," "aunt," and "uncle" for their relationships. These could be coincidental or entirely voluntary. Most of these associations remained private, enriching people's lives and improving their communities.

RELIGIONS

Like people of all cultures, Chinese people have developed religions and philosophies to help them understand the world and cope with life's inevitable tragedies and confusions. Confucianism, described above, offered a satisfying, coherent system of ethics and human relations, but it never stood alone. Daoism, also an ancient textual tradition, provided a more personal, less socially regulated vision of the good life. Daoist books and commentaries advocated freedom, passivity, and conformity to the laws of nature rather than the artificial norms of society. Over centuries of use, Daoism also developed a mystical, esoteric side, inhabited by magicians, mountain-dwelling hermits, and priests who could purify a polluted home or drive malevolent demons from their victims' bodies.

In addition, China has been a magnet for trade and migration for millennia, and people of many faiths have found their way there and propagated their religions. The most successful, Buddhism, arrived from India, beginning in the late first century CE. Through a complex process of translation, its texts and ideas became available and then dominant in China over the following centuries. By the seventh century, Buddhist institutions and values permeated religious and intellectual life. Monasteries inhabited by celibate monks—a challenge to Confucian filial piety, which demanded male offspring of every male Chinese—sat on many Chinese mountains. Every large city had temples, soup kitchens, and pawnshops operated by both clerical and lay Buddhists. Other religious traditions, including Sunni Islam, Nestorian and Roman Catholic Christianity, Manichaeism, Judaism, and Tibetan Buddhism, also built their temples and spread their faiths among Chinese people before and during the Ming period.

At the level of villages and market towns, as well as among elites, popular religion blurred the textual distinctions among Buddhism, Daoism, and Confucianism. Families performed Confucian ancestral rituals at home and at graves, attended festivals and fairs at Daoist and Buddhist temples, and called on various religious specialists for their skilled functions. Thus, most Chinese could accurately be called Buddhist Daoist Confucians.

Everyone celebrated the culture-wide holidays that punctuated the hard work of the agricultural cycle: the Duanwu festival (fifth day of the fifth lunar month), with its dragon boat races; the mid-autumn festival (fifteenth day of the eighth lunar month), on which everyone who could afford them ate round sweet "moon cakes"; and the fifteen-day New Year, or spring festival, the only extended rest from ordinary labors. Holidays brought formal and informal visiting among friends and kinfolk, special foods, and lots of noise and excitement in the form of fireworks and outdoor theatrical performances.

During the Ming, religious leaders created the Three Teachings tradition, which placed statues of the Buddha Sakyamuni, the legendary Daoist sage Laozi, and the Great Teacher Confucius on the same temple altar. In addition, some millions of Ming period Chinese were Muslims, a few thousand were Jews, and some had converted to Christianity under Jesuit missionary influence. In short, religious traditions permeated Chinese society, and their followers created communities of belief and ritual ranging in size from the family to vast transcultural congregations.

Some sorts of voluntary associations caught the attention of the law because they set themselves up, either consciously or not, as parallel to or even as rivals with state power. The Ming rulers' Neo-Confucian autocracy did not tolerate any alternatives to its own orthodox hierarchy. Not surprisingly, many of these arose in the realm of religion, for charismatic religious leaders claimed divine guidance to construct authority among their followers.

Sectarian religion flowered in periods of social chaos, central government weakness, and economic

Niujie (Oxen Street) mosque, Beijing. Originally built in 996, it has served as the core of a flourishing Muslim community. The current structure dates from 1442, enlarged and renovated in 1696. The door plaque reads, "The Pure and True Ancient Teaching," meaning Islam.

downturn, particularly in impoverished regional peripheries. When conditions deteriorated, people turned to messianic expectations—the idea that a savior will come to end our troubles. Rebels against the Ming in the 1630s and 1640s called upon popular religious traditions to build support.

Like religion, intellectual activity stimulated deep and long-lasting divisions in late Ming Chinese society. Scholars and officials who found the politics of the court frustrating or even immoral returned home—many of them to the Lower Yangzi region—and founded academies, schools where like-minded men could debate the burning issues of the day. Qualified to hold government office because of their literary skills and moral rectitude, these men complained about the influence of eunuchs and other "illegitimate" elements at the emperor's court.

ORTHODOXY, MERITOCRACY, AND THE EXAMINATION SYSTEM

The government that ruled the Ming state claimed to take its structure from antiquity. The emperor sat at the center not merely of the state but of the entire cosmos. His palace lay on the north–south axis of balance in the world, and his southward-facing gaze took in all of reality. His rituals kept Heaven and Earth in equilibrium and harmony, while his sagacious decisions maintained the human realm in good order.

Among his most important responsibilities, the emperor selected moral, self-disciplined, well-educated

HAI RUI REBUKES HIS LORD

In November 1565, Hai Rui (1514–1587), a junior secretary in the Ministry of Revenue, wrote an extraordinary letter to his master, the Jiajing Emperor (r. 1521–1566). Using the rigidly formal language required by his bureaucratic post, Hai Rui accused the emperor of numerous violations of his proper role as head of state and lord of All Under Heaven. He argued that the realm's sorry condition stemmed directly from the monarch's character and behavior. Because the emperor was selfish and immoderate, unwise and suspicious, the people suffered from high taxes and incompetent and corrupt officials. Violent bandits and criminals devastated society without fear of pursuit or punishment: "It has already been some time since the people under Heaven started to regard Your Majesty as unworthy." Hai Rui based part of his argument on strict Confucian principles: the behavior of the emperor would directly affect the behavior of his officials, whose attitudes and acts would be imitated by the common people. To solve the problems of society, Hai Rui wrote, "All that is needed is a change of heart on Your Majesty's part."

What kind of person would write such a letter, risking not only his own life but that of his family and perhaps his friends as well? Well-known in official circles as a moralist and an advocate for official virtue, Hai Rui had never passed the highest-level examination. He entered the civil service as a *juren* (second-degree holder), rising slowly through the ranks as a local official. Stories circulated that he was willing to confront anyone, no matter how exalted, who violated the law or the rigid moral standards Hai Rui set for himself. His frugality became legendary—one popular joke had a high military officer announce, "Sensational news! Magistrate Hai is providing a banquet to celebrate his mother's birthday! He has already bought two pounds of pork!" By rebuking several high-ranking officials and trying to redistribute wealth and power in his district, Hai Rui made himself popular with the general public, but he also put his career in grave danger.

After submitting his letter, Hai Rui waited to be executed; some officials believed he had already bought his coffin and said goodbye to his family.

men to perform the daily work of government. The examination system, however well or badly it might have worked in practice, did distinguish Ming China from most of its contemporary states in Eurasia (including Chosŏn Korea and Tokugawa Japan). Its officials were chosen not because of noble birth (*aristocracy*), but because of their skill in a particular kind of learning (*meritocracy*).

The Confucian texts, with their core of moral philosophy, ritual rectitude, and ancient advice to kings and ministers, became the core curriculum for these examinations. Although apparently irrelevant to official life, compared to administrative procedures, laws, and tax codes, a Confucian education theoretically guaranteed the *character* of the men governing the realm. In Confucian theory, they absorbed from ancient texts the personal qualities necessary to create good government.

Every Chinese male who could undertake lengthy and arduous study had the potential to become an official. Most poor families could not afford to support non-working sons through the many years required to prepare for the exams, so the sons of wealthy families—with libraries, tutors, and leisure to study—usually dominated the lists of successful candidates. But every so often, a poor family's son passed and became an official, earning empire-wide fame, as did widows who labored in adverse circumstances to educate sons who succeeded in the exams.

The Neo-Confucian interpretations and commentaries of Zhu Xi (1130–1200), declared *orthodox* in

---

The emperor, suffering poor health and aware that many of Hai's accusations were true, did not have him arrested for several months. In February 1566, the Ministry of Justice sentenced Hai to death by strangulation, but the emperor, who had to approve all death sentences personally, died ten months later without signing the execution warrant. The condemned man walked out of prison after a year and resumed his official career. For the rest of his life he was famous, a model official in the eyes of the public, but he never succeeded in reforming the state. When he gained substantial office—a provincial governorship in 1569—he lasted only a few months, making himself so unpopular with the wealthy landholders that they impeached him. Unable to compromise with the realities of a complex, inequitable land tenure system, he had again tried to redistribute land and wealth.

Out of office for 15 years, Hai Rui lived modestly, wrote essays, and hoped to change the world. Though recalled to office in 1585, aged 72, he could never put his high-minded Confucianism into action. Whenever Chinese people want to praise a government official as honest and "on our side," they call him "a real Hai Rui" (see p. 365 for an example of this).

Hai Rui's signature, late 16th century. This signature, at the end of an original poem, exemplifies the skills with the writing brush expected of an official. Elite men and women practiced for years to write a beautiful hand, and composed poems on any occasion of emotional or public significance.

the fourteenth century, contained authoritative understanding of the Classics. From their first days in the schoolroom, young Chinese boys whose parents desired them to succeed in public service (and elite girls who had the opportunity to study) dedicated themselves to an intense concentration on the orthodox texts. First they memorized the primers called *Three [Character Classic]*, *Hundred [Names Classic]*, and *Thousand [Character Classic]*; then they turned to the *Four Books*, the heart of the Neo-Confucian curriculum, and memorized that, too. Containing the Analects of Confucius (*Lun Yu*), the Mencius (*Mengzi*), the Doctrine of the Middle Path (*Zhongyong*), and the Greater Learning (*Daxue*), the *Four Books* had been chosen by Zhu Xi as the most profound expressions of the ancient wisdom that should animate and control individuals, states, and societies.

Memorization of these texts served a useful function in learning to read a language with tens of thousands of characters and no alphabet to indicate pronunciation (see p. 27), but it had a philosophical rationale as well. Zhu Xi believed that the purpose and meaning of "study" (c. *xue*) did not lie in simply becoming familiar with the content of a text to pass an exam. Rather, the student must *internalize* the text, make it part of himor herself, causing its moral content to penetrate to the inmost soul. Only this process constituted the transformative work specified in the *Daxue*, "fully apprehending the principle [pattern] in things," enabling a person to cultivate the inner life toward perfect goodness.

Once children completed the *Four Books*, they could (if they had the talent and the family could afford it) tackle the formidable array of Chinese literature. They studied more philosophy from the Hundred Schools of Thought of the Zhou period (first millennium BCE), the *Book of Changes* (*Yijing* or *I Ching*) and other ancient classics, the more than 20 multivolume histories of former dynasties, essays and poetry, diaries and public documents, biographies and ritual instructions. Boys had to memorize this enormous quantity of text before qualifying to take even the lowest level of examinations. In the process, many of them became skillful philosophers, philologists, historians, and literary critics. They produced not only examination essays but also a literature of commentary on the classical texts, similar to commentaries on the Bible or the Qur'an in their goal of clarifying ancient meanings for a changed world. For

over two millennia, elite Chinese concentrated on *written texts* as the core of all important knowledge.

To take the civil service examinations, young men spent several days in their county or prefectural town, surrounded by dozens or hundreds of other candidates, locked in tiny cells, writing essays on a variety of classical subjects, linking obscure passages from ancient texts to contemporary problems. They wrote in a precise form of prose, with eight rigidly defined parts, and used all their memorized resources to dazzle the examiners. Senior officials assigned by Beijing to each locale read all of the essays and ranked the candidates, specifying who had passed.

After celebrating, those who passed at the lowest level—bearing the title of *xiucai*—resumed their studies in hopes of passing the provincial exams and becoming *juren*, second-degree holders. This status would give them province-wide prestige, the right to hold some public offices, and permission to take the triennial metropolitan exams. The small number who passed that final hurdle—only a few hundred every three years from a population numbering at least 100 million—became *jinshi*, "presented scholars." The emperor personally examined and ranked them, after which they could receive assignments as government officials. Through this process, the successful candidates became the emperor's men, individually loyal to His Majesty.

Six ministries did the bureaucratic work of the central government: transmission and filing of documents, keeping of accounts and statistics, writing and distributing of reports, organization and supply of armies and navies, and many other administrative jobs. Each ministry had specific responsibilities—Revenue and Finance, Personnel, Rituals, War, Law and Punishments, and Public Works—and the bureaucrats often developed deep specialties in their official duties. To contrast this emperor-centered, Confucian system with a modern state, the Ministry of Personnel did not administer the civil service examinations, as we would expect, but rather the Ministry of Rituals. The ruler's selection of righteous officials lay at the heart of his *ritual* duty, the regulation of All Under Heaven.

Beijing sent officials to provincial-, prefectural-, and county-level posts throughout the Ming state. County magistrates and their professional staffs governed districts that varied widely in wealth and population, from poor mountain peripheries with a few thousand inhabitants to upper-level counties in regional cores with over a million. Their official roles included police chief, tax collector, judge, jailer, instructor in morality, and keeper of granaries for emergencies.

Although no "balance of powers" existed in the Ming government, it did include the Censorate to oversee the officials and, in theory, to ensure that they did not act selfishly or corruptly. Even the emperor could theoretically be rebuked by the censors, though they certainly did not do so lightly. Since the ruler possessed absolute power, it could only be regulated by his own virtue, limited by the principled remonstrations (complaints and criticisms) of his officials. A censor might risk his emperor's displeasure, his life, and his family's future by confronting an errant ruler (see pp. 38–39).

The emperor's daily work consisted of meeting with his officials in the Regular Audience (usually held at dawn, except on the coldest winter days) and handling a vast volume of paperwork presented to him by the Office of Transmission. Together with his Grand Secretaries, the supervisors and censors who oversaw the bureaucracy, and his personal attendants, many of them eunuchs, he spent hours each day reviewing proposals, reports, petitions, and accounts. The Grand Secretaries,

personally chosen by the emperor, controlled his access to information and thus his view of the realities outside his palace, the Forbidden City in the north central part of Beijing, which he rarely left.

In his capacity as the Son of Heaven, the emperor performed numerous, precisely regulated rituals, plowing the first symbolic furrows in the spring and praying to his own ancestors to maintain the peace of the realm and the smooth flow of the seasons. Destructive natural phenomena such as floods, earthquakes, and droughts called his virtue (even that of the entire dynasty) into question, so he tried to prevent them through sacrifices, prayers, and music. Some Ming rulers took their jobs very seriously, performing their tasks diligently and studying the Classics. Others did not. Their willful disregard of official business led to serious, even fatal, breakdowns in government functioning, for in a highly centralized autocracy, the personal qualities of the autocrat mattered.

TIME AND THE COSMOS

Chinese civilization lacked an indigenous creation myth, and most Chinese people did not hold any strong idea of a creator external to the cosmos. Everything that exists, visible and invisible, thus lay within

Examination hall for the imperial civil service, Guangdong province, 1873. The hundreds of cells in which the candidates took the exams flank the approach to the central hall. Locked into these cubicles, they spent days composing rigidly structured answers ("eight-legged essays") to questions on passages from the Classics chosen by the examiners. Those who passed continued their climb toward jobs as government officials.

comprehensible reality. Ancient philosophers decided that the cosmos functions through the interaction of two complementary qualities—*yin* and *yang*—that act together in dynamic tension to produce the energy and motion that animate the universe.

All things, even mountains and the heavenly bodies, contain the interaction and flow of *yin* and *yang*, not least the human body itself, in which invisible channels contain that movement. Skilled doctors can stimulate or interrupt *yin* and *yang* energy by prescribing medical herbs and diet, by applications of heat or massage, or by insertion of thin needles, a process called *acupuncture*, to restore an ailing person to healthy equilibrium. Other specialists learned to "read" the flow of dynamic *yin* and *yang* energy in hills and valleys, even in domestic space, to help people arrange their homes and the graves of their ancestors in harmonious locations, a still-living tradition called *fengshui* ("wind and water," or *geomancy*).

Lacking a creation story, the Chinese also had no initial year for counting time, in the way that Christians use the birth of Jesus, or Muslims the *hijra* of Prophet Muhammad from Mecca to Medina as Year One. Since the earliest days of Chinese civilization, a crucial facet of the emperor's power therefore lay in the regulation of time, the creation of the calendar and the almanac, even the naming of years. Anyone who privately made a calendar different from the emperor's could be executed, for the act implied a claim of competing rule over the cosmic forces.

When a new emperor took the throne, the court historians and astrologers chose an auspicious title, a *reign-name*, for the period of time he ruled. The first Ming reign-period was called Hongwu (Magnificent Martial, 1368–1398) and the last one Chongzhen (Sublime Auspicious, 1628–1644). East Asian texts count time through these titles, so 1368 would be "Hongwu 1st year," and 1640 would be "Chongzhen 13th year." We will use these titles throughout this book to name the Chinese emperors, the Korean kings, and the Japanese emperors, but not the Japanese *shoguns*. Following Japanese custom, the shoguns are called by their personal names.

AGRICULTURE AND COMMERCE

The urban markets and commercial districts of late Ming China flourished at a level far above that of Europe (London or Paris) or the Middle East (Cairo or Baghdad) at the time. Holding the Confucian view of commerce as a low profession, Chinese elites saw this as deplorable, but they lived within cityscapes rich in excitement and danger, filled with producers, sellers, and consumers eager to share in the latest fashions.

Elite families ensured continuation of their wealth and status by incorporating their lineages. High officials built luxurious mansions "back home in the country" and retired there when they left government service. Prosperous merchants linked their names to official families through marriage ties, for they shared a high culture of art connoisseurship—appreciation of fine painting, calligraphy, poetry, ceramics, and antiques—and a common desire to perpetuate their elite status through education and the examination system.

They also shared a complex currency system with all subjects of the emperor. The Ming state used gold only rarely as currency, relying instead on small silver ingots and bronze coinage. Many of their subjects still transacted barter exchanges and paid their taxes in grain. The early Ming court had followed the Mongol pattern of printing paper money, but extensive counterfeiting and unwillingness to hold precious metal reserves made the notes worthless by the mid-fifteenth century. Thereafter, officials wrestled with the problems of bimetallism—the relative value of silver and bronze, hoarding by the wealthy, and the sometimes disastrous impact on the poor of changes in the value of currency.

The state and merchants faced complex issues in foreign trade, especially with their sources of silver (Japan and Latin America). Silver fetched a very high price in Ming China, which had few domestic supplies of that precious metal but needed large quantities to monetize its domestic economy. So merchants from all over the world earned substantial profits by exchanging silver for Chinese trade goods. Europeans competed effectively in that trade once they learned to navigate from India to southeastern China and across the Pacific from Acapulco to the Philippines.

LAND AND POPULATION

Connected to the cities through marketing systems but living outside urban culture, most Ming subjects farmed the land. Some demographers estimate that 90 percent lived in villages, whether as independent freeholders, as tenants who rented land, or as laborers who worked the fields for a wage. Few generalizations about this vast population can hold true. The ecologies and economies within which peasants lived varied greatly, from the extensive plains of the northeast, with low temperatures and short growing seasons, to the lush paddies of the frost-free Guangzhou delta, in which three rice crops might be grown every year. In the dry-field regions of the north, most peasants owned and farmed their own land, while wealthy families bought up the more valuable wet-field rice lands of the south and rented them to tenants, often their own kinsmen.

Although they were rarely conscious of it, their Ming state and Chinese culture certainly united all these villagers in some ways, such as ancestor veneration, fundamental notions of human relations (such as filial piety), cosmic dynamism (*yin–yang* theory), ritual life, bronze coinage, and subjection to centrally appointed officials. In the late Ming, local magistrates organized "village compact" meetings to standardize culture and behavior, at which they or their representatives lectured the villagers on proper Confucian conduct.

But attachment to local culture and local language gave people the most immediate elements of their identities. Most Chinese knew themselves more as people of their own family and place than as "Chinese" or "subjects of the Ming." Most peasants lived their lives within the circle of village and local markets. Many of them did migrate to areas where new lands became available or for greater safety in times of trouble. This mobility indicates to modern scholars that information flowed freely around the Chinese culture area, following the same routes as commodities and merchants. For those who moved, however, becoming "local" in a new home could take many generations. To this day, the lowlanders of Guangdong province, whose local roots are deep, call the hill-country people *Hakka*, "guest families," even though they arrived from northern China in the thirteenth century.

The crops grown by late Ming peasants varied with climate and terrain. All of them relied on cereal grains—rice, wheat, barley, millet, and sorghum—for the bulk of their calories. Cooked grain (c. *fan*) remains the core of most Chinese meals, eaten as steamed or boiled rice, steamed bread, porridge, or noodles. In the sixteenth century, food crops newly imported from the New World, most of them via the Spanish colony in the Philippines, began to increase the nutritional options.

Sweet potatoes, corn (maize), tomatoes, peppers (both sweet and hot), white potatoes, and peanuts could be grown on land that had formerly been unusable—hillsides, sandy soils, and arid fields. Scholars agree that the remarkable population growth of the late Ming and the following Qing period could not have occurred without these dietary additions.

During the Ming, the population of the Chinese culture area rose steadily. All pre-1950 population statistics from China are suspect, but current estimates (with a good deal of educated guesswork) show the Ming population of around 100 million in 1500 increasing to over 400 million three centuries later, a change of immense significance in China's later history. Despite carefully considered alterations in taxation policy—reducing the number of exactions on rural families to one or two per year, for example—the state never succeeded even in counting its subjects, not to mention taxing them equitably. Like many of its predecessors, the Ming taxed agricultural land more effectively than anything else, for it was immobile and did not vary much in either value or productivity from generation to generation. Local gentry, however, usually stayed several steps ahead of the magistrates and the Ministry of Revenue, concealing their landed wealth in a bewildering maze of relationships and documents.

FRONTIERS, DEFENSE, AND DIVERSITY

Always nervous about a resurgent Mongol threat from the north and northwest, the Ming government devised many strategies to separate their vast agricultural lands from the potentially aggressive non-Chinese peoples who surrounded them. The most famous of these efforts, the Great Wall of China, has become a symbol of China's longevity and insularity. The Wall's enormous size has generated many legends, for example that it is visible from the moon (it is not) and that it is over 2,000 years old. In fact, the Ming constructed virtually all of the currently existing old walls between 1550 and 1644, with substantial reconstruction for tourism after 1978. The Great Wall's modern reputation considerably exceeds its effectiveness as a defensive barrier. With some early exceptions, it never prevented frontier peoples— Jurchens, Mongols, Turks, Tibetans—from raiding into Ming territory, and the vast expense of its construction kept the Ming from investing in other projects.

The greatest of the Mongol rulers of the time, Altan Khan (1507–1582), negotiated with high Ming officials to obtain what Mongols had always wanted—officially sanctioned trading posts where pastoral people could obtain agricultural goods, especially grain and tea, in exchange for horses, leather, and grassland products. Herding people always faced greater economic insecurity than farmers. Flocks often succumbed to severe weather, leaving people to starve if they had no access to food supplies from agricultural areas. In 1571, the Ming finally agreed to regular frontier markets.

During the Ming period, cultural and religious connections between Mongolia (north of China) and Tibet (west of China) grew increasingly intimate. The fourth reincarnation of the Dalai Lama, an important leader of Tibetan Buddhism, was Altan Khan's grandson, the only Mongol ever to hold that exalted religious position. During his early seventeenth-century reign, Mongols played important roles in the military and political life of Tibet. As we will see in Chapters 3 and 4, the next dynasty to rule over the Chinese culture area took military action to prevent a close alliance of the religious power of Tibet and the military power of the western Mongols.

Given Chinese culture's long history of conflict and interaction with Manchuria, Mongolia, Turkestan, and Tibet—now China's frontier areas—Ming defense policy focused there rather than on its long coastline. The Ming ruled none of those frontier regions during its long reign, dealing with them by defensive measures and diplomacy. They judiciously balanced the rhetoric of *tribute*, in which inferior cultures paid homage to the emperor and his superior civilization, with the realities of frontier relations. In one famous incident, Tamerlane (Timur-i Lang, 1336–1405), a Muslim conqueror from Central Asia, planned to subdue China for its wealth and its arrogant refusal to embrace Islam. Upon his sudden death, his son, negotiating with the Ming court from what is now Afghanistan, insisted that their communications reflect a relationship of equals rather than the subordination demanded by Chinese ritual. Preferring peace, the Ming officials agreed that the monarchs would call one another brothers.

In a more dramatic case, the Ming court came to the aid of its tributary and ally, Chosŏn Korea, which found itself under attack by the aggressive unifying warlord of Japan, Toyotomi Hideyoshi, beginning in 1592. Pouring out treasure and its soldiers' lives, the Ming expeditionary force marched through southern Manchuria and down the Korean peninsula to fight alongside the local armies and succeeded in blocking the invasions until Hideyoshi's death in 1598 (see pp. 54–55).

Piracy constituted a major problem for the Ming, but rather than build a vigorous, aggressive navy, the later rulers withdrew substantial populations from the coast, leaving the sea to freebooters, Chinese, Japanese, and Korean. This landward orientation later prevented effective reaction to the arrival of a persistent, technologically advanced threat from the sea—the Western Europeans—and continued to plague the rulers of the Chinese culture area into the twentieth century.

BEING CHINESE

As noted in Chapter 1, the huge expanse and ecological diversity of the Chinese culture area gave rise to considerable variation in human adaptation. What then did they have in common that made them all Chinese? Even if they could not communicate in speech, their elites all used the non-phonetic Chinese script, which enabled them to write to one another. They were all subjects of the Ming emperor, for even enterprising merchants in ports around the South China Sea continued in theory to be his subjects. Culture-wide notions of how things work, like *yin–yang* theory, *fengshui*, and the five flavors of food, had deep roots and wide acceptance. All Chinese lived in a society deeply influenced by the social, ethical, and political norms of Neo-Confucianism, and their various languages (now called "dialects") included many proverbs and quotations based on its texts.

Most Chinese held a normative prejudice in favor of patrilocal marriage, and they honored and communicated with their ancestors through ritual. They shared a complex religious heritage including Confucianism, Buddhism, and Daoism. According to one scholar, they expressed their common culture by following the same nine steps in funeral rituals. They all looked upon agriculture as the primary occupation, literacy and scholarship as the highest achievements of culture, cooked grain as the main food, and the patrilineal family as the basic building block of society. But they did not know or imagine one another as "fellow citizens." Rather, they lived as *subjects* of a distant emperor, and few of them would have placed "Chinese" at the top of their list of roles. Familial, local, and economic identities would have come first. Only later, under pressure from powerful outsiders, would ethnic unity and nationalism enter their minds.

KOREA UNDER THE CHOSŎN KINGS

THE *YANGBAN* RULING CLASS

Like the Ming, by 1600 the Chosŏn dynasty had survived for more than two centuries, ruling over the entire Korean peninsula. But unlike its giant neighbor it lasted another 300 years, making it the longest Korean dynasty. During more than half a millennium of rule, immense changes transformed the social, economic, and intellectual lives of the population. Yet throughout the entire period, a single hereditary group known as *yangban* dominated the social, political, and economic life of the peninsula and kingdom.

Literally meaning "two ranks," the term *yangban* emerged as early as the tenth century to refer to the two orders of officials, military and civil, who lined up on either side of the king (к. *wang*) at court to debate and offer advice. By the seventeenth century, however, *yangban* came to refer to a group in society claiming aristocratic status and privilege—about 10–15 percent of the population.

Like the other main social-status categories of the Chosŏn kingdom—commoners, *chungin* (middle people), and slaves—*yangban* status was hereditary, with distinctions between different status groups maintained by a multitude of laws and social rituals, many of them derived from the same Confucian texts and Neo-Confucian interpretations used in the Ming. One marker of *yangban* status, like that of the Chinese gentry, was a written genealogical record, still used in Korea today, recording the common descent of the kinship group or *patriline*, usually beginning with an illustrious ancestor. Sometimes historical, often mythical, the genealogies trace the many branch families that had moved away from their ancestral seat to settle around the peninsula. Since most non-*yangban* did not even have family names, the possession of a genealogical record distinguished *yangban* from others.

Social status governed the everyday activities of the people. Clothes, architecture, punishments, taxation, language, neighborhoods, and villages—all these and many more were articulated along status lines, always with the *yangban* at the top of the hierarchy. Any observer in 1600 could distinguish a male *yangban* by his clothes, his flowing white robe, tall horsehair hat, and pointy shoes forming a striking contrast to men of other status groups. Distinctions in fashion carried over into social interactions among individuals, all conducted according to status differences.

Whether a leading official in the capital or living more simply away from court politics in the countryside, a *yangban*'s claim to a position at the top of the social ladder rested on his training in Confucianism as well as his noble birth and gender. Various strands of Confucian thought had entered the peninsula from as early as the fourth century, but not until the general

Korea in the Chosŏn period (1392–1910)

45

Yi Sŏnggye (1335–1408) overthrew the Koryŏ dynasty (936–1392) to establish the Chosŏn dynasty in 1392 did Confucianism become the fundamental ideology, the orthodoxy, of dynastic rule. Known to history by his posthumous title King T'aejo, Yi and his chief ministers began a wide-ranging process of Confucianization that transformed life in the peninsula over the next two centuries. In launching Confucian reforms, leading officials took as their model not the actual Ming China of their day but rather the patterns of proper conduct, rituals, and institutions portrayed in classical Confucian texts and interpreted by Song dynasty Neo-Confucians such as Zhu Xi (see p. 40).

This appeal to the classical age of the sages worked only because Korean scholars had a long history of using the Chinese written characters and reading Confucian texts. Chosŏn dynasty literary men saw themselves participating in universal knowledge that transcended dynastic or cultural barriers, not the property of any one place or people (China or the Chinese). They learned a written language that differed greatly from their spoken language in order to pursue the moral truths that should order all societies at all times. They captured this commitment in one of their names for the written Chinese characters, *chinmun*, "truth script." As a result, *yangban* educated themselves in the same textual traditions as their Chinese and Japanese counterparts.

However, they also commonly believed that classical knowledge needed to be adapted to suit their particular age and the specific environment of the peninsula, giving Korean scholars license to adjust these

MS. KIM HANGS HERSELF

The historical records do not tell us much about Ms. Kim. A few thin lines and an ink sketch record her fate, published together with the biographies of dozens of other "virtuous women" in a moral handbook of 1617. As recounted in both Chinese characters and the Korean phonetic script, included so that women could read the story, Ms. Kim was widowed shortly after her marriage. Pressured to remarry, she fled to her husband's grave, where her in-laws again tried to force her to wed. Determined to maintain her loyalty to her deceased husband, as Confucian propriety demanded, Ms. Kim hanged herself rather than break her vow of marital chastity.

As presented by the editors of this state-sponsored handbook, Ms. Kim's story did not represent a tragedy but rather a celebration of a widow's correct moral commitment. As was customary, the account identified Ms. Kim only by her husband's name and her hometown, leaving out her personal name, unnecessary because the handbook's purpose did not lie in publicizing her accomplishments as an individual. Rather, her story

demonstrated how a woman, in the face of social pressure, could correctly perform the role of a virtuous widow.

Yet the very fact that this handbook was the third in a series of similar publications commissioned by the throne, each edition reprinted and distributed many times, can cause us to question the reasons for these publications. Why the need to reprint similar stories so frequently? While there may be many answers to this question, we can speculate that leading officials had grown less than satisfied with the behavior of Korean women. Reading about Ms. Kim and other virtuous women, they believed, would encourage proper behavior among women who did not yet live up to Confucian expectations. For historians today the story of Ms. Kim represents a common record for the study of gender in the Chosŏn period. Even though we suspect Ms. Kim was praised precisely because her behavior was so rare, she and other "model" women have ironically dominated our understanding of the lives of women in this era.

norms creatively. Consequently, in addition to the classical texts and the commentaries of Zhu Xi and many other Chinese literati, they developed a longstanding tradition of indigenous Korean commentaries on the Confucian Classics. Scholars such as Yi Hwang (pen name T'oegye, 1501–1570) and Yi I (pen name Yulgok, 1536–1584) offered new ways of thinking about Confucian metaphysics, focusing on some of the same problems as Chinese philosophers but finding somewhat different answers.

The challenge of adapting classical textual traditions to the contemporary Korean environment, in particular to real social lives, extended even to that most supposedly Confucianized of status groups, *yangban* families. As we have seen in the Ming, all schools of Confucian thought placed great emphasis on the family as the basis of a moral order that stretched beyond the household to include the entire cosmos. Because of the close connections between human morality and nature, scholars held that improper relationships within the family resulted in disturbances in the natural world. Following this thinking, the Chosŏn dynasty promulgated laws and offered enticements to promote proper familial relations, social controls that paid special attention to the relationship between husbands and wives.

By 1600, the conjugal relationship among the *yangban* elite had been fundamentally transformed into a patrilineal social order similar to that of Ming China. During the previous Koryŏ dynasty, women had remained in their natal homes to be joined by their husbands after marriage. This gave women considerable autonomy, including the possession of property and its free disposition. During the late Koryŏ period, marital arrangements had begun to shift toward patriliny among some elite groups. But marital relations and, more broadly, gender relations changed dramatically under Chosŏn rule. New laws made women leave their parents' homes to live with their husbands' families, a cause of much agony and a subject of many poems.

During the first half of the Chosŏn period, *yangban* women also lost their ability to transmit their property to their children, as all property became the possession of the husband to be inherited by the eldest son, that is, through *primogeniture* (unlike China's partible inheritance). Women's power to divorce and remarry disappeared, as the Chosŏn dynasty ordered that the prerogative to leave a marriage rested solely with the

Statue of King Sejong, Tŏksugung palace, Seoul. Cast in bronze by Kim Kyŏngsŭng in 1968, this sculpture sits in the grounds of the former palace of the Chŏson kings and is witness to the esteem in which Sejong is still held by the Korean people.

husband. The state urged widows, even under the most trying circumstances, to maintain their chastity by not remarrying, even if, as in the case of Ms. Kim (see p. 46), it meant sacrificing their lives.

The proper role of women, in this Neo-Confucian vision of social relations, lay in subordination to men, a truth most famously expressed in what came to be known in both Chinese and Korean cultures as the "Three Obediences." When young, women were told, obey your father; when married, obey your husband; when widowed, obey your son. Women's loss of status and growing dependence on men manifested itself in the architecture of *yangban* homes, which physically separated a room for men to receive guests from an inner room where women lived. This inside/outside divide came to represent the closing off of women from public life, as official ideology defined their roles through their relationships with the men in their lives, that is, as daughters, wives, mothers, or grandmothers.

Yangban families also maintained clear distinctions between the primary wife and any concubines who lived in the same family compound. In the judgment of Korean Confucians, maintenance of a pure family line required that only the descendants of the main wife could inherit the patriline. Even when the wife did not bear a son, a relative from within the larger descent group, usually a nephew, would be adopted to serve in this role. Discriminated against as "secondary sons," the sons of concubines did not share the *yangban* status of their fathers.

These practices denied secondary sons not only the status of their own families but also full participation as sons in any family. As secondary sons protested in group memorials (letters to the king) down to the nineteenth century, this denial violated filial piety, one of the fundamental tenets of Confucianism. In contrast, though Ming law recognized a primary wife, the children of

concubines legally belonged to the primary wife and could inherit both rank and property from their father.

In Chosŏn Korea, maintaining distinctions among wives as a means of maintaining the pure descent line of the family illustrated the power of *aristocracy* (status granted by birth) as a principle in Korean culture. Moreover, by limiting the number of children entering the ranks of the *yangban*, these distinctions sought to limit the size of the *yangban* status group and avoid diluting the group's elite power. In these ways, redefining the relation between men and women became a cornerstone for the Confucianization of Korea. This process strengthened the group status of the *yangban* even though specific social relationships might violate the norms of Confucian tradition. It also bore no resemblance to Chinese practice.

Education served *yangban* class purposes among both men and women of the Chosŏn elite. To be sure, *yangban* women did not study the same texts that male aspirants to the civil service examinations mastered, yet their proper conduct as "virtuous women" was learned, not natural, behavior. From the time they were young, females received lessons in social behavior designed

Hunmin Chŏngŭm, **1446. In this manuscript, Sejong first set forth the han'gŭl alphabet, the formulation of which he had completed three years earlier. The document is now one of Korea's National Treasures.**

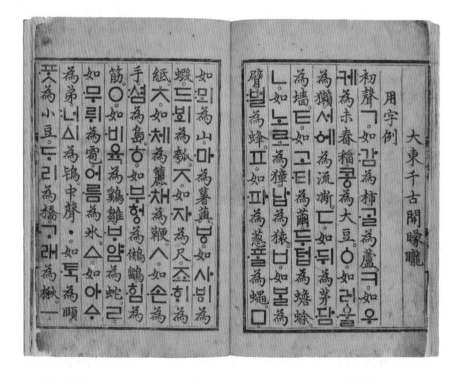

to make them act appropriately in their social roles, which also made them attractive marriage partners. They learned the four basics of womanly behavior from a manual derived from ancient Chinese texts: moral conduct, proper speech, correct appearance, and good womanly habits.

Although women were expected to learn these ideas, they were *not* expected to learn to read Chinese characters. Many likely did, but Korean women had an alternative; Korea's famous system of vernacular writing. In 1443, after much research and investigation of other writing systems, King Sejong (r. 1418–1450, also called Sejong the Great) proclaimed the invention of a new alphabet based on the sounds (*phonetics*) of spoken Korean. This did not imply rejection of the Chinese characters, which continued to be the dominant mode of writing, but rather was specifically designed to meet the need of the people, as the king explained, to write down their words as they spoke them (see p. 26).

Many *yangban* scholars objected, referring to the new system as "vulgar writing" in contrast to "truth writing" in classical Chinese. In fact, the announcement of the project caused a heated debate between Sejong and his conservative advisers, led by Ch'oe Malli, the highest-ranking academician in the Hall of Worthies. Ch'oe and others believed that the Korean alphabet threatened to harm the population's morality by diverting them from the activities proper to their status. Moreover, it threatened a crucial means for drawing class distinctions—literacy in classical Chinese. Despite their objections, this way of writing came to be widely used among people not formally educated in the Classics. This writing, now called *han'gŭl*, is officially used in both North and South Korea.

Recent research has revealed that many formally uneducated people, in particular elite women, became prolific writers and enriched Korean literary culture. Some wrote in Chinese characters, but the written language of choice for *yangban* women was the phonetic *han'gŭl*. Tens of thousands of lyrical poems, in a uniquely Korean style called *kasa*, have been discovered, giving us a glimpse into the day-to-day emotional lives of women in the latter half of the Chosŏn dynasty. Mostly anonymous, these poems were authored by women about whom little, if anything, is known. The erasure of these poets and many other women from the historical record ensured that literate men stood at the center of the historical sources from which our understanding of this era derives. Consequently, our view of the Chosŏn period consistently underplays the roles and contributions of women.

EXAMINATIONS AND THE LIMITED POWER OF A CENTRALIZED STATE

As in Ming China, the civil service examination system of the Chosŏn dynasty constituted the gateway to prestige, not only for an individual but also for his entire lineage. Under the Ming, however, anyone, from any social class, could take the civil service examination, whereas in the Chosŏn kingdom strict rules limited examination candidates to the recognized (not secondary) sons of *yangban* families. This undercut the meritocratic basis of the exams and affirmed the centrality of hereditary aristocratic status in Chosŏn. *Yangban* families educated their secondary sons alongside their "legitimate" half-brothers; but they remained ineligible for the exams. So, too, did the sons of *chungin* ("middle people"; hereditary clerks and functionaries), educated at home by their families. The Chosŏn system thus reinforced *yangban* power, the prestige of successful candidates and officials providing cultural capital for some lineages to set themselves above others.

In this competition for social prestige and high office, a few lineages with long histories of scholarship dominated the rosters of successful candidates. In the latter half of the dynasty, only 39 lineages produced an incredible 63 percent of the students who passed the highest-level exam. Unlike Ming China, where elite families struggled to preserve their status and wealth over time, in the Chosŏn system the examinations combined with hereditary *yangban* status, tax privileges, and primogeniture to allow dominant lineages to maintain their position at the top of social and political hierarchies for generations.

Headquartered for the most part in the vicinity of the capital, these powerful lineages had all the advantages of wealth, their money enabling them to hire the best teachers for lineage schools designed specifically to train their young men for the examinations. Of course, such high success rates also translated into political power with official appointment. Rather than broadening access to power, the examination system in the Chosŏn kingdom enabled a limited number of lineages to exert enduring power in both state and society.

The royal bureaucracy of Chosŏn provided the basis for one of the most centralized states in the world. Established at the beginning of the dynasty as part of the Confucianization of political life and institutions, and structured very much like the Ming state, the bureaucracy revolved around the capital of Seoul. Its central power extended throughout the kingdom through a hierarchy of officials, from the Six Ministers at the top to county magistrates at the bottom, the lowest officials appointed directly by the court. Connected by a centralized road and communication system, the state depended on a peninsula-wide tax on agricultural land—strongly resembling the Ming revenue system—and collected revenues on the basis of relatively regular, though imperfect, land surveys. Since *yangban* filled almost all official posts, the state, in turn, implemented policies that protected the group interests of the *yangban*.

Virtually all officials had passed the civil service examinations, but not all successful candidates could receive bureaucratic appointments. With the most numerous official appointments, the county magistracies, numbering only slightly over 300 for most of the dynasty, the bureaucracy could not absorb the roughly 30 candidates who annually emerged from the examination system. This resulted in a struggle for office among the powerful lineages of Seoul, which erupted in 1575 over the position of the Minister of Personnel, leading to the division of officialdom into two large, enduring factions, the Easterners and Westerners. Over time the Eastern faction split to produce Northern and Southern factions, and through the centuries these four basic alignments continued to divide and re-align in a bewildering array of groupings.

After 1575, factional strife remained a feature of bureaucratic politics and decision-making for the remainder of the dynasty, over 300 years. Like so many other features of Korean social life, even factional membership became hereditary. Sons adopted the factional allegiances of their fathers, allegiances further enforced by the teachers hired by lineage schools both for their intellectual abilities and for their factional commitment. This extended to the creation of marriage ties and social networks based on factional affiliation.

To be sure, factions constituted the means to political power at court and within the larger bureaucracy, yet factional struggles also involved divergent ideological stances and approaches to the philosophical and political issues of the day. As a result, highly charged issues—such as a seventeenth-century case on conducting the proper mourning rituals for the king's deceased mother, discussed in Chapter 3—could result in a refragmentation of factions, leading to new configurations that removed a dominant group from power. But the loss of power was never permanent. Vanquished factions retreated to their rural estates and lineage schools, living the life of retired scholars outside of bureaucratic politics, waiting for the opportunity to regain power and position in Seoul.

This endemic court factionalism weakened the centralized rule of the Chosŏn king. Without the ability to control, let alone eliminate, factions, most later monarchs worked through the factions, seeking to play one off against another but always needing to consider how their decisions would shape and be shaped by factional court politics. Thus, despite the centralized power of the state, expressed in a well-organized bureaucracy and the theoretical power of the king, factionalism severely limited royal prerogatives.

The difficulties faced by county magistrates even more vividly illustrated the limits of royal power at the local level. Ostensibly omnipotent in controlling the common people, each magistrate supervised a numerous and widely dispersed population. Living in isolated villages, spread out over hundreds of square miles often obstructed by mountains and valleys, the villagers could not easily be governed by a lone official who, according to dynastic law (similar to a Ming statute), could not be a native of the county.

Consequently, magistrates relied on local *yangban* to act as intermediaries. Like the local gentry of the Ming countryside, local *yangban* could use their community prestige and power to fulfill the magistrate's two most important objectives: the maintenance of peace and the collection of taxes. Such arrangements were mutually beneficial. The sponsorship of the local magistrate enhanced the status of rural *yangban*. At the urging of the magistrate, for example, they might hold special village meetings, like the Ming "village compacts," designed to promote Confucian values such as loyalty to the king and filial piety. This legitimated *yangban* status and prestige while inculcating state orthodoxy among commoners.

Such arrangements could also be fraught with tension, however, since the economic interests of local elites might very well run counter to those of the central government in the area of taxation. The Chosŏn state derived all of its revenues from collecting local economic resources into state coffers in the form of taxes, whether land tax, military tax, *corvée* labor demands, the grain loan system, or sundry taxes on specific goods.

Unable to collect all these taxes on their own, local magistrates depended on the cooperation of prominent *yangban* families to ensure the smooth running of the system. Yet such cooperation had its limits. After all, prominent local families often desired to keep economic resources in their localities and to use the revenue collection system to protect, if not expand, the wealth of their lineages and the privileges of their status group. This self-interest always guaranteed, for example, that state surveys of population and landholdings would be undermined by local elites, who often underreported the size of their estates to avoid paying their share of the land tax. The constant shrinking of the tax base required the government to conduct frequent, difficult, and expensive surveys.

LAND, SLAVES, AND COMMONERS

Asked about his wealth, a seventeenth-century *yangban* would likely respond by listing the amount of land and the number of slaves owned by his family. In the agricultural society of the Chosŏn dynasty, land and slaves were the basic sources of fortune and the main means of economic production. By 1600, most of the fertile land in the peninsula, with the exception of the far north, was already under cultivation, leaving Koreans few opportunities to open up new land.

In theory, the king owned all land, but in practice both law and custom recognized private landownership. Although many independent farmers tilled their own small plots, most agricultural laborers worked for *yangban* families or landowning government agencies as tenants or slaves. Historians disagree on the exact distribution of land and the extent of tenancy versus individual ownership, yet the laws on taxation favored the *yangban*, who used the state apparatus to protect their economic interests and shift the burden of taxation onto freeholding commoners.

Confucian ideology justified the economic privileges of the *yangban*. Serving as the exemplars—the models for emulation—for the transformation or maintenance of the moral fabric of society, they could pursue their moral self-cultivation only through everyone else's economic support. Such reasoning underlay many policies and laws, especially with regard to taxation. Using their control of the state, *yangban* granted themselves exemptions from virtually all taxes with the exception of the land tax. Moreover, slaves provided much of the labor in *yangban* households and enabled them to maintain sizable estates over generations without their own direct labor. Scholars have commonly estimated that by the seventeenth century somewhere around 20–30 percent of the population belonged to the slave class. As chattel property, slaves could be bought and sold or given away as presents by their owners, who for the most part were wealthy *yangban* or government bureaus.

Slaves' social lives varied tremendously. Some worked for government offices, tilling land that belonged to the local post station, for example, or carrying out duties for a local magistrate. The majority of private slaves lived far away from their owners, tilling a distant piece of the owner's land and returning 50 percent or more of the annual harvest to their owners. These slaves possessed a great deal of autonomy in their day-to-day lives, residing in their own houses and working according to their own schedule. Despite being owned by another person, their living situation in fact closely resembled that of a commoner farmer. Not liable for any tax burden, on rare occasions slaves accumulated enough wealth to buy land and other slaves or even to buy their own freedom. Other slaves worked and lived in the homes of their owners, a position considered the least fortunate since these household slaves had little distance from the often whimsical demands of their owners.

With *yangban* exempt from paying almost all but the land tax and slaves not liable for any taxes, the main burden for providing state revenues fell on the shoulders of the commoner farmers. Their lives were not easy. In addition to land taxes and the heavy military tax, every year the Chosŏn state required commoners to provide several weeks of *corvée* service. Pulled away from their regular occupations by the needs of either central or local officials, *corvée* laborers could find themselves far from home building, dikes, constructing roads, or merely shoveling the manure from a magistrate's stable.

Vulnerable to the whims of the magistrate and his tax collectors, who often added supplementary fees to the legally mandated tax burden, commoners had little recourse but to pay the levies demanded of them. So onerous was the burden that some commoner families sold themselves and, by consequence, all subsequent generations into slavery in order to gain the tax-free benefit of this lowest-status group. Other commoners abandoned their land and fled. Over time, the shrinking number of taxpayers became a serious problem.

The economic fragility of commoner families made it difficult to conform to the ideals of Confucian social life. As we have seen, the Confucian emphasis on family caused the Chosŏn state to pay special attention to household relationships. Yet commoners, like slaves, did not have surnames and did not have the resources to maintain the expanded lineages that were so crucial for *yangban* in living out the Korean version of Confucian ideals. Gender relations also differed enormously across status lines. *Yangban* could afford to cloister their women and by seclusion protect their virtue. Commoner women, however, worked and lived side by side with men.

Yangban women were encouraged to stay at home, practice their weaving, and manage household affairs. In agricultural families, women worked in the fields. In fishing villages, women helped process the daily catch. Gender thus became one more way of marking status, since only well-off families could afford the houses that enabled women to perform what Confucians had come to consider their proper roles in the inner chambers.

For these reasons, it is not at all clear how deeply Confucian morés penetrated the lives of people outside the *yangban* status group. The process of Confucianization that had been launched early in the Chosŏn dynasty had certainly transformed the life of the elite. A Confucian state had been built, as witness the resemblances between Chosŏn and Ming government. But even among the *yangban* elite, as we have seen, aristocracy and the direct descent of the lineage coexisted uneasily with the meritocratic impulses of Chinese-style Confucianism. The state and *yangban* exerted much effort in promoting "proper" social relations among the non-elite, and they succeeded to a degree. Nevertheless, in a variety of ways, including many popular religious practices, the non-elite population of the Chosŏn kingdom was never completely Confucianized.

The continued existence of Buddhism, despite centuries of repression, exemplifies the limits to the spread of Confucianism. Long considered the main rival of the state-sponsored ideology, Buddhism became the target of official attacks from the very beginning of the Chosŏn period. As in China, leading officials and scholars inveighed against its political and social evils. They designed policies to eliminate Buddhism completely from public life and even to restrain its influence in the private realm, banning Buddhist rituals from court. The state confiscated monasteries and their lands, while reducing the number of monks allowed to practice and study. By the early sixteenth century, Chosŏn law prohibited monks from entering the capital city, relegated the few remaining monasteries to distant mountains, and even banned the incantation of Buddha's name in the cities.

Despite these repressive measures, Buddhism survived, especially in the countryside. Some scholars continued to write commentaries on Buddhist theological issues, monasteries still received donations from their lay believers, and funerals were often conducted according to Buddhist rituals. Commoners, in particular, still celebrated Buddha's birthday as a festival in the villages, and groups of women undertook pilgrimages to popular Buddhist temples.

The state also failed entirely to eliminate widespread belief in spiritual mediums, or *mudang*—the people today referred to as shamans. Known for their ability to communicate with spirits, *mudang* retained their audiences among all status groups. Through their services, people sought to commemorate ancestors, obtain extra-worldly advice, learn propitious dates for weddings, divine their fortunes, and pray for good luck. Attempts to eradicate the influence of *mudang*—banning them from the capital and prohibiting them from participating in all state functions, among others—failed, since even the highest levels of society, including women inside the royal palace, demanded the skills of *mudang*.

Elite men may have shunned *mudang* as part of their commitment to Confucian teaching. But they were unable, and perhaps unwilling, to deny the women in their households the pleasure of observing a *mudang*'s ecstatic dance as she communicated with famous figures of the past in an effort to aid and comfort her clients. Indeed, participation in *mudang* rituals and observing Buddhist customs emerged as cultural markers that distinguished participants by status and gender from male *yangban*, who considered themselves the exemplars of correct social behavior. Male *yangban* sought to replace popular beliefs with more properly Confucian ideals. In fact, their status as a special, moral group committed to Confucianism depended on the presence of others—women, commoners, and slaves—who did not fully adhere to the *yangban* conventions. The continuing existence of these imperfectly cultivated groups confirmed the male *yangban*'s own moral superiority and the need to continue the process of Confucianization.

TRIBUTE AND INVASION

Chosŏn's relations with various dynasties in China went through cycles of harmony and conflict, but after the seventh century the two cultures had communicated primarily through the rituals, rhetoric, and institutions of the *tribute system*. At the core of the tributary relationship lay the personal bond between the two monarchs. As the sole possessor of Heaven's Mandate, the ruler in Beijing assumed the title of emperor, defining his sovereignty over "All Under Heaven." Just as there is only one sun in the sky, the saying went, there could be only one emperor. All other rulers were thus expected to accept the title of king. In the ritual vocabulary of tribute, this implied that the legitimacy of the king's rule depended on the good graces of the emperor.

Often characterized as kinship between an elder and younger brother, tribute relations were seen as mutually beneficial, like the Confucian principle of brotherly reciprocity. The Chosŏn court's recognition of the Ming emperor's claim to the Heavenly Mandate served as proof of Beijing's moral leadership. In return, the emperor's acceptance of the Chosŏn court confirmed the legitimacy of Korean kings. By 1600, Chosŏn had eagerly participated in this subordinate relationship to the Ming dynasty for almost two centuries.

Subordination in tribute relations expressed itself in a number of ways. Most famously, the Chosŏn court regularly sent tribute missions to the Ming, traveling the 600 miles (965 km) from Seoul to Beijing to celebrate the emperor's birthday, for example, or to offer congratulations and fraternal best wishes on the New Year. When a new Korean king ascended the throne, an envoy journeyed to Beijing to receive approval for his investiture. The emperor, as the Son of Heaven, sent a calendar to Korea every year, and the Chosŏn court officially used Ming reign-names to calculate time.

In practice, however, these testaments to subordination were often merely symbolic and frequently ignored. No Ming or Qing emperor, for example, ever tried to overturn a Korean decision about who would next assume the Chosŏn throne. Officials in Chosŏn often dated their documents with Chosŏn's own reign-names, and generally the Seoul court made decisions without any communication with the court in Beijing.

The Ming emperor did not overly concern himself with the internal dynamics of the Chosŏn court or its administration, so long as tribute missions arrived in Beijing to offer their uninterrupted obeisance to his rule. Unlike many other tributaries, Chosŏn rarely disappointed, sending an average of four missions a year; more than any of the Ming's other neighbors. This earned Chosŏn the top rank in all hierarchical lists of Ming tributary states. Even during periods of tension, tribute missions arrived, smoothing conflict or easing pressures. After all, the two courts communicated and negotiated difficulties through tribute relations.

Tributary relations with the Ming also became a factor in the internal political dynamics of Chosŏn. While the Ming never interfered in Chosŏn politics, the subordination of the king, however symbolic, acted as a

Admiral Yi Sunsin's turtle ships were among the world's earliest ironclads. This reproduction is housed in the National Military Museum in Seoul.

limit on a king's power. When some of the early Chosŏn kings tried to conduct sacrifices to Heaven, for example, court ministers pointed out that this ritual was the prerogative of the Son of Heaven alone. To undertake it would imply the usurpation of the Ming emperor's duty by the Chosŏn king. The theoretical dependence of the king on the emperor, then, offered one means for officials to fetter the growth of unrestrained monarchical power. The bureaucratic power of factions and powerful families as well as the tributary subordination of the king to the Ming emperor created a balance between the Chosŏn kings and their officials.

Seoul and Beijing also shared a strategic bond. As one proverb put it, Korea was to China as lips are to teeth; when the lips are gone, the teeth get cold. Seldom was this metaphor about the geopolitical importance of Korea to China more appropriate than in the late sixteenth century, when the new ruler of Japan, Toyotomi Hideyoshi, invaded Korea on his way to attack the Ming. En route to the north, the fleeing Chosŏn court sent a mission to Beijing, warning of Hideyoshi's ambitions and requesting military assistance. At first skeptical, Beijing could not believe that distant Japan would dare launch such an attack and worried that the Chosŏn court would side with the impudent (but very dangerous) Hideyoshi. The long history of tributary loyalty did not translate immediately into Ming assistance, and the initial requests were denied.

In the meantime, more than 20,000 irregular Korean soldiers, or *ŭibyŏng* ("righteous armies"), as they have come to be called, harassed Hideyoshi's troops throughout the peninsula in guerilla actions. Admiral Yi Sunsin (1545–1598) led what little remained of the Chosŏn navy to interfere with Japanese supply lines. Impregnable armored ships of Yi's own design—the so-called "turtle ships"—determined the Chosŏn fleet's control of the coastal waters. In one battle, Yi's three armored ships sank 39 of Hideyoshi's. But the Ming court continued to receive alarming reports about the peninsular war. In mid-summer 1592, when Hideyoshi's forces reached the Ming–Chosŏn frontier along the Yalu River, the Beijing court acknowledged the imminent danger of invasion. By January 1593, more than 50,000 Ming troops had crossed the frontier to confront Hideyoshi's armies on Chosŏn territory.

The war devastated the peninsula. Armies trampling over delicate irrigation networks ruined the water-dependent paddy rice fields. Farmers fled into the hills from advancing armies, often not returning and leaving their land fallow for years. Famine and disease led to a decrease in population, especially in the hard-hit southeastern part of the peninsula (Kyŏngsang province). Government records, documenting taxation rates and permanent slave status, went up in flames, as did homes and government offices, including much of Seoul. By the time the war ended with Hideyoshi's death in 1598, the economy of the peninsula had been ravaged, and it took decades to recover.

THE ORIGINS OF TOKUGAWA JAPAN

THE INTERNATIONAL CONTEXT

Toyotomi Hideyoshi (1536–1598), one of Japan's powerful sixteenth-century leaders, turned his sights to continental glory in 1586. He had already conquered all but a few provinces on the islands of Honshū, Shikoku, and Kyūshū and acquired the surname Toyotomi (Bountiful Minister). "I shall extend my conquest to China," Hideyoshi declared, beginning overtures to Chosŏn's King Sŏnjo to enlist his support in making the Toyotomi "name…known throughout…[Japan, China, and India]."[4]

Diplomatic missions to Chosŏn between 1587 and 1591 failed to obtain the king's agreement to support Hideyoshi's thrust into China, so Hideyoshi called up his troops in the fall of 1591. That was a busy time for him. Grieving the death of his toddler son and, soon thereafter, of his half-brother, he adopted his nephew as his heir. This adoption set off what would become a bloody succession dispute after the birth of his second son in 1593.

For Hideyoshi, glory outweighed mourning. His rapid assembly of 200,000 samurai warriors from the ranks of his *daimyō* (feudal lords) permitted him to launch his first overseas invasion in 1592. This ability to call on vassals indicated his growing legitimacy as a ruler of the *tenka* (the same term for "realm" as Ming China's "All Under Heaven"), the term used at that time rather than "state" or "nation," for which there were no Japanese equivalents until the nineteenth century. Hideyoshi's generals seized Seoul before being stopped by Korean resistance fighters, Ming armies assisting Chosŏn, and the Chosŏn navy under Admiral Yi Sunsin. Hideyoshi withdrew his forces to the far south of Korea in 1593, in return for a Ming promise that a daughter of the Ming emperor would be sent to marry the emperor of Japan.

In 1597, angered that the Ming had not yet sent a princess to Japan, Hideyoshi sent his army back to the peninsula. The Chosŏn navy again cut off Hideyoshi's ground forces, forcing them to sustain a siege that lasted until the invasion's abrupt termination when Hideyoshi died in 1598. In addition to the devastation of the peninsula and the weakening of the Ming state, Hideyoshi's ill-conceived adventures undermined his ability to transform his domestic battlefield successes into sustained government dominance by his family. Not only had he squandered the decade following his 1591 conquest of Japan with dreams of foreign glory, he also bled his most loyal *daimyō* supporters by sending their men overseas while allowing *daimyō* who would later compete with his son to build their strength at home.

Hideyoshi's invasions of Korea, destructive as they were, constituted but one part of Japan's much larger international posture in the sixteenth century. During the first half of the century, Japan had exported vast quantities of silver to China, whose immense domestic economy and international trade were based on silver (see p. 42). Legitimate merchants conducted some of this trade, while Japanese, Korean, and Chinese pirates known in Japanese as *wako* (c. *wokou*; κ. *waegu*) undertook the rest. By 1557, these pirates had so ravaged China's coastal towns that the Ming government suspended even officially authorized trade with Japan. Legitimate Japanese traders then sought additional markets throughout East Asia, including the Philippines and the Malay Peninsula. Sixteenth-century Japan exported silver, umbrellas, fans, and metal products (including swords) and imported silk, tropical foods, woods, medicines, sugar, and saltpeter (used in gunpowder).

China continued to be a major trading partner at century's end, but Portuguese and, later, Spanish ships carried most of the goods. This trade was global. A Portuguese ship would depart that country's colony of Goa (on the west coast of India) with cargo to be sold in the Portuguese colony of Macao in southern China. There it would take on silk to haul to Japan, where it traded the

Toyotomi Hideyoshi rose from a humble background to conquer Japan and invade Korea before his death in 1598. This woodblock print is based on a 1598 portrait by Kanō Sanraku (1559–1635).

silk for Japanese silver destined for China, then return to India laden with Chinese trade goods. Spanish ships, called Manila galleons, undertook a different triangular trade that embraced Mexico (its silver competing with Japan's), the Philippines, and Japan. Hideyoshi's suppression of piracy after 1587 eased trading for legitimate Japanese merchant ships, and until the early decades of the seventeenth century, they also took part in this lively system of trade in the western Pacific, based in part on the high price of silver in Ming China.

On the eve of the seventeenth century, Japanese trade lay primarily in private hands, though officials also took part. Like the Chosŏn kings, the fifteenth-century shoguns had official tribute relations with the Ming that continued till the middle of the sixteenth century. Several Japanese port cities grew from this trade. Profits from trade in non-tribute goods, shipped together with tribute items, far surpassed other types of income earned by the port city of Sakai (now a suburb of Osaka), for example. Sakai, with its commerce-based economy and opportune location at the eastern end of the Inland Sea, emerged as one of Japan's leading sixteenth-century cities.

In a still overwhelmingly rural Japan, several cities blossomed culturally. In the 1580s and 1590s, Hideyoshi, when not on the road to battle, moved between the imperial capital at Kyoto, where he studied tea ceremony and poetry; Osaka, where he performed in laudatory plays about himself; and Nagoya, his headquarters during the first Korean invasion, where he persuaded other *daimyō* to join him on stage. He patronized the arts ostentatiously. In 1585, he hosted a massive tea ceremony with thousands of guests—a flamboyant rendition of a ritual intended to be quiet and contemplative. In 1588, he invited the emperor to a series of banquets, at which this peasant's son read his own classical-style poetry and earned political legitimacy in exchange for generous funding that restored glamour to the emperor's rundown court. In addition, Hideyoshi built himself three elegant castles, a golden teahouse, and beautiful gardens.

Accompanying the newfound glory of the warrior elite, urban life took on a more artistic tone. Artworks in bright colors and gold leaf decorated cosmopolitan homes. The popular *samisen*, a musical instrument viewed today as a classic Japanese instrument, was at the time newly imported from the Ryūkyū islands (now Okinawa Prefecture). European fashions copied from sailors and merchants, like pantaloons and hats, as well as imported and locally produced Korean-style ceramics, became hot trends.

These two gold lacquer *tenmoku* teabowls were given by Hideyoshi's family to the abbot of Daigoji (near Kyoto) in thanks for the latter's prayers for Hideyoshi's wellbeing in the last year of his life. These bowls represent both Hideyoshi's flamboyant taste and his devotion to the tea ritual.

Hideyoshi's commanders also brought innovative Korean printing presses, with movable metal type, back from their mainland invasions. As Portuguese Jesuits in Japan at the time wrote, trade and temporary peace restored wealth throughout the realm.

THE END OF THE WARRING STATES PERIOD

Civil warfare was not entirely over at the end of the sixteenth century; in fact, major warfare broke out after Hideyoshi's death and continued as his successors, the Tokugawa family, consolidated power. Japan owed its

decade of political stability in the 1590s to its form of governance, which differed greatly from the monarchical systems in Ming and Chosŏn. Japan did have a monarch, whose dynasty had already reigned for more than a millennium. But the emperor had not held the reins of power since the late twelfth century, though twice attempting, in the thirteenth and fourteenth centuries, to reassert his authority.

Instead, military lords and their vassals created a political system that resembled medieval European feudalism. The erosion of the emperor's centralized economic and political control led to a war among samurai warriors in the late twelfth century. From this war the most powerful military family (Minamoto-Hōjō) emerged as de facto rulers, gaining legitimacy through being invested by the otherwise impotent emperor with the title of shogun (great general).

Samurai were arranged in hierarchical relationships of vassalage (a vassal vowed loyalty and service to a lord in exchange for protection of life and property) with the shogun as the highest feudal lord. The system was not entirely stable, and internal and external pressures, especially from the Mongols in the late thirteenth century, undermined the shogun's dominance.

Renewed warfare in the fourteenth century ended with a shaky balance of power among dozens of provincial lords and a new family, the Ashikaga, invested with the title of shogun from 1336 to 1568. That balance crashed in 1467 amid succession disputes and a struggle for power among newly emerging provincial forces. During the next 130 years—the Warring States era—coalitions of samurai, supported by villagers whose output they could commandeer, fought their samurai neighbors for increasingly larger areas of control. By the mid-sixteenth century, the largest of these feudal lords came to be known as *daimyō*, and from those ranks arose three powerful warriors, Oda Nobunaga (1534–1582), Hideyoshi, and Tokugawa Ieyasu (1544–1616), who unified the realm.

The villages provided most of the wealth for the rise of powerful *daimyō* lords from among the hundreds of small-scale samurai lords. Not all samurai lords survived the rough-and-tumble warfare of the early sixteenth century. Those who enjoyed good relations with villagers, either by being trusted land stewards or part-time samurai-farmers, were more likely to mobilize the villages' output for their own benefit, which, in turn, permitted the consolidation of larger territories under their control. Oppressed villagers voted with their feet, absconding to areas under the control of lords who either taxed at lower rates or accorded greater autonomy to village leaders. Valuable though land was, it was worthless without peasants to farm it. Thus, in many areas of Japan, villages gradually developed methods of self-government, because feudal lords who recognized the value of harmonious villages won larger territories.

This does not mean that sixteenth-century villages were democratic. Local governance varied from village to village, and many had some type of process whereby all long-established households had a voice in decisions that affected the community, including allocating wood, fodder, fertilizer, common land, and irrigation water, as well as deciding on codes and regulations. Many villages had a Shintō or Buddhist association in which all households had a stake.

At the same time, however, household wealth and prestige varied greatly, as did village leadership roles. Large households might include not only the family head and his immediate family, but also the heir (often but not always the eldest son—and on rare occasions a daughter) and his family, adult unmarried children, siblings of the heir and their families, hereditary servants, and others. Some of these extended-family households, genealogical records indicate, had dozens of members.

Just as differences among households meant that villages were not run democratically, differences within households also gave greater status to some members over others. By the end of the sixteenth century, females, in most cases, could become household heads or heirs only in the absence of a competent male, although in earlier centuries women had not only inherited property but could also serve as family heads.

Official documents do not offer much comment on peasant activities as gendered, but they do indicate that men, women, and children all participated in communal social activities like dancing and singing at religious festivals. Women were neither sequestered nor prevented from having relationships with men, including intimate relationships that might lead to marriage. Some records noted the presence of women's community halls, which became commonplace in later centuries. In the medieval period, these halls had both recreational and economic functions. Women could relax with other women and take part in community food preparation for festivals or survival.

Women were responsible for most of the spring rice planting and the fall threshing and hulling. They went out to sell vegetables, wood, and farm products. Popular plays depict rural husbands as lazy carousers and wives as hardworking and reliable. The effective functioning of the village household required both men and women, so the sexual divisions of the samurai warrior class (see p. 63) were not as evident in the villages. Nevertheless, men increasingly played superior ceremonial and political roles on behalf of the family, including participation in village associations.

Heads of the largest extended households in the Warring States period often were part-time samurai-farmers, elevating them not only above other members of their families but also above the heads of less prestigious families. They mediated village disputes or oversaw some of the farming activities of their less wealthy neighbors. They might supply tasty foods at village festivals, in exchange receiving a few days of labor from other village families. The latter remained in a subordinate relationship to the leading families, who met more of the village's economic needs while the average families supplied more of its labor. Though mutually beneficial, this relationship remained hierarchical, and the leading families had greater though not exclusive voice in village matters. Canny *daimyō* took advantage of village hierarchy, coopting leading families by acknowledging their ability to run their villages autonomously.

Similarly, some villages were more independent than others, particularly villages organized around Buddhist temples. Buddhist teachings hold that life is full of suffering caused by selfishness and greedy attachment to worldly things, and that human beings

57

must undergo rebirth in this suffering world until they end their selfishness. "Salvation," often called "enlightenment," occurs when one ceases to be reborn and blends, like a drop of water into a great sea, with the cosmos. Japanese Buddhism in its earliest days (from the sixth through the twelfth centuries) had been centered in monasteries where monks and nuns, often of the privileged classes, practiced a secret, intellectual religion aimed at personal salvation. In the thirteenth century, Buddhist scholars in Japan, basing themselves largely in ideas imported from China and Korea, had developed faith-based sects that appealed to common folk and elites alike. These new sects included *Zen* (c. *Chan*, k. *Chon*), which attracted the warrior elite with its emphasis on self-denial, meditation, and sudden enlightenment; *Hokke*, which advocated salvation by faith in the Lotus Sutra (a principal Buddhist scripture) alone; and Pure Land, which emphasized salvation through faith in Amida (SANSKRIT *Amitabha*), the Buddha of the Western Paradise, a kind of heaven where the faithful would be reborn.

Villages organized around *Hokke* and Pure Land temples constituted lay congregations that became increasingly militant in the defense of both their faith and their livelihoods during the Warring States period. Oda Nobunaga found these villages to be one of the greatest challenges to his rise to dominance. After sending the last Ashikaga shogun packing and thereby ending the shogunate in 1568, Nobunaga began his program of conquest, systematically absorbing other *daimyō*'s territories. But Pure Land and *Hokke* villages, communally organized and motivated by religious ideals, put up strong defenses against Nobunaga, who attacked them with extreme violence. His forces killed 20,000 men, women, and children in one brutal struggle in 1574. Three years before, he had attacked the 600-year-old temple community on Mt. Hiei, northeast of Kyoto. Burning 300 monastic buildings, including residences, libraries with irreplaceable treasures, and prayer halls, he then slaughtered those who managed to survive the battle—3,000 women, men, and children.

As an emblem of his power, Nobunaga built the enormous Azuchi Castle (1576–79). He filled it with art intended to glorify his rule and call attention to his understanding of proper sovereignty. In the castle's great keep, he had each floor lavishly painted by the great master Kanō Eitoku (1543–1590), using fine colors and gold leaf. The sixth floor contained Buddhist images, but the highest floor, the one that superseded the spiritual realm of Buddhism, contained paintings of Chinese culture-heroes and images of Confucian government, as if Nobunaga himself were worthy of Heaven's Mandate. Despite his propaganda and self-aggrandizement, however, Nobunaga died in a most ordinary way, assassinated by one of his vassals in 1582.

HIDEYOSHI'S PACIFICATION

Nobunaga's assassination afforded Hideyoshi the opportunity to seize power. Intercepting a message, he learned of Nobunaga's death and mobilized his forces secretly to attack the assassin. He then began his march to conquest. His successes stemmed both from his ability to deal with *daimyō* whom he either conquered or controlled as vassals and from his superior understanding of the villages.

Like Nobunaga, he had to neutralize the rural areas, but he viewed their power in a more nuanced and political way. Nobunaga had gone after uppity villagers with his sword. Hideyoshi, on the other hand, approached them creatively. He recognized that some rural samurai-farmers might become leaders, as he himself had, and so they had to be deprived of that opportunity. He also saw that taxation of farm production was the basis of *daimyō* power and must be preserved through accommodating the producers. Finally, he knew that farmers mostly wanted to get on with their lives and the autonomous running of their villages. To those ends, he issued in 1588 the famous "Sword Hunt" edict, disarming all villagers:

> *The farmers…are strictly forbidden to possess…
> any form of weapon….Swords collected…shall
> be [melted down and] used…in the forthcoming
> construction of the Great Buddha….If farmers
> possess agricultural tools alone and engage
> completely in cultivation, they shall [prosper]
> unto eternity.*[5]

Hideyoshi's Great Buddha had an ill-fated history: earthquakes, fires, and other natural disasters destroyed wooden and bronze versions in 1596, 1602, 1622, and 1789. In 1591, Hideyoshi followed the Sword Hunt with the Edict on Changing Status, which stipulated that any samurai who returned to settle in his native village should be expelled, that no villager could become a town merchant, and that samurai who left their *daimyō* could not be hired by other *daimyō*. To maximize the efficiency of taxation, he ordered surveys of villagers' land and its productivity.

By the time he began showing signs of what would be his fatal illness, Hideyoshi had established, with these edicts, what he believed would be peace, prosperity, and stability. His edicts created hereditary social statuses (samurai, farmers, and townsfolk) specifically charged to carry out prescribed functions. All of the *daimyō* fell nicely under his control. He could tax the farmers, who could live in peace without the threat of a militarized countryside. Although the division into status groups of samurai, farmer, and townsfolk (artisans and merchants) was never as rigid or permanent as Hideyoshi had intended, the countryside never rearmed, and farmers were able to manage their own affairs without the samurai. This removal of the elite from the villages distinguished Japan very clearly from Chosŏn Korea and Ming China, where many *yangban* and gentry continued to own agricultural land and live in rural areas.

Hideyoshi's edicts applied only to lands under his own direct control, but *daimyō* throughout the realm soon emulated them. When Hideyoshi removed his samurai from the countryside, he housed them in barracks surrounding his castles. *Daimyō* did likewise, moving their own samurai into the areas surrounding their castles. In the last decades of the sixteenth century, when European-style cannon, some cast by Jesuit scientists, joined the Japanese arsenal, castle architecture had been transformed. Since an enemy might have artillery, a proper castle required a huge stone base capable of protecting the samurai defenders against cannon fire, topped by a central tower made of wood, in which the *daimyō* and his family lived. The lodgings of the vassal samurai formed a defensive perimeter around the castle.

Hideyoshi and the *daimyō* mobilized thousands of workers to build castles, roads, drainage ditches, bridges, port facilities, and temples, and each castle became the center of a town. Military quartermasters, accustomed to filling orders for weapons, food, and other logistical needs during wartime, organized these massive peacetime construction efforts. In time professional artisans replaced the quartermasters. Most of the labor force came from the countryside.

Kanō Shigenobu, *Bamboo and Poppies*, c. 1625 (detail). Works of the Kanō school combined Chinese-style ink painting with bright colors and rich use of gold. Large works like this screen decorated walls and rooms in samurai and shogunal buildings.

HOSOKAWA GRACIA TAMA

Honored as a model samurai wife in the seventeenth century and pronounced a Catholic saint in 1862, Hosokawa Gracia Tama (1563–1600) has usually been presented as a perfect woman. While embellishment may have made some of the details of her life a bit murky, we do know that Hosokawa actually lived a complex and very human life. Born to great privilege in 1563, Tama was the daughter of Akechi Mitsuhide, a high-ranking *daimyō* and vassal of Oda Nobunaga. Apparently beautiful and well educated—Jesuits with whom she later studied Christianity claimed she had studied Buddhist texts seriously as a young girl—at age 15 she married Hosokawa Tadaoki, a powerful and wealthy *daimyō* who, like her father, was allied with Nobunaga. Tama moved to her husband's castle near Kyoto in 1578.

The grave of Hosokawa Gracia Tama at Daitokuji in Kyoto.

Depicted as the perfect *daimyō*'s wife, Tama raised two children in the years from her marriage until 1582, when her father Mitsuhide assassinated Oda Nobunaga at Honnoji Temple in Kyoto. Toyotomi Hideyoshi immediately set out to fill Oda's shoes as overlord of the realm, and Hosokawa Tadaoki—like Tokugawa Ieyasu and other powerful lords—joined Hideyoshi and turned on his father-in-law. Within days, Mitsuhide was killed by peasants, and his forces scattered. Surrounded by hostile forces in the Akechi family's castle, Tama's mother, sisters, and brothers set the building on fire and died. Living with Hosokawa, Tama survived, but as a daughter of a treacherous vassal, she was soon divorced and sent into exile in a remote area of Japan, rejoining her husband two years later.

In 1587, while Hosokawa Tadaoki fought under Hideyoshi's command in Kyūshū, Tama accepted baptism as a Roman Catholic and took the name Gracia. Her conversion has been variously attributed to the influence of her Christian lady-in-waiting, Kiyohara Maria Kojijo, or of her husband's friend, Takayama Ukon, a prominent Christian *daimyō*. She also maintained close ties with several Catholic priests whom she impressed with her erudition. In 1600, while her husband fought alongside Tokugawa Ieyasu at the Battle of Sekigahara, Tama was threatened with abduction by one of the Hosokawa family's enemies. In accounts depicting her as a dutiful wife, Tama committed suicide rather than allowing herself to be captured. In Christian accounts, however, she has been portrayed as being killed by a trusted retainer, who was either following Tadaoki's instructions or helping Tama with a kind of suicide-by-assistant—suicide being sinful in a Christian context.

Tadaoki was well rewarded for his assistance to the Tokugawa, and lived out his years as a successful *daimyō*, a renowned man of culture, and a master of the tea ceremony, having learned that art from Sen no Rikyū. Though she lived just 37 years, Hosokawa Gracia Tama has been constructed in multiple ways—as an upper-class daughter, a *daimyō* wife during a time of civil war, a Christian convert, and a martyr. After her death, others molded her memory as a pair of myths, creating both a Christian saint and a model dutiful Japanese wife, neither image coinciding entirely with her short but tumultuous life.

Daimyō conscripted farmers to work on their own construction projects and on those for which Hideyoshi demanded support.

For example, Hideyoshi requisitioned from his *daimyō* approximately 250,000 workers to build his grand castle at Fushimi. Farmers supplied the brawn needed for construction, learning how to make tiles and walls, roofs and brackets. After the completion of the projects for which they were conscripted, many stayed in the growing urban areas as artisans and laborers, disregarding the edict prohibiting individuals from changing their status-based residences and professions. These new urban settlers built shops large and small, as did merchants drawn from other towns by offers of trade benefits and free land for stores and warehouses. By the end of the sixteenth century, there were—in addition to the emperor's capital of Kyoto, the port city of Sakai, and the towns that had sprung up around temples—at least 90 new "castle towns." They grew rapidly in the next century, and virtually all of the 100 largest cities in contemporary Japan (except Kyoto and Osaka) got their start as castle towns.

Like Nobunaga, Hideyoshi used grand architectural monuments as symbols of power. Legions of conscripted laborers built castles and temples, decorated in the most ornate and often ostentatious styles. The bold and lavish paintings of Kanō Eitoku and his followers (the "Kanō School"), patronized by the rich and powerful, continued to dominate painting for several decades into the next century. Europeans, with their odd clothing, appearance, and strange objects of daily life, became another popular theme in artwork patronized by urban connoisseurs, a style called *nanban* art, pictures of the "southern barbarians."

Townsfolk, whether merchants, samurai, or the highest level elite (*daimyō* and the nobility), were not the only ones to patronize and enjoy artistic production. From the fourteenth to the sixteenth century, itinerant storytellers, many of them originally monks and nuns, brought their multimedia presentations to villages and mansions alike. These performances, usually presented by a single artist, included song, dance, recitation, instruments, puppets, and pictures to accompany the text or songs. The stories could be secular, religious, or a blend of the two. Traveling throughout the country, visiting rich and poor, these male and female performers helped to develop a national culture.

By the end of the sixteenth century, some of the individual artists formed larger troupes, which continued to move from place to place, entertaining all classes of society. In time, urban elites built permanent theaters to present plays with actors or puppets. Women actors disappeared in the seventeenth century, replaced with men even in women's roles, but in the sixteenth century, women were still free to perform, though often under the guise of being nuns to avoid being taken for prostitutes, which many of them were.

Hideyoshi enjoyed popular arts as well as "high culture." In addition to writing poetry, Hideyoshi studied the Dao of Tea (J. *Chadō*) with the great tea master, Sen no Rikyū, who fashioned the making and drinking of tea into the simple, intimate ritual known today as "tea ceremony." But, for reasons that historians still cannot fathom, Hideyoshi—clearly a complex and unpredictable leader—ordered this important artist to commit suicide in 1591.

One of Hideyoshi's areas of disappointment lay in foreign policy. Obsessed with self-aggrandizement, he failed to recognize the folly of his Korean invasions. His vassals did, however, and they terminated the expedition immediately after Hideyoshi's death. In part because of Hideyoshi's foreign adventures, Japan's subsequent rulers, the Tokugawa, distrusted foreign relations and maintained a strong desire to minimize and strictly control them. Indeed, the Tokugawa shogunate kept all of Japan's important port cities in its own hands, not giving them to *daimyō* as fiefs.

Christians presented Hideyoshi with a related problem. Europeans had been arriving in the islands since a shipwreck in 1543 brought three Portuguese ashore with arquebuses. These early muskets altered the course of warfare, for Nobunaga and a few other *daimyō* used firearms to great tactical advantage. Thereafter, Portuguese ships began arriving in greater numbers, bringing not only new products but also Jesuit missionaries, starting in 1549. The success of the missionaries was tied to their involvement with trade. *Daimyō* converted to Roman Catholicism to facilitate trade and often forced their vassals to convert as well.

By the 1580s, as many as 200,000 Kyūshū residents of all classes had adopted the foreign faith. Hideyoshi first noticed the divisive role played by Christians in 1586 while fighting his rivals there. He issued two edicts, one to expel missionaries and one to limit the propagation of Christianity. And yet, a few years later, Hideyoshi treated Jesuits cordially and offered land in Kyoto to the rival Franciscan order. Hideyoshi apparently did not intend his first expulsion and limitation edicts to be applied generally. Rather, he directed them at a particular group of Jesuits in Nagasaki who encouraged destruction of Shintō shrines and Buddhist temples, served as currency brokers for Kyūshū daimyō, and invested in shares of Portuguese trading ships.

By the mid-1590s, Hideyoshi increasingly worried about the missionaries, especially as the rival Franciscans and Jesuits persuasively discredited one another in the eyes of their Japanese hosts. The rivalry of these two religious orders, while Hideyoshi's representatives negotiated with the captain of a silver-laden Spanish galleon shipwrecked in Japanese waters, provoked fears that the missionaries formed the leading edge of Spanish and Portuguese colonization. This convinced Hideyoshi to execute six Franciscans, three Jesuit lay brothers, and seventeen Japanese Christian converts in 1596. But he took few other actions, as trade was too valuable to Hideyoshi to risk offending the Iberians at that time. Systematic expulsion of Christians came later, under the Tokugawa.

THE ROAD TO SEKIGAHARA

Hideyoshi, like Nobunaga before him, had taken Japan a long way toward political unity. But this unity depended on the loyalty and economic support of daimyō, who continued to maintain considerable autonomy. Japan was far less centralized than Ming, Chosŏn, or its European contemporaries. Though Hideyoshi's daimyō proved their loyalty through donations of money, labor, and soldiers, he had not yet called on them to justify their continued existence by competent peacetime administration, as Tokugawa Ieyasu and his successors later did.

Ieyasu had received a highly productive fief in exchange for military assistance to Hideyoshi. In 1590, Hideyoshi moved Ieyasu to the huge Kantō plain in eastern Japan in exchange for the Tokugawa domain in the Tōkai region, closer to Hideyoshi's own territories. The Kantō plain, Japan's most expansive rice farming area, had enormous potential productivity. It had been the home territory of Japan's first shoguns in the late twelfth century and remains the most populous heartland of Japan today.

Ieyasu collected sufficient taxes from his villagers to fund a powerful military and build a strong castle town. He set about creating a new capital, selecting a small fishing village of only 200 souls along Edo creek, mired in a swamp. In this unprepossessing spot, Ieyasu built a castle town that he called Edo, boasting 5,000 houses by 1610 and 150,000 residents ten years later. Within a century, Edo (now Tokyo) had become one of the world's largest cities, with over a million inhabitants.

As Hideyoshi and Nobunaga had done, in the 1590s Ieyasu mobilized his own and his vassals' peasants. They cleared forests; cut massive amounts of lumber needed to construct castles, barracks, temples, and mercantile buildings; laid roads and canals; dredged rivers; and built bridges and docks. He needed porters and teamsters, stonemasons, laborers, charcoal makers, silversmiths, ironsmiths, and carpenters. He made exhaustive use of natural resources, especially lumber, a despoiling of the environment that would have to be addressed later in the Tokugawa period. On the other hand, deforestation increased land for farming, thereby enhancing the domain's tax revenues.

Ieyasu's power was soon put to the test. On his deathbed in 1598, Hideyoshi appointed Ieyasu as one of five regents to administer the realm until his son Toyotomi Hideyori came of age. Hideyoshi believed the five, potentially rivals, would keep an eye on one another and preserve the peace. Within two years, however, tensions erupted into a renewal of warfare. Ieyasu and his allies among the daimyō raised an army of 80,000 men and challenged Hideyori's supporters at Sekigahara in the fall of 1600. Victory in this battle permitted Tokugawa Ieyasu to reward his followers, gain new allies, and punish his opponents by either eliminating or reducing their domains.

The process of consolidating power by transferring daimyō or taking away their territories continued until the middle of the seventeenth century, but the Battle of Sekigahara established Tokugawa hegemony. Ieyasu moved Hideyori and his family to one of the Toyotomi castles, at Osaka, where they remained until the Tokugawa eliminated them in 1615. Like his predecessor, Tokugawa Ieyasu sought legitimation from the emperor. Granting wealth (but still no power) to the Kyoto court, he felt entitled to ask for the title of shogun, which the emperor conferred in 1603.

Ieyasu rose to power for many reasons, most of them associated with clever, often ruthless governance. His productive agricultural base in the Kantō permitted him to field a large army—armies, after all, marched on their stomachs. As we have seen, Ieyasu made extensive use of natural resources, though his cutting of forests was recognized as excessive by later shoguns who undertook reforestation and by some *daimyō*, contemporary with Ieyasu, who practiced forest conservation. His construction projects surpassed even Hideyoshi's, and that meant conscripting thousands of farmers.

Ieyasu was not alone in mistreating those loyal to him, and, like Hideyoshi, he saw women as subordinate and used them in a cynical way. Samurai women, unlike village women, were seen as "borrowed wombs" (J. *hara wa karimono*) for the creation of the samurai's progeny, although they, too, in centuries past (as in Chosŏn), had been able to inherit property as well as titles and the feudal responsibilities that accompanied those titles. In the Warring States period, Nobunaga, Hideyoshi, and Ieyasu all practiced a form of marriage politics that placed wives, sisters, daughters, and even mothers in jeopardy.

Confucian veneration of parents and ancestors did not yet play a role in Japanese ideology, as it did in China and Korea. Women were often expected to act as spies for their natal or married families, and as a result women came to be seen as treacherous and untrustworthy. Early in the era of unification, Nobunaga married his daughter to Ieyasu's eldest son to cement a tie with his young vassal. This daughter reported to her father that Ieyasu's first wife was plotting to kill Nobunaga and set up the son (her own husband) in her father's place. Ordered by Nobunaga to avert this plot, Ieyasu dutifully killed his wife and son.

All three of the great military leaders practiced cruelties through marriage. Nobunaga (falsely) told his wife that her father's retainers were plotting against him. She reported this to her father, who had these (actually loyal) retainers put to death, thereby leading to his own downfall. Ieyasu's father divorced his own wife, the sister of a man against whom Nobunaga had turned, to show his loyalty to his lord. To conclude a peace treaty with Ieyasu, Hideyoshi forced the divorce of his 43-year-old, happily married sister in order to give her to Ieyasu, whereupon her first husband committed suicide.

Ieyasu also used women as hostages or spies. The most poignant case occurred 12 years after he married his granddaughter Senhime to Hideyoshi's son Hideyori. When the Tokugawa army captured her husband in Osaka castle in 1615, Senhime, though permitted to survive, had to suffer the execution of her little son at the hands of her father's forces. The status of women depended on their social class, with samurai women continuing to be more subordinate to men of their class than women in other classes were to their menfolk.

DIASPORAS

Chinese, Japanese, and Korean sailors left their homelands to trade as merchants or raid as pirates throughout the western Pacific—first in Korea, then along the Chinese coast, where the richest ports and targets could be found. The foreign trade policies of Ming, Chosŏn, and successive Japanese governments often made commerce difficult, so the seafarers turned to coastal invasion to enrich themselves. Usually referred to as "Japanese pirates," by the late Ming period most of these men were Chinese, who worked with Japanese and Korean brigands to pillage the coast, from Korea to Guangdong, when Ming sea power waned. They lived on islands, including Taiwan, and could raise fleets of several hundred small ships for concerted actions.

Despite some victories, the Ming never developed a centralized coastal defense force, so they sought alliances, in at least two cases with the Portuguese, to resist the pirates. As trade barriers came down in the sixteenth century, many of the pirates returned to legitimate commerce, and Hideyoshi's effective central government both suppressed piracy and prevented Japanese commoners from arming themselves in Japan. At their height, the pirates constituted a kind of primitive diaspora, spending their lives at their substantial island bases far from home. Apart from them, few Japanese or Koreans lived abroad before the nineteenth century, and none established what we could call overseas settlements.

Not so the Chinese. By the fifteenth century, permanent Chinese trading communities had already been established around the South China Sea, and they grew to considerable size as intercultural trade expanded over the next two centuries, in part stimulated by the arrival of the Europeans. Using fair-sized ships called *juncos* in Portuguese (from which comes the English name "junk"), merchants of southern China, most of them from Fujian and Guangdong, dominated the long-distance shipping lanes of the Malay Peninsula, Sumatra, Java, Borneo, and the Philippines. They exchanged the manufactured goods of China, for which there was demand everywhere, for Southeast Asian raw materials and foodstuffs—pepper and other spices, gold, tin, and teak wood. The shallow draft junks, which could sail only before the wind, suited the predictable monsoon winds and shallow waters of the South China Sea.

By 1600, dozens of private Chinese ships per year arrived in the newly founded Spanish colonial city of Manila, where they traded the luxury goods of Ming artisans for silver and gold brought across the Pacific by the Spaniards from Acapulco and other colonial ports of New Spain. Indeed, Chinese merchants settled from Manila to Malacca and became the trusted agents of many local states, undertaking licensed foreign trade (usually a state monopoly) as well as tax collection and production. These functions brought them great wealth but did not endear them to local populations, a pattern that continues to the present day, as the wealthy commercial Chinese communities of Southeast Asia continue to come under attack as foreign exploiters.

The coming of the Europeans—first the Portuguese and Spanish, then the Dutch and finally the British—gave these Chinese traders new opportunities, and their communities grew. Chinese merchants married into many different cultures and laid the foundations for *mestizo* (mixed-race) communities and long-term presence in places as diverse as Siam (Thailand), the Philippines, the Malay Peninsula, and Java, where some of them converted to Islam.

CONNECTIONS

The most obvious connection among the three East Asian cultures around 1600 lay in Toyotomi Hideyoshi's desire to conquer the Ming by using the Chosŏn kingdom as his road. Ming and Chosŏn troops and local *ŭibyŏng* thwarted his ambitions until his death without an adult heir (1598) turned his vassals away from mainland conquest back to civil war. The peninsular conflict laid waste Korea's economy and cost the Ming dearly in

blood and treasure, affecting both states and cultures for decades to come.

Under the obvious political, diplomatic, and military confrontations of the 1590s lay a much deeper set of linkages among China, Korea, and Japan as *cultures*. They shared a vast literature written in Chinese characters, the non-phonetic literary script ("truth script") of the classical learning, history, philosophy, religion, and poetry of the entire region. Though Korea and Japan had indigenous scripts (now called *han'gŭl* and *kana*), literate men and some women read and wrote in classical Chinese. Not only Confucianism but also Buddhism and Daoism could be imbibed through these texts, and all East Asian elites partook of their wisdom. They thus shared the theory of *yin* and *yang*, acupuncture, the idea of reign-names, ancient Chinese history, and many other cultural features conveyed in texts. By 1610, even Roman Catholicism was available in classical Chinese through the writings and translations of Matteo Ricci and his Jesuit colleagues, so Korean and Japanese readers could obtain them through land and sea trade routes, though their governments tried to prevent it.

In family and social structure, by 1600 China and Korea had been powerfully influenced by Buddhist then Confucian patriarchy (or its indigenous equivalents), and Japan had begun to absorb its principles. Treatment of women had not become identical, however, since indigenous ideas about gender continued to influence people—the power of Korean female *shamans*, for example, or of female Buddhist deities. The organization of the patriline had some common features, such as ancestor veneration, genealogies, and inheritance through the male line, but Chinese society stressed partible inheritance, while most Koreans and Japanese practiced unigeniture (single inheritance).

Ming and Chosŏn strongly resembled one another in the structure of government centered around the emperor and king who both reigned and ruled, as well as the Six Ministries, the primacy of civil over military officials, the appointment (for limited terms) of central officials to govern provinces and counties, and much more. As Japan achieved unification out of the chaos of the sixteenth century, however, its state structure took on a very different character, since it was based on the dominance of warriors (samurai), led by lords (*daimyō*) who ruled over their fiefs with considerable autonomy.

It was relationship between lord and vassal, rather than the bureaucratic loyalty to a monarch, which constituted the most powerful bond in the early years of the seventeenth century.

The elites of Ming China and Chosŏn Korea could live either in cities or in rural areas. In retirement or retreat from government, they returned from Beijing, Seoul, or other metropolitan centers to lands owned by their families, where members of their patrilines managed their estates or businesses. The Japanese elite of *daimyō* and samurai, however, moved irreversibly from their native countryside to castle towns, constructed under Nobunaga, Hideyoshi, and the early Tokugawa shoguns, leaving the villages more independent and self-governing than they could be in Ming or Chosŏn.

Chosŏn shared its preference for *aristocracy* more with Japan than with the Ming, where *meritocracy* held sway, to some extent, through the system of civil service examinations. In addition, the warriors who formed the ruling elite of Japan allowed the emperor, a venerated figure without much political power, to continue to reign (without ruling) in the old capital of Kyoto.

Finally, and perhaps most "modern" in our eyes, the three realms—all calling themselves "All Under Heaven"—traded with one another and with the rest of the world. Japanese silver and swords, Korean ginseng and pottery, Chinese silk and printed books, these goods and many more flowed in ships (with crews of many cultures) and caravans. Silver, gold, new food plants, and exotic textiles came across the Pacific from the Spanish and Portuguese New World colonies, and many products, from spices to cloth to handicrafts, returned to Europe, the Philippines, or Southeast Asia on the same ships. People also moved among the cultures—merchants, pirates, potters and other artisans, Jesuits, and diplomatic representatives.

To sum up, China, Korea, and Japan in 1600 already participated in a complex international system of trade and diplomacy, war and cultural exchange that included East Asians, Southeast Asians, Latin Americans, Africans, and Europeans. Their cultures and governments both differed and resembled one another, each unique but sharing more than our modern "national histories" usually recognize.

CHAPTER THREE

THE SEVENTEENTH CENTURY

WORLD CONTEXT

Thirty years after Tokugawa Ieyasu took the title of shogun in 1603, the Manchu Qing empire arose north of Chosŏn, northeast of the Ming. First forcing Chosŏn into tributary status, they then invaded the Ming. They gradually expanded their territory to include the cultural worlds of China, Mongolia, eastern Central Asia, and Tibet, as well as their own homeland, now usually known in English as Manchuria. Between the 1630s and 1750s, they created an immense multicultural empire, the most populous on earth, which endured for almost three centuries. At the opposite end of the Eurasian continent, equally momentous changes occurred as European kingdoms, from England (soon to be Great Britain) to Russia, also began their expansion into great empires by land and sea, first by invading and conquering the "New World" of North and South America.

The seventeenth century also saw the height of the Mughal empire in India. Under three of its greatest leaders—Jahangir (r. 1605–1627), Shah Jahan (r. 1628–1658), and Aurangzeb (r. 1658–1707)—the Mughal state displayed the complex brilliance and grandiosity of cultural synthesis, embodying Indian, Persian, and Central Asian elements from warfare to religion to architecture. Creating wonders like the Taj Mahal and a cosmopolitan literature of Turkish, Hindi, Arabic, Urdu, and Persian poetry, the seventeenth-century Mughals also laid waste to much of central India in their attempts to conquer the south, pouring out their vast wealth in those losing efforts.

The Ottoman empire suffered from incompetent or weak-willed sultans, with the central government often dominated by the women of the royal family as well as *vizirs* (chief ministers). Having lost naval control of the Mediterranean to Christian states in the late sixteenth century, Ottoman authority over their far-flung territories could only be as strong as the loyalty of their appointed governors and the power of the central armies to coerce cooperation. Only during the administration of Grand Vizir Fazil Ahmed Köprülü (r. 1661–1676) did the empire add Crete and parts of Ukraine to its territory.

In its final attempt to seize the initiative against Christian Europe and dominate its Austro-Hungarian enemy, the Ottoman army attacked Vienna in 1683 only to be driven back in disarray and finally destroyed by the Habsburgs and the Poles at Gran. Thereafter, the Ottomans gradually retreated from Hungary, Ukraine, and the Balkans, never again threatening Europe as they had for almost two centuries. Both the Ottomans and the Mughals remained effective empires, however, able to defend themselves and most of their possessions.

Europe's rulers began to realize some success in their long struggle to centralize their states. French King Louis XIV (r. 1643–1715) made the greatest strides; his absolutist policies allowed him to dominate France's nobility and improve control over his bureaucracy. The seventeenth century also saw major advances in European military technique, the result of conflicts like the Thirty Years' War, which devastated the German states early in the century. The introduction of regular, systematic military drill and strict chains of command gave European armies a considerable edge when they fought abroad.

Meanwhile, European scientists and mathematicians had begun to understand the natural world in revolutionary ways. Beginning with practical arts—astronomy, necessary for navigation, and probability, so useful for business (especially insurance) and gambling—the "natural philosophers" deepened their knowledge in anatomy and medicine, mechanics and mathematics, using the experimental, skeptical, replicable methodology we call "science." At century's end came the invention of calculus by Isaac Newton and G. Leibniz. (Leibniz was deeply impressed by Chinese culture, as reported by the seventeenth-century Jesuits, and he corresponded with several of the priests resident in Beijing.)

Already capable of lengthy sea voyages and accurate astronomical calculations, thereafter Europeans could comprehend and measure motion and energy in fields as diverse as ballistics and gunnery, mechanical engineering, and chemistry. In the seventeenth century, however, no one could have foreseen Europe's rise to world-dominating technological and scientific eminence. The Jesuits who visited China and Japan during those years commented on the sophistication and superlative workmanship of East Asian manufactures in comparison to their own.

The colonization of the New World by Spain and Portugal, whose monarchs gained unimaginable wealth from their new territories, had initiated a competition among European states and adventurers to profit equally from the rest of the world and, not incidentally, to convert its inhabitants to one form or another of Christianity. In North America, English settlers created the Virginia and Plymouth plantations, Spaniards built and maintained towns in Florida, and French sailors explored and claimed the St. Lawrence and Mississippi Valleys for their crown. The diseases they carried with them decimated the indigenous peoples of the continent, who had no antibodies to resist smallpox or typhoid (among many others), leaving only a fraction of the original population to deal with the invaders.

Meanwhile, Russians advanced across Siberia toward the Pacific and claimed territory around the Black Sea at Ottoman expense. Dutch sailors and merchants made inroads in the Spice Islands, later colonized as the Dutch East Indies. All of the European states increasingly saw the African coasts as sources of slave labor, taking advantage of their military superiority and local warfare to establish networks of slave hunters and embarkation stations from Gorée (in modern Senegal) to the Red Sea.

Whether merchants, conquerors, or slavers, all projected the power of Europeans to dominate the world's sea-lanes and coastlines, whoever might originally have possessed them. When they reached the Ming, Chosŏn, and Tokugawa realms, however, the Europeans could not act in a high-handed fashion. In East Asia, as in South Asia and the eastern Mediterranean, they faced well-organized states, with powerful armies, which more than matched them in cultural confidence.

Chinese and Japanese craftsmen quickly learned to make European-style firearms, eliminating any military advantage the Spanish and Portuguese might have enjoyed, except in shipbuilding and navigation. In the seventeenth century, Europeans in East Asia presented themselves as bearers of Christianity's unique truth, but they could not honestly say that their homelands were technologically or economically superior to China, Korea, or Japan. The Jesuits who led the Catholic missions in East Asia expressed shocked admiration for the orderly, culturally sophisticated, and politically well-organized states and societies they found there.

DYNASTIC UPHEAVAL AND A NEW RULING ELITE

THE END OF THE MING

Despite its cosmically mandated emperor, highly organized central government, carefully educated Confucian officials, military preparedness on the northern frontier, and vast, productive population, the Ming state tottered and fell in the middle of the seventeenth century. Chinese scholars have tended to see in its demise another example of an age-old cycle of dynastic rise and decay, repeated dozens of times in Chinese history—the gain and inevitable loss of Heaven's Mandate to rule. The emperor's rituals, these scholars contended, lost their efficacy as the emperor lost his virtue. The eunuchs and palace women usurped legitimate power from the Confucian officials, who squabbled among themselves rather than tending selflessly to His Majesty's business.

In this version of history, the ordinary people, sensing Heaven's displeasure through maladministration and high taxation, organized themselves against the dynasty and brought it down, confirming Mencius's old adage that the people have Heaven's permission to rebel against a tyrannical government. Certainly the Ministry of Revenue could not collect enough taxes to pay the officials and the soldiers, the palace eunuchs did wield great power, and the central government was plagued with factionalism, but these conditions had existed before. Much more critically, the state faced two large, roving rebel armies in the west and northwest, which it could not defeat. In addition, an external challenger arose outside the Great Wall in the northeast, among the people called Jurchen, Jusen, or Nüzhen, later to be known as Manchus.

In agriculturally and politically marginal Shaanxi province, in the northwest corner of Ming territory, bounded by the Mongol and Tibetan frontiers, the defense forces had been unpaid for as long as two years in the early 1630s. Demobilized soldiers and unemployed military transportation workers with some army training and weapons formed gangs to survive the hard times. Leading one such band, a junior officer named Li Zicheng gathered considerable forces against the emperor's armies. After 1638, Li's ranks included not only down-and-out ex-soldiers but also local gentry, even provincial examination graduates, and his army began

to resemble a dynasty-overturning rebellion. Another young man from northern Shaanxi, Zhang Xianzhong, also raised an army and battled the Ming for years, finally settling in Sichuan.

Both Zhang Xianzhong and Li Zicheng declared themselves to be the rulers of new dynasties, and Li marched on Beijing in the spring of 1644. The Ming's civil and military officials found themselves caught between two fires, for the aggressive Manchus in the northeast required concentrated attention. The emperor's officials advised him to place his resources there, rather than defending against the advancing army of Li Zicheng. So the Ming's most effective metropolitan forces faced the Manchus at Shanhaiguan, where the Great Wall meets the sea east of Beijing. It was a disastrous error. Li's rebels took the capital in a few days of furious fighting. As they entered the Forbidden City, the last Ming emperor hanged himself on the manmade hill outside the palace's north gate. Thus ingloriously ended the Great Ming dynasty, which had ruled over so much of the world's population and productive capacity for almost three centuries.

THE RISE OF THE MANCHUS

In 1596, between the two Hideyoshi invasions, the Chosŏn court sent an emissary, Sin Chung-il, to negotiate with the Jianzhou Jurchens, a group of agricultural and pastoral forest-dwellers who lived just across the Yalu (Amnok in Korean) frontier. Sin traveled through the prosperous villages to the stockade at Fe Ala ("Old Hill"), where he met two brothers, Nurgaci and Surgaci, lords of the Jianzhou Jurchens. They ruled over a mixed population that included Chinese, Koreans, and Mongols as well as Jurchens and people of similar culture from elsewhere in the region. Especially skilled in horse breeding and cavalry tactics, the Jurchens possessed both superior mounts and alarming accuracy in shooting from horseback with their short, powerful compound bows.

In his communications with his superiors in Seoul, Ambassador Sin described a people well organized for economic production and for war. He warned that these Jurchens posed a considerable danger, controlling much of the territory between the Ming frontier and the Chosŏn frontier. In part to allay Korean suspicions and to secure his southeastern frontier, Nurgaci gave Sin a letter for the Chosŏn court, suggesting a Jurchen–Chosŏn alliance against the Ming. After Sin returned to Seoul, bearing Nurgaci's letter and his notes on Nurgaci's personality, forces, and resources, the Chosŏn court rejected the proposed alliance, broke off trade relations with the Jianzhou Jurchens, and shut down its frontier trading posts.

This had no effect on Nurgaci, who continued his gradual rise to power, allying himself with some leaders and conquering others, becoming the first among equals and creating a council of kinsmen and allies. He rid himself of his younger brother's competitive presence by having him killed in 1611. In 1616 he declared himself *khan*, a Central Asian title associated with ownership of the land; bestowal of rich gifts, women, and slaves upon high-ranking followers; and conquest. Using both Chinese and Inner Asian languages and technologies of war, organization, and diplomacy, Nurgaci created a formidable military, centered on lightly armored cavalry skilled in mounted archery, as well as the beginnings of a civilian bureaucracy. He and his allies took the Ming city of Shenyang, the center of Liaodong province, in 1621 and made it their own capital, renaming it Mukden.

Knowing the usefulness of written communication and record-keeping, Nurgaci captured, bought, or won the loyalty of men literate in the Chinese and Mongolian scripts. Sometime during his reign (legend puts the date in 1599), he ordered his Mongolian scribes to develop a script to represent spoken Jurchen, later called Manchu. Constructing a collective identity for this expanding group of people involved, among many elements, a mythology of common descent—a claim of a single ancestor—as well as geographical origin and language. Food, clothing, hairstyle, language, and culture also distinguished the Jurchens from other groups in the region.

This portrait of Namjar, a Manchu warrior, was painted to commemorate the Qing campaigns in Central Asia. The inscription celebrates Namjar's heroic death in battle.

One of Nurgaci's crucial innovations lay in his careful organization of the Jurchen military forces and those of their allies and defeated enemies. Early in the seventeenth century, he began to arrange the Jurchen lineages in "banners," military units identified by colored flags. These included not only the fighting men themselves but also their families, servants, and slaves. Nurgaci made banner membership hereditary and installed his closest kinsmen and allies as banner leaders. The "banner system" reinforced loyalty to the leader, military success, and social stability. The number and composition of the banners changed, but Chinese sources usually refer to the Eight Manchu Banners as the heart of the conquering army from the northeast.

The Jurchens enrolled Mongols and Chinese in banners as well, and scholars are still arguing over the extent to which "banner" equaled "ethnic identity" in the seventeenth century. As historian Mark Elliott notes, the banner organizations resembled "a cross between the Marine Corps, the Civil Service, and the Veterans Administration, thickly overlaid with a combination of old-boy networks, political preferences, and partially articulated Affirmative Action policies." However we interpret their ethnic membership, the banners made up the core of the Manchu military machine, which Nurgaci created and his descendants led against Chosŏn and then against the Ming, with devastating results.

All states must deal with the problem of the succession of power—what happens when the current leader dies or is otherwise disqualified from office? Some societies, which we call *democracies*, choose new leaders by legally mandated elections, while *monarchies* rely upon inheritance of leadership within families (*dynasties*). Making the old ruler's first son the new ruler (*primogeniture*) has the advantage of predictability, but what if the ruler has no son? What if the first son is incompetent or foolish? The Chosŏn kings practiced primogeniture, while the Tokugawa shoguns, their *daimyō* and samurai chose inheritance by one male descendant to stabilize their rule and eliminate competition among brothers. Inner Asian rulers, including the Jurchens, did not automatically select their first sons as their successors. In fact, fratricidal warfare, assassinations, and plots among uncles and brothers characterized Inner Asian courts as far away as the Mughals and Ottomans, distant cultural relatives of the Jurchens.

So when Nurgaci died at the age of 67 in 1626, from wounds suffered in battle against the Ming, his eighth son Hongtaiji emerged victorious from the fraternal struggle that determined succession to power. Hongtaiji had already demonstrated extraordinary ability during his father's lifetime—he was the only literate one among Nurgaci's many sons. He proved an exceptional leader during his years of overlordship, ending the collegial rule by a group of generals that Nurgaci had practiced and becoming a new type of Jurchen ruler, a sole sovereign. In 1627 he sent an army led by three of his kinsmen to subjugate Chosŏn and secure his lightly defended southeastern flank. Guided by a number of former Chosŏn military men who had defected, the Jurchen armies easily took the main cities of Pyongyang and Seoul, demanding and receiving a treaty of tributary relations from the Chosŏn king, who officially became a "younger brother" of Hongtaiji, owing him both military and financial assistance.

Stable power in his expanded homeland and suzerainty over Chosŏn did not satisfy Hongtaiji's ambitions. He had his eye on the Ming, and he expressed his intentions with two crucial acts in 1635 and 1636. First, he banned the derogatory word "Jurchen" (in various languages) from his realm, mandating a new name to denote his army and people—Manchu, or *Manju*. Within two days he also received from the defeated Chahar Mongols the imperial seal of the long-defunct Mongol Yuan dynasty. He and his successors could then claim both their own Manchu inheritance *and* the mantle of the greatest Inner Asian conquerors of the past.

The following year, Hongtaiji ended his realm's tributary status under the Ming, embodied in the dynastic name Latter Jin, which Nurgaci had inherited from earlier Jurchen kingdoms. He named his state Great Qing, (MANCHU *Daicing gurun*, C. *Da Qing*), including under its sway not only the newly named Manchus but also Koreans, Chinese, Mongols, and others. Obviously a rival to the Great Ming to his southwest, the new ruler of the Great Qing called himself emperor (C. *huangdi*). The Chosŏn court had refused to pay tribute to Hongtaiji in 1632 and then rejected an emissary's demands for assistance against the Ming in 1636, so Hongtaiji himself led a huge army to subjugate the feisty peninsula a second time. The powerful banner forces captured King Injo and his whole family in a brief campaign, forcing Chosŏn into a much more humiliating and permanent subordinate status.

Between 1637 and his death in 1643, Hongtaiji improved the banner organization, adding more Mongol banners to his vanguard, and continued Nurgaci's use of Chinese bureaucrats from Liaodong, although he mistrusted them. He retained the Chinese martial troops who had been loyal to his father, enrolling them in Chinese banners. Over the years, he also obtained the technology to manufacture large artillery pieces. Originally cast by European gunners for the Ming court, these cannons enabled the Manchu military to take the heavily fortified cities that constituted the Ming empire's main line of defense. The successful siege of Dalinghe, in 1631, demonstrated that the Manchu banners could use artillery as effectively as the city's Chinese defenders.

When Hongtaiji died, his secondary consort Borjigid and his brother Dorgon placed his ninth son, the 5-year-old Fulin, on the Great Qing throne, giving him a Chinese-style reign-name, the Shunzhi Emperor. Dorgon served as joint regent with Jirgalang, one of Surgaci's sons. Much power lay in the hands of Borjigid, the emperor's Mongol mother, a reminder of the legacy of Chinggis Khan and of the extraordinary power of royal women, especially during a regency.

THE CONQUEST OF MING

Although he declared himself the emperor of the Great Qing in 1636, Hongtaiji's plans to subjugate the Ming did not ripen during his lifetime. His brother Dorgon, however, regent for the Shunzhi Emperor (r. 1643–1661), recognized an opportunity in 1644 when Li Zicheng's rebel forces took Beijing and the Ming emperor committed suicide. Wu Sangui, the Ming general stationed opposite Dorgon's Manchu, Chinese, and Mongol bannermen at Shanhaiguan, found himself in

The great gate at Shanhaiguan, part of the fortifications marking the eastern end of the Great Wall, where it meets the sea. The plaque over the gate reads, "The First Pass under Heaven," an indication of the importance of Shanhaiguan in the defenses of Beijing, only 185 miles (300 km) to the west. Shanhaiguan is now located in Qinhuangdao city, Hebei province.

an impossible position. Li Zicheng's army in Beijing threatened Wu Sangui's rear and had taken captive his father and favorite concubine. That May, Wu had to remain in his headquarters, caught between Dorgon to the northeast and Li Zicheng's army of 100,000 men to the west. Unable to confront either of his enemies without risking attack from the other, Wu Sangui chose the Manchus as potential allies.

Confident of his northern flank after receiving assurances from the Manchus, Wu Sangui defeated Li Zicheng then joined with Dorgon's forces to pursue Li's army back toward Beijing, which they took on June 6. Wu found his concubine alive, but his father and most of his extended family had been killed by Li Zicheng's men. Far from returning to the northeast or remaining under Wu Sangui's command, Dorgon and the other Manchu generals set their sights on "the great enterprise," taking all of the Ming's territory for the Great Qing. Dorgon had gained a foothold south of the Great Wall and a platform from which to announce, in his young nephew's name, his dynasty's "benevolent" intentions. The Qing would bring peace to the Ming's subjects, eliminate the remaining members of the Zhu family (the Ming imperial lineage), and rectify the damage done by eunuchs and greedy officials of the late dynasty.

During the regency, which lasted until Dorgon's unexpected death in 1650, the banner forces and their allies among the Ming generals moved southward from Beijing against loyalist Ming forces and an often hostile population. The Qing needed almost 40 years to subjugate the entire Ming territory, beginning with the Lower Yangzi valley in 1645. Some cities surrendered without a fight, while others resisted tenaciously. Qing troops needed only five days to take Yangzhou, one of the first lower Yangzi cities to come under siege, in May 1645. When the captured garrison commander, former Ming Minister of War Shi Kefa, was brought before the Qing commander (Dorgon's younger brother), the Manchu tried to deal with him respectfully. But the wounded Shi Kefa expressed his contempt for the conquerors and was immediately killed. In the resulting vengeful Manchu reaction, the Qing troops are said to have slaughtered hundreds of thousands of Yangzhou civilians. Shi Kefa's grave has become a pilgrimage site for Chinese nationalists, and even one of the Qing emperors later praised him as a loyal servant of the Ming.

All over the Ming territory, some Chinese rushed to make peace with their new rulers, while others retreated into private life and refused to serve or even recognize the Qing. Many Chinese men reacted strongly, even violently, to a 1645 Qing proclamation ordering all conquered Chinese males to wear the Manchu hair-style, shaving the front of the head and leaving only a circle of hair at the back to grow long and be braided into the famous *queue*, or pigtail (actually, a horse's tail was the model). Under Ming rule, elite Chinese men had worn their hair long, wrapped in a bun and tucked under a cap, so this Qing regulation forced them to violate what many Chinese saw as a fundamental textual rule of Confucianism, stated in the *Classic of Filial Piety*: "Our torso, limbs, hair, and skin we receive from our

THE XU BROTHERS, SCHOLARS OF THE EARLY QING

Relying on solid Confucian principle—that a minister should never serve two masters—the Wan brothers and Gu Yanwu had remained loyal to the fallen Ming and refused to serve the Qing, but many Chinese elites did not make the same choice. Nephews of Gu Yanwu and close friends with the Wan brothers, the three Xu brothers of Kunshan, in Jiangsu province, all worked for the new dynasty. Xu Qianxue (1631–1694), Xu Bingyi (1633–1711), and Xu Yuanwen (1634–1691) took and passed with great distinction the highest level of the civil service examination. Yuanwen took first place in 1659, at 25, while his older brothers came in third place in 1670 and 1673, respectively. All three of them held high offices, ranging from chief examiner in local and provincial examinations to presidents of the central ministries, and Xu Yuanwen briefly held the exalted rank of Grand Secretary. Both Qianxue and Yuanwen served as head of the Censorate and in the Hanlin Academy, the highest scholarly organ of the Qing state. Their careers illustrate the triumphs and dangers of the coveted path to high office, as well as the pleasures of elite Chinese culture.

Like Chinese scholars before and after them, the Xu brothers reveled in *texts*. Trained from early childhood in written classical Chinese, they read, evaluated, collected, compiled, edited, wrote, and printed books throughout their lives. They often received Qing government appointments to create works enhancing the Manchus' reputation as patrons of culture. Xu Qianxue, for example, in 1687 became the director-general of the *Great Qing Gazetteer* project, a vast compilation of geographical information about every part of the Qing territory. So huge was the amount of material, and so sensitive its handling, that the 356-volume work was not finally published until 1744, long after its first director's death.

Similarly, Xu Yuanwen worked for a time as a compiler of the *Veritable Records* of Hongtaiji, a day-by-day record of the important acts of the emperor and his ministers designed both as a historical source and as a demonstration of the court's power. The family library gained an empire-wide reputation, and the brothers spent many years there doing research—during the period of mourning for their mother after 1676, their various demotions from official life, and their brief retirements. Their students and disciples included both Chinese and Manchus.

Most significantly, both Xu Qianxue and Xu Yuanwen took part in researching and writing the *Ming History*, a comprehensive account of the Ming period. In Chinese culture, history did not merely narrate events of the past but rather functioned something like law in Euro-American culture. History encompassed the making of judgments, the illustration of good and evil behavior, the development of standards for every aspect of human life, and the clear distinction between good and bad people. Each new dynasty thus wrote the official history of its predecessor—an act with great political significance, for the overthrow of a former dynasty had to be justified and the new ruling family's claim to legitimacy supported. In 1690, the Xu brothers recruited Wan Sitong, one of the Wan brothers, a great historian and principled anti-Qing scholar, to work on the Ming history. Their successors finally finished the project in 1739, long after their deaths.

fathers and mothers; we must not destroy or damage them. That is the beginning of filial piety." Resistance stiffened thereafter, as some Chinese men chose to die rather than cut their hair in submission to the Qing.

An even more contentious prohibition imposed by the Manchus failed utterly to take hold among their newly conquered subjects. Manchu women did not bind their feet, and the Qing lords proclaimed in 1644 that no one under their control could do so, but the total unwillingness of their Chinese subjects to obey it caused them to withdraw the rule in 1668. It remained in effect, however, for bannerwomen. Most women in banner families, whether Manchu, Mongol, or Chinese, kept their feet unbound for many generations. This physical distinction acted as a deterrent on intermarriage between banner and non-banner families, for Chinese men found "big feet" singularly unattractive. Chinese men, who had to be out in public, could not avoid the Manchu imposition of the queue, but women, more secluded indoors and wearing (in many cases) clothing that covered their feet, could continue their Chinese practice of footbinding.

To develop a positive relationship with their newly conquered subjects, the Qing court immediately began to recruit members of the Chinese elite into their bureaucracy through the examination system. They held the metropolitan examination for the *jinshi* (highest) degree in both 1646 and 1647, and then on a regular triennial schedule after 1649. Hundreds of Chinese joined the pool of potential government officials with each round of the examinations, and members of the elite gradually made their peace with the conquerors and took office (see box opposite).

Many famous literary men, however, refused to consider either the dynasty or its examinations legitimate, and they resisted passively by returning to their home districts and living in seclusion. Even special examinations did not lure men such as Gu Yanwu into Qing service. They spent the rest of their lives doing research and writing—very cautiously, so as not to attract official attention—rather than undertaking the government careers for which they had prepared.

Active resistance to the Qing conquest coalesced around surviving members of the Zhu family. The Ming heirs often fought among themselves while maneuvering for advantage against the invading Qing, and some cities surrendered to the Manchus after having been despoiled by Ming troops. Beginning in the Yangzi valley, the Qing armies, their size often more than doubled by Ming forces that had defected to their ranks, pursued one Ming prince after another. The last of them initially based himself in Guangdong province in the far south. Qing armies gradually pushed him westward until he set up his last capital at Kunming, the capital of Yunnan province, in 1656. Three years later, he and his court had to flee again, and he requested assistance from the king of Taungoo (in present-day Myanmar), who allowed him across the frontier. In the summer of 1662, he and his son were captured by Qing forces under Wu Sangui, who the Manchus appointed governor of Yunnan. The Qing also successfully quelled resistance in the northwest and south, and along the coast, over the next decades.

One of the most tenacious resistance armies came from the ranks of the coastal pirates who had been despoiling the Ming coastline for generations (see p. 55). At their headquarters in Xiamen (Amoy), the Ming loyalist ships came under the command of Zheng Chenggong, known in Japan and Europe as Koxinga. He led fleets to attack the Qing all along the coast and up the Yangzi River.

Although he died young in 1662, Zheng Chenggong, whose mother was Japanese, played an important historical role by establishing the island of Taiwan as a base for his navy, driving out the Dutch (who had built a fort there) and initiating a significant Chinese presence. In 1683, the Qing finally took the island from his successors, attaching it for the first time to a China-based empire, for it had never been Ming territory. Migration from Fujian and eastern Guangdong increased thereafter, and the "beautiful island" (PORTUGUESE *Ilha Formosa*), originally the thinly populated homeland of Malayo-Polynesian peoples, became a rowdy, flourishing outpost of the Qing empire and Chinese agriculture.

To secure the southern portions of their huge new realm, the Qing rulers dispatched Chinese banner armies, led by generals from Liaodong who had joined the Manchu forces in the 1630s. Three of them received province-sized fiefs (Guangxi, Guangdong, and Fujian) as rewards for their service, with the expectation that they would establish stable, loyal government. Their unusually high rank—equal to that of princes in the emperor's family—and the hereditary nature of their fiefdoms led the Qing to call them the "Three

Feudatories" (c. *Sanfan*). With Wu Sangui in Yunnan and the Three Feudatories dominating the south, the Qing felt confident in their control over all of the former Ming empire—that is, all of the Chinese culture area.

Nurgaci and Hongtaiji's lineage, the Aisin Gioro family, retained the role of emperor in Beijing for 268 years, almost as long as the Zhu family of the Ming, despite the Manchus' small numbers and the overwhelming size of their subject populations. In the coming chapters we will try to understand this remarkable tenacity, the loyalty shown to the dynasty by its subjects, and the complex adaptation of the Manchu elites to their new role as the core of a huge multicultural empire. In part by binding the elites of conquered peoples, including the Chinese, to themselves as bannermen, bondsmen, officials, tributaries, and servants, the Qing became one of the most successful conquest dynasties in world history.

EMPIRE-BUILDING UNDER THE KANGXI EMPEROR

The Qing's first post-conquest emperor took the throne in 1661, as a boy of 6, when his father, the Shunzhi Emperor, died suddenly of smallpox. Aisin Gioro Xuanye, the emperor who reigned during the Kangxi period (1662–1722)—thus called "the Kangxi Emperor"—had already survived smallpox and was likely to reach adulthood. He grew up under the regency of four Manchu generals, led by the successful commander Oboi. They had helped the young Shunzhi Emperor to rid himself of Dorgon's domineering faction at court and were skilled at the factional politics of the Manchu military elite. A precocious, talented, patient politician himself, the young Kangxi Emperor had to decide when and how to take power away from his regents, who clearly had a vested interest in retaining their control. At the age of 14, in 1667, the emperor put together a faction of courtiers, high Manchu officials, and kinsmen including Borjigid, his formidable Mongol grandmother. They arrested Oboi (he died in prison) and executed many members of his faction.

During the first decades of his reign, the Kangxi Emperor had not only to deal with factions among the Manchus and the creation of a civil bureaucracy; he also had to face a major rebellion. The Three Feudatories had been reduced to two when the lord of Guangxi died without an heir, but the remaining two

and Wu Sangui gradually became liabilities to their Qing masters. Outside the regular system of military and civilian controls, they could pass their fiefdoms on to their heirs, who would have less personal loyalty to the emperor than the original title-holders. The Qing court worried particularly about Wu Sangui, the most talented and powerful of the three.

In 1673, when the Guangdong lord requested that he be allowed to retire to his old home in Liaodong, the court decided to solve the problem by ordering all three of the southern lords to return home to the northeast, giving up their fiefs in exchange for titles and honors. In a series of subtle communications, Wu Sangui refused to resign, despite the emperor's firm insistence. Finally declaring himself the emperor of a new dynasty, Wu Sangui became a rebel against the Qing. He moved his armies northeastward from Yunnan and within two years held much of the Qing empire south of the Yangzi.

Despite having joined the Manchus in 1644 and executed the last Ming prince in 1662, Wu Sangui successfully played on anti-Manchu sentiment—especially opposition to the queue hairstyle—to rally southern Chinese against the new dynasty. The Kangxi Emperor had to direct the Qing campaigns against Wu Sangui without overwhelming military superiority, but the Three Feudatories could not coordinate their northward advance effectively. Wu Sangui's death from dysentery in 1677 sealed the rebellion's fate, though the Qing troops required four more years to retake the whole south, including Yunnan. For the rest of his life, the emperor regretted the mistakes that had led to such widespread warfare and regarded the Three Feudatories' rebellion as the low point of his reign.

On another side of the empire, one of the Kangxi Emperor's triumphs lay in the expansion of Qing territory beyond the Manchus' homeland, eastern Mongolia, and the territory of the former Ming. As an Inner Asian monarch, he knew the importance of securing his landward frontiers against incursions by other federations like his grandfather's, and he perceived the advancing Russians as a threat from the north. Immediately after taking Taiwan, he transferred some of the Zheng family's naval officers to command Qing fleets on the Siberian rivers, and in 1685 his forces attacked the Russian outpost at Albazin, on the Amur. Neither side gained an obvious advantage in the fighting, and

Portrait of the young Kangxi Emperor in armor, on a hunting expedition with his retainers, late 17th century.

The Russians, with their distant capital, small numbers, and primary interest in the fur trade, constituted a smaller threat to the Qing than the Zunghars (also written Dzunghars and Jungars), a confederation of western Mongols. The last of the nomadic empires of Inner Asia and thus heir to the traditions of Chinggis Khan and Tamerlane, the Zunghars controlled a huge state. It stretched from the northern frontiers of Mongolia all the way to Qinghai, the lake that marks a four-way cultural frontier among the Chinese, Tibetans, Mongolians, and Turkic-speaking Muslims, at the northwestern corner of the former Ming state. Devoted adherents of Tibetan Buddhism, and particularly of the Gelugpa sect of the Dalai Lamas of Lhasa, the Zunghars could have allied themselves with the Tibetans, Russians, and eastern Mongols, creating a deadly circle around the Qing.

This threat became acute in 1671 when Galdan inherited the Zunghar leadership. Educated as a Buddhist monk in Lhasa and fluent in Tibetan, Galdan expanded his father's empire by conquering the Turkic-speaking Muslim city-states of Kashgar, Yarkand, Hami, and Turfan, making himself lord of eastern Turkestan as well as western Mongolia. The Qing, fully aware of the threat he posed, sought an alliance with the Russians against him, part of the 1689 Nerchinsk treaty.

Galdan, ambitious for further conquest, left the Muslim cities of Turkestan under the subordinate governorship of the famous Sufi Khoja Afaq, a local Muslim religious leader, and moved eastward through Mongolia, pressing on the Qing's Mongolian tributaries and banners. Qing diplomacy failed to halt Galdan's advance, and he struck southward toward Beijing in 1690. General Fuquan, the emperor's elder half-brother, halted Galdan's advance in southern Mongolia, and the Zunghars retreated northwest to regroup and continue their battles with the eastern Mongols. The negotiations that followed these battles demonstrated their international quality—the mediators between the Manchus and the Zunghars were representatives of the Tibetan religious leader, the Dalai Lama of Lhasa.

A careful strategic thinker, the Kangxi Emperor decided in 1696 that Galdan's Zunghars constituted too

four years later they concluded a treaty at Nerchinsk, fixing the boundary between the two empires in that region almost exactly where the Russian–Chinese border lies today. The Qing conducted these negotiations in non-tributary language—the czar and the emperor addressed one another as equals, the Russians being handled not through the Qing's Ministry of Ritual, as tributaries were, but through Hongtaiji's special bureau for relations with the Mongols.

Wen Zhengming, *The Garden of the Unsuccessful Politician*, 1551. Often called the "Humble Administrator's Garden," this Suzhou landmark dates from the 16th century. The famous Ming painter and writer Wen Zhengming (1470–1559) lived here during a period of retirement from public life. To celebrate its beauty, he created an album of the garden's sights, with accompanying poems. The melancholy tranquility of this scene captures perfectly the surroundings and feelings of a politician exiled from court. Much changed since 1551, the garden still exists in its late Qing form and has been proclaimed a UNESCO World Heritage Site.

other firearms) to good advantage, the Qing forces intercepted and defeated Galdan's army in a great battle at Ja'un Modu, in northern Mongolia. Galdan escaped but died the following year, abandoned by his followers for his failure to unite the Mongols against the Qing.

In the prime of his life, the Kangxi Emperor and his Manchu, Mongol, and Chinese banner armies had already created a multiethnic empire incorporating the Manchu homeland, Mongolia, all of the Chinese culture area, and the new frontier of Taiwan. Expanding northward outside the former frontiers of the Ming, he and his generals set a far-reaching pattern for Qing rule over substantial parts of Inner Asia. Inner Asians themselves, the Manchus participated in complex relationships—with the Zunghars, Tibetans, Mongols, Muslim Turkestanis, Russians, and others—not as "Chinese" but as conquering *khans* who administered a vast state.

By the Kangxi Emperor's time, the word *huangdi* had truly come to mean "emperor," for the Qing empire could not accurately be called "China," though many writers did and still do call it that. Its frontiers extended far beyond the Chinese culture area. Its eighteenth-century conquests, directed at the complete elimination of the Zunghar threat, would enlarge the empire to include eastern Turkestan and parts of Tibet. By ending the menace of the nomadic peoples of the north, the Qing would accomplish something that none of its predecessors—not even the great Han and Tang empires—had been able to do.

STATE, SOCIETY, AND THE INTELLECTUAL ELITE IN THE EARLY QING

The Qing conquest had brought widespread death and destruction, a complete replacement of the highest levels of political leadership, and a new military establishment to rule over the Chinese culture area. These radical transformations confronted Chinese people, especially elite men, with painful choices. On the outside, what attitude should they take toward the new dynasty? On the inside, how could they understand what had happened to them and the world they had known? Intellectuals accustomed to thinking, analyzing, and writing, they had to assess the causes of what appeared to be a terrible failure—the complete elimination of the Ming emperor and state to which they had been loyal. Many of them, true to the Confucian principle that a

great a danger to the Qing's northern and western frontiers, and he personally led a campaign against them, becoming the last Qing emperor to venture into battle. His letters from the army's camps reveal him as a Manchu warrior like his grandfather and great-grandfather, though he wrote in Chinese. He reveled in the Mongolian scenery, the rough life in camp (at least compared to the Beijing palaces), the taste of his food, the cleanness of the air, and the pursuit of an elusive enemy.

Planning and executing the daily movements of his wing of the army (there were two others, under Manchu and Chinese banner generals), the emperor, then in his 42nd year, also practiced the archery skills for which he was famous and marksmanship with the muzzle-loading musket. Using their numbers, carefully arranged supply lines, and mobile artillery units (and virtuous minister does not serve two masters, committed suicide or retreated into seclusion after the Qing victory. The majority, however, had to come to terms with the new order, with the Manchus at the top, because they felt overwhelming responsibility for their lives (bequeathed to them by their parents), families, communities, lineages, ancestors, and businesses.

Intellectuals' responses to the Qing conquest varied widely. Born into the family of a highly educated Zhejiang physician, Li Yu (1611–1680) mastered poetry at an early age and passed the lowest-level imperial examination when he was 24. After failing the provincial examination, in the early 1640s Li Yu encountered the turmoil and violence of the Qing invasion, suffering the death of his mother and of his hopes for official position. Depressed and discouraged, he returned to his hometown just in time to experience its devastation, first by fleeing Ming troops (1645) and then by Qing armies (1646).

In those few years, Li Yu lost much of his classical library, his ambition to serve the Ming as an official, his long hair (he shaved the front of his head and braided his hair in the Manchu queue), and his idealism, but he still faced the problem of earning a living. Fascinated with city life and its possibilities, he moved to Hangzhou, the provincial metropolis of Zhejiang, and became a professional writer of drama and fiction. He composed not in the allusive classical style he had practiced for the examinations but in the vernacular, common speech—the language of daily life.

Li Yu also wrote on culture, aesthetics, and literature, including a famous essay on womanly beauty. Although he believed that women should be educated and that a woman could be a man's equal in intelligence, he also maintained that family harmony lay in women's hands, and that they must make heroic self-sacrifices to maintain it. Distressed by the difficulty women with bound feet experienced in walking, he nonetheless found tiny feet attractive and wrote about women as sex objects. Never consistent, he behaved as an urban sophisticate, a cultured man about town. Although the Qing banned a few of his works for their potentially anti-Manchu content, he wrapped most of his opinions in complex historical analogies.

In the fluid social world of the early Kangxi period, Li Yu established a reputation as a lover of life and joined a brilliant circle of literati in the Lower Yangzi region, including a number of well-educated women. They enjoyed theater, fiction, poetry, and painting, and, like their colleagues throughout the former Ming territory, they grieved over the fall of "their" dynasty. Many of the men had passed the Ming examinations, but disillusioned with the Ming and unwilling to serve the Qing, they refused to stand for civil office and lived as poets, doctors, Buddhist monks, or landed gentry. All of them wrote poetry and admired Li Yu's prose and plays.

Li Yu managed to survive on his writing and by publishing his own and others' works, combining in his life and character (in the words of a modern biography), "individualism, moral universalism, rationalism, pragmatism, and love for life and humanity."[1] He also made many enemies, especially among the more rigid Confucianists, who held imaginative literature to be a danger to public morality. Years after his death, he was accused of having written a famous pornographic novel—its style is very similar to his, though no direct evidence links him to the book—and his reputation did not recover until the twentieth century.

The brothers Wan Sida (1633–1683) and Wan Sitong (1638–1702), also from Zhejiang but much younger than Li Yu, similarly refused to take the Qing examinations, preferring to become private scholars of history and classical learning. Unable to revive "their" Ming dynasty, which had fallen when they were children, they devoted their lives to Chinese culture, especially its ancient texts, in order to preserve what they saw as the distinction between civilization (that is, China) and barbarism (that is, the Manchus) without directly attacking their new rulers. With access to the best libraries in the Lower Yangzi region, the Wan brothers wrote treatise after treatise, expounding the rituals and hierarchies of the Zhou dynasty (first millennium BCE), especially those relevant to elite life in their own society.

They asked many questions: How many generations of one's ancestors should be venerated, and what impact does that decision have on the structure and workings of lineages? In what sort of temple should particular ancestors be housed? What ceremonies are appropriate to official families compared to those whose men hold no state rank? Which rituals may properly be conducted only by the emperor, and which by his high officials? Whose commentaries on the Classics hold the most truth—Zheng Xuan of the Han period or the Cheng brothers and Zhu Xi of the Song period?

This scholarly enterprise of classical studies, which inspired thousands of men in this period, provided the Wan brothers and their colleagues with a satisfying solution to the difficulty of living under Qing rule. Although their questions may seem esoteric and irrelevant to real problems, their work in fact had profound effects on social life in the Chinese parts of the Qing empire. For local gentry—that is, highly educated Chinese men without official positions—to build and maintain their own power, they needed to have an institutional form that was both effective and orthodox, unassailable by the Qing state. Kinship, the lineage, and the *family* provided precisely that combination. As a result, the huge, extended patrilines described in Chapter 2 flourished all over the Chinese culture area, but particularly in the Yangzi valley and the south.

Like people in many cultures, the Wan brothers and their colleagues looked to their own ancient traditions, embodied in texts, for correct answers to social problems—in their case, for the structures and rituals to bind the lineage together and create a good society. To avoid present political implications, they studied the past. To avoid tangling with a state they hated, they spent their lives writing manuals and commentaries designed to improve China, which had clearly gone astray, through religious acts. As one of the Wan brothers' colleagues wrote, "The Way of the sages is nothing but [observing] ritual."[2] Rejecting the individualistic, introspective methods of Wang Yangming and his followers, these Confucians insisted upon conscientious practice of rituals to reinforce social hierarchy—with themselves, the educated class, at the top—as the proper way to create a good society, even in bad times.

Gu Yanwu (1613–1682), a Ming *jinshi* degree holder, spent his life traveling and living in northern China, far from his Jiangsu home, in order to understand social and economic life. He designed a private banking system, operated farms, encouraged the opening of mines, and did extensive research in academic fields such as phonetics and etymology, aiming to establish (or debunk) the authenticity of ancient texts. His greatest work, *Record of Daily Knowledge*, contains his carefully written notes on classical study, government, ethics, economics, and much more.

Gu Yanwu firmly believed that the Ming had fallen in part because of Wang Yangming's emphasis on introspection rather than careful study of the real world, and he lived his life as a student of practical matters. His published works include treatises on geography, military preparedness, taxation, and the usefulness of ancient inscriptions as guides to good government. His style of scholarship—painstaking, meticulous, textual—became one of the favored methodologies of Qing intellectuals, usually called "evidential research" (c. *kaozheng*).

The Kangxi Emperor himself put a great deal of effort into intellectual problems, writing lengthy rescripts (comments on official correspondence), edicts (orders to his officials), and literary works as well as thousands of letters to his courtiers, eunuchs, and officials. Fluent in both Chinese and Manchu, he saw himself as the arbiter of good and evil, the builder of a just social and political order:

> Giving life to people and killing people—those are the powers that the emperor has. He knows that administrative errors in government bureaus can be rectified, but that a criminal who has been executed cannot be brought back to life any more than a chopped string can be joined together again. He knows, too, that sometimes people have to be persuaded into morality by the example of an execution.[3]

The emperor's many advisers included Manchus, Mongols, and Chinese, his childhood teachers, government officials, generals, eunuchs, his grandmother, and other women of his household. He also included Europeans on his staff—Jesuit priests who had come to China to advance Christianity by making it known to the highest levels of Ming and then Qing society. They had some successes among the high officials, and the Shunzhi Emperor expressed great interest in Roman Catholicism to his adviser Adam Schall von Bell (1591–1666). However, Jesuit accomplishments in science and technology generated far more enthusiasm than their religion.

The Kangxi Emperor favored the Catholic priests, giving them positions in astronomy, cartography, gunnery, and engineering. His tolerance of them and their religion, however, depended on several key issues—would the Jesuits allow their converts to practice the crucial rituals of ancestor veneration that, for the emperor, defined civilization and propriety? If not, then the emperor would not allow them to work in his realm. Would they obey his orders, recognizing him as the legitimate ruler of All Under Heaven, or insist on the Pope's primacy in matters of doctrine? When the Vatican sent an ambassador to him in 1705, the two men argued about control over the priests, and the emperor expelled from his empire any priest who denied his authority.

To avoid the seizure of power by eunuchs, palace women, and other inhabitants of the "inner court" (as compared to the "outer court" of officials, bannermen, and examination graduates), Nurgaci had established the Imperial Household Department, staffed by Manchu and Chinese bannermen, to manage life inside the palace. By the time the Kangxi Emperor came to power, this agency had been abolished by his father and then reinstated during the Oboi regency (see p. 74).

Through the Kangxi reign, the Imperial Household Department expanded its functions, gradually becoming an important stabilizing force in Qing finances. It earned substantial capital by supervising enterprises as diverse as the state monopolies on ginseng and salt, the imperial porcelain factory at Jingdezhen, the imperial silk manufacturing establishment, and the importation of silver and copper (for currency) from Japan. Imperial publication projects, especially numerous under the Kangxi Emperor and his immediate successors, also enriched the imperial household and enhanced its reputation among the literary men of the realm. By preserving its money outside the control of the regular bureaucracy, the Imperial Household Department gave the emperor a reliable source of funds. In charge of the court's relationship with the Jesuit priests from Europe, it also oversaw some elements of what we might call "foreign policy," for which the Qing had no single agency. Its importance may be judged by its size—by the end of the eighteenth century, it employed more officials (approx. 1,600, mostly bannermen) than did the realm's entire staff of county magistrates (approx. 1,300 men).

Among his many achievements, the Kangxi Emperor sponsored large scholarly projects, including the writing of the history of the former Ming—traditionally a prerogative of any succeeding dynasty (see p. 72)—and important dictionaries of the Chinese language; one, *The Kangxi Dictionary*, is still used. In order to create a stable, responsive society, in 1670 the emperor promulgated 16 moral maxims, summarizing what he saw as the crucial duties of human life: key among them were filial piety, mutual love and responsibility among kinfolk, prompt payment of taxes, and personal frugality.

The emperor's précis of morality initiated a powerful trend through the remainder of the Qing period, a movement toward orthodoxy and rigid obedience to the tenets of Song Neo-Confucianism, in contrast to the more liberal and tolerant atmosphere of the late Ming and early Qing years. In order to maintain their power and legitimacy as a conquest dynasty, he and his successors attempted to mold Chinese society according to the model of the *Daxue*, or Greater Learning (see p. 31). Every person should obey those above and instruct those below, modeling themselves on the hardworking, intelligent, virtuous character of their ultimate ruler, the emperor. Reasonable in theory, this morality came to encompass some of the most unproductive and oppressive aspects of Qing society—the cult of widow chastity, for example, and the rigidly structured, formalistic "eight-legged essays" of the imperial examinations. As Chinese society changed—its population expanded rapidly from the end of the Qing conquest years onward and its contacts with the rest of the world increased as well—inflexible orthodoxy served both court and society less and less effectively.

KOREA

After the devastating Hideyoshi wars, the Chosŏn dynasty and the people of the peninsula faced the arduous tasks of reconstruction. Warfare, diseases, and kidnapping had reduced the population by as much as 10 percent. The massive armies had ruined fields and irrigation systems, and many farmers had fled their lands to seek safety. Bringing land back under cultivation became a priority for the state to secure its finances and for the people to ensure their livelihoods.

But the early attempts to reconstruct state finances and the economy were interrupted by the growth of Manchu power to the north of the peninsula. Long before they invaded Ming China, the Manchus looked toward the strategically located peninsula kingdom to their southeast. With its symbolic importance as a leading tributary of the Ming, the Chosŏn kingdom offered a prize that would help establish the Manchus' aspirations to legitimacy. At first, the Chosŏn court, led by

Prince Kwanghae, adopted a wait-and-see policy, deciding not to choose sides in the growing conflict between the Manchus and the Ming and sending ambassadors and spies (like Sin Chung-il, see p. 68) to keep an eye on the situation. This neutral policy offended the pro-Ming sensibilities of the powerful Western faction, who successfully replaced the monarch with the more anti-Manchu King Injo. (See p. 50 for the division of Chosŏn officialdom into "Eastern," Western," "Southern," and "Northern" factions.) In response, the Manchus attacked. In 1627 and again in 1637, when the Chosŏn court refused to recognize their newly proclaimed Qing dynasty, Manchu forces invaded the peninsula, capturing the king himself. Forced to surrender to Manchu demands backed by overwhelming force, the court agreed to end all relations with the Ming, use Qing reign-names in the calendar, offer hostages to be held in the Manchu city of Mukden, and begin sending tribute missions to the Qing court to assist in legitimizing its claim to Heaven's Mandate.

Until 1895, the Chosŏn court dispatched more missions to Beijing than any other tribute-bearing kingdom—a fact that was not lost on Beijing observers, who regularly extolled the Chosŏn dynasty as the most faithful and virtuous of their many neighbors. Yet underneath this full participation in the tribute rituals of Beijing, resentment toward the Qing dynasty, if not outright hostility, flourished. The tribute of the Chosŏn court, after all, had not been induced by the superior moral behavior of the Manchus as, in theory, it should have been, but rather was coerced through two invasions. Only when the Manchus had physically seized the Chosŏn monarch and taken hostages did officials agree to submit to the Qing. One of the first hostages to be returned, the crown prince, assumed the Chosŏn throne as King Hyojong (r. 1649–1659) only five years after the beginning of the Qing conquest of the Ming.

Hyojong had returned to Seoul bitter at his experience of captivity and eager to erase his personal humiliation as well as that of the dynasty's defeat at the hands of his captors. To this end, he prepared to launch an attack against the Qing. With an economy still not recovered from the devastation of the Hideyoshi invasions, Hyojong nevertheless oversaw a massive buildup and reorganization of the military. In the ten years of his rule, more than 100,000 troops were raised and large cavalry units formed. Military officials, for the first time in the peacetime history of the Chosŏn dynasty, received royal favor greater than their civilian counterparts.

Mandongmyo shrine, Hwayang-ri. This shrine was built in 1704 to commemorate two emperors of Ming China: Wanli (r. 1572–1620), who had assisted Korea at the time of the Japanese invasions, and Chongzhen (r. 1627–1644), the last emperor of the dynasty.

These forces on their own, of course, could not hope to vanquish the mighty banner armies of the Manchus, yet the Chosŏn military strategists hoped that the still unstable situation of Qing forces in southern China would weaken the new dynasty. If the Qing could be caught off-guard, Chosŏn's revived military could be launched northward. These martial preparations, of course, remained as secret as possible, and the court continued to dispatch tribute missions to Beijing. But to Hyojong's frustration—and no doubt, to the relief of the more realistic officials—no opportunity presented itself. The Qing's political and military strength continued to grow, and the Manchus consolidated their rule in the southern parts of their new empire by establishing the Three Feudatories. Because the economic burdens of mobilization in the peninsula were heavy, many civilian officials quietly withdrew their support from the military orientation of the court. By the time Hyojong died in 1659, the scheme for a northern expedition had been abandoned, but however illusory the plan for a military attack may have been, anti-Manchu sentiment did not recede.

Underlying the desire for retribution lay the belief that the Manchus, despite their overwhelming military power, remained uncouth barbarians who had usurped the rightful Ming emperor's claim to Heaven's Mandate. Chosŏn writers of the era filled their books with insulting anti-Manchu comments that questioned their moral character and degree of cultivation. They commonly referred to the "stench of meat" emanating from the continent, a direct jab at the Manchus' "uncivilized" eating habits. Koreans also wrote of the Manchus as a people who buttoned their tunics on the wrong side, condemning their lack of the decorum crucial to the proper comportment of cultivated individuals. These everyday denunciations of the Qing dynasty—though kept well away from the eyes of Qing officials—accompanied a deep nostalgia for the Ming, which had assisted Chosŏn in its wars against Hideyoshi's forces and which, in the memories of Chosŏn scholars, had preserved and promoted Confucian teachings.

The rejection of the Qing dynasty and mourning for the Ming lay rooted in a deep commitment to the ideals of Neo-Confucianism, which virtually all Chosŏn scholars and officials believed the Manchus, as barbarians, could not preserve. With the lands of the Chinese culture area conquered by the Manchus, leading Confucian scholars such as Song Siyŏl (1607–1689) not only rejected the Qing claim to Heaven's Mandate but also began to view Chosŏn as the last bastion of Confucian values. Even their references to their own dynasty reflected this shift. Invoking the longstanding term *chunghwa* (C. *zhonghua*, J. *chūka*), "central civilization," which had been used since the distant classical age to designate China Proper, Chosŏn scholars began to refer to their own kingdom as *so chunghwa*, or "little central civilization." This usage indicated that with the fall of the Ming, the focus of civilization had shifted eastward to their own lands. Chosŏn, in their eyes, now constituted the sole remaining repository of civilized—that is to say, Confucian—practices, rituals, and thought.

Such claims placed a heavy burden on Chosŏn scholars. Self-appointed as the only true custodians of Confucianism, they spent the remainder of the dynasty maintaining orthodox interpretations of the Classics. Many scholars and officials believed deeply in this mission, yet the richness and internal complexity of Confucian thought continued to generate contending interpretations. Everyone could agree that orthodoxy was crucial, but the struggle over defining that orthodoxy fueled factional strife. After the fall of the Ming, with Chosŏn the last bastion of virtue, the stakes had never been so high.

One of the more renowned conflicts of the seventeenth century erupted upon Hyojong's death in 1659, when officials disagreed on how he should be mourned by the Queen Dowager. Should she, as a mother, perform the rituals appropriate for mourning a son? Or, should she, as a subject, mourn Hyojong as her sovereign? This dilemma crystallized a classic tension in Confucian thought concerning the relative importance of state and family, centering in this case on the status of the leading member of the royal lineage: when should he be treated as the monarch, and when should he be treated as a member of a family?

Factions quickly took up the issue, the powerful Western Faction led by Song Siyŏl arguing that the Queen Dowager should mourn a son, because of the precedence of family status. The Southern Faction, led by Yun Hyu (1617–1680), contended that Hyojong should be mourned as a sovereign, even by his mother. The debate was fierce: dozens of memorials were presented, hundreds of scholars from across the country who did not have official positions participated, and some memorialists were even banished into internal exile for their views. After the Southern Faction emerged victorious, the debate continued to rage for more than six decades as the losers sought to reverse the decision. What today may appear to be an insignificant formality—decisions regarding funerary ritual and status—were in the late Chosŏn period considered fundamental questions of morality, upon which the entire political-ethical order rested, the foundation of the sole remaining dynasty committed to preserving Confucian values.

TAX REFORM AND THE ECONOMY

One consequence of the Hideyoshi invasions had been the destruction of government records on landownership, records needed to collect taxes. The amount of land recorded in postwar government registries amounted to only one-third of the prewar total, or even less in regions where the fighting had been intense. Some local elites took advantage of this disarray to take over abandoned fields, keeping the new size of their estates secret from the government. Even government agencies participated in the seizure of land, adding to their institutional tax-free holdings at the expense of local farmers. As a result, tax revenues plummeted, threatening the continued viability of the state.

The court placed its priority on the reform of the taxation system. Previously, the central state had relied on a style of tribute tax, which required counties across the peninsula to supply the state with specific goods—rice or porcelain, clothes or paper, mountain mushrooms or falcons—necessary for its functioning. Inefficient as a way of funneling resources to Seoul, the tribute tax system also enabled all sorts of corrupt practice by local officials. Gradually over the course of the century, the county-based tribute tax came to be replaced by a Uniform Land Tax (k. *taedongpop*). Literally meaning the "Law of Great Harmony," the Uniform Land Tax required all landowners to pay roughly 1 percent of the value of their harvest to the central state in cash, rice, or cotton cloth. Officials then used this money to purchase needed goods. Such a system had been proposed well before the Hideyoshi wars, but only now that state finances were in dire straits did this means of applying uniform taxes gain royal approval. It was implemented first around the capital in 1608 and gradually extended to the outlying provinces until, by the early eighteenth century, the entire peninsula paid taxes in this form. As the new system was extended, it spurred the use of currency, which in turn invigorated the market economy. The court enhanced these trends by selecting specific merchants to receive an official license to buy the goods necessary for government offices. Known as "tribute men" (k. *kong'in*), they accumulated massive wealth, becoming some of the richest families on the peninsula.

To increase government revenue, officials also began reexamining slavery. Social critics of slavery, such as the famous scholar Yu Hyŏngwŏn (1622–1673), had criticized the hereditary nature of this status group. While Yu did not call for an end to slavery, he did object that the social stigma of slavery should not be passed on to innocent children and subsequent generations. He also worried about the moral implications of the master–slave relationship for *yangban* owners, who he believed were corrupted by the power such a relationship gave them. In the end, however, the real motive for changing the laws defining hereditary slavery lay in the desire to increase the tax base. According to earlier dynastic law, all offspring of any slave—even if the other parent were freeborn—inherited the status designation of the slave parent. A commoner who fathered a child with a slave, for example, ensured that the offspring and, in turn, all subsequent generations would be officially relegated to this bottom category of the social hierarchy. Since slaves did not pay taxes, this system decreased the potential size of the state's tax base by designating many of the offspring of commoners and even of some *yangban* as slaves and thus as non-taxpayers.

The state could thus expand the revenue base by changing the laws to ensure that not all descendants of slaves assumed this status. In 1669, the state did just that: from that date forward only the offspring of women slaves assumed the status of their mothers, a legal change that demonstrated the centrality of women to determining status in Chosŏn. Previously, the offspring of a male slave and a commoner woman would have become a slave, but under the new provisions the child of such a union became a commoner and, as a result, was required to pay taxes. This gradually decreased the proportion of slaves in the overall population. The interests of the state and *yangban* in maintaining the status system conflicted with the state's need to expand its revenues, a tension that was to arise repeatedly in the last years of the dynasty. The number of tax-paying commoners did increase, but the vast majority of the peninsula's resources remained in the hands of *yangban*, who continued scrupulously to guard their tax-exempt status.

FARMERS, RICE, AND THE COMMERCIALIZATION OF AGRICULTURE

In the sixteenth century, new methods of growing rice—the most widely planted cereal crop—transformed the rural Korean society and economy. Traditionally, Chosŏn farmers planted rice by scattering seeds across a field. But over the course of the sixteenth century, the method of transplanting rice seedlings spread through the fertile lands of the peninsula. In this technique, which had been known in central and southern China for centuries, rice seeds were planted densely in a separate, preparatory bed. As the seedlings grew, farmers winnowed out poor and diseased seedlings while selecting the strongest and most desirable.

When the seedlings reached a few inches in height, they were transferred to the water-flooded main paddy field, an arduous task requiring all members of the family to pluck out the seedlings, bundle them, carry them to the paddy, and replant them. Already healthy and maturing, the seedlings outperformed weeds, thus decreasing the amount of time needed for weeding. Transplantation increased the productivity of land, for while the seedlings were growing in the preparatory bed, another crop—most commonly barley—could be grown in the main field. In the southernmost part of the peninsula, the new technique enabled more than one rice crop to be grown in a single year. Thus, transplantation dramatically increased the yield of agricultural land, producing more wealth for farmers (and/or landowners) able to take advantage of the technique.

Known since the early fifteenth century, this technique had been discouraged by the state, for transplantation required more water control and was vulnerable in drought years. The old method, officials argued, may have been less productive, but it was more reliable. Farmers disagreed. The gains in yield and labor saving constituted a powerful incentive, whatever the risk of a drought year. Despite state prohibitions, more and more farmers adopted rice transplantation as information concerning the technique spread in the early 1600s, particularly in the agriculturally rich provinces of the south. New strains of rice were developed—some with shortened growing seasons to enable two crops a year, some with drought-resistant characteristics, and still others more suited to transplantation. As the land gradually recovered from the devastation of the late sixteenth-century invasions, these changes resulted in a boom in agricultural productivity and gradual population growth. That increased population in turn produced more food.

But transplantation also came with costs. The intensification of agriculture—growing more crops on the same piece of land—depleted soil nutrients, resulting in higher demand for fertilizers to restore the fields. A market developed for waste products, including night soil (human and animal manure), and new types of fertilizer were also sought. Most important, the savings in labor offered by this technique had a significant impact on land tenure and rural labor markets. Since a farming

Transplanting rice, c. 1969. Since the introduction of rice transplantation in the sixteenth century, the technique has continued to be used by farmers up to the present day.

family now required less time and labor per piece of land, the saved labor could be used to till even more land. With each farming family able to cultivate more land, small landowners had less need to rent out land to tenants. Moreover, the savings offered by this technique allowed some farmers to accumulate even more land, creating larger estates that relied on tenants or wage labor. In short, rice transplantation, by increasing the yield of land, raised the demand for prime, fertile fields, giving both large and small landowners tremendous advantages at the same time as the situation of tenants and wage laborers became more precarious.

These changes in the agricultural economy attracted the attention of many contemporary writers. Yu Hyŏngwŏn wrote extensively about rural conditions, basing most of his critiques on the Confucian belief that agriculture constituted the basis of the state and the economic foundation for a proper moral order. He especially criticized unequal distribution of land, as he asked rhetorically of his readers, "Why is it that you are not concerned that some individuals have accumulated vast holdings of land while the masses of men have no land at all?" Such inequities could only be remedied by having a public land system, he believed, one that provided a secure living for all the people and thus enabled them to cultivate their morality. "Under a system of public land ownership, the people have a constant source of production, their minds are secure, their moral transformation through education can be achieved, their mores and customs can be generous, and in all matters there will be no one who does not obtain his proper share."[4] Such proposals, with their expectation that the state could confiscate and redistribute all property, had their basis in ancient Chinese texts describing the state-operated "equal field system." Impractical and never implemented, these ancient plans nevertheless inspired critics who succeeded Yu, and land reform remained a crucial issue well into the twentieth century.

The increase in rice production supported the further commercialization of agriculture. Abundant rice guaranteed that surpluses were not reserved for the consumption of the grower but for the profits offered by the marketplace. Other farmers, able to buy rice to feed their families at their local market, turned some, if not all, of their fields over to cash crops such as garlic, cotton, onions, or other vegetables. Throughout the seventeenth century, the publication of agricultural manuals assisted these shifts in agricultural production. Occasionally state-sponsored, they were usually written by scholars living in rural communities who were interested in bettering the conditions of the countryside. These manuals explained the best cultivation techniques for different types of land, offered diagrams for the construction of irrigation devices, and introduced the expanding variety of seeds available to farmers.

With the entrance of New World crops into the peninsula during the sixteenth to eighteenth centuries, these manuals featured even more cash crops. During that period, Korean farmers began to plant tomatoes, corn, and squash, but the most important of the newly introduced crops were tobacco, potatoes, and hot peppers. Tobacco plants first arrived in the late sixteenth century, and by the middle of the seventeenth century smoking had become such a common habit among Korean men that farmers converted some of the most fertile lands in the peninsula to this most lucrative of crops. Sweet potatoes, brought into Korea by an emissary to Tsushima in 1763, also quickly spread around the peninsula. Able to grow in sandy soil and on the slopes of mountains, sweet potatoes were a boon to poor farmers. Agricultural handbooks regularly promoted the planting of potatoes as a famine crop since they could survive severe droughts, serving as a crop of last resort when other crops failed. Hot chili peppers arrived and quickly gained great popularity, becoming a basic condiment in a whole range of foods. Combined with a new type of cabbage imported from China, the fiery pepper pod transformed one of Korea's staple foods, kimch'i, from a pickle made of radishes and salt to one of cabbage, salt, and chilies.

The profits to be gained from these crops depended largely on location. Farmers in isolated areas or with infertile land could not take advantage of the growing diversification of agriculture, so their conditions did not change dramatically. If a farmer lived close to a market town, however, the profits to be made from cash crops could certainly exceed those from producing rice or other grains. As more land could be devoted to cash crops, the exchange economy flourished, and the circulation of currency increased. In 1678, the government issued new coins; and despite the periodic occurrence of what are called currency famines—when coin supply could not keep up with market activity, largely due to coin hoarding—the increasing availability of currency stimulated trade in many parts of the peninsula.

INTERNATIONAL TRADE

The arrival and dissemination of New World food crops demonstrated Chosŏn's trade dealings with the outside world. Interrupted by Hideyoshi's invasion and the Ming to Qing transition, trade with the peninsula's two neighbors—Ming (then Qing) China and Tokugawa Japan—recovered during the subsequent peace and began to boom by the end of the seventeenth century. With memories of the Hideyoshi invasion fresh in their minds, Chosŏn officials at first hesitated to reestablish ties with their Japanese neighbors. But after negotiations and the return of more than 7,000 kidnapped subjects to the peninsula, they reached a written agreement in 1607 that spelled out the conditions of the new relationship. The Tokugawa regime invited a Chosŏn delegation to visit their new capital at Edo. Embassies from abroad offered international legitimacy to the still shaky Tokugawa regime (it was only four years old at this point), and later embassies often arrived after the accession of a new shogun. Over the course of the dynasty, 12 Chosŏn missions, the first shortly after the resumption of relations and the last in the early nineteenth century, reached the shogun's capital.

Chosŏn authorities were less than eager to entertain reciprocal visits in Seoul, however. Instead, they restricted contact with Japan to a small walled compound of a few square miles in the southeastern port town of Tongnae—modern-day Pusan—where Japanese merchants were allowed to live. Through the gates of these walls, Korean private merchants, officials, and even smugglers offered the Japanese traders a wide range of goods, including medicines, porcelain (tea bowls were especially popular), books, writing utensils, horses, cowhides, and more. In 1651, when Chosŏn officials felt more confident about the recovery of the economy, the government again allowed rice exports to Japan. After the Qing authorities banned the export of silk to Japan, Korean merchants participated in a lucrative middleman trade, buying silk from Chinese merchants and reexporting it to Japan. Except for the embassies themselves, this trade passed entirely through the fief of Tsushima—several islands lying between Kyūshū and the Korean peninsula—ruled by the Sŏ family of *daimyō*, who became wealthy through commerce.

By far the most lucrative commodity in Chosŏn's international trade was ginseng. Widely known throughout East Asia for its medicinal qualities and reputed to be a powerful aphrodisiac, wild ginseng commanded a high price on the international market. In the otherwise economically backward mountains of the northern peninsula, where rice could not grow but the best ginseng could, anyone lucky enough to stumble across a large wild root could make a fortune by selling it into a market that could send it to the medicine shops of Seoul, Edo, or Beijing. As international demand for Korean ginseng grew, so too did the pressure and incentive to find wild ginseng. Dependent on the vagaries of nature and the luck of hunters, the supply could fluctuate wildly; sales to Japan plunged from 6,678 *kun* (8,013 lb [3,642 kg]) in one year to a measly 29 (35l b [15.8 kg]) the next. The difficulty of maintaining a consistent supply together with the gradual depletion of the wild stock made farmers and merchants search for ways to domesticate the root. Although farmers had long ago planted the seeds of wild ginseng, new techniques were developed to allow large fields of ginseng to be cultivated. New processing methods enabled merchants to produce concentrated or dried ginseng products, ideal for long-distance shipping. By the end of the century, Kaesŏng, the old capital city just north of Seoul, had become a center for ginseng cultivation and processing, its leading merchants accumulating massive wealth in international trade.

Silver and copper remained the key commodities in this trade. By the seventeenth century, Japan had emerged as one of the world's largest producers of these two precious metals, equal to or even ahead of the New World mines. In return for their ginseng, Korean merchants generally received these two metals, using them as domestic currency as well as to purchase silk, porcelain, books, and other products from China. Thus a hunter of wild ginseng in the northern mountains of Chosŏn could be, unknown to himself, indirectly linked through the global flows of silver and copper not just to consumers of his product in the rich markets of East Asia, but also to the miners of Peru, the sailors on the Manila galleons, and the European aficionados of Chinese silk and ceramics—a vast range of people around the world whose consumption and production depended on the global silver economy and the parallel regional trade in copper.

KIM MANJUNG

Born into an eminent family of scholars, Kim Manjung (1637–1692) experienced an early loss: the year he was born, his father committed suicide to protest the Chosŏn court's decision to submit to the Manchus after their second invasion of the peninsula. Educated by his mother, Kim passed the highest levels of exams before assuming a number of high official positions. Yet his career was consistently interrupted by the factionalism that divided the court in the seventeenth century. Kim lost his post on four occasions, in each case sent into internal exile for criticizing behavior at court that did not, in his eyes, fulfill the proprieties of Confucian orthodoxy.

Modern Koreans remember Kim less for his official career than for his work as one of the earliest writers of long narratives in Korea. Although he wrote more than ten narratives, only two still exist, one written in the Korean vernacular, the other in classical Chinese. The latter work, *Nine Cloud Dream* (*Kuun mong*), stands as a classic of early Korean narrative. Set against the backdrop of Tang China, the story recounts the experiences of a Buddhist monk who, after a tempting encounter with wine and women that challenges his beliefs, falls asleep, only to be transported into a new world where he lives as a leading Confucian official, brilliant in the arts and the sword, serving the emperor loyally. At the peak of this success, however, the monk awakens to discover that he had actually been dreaming and that none of these successes was real.

Scholars have long been puzzled by the clear Buddhist content of *Nine Cloud Dream*, demonstrated by its emphasis on the transitory nature of worldly achievement. Why would a scholar who, in his life as an official, had suffered because of his defense of Confucian orthodoxy write a narrative with deep Buddhist connotations? The prevalence of Buddhist elements in *Nine Cloud Dream* likely reflects how Buddhism, despite state persecution, maintained a vibrant existence even among the scholarly elite like Kim Manjung. For men who debated the proper form of ritual and the relation of principle to material existence in Confucian metaphysics, Buddhism did not undermine Confucian beliefs; rather, it complemented them in the everyday life of the individual.

Woodblock print illustration from an early edition of Kim Man-jung's *Nine Cloud Dream* (1689).

CULTURAL GROWTH AND CRITICISM

The changes in the economy, especially in agriculture, attracted the attention of many contemporary intellectuals. Alienated from the channels of power in Seoul and the regional bureaucracy, some of these writers began exploring strands of Confucian thought that had been deemphasized by the majority of officials, who remained in thrall to Zhu Xi orthodoxy and debates on metaphysics. Aware of scholarly trends in China, familiar with some of the early Jesuit writings circulating in East Asia, and turning for their inspiration to the earliest Classics, these writers published extensive observations of contemporary society together with proposals to reform its shortcomings. Later historians have sometimes referred to these scholars as students of "practical learning" (к. *silhak*, J. *jitsugaku*, C. *shixue*), a term that became popular in Japan and China as well. In all three cultures, they represented a reinvigoration and expansion of longstanding Confucian traditions, writing about social reform and political economy in response to current conditions in ways similar to Gu Yanwu and his colleagues in the early Qing. Chosŏn Confucianism, like its Chinese and Japanese counterparts, thus spanned the vast range from abstruse theoretical philosophizing to practical manuals for the conduct of daily religious, social, and economic life.

In the seventeenth century, scholars such as Yi Sugwang (1563–1628) and Ho Mok (1595–1682)—to name just two of many—pushed scholarship in new directions, revisiting traditional subjects such as cartography or delving into more original topics such as Islam or the technology of silver mining. Yu Hyŏngwŏn, with his essays on slavery and land reform, was one of the most wide-ranging. Living in a farming village, Yu's direct experiences with life in the countryside informed his critical and historical studies of the institutions and mores that governed rural conditions. His desire to improve these conditions led him to a massive study, published in 1670, that moved well beyond slavery and land reform to include military service, education, local governance, technology, and even mathematics. Late Chosŏn society was changing, and rural *yangban* writers such as Yu served as recorders of these changes, critics of the current situation, and advocates for reform.

The social changes brewing by the late 1600s stimulated not only critiques of the status quo but also the growth of new literary forms. Perhaps the most important literary development of the late Chosŏn dynasty was the publication of the first Korean vernacular novel, the *Biography of Hong Kiltong*. Written by a secondary son, Hŏ Kyun (1569–1618), this story of virtuous bandits displayed the talents of a non-*yangban* writer using the vernacular language to weave an entertaining yarn that criticized his society from within. Reserving his special ire for corrupt officials and discrimination against secondary sons, Hŏ offered a decidedly non-Confucian utopian vision, mixing Daoist elements into an ideal kingdom built by his protagonist on an isolated island. The popularity of the new genre quickly attracted other authors, even the famous scholar and official Kim Manjung (1637–1692), who chose classical Chinese to write the fantastical *Nine Cloud Dream*, a novel with deep Buddhist influences (see box opposite). The growth and spread of novels in the Korean vernacular opened literature to Koreans outside the Chinese-reading elites. The trade in books expanded, as publishing (like other sectors of the economy) became more commercialized, and private book-lending facilities arose in urban centers to serve the new audiences.

Just as the readership for literature expanded, so did authorship move beyond the confines of the *yangban* class. By the end of the seventeenth century, the gradual coalescence of a new status group, one with its roots in the early Chosŏn dynasty, had become clear. Defined by their occupations as the technical and administrative staff in the central and local bureaucracy—translators, calligraphers, medical experts, accountants, legal specialists, painters, mail specialists, land surveyors, minor officials, and the like—this status group came to be known as the *chungin*, literally "the people in the middle." While the term had several origins, it neatly captured the middling position of the *chungin*, above the commoners yet still below the *yangban*. These men were given the tasks deemed beneath a cultivated *yangban*, they were not able to sit for the exams, and they could not attain higher office. Yet as highly educated people, the *chungin* by the end of the seventeenth century began participating in the literary culture of the *yangban*, using their knowledge of Chinese to write poetry and essays that circulated quite widely. In these various ways, the literary culture of the late seventeenth century began to blossom as more people wrote a greater variety of literature for a growing audience. These trends accelerated in the eighteenth century.

JAPAN IN THE SEVENTEENTH CENTURY: CONSOLIDATING THE REALM

Tokugawa rule could have been cemented by Tokugawa Ieyasu's victory in the Battle of Sekigahara in 1600. But Ieyasu and his successors struggled until 1640 to pacify the realm. The peace after Sekigahara changed the lives of countless samurai. The daily practice of being samurai required them to become government functionaries, serving their lords in offices, and many of them resisted. Others had served *daimyō* who were defeated. In the first decades of the century, masterless samurai (J. *rōnin*) roamed the streets making trouble. Even more worrisome to officials, some *rōnin* joined resistance movements. The rowdy violence of the early Tokugawa decades subsided by mid-century with the growth of alternative jobs and amusements for the samurai.

Ieyasu's assumption of the title of shogun was only nominal until the shogunate learned to control the *daimyō*. The Tokugawa established a code of conduct for the *daimyō* houses and moved *daimyō* around to set up regional power balances. In addition, the shogunate instituted a powerful control mechanism called the alternate attendance system (J. *sankin kōtai*); assumed control of roads, ports, mines, and international relations; and favored ideologies that legitimated shogunal rule.

Ieyasu abdicated in favor of his son Hidetada, but continued to rule until his death in 1616. He thus solved the problem his predecessor, Hideyoshi, had faced on his deathbed in 1598. Hideyoshi's fear—that his son Hideyori would not be able to succeed him—had, in fact, been realized. Ironically, it was Toyotomi Hideyori, supported by other dissidents, whose existence in splendid impotence in Osaka castle challenged shogunal legitimacy and led to Ieyasu's last war in 1614–15. Ieyasu, unlike Hideyoshi, died knowing his son had already become shogun.

Japan in 1600 was not a modern state with central authority reaching to every segment of society, but Tokugawa Ieyasu did create mechanisms to control the realm. He established himself as a supreme ruler over self-regulating status categories. He recast the four "classes" of the ancient Chinese texts as Japanese status groups: samurai, farmers, artisans, and merchants. In reality, these self-regulating entities contained more diversity than homogeneity.

Villages regulated themselves, while cities and towns had a variety of means of governance, depending on their relationship to their *daimyō*. Groups that did not fit neatly into one of the four statuses—for example, outcastes or urbanites involved in the theater or sex

LEFT View of the Yōmeimon gate of the Tōshōgū shrine at Nikkō, in which Tokugawa Ieyasu was enshrined as the Shintō deity Tōshō Daigongen. During the Tokugawa period over 500 shrines were established across Japan to the deified founder of the Tokugawa shogunate.

RIGHT Regions and domains of Tokugawa Japan (1600–1868)

Regional border
Domain border
Tozama domain
Shinpan/Fudai domain

HOKKAIDŌ

Ezo

EAST SEA / SEA OF JAPAN

Akita

Morioka

TŌHOKU

Sendai

Yonezawa

Aizu

Kaga

HOKURIKU

Echizen

Mito

KANTŌ

Hikone

Himeji

CHŪBU

Edo (Tokyo)

KINKI

Kyoto

Owari

KINAI

Osaka

TSUSHIMA

CHŪGOKU

Tsushima

Chōshū

Tokushima

Kii

Tosa

SHIKOKU

Hizen

PACIFIC

Higo

KYŪSHŪ

OCEAN

Nagasaki

Satsuma

N

0   250 miles

0   400 kms

trades—had their own governing structures. If people and institutions stayed out of trouble and paid taxes, the shogunate generally left them alone, sometimes issuing a warning to behave in a moral way but rarely finding reason to enforce its decrees. The Tokugawa did control its own status group—the *daimyō*—very tightly, through a lord–vassal (feudal) relationship. The shogunate defined *daimyō* as vassals whose land produced at least 10,000 *koku* of rice (1 *koku* = 190 quarts [180 liters]), approximately the amount needed to sustain one person for one year).

THE TOKUGAWA AND THE *DAIMYŌ*

Soon after Sekigahara, Ieyasu began rearranging *daimyō* to reflect their role in the civil war. Some opponents, called *tozama*, lost everything or found their lands reduced. Some loyal vassals, called *fudai*, received more productive or strategically located territories. Many, even some who fought with the opposition in 1600, kept their domains until Ieyasu's grandson Iemitsu (r. 1623–1651) got rid of them. By Iemitsu's death in 1651, half the *tozama* domains were gone, although those that remained ranked among the largest domains. The shoguns moved the *tozama* to the outer periphery of Japan and the *fudai* to the heartland closest to Edo. A third category, *shinpan daimyō* (descendants of Ieyasu's sons), was created during the seventeenth century.

Ieyasu had additional means of controlling *daimyō*. All *daimyō* had to swear oaths of loyalty and demonstrate that loyalty with action. They could show obedience by destroying all but one castle in each domain, obtaining shogunal approval for family members' marriages, cultivating the skills of civil government, offering gifts to the Tokugawa to build the shogun's lavish castles and mausoleums, and making regular visits to pay formal submission to the shogun. In 1615, Ieyasu organized these practices into a Code of Laws for Military Households.

Lumping all the *daimyō* together as a single status group would have seemed ludicrous to people in the Tokugawa period. The three categories of *fudai*, *shinpan*, and *tozama* were treated differently. Only the trusted *fudai* held major posts at Edo. Three of the *shinpan* had a special relationship to the shogunal dynasty; their sons could become shogun if he died without an heir. But otherwise, the shogunate neither sought nor desired *shinpan* opinions. *Daimyō* also varied enormously

by wealth. The Tokugawa directly controlled about 4 million *koku* of rice output, one *tozama daimyō* over 1 million *koku*, and the next nine *daimyō* between 400,000 and 800,000 *koku* each. At the other end, 91 of the approximately 240 domains produced only 10,000–20,000 *koku*, enough to support a population of 10,000–20,000 souls—a few villages and towns. Although the domains consistently underreported output because villages attempted to hide rice from the tax collectors, these figures indicate a huge difference in *daimyō* wealth.

By 1642, the alternate attendance system required *daimyō* to spend alternating years in their domain castles and their Edo mansions. Their wives and heirs had to remain in Edo, as hostages in gilded cages, without returning to the domain. The shogunate strictly regulated alternate attendance travel to prevent the huge armies of retainers—some retinues had as many as 3,000 samurai—from clashing with one another on the road and to assure sufficient food and lodging in towns along the way. The retinues had to pass through guard posts to ensure that no firearms were smuggled into Edo and no women (wives) smuggled out.

The alternate attendance system controlled the *daimyō* in two ways. First, it reminded them of their subordination to the Tokugawa. Second, it manipulated the domains' finances. Maintaining an elegant mansion in Edo to keep up with one's *daimyō* neighbors, traversing the countryside with half the domain's samurai every year, feeding and housing those samurai both on the road and in Edo, redoing the home castle in the stylish Edo mode, and maintaining duplicate offices ate up two-thirds of the *daimyō*'s revenues. Alternate attendance expenditures built the Japanese economy as a whole but depleted many *daimyō*'s coffers. Just as the Tokugawa intended, few *daimyō* contemplated rebellion.

The *daimyō* technically ruled autonomously within their domains, with their own legal and fiscal systems. The Tokugawa collected taxes from their own lands, which produced about one-quarter of the realm's rice at the beginning of the period, while the *daimyō* retained the rice revenues from their own domains' villages. Though not taxed by the shogunate, the *daimyō* often received unpredictable tribute demands from Edo. For example, early in the shogunate, Ieyasu ordered the Satsuma *daimyō* to build 300 wooden ships to transport stone for Ieyasu's castle. Although the *daimyō* had to pay exorbitant costs, the domain developed jobs for lumberjacks, sailors, shipbuilders, and suppliers of food, clothing, and lodging. The stone had to be cut from quarries using tools made of iron, which was mined, smelted, and crafted. The workers' pay spread money around. Such examples demonstrate that the Tokugawa's political strategies to control the *daimyō* and strengthen shogunal power led to unintended economic and social growth.

THE TOKUGAWA REGIME AND THE WORLD

Hideyoshi's death ended continental adventures, but Tokugawa Ieyasu had no interest in cutting off trade with the Chinese, Koreans, and some Europeans. Although foreign trade was never more than a small part of Japan's expanding economy in the Tokugawa period, it did provide many desirable luxury products. Tokugawa mines produced gold, silver, and copper, providing sufficient cash for silk from China, herbs and medicines (especially ginseng) from Chosŏn, and exotic plants and woods from Southeast Asia. Regarding the Europeans, Ieyasu did not want to import Christian evangelism, so he sought alternatives to Iberian merchants and vessels.

Although Portuguese traders had hauled much of the cargo in the early Tokugawa years, they soon lost that trade. To expedite the replacement of the Iberians, Ieyasu issued 200 licenses to trade with China and Southeast Asia to Japanese merchants and samurai, as well as to some foreigners. His successors continued the practice, granting an additional 150 permits by 1630. Unlicensed traders, including some from China, joined the commercial fray as well. Mindful of the Ming prohibition on trade with Japan, promulgated because of the coastal pirates' depredations, the Chinese merchants met Japanese traders in the Ryūkyū Islands or in Tongnae (Pusan), in southern Chosŏn. By 1610, some sailed directly to Japan. Between 2,000 and 3,000 Chinese merchants took up residence in Nagasaki to handle the 30–60 Chinese vessels arriving annually during the early Tokugawa period.

Chinese trade also continued through the Ryūkyūs. In 1609, the Satsuma *daimyō* invaded the islands and compelled the independent Ryūkyū king to accept his demands for trade and control. While Ieyasu was happy to establish a trading relationship with the Ryūkyūs, he was disturbed by Satsuma's unilateral actions. The shogun also worried that such a large domain could become more powerful through international trade.

Handscroll of Dutch traders on Deshima, Nagasaki harbor, c. 1800 (detail), showing Dutch merchants and their African servants performing music, dining Western style, and trading. The Dutch were the only Europeans the shogun permitted to conduct trade on Tokugawa territory.

(He had no such concerns about tiny Tsushima, which dominated Japanese trade with Korea.) So he forbade the domains of the southwest from sailing ocean-going vessels with over 500 *koku* capacity, beginning what would eventually become a complete ban on all ocean voyages by Japanese.

Trade with Korea through Tsushima had predated Hideyoshi's invasions. After peace was restored, the *daimyō* of Tsushima tried to resume the lucrative business, but first he had to negotiate a peace treaty between the shogun and the Korean king. He succeeded in 1607, and the resulting treaty allowed trade to begin again in 1611 through an official trading post set up by the Tsushima *daimyō* at Tongnae, the only place on the peninsula the Chosŏn court allowed foreigners to live (see p. 85). In addition to the Edo-authorized trade, the Tsushima *daimyō* and his merchants also carried out private trade, including Korean ginseng and Chinese silks, for which the Japanese merchants paid between 25,000 and 30,000 pounds of silver per year.

Rapidly growing commercial exchanges with China exceeded even this large volume of trade with Korea. In one decade alone (1615–25), Japan exported at least 250,000 to 300,000 pounds of silver in exchange for imports from China. Japan's silver exports, entering the world monetary system through the China trade, played a significant role in global commerce until the 1680s, when the Tokugawa's silver mines began to play out.

This record of bountiful trade with China and Korea might suggest that the Tokugawa's commercial and diplomatic relations were unfettered by controls, but they certainly were not. By the 1640s, the Tokugawa severely limited relations with foreign countries. If a ship of any Japanese domain blew off-course and landed outside the Tokugawa realm, its crew had to remain in exile for life. The shogunate made returning from overseas, except from the Ryūkyūs or Korea, a capital crime. This policy came to be called "closed country," but in the seventeenth century it was simply another aspect of Tokugawa regulation.

Tokugawa foreign policy changed because they became serious about controlling Christianity. Hideyoshi had sporadically attempted to regulate the activities of Christians, but he had no systematic exclusion policy. In 1600, a Dutch ship's captain named Jacob Quaeckernaeck was shipwrecked off Japan and brought to shore. He convinced Ieyasu that the Protestant, commercially minded Dutch, unlike the Iberians, were not interested in proselytizing. The shogun commissioned him in 1605 to open trade ties with the Netherlands, and Dutch ships began to arrive in 1609. Similarly, the English seemed interested in conducting trade without bringing religion, so Ieyasu allowed commercial relations with England in 1613. English merchants, unable to compete with the Dutch, abandoned the Japanese market ten years later, choosing instead to focus on China, India, and the New World.

Ieyasu prohibited Iberian trade activities in 1614. Between 1633 and 1639, edicts prohibiting Japanese travel abroad ended most direct Japanese involvement in foreign trade. For the next two centuries, only the Chinese, Koreans, Ryūkyūans, and Dutch traded in the islands, mostly through Satsuma and Tsushima and the port of Nagasaki.

Although declining precious metal production at the end of the seventeenth century made it increasingly difficult for Japanese merchants to pay for imports, trade volume continued to be high. Diplomatic relations, however, did not proceed smoothly. Two elements characterized the Tokugawa regime's seventeenth-century international relations: the struggle to regulate the importation of Christianity, linked to domestic sedition; and the rise of the Manchus, which affected relations with both China and Korea.

At the dawn of the Tokugawa shogunate, Ieyasu worried about Christians as much as Hideyoshi had. Buddhists concerned him, too, but with the exception of one small sect, the early shoguns pacified the Buddhists. At mid-century, scholarly attacks on Buddhism by increasingly influential Confucian scholars deprived religious study of its earlier intellectual vitality. In addition, the requirement that all Japanese register as members of a Buddhist temple to show their rejection of Christianity made the Buddhist clergy an arm of Tokugawa local control. By the late seventeenth century, Buddhism no longer motivated mass religious movements, as it had earlier.

The shogunate could not control Christianity with the same tools. Since foreign governments sponsored Christianity, the religion appeared to be an instigator of domestic subversion. Indeed, some of the rebels supporting Hideyori in 1615 flew Christian banners, and Hideyori's defenders included two Jesuits and three Franciscans. Tokugawa Hidetada may have thought their defeat would put an end to the Christian problem, but the following year, a merchant/adventurer, an apostate Christian, dragged the shogunate into foreign trouble by attempting to conquer Taiwan. Though he failed, his piracy along the China coast contributed to Hidetada's concern about Christians. In the 1620s, Hidetada unleashed a brutal campaign to suppress the approximately 300,000 Christians throughout his realm, forcing them to recant and killing the 4,000–5,000 who refused.

Two decades later, a final Christian-inspired rebellion shook the Tokugawa. The establishment of alternate attendance, accompanied by devastating weather in the 1630s, produced widespread rural starvation, followed by peasant uprisings. In 1637–38, on the Shimabara peninsula, east of Nagasaki, the local peasants, joined by a number of *rōnin*, raised Christian banners. The shogunate brought its full power, plus Dutch reinforcements, to besiege the 37,000 farmers and samurai gathered at Shimabara and starved them out. This rebellion convinced shogun Iemitsu to enforce the ban on Christianity vigorously. Some surviving Christians practiced their religion secretly until the 1870s.

Tokugawa policy restricted international contacts, both diplomacy and trade, to countries and peoples they could trust. Both Chosŏn and Ming could be trusted not to invade or to sponsor Christianity, but Tokugawa relations with them differed considerably. Unlike Chosŏn, the Tokugawa rejected inclusion within the Ming tribute system. In its relations with Chosŏn, the Tokugawa forged bilateral ties between equals, establishing diplomatic contacts, separate from the trade office run by Tsushima. Between the seventeenth and early nineteenth centuries, 12 Chosŏn diplomatic embassies, each with 300–500 members, visited the Tokugawa court at Edo. The Tokugawa used these impressive meetings to remind the *daimyō* of the Tokugawa's legitimacy.

The two realms conducted their relations at Edo on the basis of equality. The Korean visitors did not prostrate themselves. Indeed, the Ming (then Qing) requirement that foreign visitors perform their inferiority to the emperor in the tribute system—the emperor sat above, and the visitors prostrated themselves below—led the Tokugawa to refuse to send diplomatic missions to Beijing. This, of course, did not mean the Tokugawa rejected trade with Chinese merchants, only that they

would not conduct formal diplomatic relations. The China-centered tribute system even affected Tokugawa relations with Korea, for the Chosŏn king did not reciprocate with invitations to the Tokugawa to send embassies to Seoul. Chosŏn did not accept the Tokugawa attempt to establish a regional diplomatic order without Beijing at the center.

Tokugawa unease with the Manchus also contributed to their reluctance to send official missions to the Qing court after the 1630s. The Manchu occupation of Seoul in 1627 raised fears that they would invade Japan as the Mongols had 350 years earlier. The Tokugawa debate over sending troops to aid Chosŏn in repelling the Manchus ended only when the latter withdrew. When the Manchus again invaded Chosŏn a decade later, Iemitsu was preoccupied with a proposal, never carried out, for a joint Japanese-Dutch attack on the Spanish in the Philippines, so he took no action against the Manchus at that time. When the Manchus entered Shanhaiguan to take Beijing in 1644, however, he gave strong consideration to aiding the Ming, but decided that their cause was lost in 1646. That decision marked the end of the shogunate's active China policy.

At the end of the seventeenth century, the Kangxi Emperor lifted the Ming's century-long restriction on trade with Japan, and the already lucrative trade grew rapidly. Once the licensed limits had been reached, merchants conducted unlicensed trade at ports throughout western Japan. The Dutch, restricted since 1640 to living and trading on Deshima, a tiny island made of landfill in Nagasaki harbor, informed the shogunate of Jesuit influence over the Kangxi Emperor. (He did have Jesuit advisers at his court.) The shogunate began inspecting Chinese books for references to Christianity in 1684, but they feared that Christian materials could be smuggled in elsewhere. As a result, in 1687 Chinese merchants had to join the Dutch on Deshima, where they could be strictly regulated.

Nagasaki's evolving monopoly of foreign trade was reflected in the city's population growth, from some 30,000 in the 1660s to 53,000 in the 1680s. Shortages of precious metals in the next several decades, however, kept the volume of trade from continuing to rise. Import substitution began to replace some foreign products in the early eighteenth century, and by the end of the eighteenth century, foreign trade and diplomacy had become peripheral to the main concerns of the Tokugawa realm. Moreover, anxiety about the environmental effects of mining to bolster foreign trade began to surface in the 1680s. One seventeenth-century scholar connected the decline in the "spirit of the national land" to the fact that Japan "has not preserved the gold, silver, copper, and iron that are the ultimate spirit of the mountains and streams [of our land], but have... shipped them to foreign lands in great quantity."[5]

ECONOMIC GROWTH AND SOCIAL AND ENVIRONMENTAL CHANGE

The seventeenth century was an era of rapid economic growth. Peace permitted farmers to anticipate reliable harvests. Villagers no longer had to contend with arrogant samurai neighbors making unreasonable demands. The shogunate and the *daimyō* began the process of regularizing weights and measures and standardizing units for products. Iemitsu formalized rules for villages in Tokugawa-held lands in 1642. *Daimyō* then applied similar rules in their own domains. These included prohibitions against the sale of people; exhortations to work one's own land without use of wage labor; requirements that the more fortunate help the less fortunate; organization of village families into mutual-responsibility groups; requirements to maintain bridges and roads; injunctions against arbitrary exactions by officials; prohibitions against luxury items (such as tea); and calls for village self-governance by landowning farmers.

Self-governance, an example of rule by status groups, lay at the heart of the system. Local officials appointed by the *daimyō* assessed taxes on whole villages, then the village leadership determined each household's annual portion of the village tax bill. Making these decisions at the local level permitted fine-tuning to maximize each family's retained produce. In addition, the fact that local government officials did not penetrate the village beyond interacting with the village leadership meant that villagers were able to hide productivity increases. The population grew by two and a half times, from 12 million to 31 million, between 1600 and 1720, but for a 50-year period at the height of growth, farmers reported only a 5.4 percent increase in taxable rice output. The opening of new fields, which doubled the acreage under cultivation, and the application of new agricultural techniques produced a productivity surge, much of it hidden from the tax collectors, which supported the 250 percent increase in population but retained the increased wealth in local hands.

Not all farmers were well off and able to stash away produce and income. Domains experiencing exploitative government or bad weather suffered while others prospered. Within villages, good administration ideally supported the weak and relied on the benevolence of the rich. But unfair behavior also occurred, though limited by the mutual-responsibility groups that drew punishment for all if any of the members misbehaved.

Peace was not the only reason for rapid rural growth in the seventeenth century. The financial needs of the *daimyō* required that each domain develop a systematic tax plan. Farmers paid their taxes in rice, but *daimyō* had to convert that rice to cash to meet the expenses of the alternate attendance system and to purchase luxury goods to demonstrate their high status. They sold their rice in two major rice markets—Edo for domains in the east, and Osaka, a commercial city under direct shogunal rule, for domains in the west and center. These cities, as well as the castle towns and the emperor's capital at Kyoto, accounted for more than 10 percent of the population by 1700. Edo had over a million inhabitants, while Osaka and Kyoto together boasted 800,000. All those urban people needed to eat.

Merchants with special ties to the *daimyō* marketed the tax rice for their *daimyō* clients. Alternate attendance forced most *daimyō* to live beyond their means, so merchants extended them high-interest loans in advance of their domains' next rice harvest. Those merchants took substantial risks, since bad weather might make it impossible for the *daimyō* to repay them. Plays and paintings depicted Osaka merchants with their eyes to the sky, scanning the weather and thus the outcome of their gamble. If the *daimyō*'s tax income was substantial, the merchants' loan paid off handsomely. Determining and selling rice futures as well as handling the transfer of cash from the merchant house to the *daimyō* turned some of these merchants into bankers. Roads, sea routes, transportation companies, and communications companies sprang up in the seventeenth century to address the need to move goods and information for the merchants, the shogunate, and the alternate attendance system.

As *daimyō* processions moved across the realm, towns along the way fed and lodged them. Money made its way from guesthouses to the hinterland that supplied raw materials, food, and labor. That cash was used to buy commercial fertilizer (human and animal waste) to replace the twigs and compost that farmers used to collect before they converted their communal woodlands to new fields. Innovative irrigation devices opened new lands to rice farming. New labor-saving tools, such as threshers that could be used by weaker members of the family, freed the labor of stronger women and men to work harder in their newly opened fields. Ironically, what appeared to be labor-saving devices—tools that permitted greater output with the same input of labor—usually led to greater investment of family labor as less skilled children replaced more skilled adults who could, in turn, take on new, more lucrative, tasks.

As in Chosŏn, new agricultural technologies and seed information spread through printed treatises to remote villages as literacy expanded for both men and women. When they were not busy with farm chores, village boys and girls would attend schools run by Buddhist priests and others, including women. Urban demands for fruits, vegetables, and natural fibers (silk, hemp, and later cotton) encouraged farm families to invest in producing those crops, thereby earning money to buy fertilizers and more advanced farm tools from itinerant merchants.

The expanding economy connected villagers to urban markets in a variety of ways. Demands for construction workers and artisans in the rapidly growing cities, for example, drew labor from the villages, which forced the remaining peasants to work more productively. Nuclear families that could mobilize the labor of all their members were more productive than the large extended families of the late Warring States period. By the end of the seventeenth century, villages nearest to the highways engaged most directly in commercial interaction with the urban markets, resulting in a breakdown of old village structures.

Growth of the urban economy was even more remarkable. Earlier, Kyoto had been Japan's only large city. Markets had developed near Buddhist temples, but all were relatively small in scale. The new castle towns had populations that were roughly half samurai, half commoner. Only Osaka held a population made up overwhelmingly of merchants and artisans. Kyoto harbored the old aristocracy and royal family as well as the realm's greatest artists, novelists, and playwrights until cultural centers emerged in the larger cities of Edo and

Osaka in the eighteenth century. Although there was plenty of overlap, the three metropolises divided the urban functions of the realm: Edo controlled politics, Osaka the economy, and Kyoto the world of culture and fashion, a division that was already becoming blurred by the eighteenth century.

Regional cities grew both in size and sophistication throughout the seventeenth century, though many experienced stagnation in the following century. Before long, interregional integration gave birth to the idea that the realm had a common culture considered to be "Japanese," despite the continuing identification of most people with their village, town, domain, or region.

Many people moved around the realm, not just officials like samurai and *daimyō*. Traveling merchants brought goods to the rural areas; maritime companies developed freight lines to haul heavy goods (especially rice) cheaply from the coastal domains to Edo and the Osaka/Kyoto region; packhorse hauling companies sent thousands of horses onto the roads each day; and pedestrian travelers picked their way carefully along the roads behind them. Express messenger services, of which there were 86 in Kyoto alone, could make a delivery from Edo to Osaka, a distance of well over 300 miles (482 km), in four days. Pilgrims and sightseers, a large number of them women over 40 years of age, added to the bustle and excitement of inter-urban travel. Local villagers along the highways sent their elders and children out onto the roads, scooping up marketable waste like horse manure and soliciting customers for a bath and a meal, lodging and sex, or local delicacies and souvenirs. Ordinary travelers carried coins, while large shippers and *daimyō* developed instruments of credit. Few people remained untouched by urban culture and goods by the end of the seventeenth century.

The long arm of the city reached into the countryside's environment as well. During the building frenzy of the first few decades of the Tokugawa period, hundreds of castles and mansions, thousands of houses for samurai and merchants, and innumerable ships, temples, and shops depleted the supply of high-quality wood throughout the realm. Fires periodically ravaged the cities, requiring constant rebuilding. The 1657 Edo fire dwarfed all previous fires, for most of the city, the homes of the rich and the poor, went up in flames, and at least 100,000 people perished. When Edo residents as well as the shogunate tried to rebuild, they found

95

timber supplies inadequate, restricting their architectural choices, so the city was not as elegant as it had been before the fire.

Even before the fire, rural areas had already been hard-pressed to balance the needs for lumber, agricultural land, and forest products like compost, for the same land could not supply all three. To make matters worse, clear-cutting of trees to open new fields or supply wood to urban areas resulted in soil erosion that clogged rivers and wiped out crops, contributing to famines in the 1630s. In the eighteenth century, planners began reforestation.

CULTURE AND SOCIETY

Urbanization in the seventeenth century produced new cultural and social practices. As artisans and merchants gained wealth over the course of the century, they came to share the role of cultural patrons and arbiters of taste earlier held only by courtly aristocrats or educated samurai. At the dawn of the seventeenth century, urban culture had been samurai culture. In consolidating their power, the first shoguns shaped the thinking and culture of urban dwellers by patronizing certain types of cultural life and scholarship.

Before the rise of the Tokugawa, the liveliest intellectual traditions in Japan were in Buddhist theology. But the new period called for a new focus, one more practical than the introspective learning of Buddhism. As we have seen in both Ming and Chosŏn, Zhu Xi's Neo-Confucian thought entranced a new generation of scholars. Hayashi Razan (1583–1657) in Edo and Yamazaki Ansai (1618–1682), who lived in Kyoto and Edo, both began as Buddhist clerics but abandoned the religion for the more secular Zhu Xi learning. As Hayashi, for whom the shogun Hidetada built a school in 1630, wrote: "[T]hose who prefer Buddhism, which is not real, to Confucianism do such a thing only because they have not heard of the Way."[6]

Like Neo-Confucian studies in both Chinese and Korean cultures, the basis of Hayashi's thought was the study of principle (J. *ri*, C. *li*, K. *i*) and its relationship to material existence, real, observable manifestations or substance (J. *ki*, C. *qi*, K. *ki*). Principle infused the natural universe and human society, ensuring conformity between cosmic reality and human social structures. This belief system rationalized the four-status structure, which placed the samurai rightfully on top. Hayashi

and the other Zhu Xi scholars contended that the Confucian Five Relationships (see p. 31) were natural and proper for all people and times.

In this Confucian system, the shogun should be elevated above all human beings, except the Japanese emperor, whose proper status was articulated in Shintō, Japan's ancient religion, which had taken a back seat to Buddhism for hundreds of years. Shintō explained Japan's sacred creation as ordained by the gods and the emperor as descended from the Sun Goddess. Yamazaki Ansai resurrected Shintō to counter the humiliating notion that the Confucian world order scholars took as natural was, in fact, not Japanese but imported from China. To naturalize Confucianism as Japanese, Yamazaki bound it to Shintō. The politically impotent emperor, then, became the "Heaven" from which Tokugawa Ieyasu received Heaven's Mandate to rule after Sekigahara. The Chinese characters used for the Mandate remained identical to those used in China and Korea, indicating that Heaven chose different rulers for the different realms.

Yamaga Soko (1622–1685), the creator of the cult of masculinity known as the Way of the Warrior (J. *bushidō*), took the Japan-centered view further, calling Japan the realm of the gods, *chūka*, the "central civilization." The shogun's glorious legitimacy and the samurai's upholding of *bu* (military values) sanctified the realm, he wrote. Small wonder the shogunate placed Confucianism on a pedestal and patronized its scholars. By the seventeenth century, Chinese, Japanese, and Korean scholars had all named their own culture the Central Civilization (C. *zhonghua*, K. *chunghwa*, J. *chūka*).

Non-samurai urban folk, with the help of samurai, expressed their cultural values through the arts. Kyoto lay at the center of the art world in the seventeenth century, but important artists increasingly worked from Edo and Osaka in the eighteenth. The boom in construction of luxurious mansions in the early part of the century sustained a legion of painters, sculptors, and woodworkers. Later, arts and culture became increasingly accessible to less elite consumers, as new materials and techniques, particularly woodblock printing, brought mass-produced literature and visual arts into many hands.

A new aesthetic began to emerge among those who wished to be cultivated gentlemen—the appreciation of *yūgei*, the polite accomplishments of highly skilled amateur poetry, painting, tea ceremony, music, and calligraphy. These refined artistic skills, called the arts of *bun* or literati culture, ideally complemented the *bu*, or military skills, of the warrior elite. Gracefully educated men and women of any status background could achieve mastery of the arts of *bun*, and the prestige of *bun* came to outweigh that of the samurai's *bu*.

Far less refined culture also appealed to the rapidly expanding market of urban consumers. Sexuality formed the heart of this great cultural outpouring. Entrepreneurs packed brothels, teahouses, artists' and

Yoshitoshi Tsukioka. *Since the crescent moon I have been waiting for tonight – Old man*, 1891. This famous print from Yoshitoshi's series "One Hundred Aspects of the Moon" illustrates the haiku by Matsuo Bashō of the title, with the poet depicted as the old man encountering two men drinking to the moon.

writers' studios, theaters, and restaurants into zones set aside for sexual entertainment, enlivened by street performances with exotic animals, jugglers, musicians, and entertainers of all sorts. These zones, called "pleasure districts" (J. *yūkaku*), had been created to control sexuality. They were aimed primarily at male pleasure, but many of the zones' inhabitants were women—sex workers, attendants, even some managers—and women attended plays and other attractions.

Uncontrolled sexuality frightened the shogunate. A woman dancer named Okuni brought a new form of sensual performance called *kabuki* to Edo in 1603, and soon female *kabuki* troupes were all the rage. Onlookers often became rowdy, leading the shogunate to remove the performers to the edges of town in 1608. A lively sex trade involving actors followed the troupes, so the shogunate outlawed all female stage performers in 1629. Women's roles were then deftly performed by attractive boys. Wooed by star-struck audience members, these boys also came to be seen as problematic by the shogunate, so in 1653 they restricted the performance of female roles to adult males. Many theatergoers believed that male actors performed femininity better than women could.

The shogunate did not mind male–male sexual relations, as long as they followed rules of proper sexual etiquette. The performance of sex was part of the respected practice of adult male mentoring of young and beautiful boys in the seventeenth century, and it was practiced by the Tokugawa family, the *daimyō*, samurai, merchants, and artisans. Many adult men also had relationships with wives and both male and female prostitutes. In this era, sexuality was not defined by sexual identity—that is, as heterosexual or homosexual—as it would be in the late nineteenth century.

Sex with a boy who was a protégé or with a serving maid, of course, could be practiced anywhere, but the shogunate confined sex for purchase to well-defined and segregated zones. Official sexuality districts were set up in Edo (Yoshiwara) in 1617, in Osaka (Shinmachi) in 1629, and in Kyoto (Shimabara) in 1641. Brothels, mostly staffed by women and girls, though some offered boys as well, had to move to those districts, and the sexuality zones became magnets for all sorts of arts and culture.

Life for sex workers was not pleasant. Moats and gates enclosed the pleasure districts, and the women sex workers could not leave. Sold to brothels as young

IHARA SAIKAKU

No author better portrayed the hardworking and hard-playing world of Genroku-period urban society than the Osaka writer Ihara Saikaku (1642–1693). Born to a prosperous merchant family, Saikaku enjoyed the wealth necessary to attend the theater and visit teahouses and brothels. Early in his career, he focused on writing *haikai* verse—Matsuo Bashō viewed him as a rival—but he also tried his hand at other genres. In the last decade of his life, Saikaku turned to prose writing.

Saikaku's family manufactured swords for samurai, so Saikaku worked in his family's business. At the same time, he honed his craft as a poet and prose writer. A gentleman amateur writer, Saikaku soon taught *haikai* poetry to a growing group of students. His passion for writing earned him the nickname of "Oranda Saikaku" ("Holland Saikaku"). Since the Dutch at Nagasaki epitomized the peculiar and exotic, the nickname suggested that his devotion to writing was somewhat eccentric. Saikaku earned several other pen names, many of them containing the character *kaku* (crane), as in Saikaku ("western crane") and Kakuei ("crane eternity"), associated with the famous Daoist immortals in Chinese texts.

Saikaku balanced his avocation of writing with his work in the family business until 1675, the year his wife died, when he was left alone to care for his child, a blind daughter who died a few years later. Saikaku then abandoned the sword-making business and threw himself into writing. His writing of 1,600 haikai in a single session in 1678 led to mass production of verse on a competitive basis, and his increasingly prodigious efforts culminated in the 1680s with a famous 24-hour total of 23,500 verses, for which he gained the nickname "Niman Okina" ("Old Master Twenty Thousand"). Saikaku next turned his hand to playwriting and short critiques of the sexual and theatrical skills of handsome young stage actors. His plays, written for *kabuki* and puppet theaters, never enjoyed success, but he developed a successful

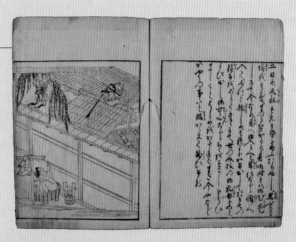

Illustration depicting the hero peering over a fence at a bathing woman from the bestselling 1682 edition of Saikaku's *Life of an Amorous Man*.

career as a prose writer specializing in the sexual lives of samurai, merchants, and actors, and later, in darker stories of the trials and tribulations of urban life.

Saikaku's keen eye for human behavior made his stories enormously popular in the Genroku era. His inaugural collection of stories, *Kōshoku ichidai otoko* (*Life of an Amorous Man*, 1682), first circulated among his friends; it was so well received that it created a demand for more and helped fuel Osaka's burgeoning publishing industry. Until his death a decade later, Saikaku wrote at a feverish pace. His first collections, including *Kōshoku ichidai otoko*, *Nanshoku okagami* (*Great Mirror of Male Love*, 1678), and *Kōshoku ichidai onna* (*Life of an Amorous Woman*, 1686), dealt with love between men and men and men and women. His collections on sex and love were witty and racy, even if their hedonistic protagonists had to atone for sometimes inappropriate sexual escapades. Saikaku's tone turned more pessimistic in his last years, however, and his tales of merchant life often depicted desperate individuals, imprisoned in social obligations and worsening their lives by making poor choices. Not long before his death, Saikaku, the son of a successful Osaka merchant, wrote a pessimistic tale of poverty, *Seken munesan'yo* (*Worldly Mental Calculations*, 1692).

girls, they led tough lives, despite their often elegant clothing and genteel bearing. Sex workers outside licensed brothels had an even harder time. The government did not tolerate unregulated sexuality, so people who engaged in unlicensed sex for hire were arrested. Burial records indicate that the leading cause of death for prostitutes was syphilis. The average age of death for serving girls at post stations, who often engaged in unlicensed sex, was 21; those in the regulated sex market presumably suffered similar fates.

Perhaps because so many found themselves buffeted by the uncertainties of life and fortune, the world of the arts came to be characterized as a "floating world" (J. *ukiyo*), a concept of life's impermanence familiar to all from Buddhism. *Ukiyo* seemed particularly appropriate during the Genroku period (1688–1704), when life expectancy, especially for entertainers, was so short; and gender, far from being "real" or "natural," was constituted through performance on stage and in brothels.

Poets, playwrights, novelists, and woodblock artists abounded, creating art for a mass-consumption market. The arts benefited from an increasingly sophisticated consumer population and the explosion of printing and literacy. During the seventeenth century, over 700 publishing companies were founded in Kyoto alone. Ieyasu had printed notices, laws, and warnings on movable-bed presses imported from Korea early in the century, and now woodblock presses delivered a seamless merging of word and text. Books, art prints, and pamphlets were found everywhere.

Contemporaries lionized the poet Matsuo Bashō (1644–1694), novelist and storyteller Ihara Saikaku (1642–1693), and woodblock artist Hishikawa Moronobu (1620?–1694). Son of a minor samurai, Bashō was the companion of his *daimyō*'s son, who introduced him to *haikai*, a form of linked verses of 17 syllables developed early in the seventeenth century. By 1677, Bashō had established himself as the major practitioner and teacher of the form. By the 1680s, he pioneered what later came to be called *haiku*—a poem of a single 17-syllable stanza modeled on the first verse of *haikai*. His *haiku* used imagery to evoke mood and suggested the linkages between seemingly dissimilar objects.

> On a withered branch
> a crow has settled—
> autumn nightfall.[7]

> A sudden lightening gleam:
> off into the darkness goes
> The night heron's scream.[8]

> On a journey, ill—
> my dreams, on withered fields
> are wandering still.[9]

In a society that enjoyed travel, pilgrimages to holy spots, and viewing scenic wonders, Bashō's poetic accounts gained a wide following, especially the nostalgic *Narrow Road to the North* (1689).

Bashō's contemporary Ihara Saikaku (see box opposite), one of the most successful prose writers of the Genroku period—he authored 25 books in the last ten years of his life—often laced his ribald tales with a touch of propriety. Saikaku was concerned with the travails of life for townsmen and townswomen and always noted the darker side of human relationships, but even these concerns were filtered through his eye for the bawdy. His novels and short stories moved from one intimate encounter to another, but even the ardent heroine of *Kōshoku ichidai onna* (*Life of an Amorous Woman*, 1686) suffered loneliness and humiliation at the end of her life.

Pictorial art was intimately connected with prose and poetry. Illustrated books brought art inexpensively to a mass readership. Woodblock prints were the breakthrough artistic form of the late seventeenth century. Earlier in the century, *shunga* (spring pictures) graphically showing techniques of love-making, gained popularity. Hishikawa Moronobu, who had studied the classical styles of painting, elevated the humble woodblock print to a major art form. Like Saikaku, many of his works dealt with average people—he illustrated Saikaku's *Life of an Amorous Man*, among other works—but he also produced picture books depicting travel scenes, handsome actors, beautiful courtesans, gardens, the bustle of Edo street life, and erotica. His work set the artistic standard for *ukiyo-e*, the "pictures of the floating world," that characterized the seventeenth century.

DIASPORAS

As Europeans colonized Southeast Asia in the seventeenth century, overseas Chinese communities took on more diverse functions. The expanding trans-Pacific trade in Spanish hands—the "Manila galleons"—brought copious silver to the Philippines, so much that the minted Mexican dollar became the standard currency of international trade in East Asia. Fujianese and Cantonese artisans, laborers, and even farmers joined the merchants to enrich themselves in and around Manila. The Dutch colonies in Java were chronically short of labor, and they planned to kidnap and import Chinese workers to increase production and tax revenues. An official wrote in 1623, "It is requisite by this present monsoon to send another fleet to visit the coast of China and take prisoners as many men, women, and children as possible…for the peopling of Batavia, Amboyna, and Banda."[10] The kings of Siam (later Thailand), never colonized and eager to participate in expanding trade, used their cultural and business connections with China to import both skilled and unskilled workers. The Siamese capital's Chinese quarter was large and prosperous, and Chinese served in many capacities at court, including physicians and entertainers.

This expansion of trade and function did not occur without conflict. In 1603, a visit to Manila by Chinese officials, mistrusted by the Spaniards, stimulated the Governor to order registration of all Chinese and regulation of their housing. The Chinese, fearful of either new taxes or violence, organized themselves to attack the main city, and mutual massacre ensued, in which the Chinese enclave was entirely looted, while hundreds of Spaniards and thousands of Chinese (some say 23,000) lost their lives. The colony, bereft of its farm-gardens, consumer goods, even shoemakers, could not survive without the Chinese, however, and new migrants soon arrived. A second Chinese uprising in 1639, this time against excessive taxation, again resulted in slaughter of the Chinese followed by a gradual rebuilding of Chinatown. In 1662, when a third confrontation threatened, the Jesuit missionaries prevented wholesale murder. For the rest of the seventeenth century, the Philippine Chinese, thoroughly intermarried with the local population but always concerned about expulsion or worse, coexisted uneasily with the Spanish authorities.

The Dutch in Java had initially desired to bring more Chinese—both kidnapped workers and traders drawn by the island's exotic goods—to their new colony. But they, too, worried about Chinese trading communities, their power and their wealth, and toward century's end

began to create laws making emigration more difficult. Enforcement of these rules gave the Dutch civil servants numerous opportunities to blackmail the Chinese merchants, and the regulations gradually became a protection racket, but they never prevented more Chinese from coming.

CONNECTIONS

Like Hideyoshi's invasions a few decades earlier, the Manchu conquests constituted an obvious seventeenth-century connection among the three East Asian kingdoms. Chosŏn and Ming both succumbed to the banner forces—the former twice, but quickly, the latter once but in an agonizing 40 years of warfare, resistance, and chaos. The Ming realm became an integral, central part of the Manchus' multicultural Qing empire, while Chosŏn Korea and Tokugawa Japan remained autonomous but could not escape from the international trading and diplomatic system centered on the enormous Qing economy, which consumed Korean ginseng and pottery and Japanese swords and metals as voraciously as it did Spanish silver and European muskets. All three cultures also shared the difficult, slow work of postwar reconstruction—China and Korea from the Qing conquest, Japan from the chaos of the Warring States.

Because they considered the Manchus barbaric, uncouth, and uncivilized—that is, not *Confucian* enough—both Korean and Japanese intellectuals and politicians began to think of their own realms as superior. Persuaded of the universal value of the Chinese Classics, the "truth texts," they saw their own civilizations as more faithful to those ancient principles than the Qing. They had always called their kingdoms "All Under Heaven," but in the seventeenth and eighteenth centuries we may find the term "central civilization" (c. *zhonghua*, к. *chunghwa*, ʝ. *chūka*), formerly reserved only for China, creeping into their self-conceptions. Scholars still argue whether this constitutes a kind of embryonic nationalism, but it certainly reflects a separation from the older, Chinese sources of universal truth.

Chinese texts remained powerful, however, and the authority of Zhu Xi's Neo-Confucianism increased as all three governments sought to establish an orthodox ideology to bolster their centralized rule. Following

Chosŏn and Ming precedents, both the Qing and the Tokugawa drew on those same ideals—especially after Ieyasu's death (1616) in Japan and the Kangxi Emperor's moral proclamation (1670). More directly, a Korean Confucian scholar captured during the Hideyoshi invasions, Kang Hang, became the teacher of many Japanese Confucians. From the content of the civil service examinations to the pressures placed on women to conform to narrowly defined, rigidly enforced notions of chastity, Qing and Chosŏn in particular used Neo-Confucian interpretations of the Classics to bolster established authority (patriarchal, aristocratic, even meritocratic).

All three states tried to persuade their millions of people to behave in accordance with their social roles and statuses—as orderly, obedient subjects, sons, wives, and daughters; as decorous, humane *yangban*, samurai, and gentry; and as productive, passive peasants, artisans, and merchants. In all three cultures, erudite Confucians debated the relationship of principle and material existence, the problems of human nature, and the relationship between their contemporary world and the values propounded in the ancient Classics.

At the same time, all three ruling elites increased in size, so their governments could not provide all of them with jobs. Some Chinese gentry who did not wish to serve the Qing, some *yangban* living in rural villages, and some lower-level samurai without access to hereditary employment had no choice but to work outside their "proper" business of government. They interpreted the Neo-Confucian imperative to "fully apprehend the principle in things" as a *practical* demand that they understand the concrete conditions of the society and institutions around them. The resulting "practical learning" (c. *shixue*, k. *silhak*, j. *jitsugaku*) produced very similar results in all three societies—treatises on agriculture, taxonomies of plants and animals, huge catalogues of medicines (pharmacopeias), guides to astronomy and astrology, geographies and maps, plans for tax relief and alleviation of famine, and more.

Qing, Chosŏn, and Tokugawa also continued to be productively connected to the world outside East Asia. International trade brought not only silver but also New World food crops. Parts of China and Korea became addicted to fiery chili peppers, while peanuts and sweet potatoes enabled even marginal land to be productive everywhere in the region. Foodways, tastes, and population growth rates all changed as these crops became ordinary parts of East Asian diets. Firearms, whether imported or homemade, transformed warfare, enabling the Manchu conquest *and* the Tokugawa victory. Jesuits preached in Beijing and Kyūshū, and their Roman Catholic ideas, translated into classical Chinese, reached even self-isolated Chosŏn, a story that will be covered more thoroughly in Chapter 4.

The Qing empire, the most expansive of the three states after the death of Hideyoshi, brought East Asia into closer contact with West Asia as well. The seventeenth-century Islamic world saw the rise of Sufism, an ideology and institutional form that connected Muslim communities to one another through loyalty to a central religious leader (Arabic *shaykh*) and his particular "mystical path." During this period, Sufis built networks in Central Asia and India, creating religious solidarities that sent missionaries in all directions, from Africa to northwest China. The Sufi leader Khoja Afaq, who ruled Kashgar for the Zunghars, had disciples in the Muslim communities of Gansu.

Finally, all three East Asian societies experienced population growth, whether gradual (Chosŏn and frontier China) or rapid (Japan and some central regions of China), coupled with urbanization and an expansion of literacy due to the easy availability of paper and the printing press. Inexpensive books stimulated popular imaginations, using not only old forms such as classical Chinese poetry but also new and revised genres—the cosmopolitan plays of Li Yu, the lively Korean vernacular tales, the *kabuki* and *haiku* and *ukiyo-e* of urban Japan. Though Chosŏn lagged behind in the size and wealth of its urban population, nonetheless the "tribute men" of the Seoul court, the ginseng merchants of Kaesŏng, and the international traders of Tongnae all gathered wealth outside the old-fashioned *yangban* professions of government service and landholding. In sum, East Asia was already undergoing some of the transformations that we associate with modernity, though in ways very different from Europe or North America.

CHAPTER FOUR

THE EIGHTEENTH CENTURY

WORLD CONTEXT

At the beginning of the eighteenth century, the Qing empire produced roughly a third of the world's goods, while India (South Asia) and all of Europe generated a little under a quarter each. China's and South Asia's great advantage lay in efficient agriculture, with farmers producing more than twice as much food per unit of land as English farmers. Artisans and wage laborers could thus be paid less, as food cost them less, so eighteenth-century Indian and Chinese workers had a standard of living equal to their English contemporaries despite their lower wages.

India used this advantage most effectively in producing inexpensive cotton textiles that competed effectively almost everywhere against local fabrics for the mass market. British textile manufacturers erased that advantage through high protective tariffs, slavery, and inventions such as the cotton gin, first built by Americans Eli Whitney and Catherine Littlefield Green. But it was only Britain's colonization of India that gave them the means to begin reversing their even larger imbalance of trade with the Qing empire.

The unprecedented transformation of Western Europe in the early modern era into the core of world-dominating empires had a profound impact all over the globe. Felt first in the Americas and in Africa in the sixteenth century, military superiority gradually enabled Europe's competing states to dominate coastal zones and river valleys on every inhabited continent. Improvements in the design and navigation of sailing ships and the weapons they carried were followed by the epoch-making development of steam engines—devices for transferring the heat of a fire into mechanical motion—and its application in both manufacturing and transportation. The harnessing of steam energy was rapidly applied to the already growing military power of England and other European countries, especially to their navies. Both manufacturing and transportation in turn demanded new efficiency and greater precision in the production of steel and tools to ensure exactness in the parts for increasingly intricate machines.

The scientific experimentation that led to these inventions often took place in the private laboratories of individual gentlemen who published their results in learned journals. Their translation into the tools of production and manufactured goods required tremendous investment in equipment and factories. The capital and risk-taking entrepreneurship—the desire to make money—for this industrial revolution came from aristocrats and merchants of the cities of western Europe and North America.

The industrial revolution began in the late eighteenth century only in England. English initiative grew from the confluence of several specific factors: (1) desire to preserve the English textile industry in the face of debilitating competition from Indian imports; (2) technological breakthroughs in the harnessing of steam for power, thereby inexpensively multiplying energy resources; and (3) discovery of very easily accessible coal to generate steam and iron ore to produce machinery and tools. These natural resources were not similarly situated in other European countries or the Qing empire, the world's technological leader at the beginning of the eighteenth century.

The persistence of slavery in the Caribbean and in the American South provided cheap cotton for British textile mills. The expansion of British colonialism in India after the Seven Years War (1756–63) added a huge market for cloth produced by the new steam-powered mills. Given these conditions, England preceded by many decades the next country to undergo an industrial revolution—the United States—and France, Germany, and Japan by nearly a century.

Other European and American entrepreneurs eventually acquired technology that rendered the initial resource factors less important than they had been for England. Moreover, the industrial revolution benefited from a transnational European and American intellectual network, connected by the printing press. They all participated in competition between companies and states to create new products and locate new sources of wealth, including natural resources, inside and outside their own borders. In other words, science and capitalism, and the dissemination of knowledge about them, lay at the heart of the highly competitive construction of the European, American, and, later, Japanese empires in the eighteenth and nineteenth centuries.

The printed word, both in Latin and in the European vernaculars—German, French, English, Dutch, and Italian—facilitated communication among scientists and engineers who followed the latest advances in their fields. It also created the groundwork for the powerful sentiment of *nationalism*, which transformed conflicts between kingdoms and their dynastic houses into competition between nation-states, the modern form of political and social organization that has gradually become universal over the past two centuries.

The mechanical printing press enabled publishers to disseminate national print-languages in the form of novels, travel accounts, history, poetry, and especially newspapers. These mass-produced publications, read by people all over a "national territory" or territories, gave rise to a sentiment of togetherness, of commonality, within what Benedict Anderson has called the "imagined community" of the nation. This sense of community differed significantly from the ancient, primarily religious, polyglot congregations using Latin (Roman Catholicism), Hebrew (Judaism), Arabic (Islam), Chinese (Confucianism), or Sanskrit and Pali (Buddhism) as their sacred scripts.

During the second half of the eighteenth century, this new version of human community became the rallying cry of dissatisfied elites in Europe's New World colonies. These Europeans, born far from their "home countries," organized themselves against the distant metropolitan empires, which discriminated against them as "colonials." They communicated with one another in pamphlets like those of Tom Paine and newspapers written in Spanish for *nuestra América*. Nationalism's first political expression in the New World, the American Revolution, was followed by the French antimonarchical movement and anti-colonial uprisings in Central and Latin America. The nation-states created by these upheavals proved so successful as political forms that they became models for national movements all over the world, even including the colonies later carved out by the European states.

Although China, Korea, and Japan later adopted the nation-state model, the successful East Asian states of Qing, Chosŏn, and Tokugawa achieved considerable stability and prosperity without it. All eighteenth-century societies, European or East Asian, faced problems of environmental limitations and degradation, particularly the constraints on production of energy using only wood and other biological fuels. By the second half of that century, England had made tentative steps to move beyond those environmental limitations, but the extent of Europe's and America's environmental advantages would not be felt until decades later. East Asian states and societies continued to be creative in agriculture, artisanship, government, and cultural life. All responded to the stresses of demographic pressure, changing socioeconomic and gender relations, and social mobility. Although all had begun to feel some tension with expanding European power by 1800, none had yet come under direct attack, and all retained their cultural self-confidence.

THE HIGH QING: TRIUMPH AND THE SOURCES OF DECLINE

The most powerful economy in the world and a stable, unified government enabled the Qing empire to provide its subjects with an "era of great prosperity" in the eighteenth century. Although tax evasion and other social problems did plague the state, three great Manchu rulers supervised political reforms, expansion of the frontiers, the destruction of their nomadic enemies, and a flourishing cultural and intellectual life. This success had many unintended consequences, including transformation of the elite, gradual changes in the status and opportunities of women, and threats to the separate existence of the Manchus. Trade relations with Chosŏn, the Tokugawa realm, Central Asia, Russia, Southeast Asia, and Europe brought vast quantities of silver, necessary for the burgeoning commercial economy, into the empire. But they also created an imbalance of trade that greatly favored the Qing and ultimately spurred the opium trade. By century's end, corruption in government began to take its toll, as domestic rebellion forced the dynasty to recognize the inadequacy of its military.

POPULATION GROWTH AND THE QING ECONOMY

One of the most popular explanations for China's nineteenth- and twentieth-century poverty and "backwardness" lies in the extraordinarily high population its land supported (and continues to support). Twentieth-century historians argued that the peace and prosperity of the first half of the Qing generated an overwhelming growth in the number of Chinese, which more than tripled from 100 million in the sixteenth century to almost 400 million at the end of the eighteenth. This explosion, in their interpretation, caused social violence and rebellion, famine, opium addiction, massive relocations of population (including migration overseas), and numerous other catastrophic consequences.

After the warfare and dislocations of the Qing conquest, the population of the Chinese culture area did, in fact, grow very rapidly during the eighteenth century. But this did not automatically lead to disaster. On average, the people of the Chinese culture area were, at least until the end of the eighteenth century, equal to or even better off than those of western Europe despite their rapidly increasing numbers. The remarkable efficiencies of Chinese farm families—using field residue for fuel, for example, profitably utilizing the labor of women and children, and not setting aside productive farmland for pasturage—and the elastic per-acre productivity of rice made some regions of China among the most successful agricultural zones in the world. Even the peripheries between regional cores contributed to the general prosperity, providing timber and other highland products to the richer valleys.

Without doubt, the eighteenth century's population growth did contribute to social transformation on a wide scale. The Qing peace allowed for rapid expansion of water-borne commerce, especially in the Yangzi valley and the south. By including more and more agricultural regions in the market nexus, this evolution allowed farmers to turn to cash crops, for they could purchase their staple grain supplies in the markets. The Lower Yangzi region, for example, imported much of its rice from the rich fields upriver in Hunan, where both population and arable land expanded rapidly at the expense of the environment. The Qing state participated actively in the drive to produce more food, more efficiently. Officials encouraged the resettlement of farmers to less populated areas, promoted New World food crops (such as the sweet potato, which produced considerable nutrition from marginal land), and extended irrigation systems to improve the yields of existing fields.

Markets for fibers and textiles also grew rapidly under the population pressure of the mid-Qing perod. The North China plain became an important site for the production of cotton, much of which was shipped down the Grand Canal to the Lower Yangzi region to be processed and woven into cloth, while silk remained an important export commodity (especially to Japan and, increasingly, to Europe). As in other parts of the world, cotton production took a heavy toll on the quality of the soil and contributed to the overall environmental degradation. Farmers sold grain and cash crops (such as vegetables, fibers, and dyestuffs) in the market and used the cash income to buy cloth, edible oils, soy sauce, and other processed necessities. The rising population placed increased pressure on producing more per acre, which resulted in a growing market for fertilizers—nightsoil, field residues, and soybean cake from southern Manchuria, to be shipped southward in enormous quantities.

The monetization of the rural economy provided more opportunities for women and children to earn cash through non-agricultural sideline production, which varied tremendously by region or even subregion. In the Lower Yangzi, a poor farm woman could add substantially to the family income by raising silkworms, reeling and weaving the thread, and selling her products to local brokers. Similarly, if a northern Chinese family could grow raw cotton, the women could support a larger family by weaving, while their young daughters could contribute by spinning the yarn for them. These possibilities played a role in gradual changes in gender relations, even for rural or artisanal families (see p. 107).

These economic changes also required a huge expansion of the money supply, including minted copper

The Qing empire (1636–1912)

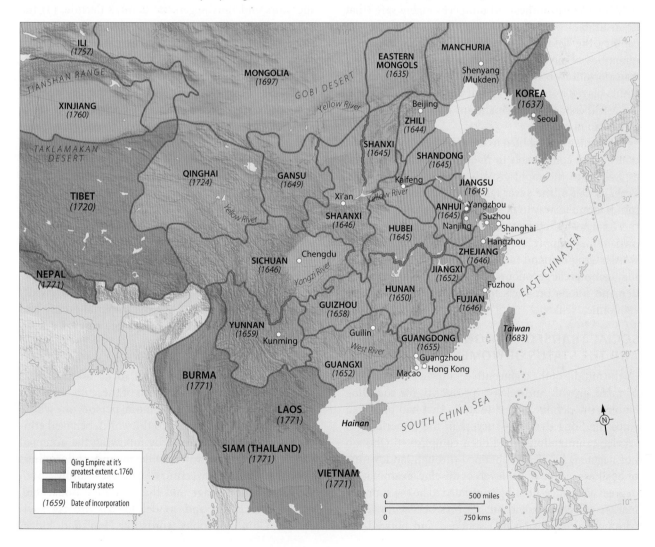

coins and unminted one-ounce (28-g) silver ingots, both used in market transactions at every level throughout the empire. Both the Ming and the Qing imported substantial quantities of both metals—from Japan and the New World—in exchange for their exports, especially silk, porcelain, and (by the eighteenth century) tea. As we have seen, foreign merchants could make enormous profits by shipping silver to China. There it commanded a much higher price than elsewhere because the Qing empire had virtually no domestic supply but used silver as the money of account for its highly commercialized economy.

Silver thus functioned as an import commodity, which Europeans could produce and transport cheaply because they commanded slave labor at the rich New World mines and built reasonably safe (that is, insurable) ocean-going cargo vessels. Early in the century, the Tokugawa, too, could profitably ship huge quantities of silver to the mainland with much lower transportation costs. Demand for the precious metal in China played as important a role in the development of the world economy as demand for East Asian goods in European markets.

This trade contributed to the rise of Europe to world dominance, comparable to the trade in African slaves, as well as to the rapid growth of China's population. Perhaps half of the silver taken out of the New World mines found its way to the Ming and Qing empires, and the Tokugawa shogunate worried about depletion of its own money supply by the trade with Qing. In other words, Qing demand for silver, fueled by its burgeoning commercial economy, combined with extensive demand for its products to create a truly worldwide economic exchange.

SOCIAL TRANSFORMATION AND THE STATUS OF WOMEN

By the middle of the eighteenth century, a peaceful time of rapid growth and relative prosperity for the Qing empire, the definition of elite status that had prevailed since the Song dynasty—success in the imperial civil service examinations—had been complicated (though not negated) by wealth obtained through landowning or business. At the upper levels of the elite, examination degrees and office-holding continued to be the supreme marker of achievement, but six or seven centuries of commercial expansion had softened and blurred the classical hierarchy of social class—scholar-officials (elite) at the top, then farmers, artisans, and merchants at the bottom.

From the provincial level downward, and sometimes even in Beijing, men who had *earned* their wealth could be seen as equals to the scholarly elite, even to office holders. The brother of a degree holder might well be a successful merchant. Riches and poverty came and went in generational cycles, and few families could maintain themselves at the top of the socioeconomic pyramid for long. The stereotype put the length of the cycle at five generations: (1) the poor, hardworking founder; (2) his equally diligent sons, who had grown up in poverty; (3) a generation raised in wealth and accustomed to it, who did not work as hard as their recent ancestors and thus began the family's decline; (4) the ne'er-do-well wastrels who squandered their inheritance; and (5) the impoverished ex-elite who might or might not begin the cycle again.

Whether they blamed wealth and poverty on fate or on the presence or absence of virtue, eighteenth-century Chinese lived in a world of private property in which magnanimous charity coexisted with conspicuous consumption. Wealth brought both opportunity and responsibility, while government could and should mitigate the worst consequences of economic inequality. Social mobility, many officials and intellectuals argued, improves society by allowing men of ambition and ability to rise to elite status, whether through acquiring wealth and property or through the "orthodox" examination system. To a greater degree than in the more aristocratic states of early modern Europe, Korea, or Japan, the Qing's relative lack of rigidly ascribed statuses (except for the imperial family and the bannermen) allowed considerable room for individual initiative.

Every individual in an idealized Confucian society properly played a number of social roles, such as "father" or "king" or "wife." Each of these involved fulfilling obligations to others. A moral person, one whose innate virtue shone forth into the world, behaved ethically and lived contentedly by following the accepted definitions of these roles. Officials and philosophers saw the eighteenth-century Chinese family, both the large-scale lineage and the economic household, as the foundation and model for an orderly society. For Chinese people, words like "kin" and "elder" were not simple descriptions but rather *prescriptions*, models or ideals that dictated correct attitudes and ritual behavior.

Women ideally lived their lives entirely within the family nexus, playing no public roles at all, but they formed an essential part of the social foundation, both as producers of the next generation and as participants in ritual and the household economy. Though secluded "women's quarters" could only be maintained by elites, women of other classes were limited in public activities by such natural truths as, "men plow and women weave," "in women, lack of talent is virtuous," and "male and female must be separated." In this vision, supported by ancient texts (some of them written by women), law, and deeply rooted custom, "womanly behavior" meant modesty, submission, service, chastity, and ritual rectitude. Women should ideally be known outside their families only because of conventional womanly virtues—remaining chaste or committing suicide after their husbands died, devotedly serving their in-laws under adverse circumstances, raising sons from poverty to examination degrees, and so on—for which they might be awarded imperial honors or a mention in local history.

But eighteenth-century social changes began to undermine these ideals. In the commercialized regions of the Qing empire, some women became known as entrepreneurs, as highly prized courtesans in the urban pleasure quarters, and most revealingly as poets. Huge published anthologies of women's verse grew popular, and women from elite families used literary work to create satisfying lives and emotional relationships or to lament an evil fate. Literate women could maintain intimate relations with their natal families, from which they supposedly separated at marriage, exchanging letters and verses with their mothers and siblings. They could create circles of friends and companions, including both kin and non-kin, to enhance their skills and express their innermost thoughts.

They could even celebrate the importance of women as active, thinking participants in their own culture. Their writing vividly reveals the connection between the Qing empire's prosperous eighteenth century and social change. In the great cities or commercial towns, anywhere that wealth coexisted with ambition, educating daughters became a socially valuable act, justified by women's importance in raising their sons to be educated and virtuous men and, not coincidentally, in building affinal relationships with other powerful families. This turned on its head the old ethic of keeping women "untalented."

These changes, whether elite women writing poetry or country women supporting their families by textile production for the market, raised the issue of gender relations among elite men. Should patriarchal tradition, hierarchy, and men's superiority be honored and reaffirmed? Or should women be recognized as equal in potential and intelligence to men? Or perhaps both? The debate involved many famous literati and came to no universally agreed-upon conclusions, but it does allow us to glimpse gender ideology in flux. Chinese writers could simultaneously believe that women shared both virtue and intellect with men *and* that they should be secluded within the family; that women constituted the foundation of society *and* that they should be subordinate to men; that they could write brilliant poetry *and* that they were incapable of the Confucian studies leading to official examinations. Some scholars see in this debate a restatement of conservative patriarchal principles, others an optimistic potential for women's liberation, and both sides have evidence for their views.

In short, we cannot see any obvious modern perspectives in eighteenth-century Chinese women's lives. They were not simply slaves to tradition, for many of them found deep fulfillment and uniquely civilized social value in their own lives. Nor were they budding feminists, for they participated—most of them willingly, as far as we know—in a social and cultural system that placed them below men in a gendered hierarchy of power. We may see this contradiction clearly in the role of "mother," simultaneously a woman submissive to her husband's patriline and a powerful authority in her children's world. According to the ancient doctrine of the "Three Obediences" (see p. 47) (c. *sancong*), a woman ought to obey her father in her youth, her husband in middle age, and her son as she grows old. The first may have been the norm; we still need to do much more research on conjugal relations to be able to analyze the second. But evidence from fiction, poetry, anthropology, and historical documents indicates that sons, heeding the doctrine of filial piety and the realities of emotional power, would be much more likely to obey their mothers than vice versa.

SHEN FU AND CHEN YUN, A QING LOVE STORY

In the spring of 1803, Chen Yun died of a broken heart because she failed to obtain the young woman she loved to be her husband's concubine. A 40-year-old wife and mother, she had not seen her children for almost three years when she died, her husband Shen Fu distraught with grief by her side. These people from the Lower Yangzi region had accomplished nothing worthy of note. He had failed the imperial examinations and become a sometime clerk in government offices; she had lived her life in the conventional roles of daughter, wife, daughter-in-law, and mother. They subsisted on the charity of relatives and friends for some time before she died, for he lost his clerical job at the Yangzhou salt monopoly office, and his parents had expelled them from home.

We know about this otherwise undistinguished couple because he chose to write a memoir, which has become a classic of Chinese prose. Although autobiographies had existed in China for millennia, they tended to be conventional, detached descriptions of offices held, virtues or vices embodied, relationships maintained, and roles fulfilled. In non-fiction writing, at least, we rarely get such a vivid view of people's interior lives as we find in Shen Fu's book, *Six Records of a Floating Life*. He recorded his emotions without conventional restraint—the joys of married life, the frustrations of study unrewarded and unemployment, the pleasures of travel, the mischievous fun of young people going out to play, the grief of estrangement and loss.

Most famously, he loved his wife, who was also his first cousin, deeply and passionately from their first meeting at the age of 12 (13, by Chinese count). He told his mother, "If you are going to choose a wife for me, I will marry no other than Yun," and they wed at 17. In her mother's house, Yun had learned to read

A nineteenth-century painting of a couple embracing in a garden. Shen Fu and Chen Yun lived as a young married couple in a garden setting like this. Shen's memoir portrays them as reveling in "the joys of the wedding chamber" as well as in poetry and art.

and write, and she, like many other well-born women of her day, loved poetry. They shared the satisfactions of literature and of making everyday life aesthetically pleasing. She insisted that they observe the minutiae of good manners, as demanded by the etiquette manuals, but their polite exchanges never negated their mutual passion.

In 1795, Yun, having met the beautiful new concubine of one of their cousins, wanted more than anything to find a concubine for her husband, a woman to share not only his bed but also her domestic life. Quite by chance, Shen Fu met a cultured courtesan-in-training named Hanyuan. Although he knew her to be far too expensive for a clerk like himself to obtain, he introduced her to Yun. The two women immediately took to one another, arranged to meet again, and soon became deeply attached.

But Hanyuan's mother had no intention of giving up her talented, valuable daughter for a poor scholar's price, so she sold the girl as a concubine to a powerful man. Yun became ill and never recovered from her loss. At death's door she cried out, "How could Hanyuan turn her back on me?" blaming her own unbridled emotions for her fatal imbalance and illness. Inconsolable, Shen Fu continued as a wandering clerk and businessman for six years after Yun's death. Sometime in 1809 he wrote his book then disappeared from the historical record, leaving us a moving, intimate, and beautiful account of eighteenth-century Chinese life.

MANCHUS AND POLITICAL POWER

Three Manchus of the Aisin Gioro clan held the cosmos in their hands from 1662 to 1799—they reigned as the Kangxi (r. 1662–1722), Yongzheng (r. 1722–1736), and Qianlong (r. 1736–1799) Emperors. All three knew China and Chinese culture intimately, from the classical texts to the lives of ordinary villagers, but none ever "became Chinese," and all three maintained their claim to rule far more than "China." Serious, intelligent, hardworking, and politically savvy, all three autocrats occupied the center of an enormous government enterprise, which employed hundreds of thousands of people and ruled over hundreds of millions more.

Certainly the Qianlong Emperor had less direct experience of warfare, of "authentically Manchu" life outside the palace, than his grandfather had, but he nonetheless worked tirelessly to maintain (even to strengthen) the identity and superior position of the Manchus within the Qing empire. He also expanded the realm, following on his ancestors' desire to secure the Qing's Inner Asian frontiers. His victorious generals created one of the largest effective empires that had ever been centered on China, their incorporation of the "New Frontier" (c. *Xinjiang*) of Zungharia and the Tarim Basin giving the realm most of the shape we currently recognize as "China."

These Manchu rulers carefully innovated, using the Ming model of government to create institutions and an intellectual basis to solidify their hold over their huge and diverse empire. Their multiple roles may be illustrated by some of the titles held by the Qianlong Emperor. He named himself with Chinese, Mongolian, Tibetan (Buddhist), and Manchu titles:

> ...the Chinese Son of Heaven [Tianzi, or Huangdi]; the successor to the rulership of Genghis Khan, and to the Jin and Yuan dynasties, and hence Khan of Khans; cakravartin king and 'Chinese Asoka Dharmaraja'...; overlord of Mongolia, Xinjiang, Qinghai, and Tibet; pacifier of Taiwan, Yunnan, Vietnam, Burma, and the Zungars and Gurkhas; the incarnate bodhisattva Manjusri; and head of the Aisin Gioro, the dominant clan among the Manchus.[1]

He could never take on Islamic titles to rule more effectively over the northwesternmost parts of his empire, but he did have Xinjiang's Muslim leaders come to Beijing and bow before him. The Qianlong Emperor and his dynastic house thus constituted the center of a multicultural empire.

All three of the great eighteenth-century Qing rulers worried about their Manchu heritage—strengthening the differences between the banner families and the vast non-Manchu population they ruled—in a period of relative peace. Remembering the rise and fall of the Mongol dynasty in the thirteenth and fourteenth centuries, they feared the dissipation of the martial spirit among the "simple, virtuous, straightforward" Manchus, always contrasted to the urbane, wily Chinese. Their Manchu, Mongol, Chinese, and other officials, in contrast, wanted most to stay out of trouble, to protect themselves in the rough-and-tumble of political power struggles. They cultivated patrons among their superiors, clients among their subordinates, and their emperor as the source of their positions and safety. When any crisis upset the ordinary routine of government, the emperor needed quickly to apportion blame and punish the guilty, while the officials scrambled to cover themselves and their friends—by strategic silence, covert resistance to imperial demands, implicating others, outright falsification, and a variety of other methods. As we will see, the emperor knew he could trust his officials only as far as their interests coincided with his.

THE LATE KANGXI PERIOD

Building upon his victories over Galdan in the 1690s, the Kangxi Emperor moved to stabilize the empire's Inner Asian frontiers, though he could not eliminate the threat of a Zunghar–Tibetan alliance. The Qing state absorbed much of eastern and northeastern Tibet, but neither at this point nor later did central Tibet, with its capital at Lhasa, become an integral part of the Qing empire. It remained a politically independent state ruled by the Dalai Lamas under Qing military protection. The Dalai Lamas maintained that their religious power gave them spiritual dominion over the emperor, while the Qing rulers claimed that their secular power was supreme, joined as it was with the spiritual legacy of the Buddhist cakravartin king—the universal Buddhist ruler—and the god Manjusri. Never settled, the debate continued as a distant precursor to today's conflict over the sovereign status of Tibet (see p. 19).

The seventeenth-century rebellions and Manchu conquest had depopulated many fertile agricultural regions of China, so the Kangxi period saw the rural areas struggle to regain their productivity. Thorough surveys of land and landownership, necessary for any effective land tax system, had the unfortunate effect of stimulating rural resistance, for the farmers believed that careful measurement of their land would result in higher taxes. Reluctant to antagonize the rural population, the Kangxi Emperor and his finance ministers opted for the status quo and rarely pursued tax delinquency cases. The court obtained sufficient extra revenues through the Imperial Household Agency to meet its expenses comfortably, and in 1712 the emperor decided permanently to fix the most recent land survey figures and census of able-bodied men liable to taxation. Filial descendants should ideally not change their ancestor's policies, so this left his successors unable effectively to tax either increased population or expanded arable land.

Although he had succeeded in enlarging the empire and stabilizing its social order, the Kangxi Emperor failed in a crucial family task: the selection and legitimization of an heir. He chose his second son Yinreng, the first son born to an empress, as heir apparent early in his reign and schooled the boy conscientiously in both the Chinese and Manchu cultures. After being given both the best possible education and heavy responsibilities as a young man, Yinreng grew into a violent and tyrannical prince. Deeply conflicted by his own complicity in his son's degenerate character, the emperor imprisoned his heir, reinstated him, then finally in 1712 removed him entirely from the succession.

Discouraged by this failure, the emperor never named another heir, leaving his surviving adult sons to compete over the throne in the old Manchu fashion upon his death in 1722. The dynastic archives report him telling them, "…later, when I am dead, you can lay my body out in the Ch'ien-ch'ing [Qianqing] Palace, strap on your armor, and fight it out."[2] Despite the glory of his military victories, the totality of his autocratic power, and the wealth of his empire, he approached the end of his life without a sense of triumph, anticipating the chaos of a succession struggle to come.

FISCAL REFORM AND YONGZHENG PERIOD ECONOMICS

Fortunately for the dynastic house, upon the Kangxi Emperor's death his very able fourth son Yinzhen

Portraits of the Kangxi Emperor (left), wearing formal state robes (early 18th century) and the Yongzheng Emperor (right), in Manchu dress (1720s?).

effectively organized his supporters and had himself declared emperor, choosing the reign-name Yongzheng. Already 44 years old and an experienced politician, he earned a reputation as the Qing's most meticulous, conscientious ruler. His workday lasted from 16 to 20 hours, including early-morning study, audiences with officials, and lengthy sessions with piles of incoming reports, memorials, and secret communications.

Realizing the defects of his father's style of rule, especially his laxness in bureaucratic supervision and playing favorites among officials, the Yongzheng Emperor focused much of his attention on gathering information, a difficult task for a monarch who spent most of his time in a closely guarded palace compound. He inherited and expanded his father's system of "palace memorials," letters from selected high officials that bypassed the ordinary palace secretariat and came sealed to the emperor's desk. Since no one knew who was entitled to submit such secret reports, they served not only as a source of information but also as a deterrent to corruption and plotting.

By expanding the number of officials allowed to submit palace memorials, the Yongzheng Emperor could keep a closer eye than his father on the bureaucracy, the Manchu clans, and the world outside the palace. He read dozens of these letters every evening and responded to each with a personal rescript, written with the emperor's unique vermilion ink, which was then returned in secret to the memorialist (letter writer). These lengthy back-and-forth communications in the Qing archives reveal the Yongzheng Emperor's skillful use of his relationships with individual officials, balancing his knowledge of their self-interest and desire to please him with a clear-headed assessment of their accomplishments.

Concerned about the palace treasury and corruption in the revenue departments, the Yongzheng Emperor turned his attention to the empire's taxation system and found it riddled with inconsistencies, inequity, and fraud. Two taxes constituted the main revenue base of the government: one on productive agricultural land, the other on adult males liable for labor service, *corvée*, which was always converted to a cash "head tax." Since government salaries were extremely low, insufficient to maintain an elite household, regional and local officials added illegal surcharges to the relatively low taxes frozen by the Kangxi Emperor, and none of that extra revenue found its way into government coffers.

To plan the reform of the empire's revenue systems, the emperor appointed his trusted brother Yinxiang to head an office of financial oversight. Acting on information gathered by Yinxiang and through the palace memorials, the emperor legalized a 10–20 percent surcharge on all tax collections but threatened dire punishment for any official who exceeded that limit. Some of that surcharge was assigned to officials at all levels as "bonuses to encourage incorruptibility," in some cases increasing official income by 20 times. The remainder stayed in the provincial treasuries for public works, disaster relief, schools, and other expenses, immune from the high levels of graft and embezzlement in Beijing.

These and other reforms improved the empire's financial situation considerably, but even a hardworking reformist ruler could not penetrate the dense, self-protective arrangements of the wealthy elite (like the Xu brothers, see p. 72) of the Lower Yangzi valley. Some of them retired officials with long experience of government methods, others successful businessmen, they had developed intricate patterns of tax avoidance, including multiple levels of ownership and land registration, to retain land rent income and shift the tax burden onto the small farmers or avoid it altogether. Even the emperor's team of 70 central government accountants, specially assembled for the task under a Manchu bannerman, could only scratch the surface of this elaborate

scheming. When they tried to question suspected tax cheats, they met with riots, jailbreaks, multiple ledgers, and collusion between officials and landholders. In the end, only a fraction of the tax arrears could be collected, and the emperor discovered one of the many limits to his theoretically absolute power.

The Yongzheng Emperor also tried to continue the westward Manchu conquests, the basis of their power as a military aristocracy. Qing armies commanded by Chinese and Manchu generals advanced to attack the Zunghars through both Mongolia and the Gansu corridor, but the northern route suffered a disastrous defeat in 1731, and the Zunghar threat—with its potential for alliances with the Russians, the Tibetans, and even the eastern Mongols—remained acute. The Yongzheng Emperor died in 1736, having ruled only 14 years, without completing his reform of the Qing's finances or the conquest of the Zunghars. Despite his painstaking attention to detail and strengthening of personal authority over his officials, he could not force the Jiangnan gentry to pay their share of taxes, and his moralizing did not persuade all the inhabitants of his multicultural empire to behave in accordance with official doctrine.

THE QIANLONG EMPEROR

Within a few months of his death, his choice as successor, 25-year-old Aisin Gioro Hongli, took over the Qing throne as the Qianlong Emperor. His instatement inaugurated one of the great ages of East Asian history, during which the Qing became one of the largest coherent states ever to be ruled from China, and one of the wealthiest and most populous empires in human history. Ironically, this reign also began the Qing's fall from its height of power and prosperity, a process Chinese historians identify with a quotation from the *Book of Changes*: "When the sun is at its peak, it begins to set."

The Qianlong Emperor's reign extended 63 years, from 1736 to 1799, longer than any other in China's long history. Like his father and grandfather, he had to balance the dual tasks of an alien monarch: ruling the cosmos, the universal empire mandated by Chinese political philosophy, through both imperial rituals and a huge bureaucratic state; *and* maintaining the uniqueness, élan, and position of the tiny Manchu ruling elite over the vast, multicultural state they had conquered. He labored to keep the Manchu banners separate from

Portrait of the Qianlong Emperor dressed as a Chinese scholar in his study (before 1767). Images of the emperor vary as much as the titles he took (see p. 109), ranging from this academic aesthete to a mounted Manchu cavalry general to an enthroned monarch.

the Chinese, though most of the bannermen had already become impoverished garrison-dwellers who routinely disobeyed the regulations against intermarriage with local women and let their military skills lapse.

At the same time, the emperor demonstrated his Chinese cultural credentials through immense imperially sponsored publication projects, a dazzling collection of arts and artifacts from every age of Chinese history, and a personal literary production that included over 1,200 prose pieces and 43,000 poems, none of them very good. Like any Chinese literary man, he painted conventional subjects, such as "flowers and insects." His red seal of ownership and uninspired calligraphy appear on thousands of paintings and his likeness in numerous popular cartoons, informal and formal portraits, and illustrations of both his military and cultural skills. As Manchu overlord, he could both *produce* and *own* Chinese culture, enjoying its delights and affirming its universal truths, while decrying its "effete decadence" and urging his bannermen not to give in to its charms.

Like his father, the Qianlong Emperor saw the Lower Yangzi region, the richest and most cultivated part of the Chinese world, as a source of both cultural glory and corruption. He went to that southern region six times in extravagant imperial journeys—four times accompanying his mother as a sign of his filial devotion—and he built replicas of southern towns in at least

two of his palace complexes. Never forgetting the importance of Inner Asia, however, he also ordered the construction of a gigantic scale model of the Dalai Lama's Potala Palace to be constructed at Chengde, his summer residence north of Beijing, and ordered his Manchu bannermen and generals to join him there for grand hunts and military exercises.

The Qianlong Emperor thus fulfilled his role as ruler, the arbiter of Chinese culture and pivot of the cosmos, without becoming Chinese in the process, remaining self-consciously an Inner Asian monarch and viewing his Qing empire as the core of the East Asian cultural region. To this dual end, he graciously received tributary missions from Chosŏn and Burma (among many others), allowed considerable trade with the Tokugawa realm, staged elaborate rituals of greeting for Mongol princes, and ordered major campaigns against the Zunghars.

ENDING THE NOMADIC THREAT AND CREATING "CHINA"

For two millennia, nomadic and sedentary peoples coexisted across a vast stretch of Eurasia. From Hungary to Korea, agricultural regions suffered from the raids of horse-riding, martial nomads, cursed by the farmers and their rulers as "the scourge of God," "unruly barbarians," and other colorful epithets. The pastoral economy of the deserts and grasslands, inhabited largely by small kin-centered groups (sometimes called "tribes"), was far more vulnerable to climate variation and natural disaster than farmers' fields. So the nomads relied on sedentary people and their states to supply food, artisanal goods, and textiles.

This nomad–farmer relationship resulted in lengthy cycles of competition and cooperation. Sometimes the nomads submitted to the trade regulations of sedentary states, at others they used their martial culture and swift cavalry to establish vast empires, conquering the cities and fertile plains that could produce so much wealth. Attila (406–453), Chinggis Khan (1162–1227), Qubilai Khan (1215–1294), and Tamerlane led federations of nomads to build "nomadic superstates," the largest of which stretched from the gates of Vienna to the tip of the Korean peninsula.

The Manchus were not nomads but sedentary people who both tilled fields and kept herds. Nonetheless, they participated in an Inner Asian culture shared with Mongols, Turks, Tajiks, and many more. They developed close relationships with their nearest nomadic neighbors, the eastern Mongols, with whom they shared linguistic and cultural affinity. Once they founded the Qing empire, the Manchus gradually incorporated these nomads into the banners and their administrative system. In exchange for peaceful relations, the Mongol chieftains gave up some measure of independence to take Qing titles and division of their vast grazing lands into stable units, as well as ceding the legacy of Chinggis Khan to Hongtaiji, after he defeated them in battle.

To the west of their Mongolian dependents and the Chinese culture area they had conquered, however, the Qing faced more complex challenges—the Tibetan peoples and state, based at Lhasa; the Tarim Basin oases, city-states populated by Turkic-speaking Muslims; and, most significantly, the western Mongols—the Zunghars. None of these peoples had been subject to the Ming, and the Qing faced the same dilemmas of frontier control as other sedentary empires.

All three of the eighteenth-century Qing rulers strove to expand their state to prevent alliances among the Tibetans, Turkic Muslims, Zunghars, and Russians, and to stop the eastern Mongols from drifting away from allegiance. Because of its proximity to Qing territory, its wealth, the extent of its empire, and its skill in warfare, the Zunghar empire constituted a threat to Qing power and required careful diplomatic and military attention.

In the late 1740s, a rebellion in Tibet caused the Qing to forbid Zunghar representatives to visit Lhasa. The Zunghar leaders feuded among themselves, and in 1753 one of the most popular and talented among them, Amursana (d. 1757), submitted to the Qing and became head of a tributary state. The Qing accepted his surrender, but three years later Amursana defected, "rebelling" against his erstwhile patron. A similar defection among the previously loyal eastern Mongols once again raised the specter of an anti-Qing alliance.

Frustrated with his ineffective field commanders and betrayed by Amursana, the angry Qianlong Emperor declared a new policy from Beijing. The Zunghar threat should be exterminated—all the young men massacred, and the women, children, and old men given as slaves and servants to the Qing military or other loyal troops. The Manchu general Jaohui led the attack, slaughtering thousands of Zunghars and depopulating the grasslands. Amursana fled to Russian territory, where he died of smallpox. Chinese historians recognized the importance of this victory and of the Qing army's subsequent conquest of the territory south of Tianshan. By 1759, for the first time in history, all of this territory—which the Qing named Xinjiang (New Frontier)—came under Beijing's control. With banner armies in charge of Zungharia (north of Tianshan), the Qing enlisted local Muslim nobles to manage the Tarim Basin in the dynasty's name.

The Qing had ended the nomadic threat permanently and, in the process, created the entity we now recognize as "China," including not only the Manchu and Chinese culture areas but substantial parts of the Mongolian, Turkic, and Tibetan culture areas as well. Except for the existence of the Republic of Mongolia as an independent state, a map of the twenty-first-century People's Republic of China traces the western and northern frontiers of the Qing empire, not those of the Ming or any earlier state. The Qing fixed most of the long border between China and Russia, the Pamir Mountain divide between China and western Central Asia, and the outline of Xinjiang, a province since the late nineteenth century. Only Tibet retained an independent government, headed by the Dalai Lama. But Qing military presence in Lhasa after the late Kangxi period provides the basis for modern Chinese nationalists' claim that Tibet "has historically been part of China."

INTELLECTUAL LIFE AND THE LITERARY INQUISITION

The eighteenth-century Qing state tried to control social morality and the effects of commerce with conservative Confucian government regulations, but they could not stop the growth of a lively, controversial, and sometimes satirical urban culture. Like the Korean *p'ansori* (see p. 118) and the arts of the urban "pleasure quarters" of Tokugawa Japan, the plays, novels, poetry, and visual arts of the empire's cities served diverse audiences of men and women, cultured and unlettered people, rich and poor. In elegant poetry salons, elite men and women ate rare delicacies and drank fine wines while composing verses on plum blossoms, the joys of friendship, the sorrows of parting, or the harvest moon. Out in the street, ordinary urbanites—artisans and their families, transportation workers, salesmen and con men, indigent scholars, and vagrant monks—rubbed elbows as they listened to street singers or watched puppet shows taken from the great historical novels, such as the *Romance of the Three Kingdoms*.

Booksellers did a thriving trade as a flourishing economy brought literacy within the reach of millions of Chinese. Fiction, despised by strict Confucians as vulgar and immoral, continued its late Ming success and culminated in *Dream of the Red Chamber*, Cao Xueqin's (1715?–1764?) immortal tale of elite family life. Both a novel of social description—the novel's protagonists resemble Cao's own family in many ways—and a religious allegory, this lengthy book became an instant bestseller whose popularity has continued to grow over the centuries. It now stands with the Bible as one of the most-studied books in any language. Cao Xueqin, reacting to the changing gender relations of his society and the corruption of male-dominated public life, made every single interesting character in his novel a woman, with only one exception. All contemporary Chinese know his characters and stories, for they have been converted to film, television drama, comic books, and many other media.

The Qianlong Emperor worried that the Manchu heritage would be lost through acculturation to Chinese ways and that Chinese anti-Manchu resentment would boil over into rebellion. He had some evidence for this anxiety in the "sorcery scares" that occurred in the 1760s. In some parts of the Lower Yangzi "queue clipping," an obvious attack on the Manchu hairstyle imposed on Chinese males, combined with the black arts in the public imagination. More dramatically, in 1774 an explicitly anti-Qing uprising exploded in the North China plain, close to Beijing, led by a martial-arts teacher and inspired by a sectarian Buddhist doctrine of apocalyptic catastrophe. The Qing military destroyed the rebels with savage thoroughness.

The emperor attempted to cement Manchu ethnic solidarity by sponsoring studies of their origins and homeland, language, folk religion (shamanism), and military traditions. To discourage heterodoxy and manage intellectuals, he also initiated a massive compilation project, modeled on one undertaken during the Ming, to collect all legitimate texts into a single encyclopedic collection. This project enabled his officials to examine and eliminate any book circulating in the empire, especially those expressing subversive anti-Manchu ideas. Called the *Complete Book of the Four Treasuries*, this collection arranged all approved works into the conventional categories of the Classics, poetry, history, and belles-lettres and ferreted out thousands of titles to be banned and destroyed.

The emperor also sponsored geographical research, some of it undertaken by Jesuit cartographers using the latest European methods. Some of their gazetteers and map collections were published in five languages—Manchu, Chinese, Mongol, Tibetan, and Turkic—to demonstrate the Qing's control over the five cultural zones. Those same five languages and cultures later became the Five Ethnicities or nations of late nineteenth-century nationalists, who claimed the entire territory of the Qing empire as their *Chinese* patrimony.

In the realm of religion as in literature, the Qing state clearly distinguished between legitimate belief, compatible with the orthodox Way of Neo-Confucianism, and heterodoxy (or sectarianism), which was potentially subversive of political authority and therefore illegal. The officials supported orthodox empire-wide rituals, performances on Confucius's birthday and honors for Guandi (the god of war), as well as worship of local gods who had particular efficacy in their own places. Although Buddhism could be considered heterodox and was often denounced by Confucian scholars, popular Buddhist piety flourished. Pilgrimages to important Buddhist sites provided men and especially women with delightful social occasions, as well as hope in desperate situations, such as inability to bear a son or the death of a loved one. Daoist religious specialists provided many Chinese with satisfying community rituals and effective exorcism of marauding spirits, which might take over the body of an unsuspecting victim and produce symptoms of disease or insanity.

In the late Ming, Jesuits attempted to convert the highest classes of Chinese society to Roman

Catholicism, adding to this complex mixture of faiths. Communicating in classical Chinese, men such as Matteo Ricci (1552–1610) contributed the possibility of monotheism to Chinese religious life, which had never been part of any indigenous East Asian religious ideology. The Jesuits insisted that their faith was entirely compatible with the morality of Confucianism. Their books found their way to Chosŏn and Japan, where they were banned in the seventeenth century, playing a part in rebellions, persecutions, and martyrdoms. The Kangxi Emperor debated doctrine and authority relations with the Jesuit representative in Beijing and ordered all Christians to observe ancestor veneration rituals and honor Confucius. Pope Clement XI's representative forbade missionaries and their converts from performing these rituals, and the Catholic effort in China collapsed.

Literate Chinese Muslims, too, attempted to explain their religion's unique beliefs by demonstrating their resonance with the Confucian Way. Educated members of Qing society, Muslim literati used impeccable classical Chinese sources to demonstrate Islam's orthodox, socially productive qualities and created an entire literature, in Chinese, justifying Islam within the vocabulary of conventional Neo-Confucianism. Unusual in world Islamic history, these texts cited the *Book of Changes* as well as the Qur'an, Confucius as well as the Prophet Muhammad. The Qing rulers proclaimed Islam's legitimacy, but the arrival and rivalry of Sufi orders among the Muslims of the northwest created conflict and violence toward century's end.

CORRUPTION AND REBELLION IN THE LATE QIANLONG PERIOD

Beginning around 1775, the Qing state gave its subjects increasing reason to be discontented. The commercial economy of the regional cores continued to thrive, and many people did very well for themselves. But such a competitive economy also produced plenty of losers, both in the wealthy cores and the less fortunate peripheries. The poor had fueled the violence that accompanied the "sorcery scares" of the 1760s and the 1774 rebellion.

State management of society and the economy declined further after the 1770s under the corrupting influence of the emperor's favorite, a Manchu named Hesen, and the malign influence his followers exerted at every level of the bureaucracy. Personally attractive, intelligent, and charismatic, Hesen gained the emperor's favor and rose to powerful positions in the bureaucracy in his 20s—vice-minister of revenue and lieutenant general—then began to amass an unprecedented personal fortune through control of access to the monarch. Anyone wishing to have a policy implemented or to achieve office had to give Hesen an appropriate bribe. Historians have debated the sources of Hesen's influence over the aging emperor, but the old man protected his corrupt favorite for over 20 years.

This sleaze spread very rapidly throughout the bureaucracy, for lower-level officials needed funds to bribe officials at higher levels, and the only sources lay in the people over whom they ruled. In one famous case in Gansu province, provincial and local officials collaborated to embezzle millions of ounces of silver (and Gansu was a *poor* province!) from famine relief funds to line their own pockets. Although the malefactors in that case were caught and punished (some were executed), the necessity to purchase political advantage became more and more pressing in the last quarter of the century.

We may be tempted to blame Hesen personally for all this—and many Chinese historians have—but the factionalism and greed that underlay his power constituted a crucial weakness of the Qing system. Without selfless, upright officials, the empire could not function smoothly, but in the late eighteenth century success often went not to the virtuous or able but to the well connected and wealthy. This tension, exacerbated by Hesen's leadership in corruption, led to social disorder on a vast scale. By century's end, the empire had grown too large, too populous, and too complex for its autocratic ruler, its bureaucrats, and its technological capacities.

The end of the Qing wars of expansion also played a part in the degeneration of administrative competence. The delimitation of a border with Russia, the elimination of the Zunghars, the final subjugation of the Mongols, and the shrinking of the Dalai Lama's sphere of power allowed the Qing court and military to complete their work of centralization of power and domination of the empire's frontiers. In place of mid-century official activism, a few decades of peace, corruption, and rapid population growth created a bureaucratic state and army far less able to react to new opportunities or dangers. Into that potentially disastrous condition came the Europeans, arrogant and powerful, ignorant of Qing politics or Chinese culture, and eager for profits, converts, and colonies. The timing could not have been worse for the Qing and its subjects.

THE HIGH QING AND THE EUROPEANS

We have already seen how the Qing, through its insatiable demand for silver and vast production of consumer goods, had been one of the driving forces of the world economic system in the eighteenth century. As long as the Europeans, Koreans, Muslims (whether Malays in the south or Turks in the west), and others were willing to participate in the fictions of the tribute system and to trade according to the rules set by the court—or negotiate different rules for more limited trade, as the Japanese and Russians did—they could partake of the huge profits.

Western European merchants (as distinct from Jesuit intellectuals) did not stand out as exceptional among the foreigners the Qing permitted to buy and sell in their empire's markets. The Russians had signed treaties with the Qing (in 1689 and 1727) on a basis of equality between monarchs to fix their borders, regulate their trade, and allow a small Russian Orthodox church in Beijing (though not missionary activity). The British,

however, needed to be controlled very differently, for their sea-faring merchants resisted the exactions of local officials (many of them illegal) and wanted, in good mercantilist style, to have direct access to the Qing court through an ambassador and trade representatives.

By 1760, the Qing had determined that these pesky foreigners could best be controlled by confinement in one port—Guangzhou (then called Canton in English)—and entrée into the domestic market through officially appointed merchants (called *cohong* in Cantonese) and a superintendent of maritime customs. Unfortunately, both the *cohong* merchants and the Europeans found this "Canton system" unsatisfactory, despite the flourishing trade in porcelain, silk, and the mountains of tea necessary to supply the Britons with their new favorite drink.

Merchants of the East India Company—which had been granted a near monopoly of the China trade by the British court—chafed under a system they saw as condescending and constrained. They also had to pay for everything in silver, for the Chinese steadfastly refused to buy British products in any quantity. Britain's loss of many North American colonies in 1776 increased competition and decreased profits in the tea trade, so the Company desperately sought another commodity to replace silver, and they found it. Britain's Indian colonies had been producing small quantities of opium—the highly addictive, dried latex of a poppy flower—for export to China since the 1760s, but in the 1780s the Company began a concerted program to replace silver with opium to pay for the China trade, and it worked.

William Alexander. The Qianlong Emperor receiving the Macartney Embassy, 1793. Lord Macartney appears in the center, presenting a gift to the aged, enthroned Qing monarch, surrounded by his courtiers.

A procession of foreigners bearing gifts. This image was created by the Qianlong Emperor's court as a present for Lord Macartney and his master, George III of Great Britain.

In order to place the China trade on a more mercantilist, European-style footing, King George III sent Lord Macartney to Beijing in 1793 with gifts for the elderly emperor on his birthday, "specimens of the best British manufactures," and a request that diplomatic and economic relations be reorganized, with an exchange of ambassadors, opening of more ports, and fixed tariffs. The Qing and British delegations, including Macartney and the emperor, engaged in elaborate ritual performances and a series of personal negotiations, during which they thoroughly misunderstood one another. Although the Qing, and Chinese culture, had gained a great deal from their interactions with the Jesuits—especially in the fields of astronomy, ballistics, and mathematics—the court saw no reason to alter either its lofty (and undiplomatic) condescension toward these foreigners or the Canton system that kept them well out of the way.

The British, on the other hand, saw no sense in the system's constraints, which brought them no liberty to expand their market or to establish equality in interstate relations. The emperor's famous letter to King George III, in which he expressed disdain for the manufactures of all other peoples, reflected not the timeless arrogance of the Celestial Empire (as British critics believed) but the recent triumphs of a universal monarch. He did not mention that the Qing continued to need foreign silver to fuel its burgeoning economy, nor could he know that within a few decades, that economy would hemorrhage silver to pay for British opium.

CHOSŎN IN THE EIGHTEENTH CENTURY

Seventeenth-century trends toward a more diversified and commercialized economy in Chosŏn continued well into the eighteenth century, leading to significant changes in the status system. Chosŏn scholars' identification of their country as the sole repository of civilized values continued to set the contours of many debates in intellectual and political life and also caused a gradual domestication of the cultural imagination. Knowledge of what came to be known as "Western learning"—including Roman Catholicism—spread among many scholars and commoners, resulting in a crisis that questioned the compatibility of the Christian teaching of the "Lord of Heaven" with state-sponsored Confucianism.

ECONOMIC GROWTH AND COMMERCIALIZATION

Like all social elites, the *yangban* aimed to maintain the power and status of their class. Their claim to social and political leadership rested on the idea that they provided moral guidance for the entire population as a result of their commitment to the cultivation of personal propriety. This social vision enabled them to enjoy many privileges; for example, they received tax breaks through their control of the state, ostensibly to support their especially virtuous lifestyle. The legal system and sumptuary regulations favored them, ensuring that punishments and clothing styles would remind others of their status. *Yangban* conformity to ideals about the seclusion and behavior of virtuous women, which could be practiced only by the elite, elevated them above other status groups. Finally, strict inheritance laws, though running contrary to the meritocratic impulse in Confucian thought, sought to keep the numbers of *yangban* small enough to avoid the dilution of their status.

Yet this ideal of a society led by *yangban* rested on an economic foundation that by the eighteenth century was far removed from the realities of life on the peninsula. In the idealized vision, the population consisted largely of simple farmers, whose labor in the fields both provided for their own livelihood and produced enough surplus to support the *yangban* in their special way of life. Through the tax system, the farmers were also to contribute most of the revenue for the state. While this vision continued to shape state policy as well as many of the reform proposals advocated by scholars in the countryside, its assumption of a simple agricultural economy based on self-sufficient farm families did not correspond to the commercialized economy that had transformed the richer agricultural areas of the peninsula. As the economy changed over the course of the century, the economic basis of the social order continued to shift, disturbing the hierarchy ordering Chosŏn's social groups.

In fact, the forces unleashed in the last half of the seventeenth century—the implementation of the Uniform Land Tax and the rise in productivity achieved by rice transplantation (see p. 83)—continued to shape the economy. Now that the state no longer collected specific tribute goods as taxation but received payment in the form of rice, cloth, or cash, it needed to purchase the goods that previously it had received directly from the population. A new merchant class, called *kong'in*, emerged with the special responsibility to supply the state with the goods the court and government needed. Official licenses enabled these merchants to dominate the market in particular commodities, allowing some of them to amass considerable wealth.

At the same time, the number of smaller merchants increased, some organizing handicraft production such as the manufacture of horsehair hats, others distributing medicines, still others shipping fish from the coast to market towns. In 1791, the court abolished the official licenses of the tribute merchants, creating opportunity for other merchants to sell their goods to the state. Gradually they became independent producers, their relation to the state reduced to paying artisan taxes. Some became purveyors of their own goods in local, regional, and even peninsula-wide markets, while others worked under the supervision—and with the capital—of merchants.

An expanding exchange economy led to greater urbanization, as more merchants and artisans gathered in commercial centers. With more goods circulating, a booming transport business emerged in many towns. Communities that previously had been largely administrative in nature began to change as their most prominent feature, a magistrate's office, came to be overshadowed by the marketplace. Population figures for towns during the Chosŏn dynasty are problematic, yet we know that cities such as Kaesŏng, Uiju, Pyongyang, and Tongnae (Pusan) grew because of their role in regional and international trade. Market towns sprouted throughout the peninsula, numbering over 1,000, according to a contemporary observer.

A large percentage of this growth occurred in Seoul, the city that had become the commercial heart of the peninsula, as well as its political center. Official figures show population growth in Seoul to have boomed from around 80,000 in 1657 to 194,000 in 1669, a rapid growth that slowed but continued into the eighteenth century. Government records claim only 200,000 at century's end, but some scholars estimate the actual figure to be closer to 300,000. To feed this population, merchants shipped rice along the coast, largely from the southern provinces, and up the Han River to the capital. Providing Seoul households with such everyday needs as wood for their stoves required a large supply network. Goods arrived from around the peninsula, even from Beijing and Japan, to satisfy the needs and desires of Seoul's urban consumers. By the early eighteenth century, markets sprawled outside the eastern and southern gates of the city. Yet despite the growth of Seoul and outlying commercial centers, they still represented less than 10 percent of Chosŏn's total population. As dramatic as the commercial growth was, the peninsula's economy (like that of China and Japan) remained agricultural.

Because of the continued dominance of rural life, even Seoul did not develop an entirely distinctive urban culture, though new cultural forms did arise to serve town-dwellers. Mask dances, a time-honored festival performance in the countryside, became a staple of urban marketplaces, as did a new form of musical storytelling known as *p'ansori*. Featuring a lead male or female singer accompanied by dramatic drumming, *p'ansori* performances lasted for hours, even several days. Singers entertained gatherings with a lively mélange of ribald humor, love stories, and social satire, often using the plotlines of new novels to improvise extra storylines and, in the hands of the best singers, to offer laugh-inducing puns.

One of the most famous *p'ansori* stories from this era is the tragic love story of Chunhyang, the daughter of a low-class entertainer. Many of the themes in "The Story of Chunhyang" reflect the world of its eighteenth-century audience. The story affirms ideals of female loyalty and chastity, goals suitable for all women, even a lowly entertainer. The villain, a corrupt governor, highlights contemporary concerns with the abuses of state officials at the same time as it confirms the idea that a truly moral official, the man Chunhyang loves, could through his individual virtue resolve the socio-economic concerns of the people. Most shocking to the audiences in the market towns was surely the love alliance—unthinkable 100 years earlier—between a low-status entertainer and a highly educated man from a prestigious *yangban* family, and the tension in the story depended on the social distance between these two statuses.

THE *YANGBAN* PUZZLE

These changes reached to the top of the social hierarchy. Indeed, one of the more puzzling phenomena of Chosŏn social history lies in the steady rise of the number of *yangban* listed on government registers, despite all the ways the *yangban* had tried to prevent the growth of their status group. Only a few local records giving official classifications of the population exist for the late Chosŏn dynasty, but they show similar trends in the rise of the number of *yangban* compared to the overall population. In one case (repeated elsewhere), in Taegu county in the southeast of the peninsula, the percentage of *yangban* rose from 9.2 percent of the total population in 1690, to 18.7 percent in 1729, to 37.5 percent in 1783, to just over 70 percent in 1858.

By the mid-1800s, according to these records, well over half of the local population belonged to this elite, ruling group. This region was famous for its sizable *yangban* populations, so these statistics can hardly be seen as "typical." Yet this region also included areas of substantial commercial activity and, despite its culturally conservative reputation, it illustrates that the new wealth created by the growing exchange economy resulted in a steady rise in the number of *yangban* registered at the county office.

One of the major causes for this growth in the number of registered *yangban* lay with the fiscal difficulties of the state. Ever since the Hideyoshi invasions, the central state had offered special titles, low-level administrative positions, and *yangban* status in return for large contributions to the government treasury. With revenues never sufficient, the sale of titles accelerated, becoming a common means of shoring up the budget. We also know that some wealthy families simply bribed local officials to make a discreet change of status in their household records.

Still other families made great efforts to emulate the ideal standards of *yangban* life. Usually rich merchant families who could buy the best Confucian education for their children, they built houses in the countryside, with inner rooms for household women and ancestral shrines for the proper conduct of rituals. By the eighteenth century, a *chokpo*, the genealogical record of the descent group or lineage that had long served as a marker of *yangban* status, could easily be forged and bought. As the commercial economy expanded, more non-*yangban* parlayed their newfound wealth into acceptance in the top status category.

The rise in the number of *yangban* might have indicated a gradual collapse of the traditional social order, but the official status classification did not necessarily translate into actual status distinctions in local society. As we have seen, *yangban* status had conventionally been socially derived, acquired over generations through family ties, government office, and lifestyle. Memories of social status in villages lingered, so that someone who managed to buy a title was not likely to be accepted as an equal by longstanding local *yangban* regardless of that person's official status. Not surprisingly, many *yangban* writings from this period note these social changes, commenting disparagingly on the new claimants to *yangban* status and the disrespectful attitudes of the population toward their status group.

The upper echelons of *yangban* society, however, remained closed, dominated by the few families that controlled access to bureaucratic positions. These families intermarried among themselves and felt little threat to their social position from the increasing numbers of *yangban*. Indeed, these highest families, by virtue of their control of the state apparatus, actually undertook the selling of titles that inflated the number of *yangban*. The gap that had long existed between the high and low ends of the *yangban* elite grew wider and more complex. The powerful upper stratum, engaged in the politics of the Seoul-centered bureaucracy, had little to do with the politically disenfranchised *yangban* dispersed throughout the country, who had to deal much more directly with the social consequences of the expansion of their status group.

Local *yangban* responded by promoting "village covenants," among other methods. Village covenants had a long history in the peninsula, as they did in China. They began in the sixteenth century to promote virtuous behavior among villagers, to pool resources for the building of a water reservoir, or to pay the funeral expenses of a poor family. As part of these covenants, all the men in a village agreed to protocols outlining proper behavior and specific responsibilities for which they could be held to account. In village meetings, males gathered in a common space to hear a leading member exhort them to better behavior, praise virtuous individuals, or mete out punishment to miscreant members. By the eighteenth century, village covenants had proliferated at the local level, where true status was determined. Local *yangban* used them to reinforce status distinctions at a time of blurring social categories.

Tiling a roof, from a nineteenth-century copy of Kim Hongdo's album of paintings, *Scenes from Daily Life.*

Although more eighteenth-century Koreans could transfer their wealth into *yangban* status, many *yangban* could no longer afford the lives expected of their status. The ideal vision held that *yangban* owned land to sustain themselves appropriately, but through negligence, personal disaster, or simple incompetence, some *yangban* families lost their land. Without any other income, these "fallen" *yangban* turned to a variety of occupations, sometimes depending on their literary skills—reading and writing letters for illiterates, for example—or taking up menial tasks with a literary tinge,

such as making and selling ink brushes. In the most extreme cases, *yangban* became tenant farmers. With the rise of newly rich merchants, the fall of some *yangban* demonstrates that by the eighteenth century there was no longer necessarily a correlation between social status and wealth.

STATE AND COUNTRYSIDE

Factional politics had obsessed and divided the Chosŏn court throughout the late seventeenth and early eighteenth centuries. These struggles could be fierce, with losers often impeached, convicted, and executed. The grip on power of successive factions alienated many aspiring *yangban* who, without factional affiliations, had virtually no hope of advancing into bureaucratic positions. This led to an ever-widening gap between the metropolitan *yangban* families, who monopolized power in Seoul, and those in the countryside.

Although officials and scholars had criticized factionalism for centuries, only in the 1720s did King Yongjo (r. 1724–1776) quell this divisive form of politics. In the never-ending struggle for power between the bureaucrats and kings, Yongjo became a master at manipulating his *yangban* officials, making him one of the most powerful rulers of the Chosŏn dynasty. He pushed through a plan to limit factionalism, a policy called "Magnificent Harmony," which sought to create a balance of power among court factions by appointing roughly equal numbers from each faction to positions of power. The resulting equilibrium strengthened royal rule for Yongjo and his grandson and successor, Chŏngjo (r. 1776–1800). Together, these two monarchs ruled for 75 years, leading two of the most activist courts in the dynasty.

Yongjo's and Chŏngjo's legacies included sponsorship of large literary projects, similar to those of the Qianlong Emperor. Using an improved form of metal moveable type first used in the thirteenth century, the court printed massive encyclopedias detailing the history of institutions, lands, and customs of the peninsula. The court published new compilations of the legal code; geographic studies and maps of the entire peninsula; histories of martial arts and rituals, including detailed illustrated accounts of royal processions; and compendia of diplomatic documents. King Chŏngjo also established a new royal library, the Kyujanggak, as a major repository for books and manuscripts collected from around the peninsula as well as from China. He even took the unprecedented step of appointing talented *chungin*—non-*yangban* "middle people"—to official positions in this library, new ranks that allowed scholars like Pak Chega (see p. 123) and Yu Tŭkkong (1749–?) (see p. 124) to write highly influential reformist political and historical essays.

The enhanced power of the royal throne also offered King Yongjo, like the Yongzheng Emperor a generation earlier, an opportunity to examine the inequities and inefficiencies of the tax system. He focused especially on the military tax, which, together with *corvée* and land taxes, was one of the three main taxes paid by commoners. Designed to cover the expenses of soldiers, the military tax was calculated on a quota basis by county. By the eighteenth century, however, this had become one of the most burdensome taxes, as the number of taxpaying commoners in some counties had declined considerably because of increasing tax avoidance. The obvious solution to this dilemma lay in spreading the burden more equitably by removing the military tax exemption enjoyed by the *yangban*.

In the 1750s, Yongjo did precisely that. With the help of some of his ministers, he did succeed in halving the tax for the commoners, but he was unable to overcome bureaucratic resistance to his plan of extending the military tax to the *yangban*. Instead, he reached a compromise: a new, much smaller household tax would be paid by each *yangban* family. Although this did increase the amount of money flowing into the state treasury, the compromise shows that even this most powerful of Chosŏn kings could be stymied by the *yangban* when it came to control over economic resources. Moreover, these limited reforms still did not take into account the growing wealth of the commercialized economy. With a vision of the economy still based on simple self-sufficient agricultural communities, the state made little effort to tap into the new sources of money emerging in the exchange economy,

a situation similar to that in both Qing China and Tokugawa Japan. In fact, none of the East Asian states ever created a viable commercial tax system before the late nineteenth century.

The commercialization of the economy, however, transformed the countryside during the eighteenth century. As population continued to rise and available agricultural land remained constant, the demand for land drove prices higher, making the purchase of land more difficult for the less wealthy. Land exchanged hands more often, as the burgeoning money economy commodified the most basic agricultural resource—arable fields. Lands on which cash crops could be grown were in special demand, since they were the most lucrative for owners. High prices supported the trend toward the concentration of land in large estates. Historians estimate that in prime agricultural areas, wealthy families and government institutions owned more than 50 percent of the land, and the remainder was broken up into smaller estates, with some land in the possession of owner-cultivators.

Tenants suffered in this changing economy of landownership. Larger estates meant that more people could not afford their own land and could survive only by renting and tending the fields of others. As the number of wholly or partially landless farmers increased, landlords could profitably replace slaves with contracted tenant labor. Unlike a slave, a tenant could work anywhere his family could find land to rent, and landlords had the freedom to evict tenants at their own discretion to find new ones. With the increasing number of farmers seeking land, rents increased and tenants' lives became much less secure, their labor now just another commodity in an increasingly commercialized agricultural economy.

Criticisms of the land system continued throughout the eighteenth century, led most notably by the reform scholar Yi Ik (1681–1763). Like Yu Hyŏngwŏn before him, Yi Ik lived in the countryside and used the Classics as a standard for advocating land reform. He deplored the growth of large estates and saw them as a source of peasant misery.

One of the greatest teachers of the century, Yi Ik passed on to the next generation of scholars his opinions and research on land reform as well as commercial development, theories of the earth's position in the solar system, religious thought, and Confucian metaphysics.

A TRAGEDY AT COURT

In 1744, a 9-year-old girl known to us only by her title (Lady Hyegyŏng) and her natal surname (Hong), joined the Chosŏn royal family, betrothed to Crown Prince Sado, also 9 years old. Her husband became a central, tragic figure not only in her life but also in the history of the royal house. As Sado entered his teens, he began exhibiting signs of madness, tearing through multiple suits of clothing every morning as he dressed, sleeping in a coffin in a bedroom decorated as a tomb, and killing several servants in fits of rage.

His father King Yongjo, one of the most eminent monarchs of the dynasty, deeply distressed over his son's illness, could not countenance the possibility of his mad son taking the throne. In 1762, after the young man had threatened to kill members of the royal family, Yongjo resorted to a most un-Confucian act—filicide—in a dramatic fashion. After formally deposing Sado as Crown Prince, he locked his son in a rice chest and left him there to die eight days later. To fill the vacant post of Crown Prince, the king appointed the son of Prince Sado and Lady Hyegyŏng, the boy who in 1776 ascended the throne as King Chŏngjo (r. 1776–1800). For many years thereafter, the Chosŏn court split into two factions, divided on the question of whether the son of a man executed (or murdered) by the king could legitimately sit on the throne as a moral ruler.

Royal procession on the occasion of King Chŏngjo's state visit with his mother, Lady Hyegyŏng, to the tomb of his father Crown Prince Sado at Hwasŏng. Seventh panel in an eight-panel screen, 1795.

These events clouded the remainder of Lady Hyegyŏng's long life (1735–1815). Fated to live for another 14 years under the rule of her father-in-law, who had killed her husband, she sought to defend her son and the honor of her family from the incriminations and rumors that circulated for decades after these events. Toward the end of her life she composed in the Korean vernacular script four remarkable memoirs known as *Records Written in Silence* (*Hanjungnok*), recounting her life at court and the terrible events surrounding the killing of her husband. Addressed to various members of her family, including her son and grandson (who also became king), these constitute our only "insider" accounts of the late eighteenth-century Chosŏn court, for the conventional historical records either eliminated or distorted Prince Sado's story. For a woman, who in typical Chosŏn fashion did not even leave her personal name for posterity, Lady Hyegyŏng broke with convention to create a masterpiece of vernacular writing that offers the most intimate details of a momentous drama at the highest levels of power.

RELATIONS WITH QING

Yi Ik wrote at a time of lingering anti-Manchu sentiment. In 1704, one 60-year cycle after the fall of the Ming, the kingdom erected an "Altar of Great Gratitude" to the Ming on the grounds of the main Chosŏn royal palace. Officials conducted commemorative rituals at this altar for the Ming's Wanli Emperor, who had dispatched troops to help Chosŏn defeat Hideyoshi, and for the Chongzhen Emperor, who had hanged himself from a palace tree. In the eyes of many scholars, these rituals implied that their dynasty had inherited the Ming line of legitimacy. The belief that Chosŏn served as the sole guardian of proper Confucian thought and practice spurred scholars around the peninsula to set up rural academies of learning (K. *sŏwŏn*). Often legitimized by royal decree, rural academies increased by more than 300 in the late seventeenth and early eighteenth centuries. They became centers for the continued study and teaching of Confucian thought as well as rural retreats for powerful families and factions out of power.

By the late eighteenth century, however, a number of writers began questioning the dominant anti-Manchu sentiment in Chosŏn. Pak Chiwŏn (1737–1805), a *chungin* who had traveled to Beijing on tribute missions, had been impressed by the wealth and commercial activity he observed there. He wrote essays calling for officials and scholars not to let their anti-Manchu biases interfere with the opportunity to learn new technologies and administrative practices from their powerful neighbor.

Pak Chega (1750–1815), another *chungin* traveler to the Qing capital, also picked up this theme, pointing out that even though Chosŏn lagged behind the Qing dynasty in many areas, "Nowadays…when someone suggests that the ways of China should be studied, people rise and laugh at him." Entitling his main work *Northern Learning*, Pak urged officials to study Qing methods for promoting commerce and trade. Going even further, he called for the development of technology and an infrastructure for economic growth. "If we trade with far lands," he wrote, "our wealth will increase and hundreds of industries will rise…How can there be in the world a country which does not wish to be rich and strong?"[3]

DOMESTICATING LETTERS AND ARTS

The eighteenth century also witnessed the domestication, or turning inward, of the Korean cultural imagination. Partly a reaction to the Manchu occupation of China and partly a result of the broadening social background of artists and writers, this trend in arts and letters featured a greater emphasis on local themes and issues. Few exemplified this trend better than the famous painter Chŏng Sŏn (1676–1759), who dispensed with conventional landscape themes based on Chinese traditions in favor of seeking out beautiful locations in the peninsula for his ink and brushes. His composition of Mt. Kŭmgang, one of the most famous paintings in the Korean canon, mastered what has come to be known as "true-view landscape painting," a style that sought to capture the sensations of on-the-spot observations of mountain and river panoramas.

Other painters, such as Kim Hongdo and Sin Yunbok, also turned their artistic talents to local cultural themes. Appointed to the bureaucracy as official portrait painters, both belonged to the *chungin* status group, reflected in their choice of unconventional subjects that had been ignored by *yangban* literati painters. Kim, though an accomplished landscape artist, enjoyed capturing the flavor of everyday life in his folk paintings of wrestlers, school groups, and similar topics. Sin's art featured a humorous and erotic side, such as a risqué scene of semi-clad women washing their hair in a stream while a pair of mischievous boys peek through the bushes. His paintings reveal the romantic life of the Chosŏn dynasty.

Following this same inward trend, new histories and geographies of the peninsula appeared. In the immediate aftermath of the Hideyoshi and Manchu invasions, studies of the peninsular past had become popular, a trend that accelerated in the eighteenth century. Many of these—Hong Manjung's *Outline of Eastern History by Dynasty* (1705), the more famous *Annotated Account of Eastern History* (1778) by An Chŏngbok (1712–1791), and Han Chiyun's *History of the Eastern Sea*—used the term "east" (K. *tong*, C. *dong*, J. *tō*) in their titles and text. A traditional name for the peninsula, this device served to organize their accounts of the courts that had ruled Korea and place them in relation to China.

These Confucian histories centered on the court and dispensed judgments—in the old "praise and blame" style of history-writing—on the moral worth of the actions of monarchs and officials from the earliest legendary reigns right down to the Chosŏn era itself. Some recounted stories of the mythical founder of the

Korean people, Tan'gun, who, according to twelfth-century accounts, established the first kingdom in the peninsula in 2333 BCE. These authors also emphasized the figure of Kija, who (according to Chinese myth) had fled to the peninsula at the fall of the Shang dynasty in 1122 BCE. By highlighting Kija, they reaffirmed a direct line of legitimacy from the current Chosŏn monarch, back through Kija, to the sage-kings of ancient China, thus implying their moral superiority to the Manchus.

Some of these histories also devoted considerable attention to Manchuria. As the Qianlong Emperor turned his court scholars' attention to the Manchu homelands and history, attempting to preserve Manchu identity, some Chosŏn historians reflected on the role of the northern territories in Korean history. Yi Chonghwi (1731–1797) in his *History of the East* emphasized the significance of the ancient kingdom of Koguryŏ, centered in Manchuria. Yu Tŭkkong wrote a historical account of the northern kingdom of Palhae, noting its coexistence with the kingdom of Silla in the peninsula and seeing Palhae's demise in 926 as representing a significant loss.

Geographical studies of the peninsula also emerged in profusion. Often historical in nature, studies such as Sin Kyŏngjun's *Investigations of Territory* and Han Paekkyŏm's *Study of the Eastern Kingdom's Geography* narrated shifts in frontiers and administrative boundaries over time, investigated the origins of place names, and traced the development of roads. Mapmaking became more precise and used techniques from landscape painting to produce maps of beauty, giving cartography an artistic flourish.

Finally, despite the continued dominance of classical Chinese in public and official writing, the Korean vernacular alphabet received considerable intellectual attention. Scholars devotedly studied King Sejong's invention, disagreeing among themselves about the origins of the letters—some contended they were patterned after Mongolian, others that they took the shape of heavenly patterns, and still others that they imitated the movements of the mouth when pronouncing sounds. The earliest dictionaries of the vernacular

Sin Yunbok. *Women Bathing during the Tano Festival*, late 18th century. Sin's lively depictions of everyday life departed from the orthodoxy of literati painting.

script appeared, and it came to be used in poetry, such as the *kasa* genre popular among *yangban* women. Vernacular novels continued to appear, including famous stories such as the *Tale of Sim Chŏng* and *Tale of Hongbu* and accounts of military gallantry like *The Record of the Imjin Wars*.

Scholars and writers of the eighteenth century thus examined more closely than ever before the various traditions and features of life in the peninsula, following both the trend toward "practical learning" (away from Neo-Confucian metaphysics) and their desire to separate their culture from China's. These studies would later be taken up by nationalist writers in the late nineteenth and early twentieth centuries to define what they came to call, in their modern vocabulary, the essence of the Korean nation.

THE COMING OF "WESTERN LEARNING"

Unlike China, where missionaries and traders had directly introduced European theories of astronomy, military technology (such as firearms), and Roman Catholicism, and Japan, where Dutch traders introduced

European scholarship after 1720, eighteenth-century Korea had no resident Europeans, with the exception of a few shipwrecked sailors, to familiarize scholars with European knowledge. Instead, the wide range of knowledge that in Chosŏn came to be known as sŏhak (Western learning) entered the peninsula indirectly, mainly via Chinese books bought in Beijing by members of tribute missions. These travelers also met with Jesuits stationed in Beijing, questioning them about the sciences and religion revealed in those books. Chinese translations of European books began circulating on the peninsula by the early 1600s, intriguing scholars outside of officialdom who were advocating social reforms and "practical learning."

Although the term "Western learning" grouped Catholicism with mathematics and cartography, it was scientific knowledge that most fascinated Chosŏn scholars. The teaching of the "Lord of Heaven," as Catholicism came to be known, received only rather bemused attention, for the majority of scholars saw it as heterodox. Yi Ik, one of the first scholars to examine "Western learning" extensively, enthusiastically accepted and expanded on European calendrical science and astronomy but rejected outright any Jesuit religious teachings, equating them with other heterodoxies such as Buddhism. By the late eighteenth century, one writer commented that the translations of Catholic books had become popular playthings among young scholars, indicating both the widespread dissemination of these writing and the fact that he, at least, did not consider them worthy of notice.

Some scholars, however, took Christianity seriously. Yi Sŭnghun received baptism from a Jesuit priest while on a mission to Beijing in 1784. On his return, Yi formed a small congregation of converts and took the remarkable step of baptizing other enthusiasts himself—a step that unknowingly violated church doctrine but that ensured the continued growth of the nascent community. Some intellectuals set up study groups, organized like church parishes, and a growing number of women became involved. With no missionaries within hundreds of miles of the peninsula, this early community of believers grew through their own efforts, interest, and enthusiasm, becoming one of the only self-evangelizing communities in the history of Roman Catholicism.

In these early days, with the number of believers in Korea still small, the Chosŏn state did not take any official action to suppress the religion. But in 1785, when one of these unofficial church organizations was discovered, King Chŏngjo branded Catholicism as heterodox, banning the importation of all sŏhak books. An investigation aimed at burning all Christian books within the kingdom even discovered heterodox books in the royal library, to the dismay of the court. Scholars who continued to study Roman Catholicism were sent into internal exile.

Alarm at the spread of the religion reached new heights in 1791. The previous year, the Catholic community learned from French Jesuits in Beijing that the Pope had forbidden believers from performing ancestor rituals—the same prohibition that had caused so much turmoil during the Rites Controversy under the Kangxi Emperor many decades earlier (see pp. 78–79). Learning of this, Paul Yun, an early convert and leader of the community, together with his cousin, James Kwŏn Sangyŏn, burned his family's ancestral tablets. His timing could not have been more unfortunate, for the next year his mother passed away. During her funeral, other family members realized that the usual mourning rituals were not being conducted, and no ancestral tablets were present. Word quickly spread to officials that this most basic of Confucian rites, the pillar of filial piety, had been neglected, and they arrested the two cousins. Both were executed for following "superstition." Despite this violent suppression, the Catholic community continued to grow, to approximately 4,000 believers by 1794. With the arrival of the first foreign missionary, the Chinese priest Father Zhou Wenmo, the religion spread further, reaching around 10,000 adherents by the turn of the century and setting the stage for fierce persecutions in the nineteenth century.

THE EARLY MODERN TRANSITION IN TOKUGAWA JAPAN

The eighteenth century opened just as the Tokugawa realm reached the height of its population growth and of the expansion of its great cities—Edo, Osaka, and Kyoto—and closed as Western nations revived their interest in the shogun's realm. The seventeenth century's remarkable economic expansion gave way to a slower pace of development. The population of the great metropolises decreased, and international trade declined with the replacement of imports by domestic products.

But any calculus of change would have to consider such trends as the expansion of literacy and culture to the hinterlands, the increasing sophistication and diversity of intellectual discourse, the adoption of new technologies of production, the rise of non-farm production in areas outside the biggest cities, the replacement of the old extended family by the nuclear family, the ongoing revision of gender roles, and the development of consumption, marketing, and banking networks throughout the islands. Confronting the limitations of a preindustrial economy based solely on renewable resources—human and animal energy for most transportation needs, immediately available resources like firewood for thermal energy, and grasses and human and animal waste for fertilizers—inhabitants of the realm made choices about limitations in the social, natural, and economic environment.

JAPAN IN THE EIGHTEENTH-CENTURY WORLD

The shogunal reign of Tsunayoshi (r. 1680–1709) encompassed the cultural glories of the Genroku period (see p. 99), but also confronted the Tokugawa era's first major fiscal crisis. The great silver mines, whose output had helped to fuel East Asia's international commercial engine in the seventeenth century, had begun to play out by 1680. Copper still seemed to be plentiful, but Tsunayoshi believed that using currency to pay for imports would sap the strength of the realm. Tsunayoshi's attitude toward foreign trade paralleled his belief in a well-ordered society where each status behaved as was proper to its station. He strengthened regulations on the clothes, homes, and foods the various classes could consume; aided the poor, sick, and homeless; forbade infanticide; improved prison conditions; and built shelters for stray dogs, for which he earned the nickname of "dog shogun."

While the shogun called for restraining international trade, his officials permitted bartering between Chinese and Japanese merchants in exchange for considerable fees. They also allowed trade with Chosŏn and the Qing to exceed Tsunayoshi's limits. Large exports of

Contemporary depiction of starving people during the Great Tenmei famine (1782–87). This family attempts to eat leather and an animal carcass. Hundreds of thousands died.

copper also continued, as the Qing government needed copper to support its burgeoning economy. Eventually, official Tokugawa limitations on exports of gold, silver, and copper led to reductions in international trade in the early eighteenth century.

Arai Hakuseki (1657–1725), advisor to the child-shogun Ietsugu (r. 1713–1716), shared Tsunayoshi's sense that foreign trade depleted the realm's monetary supplies. He reversed the practice of lax enforcement of trade regulations. No longer would Chinese ships be ignored as they unloaded the goods Japanese consumers craved at unofficial landing sites.

When little Ietsugu died in 1716, a *shinpan daimyō* assumed the position of shogun. Tokugawa Yoshimune (r. 1716–1745) faced several crushing economic downturns and famines and experimented with fiscal and economic policy. In 1730, as part of a comprehensive program to deal with violently fluctuating rice prices, Yoshimune allowed *daimyō* to issue paper money—but their bills could not be used in international commerce. Yoshimune also formed chartered trade associations, which enrolled all merchant enterprises. He intended to regulate all domestic trade, but the list of products covered by this policy included many imported luxury goods as well.

The domestic economic concerns that led to changes in foreign trade had a variety of causes, the most important being the devastating crop failures of the eighteenth and nineteenth centuries. Localized crop losses and famines normally occurred every few years, but a few stand out as extraordinary in their geographic extent and number of deaths. Natural disasters, including eruptions of Mt. Fuji in 1707 and Mt. Asama in 1783, earthquakes and typhoons throughout the century, and periodic extremes of cold, rainy weather during the growing season, exacerbated by human influences on the environment, led to crop failures.

The human contributions to crop failure included agricultural practices that enhanced productivity in good years—such as single-cropping of lucrative non-food cash crops, planting in steep ravines and other marginal lands, and relying on an exquisitely integrated system of irrigation, fertilization, and labor (a preindustrial "just-in-time" system). But this system had little tolerance for small yet unpredictable shifts in the balance of water, fertilizer, and labor. Yoshimune's requirement that *daimyō* balance their accounting books led to more efficient taxation of farmers' rice output. So in the 1720s the *daimyō* ferreted out rice that farmers had hidden away for a poor crop year. When bad weather and insect infestation led to crop failures in 1731 and 1732, rice-producing farmers had little surplus to cushion the blow.

Fortunately, some granaries still held rice when famine hit the southwest in 1731. Large harvests in the late 1720s had threatened to undermine rice prices and thereby impoverish the samurai—whose stipends were calculated in rice—so Yoshimune warehoused substantial quantities of rice to stabilize prices. In 1731, the shogun ordered shipments of rice from these granaries to areas of poor harvests, but they were no match for the famine, and thousands died. At the same time the decreased supply and consequently higher prices of rice in the cities led to urban riots.

Meanwhile, Yoshimune continued the promotion of new crops, many of them from overseas. He lifted the ban on foreign books (except for those that specifically propagated Christianity) in 1720 and created a botanical testing facility in Edo to study Chinese and other foreign botanical data. He also ordered officials to request information about sugar and other desirable products from Nagasaki-based Chinese merchants. When he discovered that potato consumption had saved numerous lives during the famine, he supported test plantings and propagation of the sweet potato in 1733. The humble tuber had traveled to the Ryūkyū Islands before being introduced to Satsuma domain in the seventeenth century—hence one of its Japanese names, Satsuma potato.

Yoshimune's support of zoological and horticultural experiments also led to the substitution of domestic products for imported goods like ginseng from Chosŏn and high-grade silk from Chosŏn and China. The promotion of scientific experimentation, undertaken to improve agricultural production as a function of good government, resulted in reduced Japanese demand for imported sugar, silk, and ginseng. Japan gradually withdrew from the lively Northeast Asian trading networks.

The decline in trade did not mean the shogunate lost all interest in neighboring lands, however. New Japanese trends in the sciences and political theory were influenced by both Chinese and European scholarship. Economic interest in Ezo (now Hokkaidō) led to contact with Russians in the north.

Yoshimune's grandson Ieharu (r. 1760–1786) stepped into power at an opportune time, greeted by good harvests, stable commodity prices, and an expanding fish catch used for both human consumption and fertilizer. Ieharu welcomed diplomatic delegations from Chosŏn and the Ryūkyūs. By the mid-1760s, however, he faced serious domestic challenges: regional crop failures; rebellions by 200,000 farmers in 1764 against excessive demands for *corvée* labor; and scholars railing against social injustice. These uprisings and seditious writings led to a tightening of regulatory policies under the shogun's advisor, Tanuma Okitsugu (1719–1788).

Many contemporaries initially accepted Tanuma's regulations because the economy seemed to have recovered by the 1770s. These policies included shogunal monopolies on consumer necessities and forced contributions from wealthy merchant houses. Tanuma also negotiated agreements with Dutch and Chinese traders, requiring them to pay for Japanese goods with gold and silver. The economic good times lasted but a decade, however, before massive crop failure again hit several regions. Cold rains from central to northeast Japan destroyed the planting season in 1783, and a few months later a massive eruption of Mt. Asama killed thousands. Famine from 1783 until 1787 claimed at least 1 million lives and led to homelessness and abandonment of fields, outbreaks of violence, and reports of theft and even cannibalism. Northeasterners, who suffered most acutely from the famine, became interested in migrating to the "frontier" of Ezo (Hokkaidō).

Until the end of the eighteenth century most Japanese had ignored Ezo, the home of non-Japanese indigenous Ainu peoples, although a few Japanese migrants, numbering about 30,000 by the late eighteenth century, gradually settled in southern Ezo. Some shogunal officials of the 1780s thought Ezo should be developed to enable resource-poor northern Japan to trade with the Russians. The shogunate hoped to cultivate the goodwill of the Ainu. They attempted both to build roads and to refashion the Ainu in the Japanese manner—that is, to change their hairstyles and force them to abandon tattooing and ear-piercing. These cultural pressures caused a significant number of Ainu to flee to Russian-held areas. In the meantime, Russian Empress Catherine the Great (r. 1762–1796) sent Lieutenant Adam Laxman to Ezo in 1792 to establish commercial relations. The shogunate offered Laxman the possibility of trading in Nagasaki.

Temporarily placated and preoccupied with European events, the Russians did not return until 1804. The previous year, one American and two British ships had entered Nagasaki harbor in search of trade opportunities, and all were refused. When Russian official Nikolai Rezanov entered Nagasaki harbor with the permit Laxman had received over a decade earlier, shogunal officials could not be so hasty in turning him away. Eventually rebuffed, Rezanov had two Russian naval officers attack Japanese and Ainu settlements on Sakhalin Island. After the unprecedented Russian attack, Edo strengthened its northern defenses. They captured a Russian captain and part of his crew who tried to force Japan to trade in 1811, and in the following year, Russian forces seized a Japanese merchant. The captives strongly supported trade and persuaded their captors' governments to come to terms in 1813,

ending the "Russian issue" until the late nineteenth century. The shogunate dropped its attempts to expand into Ezo in the early 1800s, and the Russians lost interest in 1818.

SCHOLARS AND ARTISTS

The early years of the eighteenth century continued the cultural explosion of the Genroku era. Edo and Osaka grew as cultural centers and overtook Kyoto as the heart of Japanese arts and scholarship. Merchant-status men and women in Osaka and Edo became the major consumers of the arts. Playwrights created theatrical works with commoner audiences in mind. Puppet plays (*bunraku*) and plays performed by all-male casts (*kabuki*) graced stages in the three largest cities. Tokugawa-era audiences were comfortable with the idea that gender was constructed through performance.

Chikamatsu Monzaemon (1653–1724) became Japan's most beloved playwright, writing about 100 puppet plays and 30 *kabuki* plays during a 40-year career. Some of his works treated political or historical events—"The Battles of Koxinga," for example, a tale of Zheng Chenggong's Ming loyalist resistance to the Manchus. Chikamatsu's historical plays skirted official censure by avoiding direct mention of the Tokugawa.

Okumura Masanobu. *Large Perspective Picture of the Kabuki Theater District in Sakai-chō and Fukiya-chō,* c. 1745. Museum of Fine Arts, Boston. In this bustling scene of streetlife there are two theaters, three puppet theaters, as well as a plethora of teahouses, restaurants, and shops—all catering to the sophisticated and varied tastes of Edo's citizenry. Mt. Fuji looms in the background.

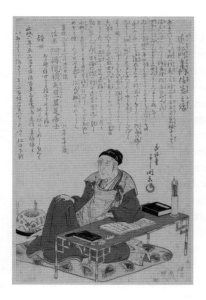

Jukōdō Yoshikuni. *Portrait of Chikamatsu Monzaemon,* c. 1804–43. Museum of Fine Arts, Boston. An extraordinarily prolific playwright of the Genroku era, Chikamatsu set the standard for later Japanese writers. His works are still performed on stage and screen.

His most popular plays were dramas of suicide. His protagonists—ordinary people such as prostitutes, small shopkeepers, and long-suffering wives—confronted great moral dilemmas. For Chikamatsu and his audiences, the elite held no monopoly on emotions and ethics. Chikamatsu's characters struggled with the conflict between human emotion and duty to a higher cause, usually a Confucian principle like filial piety or loyalty to one's superior. Tokugawa law forbade love suicides, but sometimes no other solution existed to resolve struggles involving restrictive social principles. In Chikamatsu's plays, the lovers' double suicide was preceded by a final journey during which the couple expressed their love, confessed their guilt for the sorrow their parents and other loved ones would feel, and professed their religious faith in Buddhist salvation. Chikamatsu believed in the human agency of ordinary men and women. In this, he mirrored the gradual substitution of commoner culture for elite culture.

Commoner culture spanned a wide spectrum in the eighteenth century, from pornographic or scatological writings and graphic arts to the refined world of *bunjin* culture. *Bunjin* (literati) arts entered Japan through Nagasaki in the hands of Chinese art importers, Zen priests, and political refugees from the Manchu conquest. Copying and learning from them, Japanese achieved extremely high levels of accomplishment in painting, calligraphy, poetry, prose, and the tea ceremony.

Some *bunjin* were samurai who tired of bureaucratic life and retired to become men of leisure. Others came from merchant or farmer backgrounds and simply followed their muses. Although outnumbered by men, women also joined the ranks of *bunjin*. Inspired by the mid-Qing practice of encouragement of female learning, Japanese *bunjin* masters delighted in the cultural growth of their daughters and wives. By the late eighteenth century, even girls without family ties to male *bunjin* could aspire to cultural development. Ema Saikō (1787–1861), a child prodigy, developed a national reputation as a *bunjin* artist, and her life and work epitomize the regional spread of *bunjin* culture, the cross-class nature of its practitioners, and the appeal of an artistic vocation for both men and women (see pp. 130–31).

MOLDING CLASS, STATUS, AND GENDER

Bunjin represented the most erudite end of the Japanese cultural spectrum during the eighteenth century. Millions of Japanese remained completely unschooled in reading, mathematics, or the arts. Most samurai men and women (5–10 percent of the population) became literate, and many merchant-status urbanites (another 5–10 percent) could both read and do the math necessary to maintain their businesses. Samurai studied at government expense in schools run by the shogunate or by the domains for samurai under their jurisdiction, and by the late eighteenth century some of those schools encouraged scholarly excellence over a blind respect for hierarchical status. Children of non-samurai urban families attended schools run by Buddhist priests or by married or unmarried women. Older boys often continued their education through apprenticeships, and in some cases married the bosses' daughters, with whom they jointly inherited and ran the businesses. Other urban boys attended private lessons with famous teachers, studied to become doctors, or were sent to one of many private schools run by intellectuals for anyone who could pay the tuition, regardless of their status.

Some academies stressed Confucian studies for merchant sons, while others focused on science and mathematics. The founder of the Kaitokudō Academy, chartered in 1726, stressed the importance of virtue for merchants as well as samurai. The Academy taught that the government functions of samurai and the economic functions of merchants shared equal importance in the community and larger society. This Confucian emphasis on public virtue, rather than a pure profit motive, affected economic and business thinking even after Japan began developing modern enterprises in the late nineteenth century. Many boys took the Kaitokudō's courses in reading, simple Confucianism (loyalty and filial piety), and accounting and abacus use. Those who advanced to further study analyzed Confucian texts written in classical Chinese.

Merchant and artisan-status daughters received a less extensive education than their brothers, although an unlettered young woman would not likely make a good marriage. Many girls learned to read and write and especially to use the abacus and do simple math. Urban women, like farm women, were expected to

work, and even the most privileged among them had to serve their parents-in-law, even if they did not have to dirty their hands with mundane chores. Young girls' education, like that of boys, often started in small schools run by priests or women teachers. Girls studied texts called *jokun* (precepts for women), which stressed filial piety and obedience to one's husband and in-laws.

After learning basic literacy and arithmetic, some girls acquired skills from their mothers or the families into which they were apprenticed. Daughters of well-to-do farm or merchant families commonly paid to work as servants in upper-class samurai families in order to learn manners, sometimes joined by a chaperone to ensure the girl would be well cared for despite her servant status. A daughter's education could cost 5 percent of

EMA SAIKŌ

Japanese *bunjin* took the artistic traditions of Chinese literati painting and *kanshi* (Chinese poetry) in lively new directions in the late eighteenth century. One of the finest *bunjin* artists was Ema Saikō (1787–1861), whose pen name, Saikō ("Breeze through Bamboo"), derived from a poem by the Tang dynasty Chinese poet Du Fu (712–770). Like many other *bunjin*, Saikō grew up in an intellectual household—her father, a student of both Chinese and Dutch studies, served as official physician to his *daimyō*—but unlike the majority of *bunjin*, she was a woman. She composed poetry in *kanbun*, a Japanized form of Chinese favored by male intellectuals, rather than the Japanese verse for which women writers were celebrated by "national learning" scholars as representative of Japan's true essence.

Saikō was an amazing child prodigy. Her skills in painting, calligraphy, and creative writing were already well developed by the age of 13, when her

Izuhara Maseki (copied by Kodama Seihō). *Group Portrait of the Hakuō Sha Literary Society*, 1823 (copy 1888). At top center is the great *kanshi* poet Yanagawa Seigan. In the foreground Ema Saikō is depicted kneeling and behind her is Yanagawa Seigan's wife Kōran who was also an accomplished painter and poet.

father arranged for her to receive, via correspondence, instruction from a well-known painter in Kyoto. Saikō focused herself completely on the development of her talents. At age 18, when her father tried to arrange her marriage to a bright young doctor he hoped to adopt as his heir, she refused in order to pursue her studies, so the young protégé married Saikō's sister instead.

A few years later, Saikō met the love of her life, the renowned poet Rai San'yo, seven years her senior. The attraction was immediate and mutual. Invited to help Saikō with her *kanshi* poetry, he wrote to a friend after his first meeting with the brilliant Saikō, the family's disposable income—not a trivial expense. Poorer families, particularly in the countryside, sent daughters to "girls' rooms," where more senior girls and young women guided younger girls in sewing, manners, and practical skills. Girls enjoyed these opportunities to learn alongside their female friends and to socialize at festival time, away from their parents' watchful eyes, with the "boys' rooms" in the village. In some areas of Japan, this socializing led to romance and marriage. At the end of the Tokugawa period as many as 50 percent of men and 15 percent of women throughout Japan were literate.

Education has long been linked to women's status, and eighteenth-century Japan was no exception. With rare exceptions, village women took part in communal associations as representatives of their families only in the absence of a suitable male relative. By the eighteenth century, women were more likely than men to enter a village through marriage, and few villages allowed "outsiders" to attend meetings of the village shrine association, an important sign of inclusion. Women did play an important role in politics at the top of the hierarchy, however. As wives and concubines in *daimyō* mansions and the shogun's palace, they jockeyed for position, passed messages to their brothers and fathers in public service, and used their ties with their male consort or the female head of the women's quarters to elevate their families' standing.

Despite these important functions, women had lower legal status than men. The *jokun*—the most famous

---

"I've been asked to touch up her poems, but I'd love to touch up her whole body." Rai San'yo may have, in fact, asked Dr. Ema for permission to marry his daughter. The poet certainly wrote a friend saying he wished to do so, but it is unclear whether he ever did. Although they did not marry, Saikō continued to visit Rai and the woman he later married, with whom she developed a close friendship.

She traveled with Rai and stayed at his family home in Kyoto on numerous occasions. Saikō gave serious consideration to his invitations to move to Kyoto, but her brother-in-law's death in 1820 made any move impossible because she stayed home to help her widowed sister with the household. We do not know whether or not she had a romantic relationship with Rai, who actively and proudly promoted the work of his most talented "student," but one important biographer writes convincingly that the witty, sensual poet, raised in a strict and proper family, would not have had a sexual affair with a married man.

As artists, women *bunjin* could study, read, and meet in poetry groups that included men and women. Women achieved respect and generally equal treatment in their artistic lives—though it remained rare for women to compose poetry in *kanbun*. In their social lives, however, men and women had different opportunities. Although many of Saikō's poems express her delight in a comparatively free life as a female *bunjin*, other poems express regret that women poets were often forced to choose between a life of marital love and a creative life as an artist. Commenting on an anthology of verse by Chinese women poets, Saikō lamented her solitary bed:

> The hushed night deepening, I can't take to my pillow:
> The lamp stirred, I quietly read the women's words.
> Why is it that the talented are so unfortunate?
> Most are poems about empty beds, husbands missed.[4]

An "amateur" *bunjin*, Saikō shared her works with her *bunjin* friends. It remained for her niece and nephew to publish her works after her death. Her paintings today hang in museums and private collections throughout Japan and elsewhere.

being the *Greater Learning for Women* attributed to Confucian scholar Kaibara Ekiken (1630–1714)—described women as ideally passive, submissive, cheerful, loyal to their husbands and parents-in-law, and hardworking in their role as wives. Japanese feminists in the late nineteenth century attacked Kaibara and his work as the reason for women's subordination, yet scholars today point out that he may not even have written it. It was first published in 1716 (two years after his death) as part of a larger work called *A Treasure Chest of Greater Learning for Women* that discussed numerous occupations for women, practical skills, training of children, tips for dealing with medical emergencies, and training in literature and poetry. Generations of schoolgirls studied this book, but its message of subordination paled by comparison with the empowering role of literacy promoted by the use of *jokun* as textbooks.

Despite the stereotypes about Japanese girls, families welcomed female infants with birth celebrations and feted them on particular birthdays, like their brothers. While farm families did (illegally) practice infanticide, girl babies were no more likely than boys to be targeted, as families sought gender balance as well as optimal family size. In fact, the effects of gender were always tempered by other considerations, particularly status and wealth. Women of the samurai status had to be bearers of their husbands' heirs because payment of the family's stipend required an heir. Samurai wives suffered the risk of divorce or the presence of a concubine if they could not produce a son. Merchant-status women had business roles to play in their families. Their parents often allowed them to express their opinions about prospective husbands because of the importance of family harmony to the economic success of their firms.

Farm women's roles depended on their families' wealth and on local customs. Throughout the realm, farm wives, husbands, and children contributed to the family's wellbeing and continuity. Mothers bore children but also had the primary responsibility for planting and threshing rice, spinning thread, and sewing clothing. Fathers took charge of early childhood education and even infant care, and children of six or seven years carried their siblings on their backs while their parents and their grandparents worked in the fields. No member of the average farm family could shirk either reproductive or productive functions. Some tasks were more likely to be performed by one sex or the other, but if a woman was not available for planting or a man for harvesting, no one sacrificed family welfare and continuity on the altar of sex difference.

DEMOGRAPHIC CHANGES IN THE EIGHTEENTH CENTURY

Edo emerged as the dominant city in the Tokugawa realm by century's end. By 1780, Osaka, under Tokugawa control though essentially managed by merchants, had begun a steep decline that would leave it with just 60 percent of its 1700 population by the mid-nineteenth century. The eclipse of Kyoto and Osaka, the stagnation of population growth throughout the Tokugawa realm, and a turning away from foreign trade have all given rise to the notion of "Japan in decline" after the early years of the eighteenth century.

But rather than decline, it might be more accurate to view the changes as demographic and economic shifts responding to Japan's reaching the outer limits of what historians call the "biological old regime"—that is, the relationships between cities and countryside, people and their environment in the context of humans' use of the renewable energy supplied by the sun. England first made the transition away from the biological old regime by harnessing energy locked in the earth as coal, breaking its reliance on solar energy captured annually by plants. Coal was available in Japan but was used only sparingly during the eighteenth century because its potential users—potters, salt-makers, and others—preferred fuel sources that produced less intense heat, and because farmers complained about the pollution produced by burning coal.

As in most other countries in the eighteenth century, the available energy in Japan remained mostly in the form of annually renewable sources. Thus, people made decisions about resource use and population growth within the constraints of the biological old regime. Eighteenth-century Japanese were aware of the limits of their resources—*daimyō* and villagers alike devised reforestation programs to counter the effects of the previous century's overuse of forest products for fuel and construction. But the limits imposed by reliance on annually renewed energy sources may have played the greatest role in the shriveling of Japan's cities.

Cities had grown rapidly in the seventeenth century. Most owed their existence to the political decision to remove samurai from the countryside and concentrate them near *daimyō* castles. By the beginning of the eighteenth century, urban merchants created lines of credit, commodities futures markets, and means of transferring assets that resembled banking systems. Improved roads and coastal shipping moved goods and people from farm to city and back, and the alternate attendance system spread commerce through the realm.

Farmers, especially those living near the routes used by the great alternate attendance processions, were also drawn into the network. Cash poured into post towns and way stations, permitting rural folks to buy goods they had previously made at home or done without. Farmers who had easy links to transportation and markets planted cash crops that yielded greater return on their investments of energy and cash. Farmers purchased human waste as fertilizer, a trade that relied on the growing urban–rural nexus. Food was shipped to the cities, consumed, and returned to farms as manure to supply energy for plant growth. Farmers also purchased ground fish, technically a renewable source of energy, as fertilizer.

Farmers had cash for these purchases because they shifted from staple grain production to cash crops, a trend that, as we saw above (and in Chosŏn), had a severe downside. In good times, these crops produced wealth; in bad times, single-cropping of cash crops turned crop failures into famines. Farming was always a hopeful gamble, and most farm families took advantage of opportunities to produce more lucrative crops when possible. They were aided in this by improved transportation as well as by technological advances, such as threshing machines, better irrigation, and dissemination of optimal farming practices through printed handbooks. Most farm families had at least one literate member.

These changes all made it possible to farm more intensively and to make use of all members of the family. For example, "labor-saving" devices such as the rice-threshing machine allowed children to carry out a task that had previously required the strength of an adult. Adult women redirected their saved labor to a winter crop, or to spinning and weaving in the home. "Labor-saving" did not imply leisure. Large extended families began to break apart, with servants and more distant relatives becoming tenant farmers or working in the cities and towns. By the end of the eighteenth century, the nuclear family had replaced the extended family in many rural areas of Japan.

To maximize output, families made decisions to limit their size and gender composition by careful timing of marriage, childbirth, and, at times, fertility control through infanticide. Some solved the problem of limited resources by sending adolescent children out to work. As villages developed small spinning and weaving sheds and other facilities for the production of consumer goods, teenage girls and boys worked as hands in mills set up by rich neighbors.

Some of these rich neighbors descended from seventeenth-century extended families that had let their distant relatives go as the cost of labor increased. They often maintained connections to former extended family members, many of whom became their tenants. This gave the former leading families rental income that could be invested in enterprises like small mills and soy sauce or sake breweries. Social relations in the countryside began to change, with new concentrations of wealth in the hands of these farmer-entrepreneurs. Japan's economy and population overall did not grow; rather they shifted to make different uses of limited resources.

The transfer of economic momentum to rural areas and small towns did not mean that all was peaceful in the countryside. Crop failures led to famines, and smallpox broke out frequently in the eighteenth century. As differences between the richest and the poorest rural folk increased, the target of some rural protests shifted from tax collectors and government officials to local moneylenders and others who symbolized rural privilege.

THE BLOSSOMING OF INTELLECTUAL DIVERSITY

Scholarship and ideological production flourished in the eighteenth century. Politically favored schools of thought contended with marginalized schools, champions of different views of Confucianism undercut one another, and proto-nationalist ideas emerged to challenge the dominance of Chinese scholarship in Japan. Meanwhile, mathematics and medical sciences developed, and rural sages as well as devotees of European learning propagated new ideas. Expanding literacy made scholarship accessible to larger numbers of Japanese, and common folk joined samurai, priests, and educated merchants in expressing their ideas. Even the illiterate could be drawn into new discourses by attending lectures offering practical solutions to contemporary problems.

Hayashi Razan and Yamazaki Ansai had developed Confucian-based ideologies to justify shogunal rule in the seventeenth century. Other scholars put forward ideas that irritated the authorities; the lucky among them established respected schools, while the less fortunate were punished with detention or exile. Nakae Tōju (1608–1648), for example, though not punished for his ideas, strayed from Hayashi's orthodoxy. A prolific reader of classical Chinese, well versed in the Zhu Xi school of thought propounded by Hayashi, Nakae rejected Hayashi's stress on hierarchy. He turned to Ming scholar Wang Yangming (pronounced Ōyōmei in Japanese, see pp. 32–33), asserting that adherence to old principles stifled creativity and that acting appropriately in one's own time and place was far superior. Thus he directly articulated the practical learning approach common in both Qing and Chosŏn and admired by most Tokugawa-era Confucianists, regardless of their doctrinal differences.

Somewhat younger than Nakae Tōju, Itō Jinsai (1627–1705) had no interest in serving the political authorities and denounced Zhu Xi-style thought, which elevated principle over material existence (*ri* over *ki*), echoing a contemporary debate in Qing and Chosŏn (see p. 101). Those who focused on the practical and cultivated a "mind of compassionate love" would draw talented people to follow them. Anyone, Itō noted, could succeed. Although he based his scholarship on ideas developed in China, he held that Japanese were in no way inferior to Chinese.

Kumazawa Banzan (1619–1691), a student of Nakae Tōju, had the misfortune to be named as an inspiration by disgruntled *rōnin* plotting an insurrection in 1651. For a while, Banzan, who also advocated the intuitive approach of Wang Yangming, avoided arrest by staying away from Edo, but he spent most of the last quarter-century of his life under house arrest.

Wanting to promote practical solutions to contemporary problems, Ogyū Sorai (1666–1728) decided to read the ancient Chinese Classics directly rather than studying Zhu Xi's commentaries. Ogyū believed that successful rulers must govern in light of contemporary conditions and consider diverse perspectives. The ancient texts, he declared, showed that shoguns should govern energetically. This required a sound economy, for impoverished people would lose respect for propriety and rebel.

Ogyū, an advisor to shogun Tsunayoshi, sent reform proposals to Yoshimune upon his accession to the shogunate. While Ogyū Sorai may not have directly influenced Yoshimune, he worked in that shogun's spirit of practical learning. In 1723, Yoshimune did, in fact, offer supplemental stipends to samurai appointed to higher posts than their rank allowed. He also set up complaint boxes in Edo (1721) and in Osaka (1727), where anyone could drop off petitions, and ordered the compilation of a massive compendium of shogunal and *daimyō* law, called the *Ofuregaki* (1742).

Rangaku—Dutch learning, because this European scholarship entered Japan through the Dutch traders at Nagasaki—was also considered useful because it addressed practical concerns. Only a small number of European books on medicine and navigation had been permitted in the realm before 1720, when Yoshimune opened the door to "Dutch" books on anything except Christianity. Initially, scholars studied Chinese-language treatises on European science, but by the end of the century, Japanese scholars could translate books directly from the Dutch. Physician Sugita Genpaku railed in 1775 against "hidebound Confucians and run-of-the-mill doctors of Chinese medicine [who] don't know how large the world is," stressing a practical learning attitude toward scholarship.[5]

Other scholars adopted ancient Japanese learning, called national learning (J. *kokugaku*). Kamo no Mabuchi (1697–1769) attacked Ogyū Sorai's ancient learning and practical Confucianism as wrong-headed. Far better, he asserted, would be the study of Japan's own ancient arts and texts. The leading eighteenth-century national learning scholar was Motoori Norinaga (1730–1801), son of a merchant. His writings did not appear explicitly political, nor did he ever serve as a scholar-in-residence to government officials. Motoori asserted that Japan's originally "feminine" nature, binding the people intuitively to the emperor and the ancient Shintō gods, had been corrupted by the importation of "manly" Chinese rationalism. In the nineteenth century, his scholarship would develop into a rationale for the overthrow of the Tokugawa system.

Even farmers could share in the eighteenth-century blossoming of thought, especially practical learning. Beginning with Miyazaki Antei's (1623–1697) encyclopedic 1697 treatise on farming, numerous eighteenth-century manuals by farmer-scholars explicated planting schedules, seeds, best practices for dozens of crops, optimal clothing for farm work, labor-saving technologies, and even Chinese ideas of right conduct.

Finally, where did religion fit in? Buddhism was the "impractical" straw man against which practical learning Confucians fought, but many Japanese continued to have faith in Buddhism. In addition, the prohibition of Christianity, accompanied by the requirement that all Japanese register with Buddhist temples, created a space for organized Buddhism. For example, Ishida Baigan (1685–1744), son of a farming family, migrated to Kyoto, became a merchant, and developed "heart learning" (J. *shingaku*). This religion blended Buddhist, Shintō, and Confucian ideas and stressed the equal worth of people of all status groups. If the merchant class were eliminated, as Ogyū Sorai suggested it should be, who would transport crops from farmers to samurai or tools from artisans to farmers? Ishida's ideas found a ready audience. Long after his death, "heart learning" schools spread throughout Japan, and men and women from all backgrounds attended lectures. One nun noted that her free lectures were attended by up to 1,200 listeners.

DIASPORAS

Advancing European colonialism of the eighteenth century, especially that of England, stimulated the Chinese trading communities around the South China Sea to new and innovative activity. Local rulers in Malacca and Siam had employed Chinese merchants not only as traders but also as tax collectors through a system known as *tax farming*. The rulers, unwilling to expend the resources or organize the officials to collect revenues from the population, rented out the right to collect taxes to private individuals, in this case Chinese merchant corporations, usually called *kongsi* (C. *gongsi*) in Southeast Asia. That guaranteed the rulers a fixed income (the rent paid by the tax-farmers), while the tax-farmers could then keep whatever revenues they raised, often far beyond the ordinary tax rates. This suited the financial needs of the states, and it also distanced the ruler from that most unpleasant of government functions, the collection of taxes. The hostility of the taxed population could thus be directed against the Chinese, not the rulers. The European colonial rulers also made use of Chinese expertise at tax farming, especially after the opium trade gave them a large and expanding market to tax (see p. 144).

As European and local demand for raw materials grew, Chinese merchants also invested in productive enterprises geared to international trade, especially mining and plantation agriculture. An eighteenth-century Sumatran sultan, for example, developed tin mining in his realm with Chinese miners—recruited, imported, and managed by Chinese merchants who had converted to Islam and served at court. All over the tropical islands and the Malay Peninsula, Chinese invested in pepper plantations to serve the European trade, using Chinese labor imported from Guangdong and Fujian. They planted less well-known products, too, such as gambier—a tropical vine from which a powder may be made for tanning and dyeing—and they paid particular attention to the extraction of mineral wealth. The British empire needed tin, and many of the Malay Peninsula's small states had rich sources of that metal. By 1780, Chinese corporations, using Chinese labor, had opened mines throughout the region and exported ore on a large scale.

Individual entrepreneurs undertook some of these enterprises, but most Chinese merchants preferred to spread the risk by creating joint shareholder companies. The ancestors of today's huge Chinese international trading firms, the Southeast Asian *kongsi* played a crucial role in both the expansion of China's overseas commercial network and in the success of European colonial occupation. Beginning as family businesses, with individual kinsmen holding shares of the company, the *kongsi* became multinational corporations investing in tax farming, transportation, plantations, mining, and banking, among other enterprises. The *kongsi* also had underworld connections with the sworn brotherhoods or secret societies (often collectively known as Triads) of southern China, which spread along with Chinese labor to Southeast Asia.

Meanwhile, the China-to-Java trade continued to flourish in Chinese hands, but the presence of so many Chinese, making so much money, irked the Dutch authorities. In 1740, they threatened to deport all unemployed Chinese to the plantations of Ceylon, and rumors spread that the unfortunate deportees would be thrown into the sea. The Chinese of Java rioted, but the Dutch disarmed them and turned loose the local population in a week of slaughter that took over 10,000 lives, a sad presaging of the anti-Chinese riots of late twentieth-century Indonesia. Thereafter, Chinese could only live in ghettoes, under the guns of Batavia (later Jakarta), not in the Javanese countryside or towns.

But Chinese continued to gather in less populated places—Borneo's gold fields, for example, where fortunes could be made. There the miners were mostly Hakka (see p. 43), and their headmen belonged to the Heaven and Earth Society, an important secret brotherhood. Lo Fong-pak, who arrived in Borneo in 1772, expanded his *kongsi*'s wealth and territory, opened new mines, recruited more labor, and created a little world of Hakka far from their homes in Guangdong. Two patterns thus emerged in Southeast Asia. In one, Chinese intermarried with local populations and became ordinary members of society and government; in the other, they lived separately and remained different, resented for their solidarity and their wealth. Both continue to the present day.

CONNECTIONS

For more than two centuries, European and North American historians have described their own cultures as active, restless, ambitious, scientific, and advanced. The cultures of the "non-white" world, in contrast, they have portrayed as passive, stagnant, reactive, and backward, waiting to be "discovered," "explored," "modernized"—usually through conquest and colonization or economic domination. This essentialized division of the world into two zones, progressive "we" and primitive "they," can no longer stand as a description of historical reality. The East Asian cultures were not passively killing time until the white people arrived, bearing "modernity" in the form of machines, ships, and guns, nor were late eighteenth-century European cultures coherent bastions of progressive, scientific rationality. Rather, the three East Asian civilizations, and the states that ruled over them, faced very similar problems to those of European kingdoms, at very much the same time. This vision of parallel evolution has led some twenty-first-century historians to call the seventeenth and eighteenth centuries, all over Eurasia and North America, the "early modern" period.

Most obviously, all of the Eurasian states worried about one another, about geopolitical competition for resources, territory, power, wealth, and profits. As we have seen, the Qing, Chosŏn, and Tokugawa states did not isolate themselves (as Europeans often claimed) from world markets. All three contributed to, and benefited from, the commerce that flowed around East Asia, including New World food crops, textiles, and precious metals. The international trade in silver, with its main sources in Japan and the Spanish empire, touched every continent by the eighteenth century, with powerful effects in East Asia, where Chinese demand fueled a worldwide commodity trade.

The British, suffering from a severe imbalance of payments with the Qing, began to cultivate opium in India and ship it to the south China coast. The Russians, seeking to secure their giant eastern empire and gain a foothold on the Pacific, pushed eastward. Anxious about Russian intentions and aggression in the north, both the Qing and the Tokugawa acted diplomatically and militarily to secure their frontiers. Facing the threat of an alliance between the Zunghar empire and Russia, Tibet, and Mongolia, the Qianlong Emperor and his generals finally ended the 2,000-year confrontation between nomadic and sedentary states in Eurasia by decimating the Zunghars.

All three East Asian states learned in the eighteenth century, sometimes late and often inaccurately, about the worldwide depredations of the Europeans, and they acted to protect themselves. The Chosŏn court reaffirmed its role as the last bastion of Confucian rectitude and refused to trade directly with Europeans. With its silver production declining rapidly, the Tokugawa shogunate detached itself from the flourishing trade in precious metals in order to protect its domestic money supply, limiting European visits to single Dutch merchant ships. The Qing established the Canton system to keep the Europeans at a distance from the court, supervised by merchants.

All three East Asian states also worried about the potentially subversive effects of Roman Catholic missionary activity and the divisive presence of converts within their societies. The Tokugawa shogunate had proscribed the faith in the 1630s and enforced a ban on all European writings to keep Christianity at bay. In the 1720s, however, Yoshimune permitted medical and other scientific books to enter through Nagasaki, stimulating the evolution of *Rangaku*, Dutch learning, as an alternative to Confucianism.

The Qing had permitted active missions in their realm, but the Kangxi Emperor's insistence on Catholics' adherence to Confucian rituals, and the Pope's equally dogmatic requirement that Catholics *not* venerate their ancestors or Confucius, had ended their effectiveness. Chosŏn, which saw no active foreign missionaries until late in the eighteenth century, nonetheless forbade Catholicism and persecuted its adherents if they dared violate the accepted rites. This anti-Catholic attitude did not, as we have seen, prevent East Asians from studying and using European scientific developments as they could. Nor did it prevent them from adopting New World food crops to their own ecologies; peanuts, chili peppers, and especially sweet and white potatoes became crucial elements in their agricultural repertoires.

Beyond these obvious connections lay more fundamental patterns of social and cultural change that we may call "early modern." Many Eurasian societies experienced rapid growth in literacy and the reach of print culture, which historians consider fundamental in uniting peoples to form "nations" in the modern sense. Literacy and print culture flourished in part because all of western Europe and East Asia underwent (albeit unevenly) similar processes of urbanization, commercialization, and monetization. They faced similar constraints, including population growth—here Japan differed considerably—decreasing per capita arable land, reliance on annually renewable energy sources, and environmental degradation.

In the eighteenth century, Beijing and Edo were two of the world's most populous cities; Seoul, though much smaller, grew rapidly after the Manchu conquest. Small and medium-sized market towns proliferated in their fertile agricultural regions and along domestic and international trade routes. These economic changes stimulated greater occupational complexity, a new respect for merchants and wealth, even in hidebound Chosŏn, and accelerated social mobility, both upward and downward. Traditional elites lost some of their inherited power and status to new groups—British manufacturers, French *bourgeoisie*, Chinese and Japanese merchants, Korean *kong'in* and *chungin*—and notions of fixed hereditary status hierarchies began to erode, at different rates in different places.

Gender roles in particular, often perceived to be a culture's stable and inviolable foundation, became the subject of impassioned debate as women took part in public life, whether as active participants or as objects of renewed scrutiny and control because established patterns were threatened. Parisian *salonnieres*, Lower Yangzi women poets, female *bunjin* in Edo or Kyoto—these women partook of new urban possibilities created by expanding commerce and the creation of new wealth. Even Lady Hyegyŏng, writing her memoirs in silence, opened her life to the future through literature in a way that no male could and no royal woman had before. The Qing debate about the status of women was only one of many fervent confrontations over women's proper place in a changing world. Should they be in public or secluded, seen or invisible, heard or silent? No Eurasian society experienced what we would call women's liberation in the eighteenth century, but they created a respect for women's learning that would become one of its antecedents.

Finally, and perhaps most subtly, we may place the European Enlightenment, usually seen as a unique, irreproducible triumph of scientific rationality in a world otherwise devoted to superstition and error, in parallel with its contemporary, East Asian "practical learning." In the hands of its scholarly practitioners, this offshoot of Confucianism produced massive encyclopedias, technical manuals for agriculture and artisanal production, new and critical readings of the ancient canonical texts, innovative thinking about political issues from taxation to village solidarity to ethnic diversity—in short, the same sorts of products that we associate with the Enlightenment.

We might then ask, "Why did the East Asians not advance into industrial capitalism when the Europeans did?" That question assumes that only one normal path leads from the eighteenth century to the present, the same erroneous standard of judgment that leads us to evaluate societies by the quality of their machines. East Asians did participate in "the early modern," and their solutions, though not including steam-powered industrialization or imperial domination of the globe, did answer some of the needs of their own eighteenth-century societies.

CHAPTER FIVE

INTERNAL CONTRADICTIONS, EXTERNAL PRESSURES (1800–1860s)

WORLD CONTEXT

The first half of the nineteenth century marked a crucial watershed in world history. In 1800, the Qing empire still took in vast quantities of silver in exchange for tea, porcelain, silk, and other manufactures, purchasing relatively few foreign products. The Indian subcontinent, major cotton cloth supplier to the world, was ruled primarily by local states, for the British held only Bengal, Bihar, and some stretches of the coasts. Europe was locked in internecine combat—the Napoleonic wars—accompanied by political revolutions, huge expenses, and rapid military and technological innovation. The United States, overwhelmingly agricultural, consisted of the original 13 states plus federal lands extending barely to the Mississippi. Russia had conquered little of Muslim Central Asia, the north of which remained in the hands of Kazakh nomads and the south under khanates based in Bukhara, Kokand, and Khiva. The Ottoman empire, though weakened by

Russian victories on the Black Sea and in the Caucasus, still ruled Greece and the Balkans, as well as Mesopotamia (Iraq) and Syria.

Only six decades later, the British empire had taken all of India as the "Jewel in the Crown," and cotton cloth from English mills had replaced Indian textiles in many world markets. The British had also reversed the Qing's economic hegemony through the sale of Indian opium and obtained important political and economic concessions, including the colony of Hong Kong, through military victory. France had begun to establish a long-term empire in Africa. The United States had spanned an entire continent and pushed deep into the Pacific basin with its naval and commercial power. Russia, too, had expanded considerably, mostly at Ottoman and nomad expense, and was poised to conquer the remaining independent khanates of Muslim Central Asia and threaten British India as well as the northern and western frontiers of the Qing. The once-great Mughal empire had disappeared, replaced by the British *raj*, which gradually extended its territory into Burma. The Qajar dynasty of Persia had lost its northern provinces to Russia and was blocked to the east by British influence in Afghanistan.

How did the Europeans do it? And why? These questions have challenged historians since the events took place. The explanations of *how* almost all involve the industrial revolution, the British-led capacity to overcome the biological old regime through the use of coal as an energy source for mechanical power, and the scientific advances that both allowed and followed from it. The *why* has been much more controversial, often including expansion of markets; access to productive resources and luxury goods (such as tea and spices); the desire to spread Christianity's version of ultimate truth; the need to export both goods and productive capital; the flourishing competition among European states; and, saddest to say, the notion that Europeans and other "white" folks were simply superior to all other human beings and *should* hold world dominion.

Roman Catholic thinkers of the Renaissance had conceived of all living things as arranged in a "great chain of being," from the lowest creatures to humankind at the apex. In that vision, Christianity constituted humankind's exclusive access to divine truth. Continuing that hierarchical tradition after the Enlightenment, influential nineteenth-century Europeans and North Americans moved outside the realm of religion to explain and justify their dominion over peoples of non-European origin. Their theories utilized physical appearance—skin color, texture of hair, facial features, skull shape, and more—to "prove" the superiority of people who look like "us" over people who look like "them."

Summarizing these differences in the word "race," many of them concluded that human differences expressed in language, culture, and way of life actually constitute a biologically (that is, genetically) determined hierarchy of peoples. Enslavement of Africans, for example, could be justified and encouraged by this perception of inherent difference. Eager to place themselves at the top, Europeans and Euro-Americans took technological capacity, the ability to make and use machines, as their most sensitive measure of racial

ranking, a bias that continues to inform opinion in the "developed world" today.

One version of this theory, used in the United States to rationalize westward expansion, held that Divine Providence had given the entire North American continent to white people as their "Manifest Destiny." They could thus virtuously remove (or eliminate) the "savages" who unjustifiably occupied its rich and otherwise "empty" lands. The British used similar notions to justify their domination and eventual elimination of the indigenous peoples of Australia. In the first half of the nineteenth century, the industrial revolution produced a new array of tools for this task, chief among them the steamship, the railroad, and more powerful and accurate guns. The opening of the American Midwest to agriculture coincided with vast in-migration of land-hungry Europeans. At the same time, the discovery of gold in California in 1848 drew 300,000 people to the Pacific coast. California's statehood in 1850 made the United States a Pacific Ocean nation. American ships' quest for fuel made coal-rich Japan a prime target of economic expansion.

Unconquered kingdoms and peoples, including Qing, Chosŏn, and the Tokugawa shogunate as well as the lands of Southeast Asia and the Ottoman empire, had no choice but to confront the Europeans. England, Holland, France, Russia, Austro–Hungary, and the United States competed to divide the world's territory, markets, and riches among themselves. The Ottomans, closest of the Muslim states to Europe and thus most vulnerable, managed to survive into the twentieth century by gradual reform and adaptation, giving up territory slowly to Russia, Austro–Hungary, and Greek and Balkan nationalists.

To stem the tide of European victories, some members of the Ottoman elite learned French, traveled to Europe as ambassadors or merchants, and reported on its technological advances to the sultan's court. Sultan Abdülmecid I (r. 1839–1861), depending on an adviser who had lived in Europe, proclaimed structural reforms, which brought more power into the hands of the central government. A few new schools taught mathematics, science, and foreign languages in addition to the conventional Islamic curriculum. But the reformists at court could not reorganize the empire's financial system in the face of entrenched corruption and localism, nor could they prevail against conservative opposition. Like the Ottomans, the Qing and Chosŏn survived into the twentieth century, but only by making concessions to the foreigners. The Tokugawa fell more quickly, giving Japan a valuable lead in establishing a new political system, one that could endure in a very dangerous world.

THE QING IN DECLINE

END OF AN ERA

In 1796, having reigned for 60 years, the Qianlong Emperor abdicated his throne in favor of his fifth son Aisin Gioro Yongyan (1760–1820), for whom the reign-name Jiaqing was chosen. The old ruler refused to hold the throne longer than his grandfather had, although he had no intention of giving up any real power. Unfortunately, age had severely limited his capacities, so during the three years between the Qianlong Emperor's abdication and his death in 1799 neither he nor his son ruled. Rather the realm lay entirely in the hands of Hesen and his faction. The Jiaqing Emperor, powerless to oppose his father, could only perform his ritual tasks out of filial piety, while Hesen spoke and directed policy for the retired emperor.

We know the new monarch hated this situation, for the day after his father's death he removed Hesen from all of his positions, stripped him of his titles, and arrested several of his closest allies at court. In two weeks Hesen was dead, graciously permitted to commit suicide because of his high former posts. The investigators sent to confiscate his property found movable goods to the value of 80 million ounces (2.2 billion g) of silver, more than the Qing treasury contained at the time. One official wrote, "…for almost thirty years, officials high and low have covered up for one another, and have thought only of grasping for bribes and personal gain."

When a major uprising—the "White Lotus" rebellions—broke out in 1796, systemic corruption prevented the Qing from reacting effectively. The White Lotus rebels, millenarian Buddhists, had formed antigovernment armies to defend themselves against what they perceived as Qing persecution, proclaiming that, "the officials have forced the people to rebel." The Hesen-dominated government responded slowly to the rebellion. Incompetence in the army, falsified reports, embezzlement, and massacres of innocent civilians marked its initial campaigns. Following the fall

of Hesen and his cronies, the Jiaqing Emperor capably redirected the military effort. He allowed local elites to organize local militias where central armies had failed, a tactic the central government would use until the twentieth century. Even with these new tactics, the pacification of the White Lotus required another four years, great expense, and high human costs.

Hesen and his protégés were not the rebellion's only cause. Apart from official corruption, modern scholars have identified other reasons: population growth and its consequent social dislocation, shortages of arable land in the regions in which the Buddhists rebelled, high taxes, merchant affluence in contrast to peasant misery, and increases in the price of grain. Ideology also mattered, though it never represented the sole cause of rebellion. The numerous preachers who led the 1796–1804 rebels testified that a new Buddha, usually Maitreya (the Buddha of the Future), would soon descend to earth and bring an era of great peace in contrast to the current chaos. Many of them worshiped the Eternal Venerable Mother, espoused conventional Confucian social ethics, used the Daoist terminology of "inner elixirs," and practiced meditation, demonstrating the multiple origins of Chinese popular religion. The rebels never had a centralized command nor constituted a single movement but rather responded to local distress with local resources.

SOCIAL PROBLEMS AND STATECRAFT SOLUTIONS

Many parts of the empire felt the distress of population pressure, but not everyone rebelled against the state. Rural people also moved, from crowded areas such as the Lower Yangzi and south coast to newly available land in Sichuan or Hunan and to areas of Chinese settlement overseas (see pp. 170–71). Others made their way to southern Mongolia, the "New Frontier" of Xinjiang, the island of Taiwan, the highlands of Yunnan, and the northeast, which had been reserved by the dynasty as its Manchu homeland. In these frontier zones, they found the land already inhabited by non-Chinese peoples. In some places the new migrants ceased being culturally Chinese after a few generations, while in others, the local cultures gradually disappeared, and non-Chinese became Chinese.

Sometimes proximity led to conflict. The population of Yunnan province, for example, more than doubled between 1775 and 1850, mostly through Chinese in-migration. The early nineteenth century saw a disturbing increase in violence between local Chinese-speaking Muslims (Hui) and the new migrants, who competed with the locals for jobs, trading opportunities, and farmland. Both officials and local gentry sided with the non-Muslims, and rivalry escalated to the point of armed clashes. In 1839 at Mianning and 1845 at Baoshan, local militias massacred thousands of Muslims, including women and children. These incidents led directly to a major rebellion against the Qing in the 1850s.

In the northeast, both the population and the amount of farmland increased dramatically, as migrants from overpopulated Shandong moved onto the rich plains to grow soybeans, sorghum, wheat, and other crops that could ripen in the short growing season. Many criminals were exiled to this rowdy frontier, 100,000 of them by 1735. Similarly, Taiwan became the site of intense feuding between the indigenous non-Chinese peoples and farmers from Fujian and Guangdong, and then among the Chinese settlers. In all of these areas, the Qing, using a combination of banner forces, locally recruited militias, and Green Standard troops—Chinese military units created to supplement the banners—managed to prevent widespread violence,

China in the nineteenth century

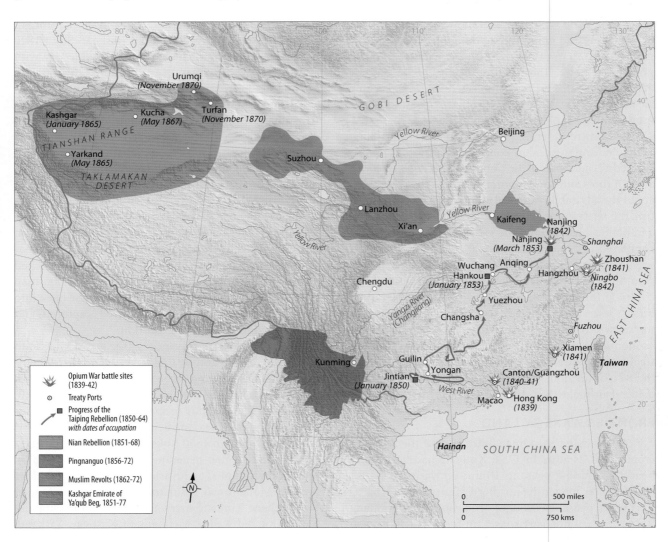

but clearly the domestic peace of the "Age of Prosperity" had been shaken.

In the face of this domestic and frontier violence, and other evidence of dynastic weakness such as falling tax revenues, continued corruption, and the collapse of the empire's internal waterways, one group of officials turned to an intensive examination of practical politics. Never abandoning the moral norms that distinguished the "cultivated man," these officials focused not on philological research or Confucian metaphysics but on economic, social, and political reform through technical expertise; the "practical learning" we have already encountered.

One such official was He Changling (1785–1848), financial commissioner of Jiangsu province in 1825, who collected a wide variety of essays on solutions to public problems and employed a young provincial degree holder, Wei Yuan (1794–1856), to expand the collection into a book. The resulting *Compendium of Qing Period Statecraft Writings*, published in 1827, became an instant bestseller, often reprinted and a model for multivolume supplements for 80 years.

Far from representing a new trend, He Changling, Wei Yuan, and their many colleagues and admirers constituted a crucial part of the Confucian heritage, one with ancient roots and contemporary echoes. They disagreed about the advisability of local autonomy vs. central control, the relative importance of personal self-cultivation and political action, and the value of piecemeal reform compared to radical institutional change. But they always returned to politics, to the roles of the state and community in improving the world. Historians find two common threads in this long and important literature. First, these scholar-officials valued practical solutions to real-world problems. Second, they despised neither economics nor military science—that is, the study of wealth and power—as government methods. Even in the face of turmoil, Chinese elites could use their own cultural arsenal to reform their society.

FRONTIER WARS BY LAND

For 60 years after the Qing elimination of the Zunghar empire and its allies in 1759, Xinjiang had been fairly peaceful. Chinese peasants from impoverished Gansu and Shaanxi moved to northern Xinjiang to farm, as did Turki peasants brought from southern Xinjiang to supply the Qing garrisons with food. The Qing also used Xinjiang as a destination for political exiles—including officials and gentry—who studied the region during their enforced residence there and created an important store of knowledge about it. Merchants from the Chinese heartland also arrived, bringing silks, artisanal goods, and especially tea (500,000 cases per year in the 1820s) to exchange for livestock, leather, raisins, medicinal herbs, cotton cloth, and other local products. The Qing state tried to turn Xinjiang's commerce eastward, but merchants continued to trade west and south.

Trouble began in the 1810s as the khanate of Kokand, west of the Pamir Mountains (now mostly in Uzbekistan), asserted its commercial and religious influence over some of the Turki-speaking Muslims of southwestern Xinjiang. The Qing refused Kokand's demands for an end to customs duties and the presence of a Kokandi trade representative in Kashgar. So in 1820 Kokand sent Jahangir Khoja, an exiled Sufi leader, with a few hundred horsemen over the Pamirs in a *jihad* to liberate southern Xinjiang from non-Muslim Qing rule.

Halted by Qing forces, Jahangir harassed the frontier, allying himself with mountain-dwelling nomad cavalry (who would now be called Kirghiz) interested in loot and open trade routes. Jahangir expanded his attacks in 1826, and the Qing faced a much more serious invasion when the *khan* of Kokand himself brought nearly 10,000 troops over the mountains to besiege Kashgar. Despite a sustained defense by the Qing garrison, the invaders took the fortress with great slaughter, and the indigenous populations of several other oases arose in rebellion. For a year, the *jihad* detached southern Xinjiang from Qing rule, but a 22,000-man relief army arrived in 1827, driving Jahangir back into the mountains, where he was betrayed, captured, and transported to Beijing for execution.

The emperor sent Nayanceng (see box opposite) to pacify the region, and he took a very hard line. Beginning in 1828, the Qing forbade all trade with Kokand, deported or naturalized all Kokandis in the realm, and seized all Kokandi property in Xinjiang, including warehouses of tea, medicines, and textiles. But this policy backfired. In 1830 Kokand, deprived of the east–west trade that had generated so much of its wealth, once again mounted an invasion, led by Jahangir's older brother, Muhammad Yusuf, to force the Qing to reopen the southern Xinjiang markets. This time the Qing defenders of the walled garrisons of Kashgar, Yarkand,

A LOYAL MAN OF QING

Nayanceng (1764–1833) was born to serve the Qing. A Manchu of the high-ranking Plain White Banner, grandson of the famous frontier general Agui of the Jangiya clan, he excelled in both military arts and the demanding Chinese examination curriculum. Achieving the highest degree at only 25, he won rapid promotions and earned his mother an imperial award for raising such a successful son. After the purge of Hesen in 1799, he found his place in the Qing bureaucracy as a frontier general and a judicial official, cleaning up messy cases of rebellion and official misconduct all over the empire. His skills included command of troops in the field, investigation and punishment of corrupt officials, and the pacification of frontiers in the wake of violent conflict. High office came his way early—by his 40th birthday he had served as President of the Board of Rites, Grand Councilor, and Governor-General.

Nayanceng's biography reads like a guide to Qing government and a travel account of the Qing empire. He dashed from office to office, from Guangzhou to Heilongjiang on the Russian frontier, from Beijing to Xinjiang. His assignments included suppressing rebels in Shaanxi, Sichuan, Guangdong, Kokonor (now Qinghai), Henan, Zhili (now Hebei), and Shandong, as well as the far northwest.

His enemies often accused him of misconduct, and he was regularly demoted then reinstated when the emperor needed his particular talents. Sentenced to death at least once, he often faced the wrath of his imperial master when he failed to deliver immediate results, but his illustrious lineage and personal record of success always brought him back to office. Nayanceng died in 1833 during a period of disgrace, degraded to commoner status, but the Daoguang Emperor returned all of his titles and showered posthumous honors on him and his family.

One key to Nayanceng's success lay in the extraordinary amount of work that the early nineteenth century provided for him and his fellow officials. No longer expanding as it had until 1759, the Qing instead had to put out fires all over its huge territory, wherever dissatisfaction with the state, the economy, the officials, or the local conditions inspired people to violence. In addition, the huge bureaucracy had been factionalized and corrupted by the domination of Hesen and his faction, so innumerable cases of official transgression—both real and invented by factional enemies—had to be investigated.

Even before the great rebellions of mid-century broke out, loyal officials like Nayanceng were sent to every part of the empire, including even the gates of the Forbidden City itself, to defend its integrity and dominion against internal enemies (White Lotus or Eight Trigrams) and external threats, such as the Khanate of Kokand and the British. They often succeeded, a tribute to their loyalty to the dynasty, their quality as leaders, and the political, military, and social resources they brought to their tasks.

紫閣元勳

Portrait of the famous frontier general Agui, grandfather of Nayanceng.

and the other oases held out, but the invaders took over the main markets, killed many Chinese merchants, and took large supplies of booty before being driven off by another Qing relief army.

To strengthen its hold, the Qing court encouraged Chinese farmers to migrate to Xinjiang and reinforced its army with thousands more troops. Kokand recognized that it held the stronger position, despite the defeat of its invasions, for the Qing could not afford to continue sending massive relief armies to the remote frontier, over 2,500 miles (4,000 km) from Beijing. By 1835, an agreement had been concluded that reopened trade. It also allowed Kokand to keep a political representative permanently at Kashgar and commercial agents at five other cities, empowered these representatives to regulate and control foreign merchants who came to the region, and gave the Kokandis responsibility for levying customs duties on foreigners' goods. This agreement granted, in effect, extraterritorial rights to the Kokandi representatives, a clear precedent for concessions made to Europeans along the coast more than seven years later.

These clashes stimulated a spirited debate among officials and literati concerned with frontier policy. Some, including experienced Manchu frontier officials, argued that most of Xinjiang could not be defended and cost too much, so it should be returned to local rulers in exchange for frontier security. Some statecraft scholars advocated complete integration of Xinjiang with the Qing empire. As Wei Yuan wrote some years later:

> The Western Regions have been disordered for several thousand years, from high antiquity until the present. It is Heaven's wish that the thorny thicket be transformed into busy highroad, the canyon's gloom into brilliant daylight, the teeming jungle into [a populace dressed in proper] caps and robes, the felt tent into village and well…To call in Chinese people (huamin) and turn this rich loam into China proper (neidi) would greatly ease the exercise of our authority and greatly increase our profit.[1]

These men argued that the Qing-ruled part of Muslim Central Asia should be made into *China*, the realm of agriculture and civil officials, in order to prevent further troubles with its non-Chinese population and invasions by outside powers. Opposed to the multicultural conception of the Qianlong Emperor, with separated culture zones and statutes against cultural mixing, these Chinese literati argued that Xinjiang and other frontier zones—conquered by the Manchus and inhabited by non-Chinese—should become Chinese in politics, economy, population, and ecology.

FRONTIER WARS BY SEA

The rapid growth of the opium trade between 1800 and 1835 had profound effects in many places. In India, it provided jobs for numerous farmers and processors of the drug, and some Indian merchants (mostly Parsis) owned ships and brokered international deals. In Great Britain and the United States, opium became the basis for huge fortunes and important merchant houses. Along the southeastern coast of the Qing empire, however, the effects looked far less positive, and indeed were economically catastrophic. From a position of dominance in 1800, the Qing experienced drastic reversal. Silver flooded out of the empire, official and private corruption became entrenched (especially in the south), and a variety of social dysfunctions emerged due to mass drug addiction.

The shortage of silver caused particularly dire consequences, for it created an imbalance in the crucial relationship between silver and copper, the two metals used for currency. As the silver supply fell and its price rose, the value of copper coins dropped correspondingly, from 1,000 copper coins per ounce (28 g) of silver in the late Qianlong period to 2,700 by the 1830s. Poor people transacted their daily market business in copper coins, but the land tax had to be paid in silver. So farmers experienced an effective rise in taxes, though the dynasty had not changed the official rates. Farmers had to pay a lot more of their copper coins to reach the value of the taxes, set in silver.

These developments caused considerable anxiety in Beijing, where the Daoguang Emperor (r. 1821–1850) asked his officials for solutions to the opium problem. Opium smoking had penetrated even into the interior of the imperial palace, and domestic production of poppies had also begun to provide cheap opium to poorer people. The officials' contradictory policy suggestions sound strikingly modern: (1) Some advocated more effective enforcement of existing regulations against opium (which had been generally ignored); (2) others argued for legalization and systematic taxation of the drug trade; and (3) a third group recommended driving the foreign merchants away entirely. The court allowed the situation to degenerate until the mid-1830s, partly misunderstanding its significance and partly because workable solutions had not been offered. By 1835, the silver outflow had become critical, as over 30,000 chests of opium averaging 140 lb (63.5 kg) each—at least 4.2 million lb (1.9 million kg) of the drug—entered the empire that year.

The opium influx expanded especially rapidly after 1834, when the British government ended the East India Company's formal monopoly of British trade in Asia. This allowed private companies to enter the opium market which in turn required the British government to send an official representative to Guangzhou to replace the Company. The *cohong* merchants (see p. 116) and Qing officials no longer dealt with a private corporation but with the British state as protector of its subjects.

In the post-Napoleonic world of European competition, British merchants and politicians became increasingly unsatisfied with Qing arrogance and "obstruction of international trade." Although some Britons objected to the opium trade on moral principle, most saw no inconsistency in equating opium with tea, cotton cloth, silk, and other internationally exchanged commodities. In this view, nations could set reasonable conditions for trade, but the Guangzhou system imposed unreasonable obstacles: commerce limited to one port, prices and conditions set by imperially sanctioned trading companies, no direct communication with imperial officials.

After years of debate and divergent policy recommendations for dealing with the opium trade, the emperor finally made up his mind in late 1838. The court chose Lin Zexu (1785–1850), an experienced provincial official and anti-opium advocate, as imperial commissioner to the Guangzhou region and ordered

Scene from the war against the Zunghars, from "The Conquests of the Qianlong Emperor," 1769–74. One of twenty-four engravings of the Qing campaigns to subdue the west done by a French printer from drawings made by four Jesuits attached to the Qing court. Note the row of camels on the left, each carrying a small cannon mounted on its saddle.

him to end the opium trade. A fine calligrapher, well liked and incorrupt by reputation and a reverent observer of the Confucian rituals, Lin Zexu allied himself with the statecraft enthusiasts in the Qing bureaucracy. His friends and advisers included Gong Zizhen (1792–1841), who had advocated the retention of Xinjiang in the 1820s and now stood with the most aggressive statecraft intellectuals, demanding an end to all foreign trade.

Arriving in Guangzhou in March 1839, Commissioner Lin (as the British called him) focused quickly and effectively on opium. He met with the *cohong* merchants, who served as the buffer between the Qing state and the foreigners, demanding that they stop aiding the British and help him to collect all the opium in the region, much of it stored in British warehouses. Domestic users and dealers also came under his writ, and he organized local students, military personnel, and gentry to enforce the eradication edict, confiscating pipes and supplies of the drug.

Most significantly, Lin wrote (via the *cohong*s) to the British merchants, requiring them to turn over all the opium currently in their possession and end the drug trade, lest they risk the death penalty. Within three weeks of his arrival, Lin Zexu bottled up the foreign merchants in their warehouses, deprived them of assistance from the local population, ordered the surrender of Lancelot Dent (1799–1853)—reputed to be the worst of the opium dealers—and threatened to end all commerce if they did not comply.

Charles Elliot, the Superintendent of Trade at Guangzhou, a government official rather than an employee of the weakened East India Company, decided to put himself, and thus the British crown, between the merchants and Commissioner Lin. He offered the opium merchants a deal. He would take all the opium stocks in the region under his own care and guarantee that the British government would pay for them. Delighted to have their income assured, all the merchants, including a couple of Americans, agreed.

Elliot then delivered over 20,000 cases (almost 3 million lb [1.3 million kg]) of opium to Commissioner Lin, who organized a secure system for receiving and guarding it, then had it destroyed by mixing it with lime, salt, and water and washing the resulting sludge out to sea. He prayed to the god of the ocean, apologizing for the mess, then allowed the Chinese servants, interpreters, *cohong* merchants, and others who lived on the foreign trade to return to their work. Confident in his victory, he concluded (wrongly), "I should judge from their attitudes that they have the decency to feel heartily ashamed." The Qing court issued a strict new opium law that summer, and Lin Zexu continued his prosecution of both foreign and domestic opium traders and users.

During the lull following the destruction of the opium, Lin Zexu also wrote a famous and controversial letter to Queen Victoria, asking her to command the British merchants to engage only in legitimate trade. In an 1840 missionary translation, it read, in part:

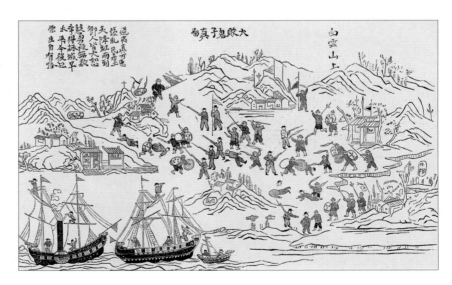

Print depicting a land battle of the Arrow War, also called the Second Opium War (1856–60), probably copied by a British printmaker from a Chinese original. The inscription claims that the Qing forces and locals defeated the British in this engagement at White Cloud Mountain.

Now, out of the wealth of our Inner Land, if we take a part to bestow upon foreigners from afar, it follows, that the immense wealth which the said foreigners amass, ought properly speaking to be portion of our own native Chinese people. By what principle of reason, then, should these foreigners send in return a poisonous drug, which involves in destruction those very natives of China? Without meaning to say that the foreigners harbor such destructive intentions in their hearts, we yet positively assert that from their inordinate thirst after gain, they are perfectly careless about the injuries they inflict upon us! And such being the case, we should like to ask what has become of that conscience which heaven has implanted in the breasts of all men?[2]

Here Lin appealed to that fundamental goodness in all humankind, which the *Daxue* called "inborn luminous virtue."

Queen Victoria never received the letter, but reports of these events did reach Lord Palmerston (1784–1865), the British foreign secretary. The opium merchants in China, India, and England collectively used their political connections and money—they raised a lobbying fund of several thousand pounds while still confined in their warehouses—to be sure that the issue of payment of the vast sum of 2 million pounds sterling for the destroyed opium stayed on the British government's agenda. Dozens of firms, including tea and cotton merchants, demanded armed intervention to insure the immensely valuable China trade and to recover the value of the opium.

The opium trade itself was, as the London *Times* argued in October, indefensible, but the seizure of British property, even contraband, could not be tolerated. How much better if the Qing could be forced to revise or abolish the Guangzhou system, a goal devoutly wished by the entire merchant community? Palmerston told the merchants that the government could not pay for the opium, for Parliament had not voted (nor would it ever vote) to provide the money, so the Qing had to be compelled to compensate them. Without consulting Parliament, Palmerston accepted plans for attacking the Qing developed by the merchant William Jardine and ordered the army and navy to carry them out.

Fighting had already begun around Guangzhou, including an unsuccessful attempt by a Qing admiral to drive British ships away from the entrance to the city's harbor, and it continued for over two years, up and down the coast. The war did not follow conventional lines; neither side formally declared war, and negotiations continued throughout the fighting. It became immediately obvious to any who had not realized it before that the British could move at will along the coast of the empire by ship. Qing coastal defenses, including walled towns and forts, had thick walls but few cannon and even fewer cannoneers capable of damaging the enemy fleet. The British also made good use of the new paddle-wheeled steamships, which could travel against the wind and maneuver in shallow rivers and harbors dangerous for sailing ships.

The Qing troops often fought courageously, but from a military standpoint there could be no doubt of British technological and tactical superiority. Many defeated Qing officers committed suicide, and morale among the regular forces plummeted. Locally recruited militias, however, made some difference, as they had in putting down the Buddhist rebels a few decades earlier.

On one famous occasion, as a British force besieged Guangzhou, thousands of outraged peasants confronted them, motivated primarily by hatred of the British troops, who had desecrated graves, looted farms, and attacked women. A rainstorm rendered the British flintlocks temporarily useless, and the redcoats found themselves thrashing through flooded rice paddies, surrounded by angry villagers armed with farm tools and handmade spears. Qing officials disbanded the militant peasants and persuaded the British to withdraw with light casualties. At the next prefectural examination in September, the Guangzhou prefect, who had led the Qing delegation, felt the loyal anger of the candidates, who shouted and threw inkstones, forcing his resignation. The city of Guangzhou remained hostile to the British long after the war ended, and the battle became a rallying cry for popular Chinese resistance to the foreigners.

The British fleet sailed up and down the coast several times, taking and retaking islands and coastal cities—Ningbo, Hangzhou, and Shanghai among them—making and then rejecting peace agreements with several imperial envoys. In August 1842, they finally struck decisively at the Qing by entering the Yangzi River, the empire's most important waterway, and besieging Nanjing. To prevent collapse of the entire

Yangzi valley trading system, the court ordered imperial commissioner Qiying (1787–1858) to accept British terms and conclude a peace. The Treaty of Nanjing (1842) opened four more treaty ports (Fuzhou, Xiamen, Ningbo, and Shanghai, all in the south and far from Beijing); ceded the island of Hong Kong, at the eastern entrance to Guangzhou bay, in perpetuity to Great Britain; awarded the British a US$21 million indemnity; guaranteed fair and predictable tariffs on imports into the Qing empire; and required equality in language and status between the British and Qing empires. The only mention of the opium trade came in Article 4, which reserved US$6 million of the indemnity to repay the merchants for the opium confiscated by Lin Zexu.

Taking advantage of the Qing defeat, the United States sent Caleb Cushing (1800–1879) to obtain a similar treaty, bargaining with Qiying and reaching even more far-ranging conclusions. By the Treaty of Wangxia (1844), Americans could open hospitals, churches, and cemeteries in the treaty ports and learn Chinese, which had previously been forbidden. Most important in the eyes of the merchants and missionaries, Americans could not be tried under Qing law for crimes committed there, only by an American consul using American law. Similar to the Qing–Kokand agreement of 1835 and earlier European treaties with the Ottomans, this condition of "extraterritoriality" freed Americans from their fear of what they saw as barbaric Qing practices such as judicial torture and guilt by association. The French, too, negotiated a treaty with all of these provisions, plus full tolerance for Roman Catholicism in the Qing empire. By the principle of "most favored nation," the British claimed all the benefits that the Americans and French had obtained as well.

These agreements, and their subsequent revisions, constituted the core of the "unequal treaty system," which subjected Qing international relations, and its economy to some extent, to foreigners until the end of the dynasty in 1912. Europeans and Americans came to perceive the Qing and the Chinese as weak, effeminate, incompetent, and ripe for domination. This new view entirely replaced earlier notions of a powerful economy, wise Confucian government, and "the wisdom of the east" that had been transmitted by the Jesuits. Recent research has shown that Qing engineers actually made strides toward effective military technology, including construction of paddle-wheeled steamships and

casting of large, accurate cannon. Their diplomats demonstrated considerable skill in handling the foreigners. But they remained far behind the Europeans, and their political traditions had not prepared them to be one nation in a world of competing states, a long way down from being the center of the cosmos.

MAPPING THE WORLD

As enjoined by texts like the *Daxue*, the statecraft scholars focused on *study*, but Euro-American trade and aggression expanded their ideas about what was worth studying. Statecraft scholars had generated practical solutions to problems of grain transport, irrigation, taxation and currency, and industrial production, but by the 1830s some had recognized that they lacked knowledge of the world outside East Asia. Gong Zizhen wrote essays about Xinjiang and the opium trade, then Lin Zexu confronted the Europeans at Guangzhou and compiled a store of information about them. But even these sophisticated intellectuals had only limited acquaintance with England's industrial revolution and its political and economic consequences. Although the Qing court had long employed Jesuits as astronomers, cartographers, mathematicians, and metallurgists, neither the Daoguang Emperor nor his officials had good contemporary data on Europe and the United States, so some of the statecraft intellectuals plunged into the study of the human world in new ways.

Xu Jiyu (1795–1873), son of a high-ranking degree holder from Shanxi province, grew up reading the Classics, preparing for the imperial examinations, and learning the diverse interpretations of Qing Neo-Confucianism. He married at 16 and loved his wife very much. Although she never bore a son, he refused to take a concubine until after her death. A prodigious student, he passed his provincial examination at 19, then studied for 13 more years before achieving the highest degree in 1826. His reform-minded reports impressed the young Daoguang Emperor, so in 1837 he obtained a position in Fujian, on the southeast coast. There he first encountered the British in a dramatic fashion—the nearby port city of Xiamen (Amoy), governed by a close friend of Xu's, was taken by the British fleet. By early 1842, Xu had become convinced of the importance of understanding the British better.

Shortly after the signing of the Nanjing treaty in 1842, Xu became financial commissioner of Fujian and thus deeply involved with the new treaty ports of Xiamen and Fuzhou, where he lived and worked. There he met David Abeel, an American missionary who spoke Fujianese and found Xu Jiyu to be a unique official. Other missionaries followed Abeel in helping Xu Jiyu to gather materials on the nations of the world.

By 1845, Xu could impress a visiting missionary with his knowledge of Britain's troubles in governing Ireland and the sovereign status of Afghanistan. In 1849 he published his *Short Account of the Maritime Circuit*, a summary of all he had learned about the world outside East Asia. By no means entirely accurate (he defined democracy as "control of affairs by local gentry"), it was nonetheless the most comprehensive description available in Chinese. Xu concluded that the Qing empire, its emperor, and its supremely moral Confucian learning no longer constituted the sole civilization on the planet.

A statecraft scholar and a practical man of government, Xu posed the question for the Qing empire that has troubled every culture confronting Euro-American power since the eighteenth century: How can we deal with these powerful, aggressive, expansive foreigners and still preserve our own valuable heritage? How can we change to meet their challenge and still remain ourselves? Answered differently in each place, this question forced not only innovation in technology and science but also a cultural interrogation—what constitutes our indispensable core? What must we *not* change if we wish to stay "us"? This dilemma plagued Chinese, Korean, and Japanese intellectuals, politicians, and ordinary folks from that time onward, and it continues to be an issue today.

IMAGINING OTHER WORLDS

If Cao Xueqin's *Dream of the Red Chamber* (see p. 114) represented eighteenth-century Chinese life by portraying a wealthy, powerful family on the verge of decline, the more precarious early nineteenth century may have been captured best in another novel, *Destinies of the Flowers in the Mirror*, published by Li Ruzhen in 1828. A series of fantasies rather than social realism, Li's fiction has been compared to Jonathan Swift's *Gulliver's Travels* (1726), for it satirizes Li's own society by creating incredible worlds of reversal: a Country of Women, for example, with upside-down gender roles; and a Country of the Two-Faced, in which every charming and elegant person has an ugly, vindictive countenance

in back. Li's broad-ranging, disjointed plot observes Chinese society in all its complexity—commercial life, Buddhism and Daoism, food, sex, even the Confucian Classics themselves—with a detached, critical vision.

The novel did not espouse any revolutionary solutions to the problems it illuminated. Rather, Li Ruzhen, like Swift or Montesquieu in Europe, wanted to show his fellow Chinese who they were, with all their absurdities and pretensions. Committed to a conservative Confucian moral framework, Li Ruzhen saw much to criticize in early nineteenth-century Chinese culture. He placed his characters in harsh and competitive worlds like those in which most Chinese, elite or commoner, actually lived.

SHAKING THE FOUNDATIONS

Qing repression had not solved the social dysfunctions that had caused the millenarian Buddhists to rebel in the 1790s. Population pressure in the crowded regional cores had not eased, so migration outward to peripheries and frontier areas continued, as did conflict between new migrants and indigenous peoples over land, jobs, commercial profits, and mineral wealth. As silver continued to flow out of the empire and its price to rise—the Qing had to pay its Opium War indemnity in silver—so too did the burden of taxes. Opium addiction took a heavy toll on the economies of the southern provinces and spread to the north. The banners and Green Standard armies, ineffective in the 1790s, had become even more demoralized by drug use, poor pay, corruption among the officers, and defeat in the Opium War.

New social problems arose as well. The Grand Canal system, the main transport route for Yangzi valley grain to the capital and much of the north, silted up, while mismanagement of water control works on the Huai and Yellow rivers caused both transport stoppages and flooding. The boatmen and haulers along these waterways, many of them single young males, formed secret societies to protect their jobs and, in some cases, to terrorize the local population. In the south, groups such as the Heaven and Earth Society (also called Triads), already powerful in the Chinese communities of Southeast Asia, organized bands of young men to protect businesses, villages, and towns from bandits or foreigners. Local militias, formed in response to local violence that the Qing's armies could not handle, often became tools of corruption as well as self-defense, preying on nearby farmers and merchants. The inefficient empire-wide system of salt distribution, a monopoly of the Qing government, provided powerful incentives to smuggle and an inexhaustible source of corruption.

Many of these problems caused ordinary people to act against the authority of the state, breaking the law covertly (smuggling salt, for example) or more openly. In 1812, another millenarian Buddhist group, the Eight Trigrams, organized an uprising in the name of the Maitreya Buddha and managed to reach inside the Forbidden City itself, where some eunuchs and bannermen joined the believers. Their abortive attack on the imperial palace in 1813 did not manage to assassinate the emperor, but it did demonstrate the ineffectiveness of the Imperial Guard and the vulnerability of the throne. (An arrow from this attack remains imbedded in one of the inner gates of the Forbidden City, a small but powerful tourist attraction.)

The most devastating nineteenth-century uprisings came in a wave, beginning in 1850 and lasting almost three decades, bringing hideous violence to most of the empire. Although uncoordinated, these anti-Qing movements nearly brought down the dynasty and certainly weakened it in the face of continuing foreign pressure. All these movements began as local conflicts, with specific local causes, but several of them spread to encompass huge areas, and their impact on the empire's population and economy cannot be underestimated. At least 30 million people died, large regions lay deserted, and the Qing state never recovered, though it survived some decades after suppressing the rebels.

The first and largest of these uprisings began as a conjunction of two local processes: extensive local feuds in Guangdong and Guangxi provinces, involving Hakka people; and the presence of Protestant missionaries. The Hakka, originally refugees from the north, had for many centuries inhabited the hills and other undesirable peripheries of the rice-growing plains of southern China, living in the poorest parts of the region. Clearly distinguished by their language (incomprehensible to their neighbors), by their folkways (including *not* binding women's feet), and by their scattered hill country settlements, they were perceived as enemies by lowland people, who the Hakka often called Punti (MANDARIN *bendi*), or "locals." Hakka–Punti feuding, sometimes involving thousands of armed men on each side, erupted

periodically in an arc of territory from Guangxi all the way to Taiwan. The feuds even spread to overseas communities in Java, the Malay Peninsula, and Madagascar.

In the 1820s, Hong Xiuquan, a promising and well-educated young Hakka from a poor family in western Guangdong, started to climb the ladder toward officialdom. Working as a village schoolteacher to support himself, he traveled three times to Guangzhou to take the official examination, and three times he failed. After his second failure in 1837, he suffered a mental breakdown.

During his illness, he saw many visions, but he had no clear understanding of their meaning until 1843, when he read a pamphlet he had picked up from a Chinese Protestant missionary in Guangzhou. It enumerated the Ten Commandments, briefly told the story of Jesus of Nazareth as the Son of God, described the Kingdom of Heaven, and warned its readers never to worship devils or idols. In this simple explication of Christianity, Hong Xiuquan found the meaning of his hallucinations. They had been religious experiences, persuading him that he had a special mission in life, indeed that he was Jesus's younger brother, God's second son, chosen to cleanse the world of demons and bring people back to true religion.

Unwilling to serve in a village school, performing rituals he now viewed as idolatry, Hong and a close friend whom he had converted to his version of Christianity left their home district in 1844 and settled in Guangxi. There they founded the Society of God Worshippers to propagate their new faith. At precisely that time, Hakka–Punti conflicts in southeastern Guangxi created large numbers of Hakka refugees, banditry ravaged the Hakka villages, and several local mines closed, leaving many young miners unemployed.

These circumstances enabled Hong and his colleagues, including Yang Xiuqing (d. 1856), a brilliant ex-clerk and charcoal merchant with a band of loyal followers, to recruit thousands of adherents, mostly Hakka. In 1850 they fought several times with local militias and defeated them, giving Hong confidence that he could realize his apocalyptic vision of overthrowing the rule of the demons, whom he increasingly identified as the Manchus. In early 1851, Hong Xiuquan declared himself the Heavenly King of the Heavenly Kingdom of Great Peace (C. *Taiping Tianguo*) and became a rebel under Qing law.

Felice Beato took this photograph of one of the Dagu forts, near Tianjin, after it had been taken by the British in the Arrow War, 1860. Overwhelmed by British bombardment, the Qing forces had been decimated.

The Taipings, as Hong's group came to be known, formed a religious army, abandoned the Manchu queue and let their hair grow out (a capital crime), prayed daily to *Shangdi*, their name for the Protestant God, and created a system of collective property. Obeying both Christian and Chinese dictates on gender relations, they organized men and women in separate military units, the latter under Hakka women commanders not hobbled by bound feet. Sexual relations, even between husbands and wives, became a capital crime, except for the Taiping leaders themselves. They based their religious activities firmly in Christianity, especially the Old Testament, but not in a form acceptable to Europeans. Although Protestant missionaries welcomed the Taiping proclamation of the Ten Commandments and their destruction of "pagan" temples, they could not tolerate Hong's claim to be the younger brother of Jesus.

In a remarkable series of campaigns, the Taiping army, increasing in size as it advanced, defeated inept Qing generals from Guangxi all the way to the Yangzi River. Only 18 months after taking their first city in the southwest, the Taipings swept into Nanjing, the great metropolis on the south bank of the Yangzi, and made it their Heavenly Capital. To preserve their momentum and finish off the beleaguered Qing dynasty, they sent an army north toward Beijing and another west into the central Yangzi region. Neither army achieved its objective. The Taiping military then became embroiled in internal conflicts that culminated in the assassination of Yang Xiuqing, the Heavenly Kingdom's finest general, and 20,000 of his followers in 1856. Qing forces counterattacked, and for eight years the fertile, densely populated Yangzi valley burned, killing millions and uprooting millions more. Initially dedicated to the welfare of the common people, the Taiping Kingdom became a tyrannical, tax-grasping autocracy with a religious veneer.

The Taiping incursion into North China stimulated a second rebellion that remained more local than the Taiping uprising. For decades, the northern part of Anhui province, an impoverished periphery subject to both drought and flooding, had been home to predatory bands of cavalry called Nian, which looted and feuded without effective interference from the Qing state. Beginning in 1851, a series of natural disasters, including major floods of the Yellow River—due primarily to neglect of the complex dike system—struck the region, and the small, independent Nian bands gradually amalgamated into larger armies.

When the Taipings passed through northern Anhui, heading north toward Beijing, these Nian armies took on the ambitions of a dynasty-overturning rebellion. Their leader called himself "Alliance Commander of the Great Han," an explicitly anti-Manchu title, and cultivated links with secret societies, powerful lineages, and the commanders of fortified villages, combining his rapidly moving Nian cavalry with well-defended stockades. In the late 1850s, rivalries between Nian commanders weakened their anti-Qing unity, and the movement returned to its original form, roving bandits trying to plunder scarce resources in an impoverished, unstable region. The Qing commanders could not finish them off for almost a decade.

Simultaneous with these wars, ethno-religious hatreds in distant Yunnan heated to boiling point. Indigenous peoples, Chinese-speaking Muslims, and recent Chinese immigrants competed for jobs and land. Officials and militias sided with the Chinese, arguing that the Muslims endangered public order by virtue of their ferocity of character and intractable solidarity. Increasing tension and animosity followed massacres of whole Muslim communities in the 1840s. In May of 1856, as the Taiping and Qing armies faced off in the

Yangzi valley and the Nian rebels rampaged in Anhui, the governor of Yunnan authorized the killing of all Muslims in Kunming, the provincial capital. For three days local militias, gangs, and neighborhood protection groups burned, looted, and killed in the city's Muslim quarters. Five mosques were destroyed, and thousands of people perished.

Later that year, as a direct reaction to the massacre in Kunming, a Muslim examination graduate named Du Wenxiu (1823–1872) declared the establishment of a new state in western Yunnan, *Pingnanguo*, "the state that pacifies the south," naming himself both general-in-chief and commander of the faithful. Du, a native of Baoshan appalled by the massacre of Muslims there in 1845, traveled to Beijing to protest to the Qing government—which took no notice—then became a wandering trader. His routes followed the extensive Chinese-speaking Muslim commercial networks of western Yunnan and its frontiers with Burma, Siam, and other Southeast Asian states. He imagined Pingnan Guo as a multiethnic state in which Islam held a privileged position but Chinese-style government prevailed. At his capital in Dali, Du used eclectic imagery and ritual—Ming, Qing, Taiping, and Muslim—to unite the diverse peoples of Yunnan in an anti-Qing movement. So well did he succeed that not only local Muslims but also indigenous peoples, Chinese, and even a few Manchus joined him.

The Europeans and Americans took swift advantage of the chaos wrought by these rebellions. In 1854 the British, with the agreement of the Americans and French, presented a long list of demands, including (1) access to more of the Qing's interior, (2) permanent stationing of an ambassador in Beijing, and (3) legalization of the opium trade. Receiving no satisfaction from the struggling Qing, the British seized Guangzhou in 1857, then the Dagu forts east of Beijing the following year in a conflict known as the Arrow War (see illustrations on pp. 146 and 151). The 1858 Treaty of Tianjin granted almost all of the British demands, but the Qing refused to allow their implementation.

The British commander and negotiator, Lord Elgin (1811–1863), invaded northern China, taking the Dagu forts near Tianjin then marching his troops to Beijing in 1860. In a gesture designed to break the dynasty's resistance, he burned the emperor's Summer Palace outside the city—much of it designed by eighteenth-century Jesuits—and enforced further punitive conditions. Tianjin, a coastal city only a few dozen miles from Beijing, became a treaty port. Qing subjects could legally emigrate in British ships, and the Kowloon peninsula opposite Hong Kong became part of the British colony. This humiliating defeat for the Qing resulted in more extensive foreign presence, less Qing control over foreign trade, and further erosion of sovereignty for the dynasty. Truly, the Qing had suffered *nei luan wai huan*—domestic chaos and foreign catastrophe.

KOREA

AN END TO SLAVERY

The last century of Chosŏn rule ushered in enormous social change. In 1801, by Chosŏn royal decree all government slave records were burned in front of the main gate of the Seoul Palace, officially freeing all state slaves. In the decades that followed, the trend toward manumission continued apace. In 1886, another royal decree announced that children would no longer inherit the slave status of their parents. And finally in 1894, the institution of slavery was itself banned. In many ways, these decrees simply reflected the gradual erosion that had taken place over two centuries in the distinctions drawn between slaves and commoners, as ever growing numbers of slaves found ways to shed the hereditary status of their servitude.

The late Chosŏn rise in the number of *yangban* closely paralleled a spectacular decline in the number of slaves. In the same records of Taegu county that charted the growing *yangban* population, the proportion of slaves in the total population in 1690 stood at 37.1 percent, a figure that gradually slipped to 26.6 percent in 1730, 5 percent in 1786, and only 1.5 percent in 1858. Slavery, an institution that had existed for centuries, virtually disappeared in 150 years.

The decline resulted partly from slaves fleeing their owners at a time when the government office supposed to capture and return them became dysfunctional. By the late eighteenth century, escaped slaves were rarely forced back to their owners. More significantly, slaves risked fleeing because the more commercialized economy increasingly offered them independent livelihoods. This might mean working in a mine, participating in craft production, or gaining the status of tenant farmer rather than slave. Recognizing this situation, the state in 1718 passed a law allowing state slaves to purchase commoner status if they could pay all the tribute that they would have owed to the age of 65—a heavy price, to be sure, but one that released a slave's descendants from lowly status.

Such measures satisfied those few slaves who had managed to enrich themselves in the exchange economy, but self-liberation cannot explain the dramatic decrease in the number of slaves over the course of the eighteenth and nineteenth centuries. Like the families who reached *yangban* status, those who shed their slave status erased all record and memory of their social past. Few families in Korea today trace their heritage back to this unfree group, one that constituted 30 percent of the population, making it difficult for historians to analyze strategies of status change.

One of the more convincing explanations connects the wholesale flight of slaves to changes in landholding patterns and the rural labor market. Many historians conclude that it became both cheaper and more convenient for landlords to contract tenants to cultivate their land rather than to buy and manage slaves. This pattern resembled, to some extent, the commercialization of labor in eighteenth-century Japan. When the Chosŏn court changed the inheritance laws to make more offspring of slaves into taxpaying commoners, many rich families resisted, since slavery was a key to their wealth. But by the nineteenth century, switching from slave labor to tenancy may have increased the profit from agricultural land. Both landlords and slaves thus had incentives, in the growing exchange economy, to find alternative relationships.

So, too, did *chungin*, technical specialists serving the state as copyists, translators, doctors, and magistrates' assistants, who sought to shake off the restrictions imposed on them by their status. This trend was already well under way in the late eighteenth century. Many *chungin* took advantage of their special training to accumulate great wealth. In particular, the translators who accompanied missions to China simultaneously traded in ginseng, books, and fashions, earning the wealth to live above their inherited station. With the increased

Kim Hongdo. Scene of a *yangban* being carried in a sedan chair, while people from the lower classes bow and kowtow at his passing, late 18th century.

size of this status group, together with the growth of publishing, highly educated *chungin* developed a new literary style that both built upon their classical education and appealed to a non-*yangban* audience. Like Li Ruzhen's *Destinies of Flowers in the Mirror* (see p. 149),

their stories and themes often satirized contemporary social conditions, poking special fun at the arrogant airs of *yangban*.

The *chungin* followed their acquisition of wealth with petition movements, seeking to convince the king

PRACTICAL LEARNING IN A CHANGING WORLD

Chŏng Yagyong (also called Chŏng Tasan, 1762–1836), the greatest of the Korean *silhak* ("practical learning") scholars, exemplified many of the strengths and conflicts of early nineteenth-century Korea in his own life and personality. A brilliant and widely read scholar of Neo-Confucianism, he wrote on the mainstream philosophical issues of his day—the debate over principle and material existence, self-cultivation, and human nature—and he studied the classical texts with great devotion. Nonetheless, Chŏng rejected the empty rhetoric that dominated elite Korean discussions, and much of his writing focused on practical matters—agriculture, fortifications, technology, medicine (including a treatise on smallpox), economics, politics, law, administration, and music, which he held to be essential to practicing the Way of the ancient sages.

For him, the morality that Koreans had learned from Chinese texts stood as unquestionable truth, but the government and elites had to address the public issues that pressed on Chosŏn (as they did throughout East Asia at this time): "If we do not keep abreast of the latest technological advances, then we will never be able to break free of the impasse our ignorance has left us in and will never be able to improve the living standard of our nation." To that end, he embraced many teachings, including European works, which he read in Chinese.

Born into a scholarly family, Chŏng seemed destined for a distinguished official career. He served in the National Academy, where he attracted the attention of King Chŏngjo, Lady Hyegyŏng's son. The king particularly praised his willingness to be objective among the factional wranglings of the Chosŏn elite, and the two men became friends. Chŏng placed first in the highest civil service examination of 1789, and his close relationship with the king and many important officials brought him success. Using his *silhak* skills and Chinese texts, he supervised the construction of a pontoon bridge across the Han River and built the pulleys and cranes used in royal construction projects.

Like some other members of his family's Southern faction, Chŏng and several relatives were much attracted to Roman Catholicism, and he was baptized as John. After King Chŏngjo's unexpected death in 1800, the transition to the young Sunjo's reign doomed the Catholics to criminal status. In a kingdom-wide persecution, led by the Andong Kims—the new royal in-laws—Chŏng's brother was executed, and Chŏng, despite his political connections and success, suffered 18 years of exile in the remote south.

As an exile, Chŏng Yagyong had plenty of time to think and write, and his collected works fill hundreds of volumes. Some of his proposals seem detached from the realities of government—in an essay on land reform, for example, he advocated a collective ownership system reminiscent of the idealistic "equal field system" of ancient China—but his scholarship never strayed far from the two deepest concerns of the Confucian gentleman: self-cultivation and the orderly management of state and society. In 1818, intercession by a highly placed ally allowed Chŏng to return to his hometown, but he never again held public office, and he died peacefully in 1836.

to eliminate discrimination against them in state service. Arguing that *chungin* matched the *yangban* in loyalty, these petitions appealed to the meritocratic impulse in Confucianism that sought to recognize people on the basis of their talents. Because it threatened the hereditary nature of *yangban* power, however, it had never been fully implemented in Chosŏn. Certainly some kings were sympathetic. Chŏngjo, for example, managed to appoint some leading *chungin* scholars—such as Pak Chiwŏn and Pak Chega (see p. 123), and Yu Tŭkkong (see p.124),—to his new royal library, positions that enabled them to write their well-known works. Yet the official examination and appointment system still remained closed to these men.

This push for greater openness and resultant strengthening of collective identity continued into the twentieth century. Some *chungin* wrote histories of their status group, highlighting their struggles and their achievements. *Chungin* set up poetry groups and published collected works, demonstrating the high level of non-*yangban* cultural erudition. By the mid-nineteenth century, despite their many efforts and rich cultural life, the *chungin* had failed to end official discrimination. As a result, many of these men vented their frustration with their marginal social position by turning eagerly to the new knowledge introduced by the arrival of the Europeans and Americans.

THE ESCALATION OF RURAL RESISTANCE

As in all agricultural societies, Chosŏn farmers countered the disadvantages of their socioeconomic status through initiative and resistance. As we have already seen, farmers took the lead in adopting rice transplantation despite official disapproval. Farmers developed a wide range of strategies, some of them violent, to improve their lives. In years of famine, flood, epidemic, or other hardships, groups of farmers often protested the collection of regular taxes, demanding—sometimes with their hoes in the magistrate's face—that taxes be suspended until the agricultural cycle returned to normal. Landlords who suddenly raised rents could find themselves confronted with a rent strike.

Less aggressive strategies included hiding some part of the harvest from the landlord if rent constituted a percentage of the produce. If a tenant's land bordered a palace estate or some other form of crown land, the tenant could gradually extend the boundary of his land, nibbling into the unsupervised royal holdings. Contemporary observers also wrote of villages that bribed local officials or powerful local families to have their lands registered as fallow. They could also place their land under the supervision of a crown agency to remove it from the tax rolls. Options abounded, but though a clever farmer could reap substantial rewards by resistance, these short-term measures could not overcome either the inequities of the land system or the tenants' vulnerability.

According to an 1810 survey, in Chŏlla, the southwest part of the peninsula—an area with particularly high productivity and land value—5 percent of the population belonged to landlord families, 25 percent cultivated their own land, and the remaining 70 percent were tenants. While the situation of tenants and self-cultivators varied, for the most part their lives were hard. A single year of below average rain, a sickness in the family, or the spread of a crop disease could spell immediate disaster for the family.

Contemporary observers, such as Chŏng Yagyong (1762–1836; see box opposite), continued Yu Hyŏngwŏn and Yi Ik's tradition of criticizing the unequal distribution of agricultural land. Chŏng recommended a number of ways to divide the peninsula's land more equitably. Yet his proposals did not receive a hearing from officials whose families dominated the land system and had little interest in reforms that would undermine their economic power.

Under such severe conditions, farmers violently attacked local and regional officials as well as landlords, uprisings unprecedented in both numbers and scale. By the end of the nineteenth century, these uprisings constituted outright challenges to the legitimacy of the dynasty, as new religions developed to compete with Confucianism. Like China's Maitreya tradition, Korean culture had always included an undercurrent of Buddhist millenarianism, often contributing to outbreaks of violence.

While the uprisings' ideological commitments separated them from ordinary tax revolts and rent strikes, they offered no sustained challenge either to the state or to its ruling ideology. Nor could they offer any viable solutions to the poverty and misery that inspired many of their followers to join. Instead, they followed a rather predictable cycle. Against a backdrop of consistently difficult living conditions, a specific incident—the imposition of a particular egregious form of taxation, the coerced payment of an unreasonable bribe, the failure to reduce taxes when natural disaster struck—triggered a rebellion, often around the fall harvest. Rebels attacked wealthy *yangban* houses and the magistrate's office, distributing the county's stored grain reserves to the people as a symbolic redistribution of wealth.

Depending on the number of participants and their location, government troops quickly or eventually suppressed the uprisings, executing the leaders and displaying their severed heads as a warning to others. The king usually granted some form of amnesty to followers willing to return to peaceful pursuit of their occupations. Measures might be taken to remedy the specific grievance that had triggered the uprising, punishing an overly rapacious official, for example. But because *yangban*, with their entrenched economic interests, governed the state, they had little interest in resolving the persistent socioeconomic problems underlying the violence.

Serious rebellions began in 1811 in the northwest, a region that for generations had suffered discrimination. The Seoul elite considered the northwest a backwater, and this discrimination restricted the number of northerners able to pass the official exams. Even for those who did pass, the chances of bureaucratic appointment were virtually nil. As a result, almost no *yangban* families in the northwest belonged to the upper echelon of their status group, only to locally powerful alliances, creating a distinctly regional social structure. Moreover, due to mountainous terrain, climate, and scarcity of water, agriculture did not develop extensively in the northwest. Instead, a high percentage of the population engaged in trade, mining, handicrafts, and other occupations that grew with the commercialization of the economy.

In 1811, a severe famine hit the region. Taking advantage of local desperation, a fallen *yangban* named Hong Kyŏngnae (1780–1812) led an uprising to protest discrimination as well as the many illicit fees that corrupt officials demanded of the merchants. When troops finally asserted control the next year, they punished the leadership without attending to the root causes of the uprising. Smaller riots continued over the following years, often inspired by false rumors that Hong had not been executed.

In 1862, a larger outburst occurred in Chinju. Reacting against corrupt tax officials, fallen *yangban* and peasant leaders circulated a call to arms that attracted substantial support in at least 23 villages within a few days. Wearing white headbands and singing songs about protecting their livelihood, the participants first attacked the local government office, where they killed the magistrate and some of his officials. Then they sacked and burned the houses of more than 120 rich and powerful local families. Several tens of thousands of peasants took part in sporadic uprisings throughout the south before government troops restored order.

FROM FACTIONAL TO CONSORT POLITICS

A new dynamic arose in court politics in the early nineteenth century. In 1800, when Chŏngjo died, his successor Sunjo, Lady Hyegyŏng's grandson, was only 10 years old. For the remainder of the century, children ascended the throne. In 1834, the 7-year-old Hŏnjong became king, followed in 1849 by 18-year-old Chŏljong, and, in 1864, 12-year-old Kojong. The fact of the monarchs' youth changed the factional configurations that had swirled around the court for over two centuries. When 10-year-old Sunjo became king, his father-in-law, Kim Chosun (?–1831), grasped the reins of royal power. Turning his back on his faction, Kim instead pursued the interests of his extended family, appointing clansmen to key positions in the bureaucracy. The principled positions and philosophical differences that in the past had separated and animated various factions now had little relevance to the unbridled advancement of a single family. As a result, Kim's family—called the Andong Kims after their town of origin—emerged as one of the most powerful families of the century. With the succession of the next king, the P'ungyang Cho clan—the in-laws of the new King Hŏnjong—replaced the Andong Kims, but the Kims reasserted their power after 1849, under King Chŏlchong. During these years, "in-law government" undermined the ideal of meritocratic official appointments more than at any other time in the dynasty.

King Chŏlchong had no son, so when he died the royal family chose his nephew to succeed him as King Kojong, who ascended the throne in 1864 as a 12-year-old. His father Yi Haŭng (1820–1898) assumed the role of regent, a position called *Taewŏn'gun*, to rule on his behalf. A shrewd connoisseur of the rough and tumble of court politics, Kojong's father intended to reform many of the institutions that had conventionally limited royal power, including *yangban* and bureaucratic authority.

Conditions had never been more favorable for such efforts. Tax revenues had been in steady decline for decades, reaching a new low in 1861. Corruption among officials was rampant: more than 450 provincial governors, military commanders, and magistrates had been sacked for corruption between 1850 and 1862. The difficulty of suppressing peasant uprisings revealed the deep problems in the countryside, as did the spread of new heterodox religions, Tonghak and Roman Catholicism (see below). Finally, the 1866 occupation of Kanghwa Island by the French showed that Chosŏn could no longer ignore the Euro-American powers already plaguing its Qing and Tokugawa neighbors.

The Taewŏn'gun moved quickly to restore the financial viability of the state. He cracked down on official corruption while pursuing a thorough reform of the "Three Administrations": the land tax, military tax, and granary loan systems. He promulgated a series of measures that previous monarchs had been unable to implement because of *yangban* opposition. For example, the Taewŏn'gun converted the military tax—a heavy burden falling only on commoners—into a tax on all households, including the *yangban*. He also made it difficult for magistrates to lend for personal profit (at exorbitant rates of interest) the grain from county "ever-normal" granaries, originally designed to relieve famine and stabilize prices.

He moved most dramatically against the rural academies, or *sŏwŏn*, that had remained the centers of Confucian learning in the country but also served the interests of powerful families and factions, who took advantage of academy lands' tax-free status. By the nineteenth century, the academies had become a major locus of corruption, as many landowners avoided taxes by nominally registering their land with an academy for a fee. Eager to undercut the economic basis of powerful regional families and enhance the prestige of the throne, the Taewŏn'gun closed most of the academies.

Taewŏn'gun Yi Haŭng, photographed in 1898 or earlier by Homer B. Hulbert.

By 1871, he had eliminated most of the hundreds of *sŏwŏn* and returned their land to the tax registers.

The Taewŏn'gun intended to shift the balance of power away from the great *yangban* families and toward the throne. The court, however, squandered much of its increased revenue on the reconstruction of Kyŏngbok palace, one of the royal Seoul residences burned during the Hideyoshi invasions. Perennially short of funds, the royal family had used the other Seoul palaces, leaving Kyŏngbok in disrepair. The Taewŏn'gun planned the reconstruction to assert royal power, conscripting thousands of laborers and coercing huge contributions from rich families.

EASTERN AND WESTERN LEARNING

At the same time as corruption in Chinju preceded the 1862 uprising, a *yangban* secondary son from Chŏlla named Ch'oe Cheu (1824–1864) began a personal quest for security and serenity. He had received a classical education from his father, but after being orphaned at the age of 17, he spent more than a decade wandering the peninsula. Reputedly working as an itinerant peddler, he explored the wide variety of religious thought available to the lower social groups, especially Buddhism, Daoism, and Catholicism. By 1860, he had become familiar with conditions in the countryside and had learned of Lord Elgin's attack on Beijing and the destruction of the Summer Palace, which shook his generation's faith in the centrality of Chinese cultural power. Ch'oe doubted that any of the religions circulating in the peninsula offered solutions to the dual dilemmas of turmoil in the countryside and threats from foreigners, the same "domestic chaos and foreign catastrophe" that plagued the Qing.

Later that year Ch'oe found his answer in a sudden religious revelation, during which God assigned him to spread knowledge of the Way, a task similar to that of Hong Xiuquan and the Taiping Heavenly Kingdom. Ch'oe came to call this new Way *Tonghak* ("Eastern learning"). Over the next few years, he expounded his ideas in sermons and texts. Mixing ideas, practices, and vocabulary from the religious traditions he had studied, he created an idiosyncratic religion that sought simultaneously to offer personal salvation and to defend the peninsula—a dual purpose captured in his adoption of the old phrase "protect the country and succor the people." The route to personal salvation lay in Confucian self-cultivation, but Ch'oe's version included incantations, meditation, and the study of his Tonghak texts, as well as participation in rites reminiscent of shamanistic practices.

Ch'oe offered this path to all people regardless of ancestry or status. During his revelation Ch'oe had heard God say that His mind lay within all people— "Heaven within humankind." This belief eventually became the basis of Tonghak thinking that emphasized equality and challenged the hierarchical social order of the Chosŏn dynasty and Korean society. The Tonghak worship services, which Ch'oe patterned after Catholic practice, captured this urge to social equality, since men and women, *yangban* and commoner, sat together.

At first, Ch'oe had difficulty gaining an audience for his teachings, and he complained that people laughed at his efforts. But the appeal of social equality at a time of such wrenching change in the countryside—together with his attempt to link the difficulties of individuals with fears of foreign invasion—gained the founder of Tonghak a gradually expanding congregation. The best indication that his message was being heard was Ch'oe's arrest on trumped-up charges of inciting an uprising in 1864. Only four years after he launched his effort to spread the Way, Ch'oe Cheu was executed. His successor as leader of the Tonghak, Ch'oe Sihyŏng (1827–1898), spent his entire career hiding from authorities. Nonetheless, while traveling around the peninsula under the cover of darkness and in disguise, Ch'oe Sihyŏng expanded on his predecessor's beliefs, arranged for the publication of a large number of Tonghak tracts, and strengthened the organization of the church.

Ch'oe Cheu had originally chosen the name Tonghak for his new religion in opposition to *sŏhak* ("Western learning")—a term that by 1860 had come largely to refer to Roman Catholicism—which he saw as causing much upheaval among the people. His fears demonstrate that, despite its history of persecution, Catholicism had continued to spread in the peninsula. In the 1790s, the state still proscribed the religion and destroyed its books, but it also emphasized more effective dissemination of

Confucian thought as an antidote. Many officials, including King Chŏngjo, believed that the reason for the spread of Catholic heterodoxy was the lax moral education of the people. In 1801, however, with the child-king Sunjo on the throne, this policy changed, and the court undertook a violent crackdown on the Catholic church.

During this crackdown, Hwang Sayŏng (1775–1801), a convert who had escaped the deadly dragnet, wrote a long letter on a piece of white silk that he arranged to have smuggled to the Bishop of Beijing. The letter appealed for assistance to save the nascent Catholic community, going so far as to request military aid. But his letter was intercepted. Hwang paid with his life, and the court increased its effort to stop the spread of Catholicism. Previously it had been deemed primarily an ideological threat, but with the call for foreign ships, ideology became linked to subversion and the possibility of foreign invasion. In the end, more than 300 converts, including Father Zhou Wenmo (a Chinese priest), were executed, and countless other believers apostatized under coercion.

The persecution did not stop the growth of the Catholic community. Word of this growth spread back to Europe, and in 1808 the first in a long line of foreign books that proclaimed Korea as a miraculous land of conversion was published in Lisbon. By 1836, the first French priest had smuggled himself into the peninsula, followed shortly thereafter by two more. Three young Koreans escaped from Chosŏn to Macau, where they began to study for the priesthood. In 1839, all three French clergy were captured and executed in a new round of persecution, and many converts (including Chŏng Yagyong's nephew) were killed. Repression relaxed somewhat thereafter, creating an opportunity for 12 more priests to enter secretly and tend to the growing population of converts. By 1863 the size of the community reached around 20,000. Following the established pattern, rapid growth of the church caused more violent crackdowns. Under the Taewŏn'gun, nine foreign missionaries were executed, though three did manage to escape, and their reports detailing the repression and the bravery of the martyred converts circulated internationally.

THE "DISTURBANCES" OF 1866

Missionaries were not the first foreigners to come to Korea in the nineteenth century. As early as 1832, British ships arrived off the coast, their requests for trade politely declined. Sailors shipwrecked in nearby waters entered the country, in most cases staying only a short time before Chosŏn authorities arranged for them to be returned to their countries through Beijing. But the widely publicized killing of nine missionaries stirred public opinion in Europe, especially in their homeland, France, which had, under the rule of Napoleon III, styled itself the protector of Catholicism around the globe in order to expand its political, economic, and cultural interests.

The killing of the missionaries gave the French a reason, in classic gunboat fashion, to send a punitive expedition in 1866. Led by Admiral Pierre-Gustave Roze (1812–1883), seven French ships occupied Kanghwa Island at the mouth of the Han River, which led to Seoul. Seeking to blockade the shipment of grain to the capital, French troops looted the island of its silver and rice. They also stole the island's valuable royal library, carting off the books to the Bibliothèque Nationale in Paris, where they rest to this day. After 20 days, and an ambush by Korean volunteers that left more than 50 French casualties, Admiral Roze withdrew.

Officials in Seoul viewed the French retreat as a great victory, reinforcing their decision to ignore proposals to establish relations with the Euro-American powers. Envoys to Beijing reportedly boasted to their hosts of their victories, pointedly contrasting their own success at fending off the French with Qing failures. Since the French troops had arrived in part to protect the Catholic community, their withdrawal was followed by a new round of persecution. The Taewŏn'gun promised to promote any official who arrested more than 20 Christians, and he ordered the execution of an estimated 8,000 converts.

The French expedition was just one of several that challenged the seclusionist foreign policy of the Taewŏn'gun. In the same year of 1866, Ernest Oppert, a Prussian who imagined himself a buccaneer, twice tried personally to open trade relations with Chosŏn, but his entreaties were rejected. He returned in 1868 and managed to prove the old adage that a little knowledge can be a dangerous thing. In one of the more bizarre chapters in East Asian foreign relations, Oppert organized a multinational "army" including Europeans, Malays, and Chinese, and marched them to the gravesite of the Taewŏn'gun's father, situated just a few miles inland.

Armed with an understanding of the importance of filial piety in Chosŏn as well as shovels for digging, Oppert planned to ransack the tomb and use the remains to blackmail Chosŏn into a trade relationship. His plan failed, for the local population drove him and his "troops" away from the gravesite. Needless to say, his actions hardly endeared the foreigners and their exhortations to trade to the Taewŏn'gun.

Also in that invasive year of 1866, an American merchant ship under British commission, the *General Sherman*, forced its way up the Taedong River to the outskirts of Pyongyang, along the way kidnapping one official and killing more than ten Koreans while bombarding the shore. When the navigators misjudged the river tides, the *General Sherman* ran aground on a sandbar. Local men floated fireboats toward the *General Sherman* until it caught fire, killing all on board.

It took several years for American diplomatic officials to determine the fate of the *General Sherman*, but in 1871 they dispatched more than 1,200 soldiers to retaliate. During two days in June, they destroyed three fortresses and killed over 350 Chosŏn soldiers, in what the New York *Herald Tribune* called, "Our Little War with the Heathens." In resistance, Chosŏn troops inflicted roughly two dozen American casualties. Receiving no positive response to his requests for trade relations, the American commander eventually retreated, an action again interpreted by the Seoul court as a victory. This brief, inconclusive engagement—the largest military action taken by the United States in Asia up to this time and for nearly 30 years afterward—marked an inauspicious beginning to US–Chosŏn relations.

These two victories strengthened the Taewŏn'gun's resolve to keep Europeans and Americans out of the peninsula, but these victories led him to greatly underestimate the severity of the challenges facing Korea. The commitment to orthodox Confucian learning, and the belief that Chosŏn alone protected this learning, further motivated rejection of trade requests. One of the leading ministers at court, Kim Pyŏnghak (1821–1879), captured the ideological impetus behind the seclusion policy, "The nation's primal energy is in the orthodox learning; when it is full of vitality, a hundred perverse things may not burst in.[3] Yet over the next 30 years, "perverse things bursting in" combined with continued troubles in the countryside to shake the dynasty to its very core.

JAPAN ON THE EVE OF MODERNITY

Like the Qing and Chosŏn courts, Japan's leaders and pundits—though not the majority of the population—worried increasingly about the world outside their borders in the early nineteenth century. Their eighteenth-century forebears had allowed contact with Chinese scholarship and European scientific knowledge but limited international commerce to merchants from Holland, Qing, Ryūkyū, and Chosŏn. Nineteenth-century European and American diplomatic and military threats understandably dismayed scholars and officials. European gunboats and merchant vessels laden with contraband narcotics in China's harbors left an indelible impression on Japanese minds as they contemplated the escalating European and American presence in Japan's own ports and off the islands' coasts.

The new manufacturing-based wealth of Europe and the United States, the desire to sell efficiently produced goods, and the increasing ease and speed of travel led inexorably to European and American pressure on all the East Asian kingdoms for formal trade and diplomatic relations. The Dutch tried to capitalize on these pressures in the 1840s, arguing that they could help smooth Japan's transition to the Western-denominated international system of law, trade, and diplomacy. Shogunal authorities rejected the Dutch offer, and intellectuals and officials spoke out, from a wide range of perspectives, on the brave new world Japan was being called on to inhabit. Debates about foreign relations were intertwined with domestic politics, as they had been in the eighteenth century.

Compared to their predecessors, government leaders in the early nineteenth century appeared obsessed with foreign issues. But (again like Qing and Chosŏn officials) most of their concerns remained closer to home—maintaining control over unorthodox thought, keeping the arts in check, and dealing with some of the worst famines in Japan's history, not to mention urban and rural riots. In the end, these domestic troubles, combined with aggressive demands from the United States and Europe in the 1850s and 1860s, spelled the end of the Tokugawa shogunate in 1868.

THE CULTURAL SCENE, 1795–1853

Most of the archipelago enjoyed prosperity during the first half of this period. The devastating famines of the 1780s had claimed the lives of the young, old, and infirm, leaving the most productive individuals to develop the economy. A modest growth in population, from about 25 million commoners (non-samurai) in 1792 to over

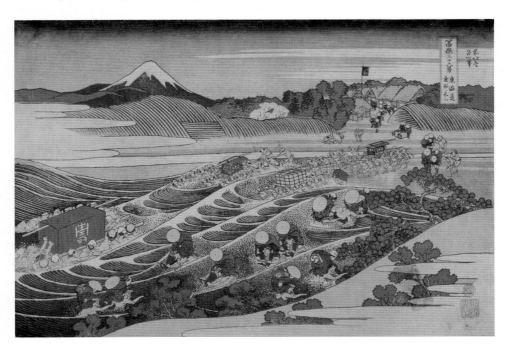

Katsushika Hokusai. *Beyond the Kanaya Ford*, from the series "Thirty-Six Views of Mt. Fuji," 1823–31. This print shows busy traffic along the Tōkaidō, a main road leading to Edo. To keep weapons from entering the city, the Tokugawa forbade bridge construction, so porters carried boxes of cargo and rich travelers in palanquins, while other travelers rode on porters' shoulders or waded through the stream.

27 million in 1828, reflected the economic wellbeing of these decades. Favorable climate conditions certainly helped, as did the growth of fishing, expanded use of coal, continued replanting of forests, expansion of education, and dissemination of agricultural and artisanal technologies in printed books. As before, prosperity remained regional, and some areas (such as the northern part of Honshū) never shared the overall good times. In general, however, relatively good economic conditions permitted a lively growth of culture in the first quarter of the nineteenth century.

Earlier trends in the popularization of the arts continued. Multicolored printing techniques made woodblock prints—of *kabuki* actors, famous courtesans, beautiful women not in the sex trades, and exciting urban scenes using European-style perspective—widely accessible. Erotic prints that left little to the viewer's imagination were popular, as were landscapes and scenes of famous places. Katsushika Hokusai (1760–1849), an artist trained in Japanese, Chinese, and European techniques, created numerous landscapes with the iconic Mt. Fuji in the background of lively human activities like samurai processions or the hauling of commercial goods.

Andō Hiroshige (1797–1858) turned out a prodigious number of landscape prints of famous tourist spots, post stations along the major roads leading to Edo (the famous "Fifty-Three Stations of the Tōkaidō"), and scenes of human activities against a backdrop of natural beauty. Both these artists appealed to connoisseurs and ordinary Japanese who yearned to travel. Their fascination continues to this day among both modern collectors and artists who base their works on Hokusai and Hiroshige themes. Western-inspired painting also developed in the late eighteenth and early nineteenth centuries. Shiba Kōkan (1747?–1818) experimented boldly with technique and by the 1790s settled on European styles, rejecting as unrealistic the Chinese approaches that were so loved by the *bunjin* artists (see p. 129). He also embraced European influences by studying Dutch-learning texts on science and geography.

Edo-based *kabuki* theater also grew, becoming increasingly spectacular, with gorgeous costumes and sets that allowed actors to move energetically. Most worrisome to authorities, sexually suggestive dialogue and gestures increased the appeal of *kabuki*, especially to young men from wealthy families who fawned on their favorite actors. Touring companies brought theatrical performances even to rural towns, knitting city and countryside together culturally.

Prose writers also had a large audience in the late eighteenth and early nineteenth centuries, indulging their readers' tastes for diverse styles and topics. Takizawa Bakin (1767–1848) mastered the writing of fiction in his 30s, following a life as an orphan, a homeless runaway, a would-be scholar, and a professional comedian. Afraid he would be jailed or suffer the banning of his works, like some writers in the 1790s whose tales satirized officialdom, Bakin always inserted a moral note in his tales. Other authors produced cheap satirical booklets that combined illustrations and text, like early-modern comic books. Two celebrated novelists favored popular prose humor: Jippensha Ikku (1765–1831), author of the "Shank's Mare" series, written in installments from 1802 to 1822 and featuring two funny, boorish rascals; and Shikitei Sanba (1776–1822), whose home was damaged by Edo firefighters because he had satirized them. Urban lending libraries made these tales even more widely available.

Shogunal adviser Matsudaira Sadanobu (1758–1829) aggressively censored novelists, humorists, and playwrights. Not limiting his censorship to producers of art, he also concerned himself with philosophy and political theory. In 1790, Matsudaira decreed that only the conservative Hayashi version of Zhu Xi learning constituted orthodox thought. Enrollments at the Hayashi school, though still only a small portion of all educated samurai, doubled between the immediate pre-Matsudaira era and the early 1800s. Matsudaira also weighed in on the relative merits of Chinese-style and Dutch-style medicine. While the former got the official nod, Matsudaira, like many other Japanese of his time, recognized the benefits of European medicine, science, and, particularly, military techniques, though it was a hard pill for him to swallow:

The barbarian nations are skilled in the sciences, and considerable profit may be derived from their works of astronomy and geography, as well as from their military weapons and methods of internal and external medicine….It might seem advisable to ban [their books], but prohibiting these books would not prevent people from reading them…. Such books should…not be allowed to pass in large quantities into the hands of irresponsible people.[4]

What kinds of works did pass into the hands of the people in the early nineteenth century? Certainly, the reading and thinking public had expanded greatly. A growing number of private schools, mostly in urban areas, educated thousands of students of all social statuses in a wide variety of subjects, including Chinese studies, Japanese studies, Dutch studies, military studies, writing, mathematics, and many other areas.

A few domain schools had been established by *daimyō* in the first half of the Tokugawa period, but numerous new schools were set up in the last decades of the period, and they trained increasing numbers of samurai. Between 1803 and 1843, 3,050 new temple schools appeared, and 6,691 more before 1867. Temple schools, attended by rural and urban children of all status groups, became increasingly secularized. By the early nineteenth century, Buddhist priests accounted for only 20 percent of the instructors and Shintō priests 7 percent. Many teachers were women. Taken together, Japan's schools—private, domain-run, shogunate-run, and temple schools—enrolled at least 1.14 million students in the early nineteenth century. And this number may be an underestimate, as schools may have underreported the number of their female students to protect their names from public exposure. Japan's population enjoyed a high rate of literacy.

This encouraged continuing advances in rural productivity, as more farmers could read the proliferating agricultural literature. The famous nineteenth-century "peasant sage," Ninomiya Sontoku (1787–1856), was probably better known for his philosophy than for his agricultural writings. He called on people of all classes to serve the community to pay back the blessings they had received. This could be done through frugality and hard work, and no one status group excelled at this over any other. This philosophy gave respect to peasants, as the Kaitokudō had done for the merchant class (see pp. 129–30). During his lifetime, officials called on Ninomiya to help restore famine-ravaged areas to agricultural productivity, and long after his death, the modernizing Japanese state continued to use his notion of "returning blessings" to promote state-centered goals.

Education could be used to raise the standing or wealth of one's family. For an ambitious samurai, it could also be a route to political office. It could allow one to escape the strictures of status-based society, as did *bunjin*, medical doctors, and professional teachers of varied social backgrounds. As we will see below, education gave some committed political commentators a foundation for their ideologies in the early nineteenth century. For others, it was the basis of the examined life—men and women of any social status could hold the Confucian ideal of cultivating and perfecting the self. This same ambition would, almost a century later, connect the notion of individual personhood to the demand for democratic rights (see p. 211).

ECONOMIC CRISES

The good economic conditions of the 1795–1825 period soon gave way to dismal harvests, starvation, and, as a result, urban and rural uprisings. The so-called Tenpō famine covered about a decade, starting with bad crop yields in the 1820s and worsening until 1836, when the overall yield for the entire realm reached only one-quarter of the usual harvest. Famine-ridden villages emptied of their residents, many of whom died or took to the roads, and cities suffered both an influx of starving peasants and drastically higher food prices. Official responses varied from domain to domain and within the shogunate. Individuals in all walks of life began to question authority, believing it increasingly irrelevant.

In response to this crisis, the shogunate ordered shipments of rice primarily to Edo and secondarily to Osaka in the 1830s, all at the expense of the rural areas. Despite this influx of food from the countryside, the cities continued to suffer as well. In 1837, Ōshio Heihachirō (1793–1837), an Osaka police official who earned an early reputation as an incorruptible crime buster before resigning to become a teacher, petitioned the Osaka city magistrate to hand out rice reserves to feed the starving. When the magistrate refused, Ōshio planned to attack officials' houses to find the gold and rice he believed they hoarded. Ōshio's plan leaked to the authorities, so he raced through town and set several merchants' and officials' houses afire before he could be stopped. These ignited large parts of Osaka, so rather than finding rice to distribute to the poor, the uprising burned down a quarter of the city, and Ōshio committed suicide. But his actions inspired other (also failed) uprisings, and in the longer term forced the authorities to take effective measures to improve the economy.

Several domains undertook drastic reforms to regain solvency. Satsuma and Chōshū—*tozama* domains that had submitted to Tokugawa authority only after being defeated in 1600—repudiated their debts, no doubt dismaying creditors but pleasing the domains' financial officers. In addition, Chōshū cut back on samurai stipends, and Satsuma increased the exploitation of oppressed sugar workers on the domain-owned plantations. Both these domains were in strong financial condition in the 1850s, when foreign pressure unhinged the Tokugawa government. The shogunate did respond to the economic crisis, but its policies came too late. Edo strengthened its control of *daimyō* and towns in the Kantō region near Edo and outlawed commercial monopolies in the *daimyō*'s domains. The famine ended in the early 1840s with the return of good weather, but the shogunate failed to regain its economic superiority over the regions, especially the southwest. This weakness continued to haunt the Tokugawa as they faced Western commercial and diplomatic pressure.

Dozens of peasant uprisings challenged the authorities and the order they had established. In addition, non-violent but boisterous religious festivals, many of them expanding to become countrywide pilgrimages, demonstrated popular disregard of the authorities. Thousands of pilgrims took to the highways in 1830, believing that religious amulets had fallen from the sky. They danced, sang, and relied on the kindness of strangers along their pilgrimage routes. In 1867, on the eve of the Meiji Restoration (see p. 174), the largest *yonaoshi* ("heal the world") celebrations occurred spontaneously, with frenzied, often naked revelers dancing while singing *eejanaika* ("Isn't it great!" meaning "What the hell!"), with no concern for the disapproval of state officials. Elsewhere, men and women had religious visions and founded new religions.

The economic scene also changed rapidly. Prosperous towns and villages began to displace cities as centers of production. Small-scale mills in the hands of rich farmers employed increasing numbers of female workers; most nineteenth-century rural girls lived away from their families during some part of their teenage years, employed as hired farm hands or mill workers (see p. 133). The men and women who worked for these entrepreneurs, as well as farmers needing to increase their family income, learned to value their time as a commodity even before the introduction of clocks to the countryside. Both the development of rural entrepreneurs and the consciousness of time undermined the old order and facilitated Japan's transition to modern industry in the late nineteenth century.

JAPAN IN THE NEW DIPLOMATIC SCENE

Russian advances in the north (see p. 128) had long concerned Edo, but by the mid-nineteenth century pressure in the south from the British and Americans had become far more worrisome. England focused its attention primarily on its Indian colonies and the huge market in China—the two linked through the opium trade—but Japan remained of interest for commercial and strategic reasons. The Americans, at first viewed

Japan's contacts with foreign countries, 1800–53

1. **Sakhalin**
   1806-7. Russian attacks on Japanese and Ainu in Sakhalin and Kuriles in retaliation for Rezanov rebuff
2. **Kurile Islands**
   1811. Russian V.M. Golovin captured by Japanese
   1812. A Japanese captured by Russians
   1813. Both men freed
3. **Mito domain**
   1824. British whaling ships

4. **Edo (Tokyo), at Uraga Bay**
   1818. British ships acquire provisions, leave Bibles behind
   1837. US ship, Morrison, enters Uraga Bay with castaways, and is rebuffed
   1846. US Commodore James Biddle enters Uraga Bay, and is rebuffed
   1853, 1854. US Commodore Perry arrives
5. **Nagasaki**
   1803. Americans, British rebuffed when seeking trade agreement
   1804. Russian Nikolai Rezanov rebuffed
   1808. Phaeton Incident, Britain
6. **Ryūkyū Islands**
   1823. British whaling ship attempts to steal livestock

anxiously as British (they were, after all, *New* Englanders), tried to nose into Japan as well. After a half-century of United States expansion across the North American continent and the Pacific, it was an American, Matthew Perry (1794–1858), who forced Edo in 1853–54 to abandon its long-held policy of restricting foreign contacts and trade to a few favored countries.

Initially, however, the British acted most egregiously in Tokugawa eyes. Although the Napoleonic wars occupied British and Russian attention in the first decades of the nineteenth century, those wars also caused British encroachment in Japan. That is, Holland, allied to France, was Britain's wartime enemy, and thus the British navy menaced Dutch merchant ships sailing to Japan. To keep trade going in wartime, Dutch companies loaded their goods onto other countries' ships between 1797 and 1817, including British ships on three occasions. When the ships entered Japanese waters, they would hoist the Dutch flag to fool the Nagasaki authorities.

This worked until 1808, when the HMS *Phaeton*, a British warship (not a merchant vessel), flying a Dutch flag, docked at Deshima. The British crew seized two Dutch merchants sent aboard by the Nagasaki magistrate to inquire about the ship's purpose. The magistrate called for reinforcements, but Japanese defenses clearly could not handle the heavily armed ship. Demanding water, vegetables, and beef from the Japanese, the British released the two Dutchmen because they had no information about Dutch vessels the *Phaeton* had hoped to capture. The Nagasaki magistrate could not deliver beef—not eaten in Japan and thus not available—but he did send water and vegetables, and the *Phaeton* sailed away. In 1809, the shogunate banned the Dutch from Deshima for eight years for their decade of deceit. Soon thereafter, British forces overran Dutch outposts in Southeast Asia and attempted to force their way into the Japan trade. The Napoleonic wars ended before the British succeeded, and the shogunate allowed the Dutch to return to Nagasaki.

The British did not entirely give up on Japan. East India Company official Stamford Raffles, the founder of Singapore, wrote approvingly (in the racist tone of his day) that the Japanese were:

a nervous, vigorous people, whose bodily and mental powers assimilate much nearer to those of Europe than what is attributed to Asiatics in general. Their features are masculine and perfectly European, with the exception of the small lengthened Tartar eye….

Kawanabe Gyōsai, *Eejanaika!* (*Isn't it great! What the hell!*), 1868. Celebrations during which men, women, and children did frenzied dancing while chanting "*Eejanaika!*" occurred throughout the country. The Tokugawa authorities were powerless to control these popular religious festivities. The artist incorporated the phenomenon into a calendar: the men in the dancing circle represent long months, and the women the short months. All wear costumes connected with monthly events or seasons and hold symbolic objects.

For a people who have had very few, if any, external aids, the Japanese cannot but rank high in the scale of civilisation….[T]he slightest impulse seems sufficient to give a determination to the Japanese character which would progressively improve until it attained the same height of civilisation with the Europeans.[5]

Following Raffles's report, the British sent ships to Japan several times to open relations, but troubles followed. In 1818, Chinese-language Bibles appeared on shore after a British ship departed, confirming Edo's fears that its policy of allowing ships to obtain provisions and depart would permit the forbidden religion to enter Japan. Edo and the coastal domains, especially those along Japan's Pacific coast, remained on alert, because they were visited by a large number of British and American whaling ships when the search for whale oil shifted from the over-hunted North Atlantic to the Pacific. The *daimyō* of Mito issued an order in 1823 to report any books or pictures of the dreaded "Kirisutan" religion. Within days, the crew of a British whaling ship stormed ashore on an island in the Ryūkyūs—its trade under Satsuma's jurisdiction rather than Edo's, while it remained a tributary of the Qing—and attempted armed theft of livestock. This led to a major shift in Edo's policy toward foreign vessels in 1825: the shogunate ordered coastal defenses to fire on and drive off all ships, with no allowance for provisioning.

These contentious relations with outsiders adversely affected scholarship, including military studies, from the 1820s until the 1840s. In 1828, a leading scholar of Dutch studies, Takahashi Kageyasu (1785–1829), traveled to Nagasaki where he had a lively intellectual discussion with Philipp Franz von Siebold (1796–1866), a German physician hired to treat the Dutch there. Shogunal authorities accidentally discovered that Takahashi and Siebold also exchanged some maps, so they arrested Takahashi and other Dutch learning scholars on suspicion of abetting Russian (!) spy activities, and Takahashi died in jail.

The attack on Dutch learning had started even before Takahashi's arrest. In 1825, Aizawa Seishisai (1782–1863), an adviser to the *daimyō* of Mito, composed his *New Thesis*, a powerful attack against the realm's weakness in facing the foreign threat. He blamed dissolute leadership, stupid commoners susceptible to foreign religion and ways, and treacherous

Artists rowed out to Perry's ships in 1853 to capture images of their diverse crews. From left, top row: Navigator, infantryman, infantry commander, depth surveyor, interpreter, Perry. Bottom row: Sailor from a nation of black people, sailor, marine. Perry's ship is depicted in the bottom row.

scholars like those who studied Dutch learning. Characteristic of the antiforeignism of that time, his work became most influential in the 1840s and 1850s when it secretly circulated among anti-Tokugawa rebels. Aizawa ranted:

The harm comes when some dupe with a smattering of second-hand knowledge of foreign affairs mistakenly lauds the far-fetched notions spun out by Western barbarians or publishes books to that effect in an attempt to transform our Middle Kingdom to barbarian ways.[6]

At the same time, more tolerant views also circulated, though they often put their proponents under a cloud of suspicion in the fearful climate of the 1830s and 1840s, especially after the Qing defeat in the Opium War became widely known in Japan. For example, another Mito scholar, Fujita Toko (1806–1855), wrote in 1834 that to "strengthen the Divine Land, information from Holland should not be cut off completely."[7] He later wrote that the ancient sages would have learned from the good points of other lands. Another scholar, Sakuma Shōzan (1811–1864), noted in 1847 that, "even Western learning is nothing more than part of our learning" and called for a principle of "Eastern ethics and Western techniques."[8] This slogan appeared in Qing and Chosŏn texts a few decades later.

Some scholars of national learning, usually considered intensely nationalistic, also allowed for consideration of foreign studies. Hirata Atsutane (1776–1843), who politicized the literary studies of his national learning teachers—"we [Japanese], down to the most humble man and woman, are the descendants of the gods," he wrote[9]—claimed that if foreign tools could help strengthen Japan, they should be borrowed. The suppression of Dutch studies continued, however, until the 1840s.

The Tokugawa authorities were not well equipped—militarily, politically, or ideologically—to deal with the

NAKAHAMA MANJIRŌ

Nakahama Manjirō, c. 1870s

Fourteen-year-old Manjirō of Nakahama (1827–1898) set sail on a small fishing vessel in 1841. The tiny craft was blown off course and, together with four other crew members, he washed up on a deserted island. Surviving for a while on the island, the five were eventually rescued by William Whitfield, a whaling ship captain from Fairhaven, Massachusetts (now the sister city of Tosa Shimizu, near Manjirō's birthplace), and taken to Oahu. Impressed with the young Manjirō, Whitfield brought the boy to New England, where he learned English and math as well as sailing techniques. In 1846, "John Manjiro" joined the crew of a whaling ship that circumnavigated the globe twice and was selected by his crewmates as second in command. In 1849, Manjirō heard about the discovery of gold in California and became the only Japanese known to have joined the gold rush. He made enough money to return to Oahu to pick up his friends. Booking passage on an American cargo ship, they arrived in Ryūkyū in 1851.

Tokugawa law forbade returning to Japan from abroad, so the castaways were arrested but only briefly jailed. The shogun's government, now eager to learn more about the West, interrogated them at great length. Manjirō, who was fond of American life and customs and who wrote glowingly of American values, apparently influenced Sakamoto Ryōma and Katsu Kaishū. Although he willingly stepped on a bronze plate depicting Mary and Jesus as a sign that he was not Christian—the only remaining issue for returnees at that time—he had attended a Unitarian Church in Massachusetts and had likely been exposed to abolitionist and other progressive ideas. When Perry arrived in 1853, Abe Masahiro (see opposite) immediately summoned Manjirō to Edo, elevated him to samurai status, and had him teach English and translate books on navigation.

Manjirō believed Japan's future lay in developing its economy, and he begged the shogunate to outfit him with a whaling ship. He briefly captained a whaler before being recalled to serve as a translator aboard the *Kanrin Maru*, Japan's first steamship, when it and the USS *Powhatan* took a Japanese delegation to the United States to ratify Townsend Harris's Commercial Treaty. Because Katsu Kaishū, the *Kanrin Maru*'s captain, was so seasick that he rarely left his room, Manjirō often navigated the vessel. In addition, he taught English to Fukuzawa Yukichi (see pp. 176–77), the leading multicultural bridge-builder of the late nineteenth century, during the voyage.

After the Meiji Restoration of 1868, Manjirō continued to teach English at the Kaisei School (later part of Tokyo University). While on a government mission to observe the Franco-Prussian War in 1870, he stopped in Massachusetts to visit the aged Captain Whitfield. The Nakahama and Whitfield descendants have maintained contact for the past 150 years.

Western threat. Some *daimyō* tried to advise the shogunate on foreign affairs, and to that end they studied Western-style military technology. But they only succeeded in offending Mizuno Tadakuni (1794–1851), a shogunal councilor until forced from office in 1843 by factional feuding, *daimyō* opposition to his reassertion of shogunal dominance, and ill-planned "Tenpō reform" construction projects. Mizuno did not know what to do when an American merchant ship, the *Morrison*, arrived in 1837, trying to trade and propagate Christianity. Gunfire drove the *Morrison* away, but that bought only a bit of time for the Tokugawa, who in 1842 reversed the strict 1825 policy of firing on foreign vessels without offering provisions.

In 1844, a Dutch warship arrived with a message from the Dutch king urging Edo to establish diplomatic relations and avoid the fate of the Qing. A power struggle had been underway in the top councils of the Tokugawa regime since Mizuno's ouster, so the shogunate dithered, finally rejecting the Dutch offer. Abe Masahiro (1819–1857) emerged as the leading shogunal councilor in 1845. Immediately facing two demands to open trade relations, one from American Commander James Biddle and one from French Admiral Jean-Baptiste Cecille, he rejected both. But he also accelerated the building of coastal defenses and did an about-face to allow the adoption of Western military tactics. Specialists in Edo and many domains began studying Western military science. Abe, while given a reprieve for the next six years from foreign pressure to open Japan's ports, knew that he would soon have to address the foreigners directly.

THE END OF THE TOKUGAWA REGIME

The European powers left Japan alone in the early 1850s. The Ottoman empire, England, France, and Russia engaged in the Crimean War, a complicated struggle that started in 1853 over the issue of Palestine and ended in 1856. It resulted in further decline of the Ottomans, limits to the imperial reach of the Austro-Hungarian empire (which facilitated unification of both Italy and Germany), and Russia's realization that it had to modernize. Across the Atlantic in the 1850s, the continental expansion of the United States exacerbated sectional tensions, leading to its temporary division in 1861. More important for East Asia, that expansion created a reason for Americans to see the Pacific Ocean as

an arena of their interest. American whaling ships had long plied Pacific waters and challenged Edo's policy of restricting trade and diplomacy. The 1848 discovery of gold in California and the admission of California to statehood in 1850 drew new populations—including many Chinese—to the "new world" of the American west coast.

Having moved westward, impelled in part by the idea of Manifest Destiny, Americans extended their sense of mission to the Pacific. In addition, Americans' desire for coal, which they believed both plentiful in Japan and the property of the world rather than of Japan itself, persuaded US President Millard Fillmore (1800–1874) to send Commodore Matthew Perry to Japan in July 1853. Not involved in the Crimean War, the new Pacific power gathered its still meager navy and demanded that the shogunate change its foreign policy. Aware of the British juggernaut in China, the Japanese had no way to know that the US navy—dubbed "black ships" by the Japanese because their hulls were painted black—was still a small force.

On his departure, Perry left a note to be delivered to the "king" of Japan in "Yedo," promising to return the following year—with a larger force—to negotiate a commercial and diplomatic agreement. Shogunal councilor Abe, facing a "perfect storm" of troubles, responded in an unprecedented way. The realm had just begun to recover from the Tenpō famine; the shogunate had been directly challenged by the autonomous powers of a number of domains; and nativist ideologies like those of the Mito school and national learning questioned the Tokugawa's legitimacy if the shogunate could not protect the realm of the emperor (All Under Heaven). The glue holding the status groups together from samurai to farmers to townspeople—that is, a sense of order, authority, and community—seemed to be dissolving through violent rural and urban resentment of growing inequality as well as non-violent sexual and religious abandon that treated officialdom as if it were irrelevant. The foreign threat in itself constituted a problem, but its importance expanded because it became the primary issue angering those who challenged Tokugawa authority.

Abe had to respond creatively. He did this by attempting to draw the *daimyō* into a common approach to the American demands. For 200 years, Edo had dictated foreign policy, with the exception of issues involving the Ryūkyū Islands (handled by Satsuma) and Chosōn, undertaken by Tsushima. Abe, hoping to build a consensus, requested that the *daimyō* present their advice to the shogun. By asking, Abe opened Pandora's box, ending the shogunate's prohibition on discussions of foreign policy among the *daimyō*. While many domains agreed to retain the traditional policy of Tokugawa control of foreign affairs, others demanded that the shogunate repel Perry when he returned.

Abe, to the contrary, decided that he had no choice but to negotiate the Treaty of Kanagawa with the Americans in 1854. This allowed American ships to be provisioned at Shimoda and Hakodate, ports remote from Edo, and permitted the placement of an American consul at Shimoda. These privileges also extended to Russia, France, Britain, and the Netherlands. Townsend Harris (1804–1878), sent as the US consul to Shimoda in 1856, pressed Edo to expand these treaty rights, warning that if the Americans could not create a model trade treaty, the British, then pushing their weight around in China, would do the same in Japan.

Abe resigned in 1855 because of criticism of his actions. His successor as shogunal advisor, Hotta Masayoshi (1810–1864), also faced intertwined domestic and international problems. As the sickly and childless shogun Iesada (r. 1853–1858) lay dying, Hotta and his allies among the *daimyō* supported an adolescent relative of Iesada as his successor. At the same time, Hotta negotiated a Japanese–American Treaty of Commerce (1858) with Harris that opened eight Japanese ports to foreign trade, gave foreigners the right to set tariffs, and permitted extraterritoriality (the exemption of foreigners from prosecution in Japanese courts for violating Japanese law). These humiliations, similar to the unequal treaties imposed on the Qing after the Opium War, angered most politically aware Japanese, and their elimination became the central focus of Japan's foreign policy until the early years of the twentieth century.

Hotta calculated that he would need the emperor's approval to remain in office after negotiating the treaty. He took the novel step of personally bearing extravagant gifts to Kyoto, but the emperor rejected both the treaty and Hotta's choice of shogun. Although the emperor increasingly had moral authority, he had no legal or political means to enforce his wishes. Nevertheless, Hotta stepped down, humiliated, without signing the treaty or appointing the new shogun. His successor as

shogunal councilor, Ii Naosuke (1815–1860), had no such scruples. Ii signed the treaty, appointed the boy shogun, and reasserted shogunal authority over the *daimyō*, which had been eroding over the past decades.

Ii's actions transformed a relatively small anti-foreign, pro-emperor movement into a violently anti-Tokugawa one. Although the emperor had not exercised political power for centuries, opponents of Tokugawa policies rallied around the emperor as a symbol of legitimate authority. Pro-emperor activists eventually struggled against any form of continued rule by the Tokugawa shogunate. Radical young men, many of them teenagers, styled themselves "men of high purpose" (J. *shishi*) and took up the anti-Tokugawa cause. Many had studied national learning and attended swordsmanship schools that taught spiritual matters alongside fighting techniques. In 1860, *shishi* cut down Ii Naosuke at Edo castle. Thousands more gravitated to Kyoto, home of the emperor, where they roamed the streets, terrorized the population, fought their rivals, and created mayhem for several years. Many of those who survived until the mid-1860s later joined more respectable anti-Tokugawa movements approved by *daimyō*. These young men abandoned their early violence and antiforeignism as impractical and foolish, but retained their pro-emperor ideology as they rose to leadership positions in the next decades.

In addition to hotheaded young men, pro-emperor women helped frame the politics of the era. Takemura Taseko (1811–1894)—known to history by her husband's surname, Matsuo, though she herself used Takemura—much older than her male counterparts, joined the pro-emperor Hirata school in 1861. In the next few years, she served as a liaison between the imperial court and pro-emperor samurai, saved the life of court noble Iwakura Tomomi (see p. 178), and wrote on the economic dislocation caused by trade relationships with Europe and the United States.

Those who complained about the negative effects of trade had reason for concern. First, trade led to a massive gold drain, as the Japanese gold:silver exchange rate was 1:5 while the world rate was 1:15. European and American traders bought up much of Japan's incredibly cheap gold before the shogunate altered the exchange rate. Second, cheaply manufactured British and American cotton cloth put small-scale handweavers out of business because the unequal treaties prevented Japan from erecting protective tariffs to build up its domestic textile industry. And third, European imports of Japanese silk drove up the price for Japan's urban consumers. In the 1860s and 1870s this turned out to be a boon for Japan, however, as silk exports saved the struggling young economy, though at a high cost to Japan's textile workers.

The shogunate altered its political course after Ii's assassination. Adopting a policy called "unity between court [Kyoto] and shogunate," Edo officials arranged the marriage of the emperor's sister with the teen-aged shogun. In addition, they ended the 250-year-old alternate attendance system, strengthened national defenses, and allowed the imperial court to order the shogunate to set a date for expelling all foreigners. On that date, June 25, 1863, pro-emperor samurai from Chōshū—the westernmost domain on Honshū and a hotbed of anti-Tokugawa sentiment—fired on an American ship. American warships, joined by French vessels, fired back, leveling Chōshū's shore batteries. The shogunate punished Chōshū by driving its radicals from the Kyoto court and followed that with a punitive expedition, joined by Satsuma and Aizu domain forces, against Chōshū. The radicals in Chōshū seemed to be vanquished.

In the meantime, the shogunate undertook important reforms. A new shogun, Yoshinobu, son of the pro-emperor Mito *daimyō*, was installed in 1866. Although a *shinpan* domain (whose *daimyō*'s familial relationship with the Tokugawa permitted it to supply heirs to the shogunal throne when necessary), Mito had long been a thorn in Edo's side because of its many links to national learning scholarship and anti-Tokugawa agitation. Yoshinobu, advised by the French minister to Edo, resolved to modify the shogunal government along Western lines. But these reforms were too few and too late for the Tokugawa to reclaim effective power.

After being bombarded by American and French warships, the *shishi* of Chōshū and Satsuma began to shift their stance concerning Western technology, especially military techniques. They abandoned their rejection of the West and adopted a new slogan with ancient Chinese roots, "rich country, strong army" (J. *fukoku kyōhei*). Chōshū radicals had not yet given up their struggle against the shogunate, despite having been driven from the domain government and advisory positions in Kyoto. Some went out to the countryside

and organized what were called "mixed militias," made up of samurai and farmers. Radical experiments because they included a status—farmers—who had not been allowed to bear arms since Hideyoshi's Sword Hunt in the 1580s (see p. 58), they became the antecedents both for the modern Japanese military and for the elimination of status divisions in the 1870s. The mixed militias defeated the Chōshū regulars in 1865 and took control of the domain's government. Flush with money due to its successful Tenpō reforms, this *tozama* fief bought modern arms from foreigners, including advanced rifles left over from the American Civil War.

When the shogunate, hoping to chastise Chōshū in 1867 for its continuing anti-Tokugawa activities, called on other domains for help, several key domains, particularly Satsuma and Tosa, ignored the call. Having made a secret alliance with Chōshū, brokered by the Tosa samurai Sakamoto Ryōma in 1866, these domains let the Tokugawa go down to military defeat. Sakamoto, originally an antiforeign, anti-Tokugawa *shishi*, had made a 180-degree ideological reversal in 1862, when a man he was attempting to assassinate, the Tokugawa naval modernizer Katsu Kaishū, persuaded him modernization was necessary. In 1867, Sakamoto worked out another deal, this time between Tosa and the shogunate, to replace the shogunate with a government based on a bicameral legislature. Satsuma and Chōshū wanted more, however, and captured Kyoto, surrounding the emperor and persuading him to declare an imperial "restoration" on January 3, 1868. The shogunal forces briefly resisted, but Katsu Kaishū surrendered. Shogunal loyalists continued insurrections for another year and a half, and 3,000 men died in these fights, but one of the world's major shifts in power and political paradigm, the Meiji Restoration (see p. 174), happened with surprisingly little bloodshed.

DIASPORAS

JAPAN

A handful of Japanese sailors and fishermen attempted in the last years of the shogunate to break the Tokugawa law that forbade any Japanese to return after a foreign sojourn. These trips were unintentional and not part of a diasporic wave, but they broke the barrier against migration and set the stage for later diasporas. Two of the returnees served as translators and intercultural bridge-builders at crucial times. Yamamoto Otokichi (1818–1867) of Onoura, a crew member on a cargo ship, and Manjirō (see p. 166), a fisherman, both sailed at age 14, were blown hopelessly off course, and took advantage of their experiences—especially their knowledge of English—to succeed in the rapidly changing world of the late Tokugawa. Unlike Manjirō, Otokichi remained abroad, married two non-Japanese women (first an Englishwoman, then a Malay), and created himself as John M. Ottoson, a British citizen. Disguised as a Chinese and fabricating a story that he had learned Japanese from his father, a Chinese trader in Nagasaki, Otokichi served as translator for the negotiation of England's first treaty with Japan.

CHINA

As the opium trade from British India to China grew rapidly, so did the tax-farming operations of Chinese *kongsi* in Southeast Asia. The numerous Chinese planters, plantation workers, miners, farmers, shopkeepers, transport workers, and sailors in the region used opium as heavily as their counterparts in southern China, and Chinese *kongsi* paid rent to various governments to operate "opium farms"—not sites of production but rather the right to tax opium sales. These powerful corporations controlled entire economic systems—they recruited labor to operate plantations or mines, they taxed the opium sold to their workers, and they ran gambling houses, thus ensuring that their workers' wages would be recycled into their own hands. Some smaller *kongsi* offered shares of the corporation rather than wages to workers to encourage their retention and loyalty, but the larger *kongsi* employed only wage-laborers. Especially in the Malay Peninsula and the rising British colony of Singapore (founded in 1819), the Chinese *kongsi* constituted a driving force of both economic growth and state expansion, bringing in large numbers of laborers and generating tax revenues and products for international trade.

Meanwhile, Guangdong—not only the Guangzhou Delta but also Shantou (Swatow) and the Hakka regions—and Fujian continued to produce surplus population. Well connected to international labor markets, Chinese merchants could provide indentured laborers, "coolies" (originally an Indian word), to work all over the world. The prohibition of the slave trade by the British in 1807, followed by the abolition of slavery within the British empire in 1833, created large demands for low-wage, efficient labor; and many European officials and merchants believed that Chinese coolies could fill the gap.

Unfortunately, the coolies did not receive much better treatment than their African predecessors. Chained, whipped, underfed, and transported under appalling conditions, their plight attracted the attention of the Qing government in Beijing as well as humanitarian Europeans. Merchants also emigrated from southern China to Latin America, Hawaii, and North America, where they traded primarily in Chinese goods and also found places in the local economy, laying the foundations for more emigration later in the century. The merchants continued to rely on secret societies, such as the Heaven and Earth Society, for protection and enforcement in their communities. These brotherhoods had long histories in southern China, including political traditions of anti-Manchu, pro-Ming violence.

At mid-century, tens of thousands of Chinese flooded to California (1848), and then to Australia (1851), when news arrived of gold strikes. Sometimes recruited as laborers but more often acting as independent miners, over 20,000 Chinese from the west side of Guangzhou Bay arrived in San Francisco in 1852 alone. The oldest functioning Chinese lineage temple in the United States is located not in San Francisco's Chinatown but in tiny Weaverville, California, near one of the gold fields, where as many as 600 Chinese lived in the late nineteenth century. In the 1850s, Chinese made up one-quarter of the population of Victoria colony, in southern Australia. This huge outflow of population created intimate relationships between villages, towns, and regions in southern China and far-flung parts of the world. It generated both wealth and conflict, because many local populations—whether Malays, Irish Californians, or Afro-Cubans—resented the presence among them of the apparently exclusive, impenetrable, and (above all) low-wage Chinese workers' communities.

As the gold fields played out, American capital found a new function for the Chinese workers. In 1861, construction began on the western end of the transcontinental railroad, and the railroad companies found that imported Irish laborers had neither the skills nor the stamina for the arduous mountain and desert conditions. Chinese did, and by the end of the project, over 14,000 Chinese worked for the Central Pacific—as laborers, dynamiters, tunnelers, cooks, and more—though at a very high cost, for more than 1,200 died along the way.

Australians, like Americans and others, often reacted violently against the Chinese—in Lambing Flat (New South Wales), white miners killed several Chinese miners and drove the rest away (1861), in the first of many anti-Chinese riots all over the world. Racism (especially fear of racial mixing) and economic rivalry provided motivation for savagery, and the Chinese retreated into their closed (and hated) settlements, Chinatowns, from Sydney to San Francisco and London.

CONNECTIONS

Historians describe all three East Asian cultures as partaking of the "early modern" phase of world history. *Social change* lies at the heart of this characterization, as do the innovative methods created to solve the problems generated by unprecedented population growth, economic growth, the rise of new classes, and the degeneration of old social boundaries. East Asia shared some of these developments with Western Europe and North America, while others seem more local in nature.

Certainly the decline of slavery in Korea, the rise of rural productivity in Japan, and an increase in the power of merchants in China all point to crucial social transformations. These trends had many positive outcomes, such as laying the groundwork for the development of modern societies in the twentieth century. But contemporaries could only notice that they were often handled badly by the state. In company with many other factors, they led to an escalation of violence in society, usually led by lower-level and disempowered elites, culminating in such upheavals as the Eight Trigrams, Taiping, and Tonghak uprisings and movements led by people like Hong Kyŏngnae and Ōshio Heihachirō. While not violent, Japan's *eejanaika* world renewal movements also rejected established authority. All of these uprisings shared a target—the existing state and its official elites—and a common ambition, to make the world a better place by reorganizing its hierarchies of power. At the same time, members of the elite took advantage of rising literacy to write popular fiction satirizing the condition of the world or imagining a better one.

One common elite reaction to societal change came in a non-violent form— "practical learning," a refocus of intellectual energy away from philosophical speculation and toward the everyday problems of society such as agriculture, public health, economics, and famine relief. Practical learning certainly prepared some members of the elite for the onslaught of European science and techniques toward century's end. It also increased rural productivity through sharing of advanced techniques, lowered mortality rates through smallpox vaccination, and allowed for more accurate mapping of the various realms, among many other advances. Another reaction to changing expectations came in the rise of Roman Catholicism in Korea, stimulated by Jesuit texts translated into Chinese and brought to the peninsula by returning tribute missions. Although Christianity remained illegal in Japan, the coming of European books inspired a small group of scholars to learn Dutch, then other foreign languages, to participate in the international world of scholarship and knowledge beyond classical Chinese.

The arrival of European power in East Asia fell heavily on all three cultures—first China, then Japan, then Korea. The foreign merchants of Guangzhou, originally only a marginal group of "ocean barbarians," began to have a powerful impact on the Qing economy when opium shipments reversed the balance of payments and created an environment of increased corruption and drug addiction in southern China. Inadequate official response and British victories over the Qing warned both Chosŏn and the Tokugawa that something new and dangerous had arrived. Perry's "black ships" in 1853 and the Chosŏn "disturbances of 1866" brought the East Asian states into direct confrontation with Europeans and Americans. Eventually, all three countries had no choice but to sign unequal treaties with foreigners, losing both sovereignty and a measure of domestic control.

CHAPTER SIX

TRADITIONALIST REFORMS AND THE ORIGINS OF MODERNITY (1860s–1895)

WORLD CONTEXT

The second half of the nineteenth century saw the imperialist countries of Europe and North America expand their realms to unprecedented size and power. Great Britain's victory over the Indian Mutiny in 1857 consolidated its hold on the subcontinent, and the completion of the Suez Canal in 1869 enabled European steamships to reach maritime Asia in weeks, rather than the months required to sail around Africa. The European nations negotiated their "scramble for Africa" at the Berlin Conference (1884–88), where they simultaneously condemned slavery and carved Africa into imperial zones. The African slave trade gradually faded, though horrific racial violence continued both in Africa and its diasporas.

After defeating the Mutiny, Great Britain found the Indian jewel in its crown threatened by rapid Russian expansion. After 1861 Russian troops conquered the Caucasus, Khiva, Bukhara, and Kokand, giving the czar's realm a long and porous frontier with Persia and Afghanistan. Thus began the "Great Game" of rivalry between Great Britain and Russia, played out from the Mediterranean to the Qing frontiers.

The Ottomans, on the ropes in the face of imperialist (especially Russian) encroachments, attempted European-style reforms, such as the founding of banks and a modern army. An elite society of bureaucrats and intellectuals, the Young Ottomans, advocated a constitutional monarchy and parliamentary government, but their empire continued to contract. Cyprus went to Britain in exchange for British support against the Russians, and the Ottoman center steadily lost power in the face of local nationalisms.

In the United States, the federal government and industrial capitalism both received a tremendous boost from victory in the Civil War (1861–65). After the purchase and absorption of California from Mexico

(1849), the agricultural settlement of the Midwest, and the completion of the transcontinental railroad (1869), Americans moved out into the Pacific. Hawaii became a site of profitable plantations, with labor provided by imported Chinese then Japanese and Korean field-hands. The planters' influence in Washington resulted in gradual compromise of the Hawaiian monarchy and annexation (1898).

Imperialism and capitalism generated their own opposition. Indian and other colonized elites, educated in European languages and acculturated to European ways, began slow processes of agitation for independence. Initially supporting British rule, the Indian National Congress (1885) demanded a greater role in government for British-educated Indians. Within Europe and America, the socialist ideas of thinkers such as Karl Marx (1818–1883) and Friedrich Engels (1820–1895) inspired radical political activists, some calling for an end to colonial empires. Organizations such as the International Workingmen's Association (1864) demanded more equal distribution of wealth and land, elimination of capitalist exploitation, and other revolutionary changes.

Responding to the success of Britain, France, and the United States as centralized nation-states, rising elites in Italy and Germany (along with Japan, as we shall see) created strong central governments to replace looser affiliations of statelets. Concerned for their own security and eager to catch up with the advanced empires, these new powers challenged the existing order in both politics and industrial production, setting the stage for World War I.

Nationalism—whether imperial or reacting against imperialism—played a crucial role throughout this period. Inspired by economic change and uncertainty, by national newspapers, by conscription into national armies, and by parliamentary elections, mass organizations emerged as important political actors. Some of them advocated change—the end of slavery or enfranchisement of the excluded—while others clung tenaciously to the status quo. All claimed the mantle of national loyalty, the obligation and right of *citizens* to participate in "our country." Entirely novel in many parts of the world, where political activity had been limited to elites, nationalism became both a powerful agent of change and a weapon in the hands of politicians who advertised patriotism and loyal martyrdom as noble aspirations.

Religion, especially Protestant and Roman Catholic Christianity, constituted an integral part of this nationalistic philosophy, as missionaries from Europe and North America spread their faiths and national cultures to every inhabited corner of the planet. Women participated eagerly in this "benevolent imperialism," for missionary work, like nursing, social work, and teaching, enabled females to build professional careers. Women's education grew in availability and quality. In the United States, Mary Lyon founded Mount Holyoke Female Seminary in 1837, followed by the rest of the "Seven Sisters" women's colleges between 1861 and 1889. At the other end of the social scale, women from poor, often immigrant families found employment in factories and joined with men in the escalating conflict between labor and capital common to all the industrializing economies.

The domestic, national, and imperial rivalries of this period gave rise to competition in science and technology. Like the Napoleonic wars half a century before, the American Civil War served as a stimulus and testing ground for many new inventions, most dramatic being that of steam-powered, ironclad, floating gun platforms such as the *Monitor* and *Merrimack*. These primitive ships rapidly gave way to more massive weapons, ancestors of the modern battleship.

Gasoline-powered internal combustion engines began their world-changing transportation revolution—the automobile and the Wright brothers' airplane (1903)—so explorers searched for petroleum from Pennsylvania to the Caspian Sea to the Dutch East Indies. Communication improved through the laying of international telegraph cables, both on land and underwater, to connect the world's cities in a network of almost instantaneous message exchange.

Non-military science also progressed rapidly, including discovery of X-rays (Roentgen); tabulation of the periodic table of the elements (Mendeleev); formalization of natural selection as the mechanism of evolution (Darwin); antisepsis (Lister) based on the germ theory (Pasteur); and isolation of the microorganisms responsible for rabies, tuberculosis, and cholera. International languages—French, English, German, and Italian—linked intellectuals in many cultures, and learned societies diffused new knowledge through journals and conferences.

Ironically, this rational science grew in parallel with the irrational power of racism. By the 1890s, *Plessy v.*

Ferguson had erased the gains of Reconstruction in the United States; legal segregation and white supremacy triumphed; and the 13th, 14th, and 15th Amendments to the Constitution became dead letters for African Americans. Social Darwinism, inaccurately applying Darwin's biological insights to human groups (usually called "races"), became both fashionable and "scientific" throughout Europe and North America. Through the works of scholars such as sociologist Herbert Spencer (1820–1903), the racial "survival of the fittest" arguments became international and obvious truths, explaining the power of "white" Europeans and Americans to dominate the planet, control nature, and win all the wars.

JAPAN'S MEIJI TRANSFORMATION

Victorious anti-Tokugawa forces, primarily samurai from four domains—Satsuma, Chōshū, Tosa, and Hizen—plus some sympathizers in the court of the emperor, emerged as the leaders of "Japan" when they proclaimed the Meiji Restoration on January 3, 1868. "Japan" did not yet exist as a nation-state but only as an imagined country under the emperor, now nominally restored to the power lost with the rise of shoguns in the twelfth century. The term "restoration" originally referred to the Chinese pattern in which a weakening dynasty reasserted its authority, but Japan's 1868 version was different, focusing on the use of the emperor as a rallying point for the new government.

The Tokugawa balance of power between *daimyō* and shogun and the socio-political structure based on statuses had both been eroding for decades, though they were still intact when Commodore Perry arrived in 1853. The shogunate's subsequent unequal treaties with the United States and European countries unleashed 15 years of turmoil: resistance by farmers whose livelihoods were ruined by unrestricted foreign trade; ideological harangues against Tokugawa control that evolved into a pro-emperor policy; antiforeign activism; ecstatic religious movements; and military opposition by *daimyō* and samurai long resentful of Tokugawa supremacy.

Although the 1868 leadership group was small and composed overwhelmingly of samurai, the fact that so many others desired change—including religious movements that called for "healing the world" (J. *yonaoshi*)—set the stage for the momentous transformation of the next three decades. Diverse proponents of solutions to the question of governance; advocates and opponents of modernization; supporters of changes in Japan's relations with Asia and the rest of the world; and enthusiasts of foreign cultures, arts, and technologies all expressed themselves in the late nineteenth century. For the first time, one did not have to be an official to voice an opinion. At the same time, government authorities severely limited free speech, and many people struggled for the right to contribute to public discussions.

Most Japanese, as most people everywhere, did not actively involve themselves in protests, government, or revolutionizing culture. But by the 1890s, even the politically inactive did not think it inappropriate that other people might do so. Was this a revolution? Or, as some historians contend, did the changes carried out by the leaders of the early Meiji years represent an "aristocratic revolution"—that is, a revolution by a single social group who discarded their hereditary privileges to create a modern Japan able to withstand Western imperialism? Or were the enormous strides toward modernity in education, economy, law, social status, and foreign policy themselves the real Meiji revolution?

Historians have spilled much ink debating whether the early Meiji transformation constituted a revolution and if so, of what type—the unleashing of ongoing, unpredictable change certainly may be called revolutionary. Many have compared the Meiji changes with European models, particularly the French Revolution referenced by Karl Marx, who defined revolution in terms of discrete stages. As this chapter will show, change always generated conflict, while progress and repression often turned out to be two sides of the same coin. Japan's bumpy road toward modernity in the late nineteenth century might be called a multifaceted revolution, but using European models to describe it obscures the enormous and often contradictory changes that occurred in Japan.

At the beginning of the new era, the leadership group was young, bold, and mostly samurai. Some scholars claim the Meiji leaders' dismantling of their

RIGHT Japan in the Meiji period (1868–1912)

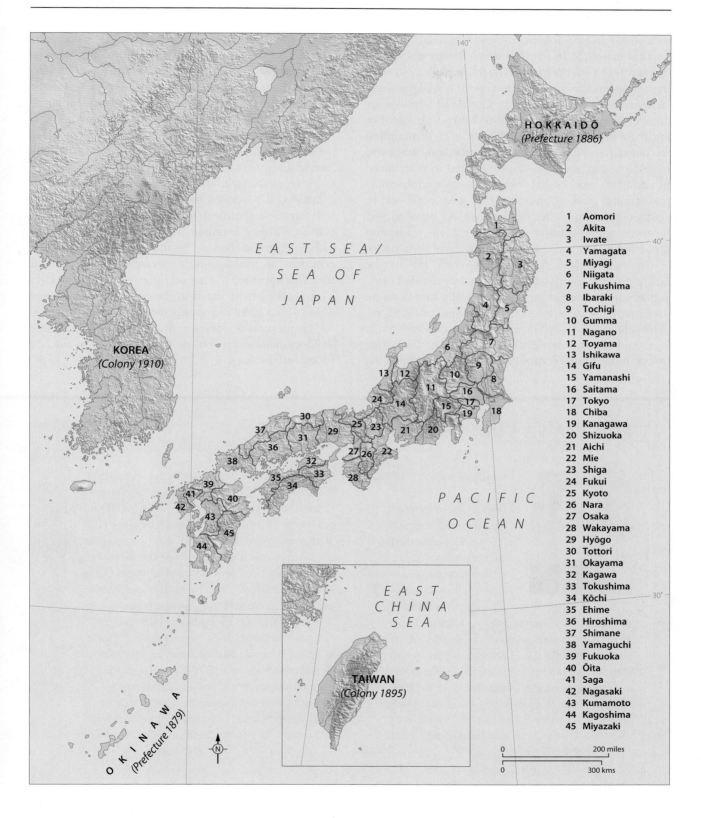

HOKKAIDŌ
(Prefecture 1886)

EAST SEA/
SEA OF
JAPAN

KOREA
(Colony 1910)

PACIFIC
OCEAN

EAST
CHINA
SEA

TAIWAN
(Colony 1895)

O K I N A W A
(Prefecture 1879)

N

1   Aomori
2   Akita
3   Iwate
4   Yamagata
5   Miyagi
6   Niigata
7   Fukushima
8   Ibaraki
9   Tochigi
10 Gumma
11 Nagano
12 Toyama
13 Ishikawa
14 Gifu
15 Yamanashi
16 Saitama
17 Tokyo
18 Chiba
19 Kanagawa
20 Shizuoka
21 Aichi
22 Mie
23 Shiga
24 Fukui
25 Kyoto
26 Nara
27 Osaka
28 Wakayama
29 Hyōgo
30 Tottori
31 Okayama
32 Kagawa
33 Tokushima
34 Kōchi
35 Ehime
36 Hiroshima
37 Shimane
38 Yamaguchi
39 Fukuoka
40 Ōita
41 Saga
42 Nagasaki
43 Kumamoto
44 Kagoshima
45 Miyazaki

0   200 miles

0   300 kms

own status group's Tokugawa-period ruling-class privileges was unique in world history. But in fact, rulers frequently change the rules of the political game in ways that appear to alter their previous positions of privilege. Moreover, the top Meiji leaders retained prestige for decades after 1868 and did not feel they were sacrificing their samurai privileges. Rather, after dismantling the old status system they could pursue commerce and manufacturing, areas previously limited to merchants. In addition, many hailed from lower- or middle-ranking samurai backgrounds, so they had not been in Tokugawa ruling circles in any case. As we shall see, however, some samurai outside the Meiji leadership group did violently resist the elimination of their status.

The young leaders' formidable task lay in the creation of a nation-state from a society divided horizontally into status groups and vertically into separate domains, all loosely linked under the shogun. With remarkable speed, they undertook political, economic, legal, and cultural changes, both to enhance their control of the imagined community that would become the nation and to strengthen the new state in the competitive international context of the late nineteenth century. These transformations brought average Japanese into new relationships with the rest of East Asia through trade and imperialism. The history of Japan's modernizing state cannot be disengaged from events in East Asia and the world.

Domestically, the changing relationship of Japan's men and women to the evolving state was perhaps even more revolutionary. The new "Japan" was created as a "nation," a governing system defined, in early modern European political theory, as coterminous with culture, identity, language, and ethnicity. "The nation" had emerged in Europe in the sixteenth–eighteenth centuries as the dominant governmental form and therefore appeared the logical form to Japanese seeking to strengthen their realm in the dangerous conditions of the 1860s. Like Europeans before the modern period, Japanese were not naturally nationalistic but came to adopt nation-centered politics and ideas in the late nineteenth century.

FUKUZAWA YUKICHI

Fukuzawa Yukichi, c. 1890s.

Emblematic of the Meiji era, Fukuzawa Yukichi (1835–1901) embodied characteristics valued by today's Japanese. Fukuzawa also represented Meiji Japan as a complicated man whose development did not follow a simple trajectory. Although known for his credo that "Heaven does not create one man above or below another man," he also denied the "lowly folk" entrance to Keiō, the university he founded in 1868. While the People's Rights Movement praised his *Outline of a Theory of Civilization*, which called for rights, civic responsibilities, and rule by intelligent leadership, he also applauded the government's repression of that movement's most radical voices. He influenced Korean modernizers like Kim Okkyun in the 1870s, but rejected Asia in his 1885 essay, "Discourse on Abandoning Asia," and jingoistically cheered Japan's 1895 victory over the Qing. His *New Greater Learning for Women* inspired generations of feminists, but he educated his daughters to be wives of gentlemen while sending his sons to Ivy League colleges.

Was Fukuzawa as contradictory as he seems? Fukuzawa had chafed at the education he observed as a child in a lower samurai family in the 1840s. He resented the privileges of those of higher rank, blaming discrimination on Neo-Confucianism. When his elder brother gave him the chance to study Dutch learning (*J. Rangaku*) in 1855, he leapt enthusiastically into his Dutch language and culture

The government of the new "Japan" resulted from the Meiji Restoration—the event that defined the emperor as the head of a nation-state encompassing old Tokugawa lands, former *daimyō* lands, and eventually Hokkaidō, the Ryūkyū Islands, and Japanese colonies and mandates. Like Chinese and Koreans, the Japanese count time by their emperors' reign-names, so the era from the Restoration until the Meiji Emperor's death—1868 to 1912—was called the "Meiji period" (see p. 42).

The Meiji leaders initiated critical nation-building projects in the first two decades of the Meiji period. They had to develop a sense of nationhood by creating and disseminating a "national" history, and they redefined relationships among men and women and the various social classes by casting off the rigid status structures of the Tokugawa era. Confronting the challenges of the unequal treaty system, Meiji leaders altered Japan's relations with the West and the rest of East Asia and selected among Western and indigenous models for military, educational, legal, religious, and artistic reform. Because their goal of "rich country and strong army" required modern industrial, financial, and commercial systems and an infrastructure of harbors, roads, and railroads, the youthful Meiji leaders began the development of Japan's modern economy.

Through stages both planned and unanticipated, most Japanese came to embrace modernity, with its positive and negative elements. The Japan of 1895 would have been unrecognizable even to the most creative dreamer of 1868. As British writer Basil Hall Chamberlain, who lived in Japan for 30 years, noted:

> To have lived through the transition stage of modern Japan makes a man feel preternaturally old; for here he is in modern times, with the air full of talk about bicycles and bacilli and 'spheres of influence,' and yet he can himself distinctly remember the Middle Ages. The dear old Samurai who first initiated the present writer into the mysteries of the Japanese language wore a queue and two swords. This relic of feudalism now sleeps in Nirvana.[1]

studies. His exposure to the post-Perry Euro-American settlement at Yokohama in the late 1850s convinced him to switch to English. Fukuzawa's youthful rejection of Confucianism for its encouragement of inequality has been viewed as progressive, while his disappointment that the Chosŏn and Qing monarchies did not quickly adopt Western learning has been viewed as imperialistic.

Modernity and progressivism were Fukuzawa's key interests. He sailed with the first Japanese steamship to the United States in 1860 and joined the translation staff of Japan's first diplomatic expedition to Europe in 1862. He used these trips as opportunities to learn about foreign customs and institutions, publishing his observations as *Conditions in the West* in 1867. A supporter of the reforms the Tokugawa had initiated in their last years, Fukuzawa's low profile during the Restoration allowed him to emerge as a progressive leader whom the Meiji leaders invited, unsuccessfully, to join the new government.

For Fukuzawa, education should first promote practical learning. It had a long history, but Fukuzawa intended a decidedly non-Confucian meaning. He wanted primary school students to learn reading, writing, and arithmetic to be able to fulfill ordinary human needs, and later learn history, geography, ethics, physics, and economics to maintain their own independence and that of their nation. In the course of their learning, students would develop public and personal virtue. Fukuzawa failed to see that his form of progressivism and education, used to strengthen Japan and the Japanese individual, could also lead to jingoism and imperialism, as they did in the modern West.

DRAFTING THE BLUEPRINTS
FOR THE NEW ORDER

The first five years of the new regime set the stage for the radical changes deemed necessary to preserve Japan from foreign dominance in the following two decades. Although imperialism of the sort inflicted by European powers on the Qing no longer worried Japan's leaders by the early 1870s, other forms of humiliation inspired them to adopt changes to convince the Americans and Europeans to renegotiate the unequal treaties. They resented extraterritoriality and the continuing economic distress caused by foreign control of Japan's international trade. They were insulted by foreign sailors' claims that Japanese prostitutes carried diseases and therefore had to be subjected to medical exams. They were angered by the inability of Japanese medical authorities to keep out a cholera epidemic, introduced by an American seaman in 1858, that killed several hundred thousand Japanese.

But would adopting European ways to achieve respect also destroy Japan's identity? While some Japanese held that point of view, others advocated "civilization and enlightenment" (J. *bunmei kaika*), viewing change as *modernization* rather than as *Westernization*. The latter consciously borrowed foreign texts, ideologies, technologies, and methods, just as their ancestors had borrowed and indigenized Chinese texts, ideas, and technologies until those Chinese ideas came to be seen as an obstacle, after which they were reidentified as foreign (Chinese) and rejected.

Advocates of "civilization and enlightenment" intended Western borrowings to contribute to creating a Japanese nation, the new word for which was *kokka* (literally, "nation-family"). One of these characters (*ka*, family) paralleled the concept of shared ethnicity theorized by European scholars as the basis for the modern nation-state and Social Darwinian racism. But in Japan, "family" suggested more than shared ethnicity; it also implied a mixed-gender, communal group of individuals. Each of these interrelated concepts—community, individual, and gender—entered into the formation of the modern Japanese nation-state. Modernization, its advocates stressed, would allow the nation-family to survive.

Japan experienced a whirlwind of change from 1868 to the mid-1870s. The young samurai directing those changes came from Satsuma (Saigō Takamori, Ōkubo Toshimichi, Matsukata Masayoshi), Chōshū (Kido Kōin, Yamagata Aritomo, Itō Hirobumi), Tosa (Itagaki Taisuke), and Hizen (Ōkuma Shigenobu), and included a prince of the emperor's court (Iwakura Tomomi). Though not part of the government, private individuals like Fukuzawa Yukichi (see pp. 176–77) also helped to frame these changes.

In 1868, the leaders asserted the centrality of the new emperor-centered government by physically moving the young Meiji Emperor from Kyoto to Edo, and renaming it Tokyo ("eastern capital"). Although Tokyo was not officially designated the capital until 1889, all administrative functions now emanated from one center rather than two. The emperor, initially represented as a "perfumed Mikado" in ancient court dress, a style interpreted by Westerners as effeminate, by 1873 was depicted in an official photograph wearing the military uniform of a European king, "arrayed," according to historian Theodore Cook, "in the symbols used to endow Western monarchs with emblematic competency and dynastic virility."

In March 1869, the new leaders persuaded the *daimyō* of several domains to bring their lands under central government control in exchange for a generous fee and the right to continue ruling those lands. Two years later, the Meiji government rescinded that right and converted all domains to prefectures with governors appointed by Tokyo. Thus, they replaced the vertical political divisions of Tokugawa Japan—the shogunate and domains—with direct central rule.

The leadership group both solidified the emperor's claim to political legitimacy and developed the framework for the rapid changes to come by issuing the Charter Oath in March 1868. Although just broad objectives, the five articles of the Charter Oath set the stage for more specific public policies and encouraged enthusiastic responses by non-governmental reformers:

> By this oath we set up as our aim the establishment of the national weal on a broad basis and the framing of a constitution and laws.
> 1. *Deliberative assemblies shall be widely established and all matters decided by public discussion.*
> 2. *All classes, high and low, shall unite vigorously in carrying out the administration of affairs of state.*
> 3. *The common people, no less than the civil and military officials, shall each be allowed to*

pursue their own calling so that there may be no discontent.

4. *Evil customs of the past shall be broken off and everything based on the just laws of Nature.*

5. *Knowledge shall be sought throughout the world so as to strengthen the foundation of imperial rule.*

IMPLEMENTING THE CHARTER OATH: CONSTRUCTING A NEW NATION

The government acted on the first article a few months later, creating a short-lived bicameral National Deliberative Assembly. Although another decade would pass before the establishment of new deliberative bodies and two decades before the seating of a national parliament, called the "Diet" in English, the government took the first steps toward creating a consultative body to decide matters by public discussion. In 1868, they established a Council of State and appointed themselves to the top posts. Reorganized in 1869 and 1871, the Council of State was staffed by men with personal connections to the ruling clique. In 1885 it was replaced with a Cabinet derived from European models, including a prime minister and ministers who headed functionally defined ministries—foreign affairs, finance, public works, and others. By the late 1880s, bureaucrats selected through impartial civil service examinations supplanted those who got their jobs through connections, a step toward substituting a merit-based system (*meritocracy*) for the Tokugawa status-based (*aristocracy*) order.

The third article of the Charter Oath underlay all the other changes. Male individuals were to be free to "pursue their own calling." The leaders decided that rule through horizontal status groups, which had characterized the Tokugawa state, prevented not only the vigorous unification of "all classes, high and low… in carrying out the administration of affairs of state" (Article 2), but also the formation of a centralized state whose authority reached directly to every Japanese.

The leaders eliminated the status system both to allow samurai and other Japanese to pursue more lucrative professions and, more immediately important, to save the government money. The continuing payment of stipends to the samurai consumed half the revenues of the financially strapped government. In 1873, the government offered samurai a voluntary deal—to exchange their annual stipends for interest-bearing bonds. When few took the offer, the government made the program mandatory in 1876. The samurai did not benefit from this exchange, and many fell into poverty. Around the same time, the government prohibited the wearing of swords. The double blow to the samurai ego was more than some could bear. Although most chose to enter new professions, some turned against the new government in spectacular rebellions.

In 1873, yet another government decision fueled samurai resistance. Concern about Japan's strategic vulnerability and irritation that the Europeans and Americans refused to revise the unequal treaties led to a desire to develop a modern military. Yamagata Aritomo (1838–1922) and Kido Kōin (1833–1877)—whose experiences in Chōshū during the pre-Restoration struggles and observation of European military might convinced them of the value of conscript armies—prevailed on their colleagues to institute compulsory military service for Japanese males. But many of those newly subject to the draft, called the "blood tax," erupted in anger—thousands of rioters attacked registration centers in 1873 and 1874—and samurai bemoaned their loss of prestige when they had to share their unique right to bear arms with "dirt farmers."

And yet, a surprisingly small percentage of young Japanese men—fewer than 5 percent of those eligible before the Sino-Japanese War in 1894–95 and about 10 percent of those eligible after that war—were actually drafted. Despite these small numbers, contemporary Japanese political observers remarked on the growth of soldiers' commitment to the larger Japanese society and their demands for citizenship rights, while foreign commentators praised Japan for making a transition from "effeminacy" to masculine martial discipline. Whether any of these observations reflected reality is debatable, but they linked the construction of Japanese masculinity through the military draft to the construction of the political system and to the carrying out of foreign relations.

The institution of compulsory public education, an attempt to strengthen Japan and further the policy of eliminating status groups, also generated conflict. In 1872, the state mandated four years of elementary education for boys and girls and created a sex-segregated system of middle and secondary schools and universities for boys, and less academic middle and secondary schools for girls. Limited funds initially made the provision of elementary schools for all children impossible, and higher schools were only gradually constructed over the next several decades. The government ordered schools to teach *practical* subjects to all children. This meant, for boys, science, math, Japanese language, history, and ethics. Girls studied these subjects for somewhat fewer hours per week, as compulsory sewing classes took time away from more academic subjects.

Not all educators agreed on the practicality of sewing classes. Tsuda Umeko (1864–1929), for one, stressed English-language training and science as important tools for women to serve society. One of five girls selected in 1871 to study in the United States, Tsuda, 6 years old when placed in an American family, returned to Japan a dedicated educator. By that time, the government's attitude toward women's education had shifted to an emphasis on creating "good wives and wise mothers," the Japanese counterpart of America's nineteenth-century "republican mothers," who should train their sons to become productive citizens of the new nation.

Tsuda's interest in science, religion, and language no longer fit the government model for education of girls, so she created a private school, now Tsuda College, to train women rigorously in the English language. Tsuda contended that developing the individual abilities of women was just; in addition, it served a practical use for the community of the nation. Like her counterparts in the government, Tsuda believed in both practicality and service to the nation; she differed from them in arguing that women could contribute through careers, not only as wives and mothers.

While many children and their parents were thrilled to be able to pursue an education, viewing it as the route to personal opportunity as well as "civilization and enlightenment," others resisted sending their economically valuable children to school and paying the 10 percent tax surcharge to fund local education. Rioters burned thousands of schools. During the 1870s, more than half of all school-age children, some too poor to pay for books and uniforms but others passively resisting the government decree, failed to attend school. The lack of teachers and buildings at that time meant that local authorities could not force them to do so. But by the end of the 1890s, 98 percent of boys and 93 percent of girls did attend, and the state had, to some extent, fulfilled its ideal of a well-educated, well-disciplined populace.

The impact of educating the entire population was enormous. A literate workforce increased productivity. The state could directly convey the responsibilities of imperial subjects to a literate public. Educated men and women could, conversely, demand rights of citizenship, something feared by opponents of universal education early on. Literacy, coupled with new printing technologies that hastened the development of newspapers and magazines, allowed Japanese to transcend regionalism and connect with like-minded people elsewhere. Education permitted Japanese to seek out and contribute to knowledge throughout the world, as mandated in Article 5 of the Charter Oath.

THE NEW JAPANESE SUBJECT

If a person was not subject to a *daimyō* and a member of a status group, what was he or she? In a modern democracy, the state defines that individual as a *citizen*, a term that implies the possession of rights, including the right to protection as a member of the national community and the right to exercise the same political rights granted other citizens. In some cases, those rights are assumed to be unconditional and inherent in the individual, although many countries have granted rights of citizenship based on service to the nation, such as military service in eighteenth- and nineteenth-century Europe. This service differentiated men (even those who had not done military service), who held full citizenship, from women and children, who held only nationality. In Japan, unlike Europe, military service did not constitute the key to male citizenship, however, as limits on male voting rights existed until 1925—and even then, Japanese military men were not entitled to vote. Japanese women in feminist movements in the late nineteenth and early twentieth centuries used the arguments developed in Europe and the United States to advocate for unconditional rights, but they, too, failed to obtain full citizenship rights until the mid-twentieth century.

Both men and women did earn the right to nationality defined by *subjecthood*, a status that stressed responsibilities more than rights. Under the Meiji government, all Japanese were subjects of the emperor, with rights of nationality modified by gender and ethnicity. In preparation for the military draft, the government defined Japanese nationality as enrollment in the family registration system (J. *koseki*). The family registration system included some minority groups, such as a Korean community in southern Kyūshū that maintained its own language and customs, or the Ainu in recently annexed Hokkaidō. It excluded some others, which suggests a variety of approaches to a multicultural Japan in the Meiji period—the myth of a homogenous Japan had not yet been constructed. Although Japan annexed the Ryūkyū Islands in 1879, their male inhabitants had to wait until 1898 to be eligible for conscription—one sign of full recognition of Japanese nationality—and until 1911 for the vote, which had been granted to a segment of Japan's male population in 1890.

The problem of inclusion in the state would continue to be debated as Japan developed its empire (see p. 210). Clearly, ending the policy of defining people by status opened a Pandora's box as the fledgling "nation-family" struggled to classify who had the right to family membership (that is, nationality) in light of diverse ethnicities and gender. Every imperial country—and Meiji Japan was no exception—must confront the issue of who may be included within "us," and who must remain part of "them."

PLANTING THE SEEDS FOR ECONOMIC MODERNITY

The Charter Oath also raised the issue of the promotion of the "national weal," that is, of economic development. In Tokugawa times, commerce had been officially disdained, although neither officials nor commoners consistently treated commerce as degraded. It took a leap of faith in modernity for some former samurai, indoctrinated in the belief that public service was nobler than entrepreneurship, to become cheerleaders for economic development. Voyages to Europe and the United States had made converts of some key leaders. Fukuzawa Yukichi, whose travels to the West in 1860 inspired his bestseller, *Conditions in the West*, was one of many influential Meiji writers, reformers, educators, businessmen, and officials whose trips overseas, sponsored by their domains before 1868 or the Meiji government thereafter, inspired new attitudes toward economic modernity.

Lest supporting economic growth appear too innovative, Meiji modernizers used a slogan from the Chinese past, resurrected during the anti-Tokugawa struggles, to support their advocacy of development: "rich country, strong army." This slogan guided policy formation, becoming the single most characteristic ideological statement of the Meiji period. By the slogan's logic, military power had to be accompanied by economic development and commerce, cleansed of their former negative meanings by their centrality in building the nation and the state.

Following the disastrous currency outflow of the late 1850s and early 1860s, Japan temporarily benefited from a silkworm blight in Europe in 1868. Finished silk as well as silkworm cocoons found a ready foreign market at that time, but revenues appeared insufficient to build the economic infrastructure. Few Japanese had great personal wealth, and, until the 1880s, most remained reluctant to take major risks to develop businesses. So the government stepped in, building telegraph lines (1869), a postal service (1871), harbors and lighthouses, and the first Japanese railroad, a short line from Tokyo to Yokohama (1872). It paid foreign advisers princely salaries to establish university curricula and run production facilities. It invested in industrial production in textiles, ships, mining, munitions, and consumer goods like sugar and beer, building factories that could serve as demonstration facilities for entrepreneurs and workers before being sold off to privileged private investors, scandalously below cost, in 1881. The government played an important role in generating modern industry and guiding the economy in its early years, relinquishing most of that role, except weapons production, to the private sector by the end of the nineteenth century.

Mandatory public education, a conscript army, and state-funded economic development cost vast sums of money. Consumer goods like soy sauce, sugar, and alcoholic beverages were taxed, but the government had to craft a more comprehensive national taxation system. The creation of prefectures from fiscally autonomous domains constituted the first step to developing a nationwide system of taxes on agricultural property. Determining land values required land surveys, which brought individual farmers, not villages as before, into a direct relationship with the government. Fixed taxes gave the government predictable sources of income, transferring agricultural surplus to industries and making a national budget possible.

Not surprisingly, many farmers protested the land tax, and its implementation represented one cause of political activism in the 1870s. The tax obligation lay on the head of household, usually designated as the senior male. When involvement in local governance extended to tax-paying heads of households, some women claimed their right to participate. As early as 1878, the government denied Kusunose Kita (1833–1920), a 45-year-old widowed household head, her right to vote in local elections. Women's rights advocates, who dubbed her the "People's Rights Grandma," supported her claim that she should not be taxed without representation and decried the use of gender in determining an individual's relationship to the state.

JAPAN'S INTERNATIONAL POSITION AND THE IWAKURA MISSION

The Meiji government acted to develop a modern, centralized nation-state—as well as social policies like decriminalizing the practice of Christianity and forbidding laborers to work outdoors clad only in skimpy loincloths—in part to convince Americans and Europeans that Japan had earned the right to revise the unequal treaties of the 1850s. Modernization was the means to diplomatic equality. In 1871, the most powerful men in the government—Ōkubo Toshimichi (1830–1878), Kido Kōin, Itō Hirobumi (1841–1909), Iwakura Tomomi (1825–1823), and others—left Japan for an 18-month tour of Europe and America, with the dual goals of renegotiating the treaties and learning how to modernize public and private institutions. Although European and American governments rebuffed the delegation's request for treaty renegotiation, the Iwakura mission certainly cannot be considered a failure. Impressed by Western life and institutions—schools and universities, factories, power plants, governing bodies, military and police forces, literature, music, and the arts—the travelers met with a broad range of citizens and came away with a better understanding of European and American perspectives.

When the delegates heard that the officials left behind in Tokyo, led by Saigō Takamori (1828–1877), planned to send a military expedition to Chosŏn to force it to expand foreign trade (as Perry had done 20 years earlier in Japan), Ōkubo and Kido rushed home to derail the idea. They did not oppose Japan's extension of its authority abroad; indeed, while overseas they had learned the benefit and prestige of imperial expansion. Rather, they concluded that Japan should not pursue an aggressive foreign policy before completing reforms at home.

Their action to terminate the proposed attack on Chosŏn was abrupt, and Saigō, Itagaki Taisuke (1837–1919), and others were sore losers. Calling Ōkubo a dictator who thwarted the legitimate voice of the new Japanese citizenry, Saigō (from Satsuma) and Itagaki (from Tosa) both left the government. Despite their petulance, Ōkubo sought to placate those who demanded aggressive foreign action. Two years earlier, Taiwanese

Hiroshige III. *Western-style stone houses in Tokyo*, from the series "Famous Places on the Tokaidō: a Record of the Process of Reform," 1875. Only seven years after the Meiji Restoration opened the country to a flood of trade and ideas from the West, the streets are filled with carriages and rickshaws and people clothed in an amalgam of styles.

aborigines had killed a number of shipwrecked sailors and fishermen from the Ryūkyū Islands. Although nothing had been done on their behalf at the time, Ōkubo now soothed the restless samurai by forcing the Qing government to recognize the Ryūkyū Islands, no longer under Satsuma's trade supervision but still a Qing tributary ruled by an indigenous king, as Japanese territory.

Saigō's proposal to attack Chosŏn had grown as much from his concern to find work for legions of depressed samurai, itching to fight but now impoverished and de-sworded, as from interest in foreign adventurism. Ōkubo knew this, and sent 3,000 soldiers to Taiwan in 1874. More than 500 died of tropical diseases, and the Japanese forces had no major battlefield victories. But the Qing payment of a small reparation sealed Japan's claim to the Ryūkyūs under the terms of the European-style international law that Japan had adopted. Japan allowed the Ryūkyū king to continue his reign until 1879, when he was forced to abdicate and his territory became Okinawa prefecture of Japan. The Japanese government had also considered establishing a "civilizing mission" on Taiwan in the European colonial mode, but decided to put that plan on the back burner for fear that war with Qing would result.

REACTIONARY SAMURAI, PROGRESSIVE REFORMERS, AND THE OLIGARCHS

The Taiwan expedition, costly in human and monetary terms, failed to placate Itagaki and Saigō. Itagaki founded a number of organizations advocating popular participation that had long-term implications for modernity. In sharp contrast, Saigō responded with armed insurrection, the last gasp of samurai resistance. Not alone in rebelling—the new conscript army quashed several other samurai insurrections between 1874 and 1876—Saigō's role as an original member of the Meiji government made his rebellion the most significant. Saigō returned home to Kagoshima prefecture (formerly Satsuma) and opened a military academy to train soldiers in the old samurai ways. In the winter of 1877, he started toward Tokyo with 15,000 armed men, picking up additional troops along the way. His army, eventually numbering 40,000, attacked the government garrison in Kumamoto. In three weeks of brutal combat, Saigō's forces suffered 20,000 casualties. Their leader committed suicide rather than being taken captive by the army of "dirt farmers" that had defeated his samurai.

Other dissenters also attacked the Meiji and its reforms. Poverty led the newly poor, many of them destitute sharecroppers, to take part in rural riots. The growth of Japan's economy through most of the Meiji period was extremely uneven, so some regions and sectors benefited from participation in the global economy, while others suffered. The printing of paper money to cover the high cost of suppressing the Satsuma Rebellion led to massive inflation. Although inflation temporarily helped farmers, who paid taxes at fixed rates, it also threatened to choke off growth and investment. In response, Finance Minister Matsukata Masayoshi (1835–1924) instituted stringent deflationary policies in 1881. These revived the industrial economy but sent agricultural prices into free-fall, so millions of farmers lost everything.

Itagaki Taisuke's response to Ōkubo's actions in 1873 had established him as an early leader of the People's Rights Movement, which grew from many roots. The ideas of Jean-Jacques Rousseau and John Stuart Mill, two of many Western philosophers whose works had been translated by the 1870s, infused the thinking of advocates for human and civil rights. By reforming Japan's political and social systems to conform to European and American liberal ideals, progressive Japanese contended, they could not only create an ideal society but also allow Japan to claim equality with foreigners.

In 1873, the sixth year of the Meiji period, Fukuzawa Yukichi and other advocates of modernization created the Meiji Six Society and began publication of the most influential intellectual journal of the decade, the *Meiji Six Journal*. The pages of this journal bristled with commentary on civil rights, political philosophies, women's role in the new Japan, family life, styles and fashions, and other issues of modernity, ideology, and daily life. Most writers recognized the foreign origins of many of their comments, yet most had already naturalized them, believing that modernity should not be seen as unique to Europe and America but rather as a stage of evolution. Europe and the United States had only recently attained modernity, and Japan and other East Asian countries would soon join them. Along with an outpouring of newspapers—Japanese rights advocates believed strongly in the power of the press—*Meiji Six Journal* inspired People's Rights discussions.

Itagaki sought to form a political movement when he left the government in 1873. The following year he established the Patriotic Party (Aikoku Kōtō) as Japan's first people's rights party. For the rest of the decade, political groups emerged in urban and rural areas, and members turned to writing essays, journals, and even drafts of ideal constitutions for the new government. Most members were men, but noteworthy women participated as well.

The People's Rights Movement had political consequences. To the government—the anti-Tokugawa rebels of the 1860s who had become the ruling establishment of the late 1870s—the movement represented unruly mobs demanding press, speech, and even voting rights and that sovereignty be vested in the people rather than in a bureaucratic state headed by a monarch. In 1875, press censorship laws limited freedom of expression, and in 1884 Kishida Toshiko (1863–1901), an inspirational feminist orator and member of the People's Rights Movement, was arrested for publicly advocating women's rights. Similar cases of repression of speech and the press occurred throughout the 1870s and 1880s. Yamagata Aritomo, by this point a dyspeptic middle-aged politician, wrote in 1879 to Itō Hirobumi, later the primary author of the Meiji constitution, urging that the rulers write a constitution as soon as possible: "Every day we wait, the evil poison [of popular rights] will spread more and more over the provinces, penetrate into the minds of the young, and inevitably produce unfathomable evils."[2]

By 1881, more than a quarter million signatures had been submitted to the government demanding a constitutional convention. Two political parties, the Jiyūtō (Liberal Party), founded in 1881, and the Kaishintō (Progressive Party), established in 1882, called for a parliamentary government. Moreover, the government leaders themselves desired a constitution, as the Western countries that served as models for Japan all had such documents. In October 1881, the government promised a constitution within the decade. Itō and his team studied constitutional law in Western countries, eventually basing Japan's first modern constitution—and the first constitution outside Europe and America—on the conservative 1854 constitution of Prussia (after 1871 a part of Germany).

The Meiji constitution was presented to the people as a "gift" of the emperor in 1889, thereby removing any doubt about the source of sovereignty. Like the national histories of many nations, the constitution itself was an exercise in historical fabrication. Although just three decades separated the constitution from centuries of shogunal rule based on self-regulation by status groups, the preamble of the constitution erased that history to claim the emperor's eternal dominion: "The right of sovereignty of the State, We have inherited from Our Ancestors, and We shall bequeath it to Our descendents." The constitution also erased a history of women sovereigns by stipulating for the first time that the emperor must be male.

The constitution established a Diet with an elected House of Representatives and an appointed House of Peers; the aristocratic men in the latter house received titles in 1885 to qualify them for their seats. It set up a powerful bureaucracy and exempted the military from parliamentary oversight. The constitution included civil rights but stipulated that they could be limited by law. The Meiji government began creating those limits immediately, with a law prohibiting women from viewing Diet sessions. They rescinded this law under pressure, though thereafter they restricted women to an upper balcony. Only a year later, in 1890, another law prohibited women from attending political rallies or joining political parties, thereby denying them the rights of speech and assembly. Feminists associated with women's schools, feminist groups that sprang up in the 1880s, and a major national organization—the Women's Reform Society, founded as a branch of the international Women's Christian Temperance Union in 1886—suffered deep disappointment. Additional limitations on rights of assembly, speech, and the press would be implemented later.

Itō wrote the constitution in part to restrict popular sovereignty, but loopholes permitted clever politicians to expand political rights. The constitution made the Diet responsible for establishing voting qualifications, and over the next three decades they expanded the electorate from less than 1 percent of the population (only rich males) to most males. The Diet also had the duty of passing the annual budget, giving it the unexpectedly useful power of the purse. The Meiji constitution was, in the end, a pliable document, which could be used both to expand and to limit popular rights.

RELIGION, CULTURE, AND ARTS

Religion had been a contested realm in the Tokugawa. The shogunate had outlawed Christianity and relegated

Shintō to small local shrines. The early Meiji government repealed the anti-Christianity statutes, and missionaries poured into Japan. The Meiji constitution granted freedom of religion, but like other freedoms, it had to be exercised within "limits not prejudicial to peace and not antagonistic to duties as citizens." The number of Christians never exceeded 1 percent of the population, but their role as activists in social reform movements belied their numbers. The government also feared the hundreds of thousands of adherents of "new religions," founded by visionaries, often women, claiming to be possessed by divine spirits, for these religions were frequently linked with uprisings of impoverished farmers.

The Meiji constitution defined the "duties of citizens" in terms of a new type of Shintō that differed greatly from the local practices of the past. The Department of Shintō, created in 1868, assumed control of all Shintō shrines for the observance of "national rites" in 1871. Later, the government set standards to certify Shintō priests, connected Shintō to the emperor, and invented a historical tradition claiming it as the religion of all ancient Japanese. This historical construction was inculcated in all Japanese subjects with the promulgation of the Imperial Rescript on Education in 1890. Read to school children on special occasions and placed in a special shrine in each school, the Rescript stated that its teachings were "bequeathed by Our Imperial Ancestors, to be observed alike by Their Descendants and the subjects, infallible for all ages and true in all places."

At the same time, other Japanese explored "civilization and enlightenment" in the arts. Some went overboard in rejecting things Japanese and adoring things European. As early as 1868, Kanagaki Robun (1829–1894) published a satire of a "Beefeater," a man who ostentatiously ate beef (not a Japanese food), wore some items of European clothing, carried a pocket-watch, and stated to all within earshot that in the "scientific West" (as Kanagaki called it), they used "telegraphic needles" to engrave plates for printing newspapers, balloons to bring air down from the sky to cool hot countries, and fires in hot pipes under railroad cars to warm passengers in cold countries like Russia.[3]

Many Japanese did indeed reject Japanese arts in the early Meiji, using woodblock prints as packing material for cheap exports sold to the West—a boon for Western collectors and an influence on Western painters, but a major loss to Japan. Some Buddhist temples were destroyed, their ancient buildings sold as firewood. The government promoted European styles of painting in art schools. In 1878, Tokyo University hired Harvard graduate Ernest Fenellosa (1853–1908) to teach philosophy. Enamored of pre-Meiji Japanese arts, he joined with his student Okakura Kakuzō (1862–1913) on a campaign to save Japan's endangered traditions, and these two men turned the tide by advocating a synthesis of Japanese and European cultures.

In literature, some Japanese writers, such as the short-lived Higuchi Ichiyō (1872–1896), the leading female author of the Meiji period, continued to develop Japanese genres, while others adopted the European-style novel. At the end of the Meiji period, Natsume Sōseki (1867–1916) perfected a style that delved deep into the souls of his characters. Most of his novels addressed the dilemmas of modernity. Only 45 years had passed since the Meiji Restoration, yet Sōseki struck a chord when one of his characters, a suicidal intellectual, claimed that, "loneliness is the price we pay for being born in this modern age."[4]

The works of European philosophers, economists, and scientists formed the core of the new higher education. Kant, Mill, Voltaire, and Schopenhauer attracted

A print from Kanagaki Robun's *Seiyō dōchū hizakurige* (*Journey to the West on Foot*) of 1876 showing (from right) an "unenlightened man," "half-enlightened man," and an "enlightened man."

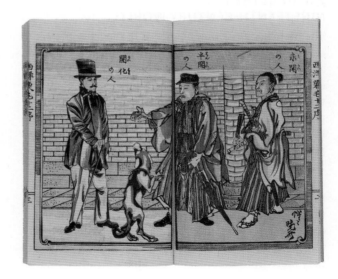

Meiji-era students and intellectuals. The works of British sociologist Herbert Spencer, particularly those dealing with Social Darwinism, influenced not only intellectuals but also framers of foreign policy. Social Darwinism applied the notion of the "survival of the fittest" to races and nations, ranking them as more or less capable of survival based on "scientific" assessment of their stages of progress. This appealed to many Japanese who saw their inferiority to Europe and America as temporary and not inherent. In contrast, European supporters of Social Darwinism saw the ranking of societies as embedded in the genes—in "race"—and as justifying white peoples' dominance and imperialism.

As Japan modernized, many Japanese concluded, it would move up on the universal scale of progress. Progressives like Fukuzawa Yukichi applauded the universalism of this theory and at first wished to lead other Asians to equality with Europe and America by helping them overcome the forces of conservatism in their societies. Conservatives also endorsed this theory, but for opposite reasons. To Yamagata Aritomo, the struggle for survival in a world of limited resources meant that Japan should pursue an aggressive, even imperialist approach to ensure survival. In the end, both conservatives and liberals, who saw their opposites' views as abhorrent on most issues, proposed an aggressive role for Japan in Asia. This helps to explain the paradox of the progressives' support for continental adventurism and colonialism.

JAPAN IN THE LATE NINETEENTH-CENTURY WORLD

The Meiji state's primary concern in the late nineteenth century lay in establishing equality with the European and American powers. This entailed revising the unequal treaties and carving out a position to challenge the Europeans in East Asia. As indicated by Ōkubo's opposition to Saigō and Itagaki's desire to invade Chosŏn in 1873, leaders linked these two goals in Meiji foreign policy. Continental advances should aid, not hinder, Japan's efforts to revise the unequal treaties. In 1872, Japan had begun colonizing Hokkaidō. They used a term that first appeared in 1862—*shokumin* (literally "settler")—for Japanese settlement in the northern island. Later, when Korea and Taiwan became colonies, they, too, were called *shokuminchi*, "settler territory," though they were both colonies of occupation rather than of

settlement as the term implied. Japan's expansion in Hokkaidō resembled white Americans' conquest of relatively sparsely populated North America, but its takeover of densely populated neighboring countries in East Asia created as much tension as Britain's occupation of Ireland. To be sure, those actions and Japan's victory over the Qing in 1895 sufficiently impressed the West that they finally revised the unequal treaties. But treaty revision driven by imperialism represented a Pyrrhic victory, as it set in motion anticolonial movements, especially in Korea.

Japan, one of several countries pressuring Chosŏn for more open trade in the 1870s, forced the Chosŏn monarchy to sign the Treaty of Kanghwa (1876), opening three new ports and giving Japanese citizens extraterritorial rights. This enhanced bilateral trade; for the rest of the 1870s, 90 percent of Chosŏn's exports went to Japan. Japan's leaders hoped to weaken Chosŏn's historic ties with the Qing. Yamagata Aritomo declared that Japan should develop a protective strategy, considering Japan's home islands a "zone of sovereignty" and its friendly neighbors, including Chosŏn, as buffers in a "zone of advantage."

To court favor with King Kojong, Japan sent military advisers to modernize his army in 1881. The following year, a coup brought the Taewŏn'gun back to power (see p. 199), and several Japanese military advisers lost their lives. Japan forced Chosŏn to pay an indemnity and allow Japanese troops to protect Japanese diplomats in Seoul. In the meantime, Japanese adventurers of all sorts—including small businessmen seeking their fortune and gangster types who thrived in turbulent situations—inserted themselves in Chosŏn. Most important, some Japan-educated Koreans (along with some Japanese) believed they could serve Chosŏn by promoting Meiji-style modernization.

In 1884, with secret assurances of help from Japanese diplomats in Seoul, Fukuzawa Yukichi's Korean student Kim Okkyun (1851–1894) attempted a coup, assassinating several government ministers and seizing the king. The Qing sent 2,000 troops to defeat Kim's coup, and angry residents of Seoul killed about 40 local Japanese. The Japanese press reacted immediately. Liberal members of the People's Rights Movement, including Ōi Kentarō (1843–1922) and feminist Fukuda Hideko (1865–1927), prepared to go to Chosŏn to fight what they considered the forces of conservatism that impeded the Korean people's freedom and their independence from Qing.

But they were arrested, and Itō Hirobumi and China's Li Hongzhang met in 1885 to agree to withdraw their countries' troops and inform the other side if they intended to send forces to Chosŏn. For the next decade, Chosŏn had advisers from the Qing, Japan, Russia, and the United States. For part of that time, Britain seized and occupied a Korean coastal island to keep an eye on their rivals, the Russians. It took little to set off a war. An uprising by the Tonghak religious movement led the Chosŏn court to call in Qing assistance. Citing the Li–Itō agreement (see p. 201), Japan dispatched an 8,000-man force to "protect Japanese residents" in June 1894, leading to the first Sino-Japanese War (see p. 203).

Japan's victories, mostly in naval battles between modern fleets of approximately equal size, impressed

Migita Toshihide. *After the Fall of Weihaiwei the Commander of the Chinese Beiyang Fleet, Admiral Ding Ruchang, Surrenders,* 1895. Museum of Fine Arts, Boston. Japanese naval officers at the surrender wore Western attire, had facial hair resembling that of the Western men standing behind Admiral Ding, and stood straight and tall, symbolizing the projection of Japanese power and modernity in Asia. Ding Ruchang committed suicide that same evening.

the world and accelerated the process of treaty revision. Most important, defeating the Qing fundamentally altered Japan's position in East Asia. The Treaty of Shimonoseki (1895) that ended this first Sino-Japanese War awarded Taiwan, some other islands, and the southern part of the Liaodong peninsula to Japan, as well as railroad rights in Manchuria and an indemnity of 360 million yen, which Japan used to build a modern steel factory. In the process of occupying Taiwan, 60,000 Japanese troops brutally suppressed a Taiwanese anticolonial resistance movement.

But before Japan's new empire could incorporate Liaodong, a strategically and economically valuable part of Manchuria, France and Germany joined Russia in a Triple Intervention, humiliating Japan by blocking it from taking control. Nevertheless, the Treaty of Shimonoseki marked a turning point in one sense—Japan had become an imperialist nation with an overseas colony (Taiwan) inhabited by non-Japanese people. In another sense, little seemed to have changed, for the Japanese had to return Liaodong under European pressure. Of course, everything changed for the Koreans, who had to accept a rapidly increasing Japanese presence; for the Taiwanese, now under Japanese colonial rule; and for the Qing, whose government came to be seen as a central problem for China following its defeat.

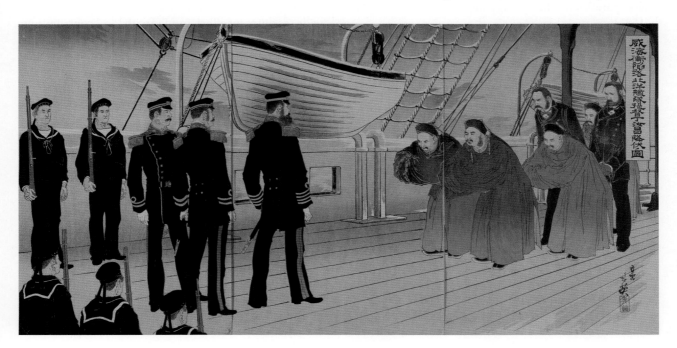

QING RESTORATION AND REFORM

Many international observers did not expect the Qing to survive the onslaught of the Taipings and other rebels in the mid-nineteenth century. Great Britain, among others, opened negotiations with some insurgents and used the Qing's obvious military incompetence as an excuse to seize further territory and privileges. But a remarkable group of high Qing officials, Chinese rather than Manchu, gave the dynasty another half-century of life by creating armies based on provincial networks and loyalties, funding them through new taxes and foreign loans, and defeating the anti-Qing rebels. Zeng Guofan (1811–1872), Zuo Zongtang (1812–1885), Li Hongzhang (1823–1901), all civil service degree holders, and their staffs and allies never wavered in supporting their Qing state and its orthodox ideology. By the late 1870s, the empire had reestablished control over almost all of its former territory and started to arm itself with European weapons under a general policy called "self-strengthening."

The Manchu rulers and their elite Chinese ministers intended to halt foreign encroachments while retaining their Confucian state and society intact. In 1860, Feng Guifen (1809–1874), an adviser to the self-strengtheners, paralleled Chŏng Yagyong's early analysis (see p. 154):

> We have only one thing to learn from the barbarians, and that is strong ships and effective guns…In the end, the way to avoid trouble is to manufacture, repair, and use weapons by ourselves. Only thus can we pacify the empire; only thus can we become the leading power in the world; only thus can we restore our original strength, redeem ourselves from former humiliations, and maintain the integrity of our vast territory so as to remain the greatest country on earth.[5]

At the beginning of this period, the self-strengtheners believed that the Qing empire and Chinese culture did not need to change radically to regain their position at the center of the cosmos. At the same time, however, the fact that the emperor's government needed to compete with others in order to take its rightful place constituted an earth-shaking admission for a Confucian official.

The empire's centrality and superiority could no longer be assumed.

Feng proposed employment of foreign instructors (as Meiji Japan did) to teach both elites and artisans how to make and use the new weaponry, as well as reform of the civil service examinations to include science and technology. With that done, he argued, the Qing could repel the foreigners without adopting their obviously inferior culture. This common reaction to European and American incursions all over the world—"let us remain as we are and defend ourselves with the Europeans' weapons"—never succeeded, even in Japan, but it provided the impetus for what the self-strengtheners hoped would be a dynastic renewal.

DEFEATING THE TAIPINGS

Although the foreigners threatened (and even invaded) the Qing in this period, domestic rebellions constituted the more immediate danger. The conventional Qing armies had failed to halt the northward drive of the Taipings to Nanjing, retake western Yunnan from Du Wenxiu's Pingnanguo, or root out the Nian from their bases in the Huai River valley. Recognizing the Qing's military ineptitude, local elites all over the south organized and equipped local militias to defend their families and communities from the rebels.

Zeng Guofan, from Hunan, undertook a province-wide recruitment effort, funded with local contributions rather than by ordinary government revenues. His troops became the Taipings' most tenacious enemy and a model for other local armies in Anhui, Yunnan, and elsewhere. The court authorized a supplementary tax on goods in transit, which could be retained by provincial treasuries and used to finance local armies. On the busy rivers of the south, where merchants moved most commodities by boat, the transit tax generated enough new revenue to buy weapons and recruit militias to fight the Taipings.

These provincial armies prevented the Taipings from holding territory up the Yangzi, and the rebels failed to take Beijing. To the east, however, lay rich cities such as Suzhou and Hangzhou, and beyond them the expanding foreign-dominated port of Shanghai. Hong Xiuquan's eccentric Christianity and the rebels' consistent stand against the opium trade eventually persuaded the foreign powers to back the Qing, so mercenary, European-commanded armies helped in the defense of Shanghai. Using shallow-draft steamships to transport troops and modern weaponry, the foreigners joined with Qing armies and local militias to besiege and take Nanjing in 1864. The victorious Qing forces slaughtered as many as 100,000 Taiping adherents, ending the most serious threat to Manchu rule since the Three Feudatories rebellion (see p. 74).

Why did the Taipings fail? Most directly, they had to confront the militias raised by local and provincial elites to defend their home territory. Zeng Guofan and his allies used statecraft methods, practical Confucian politics, to raise funds, recruit and arm troops, and to organize anti-Taiping resistance. The constant warfare left much of the formerly prosperous Yangzi valley depopulated, so the Taipings found themselves taking more and more from their diminishing tax base to support their large armies. As Hakkas, southwesterners, Christians, and outsiders, Hong Xiuquan's followers seemed utterly alien in central China, where their harsh regime of taxation, recruitment, and social regulation caused many townsmen and villagers to flee and enlist in anti-Taiping militias. During their stationary and defensive years in Nanjing, they dissipated whatever legitimacy they had earned.

THE OTHER DOMESTIC REBELS

The recapture of Nanjing in 1864 meant respite from war for the devastated Lower Yangzi region, but the dynasty's troubles continued elsewhere. Some Taiping leaders escaped and made their way northward to join with the Nian in the Huai River valley. Alarmed by the Nian proximity to Beijing, the Qing court ordered Zeng Guofan to take command of the northern China armies. After three more years, Zeng finally restricted the Nian's freedom of movement by entrenchments, walls, and defense lines at canals and rivers. His protégé Li Hongzhang, from Anhui, took general command of the campaign against the Nian in 1866, finally defeating them two years later. Thereafter, Li Hongzhang's status and power in the Qing state grew steadily.

Pingnanguo had controlled much of Yunnan province in the 1850s while the Qing fought the Taipings. Its Muslim leader, Du Wenxiu, who called himself Sultan Suleiman, utilized not only symbolism and language from Islam but also Ming dynasty court costumes and had officials of many ethnicities, including a few Manchus. Du's forces expanded Pingnanguo to control dozens of walled towns, and in 1868 they nearly took the provincial capital, Kunming. His officials corresponded with British envoys and designed an imperial palace like Beijing's.

Du's ideas included pan-Islamic, Yunnan localist, and anti-Qing sentiments, attracting a broad following that enabled Pingnanguo to persist against the Qing armies, despite the devastation of much of Yunnan. When the Qing finally took his capital in late 1872, Du surrendered and committed suicide in a vain attempt to rescue his followers, but to no avail. Qing troops massacred the inhabitants and sent 24 baskets of severed ears to Beijing as proof of the triumph. Muslims in Yunnan still remember Du Wenxiu and Pingnanguo as emblems of their resistance to Qing authority.

Portrait of Zeng Guofan (1811–1872), from an imperial album of court officials.

189

NEW TROUBLES IN THE NORTHWEST

As Qing troops fought against the Taipings, the Nian, and Pingnanguo in 1862, yet another local clash exploded into anti-state rebellion, this time in the northwestern provinces of Shaanxi and Gansu. That spring, low-level conflict between Muslim and non-Muslim militias in the Wei River valley escalated as a Taiping army approached from the south and a western Nian army fought in Shanxi, across the Yellow River to the east. Inept Qing commanders dithered between negotiations and armed repression.

Some Muslim leaders argued for a conciliatory stance toward the dynasty, while others demanded that the united Muslim militias attack the Qing directly. As rumors of impending massacres flew, Muslim militias killed a senior local gentryman and besieged the provincial capital, Xi'an, in late June 1862. The whole southern part of the province, where as many as a million Muslims lived, became a battleground for the next six years. Numerous Muslims fled westward to join co-religionaries in Gansu, where local leaders had established four independent Muslim command centers. Although Qing troops lifted the siege of Xi'an in 1863, the dynasty could not gain a military advantage until late 1868, when Zuo Zongtang, having aided in the defeat of the Nian, arrived to pacify the northwest.

He faced not only the Muslim rebels of Shaanxi and Gansu but also local uprisings in Xinjiang and another invasion from Kokand. In the "New Frontier," at least six Muslim leaders, most of them imams, declared *jihad* against the Manchus in 1864, not only because the Qing state was non-Muslim but also because corrupt officials denied peace and order to local society. About six months later Ya'qub Beg (1820–1877), a general from Kokand, brought a small army across the Pamirs to Kashgar and conquered the entire region, establishing an emirate that covered most of Qing Xinjiang. At its largest, his army numbered 35,000–40,000 troops, many of them battle-hardened cavalry.

Commanded by the Qing to retake the entire northwest, an enormous and hostile territory, Zuo Zongtang brought both military and administrative skills to the campaign. He prepared his supply lines carefully, obtained advanced weaponry (including German siege artillery), and studied both the tactics and the leadership of his enemies. Beginning with the Shaanxi Muslims, Zuo's forces broke down their communications and captured their stockades and hilltop fortifications one by one. By early 1869 Zuo had moved his headquarters to Gansu, where he attacked the Muslim strongholds separately. Responding to local conditions, he slaughtered the inhabitants of some centers while enlisting the commanders of others into the Qing army. The campaign lasted almost three years, ending with the execution of 7,000 Muslims captured at Suzhou, the last walled town on the way to Xinjiang, in late 1873.

With all the rebels in the core provinces defeated, the Qing court had to make a financial and policy decision in 1874. Should the dynasty spend its scanty resources on the retaking of Xinjiang, a territory that had depleted the imperial treasury for over a century? Or should they face the European and American imperial threat squarely and use their money to buy and build a modern navy?

Zuo Zongtang and Li Hongzhang, the two most eminent remaining self-strengtheners, took opposite sides. Li, with his base in Anhui and the north, saw the Europeans as the greater menace and argued for both naval development and construction of railroads as the Qing's highest priority. Zuo, on the other hand, had been fighting domestic rebels on the northwestern frontier since 1868. He argued that if the dynasty did not recover Xinjiang, then Mongolia would slip away and Beijing itself come under attack. Zuo believed that European threat lay not in naval power but rather in Russian or British domination of Central Asia, inspired by their Great Game rivalry. By this point, both Britain and Russia had indeed signed trade agreements with Ya'qub Beg's emirate in Xinjiang, and the Russians had occupied not only all of western Central Asia but also the Ili valley, within Qing territory, so Zuo's arguments had solid foundations.

After considerable discussion, Zuo Zongtang's view prevailed. He obtained loans of 10 million ounces (283 billion g) of silver from foreign banks in 1876 and set off to retake Xinjiang. The war, though expensive, was not a bloodbath because the Muslim leaders quarreled among themselves. Ya'qub Beg suddenly died in mid-1877—perhaps a stroke, perhaps poisoned. His armies collapsed without a major battle, and Zuo secured the entire region, including Kashgar, by December 1878. Thousands of civilians, mostly Turki Muslims, died in the process. Intensive Qing diplomatic effort persuaded the Russians to return Ili and the strategic passes of

WANG TAO,
A CONFUCIAN CHRISTIAN JOURNALIST-REFORMER

Wang Tao, c. 1890s.

Wang Tao (1828–1897) came from a declining but highly literate Jiangsu family. He learned the Classics first from his mother then his father, who prepared young men for the civil service examinations. A precocious student, Wang passed the first-level exam at 17, but he failed the provincial exam the following year and had to earn a living while awaiting his next opportunity. Visiting his father in Shanghai, Wang Tao met Walter Henry Medhurst (1796–1857), who had founded the London Missionary Society Press to produce Christian literature in Chinese.

When Wang's father died in 1849, Medhurst offered him a job as a Chinese editor; the young man, with a family to support, had no choice. Although sometimes dissatisfied with his employers, he persevered and began to build a life in Shanghai, where he found like-minded friends among the Chinese scholars who worked with the foreigners. After coming to terms with their unconventional jobs, they had to brave the contempt of their more conformist colleagues, who called them eccentrics at best, traitors and spies at worst. Some, like Wang Tao, became Christians, and all of them had to place their Chinese identity and civilization in a new world context. Personally attached to traditional ways—he wrote a nostalgic treatise on the "pleasure district" of Shanghai—Wang Tao also admitted that, "the past is gone except for some traces."[6]

During nearly 50 years of work in Shanghai, Hong Kong, and Europe, Wang Tao wrote constantly—books, translations, articles, editorials, letters, and an occasional diary. His classical education allowed him to produce commentaries on the Confucian Classics, while his experiences abroad stimulated him to write travel accounts, a narrative of the Franco-Prussian War, and essays on European intellectual history. He assisted a Scottish scholar, James Legge, in rendering all of the Confucian Classics into English, an enormous endeavor during which he lived for five years with Legge's family in Scotland. His travels also included visiting Paris (he loved the Louvre) and addressing the graduating class at Oxford.

Returning to Hong Kong, Wang founded the China Printing Company and inaugurated China's first daily newspaper in 1874. His editorials called for reform of Qing politics and Chinese education and adoption of European technology, including such controversial tools as the telegraph, which he saw as an important instrument for national defense. Wang Tao never became a revolutionary or an all-out Westernizer, however, and he continued to assert the superiority and universal applicability of Confucian ethics.

Anxious about Japan's rising power, Wang Tao spent four months there in 1879, discussing interpretations of the Classics as well as plans for reform. In evaluating Meiji Japan's achievements, he could never escape from his own ambivalence about China's simultaneous political weakness and ethical superiority. He wrote admiringly, "…[the Japanese] have adopted the West's strengths and have shown a marked ability…to rely on their own efforts." But he also believed that, "They grind down hard on their people…to impress men from afar and exhaust their riches…to acquire foreign things."[7] In this very ambivalence, Wang Tao helped to set some Chinese on the new path of nationalism and consciousness of China's place as one of many nations.

western Xinjiang. In 1884, Xinjiang became an ordinary province (by far the largest), administered by regular civil officials, and Chinese agricultural settlement accelerated, just as Gong Zizhen (see p. 146) and Wei Yuan (see p. 144) had recommended decades earlier.

During the suppression of the domestic rebellions, tens of millions had died; whole regions had been laid waste; and the dynasty had suffered further defeats at the hands of Great Britain, France, and Russia. But the Qing survived. This turbulent period, called the Tongzhi Restoration—after the reign-name of the child emperor enthroned in 1861—saw Zeng Guofan, Li Hongzhang, Zuo Zongtang, and their protégés attempt to build the Qing anew upon the conservative, well-established basis of Neo-Confucian ethics and a loyal, obedient agricultural population. Their objectives lay in "securing the people's economic security and stabilizing the people's hearts."

FOREIGN STUDIES AND THE FIRST HUNDRED

Having seen what foreign weapons and technology could do, Zeng and his allies did not deny the necessity for change—indeed, they embraced it—but they insisted that reform must strengthen the existing imperial order rather than replace it. In strong contrast to the Meiji leaders of Japan, they saw the process as restoring old methods, not changing fundamental principles. "Restoration," in this conception, aimed not at "progress" but rather at redressing an imbalance in the world.

Yung Wing (Rong Hong), 1854. A Yale graudate and naturalized American citizen (1852), he led the first delegation of Chinese students to study abroad.

Rebellions had shaken the universal empire, and the Qing had become inferior to foreigners in both technical skills and political power. If these trends could be reversed, rebels defeated, and foreigners put in their proper place, then Confucian civilization, upheld by Manchu monarchs and Chinese elites alike, would be restored to its permanent and obvious primacy. Thus although the Tongzhi Restoration differed radically from the Meiji Restoration, both centered on hereditary monarchs.

The self-strengtheners knew that the Qing had to produce its own weapons and machines in order to prevail in the new and frightening world of Euro-American power, so Zeng, Li, and Zuo built arsenals and shipyards to manufacture them. Committed to the notion of Qing centrality in the world, they nonetheless took the first steps toward changing that conception—they had no choice but to compare the Qing and the Chinese culture it encompassed to others.

In their plan to obtain and then manufacture bigger guns and faster ships, the self-strengtheners sought fundamental knowledge—science, engineering, geography—from the Europeans and Americans. Some books had been translated into Chinese, and some Chinese (like Xu Jiyu, see p. 148) had studied world affairs, but these Confucian officials recognized that Chinese people would have to study abroad in order to obtain deep understanding of foreign knowledge. A native of the Portuguese colony of Macao, Yung Wing (MANDARIN Rong Hong, 1828–1912), became the first Chinese to graduate from an American university (Yale, 1854). By 1871, he had persuaded Zeng and Li to seek a thorough European-style education for a group of Chinese boys.

In the conservative Qing political culture, this plan could not go unopposed, since it implied that Chinese culture had to compete with others as equals. Led by Grand Secretary Woren, many officials denounced Zeng and Li's plan as betraying the fundamental principles of Chinese culture:

> *Now if these brilliant and talented scholars, who have been trained by the nation and reserved for great future usefulness, have to change from their regular course of study to follow the barbarians, then the correct spirit will not be developed, and accordingly the evil spirit will become stronger.*[8]

The court nonetheless approved the scheme, appointing Yung Wing to oversee it. They chose the United States as their site because the Burlingame Treaty of 1868 had specified that people from the two countries could reside and study in the other on a basis of mutual rights, though Qing subjects could no longer become US citizens. By 1875, over a hundred young Chinese (12–16 years old), most from the coastal treaty ports, had traveled to live with American families in western New England. They rapidly learned English, excelled in their studies at the local schools, and soon abandoned or neglected their Chinese curriculum. Some of them became Christians, which their American hosts devoutly desired, and they learned baseball more eagerly than the Chinese Classics.

In 1875, Yung Wing married Louise Kellogg, daughter of a Hartford physician, unleashing another storm of criticism among Qing officials. The conservative bureaucrats who accompanied the group submitted negative accounts of the boys' rapid estrangement from Chinese ways, and the United States refused to allow them to enter the military academies. When Li Hongzhang withdrew his personal support, the Qing Foreign Ministry terminated the Mission in the summer of 1881. Most of the students (now in their twenties) went on to careers in government, business, science, medicine, and the military. High officials, including Li Hongzhang, found places for them in railroad planning, military education, and other technical fields.

The termination of the educational mission indicated clearly the limits of self-strengthening. If the students could not remain faithful to the Confucian Classics and their conservative culture and could not enhance Qing military development, the court would not support them. Thereafter, Li Hongzhang sent protégés to study in Europe, where they could receive advanced military training. For Li, *military* considerations still dominated the modernizing agenda, not any desire to emulate Europe and America in politics, society, or culture. Here we find a direct confrontation between high officials like Li and some Chinese of the coastal regions (such as Wang Tao; see p. 191), who made plans to adapt to the foreigners' power. In contrast to the Meiji reformers, who seized the central government, Chinese modernizers like Yung Wing could not exercise much influence over Li Hongzhang, Zuo Zongtang, or the Qing court.

SELF-STRENGTHENING AND FOREIGN AFFAIRS

While the Chinese boys studied in New England, political crises continued to plague the Qing and its officials. The young Tongzhi Emperor died in 1875, and his mother, the formidable Empress Dowager Cixi (1835–1908), placed her 3-year-old nephew on the throne as the Guangxu Emperor (r. 1875–1908), retaining her personal power as regent. Well-educated, intelligent, ruthless, and skilled at palace intrigue, the Empress Dowager dominated the court from a royal lady's position "behind the screen" for more than four decades, becoming the most powerful woman in Qing political history. She supported many of the self-strengtheners' proposals, but she also jealously protected Aisin Gioro prerogatives as the ruling family and Manchu privilege as the conquering elite. Recent historians have blamed her for many of the late Qing's problems, but under her leadership the dynasty managed to survive longer than many observers had expected.

On the international front, the court relied primarily on Li Hongzhang to deal with the newly aggressive Japanese, who had seized the Ryūkyūs in 1871 and invaded Taiwan in 1874, withdrawing after winning Qing concessions. The most explosive conflict concerned Chosŏn Korea, which became contested territory after 1871. Li Hongzhang sent a young official named Yuan Shikai to the Chosŏn court to support the pro-Qing faction. Yuan helped Queen Min to overcome the Kapsin coup attempt by Kim Okkyun and his pro-Japanese allies (see p. 186), and Li Hongzhang's 1885 negotiations with Itō Hirobumi concluded with both sides agreeing to withdraw their forces from the peninsula, desist from training a Chosŏn military, and notify one another before dispatching troops in future.

The Qing faced an unfamiliar world in the late nineteenth century. How could Chinese officials and scholars, Manchu princes and generals, and others who upheld the centrality of their civilization and state possibly cope with the obvious, threatening, and apparently invincible power of Europe and America? Having been defeated by the British twice (1842, 1860), by the French once (1884), and forced to compromise with all of the imperial powers (including the Japanese) over frontier and trade issues, Li Hongzhang and his colleagues recognized crucial weaknesses in their empire. Although they had annihilated the domestic rebels and temporarily ended foreign threats by the mid-1880s, they still lacked both funds and expertise to purchase or manufacture sufficient weaponry to defend their vast territory. Their efforts to centralize political power did not result in well-coordinated empire-wide communication or in unified policy.

Despite their eagerness for "strong ships and effective guns," Li and his colleagues still lacked the knowledge that had been so important for the Meiji leaders in Japan. They had not been trained in Dutch learning, had not learned foreign languages or traveled abroad, and—perhaps most telling—they worked inside a system that frustrated many reform initiatives. Their opponents included not only other examination-trained bureaucrats like themselves but also the Empress Dowager, whose maneuvers at court sometimes stymied their proposals and reduced their budgets. Products of the Qing system, the self-strengtheners perpetuated its weaknesses.

SOCIAL CHANGE

As the Qing had to cope diplomatically and militarily with the foreign threat, so too did merchants and manufacturers come to grips with the outside world. Since so few examination candidates gained official positions, more and more gentry at all levels went into business to support their families, educate their sons, and make a place for themselves in their local communities. Drawn by the presence of foreign banks, trading companies, and factories, Chinese with money moved into the treaty ports to take advantage of international trade opportunities and the domestic contracts necessary for self-strengthening to succeed.

At the lower end of society, rural Chinese heard that wages could be found in the cities, and some began to migrate toward factories and transportation labor. China's great coastal and riverine cities—including Nanjing, Guangzhou, Tianjin, Xiamen (Amoy), Hankou, and Shanghai—grew rapidly during this period of increasing investment and technological change, increasing the divide between the coastal provinces and the rest of the empire. Imports (including opium) continued to outstrip exports by a huge margin, and indemnity payments and interest on foreign loans drained wealth from the empire. But remittances from overseas Chinese (see p. 205) brought some back. Constrained by their lack of capital, Chinese industrialists could not yet compete with the foreigners, but they gained crucial

experience and knowledge of technology and markets, which would benefit them (and the entire economy) in the future.

During this period, some important economic innovation came from high officials. Zeng Guofan, Zuo Zongtang, Li Hongzhang, and other reformers invested both government and personal funds in factories, producing commodities from military hardware to standard coinage to matches, textiles, and paper. Like the Meiji leaders, they opened government mines to exploit the empire's rich resources of coal and iron, mills to transform those minerals into steel and machines, and shipyards to build vessels to carry the products. Between 1885 and 1895, Zhang Zhidong (1837–1909) made Hankou—with its wealthy hinterland and easy transportation on two rivers—into a major industrial center as well as a commercial hub. Each modern enterprise, like the foreigners' factories, required workers, so labor flowed from villages to cities, and the process of making peasant farmers into an industrial labor force began in earnest. Then as now, one reason to invest in China lay in its enormous, increasingly mobile labor force.

But the foreigners continued to control the most valuable and productive enterprises. With advanced technology and vast capital, they could undersell domestic products (such as handwoven cotton cloth) and introduce new ones (such as cigarettes and kerosene) throughout the empire, once the unequal treaties enabled their representatives, sales forces, capital, and goods to circulate freely. In the treaty ports, they dominated finance, shipping, and manufacturing. A tremendous stimulus to business and innovation, the foreign presence also drained profit and capital, stifled some important domestic industries, and competed with Chinese merchants for markets. British subjects even controlled some public functions, such as the post office and customs service.

Foreigners also came to the empire as missionaries, persuaded that China could be saved only through conversion to Christianity. Their impact, like that of the imperialist economic enterprises, varied from place to place. The missionaries undertook good works—famine relief, medicine, and education especially—in many parts of the realm. They opened schools for girls (extremely rare before the late nineteenth century) and encouraged the abolition of footbinding. At the same time, their mission demanded that Chinese culture be altered radically, that Confucian family rites (which they called "ancestor worship") and folk religion (which they called "superstition") be eliminated. They presented the European and American ideals of family life as the only decent, rational way to run a society, and they wanted, in the words of a twentieth-century American official, "to raise Shanghai up and up…until it's just like Kansas City."[9]

But most Chinese still neither knew nor cared much about foreign ways. Millions of lives had been lost, and millions more shattered, in the decades of domestic wars, so rebuilding—homes, fields, businesses, boats, the necessities of life—occupied their time and resources. Even for the literate, translations of foreign books only trickled into the empire's bookstores before the 1890s, and no trends for eating European food or wearing European clothing offered appealing alternatives to custom and tradition. Poets continued to write in established genres, and novelists (some of them also journalists) continued to write pointed satire, more openly critical of government than before.

Only in the treaty ports and overseas communities, and among the few Chinese intellectuals who went abroad, could European innovations have direct impact. The British colony of Hong Kong gave Ho Kai (He Qi, 1859–1914), for example, scope to use his talents in entirely new ways. Born in Guangdong and educated by missionaries, he earned degrees in law and medicine in England, married an Englishwoman, became a member of the Hong Kong Legislative Council in 1890, and attacked the self-strengtheners for their stubborn adherence to old ways. Rather than study Confucian ethics, he argued in 1887, Qing officials should emphasize commerce and economics, grant parliamentary representation to their subjects, and plan to compete in the modern world, as Meiji Japan was doing.

From Jiangsu on the east coast, Ma Jianzhong (1844–1900) grew up in a Catholic family, so he studied at a Jesuit school in Shanghai then went to Paris to earn a law degree. Returning home, he joined Li Hongzhang's staff as a foreign affairs adviser, represented Li in Korean plots, helped to manage Li's China Merchants Steamship Company, and accompanied his boss to negotiate with Japan in 1895. Like Ho Kai, Ma Jianzhong attempted to reform the Qing system by persuading high officials to use European technology and political institutions.

THE GREAT SHOCK OF 1895

As we have already seen, the 1884 Li–Itō agreement did not end Japanese interests on the Korean peninsula. Rather, the Tonghak rebellion (1894) gave the Meiji government the opportunity to do what Saigō Takamori had desired 20 years before—remove the Korean peninsula entirely from its younger-brother relationship with the Qing. Japan's smashing victories at sea shocked the Qing empire, leaving its military weak and demoralized. Japan forced the Qing to cede Taiwan and Liaodong (the latter returned by the Triple Intervention) and pay an enormous indemnity. Taiwan, which had only been a Qing province for a few years, became part of Japan's empire. For the next 50 years, its history diverged radically from that of the mainland in many

The arsenal at Fuzhou before the French attack, 1884. This drawing, made from a photograph, portrays the factory built in 1866 with French assistance to manufacture warships and train naval officers. The French fleet destroyed the Fuzhou arsenal in 1884 during a war over northern Vietnam.

ways—exposure to modernity, culture, and language, even personal identity. Both Chinese and indigenes on the island had to face the complex question, "What am I? Chinese? Japanese? Taiwanese?"

Reformers who had predicted the 1895 disaster found hope in defeat. Perhaps the war's appalling result would force conservative officials and the Empress Dowager to undertake radical restructuring of the Qing system. Li Hongzhang's younger colleagues, such as Zhang Zhidong, did recommend rapid construction of railways and other necessities for national defense. Politically aware Chinese found the defeat deeply unsettling and looked to international models, such as Peter the Great's Russia and Meiji Japan, for methods to change both the Qing state and Chinese society.

They learned both of the war and of possible solutions to China's problems from newspapers founded in the treaty ports by Chinese entrepreneurs and scholars, many of them trained or influenced by European and American missionaries. They aimed to correct many misconceptions about China and to stimulate the power of public opinion. Publishing newspapers and books for profit ("print capitalism") did indeed produce a greater community of identity among Chinese, what some historians call the beginning of Chinese nationalism. For the coastal newspapers did more than transmit news—they also persuaded many Chinese that the Europeans and Americans were more than just the latest barbarians to trouble the universal empire. In addition, they began the creation of a "national people," which came to be called "the Han people," including not just the politically active or well connected but *all* Chinese—a notion very different from being "a subject of the Qing." From this point on, they argued, China had no choice but to compare itself not to the idealized realm of the ancient sages but to Britain, the United States, Russia, even Japan and India.

Although many continued to cling to Chinese culture's centrality and the universal cosmic reign of the emperor, others edged away toward a more modern vision of parallel civilizations, paving the way for political activism and advocacy outside the scholar-official class. Not coincidentally, most of the latter came from the coast, from the port cities. There they had the opportunity to interact with foreigners, to travel, to hear news from overseas Chinese in Singapore, Manila, or San Francisco, to learn more about the outside world

than the well-insulated bureaucrats in Beijing or the provincial scholar-gentry whose sons became high officials. In their newspapers, written in classical Chinese, we find the early stirrings of revolutionary ideas that would, in a fairly short time, bring down the old order of emperor, examinations, and Confucian bureaucrats.

KOREA

THE "OPENING" OF KOREA TO FOREIGN TRADE

The last third of the nineteenth century was a time of extraordinary change and turmoil for Chosŏn Korea. Domestic and foreign forces gathered to put enormous pressure on the long-lived Chosŏn system, created in the late fourteenth century. From within, the dynasty faced economic disruptions caused by a series of mid-century bad harvests and, after the 1870s, the disruptions attending the penetration of global capitalism. Factional strife in the capital led to less oversight over local administration and loss of revenue due to corruption and maladministration of the tax rolls that led to the immiseration of the peasantry and rural unrest.

From without, the dynasty faced increasingly insistent demands to open Korea to the evolving trading and diplomatic system dominated by Europe and the United States. These were extraordinary problems, but the dynasty had faced crises before and survived. Indeed, given the longevity and resilience of the system, Korean officialdom remained confident that they had only to shore up the traditional system for the rocking ship of state to right itself. Unfortunately for Korea, this was not to be the case. By 1895 Korea found itself caught between Meiji Japan and Qing China, at war over the question of whose interests would predominate on the peninsula in an increasingly dangerous and violent imperialist power struggle.

During the 1860s, Chosŏn witnessed an extraordinary amount of political turmoil at the top and increasing distress at the bottom of society. In order to reconsolidate power around the throne, the informal regent (and the king's father), the Taewŏn'gun, had attacked a number of *yangban* prerogatives. Elites at the center resisted attempts to erode their traditional tax-exempt status, and they strenuously attacked the Taewŏn'gun's reforms and fiscal manipulations intended to restore monarchical power. His maintenance of the isolation policy, refusal to alter the Japan–Korea relationship after the Meiji Restoration, persecution of Catholicism, and support for military preparedness were, however, popular.

But the fragile consensus that supported the Taewŏn'gun broke down in the early 1870s as his unorthodox policies and extra-legal methods were increasingly criticized on ideological grounds. The informal institutional rationale for his rule disappeared with his son's majority and succession to the throne as King Kojong (r. 1874–1907). However, the Taewŏn'gun's successful repulse of the both French expedition of 1866 and the 1871 American attack in the aftermath of the *General Sherman* incident (see p. 159) lulled the leaders into the belief that Western barbarians were indeed paper tigers. This allowed them to continue to ignore entreaties to open their country to trade and diplomacy with the outside world, including those from next-door Japan.

In November 1868, just two years after the battles with the French on Kanghwa Island, a Japanese envoy arrived at Tongnae (Pusan) to announce the Meiji Restoration. Korean interpreters rejected the Meiji diplomatic correspondence for using unacceptable references to the Meiji "emperor," "imperial house," and "imperial" decree. In Korean diplomatic usage, such terms belonged exclusively to the emperor ruling China. The Koreans conducted relations with Japan on a wholly different, "neighborly" basis, and since 1609 Tongnae had been the only port where Japanese were permitted to trade and reside. Traditional practice circumscribed trade with quotas, and no high-level envoys had been exchanged since the early nineteenth century. While the Koreans congratulated themselves on the successful defense of their realm and the reaffirmation of their all-important relationship with the Qing, their rebuff of the Japanese set in motion forces that led ultimately to the opening of Korea.

Korean rejection of the Meiji Emperor's legitimacy—embodied in use of "imperial" language—angered Japan's new leaders, and they did not take the offense lightly. Suffering under a series of unequal treaties themselves and eager to transform Japan into a Western-style nation-state, the Japanese found the Korean insistence on the old vocabulary of inter-state relations, predicated on the centrality of China, infuriating. By

Utagawa Yoshitaki, *Leading Members of the Meiji government Discussing the Invasion of Korea*, print made 1877. The debate took place in 1873 and led to Saigō Takamori's resignation.

1872 there was a full-scale debate over what to do about this insult. One group, led by Saigō Takamori, proposed a punitive military expedition to open Chosŏn to trade and force their recognition of the new Meiji state.

Although cooler heads prevailed and plans for a military expedition to Korea were scrapped, the Japanese steadily increased pressure on the Koreans to recognize the new power arrangements in East Asia. They insisted that Korea open relations with them on the model of Western diplomatic treaty relations. By 1874, the Japanese were ominously sending warships up and down the Korean coast, purportedly to "chart shipping lanes." Finally, after creating a naval incident involving the warship *Unyō*, in January 1876 the Japanese dispatched four warships and 800 marines, landed (like foreign invaders before them) on Kanghwa Island, and demanded that Korea enter into treaty negotiations.

After heated debate, Kojong overrode the objections of the majority of his advisers and authorized a treaty with Japan (Kanghwa Treaty, 1876). He had sought Qing advice. Li Hongzhang, who had become the Qing's Japan expert, urged the Koreans to negotiate a treaty, assuring them that the "special" relationship between Qing and Chosŏn would remain inviolate. He may have believed that, but the leaders of Meiji Japan considered the treaty an opening wedge that would pry Korea away from the Qing and into the new nation-state system in East Asia.

The Kanghwa Treaty was a typical unequal treaty. For instance, Japanese merchants would enjoy extraterritorial rights, remaining liable only to Japanese laws in their settlements in the newly opened Korean ports. The Koreans, however, interpreted the treaty as a bilateral agreement with Japan and did not understand the power of the treaty to establish precedents for future agreements with other nations. The Japanese had always handled their own affairs "extraterritorially" within the Tongnae compound. The Chosŏn court desired only to provide minimal concessions, limit the export of rice, and avoid a military confrontation. Instead, the twelve-article treaty opened three ports to foreign business and set terms for commerce that included the right of merchants to trade in Japanese currency. A supplementary treaty (August 1876) gave the Japanese even more economic concessions.

The Kanghwa Treaty and subsequent treaties over the next decade, with the Western powers as well as the Qing, exposed Korea to unprecedented outside influences. Initially, it was useful for the Koreans to bring in all the various actors on the East Asian diplomatic stage in order to play them off against each other and create room to maneuver. Kojong and his government attempted to maintain neutrality by balancing the predatory interests of the foreign powers that became active on the peninsula. Such a policy grew logically from Korea's dependence on Qing influence during the early phase of its participation in the treaty system. The policy's fallacy was to think that foreign powers would inevitably avoid conflict with each other rather than striving to develop or maintain a dominant position in Korea. In addition, the Koreans misread Qing intentions in "guiding" them into the new treaty system.

The Qing, in fact, desired to stabilize their influence in Korea and limit Japanese interests there. To this end Li Hongzhang—in charge of Korean affairs as part of his portfolio as Governor-General of Zhili province and Imperial Commissioner for the Northern Ports—urged the Chosŏn court to bolster their defenses, beginning "self-strengthening" activities while simultaneously pursuing an alliance with the United States. In the aftermath of the Burlingame Treaty and the educational mission to New England, the United States appeared to be the best counterbalance to Japanese and Russian ambitions in East Asia. Qing self-strengthening had produced positive results against domestic rebels and foreign incursions. Kim Hongjip (1842–1896), returning from a mission to Tokyo in 1880, brought with him plans for self-strengthening along Li Hongzhang's lines, drafted by Huang Zunxian (1848–1905), an official at the Qing legation in Japan. By October of that year there was sufficient impetus for Kojong to approve a number of reform measures and institute the study of foreign political institutions, ideas, and technologies. The self-strengthening program that emerged after 1880 was controversial, but younger, progressive officials supported by Kojong gained power at this time and accomplished a number of significant reforms.

THE EARLY SELF-STRENGTHENING MOVEMENT

In the aftermath of opening, the Koreans scrambled to gain more information about changing conditions around them. Kojong sent representatives to Japan, China, and the United States for reports on conditions abroad. Korean students studied in the new schools in

Members of the new Foreign Ministry, 1884. In the front row from left to right: Yi Kyoyŏng, Yi Choyŏn, Min Yŏngmok, Kim Hongjip, Hong Yŏngsik, and Pyŏn Wŏngyu. The ministry was part of the self-strengthening program of 1880–84.

China that specialized in Western military technology and foreign language study. In the early 1880s the government established its own school for the training of foreign relations experts, and it accelerated the process of reorganizing and re-equipping its small army. A new branch of government, modeled on the Qing Foreign Ministry and called the Office for Management of State Affairs—established at the high level of the State Council—oversaw the self-strengthening effort. These were radical and unsettling changes for a government that had only recently considered ritual obeisance to the Qing emperor and isolation as the key elements of its foreign policy. As in China, conservatives argued that to adopt foreign methods and practices threatened the *Dao* of Confucian governance. They opposed proposals to revamp decision-making at the highest levels of government, establish new methods for the recruitment of officials, and to legislate social reforms.

Despite considerable opposition to the momentum established by the progressives between 1880 and 1884, the progressives could continue the modest reform program as long as Kojong continued to provide them with positions and limited resources. In 1881, the court created a new Special Skills Force intended as a demonstration unit for military modernization. This, however, created resentment within traditional army units, whose resources had been diverted to pay for the model unit. In 1882, disaffected soldiers rioted in Seoul demanding back pay. Opponents of reform, including the retired Taewŏn'gun, seized upon the chaos to regain power. Ultimately, the disturbances in Seoul escalated to the burning of the Japanese legation and the killing of Japanese diplomats, and they were only quelled with the aid of Qing troops. Yuan Shikai (1859–1916),

the Qing official originally assigned by Li Hongzhang to train the Chosŏn Special Skills Force, remained in Seoul for more than a decade to play an important role in both Korean history and the last years of the Qing.

The Japanese also sent troops and secured an indemnity for the destruction of their property, but they backed away from any confrontation with the Qing in the face of its superior military strength. Thereafter, the Qing court increased its influence within the Korean government by dispatching a high official directly to the Chosŏn court in Seoul, an unprecedented act in relations between the two kingdoms. Back in control of the court, conservative Chosŏn officials abolished the Special Skills Force as well as the Office for Management of State Affairs. This marked the beginning of a decade of Qing ascendancy in the Korean capital, and by 1884 the entire progressive movement was in retreat in the face of increasing Qing pressure supported by conservatives within the government.

THE KAPSIN COUP OF 1884

This set the stage for one of the most important events of the 1880s, an abortive palace coup staged by progressive forces and known as the Kapsin Coup of 1884. While some in the pro-Qing factions that led the government at this time, men like Kim Hongjip and Kim Yunsik—even members of the consort clan such as Min Yŏngik (1860–1914)—favored reform, they were gradualists, and they wished to align Korean reforms with Qing policies. A younger group of officials who had been ousted from official posts after the 1882 mutiny, some schooled in Japan like Kim Okkyun and Pak Yŏnghyo (1861–1939), plotted to seize the person of the king and effect a sweeping Meiji-style reform program. The conspirators gained the favor of the Japanese Minister (ambassador), who promised the aid of his small command of guards in support of the coup. The progressives moved in late 1884, when the Qing was preoccupied by a conflict with France over Vietnam. They seized the monarch and over a three-day period promulgated sweeping reform legislation. The Kapsin reform program sought not only to revamp the entire government along European lines but also proposed a thorough social revolution by eliminating *yangban* privileges.

Kim Okkyun, c. 1890s.

Their program, however, was stillborn. Within days, the coup was put down by Qing troops under the leadership of Yuan Shikai. The Japanese had withdrawn their support—the Minister burned the legation building and retreated to Japan with the conspirators who managed to escape, among them Kim Okkyun. A number of Korean officials lost their lives, murdered during the coup; in all over 180 Koreans, Japanese, and Chinese died in the incident. Most ominously, the coup once again brought Japanese and Chinese troops close

YUN CH'IHO

By any standard one of the great Korean reformist thinkers of the later nineteenth and early twentieth centuries, Yun Ch'iho's life (1865–1946) spanned a period of immense change and turmoil in Korea. Born in Pyongyang of a prominent military family, he received a classical education, but he is best known as one of the first Koreans to study in the United States. Yun's rise to prominence in intellectual and political circles began as a 16-year-old member of the 1881 Gentlemen's Observation Mission, a delegation of Chosŏn officials charged to investigate the progress of reforms then underway in Japan. Yun stayed in Japan to study with Fukuzawa Yukichi—who had gone to the United States 20 years earlier. In the United States, Yun acquired excellent English, which he later used in a remarkable diary that spanned his varied political career and life in retirement.

Firmly associated with progressive forces after his travels in the early 1880s, Yun was implicated in the failed Kapsin Coup of 1884. Forced to leave Korea, he studied at the Anglo-Chinese College in Shanghai (where he was christened in the Methodist Church), then returned to the United States to study at Vanderbilt and Emory. After 1895, Yun served in the

Chosŏn bureaucracy, most notably in the Education and Foreign Ministries, and as the Vice-Minister of Foreign Affairs he attended the coronation of Czar Nicholas II in 1896.

Yun's prominence in the private reform movement of the period eclipsed even his successful political career. He founded and later headed the Independence Club (1896–98), and he edited its newspaper, *The Independent*, Korea's first. Leaving government service in the early 1900s, Yun directed several modern schools, founded the Korean Self-Strengthening Society, helped to organize the YMCA movement, and was a major voice in what came to be known as the Korean Enlightenment. As a Christian and moderate politician, Yun believed firmly in education, moral reform, and a gradualist approach to social and economic change. Strongly influenced by Christian theology and Social Darwinism, he placed these twin influences at the root of his conservative approach to social change. A great admirer of Japan, Yun felt that Korea's future lay in accomplishing fundamental changes similar to those of the Meiji reformers. In the aftermath of the 1910 annexation, Yun was imprisoned as a co-conspirator in the Case of the 105, an alleged plot to assassinate to direct combat. Japanese Foreign Minister Inoue Kaoru (1836–1915), ignoring his own diplomat's complicity in the coup, sought reparations for the legation building and Japanese victims. Ultimately he sent one of Japan's leading statesmen, Itō Hirobumi, to China, where he and Li Hongzhang negotiated a memorandum of agreement known as the Convention of Tianjin (1885), or the Li–Itō agreement. This convention resolved outstanding issues including troop withdrawals, a prohibition on either party sending military instructors to Korea, and an agreement to notify each other should either party decide to send troops to Korea in the future.

Korea lay helpless between Japan and China as the two great East Asian powers negotiated their distance from each other on the peninsula. In the aftermath of the coup, the Qing strengthened their influence in Korea by appointing Yuan Shikai as "Director-General Resident in Korea for Diplomatic and Commercial Relations." Yuan held this post for a decade, during which he advanced Chinese commercial interests at the expense of Korean and Japanese businessmen. He maneuvered with his conservative pro-Chinese allies in the Korean government to purge the remaining pro-Japan progressives from their posts, limit Korea's

the first Japanese governor-general, and he served a four-year prison term from 1911–15.

In spite of this treatment by the Japanese colonial government, Yun emerged after his prison term and spent his last active years encouraging change in Korean society within the confines of colonial rule. For the remainder of the colonial period, Yun refused to criticize Japanese policies, blaming Korea's plight on its own failures and weaknesses. Yun's critique of Korean society and support of Japanese colonial reforms has sullied his reputation in Korean nationalist historiography. In spite of all his contributions, Yun is often considered one of the great collaborators of the colonial period, along with Yi Kwangsu and Ch'oe Namsŏn (1890–1951), important nationalist intellectuals in their own right. While his legacy remains clouded by his pro-Japanese statements, his tireless work in education and other gradualist reform projects establishes him as one of the greatest figures, however controversial, in the history of Korean nationalism.

Yun Ch'iho (standing) photographed with his father Yun Ungnyŏl (seated) and his brothers, c. 1905.

diplomatic representation abroad, and slow the process of reforming the Korean military.

Yuan's appointment ushered in a near decade-long period of direct Qing ascendancy in Korea. Very different from Beijing's former hands-off policy, this constituted unprecedented interference in Korean affairs, and soon even conservatives who thought the Qing would be a source of support in the increasingly brutal international politics in Northeast Asia turned against their intrusive presence. The progressive movement both inside and outside the Chosŏn court had been hopelessly compromised by their choice of tactics. The bloody coup and its association with Japanese meddling discredited the progressive cause as well as the most powerful model of modernizing reform in East Asia, Meiji Japan.

QING INFLUENCE AND INTERFERENCE

Deepening Chinese influence and the predominance of conservatives, led by the Consort Min Clan, in the Chosŏn government could not impede influences that had been put in motion by the unequal treaties, which opened the ports and interior to the world economy. While Yuan Shikai maneuvered to give Qing subjects an advantage in the Korean economy, Japanese, European, and American economic actors could penetrate Korea as well. Foreign trade brought imports of cheap manufactures into Korea that revolutionized the marketplace.

Traditional Korean handicraft industries—which produced textiles and other items of daily use—declined, helpless to compete in either quality or price against machine-manufactured items. In spite of the government's attempts to limit the export of rice, the rice market burgeoned and soon Korean peasants were selling their harvest to international rice brokers for cash. Government needs for revenue, and corruption at the center, meant proliferation of taxes and increased burden on a peasantry already reeling from the structural changes in the economy. Not surprisingly, the peasantry began to associate their worsening conditions with the increased presence of foreigners on Korean soil.

The new treaties had made provisions for the residence of foreigners both in Seoul and in the interior. After the signing of the 1882 treaty with the United States, American missionaries, soon joined by colleagues from Europe and Canada, established a presence in Korea

that would lead to the creation of the most successful evangelical Protestant movement in Asia. American Presbyterian missionaries founded a clinic and hospital in 1885 that became the leading medical school and hospital in modern Korea. A Presbyterian boys' school, the Paeje School (1885), and the Ewha School for girls (1886) both evolved into leading universities. Missionaries began to attract progressives and youth interested in Western-style education, and thereafter the various churches became focal points for new ideas, education, and a window on the outside world. Many of the early reformers of what became known as the Korean Enlightenment were Christian converts, and Protestant Christianity established itself strongly in North Korea, an area already estranged from Seoul politics because of longstanding discrimination against northern elites by the metropolitan officials.

By the late 1880s, the countryside had become increasingly unsettled. Peasant distress was particularly acute in Korea's rice bowl in the southwestern Chŏlla province, an area of highly concentrated landholding and consequently high tenancy. Rural banditry and protests against corrupt local magistrates increased as well. By this time the Tonghak religion (see p. 157) had grown to be a force in the countryside. Although its founder, Ch'oe Cheu, had been executed in 1864 and the religion formally suppressed, it had continued underground and grown under the direction of its second leader, Ch'oe Sihyŏng. Ch'oe created a unique network of "parishes" linked through a leadership hierarchy. The church grew rapidly during this time because its relatively egalitarian teaching could be effectively combined with the peasantry's deep hostility toward the *yangban* class in general. The Tonghak organization in the countryside, therefore, offered a means of mobilizing protests for diverse grievances against local and central government.

The latent force of the Tonghak emerged in 1892 when several thousand adherents rallied at Samnye in Chŏlla province and demanded the posthumous exoneration of the martyred founder, Ch'oe Cheu, and an end to the repression of the Tonghak religion. The governors of Chŏlla and neighboring Ch'ungchŏng province refused to transmit the Tonghak demands to Seoul, and nothing came either of this appeal or of a later direct entreaty to the throne. In April 1893, however, 20,000 Tonghak believers assembled at Poŭn in Ch'ungchŏng province, this time to demand the removal of corrupt officials and expulsion of foreigners from Korea. Local authorities suppressed the demonstration only with great difficulty.

Finally, in the spring of 1894, a massive uprising led by Tonghak adherents, precipitated by longstanding abuses of the county magistrate, emerged in Chŏlla's Kobu county. When the central government brutally subdued this initial rebellion, the uprising swelled to become the largest peasant insurrection in the history of the dynasty. Under the leadership of the head of a local Tonghak parish, Chŏn Pongjun (1854–1895), the greatly augmented rebel forces seized control of a number of counties, routed a government expeditionary force sent to block their northward march, and captured Chŏnju, the capital of Chŏlla province. At this point the government appealed to the Qing for military help, and both Qing and Meiji Japan sent forces to Korea in the following months. A ceasefire was established and an immediate crisis was avoided, but in July of 1894, clashes between Chinese and Japanese troops in Korea precipitated the outbreak of the first Sino-Japanese War.

THE SINO-JAPANESE WAR AND THE KABO REFORM, 1894–95

The resolution of the Tonghak uprising was obscured by the more dramatic confrontation between East Asia's largest powers. A combination of Chosŏn and Japanese troops put down a second Tonghak attempt to march to Seoul, but the real action quickly shifted to a direct military conflict between the Qing and Japan. On land, the Japanese routed Qing troops at Pyongyang and advanced down the Liaodong peninsula, attacking and seizing the strategic ports of Port Arthur and Dalian (J. Dairen), avoiding the heavy fortifications the Qing had set up to prevent an invasion from the sea. By sea, the Japanese navy destroyed the Qing fleet in the Bay of Korea, using superior tactics, training, and firepower. By the spring of 1895, the Qing had to sue for peace, resulting in the Treaty of Shimonoseki, signed on April 17. The treaty's first article declared Korea to be fully independent from the Qing, repudiating the centuries-old China–Korea relationship. The treaty also required China to cede the Liaodong peninsula and Taiwan to Japan, giving the Meiji a foothold for further expansion in Manchuria and on the continent.

The Sino-Japanese War was certainly a disaster for Korea, but more importantly it profoundly and permanently altered power relations in East Asia. Japan had established its predominant interests in Korea for the moment, and, temporarily, its first important colonial presence on the mainland. The island of Taiwan became Japan's largest colonial possession, and its administration set many precedents for later acquisitions in the coming decades. Moreover, the victory marked an important watershed in the evolution of Japanese nationalism, with the entire country—progressives and conservatives alike—rejoicing in the glow of the victory.

The Qing's defeat exposed both its defense forces and its military modernization program as hollow and incompetent. The results of the war further revealed a catastrophic lack of unity, for the Qing could not bring to bear its full military power against the Japanese in the north—southern military commanders refused to send ships or troops to participate in the war. Most important, the victory over the Qing, which surprised many international observers, established the Japanese in the eyes of Europeans and Americans as a serious regional power. The new Japanese presence in Liaodong and claims to Korea threatened Russia to the point that they immediately combined with France and Germany in the Triple Intervention, forcing Japan to retrocede Liaodong to the Qing in return for increased indemnities.

Using the war as a pretext, the Japanese had taken control of the Korean government by removing pro-Qing officials and packing the important deliberative positions with pro-Japan supporters. While occupying Seoul at the beginning of the war, they imposed a number of concessions on the Chosŏn government: the right to build a railroad between Pusan (formerly Tongnae) and Seoul, the opening of a new port on the west coast (Kunsan), a military alliance, and, more ominously, a vague agreement for the Koreans to "accept" Japanese advice on internal reforms. The latter emerged in a series of important legislative actions known as the Kabo Reform of 1894.

The Japanese helped the Korean government create a new deliberative body and packed it with moderate reformers and pro-Japanese officials. They even brought back from exile two leaders of the failed Kapsin Coup, Pak Yŏnghyo and Sŏ Kwangbŏm (1859–1896). This initiated a sweeping set of changes in government structure, fiscal organization, methods of government

203

recruitment, and traditional social norms. Much of the governmental reorganization mimicked the Meiji adaptation of Western governmental structures established in Japan during the previous 25 years, realigning responsible bureaus and departments into eight ministries to reflect new government responsibilities and interests.

The reforms also diluted the monarch's relationship to government by characterizing his role as a reigning, not ruling king. Additional provisions segregated royal financial assets within a department of Royal Household Affairs (ironically similar to that of the Qing). Ministries of Finance, Industry, and Agriculture and Commerce consolidated all central government economic functions. A new Ministry of Education became responsible for oversight of traditional educational institutions such as the Sŏnggyun'gwan (Academy for Confucian Studies) and for the creation of a new system of modern normal (teacher training) and primary schools.

The Kabo Reform abolished the traditional examination system that had been the means for recruiting officials as well as validating social status among the *yangban* class from the beginning of the dynasty. This effectively eliminated Confucian studies as the sole determinant of talent and stranded an entire generation of young scholars in the midst of their preparation for civil office. In its place, the reforms created a recommendation system that privileged new skills learned in the growing number of schools that emphasized Westernized curricula. Many younger scholars caught in the switch of credentialing systems for government service as well as a younger generation of officials already ensconced in the central bureaucracy shifted their attention to the study of foreign languages, Western history and politics, or commerce. The well-known translator and journalist Chang Chiyŏn (1864–1921) and the historians Sin Ch'aeho (1880–1936) and Pak Ŭnsik (1859–1926) belonged to this generation of transitional intellectuals.

The Kabo social legislation became significant in the long run, but as with all attempts to legislate the change of entrenched social norms and mores, the new rules could not take effect immediately. The old, fixed class structure and the institution of slavery were abolished formally, and the longstanding prohibition against the remarriage of widows, most important perhaps among the upper classes, was eliminated. The removal of traditional status distinctions in society worked in tandem with the elimination of the civil examination system (which had been open only to *yangban*) to create new avenues of social mobility in Korea. In theory, anyone could now serve in the government on the basis of education, skills, and recommendations, not only on the basis of ascribed, hereditary social status. Other, more cosmetic, pronouncements such as the encouragement of Western dress and hairstyles followed in the year after the initial Kabo legislation.

The Triple Intervention brought Russian influence to its peak in Korea and led to political chaos in its aftermath, including another reshuffle of the Korean cabinet. The ensuing struggle between pro-Japanese and anti-Japanese factions led to a bizarre and successful plot to assassinate Queen Min (1851–1895), the symbolic leader of the anti-Japanese officials. The horrible murder of the queen in October 1895 galvanized anti-Japanese forces and badly tarnished the Japanese image in East Asia.

In the aftermath of the assassination, the Korean government, especially the group around the king, leaned to the Russians for help. The viciousness of political struggles in Korea at that time led to rioting, rumors, and counterplots. Ultimately, King Kojong, fearing for his life, sought refuge for a year in the Russian embassy. The murder of the queen and the king's flight to the Russian embassy marked the nadir of Korean political agency in the maelstrom of foreign intrusion into its affairs after 1876. Moreover, it made a mockery of the last vestiges of royal prestige claimed by the Chosŏn monarchy and anticipated the demise of the dynasty itself. A decade later, the Japanese forced Kojong to abdicate in favor of his son Sunjong (1907–1910) as punishment for his plea to the World Peace Conference (1907) to consider Korea's plight as a Japanese dependency. The Western powers scarcely noticed; indeed, they were busily putting the last agreements together with Japan, covertly if not publicly to recognize its "right" to suzerainty on the peninsula.

DIASPORAS

JAPAN

When Tokugawa laws preventing overseas journeys were lifted in 1858, government-sponsored missions soon traveled abroad in search of knowledge. But few non-elite Japanese ventured overseas. The first to do so were 148 workers recruited in 1868 by an American businessman to work on sugar plantations in Hawaii and about 40 recruited to work in Guam. In the wake of the ending of slavery in the United States, this type of plantation work continued many of slavery's oppressive conditions.

The maltreatment of Japanese laborers overseas concerned the government for both humanitarian and, perhaps more important, diplomatic reasons. The Meiji government, with its focus on revising the unequal treaties, feared that the image of oppressed laborers made Japan appear to be a "pauper" nation undeserving of diplomatic equality. Policy-makers therefore differentiated between settlers in colonies (J. *shokumin*) and emigrants (J. *imin*). The former were desirable, implying the promotion of national interests through expansion. The latter migrated as individuals and were subject to discriminatory treatment that wounded national pride, so would-be emigrants could not get passports before 1885.

Hundreds of Japanese women, inhabiting brothels around the Pacific Ocean, were part of an undocumented late nineteenth-century diaspora. Some worked in Vancouver and San Francisco or as far afield as South Africa, but most labored in Southeast Asia, China, and Northeast Asia. In a pattern opposite that of European migration to colonies, Japanese women emigrants outnumbered Japanese men in Northeast Asia for several decades into the twentieth century. Many were sex workers, though some were adventurers seeking opportunities unavailable to women at home. While Japanese feminist groups railed against overseas prostitution, claiming it denigrated women and tarnished Japan's image, others praised Japan's overseas sex workers as a vanguard of civilization in frontier regions.

In 1885, Japan signed a convention with Hawaii that allowed 29,000 Japanese to enter Hawaii as contract workers. Some remained there after their contracts ended. Others, discovering that American employers sought Japanese laborers following the Chinese Exclusion Act of 1882, went on to the mainland United States. At first welcomed, within a decade they, too, suffered the discrimination earlier directed toward Chinese workers. After Hawaii, with 13,000 immigrants, the largest diaspora of Japanese before the turn of the century was to Chosŏn. In 1890, there were over

7,200 documented Japanese residents in Korea, about 850 in Manchuria and China, almost 400 in Vladivostok, about 2,000 in the United States, and about 100 each in Canada and Australia.

CHINA

By the mid-nineteenth century, Chinese had settled not only in Southeast Asia but everywhere in the world. Poverty, overpopulation, and dreams of wealth stimulated a mass exodus from the southern coast, and the European colonial regimes of the nineteenth century facilitated their increase. Bound for mines or plantations, millions of Chinese, overwhelmingly poor and male, some of them voluntary and some kidnapped ("shanghai-ed"), became an important commodity of international trade. Large numbers succumbed to harsh conditions and desperate poverty, but some of them became wealthy participants in that same system. Like migrants from many parts of the world, they considered themselves sojourners, temporary settlers, and intended to return to their hometowns once they had made enough money to retire. Many did, but many also re-emigrated back to their overseas communities and continued as transnationals.

The inauguration of regular steamship service all over the globe facilitated this great migration, as it did the movement of millions of impoverished Europeans to North America. In the days of sail, a high percentage of Chinese migrants, like Africans caught up in the slave trade, died before arriving at their destinations. But rapid steamships brought them, healthy and ready to work, to places where European capitalism had discovered raw materials and markets. In many, Chinese became middlemen between the colonial masters and the indigenous people, dominating entire local industries. They took charge of sugar cane in the Philippines, tin mining in Malaya, rice milling in Siam, and, most common of all, peddling and running small grocery stores and laundries. This pattern—often compared to the Jews of Europe and the Indians of East Africa—depended on a regular stream of cheap labor, on transnational networks of intermediaries, and on tolerance from local authorities, usually enriched by the taxes, fees, and bribes paid by Chinese merchants.

Before the end of the nineteenth century, these diasporic communities did not generally unite on the basis of shared Chinese identity. Rather, they divided, sometimes violently, along native-place and linguistic lines, organized through lineage and hometown associations and secret societies. Their head men would simultaneously be the wealthiest merchants, holders of tax and opium revenue farms, leaders of the local Triads and hometown associations, appointees to colonial offices, and organizers of labor migration through "halls" (called *tongs* in Cantonese), which brought laborers into their local markets from their hometowns back in southern China.

Since Chinese women rarely emigrated, those Chinese men who could afford to marry sought local wives. In the Philippines, Thailand, Peru, Hawaii, even in Great Britain, Chinese married locals, and their children became *mixed-race*, crucial groups all over the world. José Rizal, the national hero of the Philippines, and Corazon Aquino, its 11th president; Joseph Kasa-vubu, first president of the Congo–Leopoldville Republic; the British writer Lesley Charteris; and the Thai royal family all share some measure of Chinese ancestry dating from this age of migration.[10] In some places (Thailand, the Philippines) intermarriage dominated, while in others (Java, the United States), impeded by religious or racialist discrimination, it remained rare. But whatever their status, Chinese people became ordinary parts of the social landscape all over the world for the first time in history.

KOREA

The borders between China and Korea were only fixed by treaty in 1712 along the Yalu and Tumen rivers and along a line parallel to the Changbai Mountains between the rivers. After 1667, the Qing prohibited migration into Manchuria, the "homeland" of the Manchus, an area roughly including the northeastern provinces of contemporary China. Manchuria remained relatively sparsely populated and consequently a lure to both Korean and Chinese economic migrants. The relatively empty land and abundant resources of Manchuria, with evidence of Korean residence back into the eighteenth century, attracted Koreans from the north and northeast of the peninsula. But large-scale Korean migration into Manchuria actually commenced in the 1860s. Beginning in 1865, a series of bad harvests created famine conditions in northern P'yŏng'an and Hamgyŏng provinces, so Koreans in the border region began moving across the rivers to farm. By 1869 there were over 37,000 Koreans living in Qing territory along the Yalu, Tumen, and Hun rivers, and in the Russian Far East north of Vladivostok as well.

Attempts by the Qing to repatriate these migrants failed consistently, and in 1879 Qing and Chosŏn signed a treaty that required the Qing to safeguard and protect the lives and property of the Koreans who had already immigrated into Manchuria, while continuing the formal ban on immigration. Korean farmers brought paddy rice agriculture to parts of Manchuria for the first time and also became involved in the important ginseng trade between Manchuria and both China and Korea. Recognizing the futility of the migration ban as well as the economic advantage of putting land under cultivation, the Qing opened a stretch of territory 245 miles (394 km) long and 20 miles (32 km) wide north of the Tumen River (present-day Yanbian) to Korean immigration in 1883. At this point there was no turning back the tide, and Korean immigration into Manchuria continued into the twentieth century, accelerating after the Japanese seizure of Korea in 1910. From these beginnings, the Korean population in Manchuria grew to nearly 2 million, one of the largest minority populations in contemporary China, close to 40 percent of the entire Korean diaspora of 5 million.

CONNECTIONS

The most obvious connections within East Asia during this period focus on the Sino-Japanese War of 1894–95. This conflict pitted Qing forces against Japanese, with Korea as the cause of hostilities and sometimes as the battleground. Both the weapons and the international context had changed beyond recognition in the 300 years since Hideyoshi's invasion of Korea. Rather than bows and swords, the combatants wielded rifles, bayonets, machine guns, and artillery. Massive battleships, cruisers, and destroyers, many of them built in Europe and purchased by the Qing and Japan, replaced Admiral Yi Sunsin's "turtle ships."

On the political side, China's cultural and ritual hegemony, embodying East Asian tradition, had been superseded by a system of theoretically equal nations, competing against one another for economic success and political power. In that new and unfamiliar context, Meiji Japan seized the initiative. Rising Japan had not only purchased "strong ships and effective guns" but also hired German officers to train troops and British commanders to instruct sailors, had rapidly built shipyards and railroads for transport, and constructed a government and legal system that would meet the approval of the Europeans and Americans. Neither Chosŏn nor Qing had yet accomplished as much—indeed, many in both realms still thought that they should not—so they continued to languish under unequal treaties.

Reform dominated the second half of the East Asian nineteenth century. We must remake our state and society, to regain power we have lost, to "enrich the country and strengthen the military," and protect ourselves against aggressive foreigners. The Meiji leaders and their Korean protégés like Kim Okkyun enthusiastically advocated Westernization of government institutions, economic activity, and the military as solutions to their countries' problems. Within the Qing court, officials tended to be more cautious, though "self-strengthening" required modernization of the military, and Li Hongzhang saw the benefits of sending students abroad to study. Some elites and popular movements, on the other hand, fought *against* change—the Tonghaks appealed to the traditional virtue of the king against corrupt magistrates; the Taipings wished to overthrow the Manchus and reestablish Chinese imperial rule under the Heavenly Kingdom; the Satsuma rebels under Saigō Takamori aimed to restore samurai privileges. In their eyes, change had gone too far, and aspects of the old system were worth dying for.

During this period, all three East Asian cultures confronted the expanding, apparently invincible power of Europe and the United States. Whether brought by soldiers, diplomats, merchants, or missionaries, the "imperial west" overturned old relationships and assumptions about how things should be. In order to understand the new power system, East Asians needed new words, language to comprehend what made these outlandish foreigners so powerful. Developed mostly by Japanese scholars and journalists and written in Chinese characters, the new vocabulary had to express not only technical ideas (electrical engineering, social contract, economics), but also unfamiliar concepts such as "state" (J. *kokka*, C. *guojia*, K. *kukka*), "society" (J. *shakai*, C. *shehui*, K. *sahoe*), and "nation" (J. *minzoku*, C. *minzu*, K. *minjok*). Because all East Asian elites could use Chinese characters, these words crossed the water very quickly and became common coin throughout the region, enabling literates to share translations and conceptual frameworks. But none of them wanted to jettison their own cultures entirely.

This period divided Meiji Japan—the winner—from Chosŏn Korea and Qing China. Neither Qing nor Chosŏn had given up, but the Japanese victory in 1895 unleashed powerful currents in both societies that eventually brought down the Qing and left Chosŏn helpless in the face of expansionist Japanese power. In all three societies, however, we find intellectuals and politicians (officials) facing the same dilemmas: Can we avoid depending on foreigners for weapons or protection? Can we master their techniques without enslaving ourselves to them? By 1895, Japan had already taken steps, sometimes confused but often brilliant, toward becoming a "modern nation-state" along European and American lines. Some individuals in Chosŏn and Qing advocated those same changes, but they faced prolonged, severe opposition.

207

CHAPTER SEVEN

MEIJI JAPAN RISES, QING AND CHOSŎN FALL (1895–1912)

WORLD CONTEXT

The expansion of European and American empires continued after 1895. With its victory in the Spanish-American War, the United States took colonies in both the Caribbean (Puerto Rico) and the Pacific (the Philippines and Guam). Washington followed the lead of white plantation owners and annexed the Hawaiian Islands in 1898, finally gaining full political control over an important strategic and economic outpost. To facilitate worldwide trade and passage for its two-ocean navy, the United States began the construction of the Panama Canal in 1904, following a French failure, and completed it in 1914, two years ahead of schedule.

Germany, trying to catch up to the established British, French, and American empires, occupied parts of Africa, Oceania, the Middle East, and China, where its Jiaozhou Bay colony (Qingdao, in Shandong province) created a rich harvest of conflict. Russia and Great Britain continued their Central Asian competition, causing London to seek an anti-Russian alliance with Japan. These imperial rivalries, which culminated in two world wars, played out all over the planet; few inhabited territories escaped the attention of one or more of the "great powers."

At the same time, all of the industrialized nations experienced domestic conflict between labor and capital, between state authorities and radicals (socialists, anarchists, revolutionaries) who fought to overthrow the established order. The 1905 revolution in Russia, stimulated by the catastrophic defeat of the Russian Baltic fleet by the Japanese navy, forced Czar Nicholas II to establish a constitutional monarchy and grant limited civil rights, though he also confirmed his own status as supreme autocrat. The founding of the Industrial Workers of the World (IWW) in the United States in 1905 inaugurated a new series of labor strikes and actions for free speech, as well as a search for international connections among workers, radical intellectuals, and revolutionary political groups. In Great Britain, organizations of leftist politicians, intellectuals, and trade unionists coalesced into the Labour Party, which by 1910 had 42 representatives in the House of Commons and growing power in working-class Britain.

This period also saw intense agitation in the realm of gender. Women's suffrage had been debated, and occasionally granted, since the French Revolution—in New Jersey (1776–1807) and South Australia (1861), for example—but the worldwide movement to gain the vote for women had national-level success only in the 1890s, with New Zealand (1893) first, followed by Australia, Finland, Norway, and Denmark. In Great Britain, the United States, Canada, Germany, and many other industrialized nations, suffrage movements fought on against intense opposition for another decade and more.

Deep and tenacious nationalism also characterized this imperialist age. Often expressed as militarism— "we are a superior country and people because we win wars"—this ideology fueled international rivalries but also helped people to understand *who we are* in an increasingly complex and dangerous world. People everywhere asked, "What sort of a nation are we? Who are our enemies? What is worth killing or dying for?" They often answered these questions in racial and national terms, for those explanations of human difference had seemingly been verified by "science" and by history as fundamental.

Developments in science and technology continued, as they do now, to advance human capacity for producing, healing, and understanding *and* to enhance the murderous power of weaponry. Electricity and electrical engineering took huge leaps into recognizable forms—lighting, electric trolley cars, etc.—with the work of scientists such as Edison, Westinghouse, and

East Asia, 1880–1912

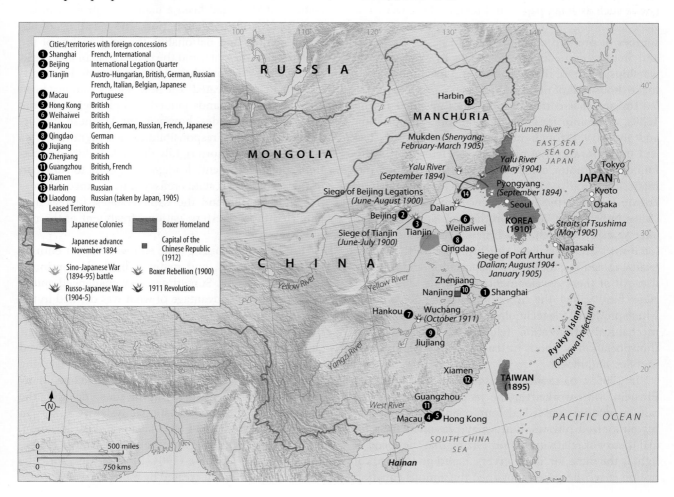

von Siemens. Electricity also transformed cultures, for the electric motor and lightbulb made possible the creation and projection of moving pictures, which rapidly became popular worldwide, creating the potential for international entertainment and stardom. Demonstrating the transcultural nature of scientific work, engineers from Russia, Croatia, Italy, England, Germany, India, New Zealand, Spain, and the United States (working separately) put together electricity, magnetism, and new technology to make possible the wireless transmission of electrical signals and eventually sound—the basic science of radio.

Along with electricity, great strides were also made in the field of chemical engineering (especially in Germany) with the invention of processes for refining petroleum, creating synthetic dyes and artificial fertilizers, and large-scale manufacturing of consumer goods such as soap, paper, and textiles. Discoveries in steel technology propelled both exploration for new sources of ore and coal (in Manchuria, for example) and improved metallurgy to create heavily armored warships, accurate rifled cannon, and machine tools to make thousands of new products.

The internal combustion engine, invented in the 1870s, came into mass production for transportation and industry through increased availability of steel and the innovations of men such as Henry Ford, who founded his motor company in 1903. Even more dramatic, that year a 12-horsepower petroleum-burning engine powered the first heavier-than-air flying machine, built by the Wright brothers of North Carolina after years of research, which flew a distance of 120 ft (36.5 m). Aircraft evolved quickly, in all of the industrializing nations, for both transportation and military use. All of these developments constitute what historians have called the Second Industrial Revolution, which produced the technology of our modern world—mechanical refrigeration, telephones, airplanes, mass transportation of goods in trucks and people in automobiles, and more.

In 1905, a naturalized Swiss citizen named Albert Einstein, who worked in the patent office analyzing new inventions, published four scientific papers that revolutionized physics. One essay presented the special theory of relativity, hypothesizing that the speed of light is the same for all observers. Based on this radical notion, a second paper contained the famous equation $e=mc^2$, which argues that tiny quantities of material might be converted into vast quantities of energy, the fundamental insight leading to the discovery of nuclear fission. The remaining essays provided direct evidence for the atomic theory of matter and an explanation of the interaction of light (energy) with matter, suggesting that energy comes in *quanta* (atom-like entities) rather than waves. Only 26 years old, Einstein had built on the discoveries of nineteenth-century mathematicians and physicists to transform our understanding of how reality works, insights rigorously tested over the following decades and largely verified through experiments and observations. The twentieth century had truly begun.

JAPAN

Nation-building had been a haphazard process in the first decades of the Meiji period. The meanings of national identity and nationality, the relationship of the individual to the state, and the place of Japan in a world dominated by nations that considered themselves modern all had to be created. The new "Japan" had just been born, and many hands guided its upbringing. By the last Meiji-era decades, however, the Japanese state itself and the rights, responsibilities, and identities of its subjects became more rigidly defined. In foreign relations, the government's leaders, struggling to rid Japan of the second-class status reflected in its unequal treaties with Europe and the United States, increasingly emulated those Western nations' treatment of the rest of East Asia.

But the modernizing state still was not yet entirely fixed in the 1890s, and many individuals continued trying to change it. Sometimes they challenged and at other times took advantage of what was defined in the law; manifested in the media, schools, economy, and politics; and embedded in Japan's changing relationship with East Asia and the world. The nation evolved as people increasingly viewed themselves as deserving a public voice, even if they did not yet have one. Many pressed for greater inclusion in the state, including the graduates of the new educational system, workers in factories that multiplied with Japan's industrialization, and soldiers returning from the Sino-Japanese (1894–95) and Russo-Japanese (1904–5) wars—in short, the new men and women created by modernization.

The nation also evolved territorially as the empire expanded. Thus, the modern nation of the late Meiji period developed both its human and its physical elements, linking economic growth, the empire, and the rise of what historian Andrew Gordon calls "imperial democracy." The inclusion of more popular voices—gradually granting the participation demanded by its voiceless members—paralleled the quest for international respect through building an empire. The pairing of democracy and imperialism, which seems so contradictory to us today, appeared natural to most late Meiji-era Japanese—as well as to the Americans, British, French, Germans, and other Europeans whose evolving democracies were also accompanied by expanding overseas empires.

This paradox of modernity in late nineteenth and early twentieth-century Japan—democracy and imperialism as two sides of the same coin—stemmed not only from impulses similar to those driving the Western imperialist democracies but also from the newly important concept of *minzoku* (C. *minzu*, K. *minjok*). *Minzoku* meant "ethnic group," but its meanings expanded in the first decade of the twentieth century. Japanese scholars and journalists published numerous works on this term, giving it a range of meanings that spread to include race (J. *jinzoku*), "the people" (J. *minshū*) in a democratic sense, "nation" (J. *kokka*) in a legal and not necessarily ethnically homogeneous sense, and "citizen/national" (J. *kokumin*).

In addition to being descriptive, *minzoku* could also be prescriptive; that is, it could be part of a call for reform. For example, it could suggest rising ethnic consciousness to combat imperialism or racial discrimination as well as popular consciousness to support marginalized people's struggles for civil rights or social respect. After World War I, *minzoku* entered popular discourse and was frequently used prescriptively, creating the multiple meanings of ethnic belonging that made the simultaneous pursuit of both democracy and imperialism possible in Japan. To be sure, the Japanese were not alone in their paradoxical uses of ethnicity—the Western democracies' acceptance of the principle of "self-determination of nations" based on ethnicity coexisted with the creation of the transnational League of Nations after World War I—but Japan's simultaneous struggle to expand the democratic rights of the "people" and build an empire that defined who belonged to the "people" had particularly strong impacts on the Chinese and Koreans, their fellow East Asians.

FROM FARMS TO FACTORIES AND MINES

As we saw in Chapter 6, Japan's leaders sowed the seeds of modern economic development in the first two decades of the Meiji period. They developed a steady revenue stream through taxes on everyday commodities and luxury goods and especially on farmers' land. Taxes on farmland accounted for as much as 90 percent of government income in the 1870s, and remained over 45 percent on the eve of the Sino-Japanese War. Tax revenues built the economic infrastructure, including the first railroads, harbors, telegraph lines, and model factories, as well as schools, government buildings, and the military. By the end of the Meiji era in 1912, no Japanese remained untouched by social and economic modernization, but these processes affected people unevenly.

The first part of the economy to grow was the most traditional: farming. Japan's population, which had stagnated during the last 150 years of the Tokugawa period, climbed from 35 million in the early 1870s to 44 million in 1900. Some of this growth occurred in cities and towns, as young women and men migrated to work in new industries. The farmers who remained behind—Japan's farm population dropped from about 80 percent in 1880 to 60 percent in 1900—increased their output by expanding cultivated acreage, using new farming techniques, and improving fertilizers. Between 1885–89 and 1910–14, Japanese farms increased their rice yield per acre by about 25 percent, a huge rate of growth. This allowed farmers both to pay the taxes that supported infrastructural development (transportation, communication, roads, government offices) and to feed the growing population of urban workers. Growth in agricultural productivity made farms more efficient, so "surplus" family members could take off to work in Japan's new factories and mines, to seek their fortune in Japan's new colonies, or to emigrate to Hawaii and North and South America. Increasing farm output allowed Japan to produce large quantities of tea and silk for lucrative overseas export.

These results of the growth of farm output contributed to modernity, though Japan's villages in the late nineteenth and early twentieth centuries would hardly have seemed modern to middle-class urbanites of the time. Exports of farm products like tea, which linked Japan to the growing global economy, and the transformation of silk cocoons into marketable fabric in factories owned by wealthy farmers and staffed by overworked farm girls were both significant examples of rural modernity. Shipments of tea and silk allowed Japan's nascent shipping companies, such as Mitsubishi—created when the Meiji government gave Mitsubishi's founder, Iwasaki Yatarō (1835–1885) 13 ships used in the Taiwan expedition in 1874—to compete with the American and British shipping companies that had dominated trade in the early Meiji decades. Wealthy farmers' roles in Japanese modernization were not limited to producing and marketing export goods. They also leveraged their wealth into upward social mobility, participating in local politics and sending their sons to the top universities, which led to elite positions in the government, society, and economy.

Poor families in the countryside were as linked to the modernizing state as the rich, but in different ways. Many worked as tenants of their rich neighbors, for government fiscal policies in the early 1880s had caused a massive deflation of rice and silk prices, causing many to default on loans and lose their farms. Tenancy rates increased from about 30 percent to 40 percent in the 1880s. Poor farmers' small, dark homes did not have the symbols of modern life, like pianos and space heaters, enjoyed by the rural rich. Their teenage daughters slogged through snow-covered mountain passes to take their places as indentured laborers in silk mills.

In contrast, the better-off sons and daughters of the countryside rode the trains that symbolized modernity. But it was the labor of the poor, especially women—in 1900, women were over 80 percent of textile workers and 15 percent of mining workers—that linked Japan to European and American markets. Some textile and mining products also went to Korea and China, along with traditional handicrafts fashioned by rural workers. Japanese farmers also received imports from the continent. Until chemical fertilizers came to be used in large quantities after World War I, fish-based fertilizers produced in Korea and China enriched Japanese farmers' yields, which, in turn, fueled national economic growth.

Japan's textile industry in the Meiji period had two sectors: silk and cotton. Both drew on the same pool of workers—young rural women—but the conditions of work and the technology of the firms differed. Many silk-reeling enterprises, called filatures, were located in the countryside, near the source of silkworm cocoons, owned and operated by rich farmers. Young girls, most in their mid-teens and with just four years of education, worked shifts as long as eighteen hours a day in peak production periods. The filatures shut down in winter, and the girls trudged home for those two months. Their fathers or elder brothers stamped their ten-month contracts—the Japanese equivalent of a contractual signature—for under Japanese civil law at that time, only male family heads could sign contracts concerning their family members.

Company recruiters combed the countryside for families willing to send their daughters to silk filatures. They paid these families an advance, often the families' largest annual cash income, for their daughters' indentured labor. When the worker arrived at the factory, she usually lived in a dormitory, wore a work uniform, and earned between 10 and 30 sen per day, between US$0.05 and US$0.15 (100 sen = 1 yen), out of which she had to pay for her own meals, usually about 2 sen each. Disease spread in the dormitories, most frighteningly tuberculosis, which was then incurable. Transmission of disease to the girls' villages was a cruel linkage of farm and factory, for factories sent sick workers home, and their families had to supply substitutes to repay their cash advances.

Silk reeling was one of the first industries in Japan to be mechanized. This allowed for the production of glossy fabric prized overseas, and exports of silk fabric to the United States jumped in value from 1.5 million yen to 21 million yen between 1889 and 1899. But the mechanization process remained highly dependent on the skilled manual labor of young girls. To reel silk, the preindustrial process had required the worker to drop living cocoons into boiling water, reach bare-handed into the water to lift them out when the worms inside had died, and then gently peel off a thread from each cocoon. The worker rolled the thin threads of several cocoons together between the fingers of one hand while placing the blended thread on a spool she rotated with the other. The first step toward mechanization was a foot treadle that rotated the spool at a more even pace. Filatures with good financial resources next replaced the foot treadle with a spool rotated by steam power and, later, electricity. But the worker still had to pull the cocoons from boiling water, find the end of the thread

Girls as young as 12 kept at least 10 cotton spindles spinning during 12-hour shifts in highly mechanized cotton mills. Tōyō Bōseki, seen here in a 1930 photo, was one of Japan's largest.

without breaking the cocoon, and roll several threads together. The even pace of the mechanized spool made for a finer product, but the difficulty of work increased, as the worker no longer controlled its pace, and mechanization did nothing to eliminate the most miserable part of silk reeling—reaching into boiling water.

Cotton spinning, more mechanized than silk reeling, did not require the same level of skill. The workers initially came from the same villages as silk workers, but as the industry grew, demanding more workers, recruiters sought girls from impoverished prefectures in the far northeast and Okinawa in the far south. Cotton workers' contracts demanded one or two years' work, with no winter break. As in the silk industry, male heads of household stamped girls' contracts and received advanced payment. Recruiters enticed teenage girls with promises of further schooling after work, good meals, clean baths, modern dormitories, the opportunity to enjoy city life, and the ability to send their wages home to help their families. Many girls who owned nothing but farm clothes were thrilled to keep the kimono they received for the journey to the factory.

But most of the recruiters' promises were deceptive. After long shifts, workers were too tired to attend classes; meals usually included just thin soup and rice, with a bit of fish perhaps once a week; baths consisted of lukewarm water covered by a film of body oil; and workers were forbidden to leave the factory until their

advance payment had been worked off, preventing them from enjoying urban life. Unlike silk filatures, cotton mills ran 24 hours a day, at least until 1929, when women and children were prohibited from working between 10:00pm and 4:00am. The expensive spinning machines, purchased in England, could not be left idle, so cotton workers worked 12-hour shifts, and companies assigned two girls on alternating shifts a single set of bedding, a prescription for disease transmission in the dormitories. Tuberculosis infected 20–30 percent of workers. Factory conditions were hard. Cotton lint filled the air, causing or exacerbating respiratory illnesses. Excessive heat in summer and cold in winter debilitated young workers who each had approximately ten spinning machines to oversee. Allowing threads to break or spindles to become clogged could be punished with a fine or beating.

But neither textile industry constituted an unremitting tale of woe. Not entirely passive victims of their families' and factories' exploitation, many girls sought out factory work despite their parents' fears for their health and safety, especially their sexual morality. Many made a hopeful gamble that their experience in the factories, especially the cotton mills, would be better than the other jobs available to poor girls and women— backbreaking farm labor, prostitution, and mining.

Once at the factory, many avoided the eyes and ears of supervisors to organize resistance. Because they ate at long tables and bathed in tubs that held a dozen workers, groups of women could talk without raising suspicion that they were organizing. Indeed, although men dominated the later labor movement, and women's contributions were long overlooked, women actually organized Japan's first industrial strike, at the Amamiya Silk Mill. After a small number of workers walked off the job in 1885 to protest managerial favoritism, a much larger group organized a strike the following year. They demanded better pay and work hours that would not require them to walk to work in darkness, which subjected them to sexual harassment.

Workers also resisted by escaping. Many factories had more than 100 percent employee turnover in a year, meaning most positions had to be filled more than once a year. Running home was harder for girls from Okinawa or the far northeast who could not afford train or boat fare, so many factory escapees remained in cities to seek better jobs, eventually marrying there and contributing to Japan's demographic shift from farm to city.

Workers' demands for fairness played out not only in strikes, but also in songs and other forms of "everyday resistance." The company taught them songs about service to the empire that compared them to soldiers—such as "Factory girls, we are soldiers of peace. The service of women is a credit to the empire"[1]—but the workers preferred their own satirical, politically charged lyrics.

Workers did not protest their conditions in isolation. Journalists' accounts of workers' abysmal working and living conditions began to appear in the 1890s, and Christian reformers raised their voices in protest. Advocates of workplace reform within the government, however, had a tougher time reaching the ears of their superiors. The government expressed its preference for economic growth over workers' rights with laws like the Public Peace Police Law of 1900 that, among other prohibitions, outlawed strike organizing. Nevertheless, government welfare officials issued a stinging report in 1903, describing the appalling health, welfare, and safety conditions in the textile mills. Parliamentary pressure and reports like these eventually pushed the government to pass the Factory Law of 1911, although businesses postponed its implementation—first until 1916, then 1926, and finally until 1929—claiming that workplace reforms would make Japanese products uncompetitive in the global market. This law finally protected women and children from the worst workplace abuses.

Textiles and other modern industries did not only affect workers. Japan's economic growth enabled the development of a middle class and political sector that demanded greater levels of democracy as well as the strengthening of the military. This, in turn, led to a shift in global attitudes toward Japan and the revision of the unequal treaties.

Many Japanese were aware of the workers' plight, but just as many viewed the captains of major industries as heroes. The most famous of these heroes was Shibusawa Eiichi (1840–1931). By the time he turned to cotton spinning in 1883, Shibusawa had already established a number of firms, introduced the idea of the joint-stock company to Japan, and founded Japan's First National Bank in 1872, setting up a branch in Korea in 1878. Shibusawa's Osaka Cotton Spinning Mill opened with over 10,000 steam-powered spindles and gas-lighting to keep them running 24 hours a day. In the next few decades, Shibusawa founded some 600 companies in varied fields such as paper, banking, mining, brewing, shipping, insurance, and textiles. In his later years, he preached industrial harmony through management paternalism toward workers. Shibusawa claimed to reject the profit motive, stressing that industrial success should not benefit capitalists but rather support the nation.

Furukawa Ichibei (1832–1903) also got his start in the textile industry—he established Japan's first mechanized silk filature in 1871—but made his reputation in copper mining. In 1877, Furukawa bought a copper mine at Ashio that produced only 33 tons (30 metric tons) annually. When he discovered a mother lode in 1884, he quickly installed advanced foreign technology and was producing half of Japan's copper by 1886. He next turned to the global market, signing a contract in 1888 with the British trading firm Jardine Matheson to export 19,000 tons (17,000 metric tons) of copper in a 29-month period. This forced him radically to accelerate output through modernizing his equipment. He set up a telephone system and established Japan's first hydroelectric plant to provide lighting and to power a railway in the mine. By 1890, Furukawa's output was almost 8,818 tons (8,000 metric tons) annually, and copper became Japan's third largest export item. In 1899, Furukawa was named one of the Twelve Great Men of Meiji by the influential magazine *The Sun*.

But not all was well at Ashio. Brutal labor bosses controlled Furukawa's thousands of overworked miners, who eventually rioted in 1907. Even more damaging, from its opening the mine generated extensive environmental destruction. A dirty industry under any circumstances, most copper mines elsewhere were located far from densely populated areas, but Ashio lay upstream from fertile farmlands. The poisonous effluents from the mining and smelting processes flowed directly into the Watarase River, which washed over fields downstream. Even before the 1888 Jardine Matheson contract, the mine had problems with flooding, and the wastewater ran an unnatural color that shocked the neighboring farmers.

The mine's new electric railway required railroad ties, and the opening of new tunnels demanded sturdy support beams, so the company denuded the surrounding hillsides to provide timber, leaving no vegetation behind to absorb the mine's run-off. The annual floods, which until then had left a fertile layer of silt, now turned deadly. Plants failed to grow, stillbirths multiplied, fish died, and odd sores appeared on farmers' hands and feet. The local representative to the Diet, Tanaka Shōzō (1841–1913), declared in a parliamentary session in 1891 that the mine's actions violated Japan's mining law and the protection clauses of the new Meiji Constitution. Tanaka's protest was one of the first uses of the modern legal and parliamentary system to address people's rights. Furukawa agreed to install antipollution technology and to compensate farmers in the surrounding villages.

But this did not solve the problem. In the next few years, floods sent new torrents of pollutants downriver. Local soldiers returning from the Sino-Japanese War questioned why their service to the nation was repaid with their families' suffering. University students organized seminars with "lantern slides" to raise awareness of the environmental disaster that pitted the poor against the industrialists. They joined church groups and women's organizations to send relief supplies to the affected area. Farmers marched on Tokyo in several mass uprisings in 1898, and many were arrested when they clashed with police. After a series of trials, the farmers were exonerated in the courtroom and vindicated in the court of public opinion—the modern newspapers spoke eloquently on their behalf. Furukawa had to make serious cleanup efforts.

The Ashio mine's story illustrates Japan's extraordinarily rapid economic growth and successful emergence into the global marketplace, accompanied by oppression of workers and destruction of farmers' livelihoods. It highlights the role of modern institutions like newspapers, the Diet, university students, and civic organizations (including women's groups) in framing the rights of individuals and communities, juxtaposed with the challenge of modern capitalism to the traditional social contract of the village. It raises the issue of who was to have a voice in the modernizing state.

Men, women, and children also worked in coalmines under difficult conditions. Until the Factory Law went into full effect in 1929—outlawing female and child labor underground—coal miners often worked as couples. The husband chipped the coal from the mine face, and the wife hauled 220-lb (100-kg) tubs of coal through narrow, low-ceilinged shafts and loaded them into coal cars. Mine managers preferred hiring married couples, believing this strengthened men's commitment to their jobs. In addition, because temperatures reached 130 degrees in many mines, male and female workers stripped down to their loincloths, so modesty demanded that married couples work together. Pregnant women hauled heavy baskets until right before childbirth, and some babies were born in the mines. Children as young as 5, small enough to crawl into the tiniest seams to find extra lumps of coal, sometimes accompanied their parents.

Young women who sought cleaner labor could work above ground sorting coal, but their pay was approximately the same as that earned by female textile workers—about one-third that of male laborers. Women who worked underground were less educated, more sickness-prone, and more likely married than those who worked above ground, but they earned up to 75 percent of their husbands' wages. Conditions in the mines were dangerous, and management control draconian, but many women chose higher wages over safety.

The largest coalmines were located in the southern island of Kyūshū. Coal was transported by rail—by 1900, Japan had 3,400 miles (5,471 km) of railroads, both publicly and privately owned until 1906 when the government nationalized most of the intercity lines—to fuel Japan's domestic industries and the many steamships in its ports. Two companies, Mitsui and Mitsubishi, dominated the Kyūshū mining operations. As in the case of copper, Japan was one of the world's leading coal producers in the late nineteenth century, a position it rapidly lost in the twentieth.

Mitsui, a long-established company, had sold fabric and lent money to the shogun in the Tokugawa period. In 1876, the Meiji government asked Mitsui to market the coal produced at the government-owned Miike mines, and Mitsui profited enormously. After Mitsui bought Miike from the government in 1888, its profits rose even more quickly, and the company opened trading offices in Shanghai, Hong Kong, and London. It later branched out into chemicals, cotton spinning, engineering, paper, and scores of other industries. As noted above, Mitsubishi got its start in shipping, but then went into mining, shipbuilding, railroads, machinery, chemicals, and more. Industrial conglomerates like Mitsui and Mitsubishi—and others including

GOTŌ SHINPEI, MODERNIST AND IMPERIALIST

Gotō Shinpei (1857–1929) exemplified the link between modernity and imperialism. A precocious student, he entered medical school at 17, served as a medic in the Satsuma Rebellion at 20, and became president of Nagoya Medical School at 25. After continuing his medical studies in Germany, Gotō returned to head the Home Ministry's Bureau of Hygiene in 1892. He used his office to advocate, unsuccessfully, for government medical insurance for the unemployed, arguing—as did his mentors in Germany—that social policy should focus on the poor.

Gotō Shinpei, demonstrating his skill as a radio broadcaster, 1920s.

The empire first affected Gotō's career in 1894–95, when he supervised the quarantining of soldiers returning from the Sino-Japanese War. His performance attracted the attention of General Kodama Gentarō. When Japan's violent suppression of anticolonial forces in Taiwan failed in 1897, Tokyo adopted more benign policies and appointed Kodama as governor-general in 1898. The general, in turn, appointed Gotō as civilian administrator, a post he held until 1906.

The cost of establishing Japanese rule in Taiwan was enormous; 11 percent of Japan's annual budget went to military and civilian expenses in Taiwan in 1896, so Gotō was anxious to run the colony more efficiently. He succeeded so well that by 1905, Taiwan was no longer financially dependent on Japan, and by 1907, the colony began to send money to the metropole.

Believing that Japan's modernization programs would not necessarily work in Taiwan, Gotō set up a committee to "investigate old customs." This led to the development of methods of modernization geared to local conditions—urban planning, sanitation, railroads, hydroelectric power plants, reduction of opium use, and scientific improvement of rice and sugar production. A household registration survey led to a modern census. Gotō made Taiwan a test lab for Japan's modernization, and the government adopted his census, urban planning, and sanitation methods

for national use. His advocacy of "gradual assimilation" received the support of some Taiwanese elites, who helped him suppress anticolonial resistance.

Gotō's success in Taiwan earned him appointments as the first director of the South Manchurian Railway in 1906, minister of communications and head of the Railway Bureau in 1908, director of the Colonization Bureau in 1912, home minister in 1916, and foreign minister in 1918. As foreign minister, Gotō supported Japan's Anglo-American allies against Germany in World War I and pushed for Japanese involvement in the Siberian intervention, which he viewed as enhancing Japan's continental presence (see p. 250).

Gotō also served as mayor of Tokyo. When the 1923 earthquake destroyed the city, the former urban planner of colonial Taiwan asked his friend, American historian and director of the New York Bureau of Municipal Research, Charles Beard, to help him plan a new capital city. Reappointed home minister, Gotō supported the right to vote for all males. The internationalist and reformist credentials of one of the framers of Japan's empire included his roles as Japan's chief boy scout and as the first director of NHK, Japan's national broadcasting system. Both an imperialist and an internationalist, a cosmopolitan and a technocrat, Gotō exemplified late Meiji Japan's modernizing elite.

Sumitomo and Yasuda—were called *zaibatsu* (literally, money cliques).

Government helped the *zaibatsu* with cheap loans, subsidies, and the sale of public enterprises at favorable rates as well as the benefits of government-supported infrastructure. By the early twentieth century, *zaibatsu* controlled hundreds of mining and manufacturing enterprises linked by overlapping management, a trading division, and a bank. They enjoyed close relationships with government and military officials. In some ways, they resembled the massive concentrations of wealth that emerged in the United States at the end of the nineteenth century. But unlike the American trusts, individual *zaibatsu* conglomerates were not monopolies or near-monopolies in a single field like oil, mining, or finance, but rather reached into virtually every sector of the economy. In addition, although the *zaibatsu*'s founding families continued to hold a majority of their shares, *zaibatsu* hired professional managers trained at Japan's top universities or overseas. After World War I, social critics began to see the *zaibatsu*'s dominant role in the economy as detrimental to smaller businesses as well as corrupting the political system.

Japan's overseas interests also played a part in its economic development. As we saw in Chapter 6, the Qing ceded Taiwan to Japan under the Treaty of Shimonoseki. Residents of Taiwan resisted their new colonial masters, declaring their independence in May 1895. The brutal suppression of their uprising continued until 1898, when Governor-General Kodama Gentarō (1852–1906) realized repression would only cause further resistance. He appointed Gotō Shinpei (1857–1929) (see box opposite) to be civilian administrator of Taiwan. Gotō's many reforms—including health and sanitation programs, development of railways, reduction in opium addiction, and scientific methods in farming—spurred the growth of Taiwan's economy, especially production of rice and sugar.

The 1895 treaty also forced the Qing to pay a 360 million-yen indemnity to Japan. Over 80 percent went to military spending, but a large amount also funded the construction of a modern steel mill at Yahata in Kyūshū. The government-owned Yahata mill helped Japan's trade balance by replacing some of the steel it had imported until then. It also trained young engineers who then diffused the Yahata technology when they founded their own firms.

Even before the Sino-Japanese War, Japanese investors had begun to set up companies in Korea. Some were "wild-east" fortune-seekers involved in less than savory enterprises like prostitution, for unlike Western nations' colonies, Japanese women outnumbered men overseas, and some of these women were sold to brothels. Some Japanese investors ran small companies, while others founded major enterprises like railroads and logging firms. A lively exchange of Japanese cotton for Korean rice emerged, and by 1900, 75 percent of Korea's trade was with Japan. Foreign trade was a vital part of Japan's economy, growing from 5 percent of GNP in 1885 to 15 percent at the end of the Meiji period, although Japan had a negative trade balance during most of these years. Savings sent home by emigrant laborers in the United States and Hawaii constituted another source of money for Japan's economy, accounting for approximately 3 percent of foreign currency earnings.

JAPAN AND THE WORLD

Japanese emigration was not without repercussions. A small number of Japanese sailed to Hawaii (141 men, 6 women, and 1 child) and to California (a few dozen) in the first two years of the Meiji period, and a few thousand more during the next decade. Although emigration was technically illegal until 1886, the government did issue some passports. Emigrants were more likely to sojourn in Northeast Asia and China than across the Pacific. In Hawaii—not part of the United States before 1898—most Japanese worked as contract laborers on sugar plantations. The work was hard and humiliating, but many saved enough money to book passage to the mainland United States. Californians had conducted a virulent anti-Chinese movement for several decades, but did not initially oppose these new East Asian settlers. When some 275,000 Japanese arrived in the United States and Hawaii around the turn of the century, however, anti-Asian prejudice extended to them. Although most were farm laborers, American labor unions considered them low-wage workers who undercut "white Americans'" factory wages. Fueled by scurrilous journalists, racist beliefs that Japanese men sexually menaced white women led to violent attacks on immigrants.

At the same time, some in Japan encouraged emigration both as a source of foreign exchange and, ironically, as a way of favorably influencing the foreign policy of host countries through the exemplary behavior of Japanese emigrants. The insulting behavior of Californians particularly shocked people who held these optimistic views, especially as it occurred despite Japan's collaboration with the Western powers in suppressing the Boxer Uprising in China in 1900, its alliance with England in 1902, and its stunning naval victory over Russia in 1905. Many Japanese thought of themselves as the modern leaders of Asia. The formation of the Asiatic Exclusion League in San Francisco in 1905 and the segregation of Japanese, Korean, and Chinese students in an "Oriental" school in 1906, after the San Francisco earthquake, led the Japanese government to protest strongly. US President Theodore Roosevelt, who had just negotiated the Treaty of Portsmouth that ended the Russo-Japanese War, also saw California's actions as insulting to the Japanese (see p. 241), though he accepted the segregation of Chinese children.

At the same time, Roosevelt needed to placate white Californians. Negotiations led to the so-called Gentlemen's Agreement of 1907, which tried to please everyone. The United States would not forbid Japanese immigration (as it had Chinese immigration in 1882), thereby saving Japan from international humiliation, as long as the Japanese government would refuse to issue passports to working-class men. By this agreement, it was hoped, only those laborers already in the United States would remain, and elite Japanese visitors and scholars could continue to enter the country.

As a humanitarian gesture, family members of Japanese men already in the United States were allowed to join their husbands and fathers. Under this agreement, signed in 1908, wives from Japan, many of them married by proxy (this was legal under Japanese law at the time), crossed the Pacific in large numbers. Their American-born children were automatically US citizens, and this rekindled racist sentiment. In 1913, the California legislature made it illegal for Asian immigrants to own land. In the following decades, the humiliation of unequal treatment engendered an ethnic sensitivity that Japan and the Japanese would never be treated as equals by the United States, a *minzoku* consciousness that later affected US–Japanese relations.

Despite the immigration issue, Japan emerged as a great power at the beginning of the twentieth century. Years of negotiations to revise the unequal treaties finally began to pay off, though not because Japan had developed modern institutions and legal systems, religious tolerance, and all the other requirements that Western powers had declared necessary and sufficient to revise the treaties. Rather, Japan had become a military power to reckon with. On the eve of the Sino-Japanese War, England became the first Western power to end extraterritoriality. Others followed in the next few years, and by 1911, Japan regained the right to set its own tariffs. As we saw in Chapter 6, the Triple Intervention by Russia, France, and Germany denied Japan the Liaodong peninsula in 1895, and within three years the Qing leased that same territory to Russia. Many Japanese felt they had been humiliated by the Russians, so it was small wonder that they turned to Britain, Russia's rival in power politics and the "Great Game," for support and alliance.

Japanese troops had been part of the multinational force suppressing the Boxer Uprising in 1900 (see p. 226). When the Russians used their own involvement in this expedition as an opportunity to expand into Manchuria and press the Japanese to abandon their interests in Korea, pro-British officials in the Japanese government raised the issue of a treaty with England. At the same time, the British, concerned about rising tensions in Europe, hoped that Japan could aid Great Britain by tying down the Russians in East Asia. The resulting Anglo-Japanese Alliance of 1902 not only elevated Japan to great power status, it also represented England's first modern mutual security alliance. Each side recognized the other's possessions and interests in East Asia and agreed to join its ally should Russia plus an additional country attack either.

Despite the treaty, Japanese diplomats did not give up on negotiating with Russia. Japanese and Russian diplomats met four times in 1903 to recognize the paramount interests of Russia in Manchuria and Japan in Korea. Neither side wished to abandon completely its claim to the other's sphere of interest, however. While senior leaders in Japan—particularly Itō Hirobumi—initially tried to avoid war, younger officers, hawkish journalists, and many politicians clamored for aggressive action when negotiations failed. Acting decisively, Japanese leaders decided to break off relations with Russia on February 4, 1904 and attacked the Russian Pacific fleet at Port Arthur (on the Liaodong peninsula) on February 8, inflicting severe damage. The Japanese government officially declared war two days later. The Japanese army moved northward in Korea, pushed into Manchuria, and defeated Russian land forces at Port Arthur in January and at Mukden in March 1905, both sides suffering considerable losses. When Russia's Baltic fleet arrived in the Straits of Tsushima in May, the Japanese navy disabled or destroyed 31 of their ships in a 24-hour battle. Only four made it to the Russian port of Vladivostok.

Despite this stunning naval victory, which gave Chinese, Vietnamese, Burmese, Indonesians, and Indians hope that they, too, could defeat Western imperialism, Japan's leaders knew they could not continue to fight. Over 80,000 Japanese soldiers had been killed or died of disease, and Japan's national debt reached 2.4 billion yen. Months earlier, US President Roosevelt had offered to mediate an end to the war, and finally diplomats from Russia, left without a fleet, and Japan, suffering terrible human losses and almost out of matériel, traveled to Portsmouth, New Hampshire, to negotiate a treaty. Roosevelt received the Nobel Peace Prize for his role as mediator.

When Japanese negotiators received little of the territory or reparations they sought in the Treaty of Portsmouth, jingoists exploded in riots at Hibiya Park in Tokyo. Many Japanese believed their sacrifices and victories should gain them prestige and power in East Asia. Although Japan received the Liaodong peninsula (the prize lost in the Triple Intervention), the southern section of the Russian-built China Far East Railway—renamed by the Japanese the South Manchurian Railway (J. *Mantetsu*)—and several Russian coalmines in Manchuria, nationalists criticized Japan's diplomats as sell-outs. Over the ensuing decades, however, these new possessions would come to have enormous importance for the Japanese empire.

Hashimoto Kunisuke. *Crowds Gathering to Read the News*, 1904. Museum of Fine Arts, Boston. Men and women, workers, soldiers, and professionals gather round a placard to read the latest news of the Russo-Japanese War. Increasing numbers of Japanese cared deeply about government affairs.

Despite widespread support for the war throughout Japan, socialists, feminists, and Christians opposed it, and many were jailed for their antiwar writings. One of Japan's leading feminist writers, Yosano Akiko (1878–1942), wrote a famous poem begging her brother not to fight: "Do not offer your life," she wrote. "The Emperor himself does not go to battle."[2] The Hibiya rioters and the antiwar activists seemed to occupy opposite ends of the political spectrum, but they resembled one another in a key way. That is, both believed that Japan's leaders—whether the delegates to the peace conference reviled by the rioters or the emperor rejected by the socialists, Christians, and pacifists—should not ignore the voices of the people, including the marginalized. All sought to be active participants in an expanding Japanese *minzoku*.

Foreign policy also altered Japan's regional role in East Asia. Two months before the Treaty of Portsmouth of September 1905, Japan's Prime Minister, Katsura Tarō, and US Secretary of War, William Howard Taft, signed the secret Taft–Katsura memorandum, recognizing each other's imperial interests in East Asia. Japan promised to respect the United States colony in the Philippines, and the United States gave Japan the green light to advance its interests in Korea. Britain concurred in August, and Japan forced Korea into protectorate status, by treaty, in November. The following year, Itō Hirobumi became Japan's first resident-general in Korea, a new position created to take over Korea's foreign relations and establish Japanese domination on the peninsula. By 1907, Itō had forced the Korean king to abdicate in favor of his son, dissolved the Korean army, and instituted a Meiji-style modernization program. Strong Korean resistance opposed these actions, and 20,000 Japanese soldiers were sent to suppress them. By the time the fighting ended, 17,690 Koreans had been killed and Itō assassinated by a Korean patriot, An Chunggun (1879–1910). Korea became a colony of Japan in 1910 (see p. 241).

Thus, by the end of the Meiji period, Japan had gained an Asian empire—most notably possessing Taiwan and Korea—revised its previously unequal treaties with Western countries, and built an alliance with Great Britain, the strongest nation on earth. At the same time, its citizens suffered disrespect and discrimination in North America. At home, the Japanese people demanded greater rights from their leaders and at the same time embarked on an international quest for power and status through imperialism.

POLITICS, RIGHTS, AND CITIZENSHIP

The first non-Western country to develop a constitutional system, Japan expressed its modernity in part through the Meiji Constitution and the bureaucratic practices that evolved in the late nineteenth century. But the citizens' rights articulated in the constitution were all circumscribed by the phrase "within the limits of the law," which gave the government the power to deny rights through regulation and legislation. This power forced advocates for rights and liberties to struggle to expand the boundaries of citizenship, just as their predecessors had done in the People's Rights Movement of the early Meiji period (see p. 184).

That struggle developed, among other places, in the new higher education system. The liberal "civilization and enlightenment" philosophies used by the People's Rights Movement became a part of Japan's secondary and university curricula, which contrasted strongly with elementary education. Elementary education, designed for the 90 percent of children who completed only six grades at the turn of the century, taught patriotism, good civic behavior, gender norms, ethics, and the basic reading and arithmetic skills helpful on the farm, in factories, or in small businesses. The curriculum did not aim to make the new Japanese subjects into independent thinkers.

In contrast, public middle schools, higher schools, and universities for boys and separate higher schools for girls offered a much more creative curriculum. Other than elementary schools and normal schools (teacher-training colleges), public schools were sex-segregated, with vastly superior schools for young men. Young women could only attend private colleges. Nevertheless, the small percentage of young men and women privileged to study beyond elementary school (about 10 percent) learned the various modern sciences, Western and Asian philosophies, history, and world literature. For many young people, going off to school represented a thrilling opportunity to prepare to contribute to modernizing Japan. Small wonder that many educated young people became involved in movements like the antipollution movement at the Ashio copper mine or, especially in the case of women, in women's rights groups.

Other Japanese already contributed to the new society through their involvement in both electoral and oppositional politics. Many of the men elected to the first few Diet sessions belonged to political parties that struggled with the small group of powerful men—an *oligarchy*—who had led Japan's Meiji government since 1868. The oligarchs (J. *genrō*) were, by the 1880s and 1890s, middle-aged and older men who, as young revolutionaries from places like Satsuma and Chōshū, had created the new Meiji state. Now they had become the establishment, trying to hold onto power and fearful of granting the rights of citizenship—voting, determination of public taxation and spending, freedom of expression, and the like—to all those Japanese who had come to see themselves as part of the *minzoku*.

The right to vote for one of the 300 members of the House of Representatives in the first national Diet in 1890 was limited by gender (male), age (over 25), and wealth (how much one paid in taxes). Most representatives were rich farmers, landlords, and businessmen, as well as a few urban journalists and other professionals. The members of the House of Peers, unelected in the early years of constitutional government, were aristocrats, former *daimyō*, top bureaucrats, and appointees from among the richest businessmen. As intended, they were far more conservative than the House of Representatives. The prime minister and the cabinet did not represent the majority party in the Diet, as in the British parliamentary system, but rather were appointed by the emperor, advised by the oligarchs. Although the Representatives were elected by less than 1 percent of the population, they struggled with the prime minister and his cabinet from the beginning. Political parties emerged from among the activists of the earlier People's Rights Movement.

Voters went to the polls six times between 1890 and 1894. The House of Representatives confronted the cabinet over taxes, social welfare (including poor working conditions in factories), and lowering the tax qualifications to vote. When parliamentary resistance made passage of the budget impossible—the government always wanted more money, and the Diet wanted to cut taxes and expenditures, especially for the military—the prime minister called for new elections. In 1894, the Sino-Japanese War ushered in a period of cooperation when the Diet rallied around the government, agreeing to higher military budgets. By 1900, the parliamentary struggle had resumed, and Prime Minister Itō Hirobumi, chief author of the constitution, conceded the need to compromise. He founded a new party, the Seiyūkai (Friends of Constitutional Government), resigned as prime minister, and left his party in the hands of Saionji Kinmochi (1849–1940), a liberal court noble, and Hara Kei (1856–1921), an effective party operative. For the next decade, the prime ministership alternated smoothly between Saionji and Katsura Tarō, the protégé of Itō's conservative counterpart and rival in the oligarchy, Yamagata Aritomo. The Diet gave the government the funds it wanted for the Russo-Japanese War, both prime ministers had a few Seiyūkai members in their cabinets, and the electorate expanded from 1 percent to 2 percent of the population.

Cooperation came to an end in 1912, when Prime Minister Saionji refused the army's requests for more money. In protest, the army withdrew the war minister from the cabinet, forcing Saionji to resign. Katsura then tried to create a new party and form a cabinet, but the Diet refused to support him. He asked the emperor to issue a rescript to force Saionji and his party to cooperate, an undemocratic action that inflamed public opinion. When the resulting Movement to Protect Constitutional Government exploded in riots in the winter of 1912–13, Katsura resigned. But in terms of constitutional government, important strides had been made. Within a few years, the party Katsura had tried to form became Japan's second important parliamentary party; and the ability of the military to bring down the government ended until the 1930s, when it returned with a vengeance.

Parliamentary government was not the only expression of the demand for citizenship or respect as part of the *minzoku*. In 1901, a small group of socialists established the Social Democratic Party. Although the party was immediately banned, socialists continued to

A woman chauffeur, 1911. Both automobiles and women's rights supporters like those in the Bluestocking Society made for exciting images of modernity at the end of the Meiji period.

publish their ideas through the *Commoner News*. After the Russo-Japanese War, the socialists intensified their antigovernment stance, staging demonstrations and taking part in riots, for which the government jailed many of them. In 1911, when a small group of radicals plotted to assassinate the emperor, 12 radicals, including some who had not been involved in the plot, were executed in what was called the Great Treason Incident. Leftist movements were temporarily stifled.

Women's rights movements also remained active in the late Meiji. Kannō Suga (1881–1911), one of the founders of the socialist feminist journal *Women of the World* (1907), was among those executed—most likely for her socialism rather than her feminism. Other women increased their activism in the face of repression. Women's rights organizations like the Women's Reform Society (founded in 1886 as a branch of the international Women's Christian Temperance Union), as well as advocates for factory workers and middle-class supporters of political rights, tried to make their views known. From the time of the People's Rights Movement, when women called for equal rights, through women's protest of the codification for the first time in 1890 of the policy that the emperor had to be male, women spoke out.

But Article 5 of the Public Peace Police Law (see p. 214), first passed in 1890 and reaffirmed in 1900, forbade women from joining political parties and attending rallies, though they could still write as journalists, and some became teachers. In 1911, Hiratsuka Raichō (1886–1971) and other feminists proclaimed in their new journal *Bluestocking*, "In the beginning, Woman was the Sun," and called on women to reclaim their lost rights. The repeal of Article 5 became the rallying cry for women's rights activists in the next decade.

By 1912, when Japan mourned the death of the Meiji Emperor, modernization had set in motion enormous changes in the economy, polity, diplomacy, and human rights.

THE END OF THE QING

RESPONSES TO THE 1895 DEFEAT

A favorite of the Empress Dowager, Zhang Zhidong had a reputation as a brilliant and incorruptible official. He rose rapidly within the Qing bureaucracy, held high offices all over the empire, and ended his career as a Grand Secretary. After the Japanese victory over the Qing in 1895, Zhang began to recommend young reformers to the emperor to overcome the stubborn conservatism of the court.

Zhang argued that the Qing could revive its former glory by renewing its foundation (c. *ti*) in Confucian ethics and Chinese tradition while adopting foreign scientific techniques (c. *yong*). Zhang's formula, with its ancient philosophical roots, created a middle option between the rejection of Western knowledge advocated by conservatives and the more radical changes desired by reformers and revolutionaries. Similar to earlier Japanese prescriptions—Sakuma Shōzan's "Western science, Eastern ethics" (see p. 165)—the *ti-yong* synthesis resembled nineteenth-century attempts all over the world to retain "our culture" in the face of overwhelming threats from "their power." From 1895 onward, this theme would run throughout modern Chinese history, as Chinese sought the secrets of "Western wealth and power" *while* drawing deeply on the resources of their own culture.

The "national humiliation" in the wake of the 1895 defeat stimulated both admiration and anger. If Japan could adopt European and American weaponry to defeat the Great Qing, then surely we Chinese can do even better—with our enormous pool of human talent, great cultural tradition, and vast economic resources—once we get our hands on appropriate techniques.

So in 1896, 13 young Chinese men arrived in Tokyo to begin a course of "Western studies." While they struggled (only seven finished), Zhang Zhidong wrote the famous "Exhortation to Study," praising Itō Hirobumi and Yamagata Aritomo for studying overseas and proposing a Qing public education system and expanded study abroad. He argued that Japan had succeeded because of:

> [1] the determination of a national policy [announced in] solemn covenant between the Emperor [J. Tennō] and his officials, [2] the establishment of an evaluative mechanism for the purpose of recruiting talented men, and [3] the creation of an office to draft regulations and the establishment of a constitution.[3]

Impressed by Zhang's stress on education, the Guangxu Emperor ordered his book distributed to all Qing students and officials.

REFORMERS AND REVOLUTIONARIES

Like Zhang Zhidong, Kang Youwei (1858–1927) argued that the dynasty had to reform in order to survive. After the 1895 announcement of the Treaty of Shimonoseki—the loss of Taiwan, the huge indemnity, the national humiliation—Kang organized over 600 examination candidates to protest against it. These elite men demanded that the Qing court repudiate the treaty, move the capital to Shanghai, modernize the military, continue the war, and reform the government.

For the next three years Kang bombarded the court with memorials and petitions, comparing the Qing with Russia and Japan, which had effectively (in his eyes) renovated their institutions. Like Wang Tao (see p. 191), he discovered that Chinese civilization had counterparts, that the Qing empire could only be one state among many. Only a decade or two before, this would have appeared monstrous, for the universal rule of the Qing emperor could never be compared to any other. To promote his proposals, Kang compiled a lengthy treatise entitled *Confucius as a Reformer* (1897), arguing that the historical Confucius had advocated reform, justifying Kang's own reformism as deriving from tradition.

By this point, many Chinese recognized the necessity to translate "Western studies" into their own language, decades after Japan's Dutch learning scholars had done the same. In an international collaboration, Chinese and foreign scientists at the arsenal in Shanghai had rendered the periodic table of the elements and many other chemical terms into Chinese, and similar translations appeared in other sciences. The telegraph and other foreign innovations had already demonstrated their usefulness and had been adopted, though cautiously at first, by the Qing government. But outside of science, a broad spectrum of elite Chinese wanted to learn the economic and political secrets of foreign wealth and power.

Yan Fu (1853–1921), a Fujianese doctor's son, had trained for the official examinations but, like Wang Tao, his father's early death drove him into the job market. Weeping at this unorthodoxy, his mother sent him to the Fuzhou naval school to study the "Western" sciences. At 25, the academically gifted young man earned a place at the naval academy in England. The Qing ambassador there shared Yan Fu's conclusion that far more than "strong ships and effective guns" underlay British success. The Qing would have to change its political and legal institutions, its social structure, even its values in order to compete for "wealth and power."

Bearing this risky reformist notion, Yan Fu returned home in 1879 and joined the Shanghai arsenal's faculty. After the 1895 defeat, he erupted in public prose, beginning with a series of essays on the state of the world and Qing weakness. During the next 15 years, he published translations of what he judged to be the key works explaining European success, including Spencer's handbook of Social Darwinism, Adam Smith's explication of capitalist economics, Montesquieu's proposal for constitutional government and impersonal law, and John Locke's fundamental text on individualism and free speech.

Yan Fu's translations—in difficult classical Chinese—stimulated a zealous and longlasting exploration of European and American ideas among elite Chinese eager to preserve their culture, as they thought the Japanese had done. Persuaded that their traditional values could no longer be the sole support of state and society, his readers sought transformation through intellectual activity, trying to comprehend Western concepts such as evolution, nationalism, and individual freedom within a cultural universe still dominated by Chinese classical learning. Although he wrote for highly educated elites, Yan Fu's work, like Kang's, nonetheless broke

with the past. He used the language of the ancient Chinese texts to propose modern ideals such as individual freedom:

> …policies to benefit people must start with the people's ability each to benefit himself, and the ability to benefit oneself starts with each one's enjoyment of freedom. If each is to have freedom, this must begin with the ability of each to control himself. Otherwise there is chaos. And those who can control themselves in freedom are those whose strength, wisdom, and virtue are truly superior.[4]

Not all Chinese favored preservation of the Qing state. They feared their culture's extinction by imperialism and colonialism and argued that a more powerful, representative government should replace the decaying dynasty. Unlike reformist elites, who wanted to change and preserve the Qing, men like Zhang Binglin (1868–1936) found Qing rule entirely illegitimate because it was *Manchu* rule, not Chinese, for which he used the "ethnic" term *Han*. He wrote to Kang Youwei in racialized language, using European examples:

> Today five million Manchus rule over more than four hundred million Han only because rotten traditions make the Han stupid and ignorant. If the Han people should one day wake up, then the Manchus would be totally unable to rest peacefully here, like the Austrians in Hungary or the Turks in the former Eastern Roman Empire. It is human nature to love one's own race and to seek gain for oneself.…[5]

Like the reformers, many anti-Manchu leaders came from the far south, distant from the Qing center and exposed to foreign influences. Sun Yat-sen (1866–1925), called "the father of the country" by most twentieth-century Chinese, came from a part of Guangdong famous for emigrants. His older brother owned a store in Honolulu, so as an adolescent Sun joined him there and excelled at English. Back in China, the young man became a Christian, gained admission to the first class at the Hong Kong College of Medicine for Chinese (founded by Ho Kai; see p. 195), and received his MD in 1892.

When Li Hongzhang rejected his reform proposals, Sun turned to revolution and the overthrow of the

Manchus. From 1894 on, he prepared numerous uprisings and spent 16 years outside the Qing empire as a fugitive. His financing came largely from the Chinese diaspora (see pp. 99–100, 135–36, 170–71, 205–6), from Southeast Asia to the Americas to Europe. Diasporic Chinese, victims of anti-Chinese racism, wanted their homeland to be strong enough to defend them, so Kang Youwei's pro-Qing reform societies and Sun Yat-sen's revolutionary insurgents competed for their substantial donations. Sun had close connections with secret societies (Triads) through their long tradition of anti-Manchu activism and deep roots among southern Chinese abroad.

Sun first attempted a coup in late 1895, trying to take advantage of the confusion of defeat by capturing Guangzhou. His tiny Revive China Society was betrayed, the Qing executed some of his comrades,

and Sun fled to Japan. There he cut off his queue, symbolically breaking with the Qing, and with the help of Japanese supporters went to the United States and England to lecture and raise funds. In London, the Qing ambassador arranged to have him kidnapped and detained at the embassy, to be shipped home for certain execution. A newspaper broke the story, the British Foreign Office demanded his release, and Sun Yat-sen instantly became an internationally recognized figure, a legitimate opposition leader rather than a terrorist.

Sun hoped to make use of Japan to forward his revolution, seeking allies among opposition leaders such as Itagaki Taisuke, but only between 1895 and 1900 did he receive significant financial support. Mainstream Japanese politicians wanted stability in the Qing, not revolution. Sun's successes came primarily among the more radical Japanese Pan-Asianists, who believed that all Asians should jointly defeat European and American imperialism. Although they had a common enemy in the imperialists, Sun and these Japanese nationalists shared little other than a romantic attachment to revolutionary violence. Sun claimed the mantle of the pre-Meiji *shishi* ("men of high purpose") who

Sun Yat-sen (front row, center) in Japan, 1916. Sun lived in Japan after 1895, recruiting supporters, monitoring developments in China, and traveling to raise funds for the anti-Qing cause in overseas Chinese communities.

fought to topple the Tokugawa, but his Chinese nationalism could not tolerate Japanese incursions on Qing sovereignty.

Like many Chinese, Sun Yat-sen envisioned the nation of "China" inheriting the entire territory of the Qing, including Manchuria, Mongolia, Xinjiang, and Tibet. But he focused his attention primarily on what the Qing called the *Han* people. These were the cultural and linguistic Chinese, composing an ethnic unity of some 400 million people. They had not yet begun, however, to imagine themselves as a "nation." As a politically radical Cantonese, Sun Yat-sen would have, in fact, seemed unfamiliar and threatening to many northerners. Having read the Euro-American theorists who saw "race" as the most important difference among peoples, Sun argued that the overwhelmingly numerous, urbanized, commercialized, cosmopolitan Han "race" should lead the backward frontier "races"—Manchu, Mongol, Turki, and Tibetan—into the modern world. Sun imagined a New China, a republic of, by, and for the Han "race," replacing the alien, incompetent Manchu Qing.

KANG YOUWEI AND THE HUNDRED DAYS OF 1898

In contrast, Kang Youwei aimed his persistent advocacy of "reform within tradition" at the Guangxu Emperor, who formally assumed personal power in 1889, began to learn English, and tried to understand the changing world. The Empress Dowager—the emperor's aunt—continued to wield substantial authority through her faction at court and her personal ascendancy over the young monarch. Holding too low a rank to address the throne directly, Kang Youwei joined new-style civic groups, sponsoring lectures, translations, and periodicals to encourage reform. His student Liang Qichao (1873–1929) popularized reformist ideas in Hunan province, a hotbed of radical politics.

A foreign relations crisis in late 1897 gave Kang a more direct opportunity to influence the court. Russia ceded to Germany its rights to Qingdao, on the southern shore of the Shandong peninsula, and the Germans then forced the Qing to grant them a 99-year lease of the city and its hinterland, Jiaozhou prefecture. After gaining ascendancy in Chosŏn, the Russians, in turn, occupied Dalian and Port Arthur, on the southern tip of the Liaodong peninsula, and demanded the right to construct a railway northward through the mineral-rich Manchu heartland to link with the already-built China Far East Railway.

After bribing Li Hongzhang and his fellow negotiators, the Russians occupied Liaodong, which they had forced Japan to return to the Qing only two years before. The British, French, and Japanese followed—in an international "Scramble for Concessions"—demanding territory and railway construction rights all over the empire. Horrified by Qing weakness, one of the emperor's intimate advisers introduced Kang Youwei's reform proposals to the monarch. Although scorned by the Empress Dowager and her allies, Li Hongzhang, and the Manchu Grand Councillor Ronglu (1836–1903), Kang's ideas appealed to the emperor, who ordered that Kang's memorials be forwarded directly to him.

In the spring of 1898, Kang wrote several powerful recommendations for wide-ranging institutional change, including replacement of the traditional six boards of the central bureaucracy with European-style ministries.[6] On June 16, 1898, the two men finally met, and Kang told the emperor:

> ...all the laws and the political and social systems [must] be changed and decided anew, before it can be called a reform. Now those who talk about reform only change some specific affairs, and do not reform the institutions...most of the high ministers are very old and conservative, and they do not understand matters concerning foreign countries. If Your Majesty wishes to rely on them for reform it will be like climbing a tree to seek for fish.[7]

Profoundly impressed, the emperor appointed Kang to the foreign ministry, and radical reform edicts followed immediately. The emperor ordered alteration of the official examinations to deal with current affairs rather than the Confucian Classics; an imperial medical school; simplification of administrative procedures; permission for Manchus to engage in commerce; teams of high officials to undertake foreign study tours; preparation of an annual government budget; and the elimination of many highly paid but low-functioning offices. For over 100 days that summer, Kang and his allies had control of the emperor's autocratic writing-brush, which in theory could have entirely transformed the Qing state.

But it was not to be. Profoundly alarmed by the reforms' potential to overturn their world, conservative officials throughout the realm ignored the emperor's edicts. In September, informed of the reformers' plans by Yuan Shikai, returned from Chosŏn and appointed commander of the Qing's New Army, Ronglu rushed to Beijing (by train!), where he and the Empress Dowager staged a coup. The Empress Dowager justified retaking the reins of government by announcing that the emperor was seriously ill, so the unfortunate young monarch became a permanent prisoner. Kang Youwei and Liang Qichao escaped to Japan, but several of their colleagues, including Kang's brother, were summarily executed, and Kang's writings were banned. The tide of reform had been temporarily halted.

"SUPPORT THE QING AND ANNIHILATE THE FOREIGNERS"

In late 1898, the Empress Dowager and her faction had to cope with the aggressive Europeans, and antiforeign sentiment remained deep and widespread. In Shandong, French and German Catholic missionaries polarized local society by protecting Chinese converts and bullying officials into favoring Christians in legal decisions. When severe drought followed disastrous floods, local leaders, already angry at official favoritism, blamed foreigners and Chinese Christian converts (called "secondary hairy ones") for their communities' misfortunes.

Some local leaders possessed skills with deep roots in Shandong popular culture: healing, martial arts, spirit possession, and worship of popular gods. In the late 1890s, economic deprivation, natural disasters, and antiforeign, anti-Christian sentiments combined to spread these skills, especially spirit possession, more widely. They became the underpinning of a movement that came to be called the Boxers. A young rural man, unemployed because of the drought, might study with a master, learn to call down a god into his body, then use his spiritual power to attack his enemies. He might even become a Boxer leader himself, especially if his abilities included invulnerability to bullets. A local magistrate heard of one leader:

Whenever he competes with the Boxers, even ten or more men cannot approach him. He boasts that "my whole body has qigong *[lit.: 'breath efficacy']; I can resist spears and guns. When the hard and precious [Buddhist guardians] possess my body, the foreigners cannot oppose me."*[8]

The Boxers assaulted Christians and their official defenders with the gods on their side. Some officials saw the Boxers as potential allies against the foreigners, but Yuan Shikai, serving as Shandong governor, suppressed the Boxers with his modern-style New Army. The spring of 1900 brought intensified drought, and the hungry, unemployed Boxers became bolder in their choice of targets. Battling Qing troops and burning churches, they organized bands in cities—Tianjin and Beijing—as well as the countryside.

The diplomatic community protested, but the court wavered because public opinion strongly favored the Boxers. In June, the Boxers besieged the capital's foreign embassies and Catholic cathedral, and a British-led relief expedition suffered ignominious defeat. The Empress Dowager, alarmed by the movement of foreign troops toward the capital, decisively allied with the Boxers and declared war against the foreigners. Qing troops killed a Japanese diplomat, while Boxers murdered the German ambassador. In some provinces, such as Shanxi, pro-Boxer governors encouraged the killing of foreign missionaries, and the foreign community of Tianjin (including future US President Herbert Hoover) suffered a month-long siege.

Elsewhere, however, anti-Boxer officials kept their regions quiet—the Yangzi valley and southern governors agreed to exclude the Boxers, and Yuan Shikai pacified Shandong. In August, an army of 18,000 troops from seven imperial nations marched rapidly from the coast to Beijing, relieved the embassies besieged there, then went on a rampage of "punitive expeditions," pillaging the capital city, devastating much of North China, and killing far more civilians than Boxers. The German contingent, arriving too late for the march to Beijing, participated eagerly in the plunder.

The Empress Dowager and emperor fled westward to Xi'an, where they remained until early 1902, while the foreigners competed for the diplomatic and financial loot. The final peace agreement required the Qing to execute a number of high officials, pay an enormous indemnity (450 million ounces [12 trillion g] of silver), send apology missions to Germany and Japan, accept foreign troops being stationed in North China, and suspend the official examinations in the Boxers' most active regions.

Coming only five years after defeat by Japan, the Boxer catastrophe not only demonstrated the Qing's continuing weakness, it also deprived the court of the resources to strengthen itself. Defeat had eroded the dynasty's legitimacy, and the peace settlement devastated the treasury. Nonetheless, following the Empress Dowager, officials undertook far-reaching reforms, and ordinary Chinese commenced remarkable transformative work. They could not save the Qing, but they laid the groundwork for a New China in the twentieth century.

TOO MUCH, TOO LATE: "NEW GOVERNMENT" AND QING REFORMISM

In the aftermath of the Boxers, many Qing officials advocated thorough reform, including constitutional government and many of the other policies that Kang Youwei had recommended in 1898. The Empress Dowager agreed reluctantly and solicited advice while consolidating the position of the Manchu elite in Beijing. The post-Boxer reforms were led by Chinese officials such as Zhang Zhidong, who had focused on education in his 1898 book; Yuan Shikai, who replaced Li Hongzhang as the leading power in North China then became a Grand Secretary; and Huang Zunxian (see p. 198), who studied Japan as a potential model for the Qing as early as 1880. Outside the government, Kang Youwei's disciple Liang Qichao, who had escaped to Japan in 1898, published a reformist newspaper in Tokyo for several years, arguing for a parliament, judicial independence, and local self-government. Although he and Kang deeply desired to participate in the reform, neither the Empress Dowager nor Yuan Shikai would work with them.

Scholars disagree on how effectively the "New Government" reforms alleviated Qing weakness. Conventional Chinese narratives insist that the Manchus acted selfishly and shortsightedly, for their own corrupt benefit, and focus instead on the revolutionaries under

A "New-Year style" Chinese print illustrating the attack on Tianjin by combined Qing and Boxer forces in June 1900.

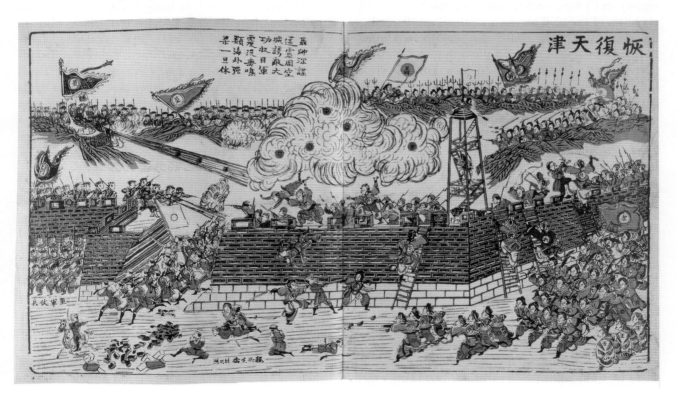

Sun Yat-sen, who continued to plot the dynasty's over-throw from overseas. Recent historians, however, argue that most twentieth-century political regimes in China owe their institutions and orientations to the late Qing innovations rather than the revolutionaries' ideas.

In either case, Japan played a crucial role in this period. Many future Chinese leaders studied there, and the Meiji state served as a model—an East Asian, Confucian society that had modified European and American technology and institutions to succeed in the modern world. Japan sent hundreds of teachers and specialists to the Qing, where they played the same role that Europeans and Americans had in Japan three decades earlier. Just as important, Japanese writers pro-vided Chinese reformers and revolutionaries with the *vocabulary* of modernity, words in Chinese characters that enabled literate East Asians to comprehend the world outside without learning a European language. From "Chamber of Commerce" to "society," from "an-archism" to "revolution," Japanese neologisms spread rapidly to Korea and China to replace the difficult clas-sical translations of Yan Fu and his colleagues.

Many New Government reforms had longlasting impact on Chinese society—none so much as the 1905 abolition of the civil service examinations. By ending the exams, the Qing ended the 1,000-year domina-tion of Chinese education by the orthodox Confucian curriculum and opened the way to a restructuring of the elite. After 1905, new schools teaching a modern curriculum modeled after Japan's—science, foreign languages, ethics, world history, and international af-fairs—gradually produced leaders very different from Zhang Zhidong or Kang Youwei. This did not happen immediately or without controversy, for classical Chi-nese continued to be an important idiom, but once the exams were gone, elites had to seek status, power, and fortune through other paths.

One pivotal figure in this transition was Liang Qichao, a Cantonese scholar who had trained for the exams but changed course to become one of China's first modern public intellectuals. Rather than concen-trating solely on reforming the state, he insisted on "renewing the people," inculcating nationalism in the population. A gradualist rather than a revolutionary, Liang called for study of Japanese to access the modern world, a radical proposal in a world dominated exclu-sively by Chinese texts. As early as 1899, Liang urged

Chinese reformers to learn Japanese, using the Japanese word *isshin* (C. *weixin*), "imperial restoration," rather than an ordinary Chinese term for government reform, indicating that he had already begun to adopt the new Japanese vocabulary:

> Those of you yearning for new knowledge, join me in learning Japanese…In the thirty years since Japan's weixin…at least several thousand useful works have been translated or written in its vast search for knowledge. These give special attention to politics… economics…philosophy…and sociology…all subjects urgently needed to open people's minds and as a foundation for national power.[9]

FREE THE MIND AND THE FEET: WOMEN AND CHINESE NATIONALISM

The new education included Chinese women. Public agitation against footbinding had begun in the 1870s, stimulated by foreigners' disdain for the practice. Girls' schools founded by missionaries slowly gained ac-ceptance, especially among the urban poor. Patronage by powerful men such as Kang Youwei, who founded a "natural foot society," and Liang Qichao, who es-tablished a girls' school after 1895, accelerated these changes, and the New Government reforms added of-ficial sponsorship of elite girls' education. Like Tsuda Umeko returning from the United States, Chinese girls who had studied in Japan came home and opened schools, using new-style curricula. This opening had a dark side, too, for young women forced into marriage now knew that other options existed, and some took their own lives in despair and anger.

Others demanded more public, more individual roles for women. The iconic heroine Qiu Jin (see box opposite), among others, returned from Japan to par-ticipate in transforming China. Some Qing women had become literate, aided their husbands' careers from "be-hind the screen," ran family businesses, or composed poetry, but the public sphere of political and social activ-ism had not been available to them before. Finally, they could attend mass rallies against China's humiliation, found patriotic societies, serve as nurses, and join the anti-Manchu associations of Sun Yat-sen and his allies. Perhaps most visibly, they became schoolteachers, and their image—militant teachers leading their students

QIU JIN, REVOLUTIONARY HEROINE

Qiu Jin's short life (1875–1907) illustrates many of the tensions and contradictions of the Qing's last years. Born into a wealthy family from Shaoxing—a city famous for its intellectuals and politicians—she studied the Classics alongside her brother and read widely in popular fiction, identifying with courageous heroines. She also learned the masculine skills of swordplay and horseback riding and prided herself on being able to drink huge quantities of rice wine, another of Shaoxing's famous products. Marriage into a conventional Hunan merchant family temporarily ended her exploits. While chafing in domestic life, including two children, she expressed her frustration in poetry as she traveled between Hunan and Beijing. She might have been another depressed, poetical, elite matron but for her remarkable personality and the late 1890s, which brought the idea of personal liberation to tempt her and the sight of foreign troops marching into Beijing to humiliate her.

Inspired by historical and fictional heroes, she resolved to use the opportunities of the post-Boxer world to make something meaningful of herself. Chinese students were going to Japan, and Shimoda Utako (1854–1936) opened her Girls' Vocational School to Chinese women. Qiu Jin was accepted in 1904, so she left her husband and children and embarked on a life-transforming three-year adventure. Quickly gravitating to radical Chinese circles in Tokyo, she joined both the Hunan and Zhejiang provincial clubs. Charismatic and hotheaded, she practiced shooting and bomb-making to fulfill her revolutionary ambitions. That fall she joined a secret society and in 1905 became the Zhejiang provincial leader in Sun Yat-sen's China United League.

When the Japanese Ministry of Education strictly regulated Chinese students in late 1905, Qiu Jin returned to Shanghai and joined the Restoration Society, a secretive revolutionary organization. Unfocused but still passionately political, she taught

Qiu Jin cross-dressed in the traditional clothing of a Chinese gentleman, c. 1905. Fond of wearing male clothing, she also had herself photographed in a European suit, in Japanese clothing, and brandishing a sword.

briefly (a model militant schoolteacher), continued her dangerous work with explosives, founded a feminist magazine, and plotted with other Hunan and Zhejiang radicals. Finally, in February 1907, Qiu Jin assumed the leadership of the Datong School in Shaoxing, where she and her colleagues planned an uprising. Poor organization and communication defeated them that July. Her co-conspirator in Anhui assassinated the governor, failed to arouse any revolutionary fervor, and was summarily executed. Qiu Jin's uprising, less than two weeks later, had been linked to the assassination plot, so the army captured her easily, discovering a cache of arms at her school. The local officials, fearing a wider uprising, requested her immediate execution, and Qiu Jin was beheaded on July 15, 1907.

A radical feminist for her day, deeply educated in Chinese culture *and* the new things of the West and Japan, a Shaoxing loyalist with a nationalist vision, an individualist who sacrificed for the cause—with her impulsive activism and early death, Qiu Jin earned her nickname, "Heroine of Mirror Lake," and became an icon of twentieth-century Chinese nationalism and feminism.

into battle or protest—formed part of the imagining of a New China. Women could see themselves saving the nation, rather than maintaining the family.

TOPPLING HEAVEN:
THE 1911 REVOLUTION AND
THE END OF IMPERIAL CHINA

The Empress Dowager, who manipulated or held the reins of power in the Qing realm for over 40 years, tried to strike a balance between reforming the government and maintaining Manchu control. Blamed in twentieth-century Chinese historiography for many of the late Qing's failures, she nonetheless presided over the beginnings of constitutional monarchy and the end of the examination system, while also increasing the power of the Manchu princes in everyday politics. In the fall of 1908, the 73-year-old Empress became fatally ill. She ensured a dynastic crisis by having the Guangxu Emperor murdered and appointing her 3-year-old grandnephew Puyi (1906–1967) the next emperor, with his father (Prince Jun; 1883–1951) as regent.

These events precipitated three years of political chaos, in which competing factions of Manchus fought veiled battles over how to run the empire. To appease the constitutionalists, in 1909 Prince Jun ordered the establishment of provincial assemblies, elected by a limited franchise of elite males (as in Japan), and the following year the provinces demanded a national parliament. The regent, however, appointed a governing cabinet made up primarily of Manchus, disappointing many reformers and adding fuel to the growing anti-Manchu fire. Provincial elites, represented for the first time in the assemblies, argued that provinces should be governed by local men, not by centrally appointed officials.

During the last few years of the Qing, foreign and domestic observers saw remarkable changes in China. They reported on the nascent electoral system, the public activities of women, the rising power of the press, the activism of students, and the influence of the military, especially the New Army trained by Yuan Shikai. Diasporic Chinese, too, played a prominent role in Qing affairs, supplying money to both reformist and revolutionary groups and returning to China to establish businesses.

Even industrial workers, though their numbers were small, participated in patriotic demonstrations and communicated the "new things" of modernity to their home villages. As a foreign journalist wrote in 1907:

> For the first time in history the Chinese have discovered a common ground of union which has appealed to men of all classes and trades, of all religions, and all sections of the community. Unconsciously, the Chinese have welded themselves into a nation.[10]

Although that judgment was premature, it predicted China's future. Chinese of many classes and places learned of their commonalty through periodicals, new translations, connections to urban areas, and education. Some did share a nationalistic sentiment, a desire to belong to a strong, united, successful China rather than a tottering Qing empire.

Sun Yat-sen and his colleagues, living in exile, continued plotting as the Qing tried Japanese-style reform and constitutionalism. In 1905, the Tokyo-based revolutionaries created an umbrella organization, the China United League. Japan's victory in the Russo-Japanese War, fought largely in Qing territory and reported widely in the Chinese press, spurred them to further efforts to renew China by overthrowing the Qing. They professed a combination of anti-Manchuism and foreign notions such as nationalism and individual freedom. Sun Yat-sen traveled from Hanoi to London, from Japan to San Francisco, building anti-Qing solidarity with students, secret societies, and merchant associations. From 1906 to 1911 they undertook ten uprisings, all in the south and southeast, and all failures.

Sun Yat-sen prescribed for China the doctrines of people's nationalism, rights, and livelihood, which became known as the Three People's Principles. These vague goals could be interpreted differently for different audiences, but all of them reflected Sun's experiences in the United States, his familiarity with European and American political theory, and his desire to overthrow the Manchus and transform China. *People's nationalism* included the end of imperialist domination; *people's rights* meant democracy and elections (after an indefinite period of elite "political tutelage"); and *people's livelihood* encompassed government restrictions on private capital and equalization of landholding. To advance this broad program, Sun made sweeping away the Qing his highest priority.

Popular support for revolution grew rapidly after 1908, in part stimulated by the "railroad rights recovery" movement, which pitted provincial gentry and their local supporters against centralizers in the Qing administration. In the spring of 1911, the Qing announced the nationalization of all railways, belonging to both foreign and provincial investors. The newly elected provincial assemblies, whose wealthy members stood to lose some of their investment, protested strongly. In Sichuan, especially, mass rallies stimulated powerful emotions, as railway rights joined uneasily with anti-foreign sentiment, anti-Manchu racialism, provincial loyalties, and revolutionary rhetoric.

Song Jiaoren (1882–1913), a Japan-educated activist, became the China United League's chief representative in Shanghai, protected by the international sovereignty of the foreign concessions. Sun Yat-sen's supporters and allies had infiltrated the Qing military, mostly through cadets returned from Japan. Song Jiaoren planned a coup in Wuchang, part of the tri-city area of the central Yangzi, making extensive contacts in the local Qing garrison and among revolutionary students. When the Sichuanese railroad rights movement broke out, the court ordered part of the Wuchang garrison westward, leaving the city vulnerable. An accidental bomb explosion alerted the police, so the conspirators decided to strike early, and on October 10, 1911, they seized arsenals and the governor-general's office, then the entire tri-city area. Since Sun Yat-sen was in the United States and his lieutenant Huang Xing in Shanghai, the rebels forced the Qing garrison commander, Li Yuanhong (1864–1928), to be their chief.

In a confusing series of battles, the Qing regained control of much of Wuhan but lost Shanghai and Nanjing to the revolutionaries, as province after province declared independence. Sun Yat-sen, who learned of the Wuchang uprising from a Denver newspaper, headed for London to secure loans for a new Chinese republic and persuade the British to abandon the Qing. Successful there, he was greeted enthusiastically in Paris and then returned to Shanghai on Christmas Day. A week later, delegates from 14 provinces elected him provisional president of the Republic of China (ROC), the culmination of his 16 years' planning to overthrow the Qing.

But for all his years of revolutionary conspiracy, Sun Yat-sen lacked an army, and control over the military remained in the hands of Qing generals. Without military unity, China would be open to imperialist encroachment, dreaded by all. As the realm dissolved, the court turned to the former head of the New Army and reformist bureaucrat Yuan Shikai, who had been forced from office in 1908, and named him prime minister. His subordinates, both civilian and military, immediately began negotiating with the revolutionaries and pressuring the Manchu princes to step down. They succeeded on both fronts. The Qing court abdicated on February 12, 1912, ending 2,000 years of rule by an emperor in favor of a theoretically democratic and constitutional Republic of China (ROC). A few months

New Army troops, newly loyal to Sun Yat-sen's revolution, cross the Yangzi from Wuchang to Hankou, October 11, 1911 (the day after the initial seizure of power). The American Francis Stafford, working for the Commercial Press in Shanghai, took this and many more photographs of the events of 1911–12.

later, Yuan Shikai replaced Sun Yat-sen as president of the Republic, the first of many military men to attempt the reunification and construction of a New China.

KOREA

The Kabo reform of 1894–96 had marked a period of renewed Japanese ascendancy in Korea in the wake of their stunning defeat of the Qing. While the governmental changes anticipated most of the modern reforms that progressives had sought over several decades—most of them taking Japan as their model—they could not be sustained. Similar to the Qing's 100 days of reform in 1898, nullified by conservative reaction, the Kabo reform was stalled by anti-Japanese forces within the Chosŏn government as well as popular opposition to the new social agenda.

The Triple Intervention led by Russia, forcing Japan to retrocede the Liaodong peninsula, began a Russian challenge to Japan for influence in Korea. Russian interests coincided with those of Korean conservatives led by Queen Min, and they collaborated to undermine the pro-Japanese cabinet behind the Kabo reform. The struggles of the summer and fall of 1895 reached a peak in October with the assassination of Queen Min. Miura Gorō (1847–1926), Japanese Minister in Korea, had aided the plotters. Knowledge of this fact emboldened conservatives to demand reparations, Miura's punishment, and removal of the pro-Japanese Korean leadership led by Pak Yŏnghyo. Assassins murdered others within the pro-Japanese camp, including Kim Hongjip, while the more fortunate of the reformers—like Kang Youwei and Liang Qichao escaping from the Empress Dowager two years later—managed to escape to Japan. In February 1896, conservatives under Yi Pŏmjin (1853–1911) smuggled the king out of the palace and brought him to the Russian embassy, where he lived for a full year, relatively safe from plotters.

Conservative forces gained the upper hand with the king's flight to the Russian embassy, and the Japanese,

Sŏ Chaep'il (Philip Jaesohn), founder of the Independence Club, 1942.

exhausted from the war as well as stung diplomatically by the Triple Intervention, assumed a lower profile in Korean affairs. The conservative ascendance and new Russian influence did not just reflect palace intrigue or the machinations of elite politicians. The second round of Kabo legislation in the fall of 1895 led to a popular backlash against the reforms and their Japan-supported sponsors. Most of this second round of reforms focused on the elimination of "backward" customs and social structures, including abrogation of sumptuary regulations intended to support the theoretically rigid Chosŏn class distinctions. For example, the reformers eliminated the detailed styles of commoner dress that distinguished them from the *yangban*. These new rules matched earlier social reforms that had banned discrimination on the basis of social class and had liberated the hereditary, lowborn classes. The new regulations also banned the "top knot," the traditional hairstyle denoting male adulthood. This order was immensely unpopular, and it rallied popular opinion against the reformers.

With the breathing room provided by the Japanese withdrawal from Seoul, King Kojong left the haven of the Russian embassy in February 1897 and moved into a new European-style palace constructed within the precincts of the still-standing Tŏksu palace. For the next few years, the king maneuvered to ingratiate himself with Russia and the United States as counterbalances to Japan.

Kojong, however, bought Russian and US help at the expense of generous economic concessions. The Russians desired logging rights in the far northeast, near their new port at Vladivostok. The chief US diplomat in Seoul, Dr. Horace Allen (1858–1932), actively brokered franchises for American businessmen, including a concession for gold-mining operations at Unsan, a franchise for building the Seoul trolley system, and rights to operate a railroad between Seoul and its port at Inchŏn. Private companies from France and Germany also received concessions during this period, further eroding Korean control over its own resources. Kojong and his advisers calculated that they were necessary to balance the strong hold Japan had on Korea's economy and transport infrastructure.

THE INDEPENDENCE CLUB AND NATIONALIST REACTION

Educated and politically minded modernizers watched with disgust the foreign powers' maneuvering to obtain the spoils of the Chosŏn economy, with the collusion of the monarch and the conservative elites. Many viewed the king's policy—to maintain a semblance of independence and territorial integrity by currying favor with Europeans and Americans—as shortsighted at best, at worst a further erosion of Chosŏn sovereignty. From this time onward, new political organizations emerged in the public sphere, headed by a generation of men who had been exposed to modern learning, educated abroad, and/or attracted to Euro-American liberal thought.

The first such group, which created the precedents for others to follow, was the Independence Club, organized in 1896 by Sŏ Chaep'il (1864–1951), a young doctor who had adopted the Anglicized name Philip Jaesohn during his medical training in the United States. Kojong favored Sŏ's organization by providing its charter, but the Independence Club remained a private organization in which officials and commoners gathered to discuss policy issues and reform proposals, similar to Fukuzawa Yukichi's Meiji Six Society (see p. 183).[11] A number of pro-Japanese officials joined the Club in its early months, including Yi Wanyong (1858–1926), Chosŏn's prime minister at the time of annexation. But as more and more non-officials joined and the tenor of its meetings became more radical, many of the members holding government portfolios resigned.

The Club broke the *yangban* elites' monopoly on political discussion, and it created precedents for the expansion of public life by holding public debates on government policy. Conservatives in the government began hounding Sŏ immediately, and they forced

The Independence Gate, with the remants of the stone pillars of the old Gate of Welcoming Imperial Grace in front, c. 1920.

him to return to the United States (he had become an American citizen) in May 1898. The Club's membership, however, included prominent intellectuals such as Yun Ch'iho (see pp. 200–1) and moderate reformers like Namgung Ŏk and Chŏng Kyo, who assumed leadership after Sŏ's departure. Besides pioneering public policy debates, the Club published Chosŏn's first vernacular newspaper, *The Independent*, lobbied for citizen participation in government, and pushed the government to expand public education. Its three principal goals were to strengthen Korean independence, promote national "self-strengthening," and advocate democratic participation in government decisions—goals very similar to those of Qing reformers such as Liang Qichao.

Initially the Club focused on symbols. It campaigned to petition the king to rename the kingdom as the Empire of the Great Han (к. *TaeHan Cheguk*) in order to make Korea's independence from the Qing more explicit. Moreover, the Club urged Kojong to adopt the title of "emperor" (к. *hwangje*, the same Chinese characters as c. *huangdi*) rather than "king" in order to assume equal status with the Qing and Japanese emperors. Kojong granted their wish, took the title of emperor, and declared the first new reign-era Kwangmu (Illustrious Strength) in a coronation ceremony in October of 1897, only months after leaving Russian protection.

The Club also raised funds to erect a monumental arch, Independence Gate, on the site of the Gate of Welcoming Imperial Grace, where the Chosŏn kings had officially welcomed envoys from Qing. This project expanded to remake the former Qing diplomatic residence, the Hall of Cherishing China, into a public meeting place renamed Independence Hall, surrounded by a park. These were popular projects both at court and with the Seoul public, and they formally ended the tributary language and behaviors of past Chosŏn–Qing relations, so normal in the past but now humiliating to Korean nationalists.

The Independence Club planned and generated a movement that encompassed public education, the creation of a national newspaper, and the beginning of language reform, all projects that anticipated the gradual emergence of a new public sphere in Korea as well as developments in China a decade or two later. The Club's newspaper realized, at least in part, all of these goals. *The Independent* used the vernacular script, *han'gŭl*, and included sections in English as well. This constituted a major break from the traditional dominance of classical Chinese, as well as an initial assault on the elite monopoly on education and scholarship.

For more than a millennium, classical Chinese had been the official written language of the court and elite communication, while *han'gŭl* had been used for publications directed at the peasantry, or at women (see p. 49), and for popularizations of Confucian and Buddhist texts. Later a proliferation of novels written in *han'gŭl* in the seventeenth and eighteenth centuries had solidified its non-official use in society. By using *han'gŭl*, *The Independent* made a deliberate statement about national cultural unity and linguistic identity. Its editorials decried the use of classical Chinese as the official language of government and literary language of the *yangban*. Twenty years later, and for many of the same reasons, language issues became prominent in China, when Hu Shi (1891–1962) and others championed the use of the written vernacular for its wide appeal and simplicity (see p. 260).

In a scathing editorial on the national language, Chu Sigyŏng (1876–1914), the founder of the modern Korean vernacular movement, asserted that perfecting and spreading the use of *han'gŭl* had to be the principal means for ending the *yangban* slavery to Chinese culture. This widened the attack, begun with symbolic arches and imperial nomenclature, on what the Club perceived to be the mindless subordination of Korean elites to Chinese culture in general.

This attack against elite identification with China began the process of transforming the very language used to describe Korean–Chinese relations. The term *sadae* ("to serve the great") had heretofore simply described the ancient tributary ritual relationship. Chu Sigyŏng turned it into a negative epithet, denouncing subservience or toadyism to foreign culture in general. Subsequently, *sadae* and its various forms, *sadaejuŭi* (the doctrine of subservience) or *sadae ŭisik* (the

mentality [consciousness] of subservience) became a synonym for antinationalism, subjection to things foreign. In postcolonial and divided Korea, this terminology still lingers in political and cultural discourse.

The Independence Club's newspaper constituted the core of a nascent public sphere that the Club helped to open in late Chosŏn Korea. Although its circulation never exceeded 3,000, it nonetheless represented a radical departure from business as usual in the tightly closed Chosŏn political arena. The paper announced public debates, editorialized on national affairs, and presented announcements, advertisements, and news items of the day. In short, it created a political agenda for discussion by people previously excluded from the narrow confines of the Chosŏn bureaucracy and state councils. The public debates organized by the Club brought together individuals from a broad spectrum of status groups and class backgrounds. Open discussion of matters of state—*yangban* officials mingling with members of secondary status groups as well as commoners and low-status outcastes—was unprecedented. Indeed, for all these participants a common cause—the crisis facing what was more frequently being called the Korean nation—overrode class and status barriers.

The Club ultimately foundered because of its radical political advocacy of a constitutional monarchy—already done in Japan and proposed in the Qing after 1898—and representative democracy. It proposed the creation of a privy council made up of both *yangban* officials and "wise and erudite men" selected from outside the government. Conservatives within the government seized upon this issue and convinced the monarch that such ideas would ultimately lead to the destruction of royal authority, and Kojong disbanded the Independence Club after barely 18 months of existence. He had initially been pleased by the Club's support and the creation of national symbols that augmented his prestige, but he was still dependent on officials who owed their power to the traditional political system. In the end, the newly renamed Korean emperor opted to uphold the theory of royal authority, however limited it was in reality, rather than risk opening the political system to public participation.

The disbanding of the Independence Club ended the brief reform movement of 1896–98, but it had a galvanizing effect on the intellectual climate of Korea. In its short life, it spearheaded the cause of intellectual inquiry into the same issues that troubled reformist elites in the Qing and Japan: seeking the fundamental sources of Western power and debating political issues such as the role of "the people" in legitimating state power, the importance and potential of public participation in government. It linked political participation with social emancipation and public education in ways that forever changed the language of politics in Korea. Thereafter, as it had in Japan, the concept of an inclusive nation of active citizens, not passive subjects arranged in exclusive status groups, framed the debates over reform. Moreover, a number of its members—Yun Ch'iho, Syngman Rhee (Yi Sŭngman, 1875–1965), Yi Sangje (1850–1927), An Ch'angho (1878–1938), and Chu Sigyŏng, among others—subsequently became prominent leaders of political or cultural movements.

EXPANSION OF THE PUBLIC SPHERE

The short-lived projects of the Independence Club laid the foundation for a burgeoning of organizations, schools, and publications. The *Capital Gazette* (1898–1910) and *Imperial Post* hit the streets in 1898 before the demise of the pioneering *Independent*. The *Capital Gazette* became the voice of moderate members of the Independence Club interested in retaining significant elements of Korea's traditional culture in the face of necessary reform. It used mixed-script, a combination of *han'gŭl* and Chinese characters that appealed to more traditionally minded elites. The *Imperial Post*, published in pure *han'gŭl*, was reputed to be most widely read among women and the less educated. Like the *Independent*, both papers published runs of 2,000–3,000.

In 1904, the *Korea Daily News* emerged in time to cover the Russo-Japanese War. Owned and operated by an Englishman, the *Korea Daily News* enjoyed extraterritorial protection and thus avoided censorship until Japanese annexation in 1910. It quickly became the most popular newspaper of its day because of its uncompromising editorial line and fearless reportage. Scholars often trivialize the emergence of a Korean press at the turn of the century because of its small circulation and poor financial situation. But it played an important role as the foundation of an expanding public discourse, in which the conversations of the Korean intelligentsia began to articulate a new collective Korean identity.

The newspapers reported on the activities of new national and regional educational and reform associations spawned by the energy of intellectuals inside and outside Seoul. Around the time of the Russo-Japanese War these organizations became very active, with their dues-paying memberships often exceeding a thousand individuals. A study of one such association, the Northwest Education Association, revealed that the membership included a range of status groups from *yangban* through the so-called secondary groups to commoners. This diversity resulted from profession and education being the criteria for membership, not formal class or status. The Association's rolls listed local officials, teachers, school principals, magistrates, technicians, and businessmen. Such a diverse membership indicated the increasing interaction between private citizens and officials, whether in the new press or face to face at Association functions.

The monthly journals of these groups revealed their competition to become the most advanced and most reform-minded, the best organizers of new schools, and so forth. Regional journals and newspapers became the medium for a unique conversation among educated Koreans, and from their disparate opinions and passionate outpourings emerged a new imagined community, the Korean nation, which people called a *minjok*, using the Japanese neologism *minzoku* (C. *minzu*). Thereafter, all East Asians used this same word to refer to their own "national peoples"—the Japanese, the Koreans, the Han Chinese—as genetically defined, familial, cultural entities, with political implications.

THE KOREAN ENLIGHTENMENT AND THE ORIGINS OF KOREAN NATIONALISM

Like the Opium wars and Perry's arrival in Japan, the opening of Korea in 1876 to trade with the outside world began the transformation of Korea's economy, but just as importantly, it initiated contact with the "the West"—Europe and the United States—and its value systems, religions, ideas, and political institutions. In the period before the rise of the Korean press, the process of absorbing these influences was slow and uneven, but the new missionary schools, returning students, traders, and diplomats all promoted and spread the new Western-style knowledge. By the late 1890s, the popular press provided the medium for an explosion of interest in and discussion of all aspects of the outside world. The lively intellectual outpouring in the new, privately owned press stood in stark contrast to the increasingly moribund Korean government's siege mentality. These processes strongly resembled the Qing's resistance to new ideas until the Sino-Japanese War and Boxer catastrophes broke down the walls.

The diverse writings of the "Korean enlightenment," as it came to be known, fell into three related sets of inquiry: discovery of and elucidation of a new universal path of social and political development; rethinking Korea as a nation within this developmental course; and a critique of Korean tradition as an obstacle to the future development of the nation. As in Meiji Japan and late Qing China, this discourse found its common vocabulary under the rubric of "civilization and enlightenment." It sought to discover how Korea fit within the new universal framework of an evolving world of competing societies and nation-states. Concurrently, Koreans became intensely interested in what defined Korea as a nation—not just a country but also as a *minjok*, a people—and what should be done to ensure its survival as a unique society.

The inquiry into a universal path of social development continued the process of de-centering China in the Korean worldview, which augured a redefinition of Korea as a nation in the modernized (and Japanese) sense of the word. For this to happen, Korean cultural and political identity had to be decoupled from China, neither an easy nor a happy task. Korea needed to become an independent polity, not one that orbited

SIN CH'AEHO, NATIONALIST HISTORIAN

Sin Ch'aeho, c. 1930.

Historian, journalist, and exiled independence fighter, Sin Ch'aeho (1880–1936) is revered in contemporary South Korea as the quintessential patriot. He was born into a fallen *yangban* family, whose self-regard as the ancestors of a powerful and prestigious Koryŏ dynasty lineage (the Py'ŏngsan Sin) far eclipsed their modest circumstances at the time of his birth in rural Ch'ungch'ŏng province. Educated locally, he then enrolled in the highest rung of Chosŏn schooling, the National Academy. After graduating in 1900, he immediately engaged as a nationalist writer in the political and intellectual ferment of the day.

The Independence Club had attracted Sin as a student, and he began contributing articles to the new newspapers. His short pieces for the *Capital Gazette*, and more famously for the *Korea Daily News*, initiated a writing career that reshaped both the political lexicon and the historiography of Korea.

Central to the project of disassociating Korean history from *sadae* (serving the great), Sin's redefinition of history as the singular story of the Korean people constituted a scathing attack on traditional elite subservience to Chinese culture. He transformed *sadae* from a phrase simply defining Korean–Chinese relations into a nationalist slur meaning "subservience to outside power." In almost Hegelian terms, Sin described history writing as the most important means of defining the national essence or national spirit. To Sin, history represented the font of national identity itself.

Sin's early historical writing, exemplified by a biography of the Koguryŏ general Ülchi Mundŏk (seventh century), emphasized the martial valor and independent fighting spirit of past Korean heroes, contrasting their independence to the Sinocentrism and pacifism of the Chosŏn *yangban* elites. In works such as *Treatise on Korean History* (1909), Sin narrated the self-determination of Korea's evolution as a people. He pioneered the use of the term *chuch'e* (*juche* in North Korean transliteration) to signify autonomy or independence, opposing it to the hated

China in a Sinocentric world order. Koreans needed to claim their own distinct culture, history, and identity as a nation among other nation-states. This task engaged the intellectuals writing in the new press and teaching in the new schools in the last years of the nineteenth century.

Chu Sigyŏng had already called for positioning the Korean language as a principal building block of identity, and at the turn of the century a young classically trained intellectual, Sin Ch'aeho, made an equally passionate call to find Korean identity in a new historical consciousness (see box below). Sin's writings complemented the case made by other contemporary writers for reifying a true, singular Korean culture. For Sin's older colleague Pak Ŭnsik (1859–1926), history served

to define or capture the national soul. Terms such as "national essence" (к. *kuksu*, ɪ. *kokusui*, с. *guocui*) appear frequently in Chinese and Japanese writings of the time as well, demonstrating that intellectuals in all three cultures shared the desire to discover what being "us" *really* meant. Knowledge of national history lay at the core of this project, gradually instilling in Korean people a strong sense of themselves as bound together as a *minjok*, not a conglomeration of class or status identities subservient to the rule of the *yangban*, who worshipped Chinese culture.

Through the last years of the Chosŏn dynasty, Korean reformers gradually accepted Euro-American concepts of progressive history, social evolution (including Social Darwinism), and the role and function

sadae and anticipating its emergence in North Korean polemics and ideology after World War II.

Active in the major nationalist organizations of the protectorate period (1905–10), Sin went into exile in 1910 to continue to work for independence. With little money and in poor health, he haunted the archaeological sites and monuments of the old Korean kingdom of Koguryŏ (sixth–seventh centuries) in Manchuria. His writing emphasized not only the glory of Korea's pre-Chosŏn past but also his belief that Korea should recover its true homeland by occupying the entire territory of trans-Yalu Koguryŏ. In Shanghai by 1920 to join the Shanghai Provisional Government (a Korean government-in-exile), Sin rose to head its consultative assembly and edit its propaganda organ.

Soon discouraged by the internecine struggles of exile politics, Sin returned to historical research. In 1923, a group of young Korean anarchists requested that he draft a manifesto for their organization, the Righteous Fighter Corps. The resulting "Korean Revolutionary Declaration" became a classic of Korean political writing. Thereafter, Sin's politics became

increasingly radical, and he refused offers to return to Korea to teach and write. In 1929 he was arrested in Dalian for subversive activities and sentenced to ten years in prison. His works remained in great demand and were reserialized in Korea, but he refused to publish new work in colonial journals dated with the Japanese reign-name.

Sin died in prison in February 1936. Despite his last wish—not to have his body returned to a colonized homeland—his family interred his cremated remains in his native village. Mindful of the symbolic value of his burial, Japanese authorities prohibited the construction of large memorials but allowed a secret burial in an unmarked gravesite known only to the family. In the postwar era, modern students still read his historical works, memorials have been raised in his honor, and a scholarly society watches over the compilation and publication of his collected writings. Perhaps more important, Sin's legacy perseveres in debates over dependence and autonomy in modern Korea—issues that continue to fuel the propaganda wars between North and South Korea in the twenty-first century.

of the nation-state. In this way, they reconfigured the "Western" knowledge that had been pouring into Korea since the first study trips and students studying abroad in the early 1880s. They conceived the new knowledge as the most highly evolved cultural and technical values that could be appropriated in the service of the nation.

By 1900, Japanese and (some) Chinese scholars had built an impressive body of knowledge about the West, and from these secondary works Koreans constructed their own programs for action. Chang Chiyŏn translated the writings of Liang Qichao, who had summarized Yan Fu's translations, indirectly transmitting Darwin, Huxley, and Spencer to Korea. Journals of the regional study societies and new national organizations—for example, the National Self-Strengthening Association (1906–10) and the New People's Society (1907–10, using Liang Qichao's term "renew the people")—devoted considerable space to European science and positivism, a tradition they believed underlay the success of European and American political institutions.

The mirror side of this fascination with foreign ideas and institutions required a growing attack on Korean tradition, echoes of which would be heard for decades in China as well, most notably during the May Fourth era of intellectual ferment (see pp. 261–63). Koreans reasoned that if the dynamism in European societies stemmed from values such as individual freedom, then Confucian social mores constituted the main obstacle to that dynamism in Korea. Their critique principally denounced the Confucian concepts of filial piety, social harmony, and social authority. Ignoring any positive valances, these iconoclasts focused on the authoritarian aspects of ancestor veneration, prohibition of widow remarriage, obligation to parents and elders, subordination of women, and excessively elaborate ritual protocols. They believed these to be destructive to individual initiative and free will. As in China, some of this writing contains a recognizable echo of Protestantism, particularly its characterization of ancestor ritual as "wasteful ceremony." They also supported freeing women from the worst excesses of Confucian patriarchy, reflecting the importance of church schools and the prominence of Christian converts within the Enlightenment movement.

Enlightenment iconoclasm also featured an attack on traditional Korean folk culture. Although the elite Confucian tradition had trickled down in Korean society and regulated family ritual, most notably ancestor veneration, peasant society remained strongly influenced by indigenous beliefs as well. With its ancient shamanistic tradition, Korea contained a rich and regionally diverse mixture of customs and values tied together with ritual, dance, music, and art. Although this folk tradition provided a repository of unique symbols of national identity, enlightenment thinkers decried folk culture as antiscientific, superstitious, and fatalistic. In their minds, belief in spirits and the powers of shamans blocked acceptance of modern science, and dependence on fortune-tellers and geomancy encouraged fatalism and passivity.

THE RUSSO-JAPANESE WAR AND THE REEMERGENCE OF JAPANESE POWER

Japan's withdrawal from Korea in the late 1890s proved to be temporary. During several years of respite, the Korean government brokered concessions in return for closer relations with the Euro-American powers, especially Russia. By the time of the Boxer Uprising in 1900, however, the growing Russian military and economic intrusion in Northeast Asia had become a transparent threat to Japanese long-term interests. So in the first years of the new century Japan moved decisively, first to counter and then to defeat the Russian threat. In 1902 the Anglo-Japanese Alliance provided British recognition of Japan's interests in Korea and Manchuria, with mutual security guarantees (see p. 218). Japan followed this alliance with diplomatic overtures to the United States. Acquisition of the Philippines had entered the United States in the complicated power politics of East Asia, and Japan needed to be assured of US neutrality in any conflict with Russia.

The Russians had occupied southern Manchuria during the Boxer Uprising with the understanding it would withdraw in 1903. As 1903 waned with no Russian withdrawal, the Japanese government decided on war. After beginning hostilities in February 1904, Japan sent an army to occupy strategic points in Korea. Not stopping there, the Japanese forced the Korean government to accept "advice" on further reform of their administration. From this point, Japan became the supreme power on the peninsula, not dislodged for 40 years.

A second large Japanese army invaded the Liaodong peninsula, laid siege to Port Arthur, and then moved north to engage the Russians. The land battles brought horrendous slaughter that anticipated the mechanized killing of World War I. In the decisive battle of Mukden, the Japanese and Russian armies altogether suffered over 150,000 dead and wounded. After the crushing destruction of the Russian Baltic fleet in the Straits of Tsushima in May 1905, the 1905 Revolution, and a stalemate in Manchuria, Japan accepted President Theodore Roosevelt's offer to mediate an end to the conflict. The war had exhausted Japanese resources, but victory legitimated its rise as a major power in East Asia if not the world, and the ensuing treaty gave Japan free rein to absorb Korea as part of its expanding empire.

THE JAPANESE PROTECTORATE

After the war, the "civilized world," which had never embraced Korea in the first place, abandoned it to the Japanese. The bellicose President Roosevelt relinquished any American interests in Korea to Japan in exchange for assurances of "non-interference" with American hegemony in the Philippines and elsewhere. Japan followed the Taft–Katsura memorandum (July 1905) with the establishment of a protectorate over Korea. During the war, the Japanese had signed two protocols with the Korean government that provided advisory powers in Korean affairs. In the war's aftermath, a system of overt control emerged, formalized in the five-point Protectorate Treaty of November 1905. This treaty required the Korean government to cede control of its foreign affairs to Japan and established a residency-general. One of the premier statesmen of Meiji Japan, Itō Hirobumi, served as the first resident-general. From this point on, Korea, unable to represent itself in foreign capitals, all but disappeared from the global community of nation-states.

A faction in the highest levels of the Japanese government, including Itō, had long argued for indirect control of Korea, preferring a formally independent, reformed, stable, and docile Korea to direct Japanese colonial rule. Nevertheless, in the face of stiff Korean resistance at all levels of society, Itō restructured the Korean government, gradually increasing the power and influence of Japanese "advisers." By 1907, the residency-general abandoned any pretext of indirect control, for continuing Korean resistance required sterner measures. That year, Japan added control of finance, home affairs, and policing to its domination of Korean diplomacy and defense. After Kojong dispatched envoys to plead for outside intercession in Korea at the World Peace Conference in The Hague, in 1907 the Japanese forced his abdication in favor of his son, Sunjong (r. 1907–1910). In the same year they disbanded the small Korean army (8,800 troops) and assumed direct control of the police and the judiciary.

ANNEXATION AND DESCENT INTO COLONIAL STATUS

The residency-general's power to direct the Korean government increased dramatically after 1907. It promulgated laws and regulations to bring the Korean press under stricter regulation as well as harsh rules for government and private schools that required pro-Japanese texts and curriculum. During the summer of 1909, hardliners in Tokyo won the debate about whether or not to annex Korea. Itō resigned as resident-general and, while on a state mission to Harbin, was assassinated by a Korean independence fighter, An Chunggun. Replacing Itō, the humorless General Terauchi Masatake (1852–1919), former war minister, arrived empowered by the Meiji cabinet to terminate Korea's independence. On August 16, 1910, Terauchi forced Sunjong to affix his seal to a Treaty of Annexation already signed by the Korean Prime Minister Yi Wanyong. For this act, Yi earned a place of permanent vilification as the worst collaborator in modern Korean history. After 518 years, the once proud Chosŏn dynasty ended.

This summary reflects only the inexorable progress of the Japanese seizure of Korea without doing justice to the turmoil and trauma of the process. In the press, Korean journalists raised a hue and cry over every Japanese move to increase their power. The Protectorate Treaty provoked outright denunciation of the traitorous officials who had collaborated in such perfidy; the editor of the *Capital Gazette*, Chang Chiyŏn, wrote a now canonical essay, "Today We Cry out in Lamentation," in a special edition distributed free of charge in Seoul. Moderates who had believed in the benign intentions of the Japanese reform propaganda expressed their sense of betrayal.

A number of officials in the Chosŏn government committed suicide in protest. Most renowned of these martyrs was Min Yŏnghwan (1861–1905), Kojong's military attaché. He left a testament decrying the treaty and enigmatically declaring that he was "dead but [had]

Guerrilla bands called *ŭibyŏng,* "righteous armies," fought the Japanese military and police after 1905. Their ranks swelled after the Japanese disbanded the Chosŏn army in 1907; note the uniformed soldier in the photograph.

not died." News of his testament spread rapidly and provoked a torrent of patriotic letters, poems, and essays that echoed Min's insinuation that the spirit of the nation must live. Moreover, the rumors that bamboo had sprouted on the spot of his death further enflamed patriotic passion. But however eloquent and impassioned the words might have been, they fell on deaf ears abroad and among the Japanese overlords.

Not all Korean resistance consisted of prose and poetry. As early as the mid-1890s, particularly after the assassination of Queen Min, small bands of guerrilla fighters emerged to harass the Japanese and other foreigners. Using the name "righteous armies" (K. *ŭibyŏng*, recalling the resistance against Hideyoshi), local literati often organized these groups, and their patriotism focused on supporting the monarch and the Chosŏn system. The movement grew rapidly after the announcement of the Protectorate Treaty.

In 1905, the venerable Ch'oe Ikhyŏn raised a force in North Chŏlla province, and Na Inyŏng gathered another small army in South Chŏlla. According to their traditionally worded pronouncements, they intended to protect the monarch, resist Japan, and restore independence to Chosŏn. The disbanding of the Korean army in 1907 further swelled the ranks of *ŭibyŏng*, as demobilized soldiers joined the guerrillas. Most bands numbered in the hundreds, but occasionally the *ŭibyŏng* put several thousand together against the Japanese army, with one army of 10,000 turned back in heavy fighting only eight miles (12 km) from the heart of Seoul.

In the last years of the dynasty, the slogans of the *ŭibyŏng* subtly shifted to contemporary nationalist language, reflecting the training and indoctrination of the disbanded Korean soldiery. The Righteous Armies activity reached its peak in 1907, with Japanese estimates of nearly 70,000 irregulars challenging Japanese forces in 1,500 clashes. The guerrilla struggle waned after 1907, but it forced the Japanese to strengthen their military garrison, and sporadic fighting continued for a year after annexation. With additional troops from Japan, the gendarmerie fanned out in encirclement campaigns to find and destroy the last bands. By 1910 the 6,100-man garrison that remained in Korea sufficed to keep order, but the colonial police expanded to 22,000 by 1920. The meticulous Japanese military ultimately numbered Korean deaths in the pacification campaigns at 17,690.

It took the Japanese several years to pacify the peninsula after 1910. In doing so they faced all manner of Korean resistance: sabotage, assassination of Japanese officials and their Korean collaborators, armed confrontation, secret political organizing, journalistic broadsides, appeals to foreign powers, and in the end all manner of daily resistance. While subduing the *ŭibyŏng* rebels, Governor-General Terauchi worked to eviscerate the intellectual leadership of the Korean nationalist movement, such as it was. In the cities the police closely watched religious leaders, nationalist politicians, and intellectuals. The press blackout imposed in 1907 continued, and arrests for political activities mounted. In 1912 alone, setting a pattern for the entire colonial period, the police arrested 50,000 people for crimes including unlawful assembly and illegal political activity.

In December 1910, Terauchi used the discovery of an assassination plot against him to move decisively against the nationalist leadership. In the "Case of the 105," the colonial police arrested 105 prominent leaders including Yun Ch'iho, Yang Kit'ak (1871–1938), and Yi Sŭnghun (1864–1930) of the New People's Society, a moderate reform movement stressing education, economic development, and cultural activities focused on building national strength. After 1910, the Japanese government declared it an illegal organization and a prime target, and many of the accused were tortured. In the end, only a few of the original group were convicted, but the case decapitated the nationalist leadership during the important early phase of pacification.

Up to 1910, opposition to the Japanese presence had been the main unifying force among those disparate groups that fought to preserve Korean independence. After annexation, anti-Japanese sentiment unified and mobilized most Koreans—conservative Confucians, radical Westernizers, and everyone in between. The fall into colonial status stimulated the movement to articulate a modern national identity and organize a struggle to regain political independence. Faced with a sullen populace and lingering armed resistance, the Japanese began the process of ensuring their domination by creating a colonial state of unprecedented reach and power in Korean society.

DIASPORAS

JAPAN

As Japan staked out a larger place in the world, its subjects sought livelihoods across the Pacific. The trickle migrating to Hawaii before 1890 turned into a wave of farm workers by 1900, and many of them migrated to the West Coast, encouraged by American labor contractors. Unlike Chinese a few decades earlier—mostly male miners and railroad workers—Japanese men often worked in agriculture or in urban homes as "schoolboys," a euphemism for middle-class servants. Others worked in salmon canneries in Alaska, sawmills in Oregon, and mining camps in Utah. Many saved their money to bring their wives and children to the United States to work alongside them.

By 1900, over 2,000 Japanese women had received passports to enter the United States, about 160 of them prostitutes in California cities and towns. This fueled a stereotype of Japanese female immorality, parallel with hysterical accounts in San Francisco newspapers of Japanese men as sexual predators. Lurid tales of "Oriental depravity," fears of economic competition from Japanese immigrants, and widespread racism led San Francisco to segregate all East Asian schoolchildren in 1906. One newspaper screamed, "[O]ur children should not be placed in any position where their youthful impression may be affected by association with pupils of the Mongolian race."

Japan's ambassador in Washington, publicly objected, and the San Francisco Japanese community responded with protests and political action. They had some American allies against the segregation policy, most notably President Theodore Roosevelt, who hoped to avoid diplomatic insult to Japan, and African American journalists, who favored an African American–Japanese alliance to end racism. The crisis ended when the United States and Japan concluded a "Gentlemen's Agreement" in 1907—less embarrassing than a treaty—prohibiting the immigration of male Japanese laborers in exchange for ending the segregation of Japanese schoolchildren. Japanese wives and children could still enter the country, however, and soon women, many of them picture brides, established families in the United States. About 800–1,100 Japanese women entered the United States annually from 1910 to 1913, and their United States-born children were citizens.

The first Japanese migrated to Canada in 1877 to work in lumber, fishing, and mining. Their number peaked in 1905–7, leading to a "Gentlemen's Agreement" there in 1908. After 1897, Japanese also migrated to Mexico, where many of them married local women. Sugar and cotton plantations drew Japanese laborers to Peru in 1899, and some went on to Bolivia to work on rubber plantations, mining, and railroads. In each of these countries, many later opened small businesses.

The largest South American emigrant population entered Brazil after the North American Gentlemen's Agreements made the south more attractive. Brazil's "whitening project" had prohibited Asian immigration before 1892, but the coffee plantations required labor. The first 790 Japanese immigrants arrived in Brazil in 1908, and most worked on plantations at first, later migrating to the cities. Unlike Mexico, few Brazilian Japanese married locals. Today Brazil has more citizens of Japanese ancestry than any country outside Japan.

CHINA

At century's end, Chinese migrants already covered the globe, living and working in French Mauritius and Madagascar, German Tanganyika, British South Africa, Spanish Cuba, and Portuguese Brazil, among many others. Apart from the students discussed earlier (see pp. 192–91). , most were plantation laborers, but they also did arduous mining and construction work and opened small shops selling everyday consumer goods. Racism prevented most of them from becoming full participants in the societies to which they migrated, but their conditions varied tremendously—from extensive intermarriage to racialist exclusion, from independent wealth to indentured servitude. Whether as laborers or as middlemen, as merchants or as managers, they formed essential elements in the economic structure of the European and American empires.

In the United States, the hostile response of "whites" to the presence of "Asiatics" narrowed the employment possibilities for Chinese men to restaurant work and laundries, urban occupations constrained by stereotype and lack of capital. Wildly contradictory ideas about the Chinese—effeminate yet predatory, highly civilized but utterly savage, simple-minded laundrymen but also megalomaniacal opium dealers—enabled images ranging from the fictional Fu Manchu ("a brow like Shakespeare and a face like Satan") to an 1871 Thomas Nast cartoon, naming the Chinese as "coolie, slave, pauper and rat-eater." Especially in San Francisco, fear of "racial mixing" combined with working-class anxiety about "cheap Chinese labor" to create hostility that cut across all classes of "white" society, from Stanford professors and mayors to railwaymen and construction workers.

The San Francisco earthquake of 1906 created an unexpected opening, for the fires destroyed the municipal records. Chinese claimed, in large numbers, to be native-born rather than immigrants, and thus gained the right to bring their wives and children to the United States. As with the Japanese after the Gentleman's Agreement, this led to the birth of American citizens of East Asian ancestry, still objects of derision and discrimination but nonetheless possessing the theoretical rights of "natural-born Americans." In Hawaii, in contrast, the mixing of indigenous people with immigrant populations from all over the world led to a somewhat more open, multiracial society, despite continuing racist discrimination.

KOREA

The Sino-Japanese and Russo-Japanese wars, escalating Japanese intrusion, and final annexation of Korea caused tremendous hardship for all Koreans. Warfare, economic dislocation caused by the penetration of global markets into the peninsula, and political instability accelerated the flow of Koreans into Manchuria, especially the Kando (Jiandao) region across the far northeastern border. By 1910, over 100,000 settlers had moved to this area, and within three years of annexation another 60,000 joined them. Another wave of emigrants waded or walked over the frozen Tumen River into the Russian Maritime province. These migrants opened uncultivated land, establishing wet-field rice agriculture for the first time. In the next generation, their numbers, particularly in Manchuria, swelled to create the basis for what later became the Yanbian Korean autonomous prefecture of the People's Republic of China.

Seeking to remedy a labor shortage in the Hawaiian sugar industry, plantation owners worked with American middlemen and missionaries to recruit Korean men, beginning a smaller stream of migration to Hawaii. Between 1902 and 1910, over 7,000 laborers made the journey. Subsequently, many of the contract laborers moved to California, where they settled around Los Angeles and San Francisco. The Korean communities in Hawaii and on the mainland provided funds and manpower for nationalist groups that formed after annexation in 1910.

While not permanent emigrants, students also participated in the Korean diaspora of the early twentieth century. With opportunity limited in Korea, advanced students went to Japanese high schools and colleges: from 791 in 1909, their number increased rapidly after annexation to 3,171 by 1912. As the colonial period wore on, increasing numbers of Koreans studied in Japan or undertook the much longer voyage to the United States and Europe. Mostly privately financed, they benefited from scholarship programs offered by churches, youth associations, and the colonial government itself. These students constituted a core of Korea's future social, economic, and political leadership, a trend that continues today, as tens of thousands of Korean students leave Korea each year to study abroad.

CONNECTIONS

During this period, Japan clearly took the lead in mobilizing its resources for defense and development. The first East Asian state to industrialize, early Meiji-era Japan transferred government-funded resources and technology to private capital—especially the *zaibatsu*—quickly ending its dependence on foreign experts and striving for control over natural materials and productive processes by the period covered in this chapter. Winning two wars against the Qing and Russia, taking Taiwan and Korea as colonies, the Japanese demonstrated that a non-white *minzoku* could play the game of empire along with the Europeans and Americans. In response, both Chosŏn (Kabo reform) and Qing (New Government reforms) took Japan's path as a model, a way for East Asian people to learn and utilize the new things of "the West" while remaining culturally and spiritually themselves.

In both Qing and Chosŏn, the concept of *reform* dominated the elite discourse of this period. Though some Chinese (notably Sun Yat-sen and his allies) advocated *revolution*—the overthrow of the Manchu Qing—many intellectuals, such as Kang Youwei and the Independence Club members of Seoul, did not want to eliminate their traditional political forms but to make them better. Formulae such as Zhang Zhidong's "Chinese learning for the foundation, Western learning for methods" and modern devices such as newspapers and public monuments represented means to a middle path. Reformers knew that East Asians had to adapt to the aggressive modernity of Europe, America, and Japan, but they also wanted to retain their traditional cultures as long as they served national purposes. In the twentieth century, this reformist position gradually lost relevance as more elites advocated thoroughgoing, revolutionary change.

Chinese and Korean elites also quickly adopted the shared *vocabulary of modernity* created, mostly in Japan, by using Chinese characters to translate European and American terminology. In addition to lexicons of science and technology, intellectuals in all three cultures used concepts pronounced in Japanese as *minzoku* (the ethnic nation), *kokusui* (the national essence), *shakai* (society), and *kaika* (enlightenment) to understand how Europe and the United States had achieved wealth and power. They also began to develop a progressive vision of history, a new way of understanding themselves as nation-states among equals, competing for profit and power, not as the Central Kingdoms, the repositories of Confucian virtue.

This new conception formed within a discourse of *race* and *evolution*, pseudo-scientific Social Darwinism, which theorized a racial hierarchy of peoples, biologically determined, with northern Europeans at the top and Africans at the bottom. Where would East Asians fit? By winning two wars and ending its unequal treaties, Japan created the possibility that the "yellow" peoples would not always be losers. Modernizers like Liang Qichao even speculated that the final winner would be decided in a race war between the whites and the Asiatics. Amid the heated imperialist rivalries of the late nineteenth century, military, political, and economic dominance over other nations demonstrated one's own superiority, so Qing Taiwan and all of Chosŏn became Japan's proofs of virtue.

Education in the new knowledge appealed to more and more East Asian elites as a key to personal and national advancement. Recognizing Japan's decades of development in curriculum and teacher training, Chinese and Koreans flocked there after the Sino-Japanese War, and especially after 1900, to gain access to modernity through Japan's experience. There, ironically, they also became more conscious of Japan's ambition to dominate the region, creating a foundation for their own nationalism—some origins of anti-imperialist, anti-Japan movements for Chinese and Korean independence lay in Japanese schooling. In Japan, East Asians also studied the radical thinking that had arisen in Europe and the United States—labor unionism, socialism, feminism, anarchism—and some returned home resolved not only to overturn the old political order at home but also the entire social order as well. Three great themes of modern history—race (*minzoku, minzu, minjok*), class, and gender—joined in the minds of these new East Asian elites as foundations for national advancement or salvation.

CHAPTER EIGHT

TRIUMPHS, REVOLUTIONS, AND HARD TIMES (1910–1931)

WORLD CONTEXT

The rivalries among the European powers—Great Britain, France, Germany, Austro-Hungary, Russia—burst into open warfare in 1914. "The Great War" raged for four years, slaughtering and maiming tens of millions of young men, forcing European industries into military production—the United States and Japan followed later—stimulating a new wave of scientific discoveries and inventions, shattering not only bodies, lives, and landscapes but also cultures and countries. The most obvious political casualties—the Ottoman and Austro-Hungarian empires—disintegrated into independent national states (e.g., Hungary and Turkey), colonies, and protectorates (e.g., Iraq and Egypt). The Russian empire remained whole but became the Union of Soviet Socialist Republics (USSR), a radically new sort of country, after the Bolshevik victory in the revolution of 1917.

Woodrow Wilson (1856–1924), the only American president with a PhD, a lifelong white supremacist, and a visionary in international relations, took a reluctant United States into the Great War in 1917, raising revenue with the newly established federal income tax. He articulated many important doctrines of the twentieth-century world system—collective security and an international body to structure it; international law and a court to enforce it; democracy as an international value; and, perhaps most dramatic, the self-determination of peoples, an idea that resonated powerfully throughout the colonized world. Domestically, Wilson presided over the constitutional amendment process that gave American women the vote in 1920 but also resegregated the federal civil service and allowed the southern states systematically to disenfranchise their African American citizens. While serving as president of Princeton University, he had refused admission to all black applicants, but as president of the United States he nominated the first Jew (Louis Brandeis) ever to serve on the US Supreme Court.

A conference of diplomats from over 30 countries, dominated by the Great Powers (Britain, France, United States), negotiated the Treaty of Versailles (1919) to end the Great War. Defeated Germany and revolutionary

Russia—the infant USSR—were not seated, while delegations from many colonized peoples (Korea, India, French West Africa) and "weak" nations (ROC, Greece, Brazil) attended to press their interests. Among these non-powers, the World Zionist Organization presented its plan for a Jewish state in Palestine, which had been Ottoman territory. Removing the Arab provinces from the Ottoman empire, the conference laid the groundwork for a British mandate in Palestine, with the long-term goal of establishing a Jewish "national home" there.

After considerable controversy, the Powers decided to punish Germany severely, restricting its military from rearmament and imposing an enormous indemnity—equivalent to US$400 billion in 2009 dollars, later reduced by 50 percent—that blocked the Weimar Republic from economic recovery and contributed to the strong resurgence of German nationalism under the leadership of the National Socialist (Nazi) Party. British economist John Maynard Keynes attacked this part of the treaty vehemently, claiming (with considerable prescience) that it would impoverish Germany for a generation and bring quick, violent retribution.

Hoping to end discrimination against its citizens, Japan proposed a racial equality clause for the treaty. Despite a majority vote in favor of the proposal, President Wilson (chairing the conference) refused its passage under heavy pressure from the British and Australians, for Japan's amendment would have delegitimized their white supremacist regimes. Many noble ideals did become part of the League of Nations charter—non-white people's rights, women's rights, soldiers'

East Asia by early 1937

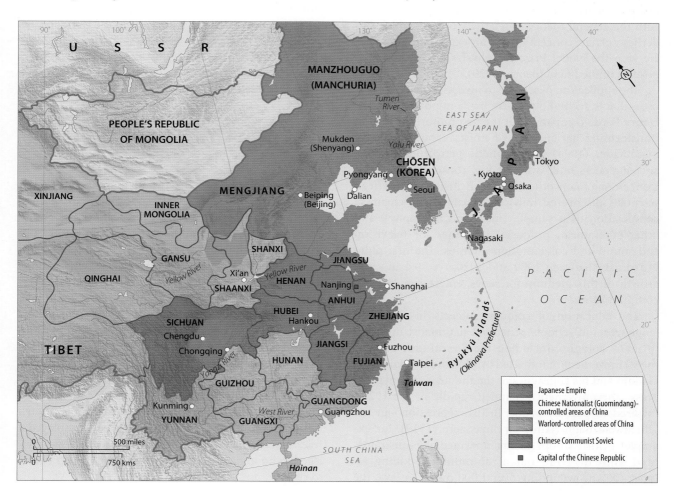

rights—but without enforcement capacity, the League failed to alter the condition of colonized, enslaved, or degraded people.

The signatories created the League of Nations to secure a permanent peace and solve the international problems that had led to war. Wilson's ideas, articulated in his "Fourteen Points" (January 8, 1918), constituted the foundation for the League, but the US Senate refused to ratify the Versailles Treaty, so the United States never joined. Over 50 nations did, but the League lacked an independent military force and could not enforce its idealistic principles.

The astonishing march of science continued during this period, including elucidation of the structure of the atom, accurate mapping of our galaxy (the Milky Way), discovery of the antibiotic properties of penicillin (1928), and creation of a vaccine for yellow fever (1930). Albert Einstein continued his epochal career with the general theory of relativity (1916), which underlies current conceptions of an expanding universe. He won the Nobel Prize for physics (1921) and proposed a unified field theory (1929).

The application of science to invention and practical use—that is, technology—also made important strides. Henry Ford's company built the first motorized tractor, transforming agriculture. Chemists created effective insecticides (1924) and synthetic petroleum (1910s), and engineers built a liquid fuel rocket and a cyclotron, among many other devices. British and American scientists discovered how to determine the chemical composition of a sample (mass spectrography), and other laboratories produced machines for television and sound and color motion pictures. The first radio broadcasts, between 1909 and 1920, resulted in rapid growth of this medium for news, entertainment, and communication.

The education of colonial subjects in European languages and schools generated nationalist upsurges in many colonies, including the *Swaraj* (self-government) movement in India, led by Mohandas (Mahatma) Gandhi and his colleagues in the Indian National Congress. The movement expanded rapidly in the 1920s, inspired in part by brutal British repression—in the Jallianwala Bagh (Amritsar) massacre (1919), for example, British troops facing unarmed demonstrators fired until they ran out of ammunition, killing almost 400 and wounding over 1,000 more. In Java, the charismatic Sukarno led the *Partai Nasional Indonesia* (founded 1927) to oppose Dutch colonialism—he and his colleagues openly hoped for a Japanese invasion to liberate them from the Europeans.

All over the world, the Great War and its senseless violence created conditions for rapid postwar cultural change. Rejecting traditional, or even recent, ideas of art, literature, music, philosophy, psychology, and politics, modernist rebels from Picasso to Stravinsky, Virginia Woolf to Sigmund Freud, undertook to turn the world on its head, to make the respectable seem laughable and the revolutionary seem ordinary. Widely available phonograph recordings of improvisational African American jazz music moved hearts and bodies in new ways. The rise of the USSR encouraged socialists, anarchists, labor unionists, and other political radicals to organize utopian societies, to dream of an end to exploitation, a world of equality and prosperity for all.

Then came the crash. Beginning in the United States in October 1929, the world's financial system came apart at the seams, plunging all industrialized and industrializing societies, and their colonies, into the Great Depression.

JAPAN: DEMOCRACY AND EMPIRE

The second decade of the twentieth century ushered in the era of "Taishō Democracy." Historians usually terminate that period not with the death of the Taishō Emperor in 1926, the endpoint of the reign-period, but with the Manchurian Incident in 1931. Millions of Japanese in the 1910s and 1920s felt that they had access to rights, prosperity, education, and culture that their parents' generation had not enjoyed. Many could take part in a government increasingly led by political parties rather than unelected oligarchs. Contemporaries often referred to the growth of parliamentary politics as the essence of Taishō democracy, but an exclusively political view of Taishō democracy is too limited. This chapter will recast this useful term to note the paradox of the Japanese people's simultaneous pursuit of civil rights and empire, including both those who played a role in parliamentary politics and those, far less privileged, who audaciously hoped they could gain access to rights.

JAPAN'S EXPANSION DURING WORLD WAR I

Japan entered World War I in August 1914, following Britain's request for assistance against the German navy in the waters off Qingdao, in Jiaozhou, Germany's Shandong leasehold. Although Japan played only a minor military role, World War I was Japan's "good war." Europeans and Americans focused their attention on the battles in Europe; the United States did not enter the war until 1917 but produced war matériel for its allies. This permitted Japan, for the first time, to compete in sales of advanced industrial products in Asian markets and to play a radically expanded role in China. The economic benefits of World War I temporarily lifted Japan's poorest from poverty and led to the expansion of Japan's middle class, who aspired to greater political and social participation.

Japan literally expanded by gaining German-held territory. Within weeks of declaring war on Germany, Japanese forces took Qingdao in early November 1914 after bombing the city from seaplanes launched from the world's first aircraft carrier. In October, the Japanese navy also seized the Marshall, Caroline, and Mariana Islands from the Germans. The British requested Japanese naval assistance in Singapore, South Africa, and the Mediterranean, and the Japanese navy obliged by escorting British troop transports and patrolling for German submarines. None of these were major military actions of the war, but they had enormous political and diplomatic significance in the region. Perhaps most important, these actions earned Japan major power status at the 1919 Versailles Peace Conference that ended World War I and allowed Japan to expand territorially in Asia and the Pacific.

Japan also expanded its political and economic influence in China and Manchuria. In January 1915, Prime Minister Ōkuma Shigenobu (1838–1922) and Foreign Minister Katō Takaaki (1860–1926) presented the Twenty-One Demands to Yuan Shikai, president of the nominal Republic of China (see p. 232). The first four (of five) groups of demands raised little concern for Japan's closest ally, Britain. These demands would:

- confirm Japan's new role in Qingdao
- extend the South Manchurian Railway rights gained after the Russo-Japanese War and grant Japanese settlement and extraterritorial rights in Manchuria and eastern Inner Mongolia

- give Japan control of the Hanyeping mines near Wuhan, a major supplier of iron ore for the Yahata steel mill
- prohibit China from granting harbor and coastal rights to any country other than Japan

The fifth group of demands, on the other hand, would have inserted Japanese advisers into China's political, economic, and military affairs, so it inspired vastly different reactions, even from Japan's British and American allies, who protested this group.

Chinese nationalists reacted to the Twenty-One Demands with mass public demonstrations and boycotts of Japanese goods and shipping. Yuan Shikai approved the popular outrage but also feared Japanese forces stationed in China and Manchuria. Japan withdrew group five under US and British pressure, but forced Yuan to accept the first four groups in May 1915. Japan's power and influence in China expanded, but any positive attitudes Chinese may have held toward Japan evaporated with this imperialist move.

When the United States joined the war alongside Britain and Japan in 1917, US Secretary of State Robert Lansing and Japanese special envoy Ishii Kikujirō (1866–1945) signed the Lansing–Ishii Agreement, recognizing Japan's special interests in China while upholding America's Open Door Policy. This agreement underscored American acceptance of Japan's increasing domination in China and the first four groups of demands.

Prime Minister Ōkuma and Foreign Minister Katō might seem ironic proponents of the imperialism represented by the Twenty-One Demands. The prime minister was a veteran of the People's Rights Movement and his foreign minister an admirer of British parliamentary democracy since his days as Japanese ambassador to England. Moreover, Ōkuma and Katō were early members of what became Japan's second—and more liberal—parliamentary political party, called Dōshikai in the early 1910s, renamed Kenseikai in 1916 and Minseitō in 1927. Katō viewed his actions as foreign minister as constitutional. Indeed, while the conservative oligarch Yamagata Aritomo did not object to expanding Japan's presence in Asia, he resented Katō's insistence that the foreign minister had the constitutional right to make foreign policy without consulting him. As we have seen before, the expansion of constitutional rights was not inconsistent with support for imperialism.

World War I also became a "good war" for Japan's economy. Industrial output increased fivefold, from 1.4 billion yen in 1914 to 6.8 billion yen in 1918, as Japanese producers filled orders for munitions from the allies and claimed former European and American markets in Asia. Import substitution in Japan's domestic market was particularly important in industries with higher levels of technology, such as chemicals and machinery. Allowed space to develop, these high-tech industries gained a foothold in Japan that they retained when the Europeans reentered the Japanese market in the 1920s. By the early 1930s, these advanced industries had expanded both in profits and technology. Many, like the chemical firm Nippon Chisso, grew exponentially in Korea, building dams, power plants, research labs, factories, and cities and serving as the economic spearhead of Japanese imperialism.

World War I also opened other, less technologically sophisticated, markets. For instance, when European match producers turned to munitions production, Japanese children in impoverished families took unskilled jobs making matches. Before the war, slums ringed every city, and their occupants worked at odd jobs such as rag picking, piecework, hauling, and street vending. Whole families of five or six, who often took in a few boarders as well, lived in single tenement rooms with one outhouse for several dozen families. Everyone worked, and most families could still barely scrape by. Having no cooking facilities, tenement-dwellers bought leftover food hawked by vendors.

Wartime labor demand opened increased opportunities in factories, offering former tenement-dwelling pieceworkers predictable incomes as part of the increasingly stable industrial working class. Some workers moved into the new middle class. As incomes rose, demand for services like medical care increased. Instead of entering a factory, a young woman might attend nursing school, pulling her whole family into the middle class as she became a professional. More children stayed longer in school, increasing the demand for teachers. The small houses of the working class—two or three rooms, a tiny kitchen, and a privy—replaced one-room tenement dwellings. The new middle class increasingly moved into Western-style homes in the uptown sections of Japan's cities. Urban and rural electrification also expanded rapidly; by the mid-1930s, almost 90 percent of Japan's homes had electricity.

FROM WORLD WAR I TO THE EARTHQUAKE: 1918–23

After the rising economic tide lifted many families during the war, the postwar crash exposed continuing social and economic inequalities that the Japanese were less willing to accept. Rapid wartime growth had fueled inflation. The first sign of trouble appeared in July 1918, when housewives in a fishing village demonstrated against the doubling of rice prices between January 1917 and July 1918. During the next two months, demonstrations called "Rice Riots" erupted all over Japan. Close to a million people took part in over 600 demonstrations; 1,000 people were killed and 25,000 were arrested. The government suppressed the Rice Riots, but Prime Minister Terauchi Masatake had to resign.

Katō Takaaki seemed an obvious choice for the next prime minister, but oligarch Yamagata hated him for his independent foreign policy decisions in 1915. Yamagata instead had the emperor appoint the Seiyūkai party head, Hara Kei, as prime minister. Although Hara, nicknamed the "great commoner," was hardly a progressive—he brutally suppressed a steelworkers' strike, using troops, in 1920—he was the first prime minister who was also head of a parliamentary majority party.

Hara supported an expansion of the electorate to 5 percent of the population in 1919, though he considered "universal suffrage" (actually only male suffrage) to be a "dangerous idea." His cabinet created a Social Affairs Bureau to handle unemployment and labor issues and persuaded the Diet to pass laws requiring companies to provide health insurance and compensation for death and injury. Hara had a mixed record on progressive issues, but historians and contemporaries viewed his selection as a step toward "Taishō democracy." Following Hara's assassination in 1921 by a right-wing worker, the next three prime ministers were not party leaders. The Seiyūkai, Minseitō, and a smaller political party banded together to demand party cabinets in 1924. They urged the public to rally for "normal constitutional government," suggesting that Hara's single term had made parliamentary cabinets "normal." When the Kenseikai won a parliamentary plurality in 1924, its head, Katō Takaaki, became prime minister. Katō's perennial opponent, Yamagata Aritomo, had died in 1922.

Despite the enthusiasm of politicians for party cabinets, the Diet and cabinet were never the only decision-makers, even during the Taishō era. Other institutions participated in the balance of power. Under the constitution, the emperor, "sacred and inviolable," was the head of state, though he rarely articulated decisions. More important, the central government bureaucracy and the military reported directly to the emperor, not to the Diet or cabinet. This allowed the military to act independently of civilian government during the 1930s. The Privy Council was also independent of the Diet. Appointed in 1888 to ratify the constitution, it continued until 1945 as a secret body of men appointed for life by the emperor. These men came from the oligarchy—the elder statesmen of the Meiji period—and were joined by other elite men when the oligarchs died. The men who replaced the oligarchs were called "senior statesmen," and though they were not part of the Meiji oligarchy, they continued to recommend prime ministers, even in the era of party cabinets. The Privy Council, senior statesmen, and House of Peers (the aristocratic house of the Diet) all came from similar backgrounds. Despite movements to expand civic participation to marginalized groups, these extra-constitutional elites remained central to the decision-making system.

The Rice Riots were just the first manifestation of a growing social divide. Soon after the war's end, thousands of small companies that had sprung up during the war failed. Many had produced the inexpensive consumer goods abandoned by larger companies in favor of higher-quality, more profitable goods, while others, just tiny in-home workshops, had served as subcontractors to larger firms. When European and American companies reentered the Asian marketplace, many of the smallest companies could not compete. The economy crashed in 1920, with bank failures, loss of export markets, and unemployment for the unskilled workers of numerous tiny workshops. Large companies, especially *zaibatsu* affiliates, also laid off workers, but belt-tightening, superior technology, and more highly skilled labor allowed some to weather the economic storm. When the wartime micro-companies died, the economy became more concentrated in a few large *zaibatsu* corporations.

Many unemployed workers returned to the countryside, where they joined an already depressed farm economy. The increase in prices that engendered the Rice Riots in 1918 had not helped tenant farmers, but it did cause the government to change colonial policy to import more rice from Taiwan and Korea. Increasing rice supply meant that Japan's urban consumers got cheaper rice, but Koreans and Taiwanese now had much less rice to eat—half of Korea's rice was shipped to Japan—and Japanese farmers suffered a steep drop in the value of their crops.

Tenants cultivated over half of Japan's farmland at the end of World War I, paying as much as half their harvest as rent. This seemed intolerable to urban workers who returned to the countryside after the war, accustomed as they were to rhetoric condemning capitalist exploitation. They joined other farmers and social reformers in organizing tenants' unions. Protests against high rents and bad conditions escalated from about 1,500 in 1921 to 2,700 in 1926. In 1922, tenant farmers formed the All Japan Farmers' Union. By 1926, 150,000 had joined the union, hoping to struggle for rights, a rural example of Taishō democracy.

Until 1921, Japan engaged in a series of costly military and diplomatic ventures. Shortly after signing the 1917 Lansing–Ishii Agreement recognizing Japan's "special interests" in China, the Terauchi government sent Nishihara Kamezō (1873–1954) to North China to make large loans to the warlord government of Duan Qirui (1865–1936), one of Yuan Shikai's subordinates and a leading contender for power between 1916 and 1920. Ostensibly a private businessman arranging loans from private Japanese banks for projects like railway building, Nishihara was actually commissioned by the Japanese government, which underwrote the loans to prop up Duan's government. In exchange, Duan secretly confirmed Japan's possession of Germany's Qingdao colony.

Japan became even more entrenched in Northeast Asia after the Bolshevik Revolution and the USSR's separate peace treaty with Germany in late 1917. The French, British, Canadians, and Americans feared that the Germans would be able to strengthen their forces on the western front and seize Russian munitions in Siberia. Moreover, a Czech military contingent, part of the allied forces, remained in Siberia, unable to return home after the collapse of the eastern (Russian) front. Hoping to rescue the Czechs, secure the Russian munitions, and restore a non-communist Russian government to reopen the eastern front against Germany, the western allies decided to invade Siberia.

Japanese generals had also been agitating since the fall of 1917 for Japanese intervention to support anti-communist (White) Russian forces in Siberia. So when US President Woodrow Wilson asked Japan to send 7,000 troops in the summer of 1918, Prime Minister Terauchi agreed, fearful of a Communist USSR so near to colonial Korea. The United States dispatched about 8,000 troops, the British 1,500, and the Canadians 4,200. By the time Japan left Siberia in 1922—two years after the other combatants withdrew, having failed to defeat the USSR—as many as 70,000 Japanese soldiers had participated in the expedition. Japan succeeded only in angering the new Soviet Union, irritating the United States and Britain by sending so many troops for so long, suffering 3,000 war dead, and engendering a peace movement at home.

The post-World War I economic troubles made curtailing the huge expenses of a growing global arms race appealing to all the powers, including Japan, so they met in Washington, DC, in 1921–22 to negotiate cost-saving naval reductions. The disarmament conference could not have come at a better time to help extricate Japan from its costly foreign policy.

The Washington Conference also dealt with the issue of Qingdao. Germany's defeat and Japan's agreements with Britain, the United States, and the warlord government of Duan Qirui left Germany's leasehold in Japanese hands when the victorious powers negotiated the Versailles peace treaty. Japan's primary goals for the Versailles Conference were confirmation of its possession of Qingdao and the Pacific Islands and insertion of a racial equality clause in the Covenant of the proposed League of Nations. The Great Powers—Great Britain, France, and the United States—refused the racial equality clause but granted possession of Qingdao and the Pacific Islands, so no one was entirely pleased. Japanese anger over the racial issue would later worsen US–Japan relations—though, of course, Japan gladly held onto Qingdao and the islands—but it was not nearly as intense as anger among Chinese nationalists, who erupted in anti-Japanese demonstrations on May 4, 1919 (see pp. 261–63). By then, Japan appeared to nationalistic Chinese to number not only among the aggressive imperialists occupying Chinese territory, but to be the worst of these imperialists.

The May Fourth Movement in China followed close on the heels of the events of March First in Korea. Inspired by Wilsonian rhetoric of "self-determination of nations" and angered by repressive treatment at the hands of Japanese colonial authorities, Korean students and Christian leaders proclaimed Korean independence before a large but peaceful crowd on March 1, 1919. This aroused a colony-wide outbreak of demonstrations. By the following year, brutal suppression by Japanese military police of 1,500 demonstrations had led to 7,500 Korean deaths and 45,000 arrests (see p. 272).

Japan's examination of its brutal suppression of the Korean declaration of independence led the government to change its colonial policy. The resulting "cultural policy" modified some of the more objectionable practices—for instance, it replaced military police with civilian police and offered limited press freedoms that permitted some nationalist and feminist expression. While the colonial authorities took small steps toward relaxing cultural expression, however, economic policies, such as increased rice exports to Japan, made life more difficult for many Koreans.

The Washington Conference represented a shift from the more aggressive policy of the 1910s to a more cooperative policy in the early 1920s. The Washington Conference began with US President Wilson's invitation to Britain, France, Italy, and Japan to negotiate arms limitations. These five powers were joined by Portugal, Belgium, the Netherlands, and China for extensive discussions about Asia/Pacific policy. A number of agreements came out of this two-month conference. The Five Power Treaty held Britain, the United States, Japan, Italy, and France to capital warship tonnage in the ratio of 5: 5: 3: 1.75: 1.75. Some other naval vessels were not covered—cruisers, for example, and aircraft carriers—and the treaty stipulated that no new naval bases be built in the Pacific. This slowed the naval arms race while guaranteeing the security of the signatories.

With the Four Power Treaty, Britain, the United States, Japan, and France agreed to respect each other's claims to their colonial possessions; the treaty also ended the bilateral relationship between Japan and England. Under the Nine Power Treaty, the signatories agreed to respect the territorial integrity of China and honor the Open Door principle of equal trade opportunity there, though they included no sanctions for violating these rules. Japan agreed to give most of Jiao-zhou back to China, while retaining the Jinan–Qingdao Railroad for 15 more years.

In the years after the Washington Conference, Japan withdrew from Siberia, decreased military spending to 29 percent of the budget in 1924 (it had been 55 percent in 1918), and cut the army and navy by a total of 100,000 men. While drastically reducing troop levels, military leaders redirected spending to retain strength. First, they modernized the military with costly new weapons. Second, because the military lost prestige after World War I—reflected, for example, in officers wearing civilian clothes when off duty, rather than the uniforms that had been so respected earlier—the Army Ministry implemented military education for boys in middle and higher schools to rebuild public support.

During most of the 1920s, Japan's foreign policy was characterized by the multilateral Washington treaty system, whose strongest advocate was Shidehara Kijūrō (1872–1951), foreign minister whenever the Kensei-kai/Minseitō was in power. He occasionally acted in a unilateral way, but that was the exception. For example,

The nine delegation heads at the Washington Conference, 1921–22. Ambassador Shidehara Kijūrō (third from left) negotiated for Japan, and naval minister Katō Tomasaburō (far right) was the nominal head of the delegation.

he opposed China's regaining the tariff autonomy it had lost in the 1840s, worried about the possible impact on Japanese textile exports to China. This sank a multilateral tariff-revision effort in Beijing in 1925. But Shidehara generally maintained a multilateral approach even when differences with Western countries emerged.

The most important of these differences derived from US immigration policy. The US Supreme Court's 1922 decision preventing Asians from becoming naturalized American citizens and the 1924 prohibition of all Asian immigration to the United States, a decision that ended the Gentleman's Agreement of 1907, were viewed as racial insults and undermined Shidehara's ability to persuade the Japanese public of the effectiveness of his multilateral approach. As a result, when he refused to send Japanese troops to China to suppress anti-Japanese boycotts and violence, the opposition called him "weak-kneed." Advocates for unilateral Japanese action in China began to gain power in policy-making circles. After 1931, unilateralists dominated Japanese foreign policy decision-making. The shift toward unilateralism doomed Taishō democracy at home as well.

Taishō democracy dominated the 1920s. Parliamentary government as well as movements of marginalized Japanese who believed they had the right to equality and respect characterized the Taishō spirit of change. Some stressed assimilation and equality, while others focused on nationalism and distinction. Women's movements of varying ideologies stressed both women's equality and difference from men in their quest for rights, respect, and inclusion. Labor organizations fought for recognition, fairness, and civil rights.

The hereditary degraded group called *eta* during the Tokugawa period, considered non-human, received legally human status and the name *burakumin* (hamlet people) in 1871. They struggled to be better educated and prove their worth in the workplace, to overcome discrimination in schooling, employment, residence, and marriage. These moderate tactics failed. In 1922, more militant *burakumin* founded the Suiheisha (Levelers' Association) to demand social inclusion and equality. Ryūkyūans (Okinawans), regarded as inferior by most Japanese, also sought inclusion. Thousands migrated to western Japan's cities in the early twentieth century. Young women became favored employees of textile mills, as it was virtually impossible for them to escape, and Ryūkyūan men frequently worked as day laborers, most paid abysmally. Despite being linguistically and culturally distinct from other Japanese subjects, many believed that hard work and adopting mainstream culture would allow them to be integrated into Japanese society.

Few Koreans lived in Japan before 1910. As late as 1889, Japanese laws strictly limited the employment of foreign laborers without permission from prefectural authorities. Intended to restrict Chinese workers from immigrating, these laws affected all foreigners. In 1911, only about 2,500 Koreans, mainly students, diplomatic employees, and a few workers, lived in Japan. This number slowly grew to about 4,000 in 1915. Soon after that, however, large numbers immigrated to meet demand for labor. From 1917, when about 14,000 Koreans resided in Japan, the number increased to over 32,000 in 1921 and 137,000 by 1925. Recruiters hired Koreans to work in textiles, mining, and other industries. Women textile workers came from throughout the peninsula, though men tended to be recruited from a few provinces in the south. At first, many workers were sojourners, returning home between jobs. A

stable residential community took about two decades to build. Male Korean workers earned much less than their male Japanese counterparts, though both earned more than women of either ethnicity.

Korean students were another story. Although fewer in number than workers, students constituted an articulate minority in Japan's Korean community. Encouraged by professors like Yoshino Sakuzō (1878–1933), an advocate of Taishō democracy and of promoting Korean national and cultural identity rather than assimilation, Korean students in Tokyo formed nationalist and Christian groups. Surveillance and harassment by Japanese authorities led many to abandon moderate approaches for more radical ones. Some students questioned whether solidarity with Japanese Marxist students should outweigh their Korean nationalism. Ironically, the articulated policy of the Japanese imperial government paralleled the leftist students' downplaying of cultural distinctions. Government policy aimed to assimilate Koreans as Japanese subjects—according to officially sponsored legends, they were to be "restored" to the "Japanese" ethnicity they had possessed before being "Sinified" hundreds of years earlier.

View of Tokyo in the aftermath of the Great Earthquake of September 1, 1923.

Many had to confront the question of nationalism versus internationalism or assimilation when the Great Earthquake of September 1, 1923 destroyed much of eastern Japan, killing between 100,000 and 200,000 people. Tokyo and Yokohama almost completely burned to the ground, and millions were left homeless. Within days of the earthquake, an estimated 3,000–6,000 Koreans (and some Japanese leftists) were killed by police and vigilantes filled with ethnic rage and fear. Despite the government's rhetoric of ethnic similarity, Koreans were targeted for their ethnicity. A decade later, Korean miners working in Japan called on Japanese miners to support their strike as fellow workers. Although the Japanese union gave logistical support, not one Japanese miner joined the Koreans. In the end, the dark, exclusionary side of *minzoku* (racial) thought trumped Taishō liberalism and class solidarity.

Japanese laborers had themselves struggled for decades for respect and dignity. Although the Public Peace Police Law made labor organizing difficult after 1900, and the execution of socialists in the Great Treason case in 1911 silenced leftists, some workers still undertook unionization and strikes. In 1912, Christian social reformer Suzuki Bunji (1885–1946) met with 13 male factory workers in a church basement to found an association called Yūaikai (Friendly Society). His organization initially stressed the harmony of labor and capital, thereby earning industrialist Shibusawa Eiichi's support. In 1916, the Yūaikai created a women's division, and in 1919, the Yūaikai transformed itself into a union—the Greater Japan Federation of Labor. The Federation developed a political agenda that included the elimination of child labor, the eight-hour workday and minimum wages for men, revision of the Public Peace Police Law, and universal male suffrage.

Labor became more militant after the war, with 497 strikes in 1919. This militancy paralleled the re-emergence of socialist activism. The labor movement included both Marxist unions seeking to overthrow capitalism and non-Marxist unions like the Federation of Labor. Over 100,000 workers had joined unions by 1921. Men far outnumbered women in unions, although women outnumbered men as industrial workers until 1933. Women formed the earliest unions of office workers and typists in 1919 and 1920.

Company owners' concerns about strikes and labor mobility led some to establish factory councils to challenge the unions' allure. Recognizing that dignity was a key reason for workers' organizing, these companies promised job security, bonuses, health clinics, and meetings where workers could air their views, in lieu of unions. Some workers accepted the conditions these paternalistic companies offered, while others preferred to demand respect and economic advancement through unionization.

Japan's feminists also focused on the issue of respect and inclusion in the body politic. As noted in Chapter 7, women activists were not a monolithic group. Christian feminists of the Women's Reform Society (WCTU), cultural feminists of the Bluestocking Society, and socialist feminists all sought to improve the status of women. But how should women earn rights? As people with special characteristics (such as motherhood), or as the equivalents of men? In the mid-1910s, feminist thinkers contested these approaches in what was called the "Motherhood Protection Debate." *Bluestocking* founder Hiratsuka Raichō argued that the state was indebted to women for reproducing the next generation and must support them financially and reward them politically. Feminist poet Yosano Akiko considered that to be "slave morality" and wrote that women must be financially independent before having children. Marxist writer Yamakawa Kikue (1890–1980) dismissed both attitudes, claiming that only socialism could guarantee protection for mothers and equality for women.

The post-World War I years saw an explosion of interest in women's civil rights, but feminists' hands were tied by Article 5 of the Public Peace Police Law, which forbade women's attendance at political meetings and membership in political parties. By World War I, middle-class women had joined their working-class sisters in the workplace, working in schools, shops, offices, newspapers, telephone exchanges, hospitals, and banks. Thousands of housewives not in the workplace belonged to women's service organizations.

In November 1919, Hiratsuka Raichō, joined by Ichikawa Fusae (see pp. 254–55), formed the New Women's Association (NWA), a group targeting both professional women and housewives. By 1922, the NWA had succeeded in overturning the Article 5 prohibition on women attending political meetings. A group of Marxist feminists formed the short-lived Red Wave Society in 1921, in 1922 contraception advocates invited American birth-control pioneer Margaret Sanger (1879–1966) to Japan, and the Women's Reform Society was considering adopting the cause of women's voting rights when the Great Earthquake struck in September 1923.

Women of many groups, from revolutionary socialists to middle-class suffragists, from advocates of rights based on motherhood to equal rights feminists, labored together on earthquake relief. Working side by side to feed and shelter families, they formed the Tokyo Federation of Women's Organizations. In late 1924, the federation's political arm founded the Women's Suffrage League.

FROM RECONSTRUCTION TO THE MANCHURIAN INCIDENT: 1923–31

The Katō government's 1925 granting of suffrage to all males over 25 not receiving public welfare was the most famous Taishō reform. Activists had been agitating for "universal suffrage" since the 1890s. Although limited to men, the extension of the vote constituted a major step toward democracy. Several days before the Diet passed the suffrage bill, Katō Takaaki appeased conservatives—worried about the possible election of leftists—by introducing the Peace Preservation Law, which outlawed criticism of capitalism and the emperor. As it turned out, the mainstream political parties,

ICHIKAWA FUSAE

Ichikawa Fusae (1893–1981), born in a farming village, was known as the "Susan B. Anthony of Japan." She first worked as a schoolteacher, but unequal treatment of women teachers drove her from the classroom. She next took up journalism in Nagoya, where she encountered feminism. Moving to Tokyo in 1918, she joined Hiratsuka Raichō and Oku Mumeo (1895–1997) in founding the New Woman's Association (NWA). Criticized by socialists for downplaying social issues and even by Hiratsuka for her single-minded focus on civil rights at the expense of motherhood protection, Ichikawa was challenged for her "bourgeois" quest for the vote in the prewar period.

Ichikawa left the NWA in 1921 for the United States, where she deepened her understanding of the diversity of Western feminisms through meetings with Jane Addams, Alice Paul, and others. She observed the lives of African Americans she met in Chicago. Rushing home following the 1923 Tokyo earthquake, she worked on women's issues for the International Labour Organization from 1923 to 1927. At the same time, she joined women from across the political spectrum to carry out earthquake relief. In December 1924, their relief work done, Ichikawa and others launched Japan's leading suffrage group, the Women's Suffrage League (WSL).

Ichikawa considered the late 1920s a "period of hope." WSL and other women's organizations gathered 20,000 signatures for suffrage in 1929, and the Seiyūkai and Minseitō, assuming women would eventually vote, vied to gain women's support. In February 1931, the House of Representatives approved a bill—opposed by feminists because it failed to grant complete civic equality—for women's right to vote in local (not national) elections. But the House of Peers rejected even this limited bill, and Japan's rightward shift after the Manchurian Incident killed any chances of women gaining the vote soon.

Japan's militarist government kept suffragists under close surveillance in the 1930s, so the WSL turned to issues like garbage collection, municipal utilities, clean elections, and the Tokyo fish market to safely involve women in public affairs. But the WSL, like other organizations, was soon swept up by nationalism. Eight women's groups formed the Federation of Japanese Women's Organizations in 1937, with Ichikawa as secretary. A Women's National Emergency Congress supplanted the annual National Women's Suffrage Convention in 1938. The WSL was

Seiyūkai and Minseitō (formerly Kenseikai), and not the leftists, won virtually all parliamentary seats in the 1928 elections. In 1928 a Seiyūkai government, however, used the Peace Preservation Law to arrest over 2,000 people accused of communism.

Katō's Kenseikai/Minseitō cabinet also pushed for reforms to help tenant farmers mediate disputes and to assist unions. Katō won passage of the tenant bill and was able to repeal the antiunion clause of the Public Peace Police Law of 1900, but failed to win passage of other pro-union measures. A later Minseitō prime minister, Hamaguchi Osachi (1870–1931), met with Women's Suffrage League members in 1929 and promised to support women's civil rights in exchange for women's help in carrying out government fiscal policy. Women called this a "period of hope," and indeed the late 1920s heralded the inclusion of marginalized groups, if only to bring social stability to a nation recovering from economic difficulties and the earthquake. The Minseitō cabinet and the House of Representatives agreed to grant women some voting rights in 1931, but the Manchurian Incident put an end to all liberal goals before they could be achieved.

Tokyo's reconstruction after the earthquake made it a more modern city. The economic stimulus from rebuilding and easy government loans helped it recover.

disbanded in 1940. When the government invited Ichikawa and other feminists to serve on government committees, most did.

Within ten days of Japan's surrender, Ichikawa found colleagues alive in war-torn Tokyo. Reestablishing the WSL, she met with cabinet officers who agreed to grant women the vote. A few days later, the American military occupation also demanded that women be given the vote; Ichikawa, who had long struggled for rights, was disappointed that the myth emerged that General Douglas MacArthur, head of the occupation, "gave" suffrage to Japanese women. Ready to claim her new civil rights, Ichikawa was instead purged by the occupation in 1947 because of her wartime service on government boards.

Following the occupation, she resumed public life, running successfully for a Diet seat in 1952. On trips to Okinawa she addressed the issues of forced suicide and institutionalized military rape. While in the Philippines to receive the Magsaysay Prize for Community Leadership in 1974, she was one of the first government members to apologize for Japanese wartime aggression. In 1975, Ichikawa brought Japan's women's organizations together in the

Ichikawa Fusae, wearing a Western-style suit at a meeting of the New Woman's Association in 1921. Hiratsuka Raichō is seated, third from the left.

International Women's Year Action Group to confront sexism. Widely popular, her historical place appeared assured. Yet, her quest for citizenship rights exposed Ichikawa—and other women and minorities who prioritized equal rights—to criticism for collaborating with the wartime state. She died while still an active Diet member.

Not all sectors recovered equally, however. Consumer goods produced in China challenged Japanese products, and an overvalued Japanese yen made Japanese products costly in global markets. Then the economy crashed when dozens of banks failed in 1927. For several years, banks had held risky earthquake recovery loans and failed to write off bad loans. Many banks were thus close to failure when speculation brought down the semi-governmental Bank of Taiwan, triggering a run on the banks.

The severely damaged Japanese economy did not recover before being hit by the Great Depression, started by the 1929 New York stock-market crash. Economic distress in the late 1920s and early 1930s fueled right-wing anger at Japan's globalized economy. Rightists who railed against the multilateral economic system targeted business leaders, including the heads of *zaibatsu*, for assassination. This paralleled the militarists' attack on the Minseitō's multilateral foreign policy as "weak-kneed."

Rightists also criticized Japan's liberal urban culture as decadent, overly Westernized, and destructive to Japanese traditions. The New Women and Modern Girls, emblems of the Taishō period, received particularly harsh criticism. The New Women of the 1910s were often educated literary and political figures like Hiratsuka Raichō and Yosano Akiko. Although frequently whispered about as overly sexual, they tended to have respectable careers.

The Modern Girls of the 1920s, however, were both more numerous and a creation of the mass media. Stylish, up-to-date, wearing daringly short hair and short skirts, the young, bright Modern Girls represented sexual liberation. They worked in modern occupations to earn the money they spent in trendy department stores and in cinemas, coffee houses, and jazz bars. Strolling down the Ginza, Tokyo's most fashionable street, they thrilled some people and frightened others. At times, they appeared with Modern Boys, less fashionable but more politically active. Despite Modern Boys' generally leftist ideology, they did not rival Modern Girls as threats to traditionalists. Even some Marxists saw Modern Girls as hedonists.

Images of modern society permeated Japan in the 1920s. Mass-market publications—newspapers and glossy magazines—appealed to every segment of society, selling millions of copies. Radio reached several million households by the late 1920s. Novelists became

sensations, selling thousands of copies of their works, and Hollywood movies and stars were as familiar in Japan as in the United States. Middle-class homes built after the earthquake, many modeled on Western dwellings and interiors, were filled with material goods, part of Japan's modern and cosmopolitan urban culture. It threatened some conservatives and angered those who saw it as shockingly materialistic when many rural people suffered privation.

Although modern ideologies, occupations, and movements characterized the Taishō era, resistance to

Japanese New Year's card of 1932 showing women in modern fashion. Museum of Fine Arts, Boston. "Modern Girls" shocked traditionalists with their seeming hedonism and materialism.

those ideas and practices always played an important role in Japanese culture, even if not the dominant one in the 1920s. Similarly, multilateral international relations as manifested in global treaty systems always had their unilateralist opponents. Even as aggressive foreign policy was replaced by more cautious policy in the early 1920s, unilateralist approaches lurked in the background. When the Seiyūkai returned to power in 1927 and the Depression discredited globalism in 1929, aggressive foreign policy reasserted itself.

Tanaka Giichi (1864–1929), an army general and head of the Seiyūkai, became prime minister in April 1927 and immediately set about changing foreign policy. He sent Japanese troops into China on three occasions, ostensibly to protect Japanese citizens and businesses but actually to stop the Northern Expedition of Jiang Jieshi (Chiang Kai-shek, 1887–1975) and the Guomindang (see p. 266). Tanaka sought alliances with Chinese warlords because he feared the rising power of Chinese nationalism that Jiang Jieshi represented. This type of unilateral China policy violated the spirit of the Washington treaty system. When Japanese officers—hoping to ignite skirmishes so Japan could take over Manchuria—assassinated northern warlord Zhang Zuolin (1875–1928) in 1928, Prime Minister Tanaka did not condemn their action. The emperor, annoyed by Tanaka's failure to punish the assassins, forced Tanaka to resign, but not before Tanaka's unilateral policy exacerbated Japan's tensions with China.

At the 1930 London Conference, the follow-up to the Washington Conference eight years earlier, Prime Minister Hamaguchi hoped to increase Japan's capital warship tonnage from 60 to 70 percent of that of Britain and the United States. The Western powers refused, and the Minseitō prime minister agreed to the lower ratio. Right-wing proponents of a unilateral foreign policy called Hamaguchi a traitor to Japan for cooperating at a multilateral conference, and he paid for multilateralism with his life in late 1930, victim of a right-wing assassin's bullet. Political assassins killed other business and government leaders, and rightist elements in the military planned two coups in 1931.

To get them out of Japan, the army shipped some of the military rightists off to Manchuria to serve in the Kantōgun (also called "Kwantung Army" in English), the Japanese army force that patrolled the South Manchurian Railway. When they got there, they plotted to take over Manchuria to develop a utopian society and economy, to support a war they predicted would occur between Japan and the United States. To provoke a war they hoped would lead to Japan's acquiring Manchuria, they staged a bombing.

Tokyo got wind of the plot and sent a senior officer to Manchuria to stop it, but he supported the plotters and intentionally arrived too late. Colonel Ishiwara Kanji's (1889–1949) troops blew up a section of railway track on September 18, 1931 and blamed the Guomindang government in Nanjing. The Minseitō cabinet tried to settle the incident locally, but the army general staff claimed the cabinet did not have the right to intervene, because the military reported only to the emperor. The Kantōgun proceeded to take southern Manchuria.

Zhang Xueliang (1901–2001), son of Zhang Zuolin and in command of the Manchurian army under Guomindang colors, appealed to the League of Nations, which called for the withdrawal of Japanese troops in November. Foreign Minister Shidehara tried to restore peace, but was forced out of government in December. The Seiyūkai's Inukai Tsuyoshi (1855–1932) headed the next cabinet, and the emperor thought the Seiyūkai could rein in the military more effectively. But Inukai also failed, assassinated by right-wing officers in May 1932. This Manchurian Incident, leading to Japanese control over the region (see pp. 282–85), ended parliamentary government in Japan and began what the Japanese call the "Fifteen-Year War."

CHINA: WARLORDS AND NEW CULTURE

YUAN SHIKAI, MILITARISM, AND IMPERIALISM

The deal that ended the Qing included a constitution, elections, and parliament as checks on the president, but Yuan Shikai, a reformist Qing bureaucrat, had little tolerance for constitutional politics. An intelligent, ruthless proponent of centralized power, he sometimes cooperated with Sun Yat-sen and the revolutionaries but always strove to increase Beijing's control at the expense of local and provincial elites. Those local elites had played crucial roles in the revolution, operating the provincial assemblies and organizing the provincial

Sun Yat-sen (center) at the Shanghai Railway Station, January 1, 1912. After arriving in Nanjing a few hours later, he proclaimed the founding of the Republic of China and assumed the office of Provisional President. Song Jiaoren was assassinated on this same railway platform fourteen months later.

chauvinism that culminated in railroad rights recovery movements and eventually secession. Ever since Zeng Guofan and his allies raised provincial armies to fight the Taipings (see pp. 150–51), the province had become an alternative political space, no longer governed by outsiders sent from the capital at Beijing but rather by local elites, who advocated balance between center and province, not a renewed autocratic center called a republic rather than a dynasty.

Nonetheless, in 1912 the revolutionaries and the provincial elites invited Yuan's presidency. With constitutional guarantees and a burgeoning press—487 newspapers and magazines by 1913—the Republic under Yuan Shikai promised a united China, capable of resisting foreign pressure. As in early Meiji Japan, almost no one advocated wide public participation in politics. Only elite males could vote or be elected to the provincial assemblies and the national "deliberative assembly," for which delegates were chosen that spring.

Yuan Shikai dominated the north, where he had served the Qing, while his opponents came overwhelmingly from the south, though his allies included Tang Shaoyi (1862–1938), a Cantonese graduate of Yung Wing's US educational mission (see pp. 192–93). Tang mediated the Shanghai negotiations that made Yuan Shikai president, and Yuan appointed him prime minister in March 1912. After joining the United League, now an open political party, Tang approved the provisional constitution drafted by Song Jiaoren along French and American lines. When Yuan Shikai violated the constitution in June, Tang Shaoyi and the other United League ministers resigned, and Yuan replaced them with more reliable followers.

In August 1912, Song Jiaoren combined the United League with several smaller parties to form the *Guomindang* (GMD or KMT), the Nationalist Party, which held a two-thirds majority in the "deliberative assembly." Song spent that fall organizing December elections for a national parliament, which gave the GMD a plurality in both houses. Although only 5 percent of the population (upper-class males) could vote, this election nonetheless stood for many decades as modern China's most open and legitimate. But Yuan Shikai could not tolerate any challenge to his position. On March 20, 1913, a gunman shot Song Jiaoren on the Shanghai railway platform, and he died two days later at the age of 31. An investigation found circumstantial links to the president's office, and Chinese historians conclude that Yuan engineered the assassination.

Impeached for taking a huge loan from foreign banks without parliamentary approval, Yuan dismissed the GMD governors of several provinces, antagonizing his southern opponents. In mid-summer 1913, seven provinces declared independence—the "Second Revolution"—but Yuan's forces quickly defeated them, and Sun Yat-sen again fled to Japan. After declaring martial law that fall, Yuan eliminated the GMD from parliament and revised the constitution, extending his term to ten years and allowing his reelection. With his men in charge of most provinces, he dismantled the remaining republican institutions and became sole dictator. These actions entailed widespread terror in which tens of thousands died.

In January 1915, when the Great War occupied the attention of the European powers, Japan seized Germany's territory in Jiaozhou (Shandong province) then presented the Twenty-One Demands to Yuan's nominal Republic. As described above, these changes would have solidified Japan's control over China, excluding the Europeans even after the war. A Japanese ultimatum forced Yuan Shikai to accept four of the five groups of demands in May, causing an eruption of nationalistic passions among politically aware Chinese. Hundreds of students abandoned their study abroad and returned home, fearing that Japan would colonize China as it had Korea (see pp. 239–41).

To Yuan Shikai, the Twenty-One Demands exposed the weaknesses of republican government, so he gathered even more power into his own hands. As part of his centralizing project, he promoted elimination of provincial autonomy, antagonizing provincial elites and revolutionaries. Most of his program consisted of gradual reforms familiar from the late Qing: monetary stabilization, consistent taxation, opium suppression, expansion of education, and industrial development. But he had neither money nor support to implement them, so he fell back on symbols. In August 1915, he initiated the rituals that would have made him emperor of a constitutional monarchy. Convinced that Chinese people desired hereditary leadership, he framed his accession to the throne as an expression of popular will. Yuan may have been right—we have no idea what most Chinese thought in 1915—but he had already destroyed his credibility with provincial and local elites, whose support might have legitimized a new dynasty.

Yuan's American adviser, political scientist Frank Goodnow (1859–1939), justified monarchy as appropriate to China's stage of development, but Yuan's enthronement pleased neither the official international community nor Chinese elites. Before he even announced his reign-title on January 1, 1916, Yuan

Yuan Shikai, 1913.

faced a military challenge from Yunnan's governor, a popular uprising for Sichuanese self-government, and many provincial declarations of independence. Official Japanese approval went to anti-Yuan forces, including Sun Yat-sen, and Japan embargoed all funds for Yuan's government. Isolated, Yuan quickly abandoned the monarchy and planned to flee to the American embassy in Beijing, but he died suddenly in early June.

Since no national figure could replace him, China disintegrated into its constituent provinces and subprovinces. The "legitimate" Beijing government fell to Yuan's generals, beginning with Duan Qirui, who accepted Japanese loans and affirmed Yuan's acceptance of Japan's demands in the name of "China." But military autonomy dominated China's politics for the next 12 years—the "warlord" period.

Some of Yuan Shikai's former officers shared North China, while a faction led by Zhang Zuolin, an exbandit, controlled the northeastern region, with its rich natural resources and close connections to Japan, Korea, and Russia. Feng Yuxiang (1882–1948), a left-leaning Christian convert, led his army all over northern and northwestern China, allying first with Zhang Zuolin, then with the Guomindang, which he sometimes supported and sometimes fought. In contrast, Yan Xishan (1883–1960) controlled Shanxi for over 30 years. Including both well-educated intellectuals and brutal thugs, the warlords all needed money for their troops, so they fought for territory and the power to tax its inhabitants. Needless to say, ordinary Chinese suffered horribly under their rule.

Although the nominal ruler of the Republic of China—whichever warlord happened to hold Beijing—claimed sovereignty over the whole country, the frontiers remained beyond central control. Tibet became an independent theocratic state under the Dalai Lamas; Xinjiang suffered under the tyrannical rule of several Chinese warlords; and Outer Mongolia, a Soviet dependency, declared its independence from China in 1924. Inner Mongolia's status varied with its leaders, sometimes leaning toward China, sometimes toward Manchuria and Japan. Nonetheless, Chinese of all political persuasions claimed that "China" included Tibet, Xinjiang, and all of Mongolia—that is, the Qing empire at its height. This remarkable consistency, so different from the fates of the Ottoman, Austro-Hungarian, and other nineteenth-century empires, has been usefully attributed to the imagined "memory," however inaccurate, of thousands of years of unity.

PUBLIC INTELLECTUALS: THE NEW CULTURE MOVEMENT

Chinese students, eager to learn about the modern world, studied primarily in Japan, but a few traveled farther. In 1910, Hu Shi, an 18-year-old student of "Western learning" with a brief classical education, received a scholarship to Cornell. Initially studying agriculture, Hu shifted to philosophy and entered Columbia, where John Dewey (1859–1952) taught him pragmatic, experimental methods that appealed to his desire to solve problems rather than build ideological schemes.

A prize-winning student and a firm believer in common sense as a guide to action, Hu Shi dedicated himself to the potential of "human intelligence and effort" to change the world. Rapidly completing his PhD dissertation, he returned home in 1917—fluent in English, individualistic and nationalistic—to find his country without an effective government, fragmented by warlords, and in danger of being engulfed by Japan. Distinguished by his doctorate, Hu Shi became a professor under Chen Duxiu (1879–1942), Dean of Beijing University (Beida), with whom he collaborated in editing *New Youth* magazine.

Hu Shi joined a remarkable and diverse faculty assembled to create a new Chinese education by Beida's president, Cai Yuanpei (1868–1940). Cai had passed the Qing's highest civil service examination, studied in Germany and France, and then took over Beida after Yuan Shikai's death. His faculty included radicals such as Chen Duxiu and Li Dazhao (1888–1927, the "father of Chinese Marxism"), moderates like Hu Shi, and even committed conservatives such as Gu Hongming (1857–1928), a Malaya-born polymath who taught English literature and retained his Manchu queue.

By this time, many intellectuals, following pioneer scholar-journalists such as Wang Tao and Liang Qichao, had reacted to China's critical condition by founding periodicals and writing proposals to improve or save their country. They advocated solutions as diverse as socialism, capitalism, Christianity, science, federalism, spiritualism, Marxism, revived Confucianism, Social Darwinism, eugenics, and physical education. Chen Duxiu had inaugurated *New Youth* magazine in 1915 with a clarion call to transformation: "Youth in society is comparable to fresh and vital cells in the human body, the new replacing the old." *New Youth* became the flagship of the "New Culture Movement," an inchoate network of intellectuals connected by new-style education, common reading, and nationalism—all deeply anxious about China's future in the midst of the Republic's failures.

With his practical inclinations, Hu Shi saw that China lacked a fundamental characteristic of a modern country: a single national language. Classical Chinese required years of intensive study and divided the elite from ordinary people. Written vernacular Chinese, however, resembled everyday speech and had been used for centuries in popular literature and drama. Hu Shi envisioned the vernacular as a cohesive force,

Members of the Beijing University (Beida) faculty in 1919 (clockwise from upper left): Hu Shi (professor), Li Dazhao (librarian), Chen Duxiu (dean), Cai Yuanpei (president).

uniting rather than dividing China, but conservative scholars and politicians reacted to his linguistic proposals with horror. Abandoning classical Chinese, they alleged, meant rejecting China's philosophy and poetry, history and literature, the pinnacle of human culture. Vindicating Hu Shi, vernacular Chinese became the standard written language within a few years.

"Western knowledge" included texts and ideas stretching from the Enlightenment to psychoanalysis, from Newton to Einstein, from the seventeenth century to the twentieth. Mostly translated from Japanese translations, this new body of knowledge bombarded Chinese students and teachers with three centuries of European and American intellectual evolution in less than two decades. Some reacted by rejecting Chinese tradition entirely, whereas others embraced new learning while continuing to value elements of Chinese culture. All compared their own country with the powerful, universalizing "modern West" of Europe, North America, and Japan. How, they wondered, can we come to terms with this invasive, apparently irresistible force *and still remain ourselves*? In order to do that, young Chinese had to articulate what constituted their own irreducible cultural core, that which made them Chinese. Like Meiji and Chosŏn reformers, they had to invent a *modern* identity using elements from a past that had failed them.

THE MAY FOURTH MOVEMENT

For over a decade, Zhou Shuren (1881–1936) and his brother Zhou Zuoren (1885–1967)—from Qiu Jin's hometown of Shaoxing—tried using literature to awaken their compatriots to China's peril. They failed until April 1918, when Zhou Shuren, under the pen name Lu Xun (see pp. 262–63), published a short story entitled "A Madman's Diary" in *New Youth*. In this brief fiction, Lu Xun created the vernacular voice of a classically educated, paranoid madman to formulate a stark critique of Chinese society and culture. To the story's narrator, confined because of his illness, the world seemed populated by cannibals; his neighbors, even his relatives, wanted to feed on his flesh. All his Confucian books, amid the words "righteousness" and "benevolence," said nothing but, "Eat people."

That same summer, also in *New Youth*, Hu Shi introduced Norwegian playwright Henrik Ibsen (1828–1906) to China with a translation of *A Doll's House* and an essay on individualism, which took China's students by storm. Describing Nora, Ibsen's heroine, trapped in her husband's house, Hu Shi argued that individuals had to liberate themselves, as Nora did by leaving her "happy" home. Nora thus became a symbol for *all* Chinese, female or male, who felt oppressed by tradition. "The woman problem" came to symbolize individuals' dilemmas *and* China's national crisis. *A Doll's House* was performed in hundreds of China's modern schools.

These voices in *New Youth* and elsewhere struck powerful chords among Chinese intellectuals. Struggling with many new concepts—democracy and science, for example—they felt trapped by family and tradition, unable to liberate themselves or China. At this same moment, news arrived of the Bolshevik Revolution in Russia, which had overthrown the Czarist empire in late 1917. The infant USSR proclaimed utopian ideals of socialism, equality, and liberation of the oppressed. These immediate influences—nationalism, rejection of family and tradition, and socialism—combined with a real imperialist threat to China, especially from Japan, to stimulate young Chinese to act for the sake of China.

The 1918 Armistice brought the victors in the Great War to Versailles. Japan argued that it should retain the German leasehold at Qingdao, in Shandong, while the Chinese delegation demanded its retrocession. Late in April 1919, word reached Beijing by telegraph that the Great Powers had awarded Qingdao to Japan. Outraged students planned a demonstration for May 7, the fourth anniversary of the Twenty-One Demands. Looking to the Korean anti-Japanese March First Movement (see pp. 271–73) as inspiration, they called pro-Japan government ministers "traitors to China." Moving the demonstration to May 4 to forestall official opposition, student leaders asked Luo Jialun (1897–1969), founder of *New Tide* magazine, to pen a manifesto. His stirring vernacular words became a crucial text of Chinese nationalism:

The loss of Shandong means the destruction of China's territorial integrity. Once territorial integrity is destroyed, China will soon be annihilated…Today we swear two solemn oaths with all our countrymen: (1) China's territory may be conquered, but it cannot be given away; (2) the Chinese people may be massacred, but they will not surrender.[1]

Over 3,000 students gathered that afternoon at the Gate of Heavenly Peace (C. *Tiananmen*) and marched toward the embassy quarter, carrying signs in Chinese, English, and French, and chanting, "Return our Qingdao!" "Protect our sovereignty!" "Down with the traitors!" Blocked by police from entering the Legation Quarter, the students marched to the home of pro-Japan Foreign Minister Cao Rulin (1877–1966). After trashing and torching the house, students beat up Cao's guest, a former ambassador to Japan, and returned to their campuses. Finally taking action, the police, many sympathetic to the demonstrators, arrested 32 students.

All over China, urban people of many classes reacted publicly to the May Fourth demonstration. Initially focused on gaining the arrested students' release, the political fervor expanded to include recovery of Qingdao and included merchants, urban workers, even rickshaw pullers and shop clerks. Teachers and professors backed their students. Just before being arrested himself, Beida Dean Chen Duxiu wrote, "There are two sources of world civilization: One is the study, one is the prison… only these provide the most lofty and sublime life."[2] By the end of June, the public outcry forced the Chinese delegation at Versailles to refuse to sign the treaty, which nonetheless gave Qingdao to Japan, and police released all of the imprisoned students and faculty.

Unable to reverse the Versailles decision, the May Fourth students and their allies created a national movement to increase the pressure for change that had been building since before 1895. Challenging the legitimacy

LU XUN, MIRROR FOR MODERN CHINA

Like Hu Shi, Shaoxing native Zhou Shuren studied "Western learning" in the Qing's last decade. In Japan for medical school, he hoped to replace traditional Chinese medicine (which he hated) with modern science, but soon realized that China's problems were deeper than even scientific medicine could cure:

> …no matter how *healthy or strong the bodies of a weak-spirited citizenry might be, they'd still be fit for nothing better than to serve as victims or onlookers… There was no need to fret about how many of them might die of illness. The most important thing to be done was to transform their* spirits…*through literature and art.*[3]

Dropping out of medical training, Zhou promoted a Westernizing literary movement but had only the classical language as a tool. His translations and essays inspired no one.

Portrait of Lu Xun, by Li Yitai (1981), in the style of the woodblock prints that Lu Xun loved and promoted.

of military government, ready to sacrifice for the nation, to learn from the foreigners *and* to defend China, that generation of intellectuals inspired all twentieth-century Chinese revolutionary and reformist movements.

After May Fourth, new political forms, including labor unions and political parties, emerged to advocate social change, national unity, and resistance to foreign control. Literate Chinese produced a flood of prose urging scientific research, new literature, national resistance, and social progress. The May Fourth Movement, therefore, is often described as the beginning of modern China. The deep roots of change lay much earlier, in the late nineteenth century or even before, but none can deny the power of 1919 in the development of Chinese nationalism.

THE FAMILY BROKEN, THE PEOPLE GONE

The May Fourth students could organize and strike in part because China had no effective central government. From 1916 until 1928, China remained an arena of regional and provincial generals—"warlords"—who created unstable alliances and networks of personal loyalty. The relations among these warlords made "China" look more like an international system than a country, with shifting coalitions, diplomacy, negotiation, and constant warfare. The unpredictable violence of that decade brought insecurity and terror to hundreds of millions of people.

Since the Taipings, violence had occurred in China on a scale without parallel elsewhere in the world, numbers so huge that we might be unable to process them—tens

---

Depressed, Zhou returned to China in 1909. He taught in Hangzhou and held a government job but did not find his vocation as modern writer Lu Xun until 1918. Under the influence of the vernacular movement, publishing in *New Youth*, he produced, in only a few years, the most powerful fiction of twentieth-century China. He had read Gogol and Chekhov and immersed himself in modernism, but he also remained deeply attached to Chinese culture, despite what he saw as its profound flaws.

Contemporary critics portray Lu Xun as holding a mirror up for Chinese to view themselves, not providing any systematic remedies but saying, "We must look honestly at who we are." His most famous fictional character, Ah Q, was a low-life Chinese Everyman: narcissistic, narrow-minded, conservative, sexist, and clueless. Ah Q's fate mirrored China's— arrested for a crime he did not commit, he died mutely before a firing squad. In the preface to his first collection of stories, Lu Xun expressed his despair in one of modern China's most incisive metaphors:

Suppose there were an iron room with no windows or doors…And suppose you had some people inside that room who were sound asleep. Before long they would all suffocate. In other words, they would slip peacefully from a deep slumber into oblivion, spared the anguish of being conscious of their impending doom. Now let's say that you came along and stirred up a big racket that awakened some of the lighter sleepers. In that case, they would go to a certain death fully conscious of what was going to happen to them. Would you say that you had done those people a favor?

Lu Xun participated in the intellectual battles of the 1920s and 1930s through *zawen*, short, pointed essays that he used as a social and political scalpel, dissecting Chinese literary circles, puncturing inflated egos, excising diseased customs and character traits, awakening the sleepers. One of China's greatest public intellectuals, he moved to the left politically but remained independent, never joining a party. A brilliant writer, compassionate critic, and nationalistic individualist, Lu Xun died of tuberculosis in 1936.

of millions dead, a hundred million left homeless—but the size of the numbers should not blind us to personal reality. Whether in famous battles or uncommemorated famines, Chinese people faced the destruction of their homes, their families, and their lives *as individuals*, not as masses. We cannot forget the human truth of suffering just because so many people suffered.

The warlord period marked an expansion of warfare in size and in geographical scope. Armies fought everywhere in China, so civilians endured not only military violence but also its social effects: disruption of agriculture, relentless conscription of men and draft animals, harsh taxation, and destruction of transportation infrastructure. Without government intervention, insurance, medical care, or social networks, people survived or died on their own, a complete breakdown of society's guarantees that would scar Chinese lives through the twentieth century. The technology of warfare also changed. Long-range artillery and explosive shells, powerful rifles and machine guns, motorized vehicles, and military aircraft expanded soldiers' ability to kill at long range. Warlords purchased weapons from abroad and began to produce them domestically, increasing their armies' effectiveness and war's horror.

Despite political fragmentation, no warlord questioned China's obvious unity, meaning the entire territory of the former Qing empire. Most nineteenth-century agrarian empires—the Ottoman and Austro-Hungarian, for example, and even Czarist Russia after the collapse of the USSR—dissolved in the twentieth century, but not the Qing, whose frontiers remained as the imagined borders of China. This ideological commitment to a unified China the same size and shape as the Qing empire survived because both Chinese and foreign actors accepted its inevitability and "naturalness." Using ambiguous terms such as "the Chinese nation," invented by Liang Qichao in 1907, politicians from the late Qing to the present have repeatedly confirmed China's singularity, with the overwhelmingly numerous Han (Chinese) *minzu* as its core. The warlords fought savagely to protect or expand their domains, but they never established sovereign states.

THE RISE OF POLITICAL-MILITARY PARTIES

By the mid-1920s, an armed Guomindang arose from the combination of warlordism and May Fourth activism. Between 1917 and 1923, Sun Yat-sen and his colleagues tried to build a firm territorial base at Guangzhou, establishing three separate governments that all failed. The GMD encompassed a broad range of political views, many inspired by the New Culture spirit, but could not overcome the provincial elites and regional militarists.

Meanwhile, Li Dazhao and Chen Duxiu gathered a few dozen like-minded radicals to inaugurate the Chinese Communist Party (CCP) in 1921, with advice from the nascent USSR and the Communist International (Comintern), established to stimulate revolutionary movements worldwide. Lacking military capacity, the Communists focused their attention on labor issues, organizing workers in cities. China's industrial workers, the "proletariat" in Marxist terms (see p. 296), formed only a small percentage of the workforce, but they were crucial in the economy. At the Anyuan coalmines in Jiangxi, Li Lisan (1899–1967), Liu Shaoqi (1898–1969), and Mao Zedong (1893–1976)—all later leaders of the CCP—organized a successful non-violent strike in 1922. Not content with higher wages alone, they created a broad education and culture program for the workers, hundreds of whom joined the CCP and made Anyuan into China's "Little Moscow."

Also enthusiastic supporters of labor, Sun Yat-sen's GMD organized China's first May Day celebration (1918) and dozens of unions, mostly in Guangzhou and Hong Kong, where they led strikes of mechanics in 1920 and sailors in early 1922. GMD leaders recognized labor's nationalist potential with the 1922 strike of the Chinese Seamen's Union, organized as both an economic action *and* an anticolonialist movement. That same year, with CCP initiation and full GMD support, unions held the First National Labor Congress, representing over 200,000 workers.

Unlike the GMD, the Communists also engaged China's overwhelming majority, the rural peasantry. Despite conventional Communist emphasis on urban workers, Li Dazhao believed that the peasants would be the vanguard of China's revolution, an idea he passed to his student, Mao Zedong. In 1922, Peng Pai (1896–1929), from a Cantonese landlord family, organized farmers into the Peasant Association, China's first peasant union. At its height, it included over 200,000 members and forced landlords to stabilize rents and cease breaking contracts and demanding gifts from tenants.

After lengthy conversations with Sun Yat-sen, Soviet ambassador Adolph Joffe (1883–1927) decided that the GMD and CCP should both reorganize and cooperate in a United Front against their common enemies—foreign imperialism and domestic warlordism. Following his recommendations, CCP members joined the GMD as individuals, without disbanding their party. Joffe and the next Soviet representative, Mikhail Borodin (1884–1951), advised both parties to establish centralized discipline and local organization to resemble the Communist Party of the Soviet Union (CPSU). Sun Yat-sen still sought British aid in reuniting China, but British anxiety about an armed GMD—perceived as "Red" allies of the USSR—precluded any substantial help.

Confirming European and American fears, Soviet advisers paid for the two parties to found the Huangpu Military Academy in Guangzhou as the training ground for the officer corps of a national army. Sun Yat-sen appointed his military protégé, Jiang Jieshi, as Huangpu commandant, a position he held until 1926, training almost 7,000 cadets. Future leaders of both the CCP and the GMD taught at Huangpu, including Zhou Enlai (1898–1976) and Wang Jingwei (1883–1944).

Their students included many famous soldiers, most notably future People's Liberation Army (PLA) commander Lin Biao (1907–1971) and future Vietnamese leader Ho Chi Minh (1890–1969). Several dozen Koreans also studied at Huangpu, hoping to organize military resistance against Japanese colonialism. Ironically, China's anti-imperialist movement established its headquarters under imperialist protection. The United Front had its main bases in Guangzhou and Shanghai, port cities protected to some extent by imperialist sovereignty, legally outside Chinese control, safe havens for radical political activities.

Based in Guangzhou, Sun Yat-sen represented both the United Front and the south in negotiations with northern leaders such as the Manchurian warlord Zhang Zuolin. Although he continued diplomatic efforts, by late 1924 Sun had concluded that only military victory could reunite China, so he planned a Northern Expedition. His health rapidly deteriorated, and Sun died of liver cancer in March 1925. His death created a vacuum at the top of the United Front, which his subordinate GMD leaders—Jiang Jieshi, Wang Jingwei, Hu Hanmin (1879–1936), Liao Zhongkai (1877–1925)—all wished to fill. Their power struggle, marked by Liao's assassination, resulted in Jiang Jieshi's control over the GMD military, with Wang Jingwei and Hu Hanmin respectively leading the left- and right-wing party factions. None trusted the Communists, but the Communists did not trust them, either.

During the 1920s, the GMD and CCP strikingly resembled one another in their idealistic striving toward national salvation, unity, and revolutionary "awakening." Seeing themselves as the already awakened elite, intellectuals and politicians—from Sun Yat-sen and Mao Zedong to village schoolteachers—worked to arouse the sleeping mass of their fellow Chinese. GMD strategists tended to focus on the whole nation, "the Chinese people," while CCP ideology excluded some Chinese—exploiters, warlords, "evil gentry and local bullies"—aiming to unite the rest through *class* identification, a Marxist category (see p. 296). The Leninist advisers to the United Front made the two parties structurally similar, and by 1927 both advocated loyalty to their own party, its leaders and its ideology, as the sole road to national salvation. Incompatible in the long run, the two parties set the stage for over 20 years of violent conflict.

Meanwhile, the labor movement, closely linked with nationalism and anti-imperialism, continued to gather strength. The largest wave of strikes began in Shanghai in 1925. During a labor action at a Japanese-owned cotton mill, guards killed a Chinese worker. A memorial meeting drew over 10,000 workers, and a protest march on May 30 even more. A British police officer ordered his Indian troops to fire on the unarmed protestors, leaving ten dead and fifty wounded. The national reaction to this imperialist incident, the May 30th Movement, included boycotts, strikes, and urban protests, which lasted until the British fired several high-ranking police officers and agreed to reparations for the dead and wounded.

ECONOMICS IN THE 1920s

Famine had been common in the nineteenth-century Qing empire, caused by endemic warfare (in the 1860s), overpopulation, catastrophic climate variations (in the 1870s), and breakdown in the government's relief system, which had prevented or mitigated many earlier disasters. In the 1920s, without any viable or unified national government and with numerous warlord regimes unwilling to send relief grain to one another's territory, hunger stalked the land just as high taxes and heavy conscription robbed the farmers of their surplus and their sons' labor. In these worst of times, farmers needed cash crops, so opium cultivation rebounded from earlier eradication campaigns and occupied much of the best farmland, especially in the north. Unmarked in most histories, the North China famine of 1927–30—by no means unique—took more than 10 million lives, created countless refugees, and contributed to a culture of callousness and brutality that dominated many parts of China through mid-century. Images from this period cemented European and North American stereotypes of the Chinese as helpless, emaciated, weak, and desperately in need of foreign assistance.

While many rural areas suffered deprivation and urban workers struck for better wages and working conditions, a middle class also took shape in China's cities. Including educated professionals, industrialists, financiers, and managers of modern enterprises, this new class flourished in cities such as Shanghai, Guangzhou, and Wuhan. Merchant organizations, including Chambers of Commerce, had been crucial in the 1911 revolution, and they continued to thrive. But the chaotic state of China's politics, especially warlord regionalism and unpredictable taxation, left this modernizing sector unsupported, isolated from the rural hinterlands and unable to innovate and invest safely.

Middle-class families had leisure for urban amusements and joined new voluntary organizations such as the Red Cross, calling for greater popular participation in the management of society. Shanghai, especially, became a modern city, partially controlled by foreign powers, in which an extensive underworld—financed by drug trading, prostitution, and gambling—coexisted with a cosmopolitan culture of universities, restaurants, race tracks, movie theaters, nightclubs, and bars. Korean nationalists gathered in Shanghai's foreign concessions to form a government in exile (see p. 272), as did Chinese seeking safety from warlord violence.

CENTRALIZATION AND ITS DISCONTENTS

Sun Yat-sen's death divided the GMD's leadership into left- and right-wing factions. Jiang Jieshi, a right-leaning Japanese-trained military man, became head of the National Revolutionary Army and the GMD in 1926. His rivals, Wang Jingwei (left) and Hu Hanmin (right), joined him in proclaiming a new Guangzhou-based "national government," in parallel to the Beijing "national government" under Manchurian warlord Zhang Zuolin. With the United Front in full swing, GMD and CCP members shared leadership in many sectors, including the army, officered by Huangpu graduates and guided politically by CCP commissars. Leaders of both parties advocated the unification of China, an end to warlordism, a strong central government, and opposition to foreign domination, but they differed radically on strategy, timing, and leadership.

Jiang Jieshi, though he had studied military organization in Moscow in 1924, had a strong aversion to Communists, expressed politically when a leftist naval officer allegedly tried to kidnap him in March 1926. He dismissed all Soviet advisers and CCP members from leadership in his own military units, and he allied with the most conservative GMD factions. Wang Jingwei also mistrusted the CCP, but he continued to support the United Front and included Mikhail Borodin and a number of CCP members in his inner circle. Although Jiang Jieshi succeeded in limiting CCP participation, Soviet leader Joseph Stalin (1878–1953)—trying to manage the Chinese revolution from Moscow—ordered the CCP to remain in the United Front.

In mid-summer 1926, Jiang Jieshi led the National Revolutionary Army (NRA), 90,000 strong, from Guangdong on a Northern Expedition to defeat the warlords and create a single Chinese government. A western column, led by Wang Jingwei, took Wuhan in September. The central column, Jiang's own, took Nanchang in November and struck north toward Nanjing, while a smaller eastward force moved up the coast toward Hangzhou and Shanghai. Either defeating or absorbing the local warlords into the NRA, the Northern Expedition succeeded within six months in unifying all of southern and central China. The CCP cadres—party operatives—attached to the NRA aimed to create a new kind of Chinese military, respecting the civilian population and striving for nationalist goals. Wang Jingwei commanded the Wuhan-based GMD government, but he depended on Jiang Jieshi for control over the military officers, mostly Huangpu graduates loyal to Jiang.

When Jiang's troops arrived at the outskirts of Shanghai in March 1927, the city was already in turmoil. The CCP-dominated General Labor Union (GLU) had called a general strike to welcome the NRA, and armed GLU workers took over the city from local warlord troops. Jiang Jieshi, however, had already decided to end the United Front and purge the CCP from the GMD. His subordinates, both civilian and military, therefore planned to retake Shanghai from the workers in alliance with local troops, police, and the Green Gang, the Yangzi valley's most powerful underworld organization. Beginning on April 12, they conducted a wholesale massacre of Communists in Shanghai. GMD troops surrounded unions' headquarters, executed their occupants, and seized their files. Thousands of Communists, leftists, and workers lost their lives, decimating the urban networks of the CCP.

To rival Wang Jingwei at Wuhan, Jiang Jieshi established his national government, based in the right wing of the GMD, at Nanjing. Intricate conflicts ensued in mid-1927, within both the GMD and the CCP, over how to react to Jiang's preemptive violence. To some extent, disagreements among the Communists reflected the power struggle in Moscow between Stalin and his rival, Leon Trotsky. Stalin ordered the CCP to reject Jiang and organize an independent military force but to remain in the United Front, secretly undermining Wang Jingwei. Wang remained eager to head the GMD government but feared CCP dominance in Wuhan, so he asked northern warlord Feng Yuxiang to mediate between the two wings of the GMD.

In late July, Wang forced Borodin out of Wuhan, and the armed Communists attempted an uprising at Nanchang, a complete failure. Finally dissolving the United Front, Jiang Jieshi took control of a unified GMD. Wang Jingwei remained his rival but never commanded sufficient military power to overthrow him. The divided, severely weakened CCP formally established its own Red Army and tried two more military coups in 1927, the Autumn Harvest Uprising in Hunan and the Guangzhou Commune, both resulting in defeat and slaughter. By the end of the year, a small remnant band of armed Communists, led by Mao Zedong and Zhu De (1886–1976) retreated to the Jinggang Mountains on the Jiangxi–Hunan border, where they established a "Soviet base area" (see pp. 295–97), leaving Jiang Jieshi and the Nanjing government victorious.

Free to continue the Northern Expedition, Jiang led his troops toward Beijing. Zhang Zuolin, who held the capital, ordered his forces back to the northeast and abandoned Beijing in June 1928. With the GMD victory, Zhang Zuolin became a liability to his allies in the Japanese army, who feared he might defect to Jiang. Hoping to replace Zhang with his son, Zhang Xueliang (1901–2001)—reputed to be a decadent opium addict—Japanese officers assassinated Zhang Zuolin. To their disappointment, Zhang Xueliang joined the GMD and brought his father's army under Jiang's command.

By the beginning of 1929, Jiang Jieshi and the GMD had succeeded in unifying much of the Chinese culture area under their Nanjing government. Stalin's United Front policy had failed, leaving a severely weakened CCP only an underground urban presence and a remnant military force in the mountains. Free to unite the Republic of China, the GMD rode a high tide of nationalism and popular approval, adopted a provisional constitution, and set up the Nanjing government. It included many nationally known figures—Cai Yuanpei, former head of Beijing University; Hu Hanmin, one of Sun Yat-sen's Cantonese protégés; and Sun Fo (1891–1973), Sun Yat-sen's son, a graduate of Berkeley and Columbia who had served as mayor of Guangzhou. Apparently, China had emerged united from the nightmares of warlordism. Just at this moment of hope, the Great Depression struck at the world economy, and the Japanese army (see pp. 282–85) took over Manchuria.

COLONIAL KOREA

When the last Qing emperor abdicated in February 1912, the Japanese were pacifying the last armed bands resisting the annexation of Korea. Sweeping arrests of intellectuals effectively decapitated the leadership of the nascent nationalist movement. This two-pronged suppression eliminated modern nationalist organizers while militarily crushing the last vestiges of the *ŭibyŏng* (righteous armies) armed resistance, which took colonial military police and Japanese army regulars until mid-1912.

At the same time, the Japanese coopted traditional elites by giving stipends and titles in the Japanese peerage to 84 high Chosŏn officials and *yangban* and pensioning off another 3,645 officials of the old government. The upper *yangban* lost all of their political power, but they retained their lands and considerable residual social prestige. While the Japanese curried favor with the traditional elite, they began arresting "malcontent and rebellious Koreans," using lists prepared before colonization. As described in Chapter 7, the police arrested 700 people, including the core leadership of the New People's Society—moderate reformers such as An Ch'angho and Yun Ch'iho among them—in connection with a blatantly fabricated plot to assassinate the Governor-General (GG) in 1911. Ultimately they prosecuted 105 people in the colony's first major political show trial. The Japanese authorities commonly tortured and abused arrested Koreans, establishing a pattern of brutal policing that continued to the end of the colonial period.

In short, Japan quickly cleared the way for the construction of a powerful, centralized colonial state. Unlike the old Chosŏn state, whose powers had been limited by its weak presence below the county level, the Government-General of Korea (GGK) penetrated society to the neighborhood level in the cities and to the village in rural districts. By the end of their rule the Japanese had left their mark everywhere. They used their Meiji state-building experience and twentieth-century technology to advance their strategic, economic, and political goals with breathtaking single-mindedness and rigor. Wanting more than simple compliance, the colonial state not only dominated Korea with the usual paternalistic logic of colonialists, they also believed they could "assimilate" Koreans culturally to Japan. Indeed, the later Japanese attempts to efface Korean culture, even its language, exacerbated colonial exploitation, repression, and racism. The poisonous memory of this experience continues to plague Japan–Korea relations more than half a century after decolonization.

Before describing the GGK, it might be useful to consider it in comparative perspective. Among non-Western nations, only Japan assembled its own modern colonial empire. The geographical closeness of Japan and Korea, a feature it shared with French North Africa and the English in Ireland, was also fairly unusual in the annals of modern colonialism. Their proximity encouraged settlement of large numbers of metropolitan émigrés and facilitated colonial migration to the metropole. By 1942, over 1.5 million Koreans lived and worked in Japan, and the Japanese population of the colony approached 800,000 (almost 3 percent of the total). Unlike France and its colonies, but like England and Ireland, Japan and Korea shared a racial and cultural affinity and a long, complex historical relationship.

The Japanese colonialists mobilized archaeology, ethnography, and historical studies to help justify their rule in Korea as a matter of lifting up a wayward sibling culture and returning it to its proper course as part of the destiny of the Yamato race. This was all the more galling to Koreans, because they had historically considered themselves culturally superior to their new colonial masters.

In the end, the Japanese created what was then a high-tech administration in Korea. They built on the colonial experience of the West, which they studied assiduously, as Gotō Shinpei (see p. 216) had demonstrated. Armed with the latest communications technology and their earlier experience in Taiwan, they established a rigid and highly intrusive administrative colonialism. The gendarmerie, swords dangling from their belts as symbols of their authority, had summary powers to enforce the regulations. This allowed the police to be both judge and jury, deciding punishments on the spot for minor infractions. The GGK even renamed the geographic features of the peninsula, including its cities and towns, and for a generation after 1945 Western maps still frequently used these Japanese names. Nothing could have prepared the Korean population for such an invasion into what had heretofore been matters of local and customary practice.

THE GOVERNOR-GENERAL AND THE COLONIAL STATE

The considerable powers of the colonial state were concentrated in the office of its governor-general. Terauchi Masatake—a high-ranking army general, protégé of the Meiji oligarch Yamagata Aritomo, and later prime minister of Japan— became the first governor-general and architect of colonial Korea. His tenure exemplified the enormous power and prestige vested in this office, and after him Tokyo appointed the governors-general from amongst the highest ranks of the Japanese military. All save one, retired admiral Saitō Makoto (1858–1936, served 1919–27, 1929–31), were high-ranking army generals. The governors-general included men who had also served as minister of war, commander-in-chief of the Kantōgun, army chief-of-staff, and even prime minister.

An appointee of the prime minister, the governor-general and his office fell nominally (at different times) under the Diet (for budgetary issues), the Home

Ministry, and the Ministry of Colonial Affairs. But throughout the colonial period, the governor-general reported directly to the emperor, like the military and the Privy Council, creating an ambiguity in the lines of authority that gave his office considerable autonomy. All of Japan's other colonies—Taiwan, Karafuto (Sakhalin), the Pacific Islands, and the Kwantung (Southern Manchurian) Lease Territories—remained more firmly under the thumb of the Tokyo bureaucracy.

The GGK was no small entity. It governed 25 million subjects, controlled enormous tax revenues, commanded Japanese military forces in Korea as well as the colonial gendarmerie, issued laws, and directed a bureaucracy that by 1945 employed 246,000 people. Compared with other colonial regimes, this constituted an enormous state apparatus. France, for example, ruled Vietnam with only 2,920 bureaucrats and an army of 11,000. The British famously ruled India with a few thousand civil servants, and the ratio of officials to population was much smaller than that of the French in Vietnam. The Japanese governor-general in Korea did not equal the prime minister in rank, but the position was almost as prestigious and autonomous.

With armed resistance crushed and the Korean leadership in exile, in jail, or under surveillance, the Japanese built the institutions that would serve colonial hegemony for the next 35 years. They investigated local conditions closely and gathered statistical data on every aspect of Korean life. They created myriad regulations governing daily life, from slaughtering a worn-out draft animal to the placement of a family grave. Other areas of regulation included new land and family registers, public health, detailed sanitation procedures in the reorganized urban administration, fisheries, water rights and irrigation ditches, operation of periodic markets, and licenses and permission forms for just about everything else. After their 35-year rule, the Japanese left an enormous archive of information—based on their colonial impulse to count, record, and control—now being mined by historians.

The GGK built upon a base of administrative law already promulgated during the residency-general (1905–10) to create a dual system of jurisprudence. Unlike native Koreans, Japanese residents in Korea retained their rights as citizens under the Meiji Constitution as well as those granted by special laws in the colony. This meant two sets of laws and punishments—one for Japanese residents, another for the Korean population. Perhaps the most obnoxious feature of this legal apartheid was the use of traditional punishment, whipping, for Koreans, while the practice was deemed too barbaric for Japanese citizens. One Japanese official fatuously claimed the practice to be "culturally sensitive," asserting that Koreans would more readily accept their own traditions in this arena. To enforce the new laws, the Japanese created an expanded judicial system, with all lower-court judges appointed by the governor-general. The emperor—actually, his advisers—directly appointed the high judges. As with most middle and high ranks in the colonial bureaucracy, Japanese occupied the overwhelming majority of judgeships until the very end of the period, when more Koreans were appointed to the courts.

The vastly expanded police force constituted the first line of control and enforcement. Initially, the Japanese simply used their military garrison as police, a colonial gendarmerie, but by 1920, a centralized, civilian police force had replaced the military. From its headquarters in Keijō (the Japanese name for Seoul), the national police oversaw and articulated with provincial, county, and district (urban ward) offices. The police grew rapidly from 6,222 in 1911, to 20,771 in 1922, to roughly 60,000 in 1940, one policeman for every 400 Koreans. If we also consider the small army of informers who worked covertly for the police to monitor political behavior, the numbers would be even more impressive. Over half the police were Koreans, and these people became the most reviled group of collaborators after the end of colonialism in 1945, which Koreans call "liberation." But for many Korean men without family connections, resources, or land, and with little education, careers in the colonial police became an important avenue of upward mobility.

LAND AND THE SURVEY OF 1911–18

The GGK extended its regulatory and legal penetration of Korea by conducting, at great expense (20.4 million yen, an amount equal to the entire annual budget of the colony), a comprehensive land survey of the entire peninsula. The survey established ownership and use of every parcel of land and created a new land registration system that remained in use until 1945. It plotted and assessed all land: wet paddy land, dry fields, upland fields, forest and mountain land, salt pans, and semi-public flood plains. It required all owners and tillers to register with the government documentary evidence of any claims to ownership or other cultivation rights.

In essence, the survey established a strict dichotomy of "owner" and "non-owner," ending a variety of age-old local practices, unofficial cultivation rights, seasonal claims on land of an ambiguous nature—in short all kinds of informal customs that had mitigated owner–tenant relations in traditional Korea. The colonial regime, in contrast, governed land by a strict and rational system of title that allowed for efficient transfers and sales. This system fixed the basis, vastly expanded from the Chosŏn dynasty registers, for taxation on land, the main source of government revenue.

Indeed, the colonial annexation itself constituted a major land-grab, because all the old public lands—government office land, part of the holdings of the old royal house, mountain land, river flood plains, tidal flats, and government salt pans—became the property of the GGK. The colonial government then sold large tracts of the agriculturally useful portion of these lands to individual Japanese and Korean investors and private corporations such as the Fuji Land Company or the huge semi-governmental Oriental Development Company. By the time they completed the land survey in 1918, the GGK controlled 21.9 million acres, almost 40 percent of all farm and forest land in Korea.

The new land system was a boon to all landowners of any ethnicity. The legal stability and predictability ensured owner control, tenants lost any informal advantages, and over time the system created a quiet acquiescence to colonial rule among the landowning class. Owners increased their holdings, and rents rose, as population pressure on the land increased. Tenants normally assumed the bulk of cultivation expenses. In good years or bad, regardless of rice prices, tenants owed 40–50 percent of the harvest in rent, leaving little to cover expenses and to finance the next year's crop. Population increase also drove up demand for land, resulting in correspondingly higher rents. Rice prices, tied to the volatile world market, declined rapidly with the worldwide depression after 1930, further increasing peasant indebtedness. Exposure to the extractive effects of world capitalism and upward pressure on rents caused an alarming rise in landlessness during the 1930s, and tenancy rates in some areas reached 80 percent by the end of colonial rule.

CULTURAL CONTROL, POLITICAL REPRESSION, AND THE IDEOLOGY OF EMPIRE, 1910–19

The Japanese restricted cultural and political activity with laws governing the press, voluntary association, and publishing, most of them originally created during the protectorate of 1905–10. Seoul became a dour and lifeless place, in contrast to the freewheeling and burgeoning urban culture of Tokyo or the coastal cities of China. During the first decade of colonial rule, the GGK closed all privately run newspapers and severely restricted permits for magazines and journals. The only daily newspaper, the official organ of the GGK, used the presses of the formerly important Korean language *Korea Daily News*, now defunct.

Creating a system of permits for public groups of any kind, the colonial regime abolished all private, voluntary associations. Because they exempted religious organizations from this crackdown, as we shall see below, Christian, Buddhist, and Chŏndogyo (the established church of the Tonghak movement) groups provided some cover for political activity. A limited number of publications did, however, see the light of day. Small and short-lived academic, literary, and religious journals survived the GGK's licensing system. Perhaps most notably, Ch'oe Namsŏn's magazine *Youth* (1914–18) continued the project begun with *Boys* (1908–11)—to pioneer new-style Korean vernacular prose and poetry as well as politicized "educational" features on national heroes in history.

Such cultural repression conformed to Japan's emerging policy of cultural assimilation of Korea into Japan. From the beginning, the Japanese intended that Korea would not just be politically absorbed like Taiwan but also culturally assimilated. At first glance such a policy seems ludicrous, but Japanese belief in the racial and ethnic "affinity" of Korea and Japan allowed such thinking to be woven into colonial ideology and practice. Assimilation of Koreans expressed the theory of the "common ancestral origin of the Korean and Japanese races."

This logic rested on the scientific racism of the turn of the century, including Social Darwinism, and the emerging discourse of Japan's manifest destiny to lead Asia against the white race. Japan had already invoked this shared background to legitimate their late nineteenth-century drive for ascendancy on the Korean peninsula. With the advent of colonial rule an array of research institutes, both private and GGK-sponsored, arose to "prove" the racial, cultural, and historical links between the two cultures, with Japan the more advanced culture and thus naturally the one to absorb backward Korea.

Education was to be the prime engine of cultural assimilation. Nevertheless, the Japanese only slowly expanded educational opportunity in their new colony, showing their interest in cultural assimilation to be more theoretical than real in the first decade of their rule. The GGK created separate schools for Japanese and Koreans. Japanese residents in Korea could send their children to school in Japan proper, or they could choose equivalent schools established for Japanese in the colony. For Koreans, the GGK created a separate, unequal system of four-year primary and four-year secondary schools for boys (three years for girls).

The Educational Ordinance of 1911 also regulated the roughly 1,200 private schools established before the Japanese takeover, requiring them to use GGK-approved textbooks. Strict decrees reduced the number of these schools to less than 700 by 1920. Japanese language study was compulsory in all accredited schools, and the Korean secondary system stressed vocational and technical education. Koreans could only study the higher liberal arts in private religious or secular colleges. In short, opportunities for Koreans in Korea to study law, medicine, engineering, and the humanities remained very limited. Ambitious students with financial backing began to go to Japan for upper-level schooling in increasing numbers during the 1910–18 period. The GGK built the education system for Koreans so slowly that after a decade of colonial rule, in 1919, only 84,306 Koreans (3.7 percent of eligible children) attended primary school.

By then the Japanese believed that they had created stable control mechanisms, pacifying and breaking the political will of the Koreans. In reality, increased

Admiral Viscount Saitō Makoto, chief Japanese delegate at the naval armaments conference in Geneva, 1927. Saitō served as the 4th Governor-General of Korea between 1919 and 1927.

literacy, economic development, and increased physical mobility stimulated Koreans' awareness of a national community. But severe military rule, blatant legal and educational discrimination, and arrests of political and intellectual leaders ensured that most members of the Korean imagined community shared resentment and loathing of Japanese colonialism. Even among the peasants, ten years of colonial rule had galvanized anti-Japanese consciousness. Colonial power intruded into daily life, heretofore governed by local custom, and the arbitrary use of whipping by the hated police also created an increased sense of collective discrimination.

THE MARCH FIRST MOVEMENT AND JAPANESE REFORMS

The new sense of the Korean nation created fuel for a massive outpouring of nationalist sentiment, which only needed a spark to explode. That spark came in the form of a coordinated, nationwide demonstration for independence on March 1, 1919. The depth of support for a demonstration demanding independence from Japanese rule—planned to appeal to world opinion and the Allied Powers convening at Versailles to end the Great War—surprised even its organizers. Spurred by coordinated readings of a "declaration of independence," known now as the March First Declaration, in school yards, marketplaces, and parks all over the country, Koreans from all walks of life poured into the streets, marching and chanting "Long live Korea!" The Japanese police reported demonstrations in 217 counties, involving over a million people.

Leaders of the main religious groups—Christian, Buddhist, and Chŏndogyo—worked in secret with students to organize the demonstrations, coordinating the movement with the funeral of the late monarch Kojong. The March First Declaration itself was a moderate document, authored by Ch'oe Namsŏn, a young writer and publisher of *Youth* magazine. In contrast to the idealistic, radical motivations of the movement's student organizers, the March First Declaration expressed the ideas of the senior religious leaders who became the public faces of the movement—men such as Son Pyŏnghŭi (1861–1921), Yi Sŭnghun, Pak Hŭido (1889–1951), and Han Yong'un (1878–1944). Directed to the Versailles Peace Conference, it appealed to the "self-determination of nations," part of Woodrow Wilson's idealistic rhetoric and supposed linchpin of the reordering of new nations liberated after the fall of the Austro-Hungarian and Ottoman empires. It also enjoined demonstrators not to engage in violence toward authorities or property. Unfortunately, the appeal to Versailles—like that of the Chinese delegation regarding Qingdao—fell on deaf ears. While initially pacifist, the demonstrations turned violent in the face of brutal police repression.

The Japanese response bordered on hysteria. They used overwhelming force to contain the demonstrations, and Koreans fought back. By mid-April, rioting was widespread, and police violence led to a number of well-documented atrocities: the burning of villages, shooting into crowds, mass searches, arrests, and the disappearance of known demonstrators. The police also seized printing presses, closed schools, and declared a colony-wide curfew. Still the rioting continued sporadically into the summer of 1919, controlled and completely suppressed only after additional troops arrived from Japan.

Scholars estimate that over 7,500 people died, 15,000 were injured, and over 45,000 arrested in the March First Movement. The GGK itself admitted to 553 deaths, 1,409 injured, and 12,522 arrests, a serious conflagration by any estimate. Notably, the statistics list 471 arrests of women and girls participating in the movement. Women leaders who become prominent in the 1920s, both moderate and radical— Kim Maria (1891–1944), Hwang Hedŏk (Esther Hwang 1892–1971), and Na Hyesŏk (1896–1948) (see p. 310)—all helped to mobilize women during the demonstrations.

The March First Movement failed to overturn the colonial status quo. It did, however, demonstrate that Korean nationalism had matured from its elite intellectual origins and was now a mass phenomenon, inspiring Chinese students protesting against the Versailles treaty on May 4. Moreover, the demonstrations, which continued into the summer of 1919, stimulated the Korean independence movement outside Korea. Within months a number of separate and politically incompatible Korean nationalist groups—socialists from Vladivostok, conservatives from the United States, exiles in China with various political goals—came together to form a government in exile based in China, the Shanghai Provisional Government (SPG). The SPG hoped to create, for the first time, a unified and powerful organization to mount resistance to colonial rule and regain Korean independence.

While the demonstrations failed to unseat the Japanese, they did force a reassessment of colonial policies and amelioration of their most obnoxious features. The Japanese lost face internationally as word leaked out of atrocities and the killing of young students, both boys and girls.

Government General of Korea Capitol Building, c. 1926

Missionaries published eyewitness accounts in the American press, and churches collected funds to help Koreans injured in the riots. That summer, the newly elected Japanese party cabinet, headed by Prime Minister Hara Kei, met to assess the situation in Korea. Hara appointed a new GG, Admiral Saitō Makoto, and charged him to reform colonial policy under the softer slogan of "harmony between Japan and Korea." The success of March First was, however, a Pyrrhic victory. With their will to hold Korea unchanged, the Japanese replaced naked coercion with a softer but more effective policy of manipulation and cooptation.

THE CULTURAL POLICY AND NATIONALIST RENAISSANCE

Saitō and his new team arrived to find the colony in turmoil. While working to pacify the riots and demonstrations, he began a series of meetings with prominent Korean leaders to assess the situation and solicit advice. Ultimately, he embarked on a reform program that softened Japanese policy and provided concessions to Korean cultural and political sensibilities in a number of areas. In the legal arena, Saitō revoked some of the most hated practices, laws, and regulations, concessions that came to be known as the Cultural Policy. The Cultural Policy abolished whipping as a punishment and modified unpopular laws regulating traditional burial practices as well as police interference with rural markets. A new pay scale for civil servants responded to Korean demands to reduce the difference between Korean and Japanese employees of equal rank in the GGK's bureaucracy.

Perhaps most significant, Saitō relaxed colonial policy toward publication and voluntary association. He allowed permits for the first time for two Korean-language newspapers, the *East Asia Daily* and *Korea Daily News*. Political journals received licenses to publish, greatly broadening the public sphere and allowing for political debate and commentary. The GGK also lifted some organizational restraints, and a host of new associations emerged, including many—such as youth groups—on a national basis. The Cultural Policy in effect allowed a new arena for Korean voices, and the 1920s witnessed an outpouring of pent-up literary and journalistic production.

The Japanese searched for ways to blunt Korean resentment while including influential Koreans within the frame of colonialism. This strategy included the creation of advisory boards at the national and provincial level, while changes in economic policies brought more Koreans into the world of commerce. The GG altered the 1910 Company Law to allow more permits for Korean-led corporations while simultaneously removing tariff and regulatory barriers that had limited Japanese companies from doing business in the colony. From a Korean nationalist perspective, this was taking with one hand and giving with the other, for these moves increased competition that hurt fledgling Korean companies. But Saitō also provided subsidies and easy credit to some Korean companies, with Kim Sŏngsu's (1891–1955) Kyŏngsŏng Spinning and Weaving Company as a prime example. With high demand in Japan for more inexpensive rice in the aftermath of the 1918 Rice Riots, the GGK began building up rice-growing infrastructure in Korea. The 1920s turned out to be a relatively good decade for Korean farmers, a fact that also helped the Japanese reestablish stable colonial hegemony.

The Cultural Policy provided a new space for Korean cultural and political activity, but it came at a price. While altering policies to create the surface illusion of more benign civilian rule, Saitō's brain trust also reorganized the colonial control apparatus. The police changed into civilian uniforms, but by the mid-1920s the force had been greatly augmented in numbers and equipment. A new censorship system monitored the emerging press, and a new police bureau secretly penetrated Korean organizations with a new army of informers for thought control. Thus, the Cultural Policy stabilized Japanese rule by placing it on a more secure footing. The new freedoms blunted overt dissent and encouraged a cooperative attitude toward the colonial regime. Given the ferocity of the disturbances that had precipitated the reforms in the first place, the Japanese took considerable risks. Over the decade of the 1920s, by trial and error Japan replaced the harsh repression of the 1910s with a more flexible policy of divide and conquer.

The new cultural and political freedoms had clearly circumscribed boundaries. Any direct denial of Japanese rule—whether in the name of social revolution, anticolonialism, or national independence—met with fierce repression. Radicals of all stripes had to tread carefully lest they find themselves in the still overflowing colonial prisons. Interestingly, leftist discourse did not disappear from the new Korean press, but only insofar as socialism or other radical ideas remained theoretical could they see the light of day. The censors cracked down on anything that could be construed as denying the legitimacy of Japanese rule or the sanctity of the Japanese emperor as sovereign of Korea.

This selectivity of Japanese controls over the press and voluntary association led to an odd dichotomy within Korean political and social movements. More conservative or moderate Korean intellectuals found freedom to speak and organize, but the left had to operate under constant duress. The younger generation of Korean intellectuals—their ranks swelled by students returning from post-secondary schooling in Japan—was more radical than the older publicists, ideologues, and organizers. Indeed, during the 1920s, socialism and a host of other new "isms" dominated public discourse throughout East Asia. As a consequence there was a constant tension within Korean organizations between the older leaders of legal, moderate organizations and a more radical, more youthful rank and file.

This tension appeared almost immediately within the Korean youth movement. In 1920, 600 new youth organizations joined together to form the Korean Youth League, but within two years leftist students broke away to form a socialist Seoul Youth Association. By 1924 this organization folded into a broader Socialist Alliance. The rising popularity of socialism among youth also affected the burgeoning women's movement that had grown from modest beginnings in the Patriotic Women's Associations at the turn of the century. By 1924 women had their own Korean Women's Socialist League.

Splits within the women's movement became more complicated. Most of the early women's groups, Christian and fairly conservative in their orientation, had long been associated with the nationalist movement, often formed as "sister" organizations. In the early 1920s more radical feminists like Na Hyesŏk and Kim Wŏnju emerged. Na and Kim directly confronted the inequity and oppression of Korean patriarchy for the first time. Radical feminism, however, was ultimately marginalized, while the less confrontational agenda of Christian-dominated, reformist women's groups continued to find favor within the male-led nationalist movement.

Even working within moderate groups, leftists found themselves hounded by the police. Given the levels of police harassment, it is not surprising that the first Korean Communist Party formed only in April 1925, four years after China's and three years after Japan's. Unfortunately, this coincided with an increase in Japanese police pressure on radical organizations of all types. The police crushed the first Communist Party, and four successive attempts to create a formal party apparatus met the same fate in succeeding years.

CULTURAL NATIONALISM AND LITERARY ACTIVITY

With the new freedoms of the Cultural Policy, Korea experienced a renaissance of national movements and cultural activity in the 1920s. A number of ventures emerged that focused on cultural and national self-strengthening. These educational, literary, and economic projects avoided direct confrontation with the authorities in favor of strengthening society from within. The contemporary press used "cultural movement" to describe them, and "culturalism" became the code for the movement's generally shared ideology. Another code word for this nationalist self-strengthening ideology was reconstructionism, a term derived, probably, from the title of a well-known tract, "On Reconstructing the Nation" by Yi Kwangsu (see box opposite), a student returned from Tokyo. Yi's belief that long-term social and economic reform should precede independence outraged radicals and leftists because it seemed a tacit acceptance of colonial rule—close to collaboration. But the ideology did motivate a considerable amount of activity from moderate and conservative groups.

Moderate nationalists mounted three major projects between 1922 and the end of the decade. The first was the National University Movement (1922–25) to raise funds for the creation of a Korean national university, a reaction to the dearth of educational opportunities at the higher levels in the colony. Wealthier Koreans could and did send their children to colleges and universities in Japan, but many others considered this a disgrace, and they collected considerable sums to establish a truly Korean center for higher learning. Unfortunately, the Japanese announcement that they would open an imperial university in Seoul (Keijō Imperial University) coopted the movement, and scandals within the

YI KWANGSU

Yi Kwangsu (1892–?), novelist, essayist, nationalist leader, and public intellectual, remains a controversial figure in Korean literary and political history, because he collaborated with Japanese assimilation programs during the 1930s and supported the Japanese war effort in the last decade of colonial rule. Yet the early and middle portions of Yi's life as writer and political activist left a legacy of enormous literary achievement and successful nationalist organizing.

Born in what is now North P'yŏng'an province in northern Korea in 1892, Yi was orphaned aged 10 and raised by relatives. His foster parents introduced him early to the Ch'ŏndogyo religion, the modern church of the nineteenth-century Tonghak movement (see pp. 157–58), and through Ch'ŏndogyo contacts he earned a scholarship from the Pan-Asianist United Progress Society to study at Meiji Gakuen in 1905, becoming one of the first Korean graduates from a Japanese university (Waseda, 1918).

Even as a young student Yi became involved in the world of letters, and by extension, nationalist politics. He worked with Ch'oe Namsŏn on the magazine *Boys*, publishing his first essay at the age of 16. After annexation, Yi leaped to prominence with the publication of *Heartlessness* (1917), usually considered Korea's first modern novel, and *The Pioneer* (1918). In these overtly didactic early novels and essays, he began his lifetime's work of championing Western values of individualism and free will as antidotes to Korea's social ills, struggling against the confining influences of Confucian tradition. In subsequent work, both essays and novels, he laid the foundation for a Korean vernacular prose literature.

In the 1920s, Yi stood out within the conservative Korean nationalist reform movement. His major essay "On Reconstructing the Nation" published in the *East Asia Daily*, where he was later editor-in-chief, became a template of moderate programs to build Korean social and cultural strength for future independence. The Korean left blasted him for accommodationism, and critics pointed out that the moderate programs he espoused served only to strengthen the Korean upper class in league with the Japanese. In the 1930s, Yi drifted toward an engagement with Buddhism that figures prominently in his novel *Earth* (1937).

By that point, his journalism had become more conciliatory toward Japan, and during the war he gave speeches to recruit young men for the Imperial Army. These activities overshadowed the major contributions of the first two-thirds of his career, and he was charged with "antinational crimes" after liberation. In 1950, during the Korean War, the North Koreans seized Yi Kwangsu and took him north. The circumstances of his death are unknown, but he is presumed to have perished along with many other kidnapped moderate and conservative intellectuals in North Korean purges of "enemies of the people."

Yi Kwangsu in his study, c. 1925

organization diluted public interest—by 1925 the National University idea had died.

Moderates organized another movement focused on strengthening Korean capitalism. The so-called Buy Korean Movement emerged out of a growing concern that Japanese capitalism would smother Korean-owned companies. Organizers came together from the earlier Repay the National Debt Campaign of the 1910s, the Gandhi-inspired cooperative movement already in place, and the small Korean business community. At its height in the summer of 1923, the movement became the most successful mass mobilization of Koreans since the March First demonstrations. Consumption of Korean-produced goods increased to the extent that some items became unobtainable. Understandably, prices of Korean-made goods rose, ironically demanding further financial sacrifice from the patriotically inclined.

The Buy Korean Movement heightened mass awareness of economic issues, and it altered, at least temporarily, Korean consumption habits. However, economic and political realities blocked its sustained growth, and after 1924 the movement declined steadily. The discovery that Korean merchants had marked up cheap Japanese cotton cloth and sold it as "Made in Korea" dealt a serious blow to the movement. Such gouging and exploitative practices demoralized people otherwise predisposed to sacrifice for the nation.

Radical nationalists excoriated both movements as ineffectual and even exploitative of ordinary Koreans. Why should peasants contribute to a university to which they could never hope to send their children? A university served only the small elite minority in the first place. They charged that economic movements could never succeed in a colonial situation and that only Korean capitalists would profit in the struggle with Japanese monopoly capitalism. The criticism of the Buy Korea Movement reached its peak in 1924 and became the focus of a bitter ideological struggle within the Korean nationalist movement. The polemical warfare ended in stalemate, but the damage had already been done to the morale of the movement, which faltered and declined by the end of the decade.

Perhaps the most important nationalist project of the 1920s lay in the realm of language. The struggle to develop the Korean vernacular by standardizing its grammar and orthography directly confronted Japan's goal of increasing use of Japanese in the colony.

Nationalist intellectuals knew the cultural importance of what might appear at first glance to be a highly specialized and arcane activity. But with the widening of outlets for Korean writing in newspapers and magazines, standard usage became a vital national priority. Moreover, the linguists responsible for this movement, gathered in the Korean Language Research Society, also worked with students and the Korean-language newspapers to create literacy programs—night schools, summer outreach programs for students in the countryside, and more—for ordinary Koreans. This activity brought together conservatives, moderates, and radicals within the nationalist movement, coming to fruition with the standardization of grammar and orthography in 1933 and the beginning of the compilation of a comprehensive Korean dictionary.

Literary output exploded in tandem with the language movement. Modern Korean literature traces its origins to the 1910s and the experiments in new-style vernacular poetry, short stories, and essays that filled the pages of magazines such as *Boys* and *Youth*. The first Western-style realist novels also appeared in the 1910s. Soon a number of literary groups published their own journals as well as serial works in the newspapers. Besides Yi Kwangsu, major writers who emerged in the 1920s included Yŏm Sangsŏp (1897–1963) and Kim Tong'in (1900–1951). Socialist writers, who believed that art should serve the cause of class liberation, formed the Korean Artists Proletarian Federation (KAPF) at this time. Among their well-known works were Cho Myŏnghŭi's *The Naktong River* and Yi Kiyŏng's *Fire Field*.

Repression returned to Korea in the second half of the 1920s. The 1925 Peace Preservation Law—parallel to a similar law in Japan—gave police broadened powers to control political life in the colony. In 1926, anti-Japanese riots around the funeral of the last Chosŏn ruler, Sunjong, precipitated further police reprisals against nationalist organizations. Some Koreans tried to bridge the differences between leftist and rightist nationalists through a united front organization, the New Korea Society (*Sin'ganhoe*), formed in 1927. For four years the Sin'ganhoe gathered forces across the political spectrum in an attempt to unify Korean nationalists, but in the end a combination of police harassment and internal ideological strife doomed the organization, the last major nationalist movement of the colonial period. Its death throes coincided with the Manchurian Incident in the fall of 1931, ultimately leading to the Japanese takeover of northeastern China and a wholesale change of direction of Japanese rule in Korea as a consequence.

DIASPORAS

JAPAN

Anti-Asian bigotry limited Japanese migration to North America. California's 1913 Alien Land Law prohibited aliens "ineligible to citizenship" (Asians) from owning land. In 1920, California passed a law forbidding them from being their children's guardians, and in 1924 the federal government outlawed all Asian immigration. Canada limited Japanese immigration to 400 annually in 1908 and 150 in 1928. Trans-Pacific migration shifted to Brazil, where coffee plantations needed workers. Despite abysmal labor conditions, 20,000 Japanese migrated to Brazil from 1914 to 1923 and 110,000 more by 1933.

The most significant Japanese diaspora in this period lay in Japan's expanding empire. Thousands of Japanese sought their fortunes where the Japanese flag was planted—Korea, Micronesia, and Taiwan—as well as China and Manchuria. Unlike Westerners' colonial migrations, Japanese migration to Korea and Manchuria was initially more feminine than masculine. Many women worked in the sex trades; Japanese newspapers in colonial Korea lauded sex workers in Manchuria for bringing civilization to their rough Russian customers. Other women sought work as professionals, because opportunities were limited in Japan. Some were administrators, including an immigration official in Harbin (1898–1901), while others worked as journalists, teachers, and shopkeepers. Interwar Japanese colonial migrants differed from their Western counterparts in their choice of intimate partners. Japanese women were more likely to marry Korean men, but Japanese men preferred liaisons with Japanese rather than Korean women.

The population of Japanese in Korea rose from 20,000 (55 percent male) in 1907 to 170,000 in 1910, 340,000 in 1919, and over 500,000 in 1930. Although most emigration to Manchuria came after 1932 (see p. 314), by that year over 200,000 Japanese (and many more Koreans) already lived there. Thousands of Japanese families planned to reside permanently in the colonies. Japanese men would serve as government officials, police, teachers, farmers, shopkeepers, laborers (and not a few as ne'er-do-wells), and were increasingly accompanied by their wives and children.

Just a few hundred traders and fishermen had settled in the Micronesian islands before Japan's League of Nations mandate after World War I. Development of sugar plantations on Saipan led to a Japanese population of 20,000 in 1930 and 50,000 in 1935. In addition, Japanese migrated to cities throughout East Asia, most significantly to China's commercial centers. In Shanghai, Japanese businessmen played a large role in banking and textiles. That community, which had its own newspapers, women's groups, and medical clinics, grew from 650 in 1890 to over 26,000 in 1935.

CHINA

The Qing government had solicited the loyalty and remittances of the overseas Chinese and in 1909 declared them Qing subjects if they had a Chinese father *or* mother. The GMD, whose 1911 Revolution had been funded by overseas Chinese donations, paid close attention to the diasporic Chinese, promoting the use of Mandarin among them. In the 1920s, the GMD sent schoolteachers to Southeast Asia to keep the Chinese there actively connected to the "homeland" through language and nationalism. This worked very well where the Chinese suffered racial discrimination—in Malaya and the United States—but somewhat less successfully elsewhere (e.g., Thailand, the Philippines).

Some Chinese living under European colonial regimes in Southeast Asia became wealthy, cultivating good relations with British, Dutch, and American officials and building prestige through education, philanthropy, and (many non-Chinese claimed) corruption. These included the Aws of Burma, a Hakka family whose members invented Tiger Balm liniment and owned dozens of newspapers; and the Fujianese Tan family of Singapore, directors of a transnational conglomerate including rubber manufacturing, canneries, transportation, and timber.

The heads of these clans ranged from Anglophilic literati to puritanical capitalists to debauched playboys. Not surprisingly, the daughters often surpassed the sons in business and became magnates in their own right. They might also marry influential men—one fairy-tale marriage joined Wellington Koo (Gu Weijun,

1887–1985), a brilliant Columbia-educated GMD diplomat, with Oei Hui Lan (1899–1992), daughter of Oei Tiong Ham (1866–1924), a Javanese-Chinese sugar magnate.

The United States continued its ignoble history of discriminatory legislation against Asians, culminating in 1917 and 1924 laws barring all immigration from Asia and prohibiting naturalization, landownership, and intermarriage for any Asian except Filipinos, whose country belonged to the United States. The Cable Act of 1922 stipulated that any white woman who married an Asian man would lose her US citizenship. Under these conditions, Chinese living in the United States naturally cultivated their connections to China rather than live isolated in a hostile land.

KOREA

People go abroad for many reasons. Among significant migrations in the twentieth century has been the movement of students studying abroad. For example, since World War II, the United States has been a net importer of foreign students. Japan and its relatively advanced educational system similarly drew students from its colonies. Korea, Japan's most important and populous colony, experienced an exodus of young people that began slowly after 1900, increasing to a torrent after annexation. Most of these students stayed abroad only for education, returning to Korea with prestigious credentials to make their way in the colony.

While the Japanese took the creation of a mass education system in Korea seriously, lack of resources slowed their efforts. In the first decade after 1919, they focused on establishing primary schools. Upper education remained limited to the few foreign-run institutions and schools established for Japanese citizens, to which few Koreans gained admission. Koreans constituted only 10 percent of all common higher school students in 1940. Similarly, only 30 percent of Keijō Imperial University students were Koreans. This forced Koreans to seek higher education in Japan, with serious implications for the culture and politics of the colony.

The first large cohort of Korean students in Japan included the intellectuals who led the nationalist renaissance after 1920. Studying abroad put them in contact with radical political ideas; indeed, most of the leaders of the Korean socialist and communist movements were trained in Japan. Unlike the returning students

in the late 1910s and early 1920s, who formed the nucleus of nationalist political leadership, after the political crackdown of 1925 the larger group of returning students avoided politics and sought jobs in the burgeoning modern sector of the economy. In the 1920s, an average of 2,000 Korean students studied in common higher schools and colleges in Japan every year; by 1940 the number had increased to 21,000. While relatively few in number, these students became the educated elites in the colony and the leadership class of the postcolonial era.

CONNECTIONS

The most obvious connections between Japan, China, and Korea in this period lay in the power and actions of the Japanese empire on the mainland. Taking Korea as a colony and establishing the GGK; expanding Japanese influence in Manchuria through the Kwantung Leased Territory and South Manchurian Railway; taking control of Germany's Qingdao leasehold; extending control over the infant ROC with the Twenty-One Demands—all of these and more demonstrated Japan's dynamic, aggressive foreign policy, aimed at competing with and eventually defeating European and American imperialism in East Asia. Seeking to become a regional great power, Japan participated in the Versailles Conference, the League of Nations, and the Washington Treaty system, meanwhile brutally suppressing any overt expression of Korean independence and running roughshod over China's sovereignty.

But, as Steinbeck wrote, "The people don't like to be conquered." Beginning with the astonishingly widespread March First Movement in Korea, continuing with the May Fourth Movement in China and the founding of political parties and a Korean government in exile (SPG), many Koreans and Chinese reacted to Japanese imperialism with their own nationalism. During this period, elite nationalists spread their message outside their own ranks through mass media—especially newspapers—and organizations such as chambers of commerce, labor unions, churches (especially in Korea), and schools. Like nationalists elsewhere in the colonized world, East Asians responded enthusiastically to Woodrow Wilson's doctrine of "self-determination of peoples," but suffered grave disappointment when the Versailles Conference largely confirmed their subservient status. The rejection of Japan's proposed "racial equality clause," plus heightened discrimination against Asians in North America, reminded East Asian people that they remained, in European and American eyes, racially inferior and irremediably alien.

Nationalism could function as a unifying ideology—as it did on March 1 and May 4, 1919—but it also created conditions for division and conflict. The Russian Revolution of 1917, and the founding of the Comintern to encourage world revolution, broadcast the utopian vision of socialism and the inevitability of class struggle. By 1925, Japan, China, and Korea all had Communist parties, though Japanese repression prevented any effective organization in the Korean colony. In the 1920s, East Asian nationalists thus had to choose whether to support militarists, moderate nationalist movements, or left-wing movements, including the Communist parties and Wang Jingwei's left wing of the GMD. Japanese, Chinese, and Korean students met at Japanese schools and universities, where they were all exposed to both conservative and radical political ideas and had to choose how to use their hard-won educations in their own societies. Korea's Sin'ganhoe attempted to bridge the political gaps but failed under police repression and internal strife.

Korean and Chinese nationalists, observing Japan's apparent unity and strength of purpose in the world, attempted to build those same qualities at home. Hu Shi advocated the vernacular as the language of the Chinese nation; and under the Cultural Policy after 1920, Koreans of all political persuasions could unite in research and standardization of their native Korean. After studying in Japan, Lu Xun wrote modern stories attacking Chinese tradition, while Yi Kwangsu's groundbreaking modern novels introduced Koreans to individualism and free choice as essential personal qualities. In both China and Korea, modern ideas—translated or adapted from Europe and America—arrived initially as translations from the Japanese.

An indirect economic connection among the three societies lay in their rising rates of rural tenancy. Although parts of China did not experience it, this phenomenon was widespread enough that observers noted immiseration of the peasantry and concentration of landholdings as characteristic of rice-growing agricultural systems in general. In Japan, tenancy strengthened the left-wing movement and encouraged colonial emigration, but later, in the 1930s, it also provided fodder for military conscription, the rural army recruits who obediently expanded and defended the empire. Korean tenant farmers might flee to Manchuria, but they could also join the imperial police force, an important means of upward mobility as well as repression. Guangdong tenant farmers might have joined Peng Pai's Peasant Association, but they could also have been caught up in warlord conscription. In all three cultures, tenant farmers' daughters and sons made up a significant part of the new industrial labor force, moving to cities to work for wages, perhaps joining a union (whether right-wing or left-wing), and certainly experiencing a totally different rhythm of life.

The 1920s brought a new wave of modernity to the cities of East Asia, with its icons of daring and innovation—the Modern Girl and Modern Boy, the New Woman, the movie star, and the international businessman. Shanghai and Tokyo became the emblems of shocking, experimental cultures, where Coney Island coexisted with Confucius, while repressed Seoul/Keijō only slowly became a cosmopolitan modern city. At the same time, all three cultures remained overwhelmingly agricultural, and the trendy elites knew that they represented only a tiny minority. The 1929 stock-market crash and Great Depression affected all three societies by eliminating their overseas markets, weakening their currencies, and throwing them back on their own resources.

CHAPTER NINE

THE FIFTEEN-YEAR WAR AND ANTI-JAPANESE WAR OF RESISTANCE (1931–1945)

WORLD CONTEXT

The Great Depression of the 1930s endured for years in some countries (e.g., the Netherlands) but ended much more swiftly in others (e.g., Japan). Food prices fell by as much as 60 percent, bankrupting farmers worldwide. Canada and Australia, hard-hit because they depended on agricultural and forest products, reached unemployment levels above 25 percent. The German economy, severely handicapped by the immense World War I indemnity and the debilitating hyperinflation of the 1920s, suffered near-fatal shock with 33 percent of the workforce unemployed. A prolonged drought in the great plains of North America coincided with the Depression, so hundreds of thousands of US and Canadian farmers had to leave their homes as migrant laborers.

The Depression deprived people of cash—prices for their products fell or they lost their jobs—so world trade plummeted, with especially serious consequences for export-oriented economies such as Japan and China. Sales of luxury goods, including silk and automobiles, suffered steep declines, wrecking the silk-producing areas of East Asia and auto factories in Detroit and Stuttgart. Less than 15 percent of Germany's automobile companies survived the 1930s. Governments protected domestic economies by creating or maintaining protectionist barriers; in 1930 the US Congress passed the Smoot–Hawley Tariff, taxing imports at very high levels. But American farms and factories continued for years in the grip of the Depression, while overall international trade fell by 66 percent between 1929 and 1934, so most economists believe that protectionism failed.

The protectionist strategy also operated in politics as *unilateralism*. With each country willing to impoverish its neighbors to protect its domestic economy, governments saw less reason to cooperate in the League of Nations or other multilateral bodies. Despite some early successes in conflict resolution, the League's effectiveness declined rapidly in the early 1930s. Unable to raise a military force, it could not act when Japan annexed Manchuria (1932), Bolivia attacked Paraguay (1932), Fascist Italy invaded Ethiopia (1935), or Germany and Italy supported rebels against the Spanish government (1936). The United States tried to sustain multilateral economic and political agreements after 1932, under President Franklin Roosevelt (FDR), but effective international cooperation remained elusive until World War II.

The Fascists had governed Italy since the mid-1920s. The Depression gave them the opportunity to nationalize the economy—by 1935, Mussolini claimed state control of 75 percent of Italian industry—and to advance Italian colonization in northeastern Africa. Even more dramatically, the dire effects of the Depression in Germany led to the ascendancy of Adolf Hitler (1889–1945) and the National Socialist (Nazi) Party, voted into power in a special election in March 1933. Hitler immediately began dismantling German democracy and investing heavily in industrial production, defying the punitive Versailles decisions and unilaterally rebuilding Germany's military.

In the USSR, the Depression coincided with Stalin's First Five-Year Plan, including a nationwide collectivization of agriculture, the elimination or deportation to Siberia of millions of *kulaki*, "rich farmers," and the expropriation of their land. This vast disruption of rural society led to a catastrophic famine in 1932–33. Scholars estimate that more than 11 million people starved or were executed in those years. To silence domestic dissent and consolidate his supreme position, Stalin undertook massive purges between 1936 and 1938, with as many as 2 million people sent to labor camps or executed.

Having spent years vilifying one another, the Soviet Union and Nazi Germany undertook secret negotiations in the summer of 1939. Germany needed Russian raw materials for rearmament, while Stalin's ambitious industrialization plans required German technology. The two countries also negotiated a ten-year non-aggression pact—announced on August 24, 1939—and delineated spheres of influence in Central and Eastern Europe, including the division of Poland. Less than a week later, Germany invaded Poland, and the Soviets followed on September 17, having secured

their eastern front by signing a non-aggression agreement with Japan. The German occupation of Poland included massacres of Poles and Jews—the death camp at Auschwitz (Oswiecim) opened in June 1940—while the Soviets arrested and executed many Poles as "counter-revolutionaries."

Bound to Poland by treaty, France, Britain, and the Commonwealth countries declared war on Germany in September 1939. This despite their fears of Germany's Soviet allies, who had expanded their trade with Hitler's government. However, Great Britain moved troops to mainland Europe too late to prevent Germany's capture of Norway and Denmark or the successful invasions of France, Belgium, and the Netherlands on May 10, 1940. By late June, their principal ally, France, had surrendered, Italy had attacked British colonies in Africa, and Germany had begun bombing Britain in preparation for an invasion.

Americans remained reluctant to enter the war, though FDR did manage to increase the size of the navy and protect British convoys in the Atlantic, an undeclared war against German submarines. Hitler attacked the USSR, his ally by treaty, in June 1940, opening a two-front war, dooming millions of soldiers and civilians, and forcing the United States, Britain, and USSR into an anti-Fascist alliance. The European war also encompassed the slaughter of millions of Jews, Poles, Romani (gypsies), homosexuals, and other "subhumans" defined by the Nazis.

Many Indians did not agree to fight for their British colonial masters. Some tens of thousands joined Subhas Chandra Bose's Indian National Army, which allied with Japan against Britain. Many more agreed with Gandhi—Indians should resist fascism, using the opportunity to gain independence. Following Gandhi's call for massive civil disobedience until Britain promised decolonization, the Quit India movement (1942) resulted in the jailing of most Indian nationalist leaders until 1945.

As war always does, World War II produced scientific and technological advances—Sikorsky's helicopter (1939), plutonium (discovered 1941), the electronic computer (1942), synthetic quinine (1944), and the atomic bomb (1945), among many others. In the world of culture, Rogers and Hammerstein wrote their first musical plays together, *Oklahoma!* and *Carousel*, and the movies followed current events in *Grapes of Wrath* and *Casablanca*.

African Americans fighting in the segregated US military resented the contradiction between American war objectives—freedom and equality—and the realities of racial segregation. A. Phillip Randolph (1889–1979) and Bayard Rustin (1912–1987) proposed a march on Washington, protesting discrimination in defense industries and the armed forces. Pressure continued from African American labor and civic groups to bring American racial realities and political ideals closer together.

JAPAN AT WAR

The year 1931 is frequently called a turning point in the history of Japan and Northeast Asia. The Manchurian Incident that began in September expanded Japan's continental incursion, and domestic terrorism stifled pro-democracy movements at home. Because repression and warfare did not end until 1945, postwar Japanese historians designated 1931 as the beginning of a "Fifteen-Year War," and other scholars viewed that period as a "dark valley" between Taishō democracy and postwar democratization. To be sure, those 15 years were extraordinarily painful for Japan and the rest of Asia. Yet, to describe the period as disconnected from what came before and after would be a mischaracterization.

Historians today view Japan's war years as part of the "transwar" period that pioneered conditions in postwar East Asia: the end of formal colonialism; development of the "puppet state" model that replaced colonies with "satellites" in the Cold War period; development of "industrial policy" states in Japan and South Korea; the end of agrarianism and extreme rural inequality; and changed labor–management relationships in the Japanese workplace. Ironically, given the attack on "modernity" as individualistic and "Western" by Japan's right-wing factions, modernity continued to be promoted in Japan and areas under Japanese control, particularly Manchuria.

THE MANCHURIAN INCIDENT

When Japan's Kantōgun (see p. 257) blew up a section of the South Manchurian Railway that they were charged to protect and then blamed that deed on Chinese troops, this was not a spontaneous action. Colonel Ishiwara Kanji, the Kantōgun's operations officer, had planned to take control of Manchuria, to gain its resources for an anticipated war with the United States. Manchuria would also serve, he asserted, as a model state without the social inequalities and capitalistic selfishness he and his fellow conspirators observed in Japan. The great open spaces they claimed existed in Manchuria would offer opportunities to Japan's huddled rural masses.

In some ways, Ishiwara's predictions did come to pass. Manchuria's mineral resources allowed the Japanese government to consider war with the United States a decade later. New corporations took root in Manchuria, although the *zaibatsu* that the right-wing officers criticized also planted themselves there. At the same time, the economic control structure set up in Manchuria was transplanted from the puppet state to the metropole, so Manchuria did serve as the laboratory the young officers envisioned. But Manchuria was never as successful as planned in attracting Japanese settlers (see p. 314), and the colonizers never achieved racial and economic equality.

Right-wing groups and even some respectable politicians agreed with the Kantōgun's ideology and actions, but the Minseitō cabinet did not. Prime Minister Wakatsuki Reijirō (1866–1949), Foreign Minister Shidehara Kijūrō, and Finance Minister Inoue Jun'nosuke (1869–1932) called on the military to localize the fighting that followed the railroad bombing. But the Kantōgun pressed ahead, conquering much of Manchuria in fall 1931, claiming to be "pursuing bandits." Japan's military remained independent of civilian government, answerable only to the emperor under the "right of supreme command." Although Shidehara promised the League of Nations, to which China's government appealed for help, to control the military and commence peace talks, he could not. The League appointed a fact-finding team headed by Victor Bulwer-Lytton (1876–1947) to investigate. Shidehara resigned from the cabinet two days later, on December 12, bringing it down with him.

Seiyūkai politician Inukai Tsuyoshi took over as prime minister, and the emperor charged him with controlling the military. He failed, and the Kantōgun grabbed the rest of Manchuria. This thrilled the depression-weary Japanese public and angered the war-weary Chinese. In response to a boycott of Japanese goods and attacks on Japanese residents in Shanghai, Japanese forces carried out an aerial bombardment of Shanghai in January 1932, hardening Chinese sentiments and turning the United States against Japan. When Kantōgun officers found former Qing officials willing to form an "independent" new state of Manzhouguo in March, American Secretary of State Henry Stimson declared his doctrine of "non-recognition." (The Japanese used the Chinese romanization of the day—Manchukuo—to suggest this state was indigenous and legitimate.) Former Qing child-emperor Puyi became head of the new state, but the leaders of Manzhouguo could hardly be independent. Rather, they were puppets of the Kantōgun, imbued with notions of Pan-Asian anticolonialism, which claimed that Manzhouguo was not a colony, thereby pioneering the type of client state common during the Cold War.

The Inukai government did not formally recognize Manzhouguo, either, adding to the evils Inukai manifested in right-wing eyes. Rightists had killed Finance Minister Inoue and Mitsui *zaibatsu* head Dan Takuma in February and March, and on May 15, 1932, a group of terrorists killed Inukai and attacked Seiyūkai headquarters and the Mitsubishi Bank. They hoped this would lead to an uprising against the modern state and the creation of a communitarian rural utopia under the emperor's direct rule. Although no uprising occurred, Inukai's assassination signaled the end of party cabinets.

Inukai's assassins were inspired both by a desire to expand Japanese domination in Asia and by their view of domestic conditions. Many rightists shared an agrarianist ideology that held modernity, which they

East Asia, 1937–45

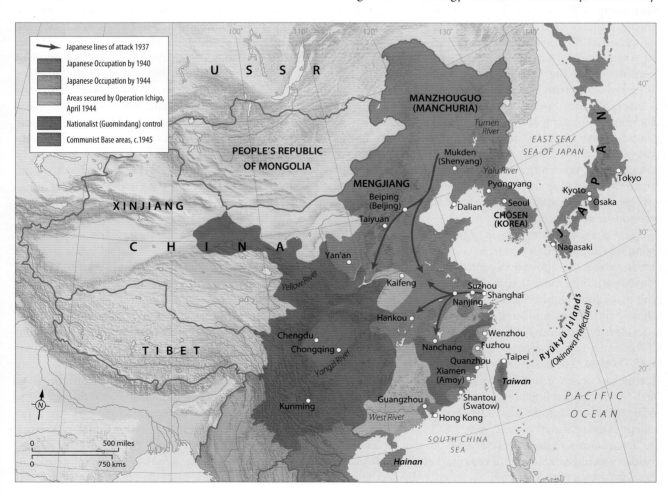

saw as Western, individualistic, and selfish, responsible for the plight of desperately poor farmers, some of whom were forced to sell their daughters into prostitution. Agrarianist rhetoric also blamed modernity, rural class conflict, and cities, with their Modern Girls and hedonistic lifestyles, for the destruction of rural harmony. They credited that harmony, viewed through rose-colored glasses, with maintaining healthy rural communities in the past. The government did not discourage traditionalist discourse, even as it developed modern means of helping farmers, such as disseminating information about scientific farm management and budgeting. Officials urged farmwomen to modernize their kitchens and improve hygiene. These efforts did improve farm families' lives and helped modernize the countryside.

Not all right-wing groups focused on agrarianism; some of the most violent were cabals of rightists in the military who scorned the civilian government as impotent. Prime Minister Hamaguchi's acceptance of American and British limits on Japanese naval expansion under the London Naval Treaty (see p. 285) incensed some army officers, leading them to create the Cherry Blossom Society (J. *Sakurakai*) in 1930. After these officers attempted two failed coups in 1931, the Blood-Pledge League (J. *Ketsumeidan*), made up of naval officers and students and led by a Buddhist priest, decided that even more drastic action was necessary. In 1932, the League assassinated government and business leaders, terrorizing Japan's elites into changing the economic and political system.

The paradoxical attack on modernity that led to what one contemporary journalist called "government by assassination" allowed violent right-wing groups to thrive with little more than a slap on the wrist. Against this backdrop, public opinion, with the exception of some peace, labor, and women's groups, applauded the successes of Japanese troops in Manchuria. The police intimidated reform groups into abandoning their liberal rhetoric. Newspapers were censored, and many learned to practice self-censorship. Government censorship had stifled liberal newspapers in the 1880s and Marxist newspapers in the 1920s, but the 1930–1940s censorship was far more repressive.

Even some socialists expressed delight that Japanese workers would be able to find new markets in Manchuria. The world, they asserted, was being divided into trading blocs like the British Commonwealth, and trade was restricted by protectionist policies like America's 1930 Smoot–Hawley Tariff. Even the Social Masses Party, created in 1932 by uniting several socialist parties, supported continental expansion because they believed it helped workers, challenged capitalism, and aided East Asian self-determination against Western imperialism.

The best way to effect change, many rightists believed, was to focus on Manzhouguo, a focus facilitated by the appointment of Admiral Saitō Makoto, former governor-general of Korea (GG), as prime minister in May 1932. Top military brass refused to allow Saionji Kinmochi (see p. 221), Japan's last "senior statesman," to appoint a party politician. Both sides could accept Saitō, who had a relatively benign tenure in Korea. By September, however, he acceded to pressure to recognize Manzhouguo as an independent state.

On October 2, 1932, the Lytton Commission reported that the Kantōgun had not acted in self-defense against "bandits" on September 18, 1931—as Japan claimed—and that no independence movement had created the state of Manzhouguo. The report called for an autonomous state under Chinese sovereignty, the withdrawal of all Chinese and Japanese forces, and a Sino-Japanese treaty that would safeguard Japanese participation in Manchuria's economic development. When the League of Nations adopted the report in February 1933, Japan's delegation walked out of the meeting. Over the objection of Finance Minister Takahashi Korekiyo (1854–1936), Japan formally withdrew from the League on March 27, 1933. This fatally undermined the League, indicating its impotence in policing its members.

Japanese forces continued clashing with Chinese forces on the southern border of Manzhouguo, and in February, the Kantōgun entered the province of Rehe and annexed it to the puppet state. Under the Tanggu Truce (May 1933), Jiang Jieshi's Nationalist government allowed the Kantōgun to hold Rehe and the Shanhaiguan pass, but not to enter North China. The treaty also formally demilitarized the territory from the Great Wall to Beiping—the Nationalists' name for Beijing—and Tianjin. Despite demilitarization, over the next two years, the Kantōgun kept triggering clashes with Chinese troops. In June 1935, the Kantōgun pushed Nationalist forces from Beiping and Tianjin and, in November, created another pro-Japan puppet state. At the same time, the refusal of Japan's former allies, the United States and Britain, to condone Japan's continental aggression—though active trade continued and many British and American businessmen supported Japan over China—led Japan to announce that it would terminate its participation in the London Naval Treaty in December 1935.

During the first half of the 1930s, Japan's role in its colonies also changed. The appointment of General Ugaki Kazushige (1868–1956) as GG in 1931 had profound effects on Korea. His harsh policies as well as those of his successors will be discussed below. In Taiwan, Tokyo similarly overturned the more moderate policies of the 1920s, appointing military officers as governors-general.

Rightist groups began to grow restive, however, viewing Saitō as weak. Forced out in July 1934 due to a bribery scandal, Saitō was replaced by another moderate admiral, Okada Keisuke (1868–1952). During Okada's term, civilian government suffered its strongest blow with a coup attempt, beginning on February 26, 1936 (see p. 286).

DOMESTIC POLITICS AND ECONOMICS

During the half-decade before the so-called "2-26 Incident," some of its victims had been developing policies that should have pleased the rebels. For example, the Japanese government, like every other Depression-era government, experimented with fiscal and economic policies to stimulate the economy, and Japan's recovered most rapidly. Economic development of Manzhouguo and Korea paid dividends, despite the expense of military action and government assistance to "new *zaibatsu*" like Nissan in Manzhouguo and the chemical firm Nippon Chisso in Korea.

Finance Minister Takahashi's removing Japan from the gold standard allowed the yen to drop to less than half its 1931 value by 1932. This stimulated exports so effectively that trading partners like the United States complained about Japanese "dumping," that is, selling below cost of production. But most important, Takahashi pioneered in 1931 what later came to be called "Keynesianism"—John Maynard Keynes published his famous work on the subject in 1936— that is, government deficit spending to stimulate a stagnant economy.

Between 1930 and 1936, Japan's economy grew by 50 percent, exporting an array of consumer products

Men, women, and children in an impoverished village in the destitute northeast of Japan, at the height of the Depression in 1934, discuss how to survive without illegally selling their daughters.

to Europe, Asia, and the United States. In 1935, total exports surpassed imports for the first time in 17 years, and Japan became the world's leading exporter of cotton textiles. Japan grew most quickly in heavy industry, chemicals, and munitions—the latter grew 250 percent from 1931 to 1935. The government footed much of the bill, and Japan's economy recovered by mid-decade. By 1940, industrial employers complained about labor shortages. In a few areas, however, growth declined. Cotton surpassed silk as Japan's leading textile export when Depression-era American women gave up silk stockings, plunging Japan's silk-producing countryside into the deep poverty that fueled right-wing anger.

In addition to fiscal stimulus, Takahashi and other officials developed guidelines to "rationalize" the economy. Concerned about wasteful duplication of effort and expenditure and never quite trusting that capitalism would serve the nation, finance ministers developed "rationalization" policies and government bureaus that would be the basis of "industrial policy" after World War II. These included the Industrial Rationalization Bureau (1930), the Major Industries Control Law (1931), and the Cabinet Planning Board (1937). The Major Industries Control Law mandated cartels in key industries to control cartel members' prices and market shares. But the government left much of the administration of these policies to private capitalists;

the *zaibatsu* controlled the cartels that regulated their industrial sectors. Additional laws expanded rationalization and control policies during World War II, but government never gained control as completely as policy-makers hoped.

Government "rationalized" other aspects of Japanese society and politics as well, though the objects of that rationalization considered it repression. Non-socialist labor unions like the Federation of Labor tried to cooperate with the government in the early 1930s by refraining from striking and collaborating with management to increase productivity. In the second half of the decade, the military considered these efforts insufficiently "rational." They forced arsenal workers to quit the Federation and asked companies to experiment with "discussion councils" as a substitute for unions. The termination of independent unions came later, after the escalation of hostilities in the second Sino-Japanese War in 1937.

The political parties, already weakened by the replacement of party cabinets with military-dominated cabinets, suffered another blow in 1935 with the Home Ministry's campaign for "election purification." The parties were admittedly "impure," with vote buying sullying the electoral process. The Women's Suffrage League (see pp. 255–54), unable to work for women's political rights, aided the government in weeding out political corruption. After 1937, "purification" took on a new style. Police monitored speeches to silence criticism of the military or bureaucracy. Voters continued to support the Seiyūkai, Minseitō, and Social Masses parties until the government dissolved them in 1940, but voter turnout plummeted.

THE 2-26 INCIDENT

Government also tried to control free thought. Viewing the "new religions" of the nineteenth century as seditious, the government disbanded several new religions in the 1930s. Universities fired leading professors for their liberal views, warning others who might deviate from emperor-centered ideology not to stray. Minobe Tatsukichi (1873–1948), professor of law at Tokyo Imperial University and member of the House of Peers, became the most famous victim. For decades, Minobe had taught Japan's top young scholars that the Meiji Constitution defined the emperor as an "organ" of the government. Members of the army's "Imperial Way"

faction, some scholars, and members of the House of Peers violently denounced this unremarkable notion, and Minobe was forced to resign from teaching and the Diet in 1935. He survived an assassination attempt the following year, effectively silencing other intellectuals.

The Imperial Way faction included sympathizers with the early 1930s terrorists, mostly young officers not trained at the elite Army War College (prewar Japan's "West Point"). Their nemesis was the Control faction, many of whose senior officers had graduated from the War College and hailed from one region of the country—the region that had been pre-Meiji Chōshū. Unlike the Imperial Way faction, who believed that the Japanese soldier's spiritual superiority and loyalty to the emperor constituted the basis of Japanese military strength, the Control faction believed that modern weaponry and "total war" (mobilizing the civilian economy) brought military success. When the Control faction's leaders cut troop strength to redirect funds to modern weapons in the 1920s, the Imperial Way faction reacted furiously.

At the height of a trial of an Imperial Way officer for murdering a leading Control faction general, the Imperial Way faction decided it could no longer tolerate the government. On the snowy morning of February 26, 1936, 1,500 soldiers occupied downtown Tokyo, declaring a "Shōwa Restoration" to parallel the Meiji Restoration and calling for a military government. Claiming to cleanse the government of those who prevented the emperor from expressing his will, the rebels murdered key leaders. Prime Minister Okada hid in a shed while the rebels mistakenly killed his brother-in-law, but the rebels cut down former Prime Minister Saitō, Finance Minister Takahashi, and a top Control faction general. Ugaki Kazushige—the former GG who had cut troop size to enhance modern armaments in the 1920s—was targeted but survived, and another politician who later served as prime minister was wounded.

The revolt was put down on February 29. The navy brought a fleet into Tokyo Bay, and the emperor ordered the rebels to return to their barracks. In the end, 20 rebels were sentenced to death, including Kita Ikki (1883–1937), a civilian who did not participate but whose work, *A Plan for the Reorganization of Japan*, influenced the rebels' ideology. The government crushed the Imperial Way faction, but the military's role in politics escalated. Until 1945, cabinet appointments had to earn military approval, and the military played the dominant hand in foreign and domestic policy.

Repression and assassination silenced reformers by the end of the 1930s, but average Japanese continued to live a good life, enjoying movies, radio, music, and books. Subway trains, trams, and buses transported people quickly throughout Japan's cosmopolitan cities. Although the *Fundamental Principles of the National Polity* (1937)—a book lauding the emperor and attacking Western modernity and individualism—became a basis of education, most urban Japanese continued to enjoy entertainment and wear Western styles. Average Japanese did not yet greatly modify their daily lives, despite changes in politics, the economy, and foreign policy.

THE SECOND SINO-JAPANESE WAR, 1937–45

Unlike the Manchurian Incident plot to blow up a section of the South Manchurian Railway, the start of the Second Sino-Japanese War was unplanned. A Japanese soldier near the Marco Polo Bridge in North China went missing on July 7, 1937. Chinese troops agreed to help find him, and that would have ended the event except for some hotheads firing shots. Still, the local Japanese and Chinese military officers, as well as the cabinet of Konoe Fumimaro (1891–1945), tried to keep the event local, a policy called "non-enlargement." In little more than a month, however, the attempt by both Nanjing and Tokyo to contain hostilities failed, and full-scale warfare broke out in Shanghai in mid-August.

Following the Tanggu Truce (1933), northern Chinese warlords and GMD generals signed several additional agreements with the Kantōgun generals who had been harassing them throughout North China. These agreements, which replaced Chinese officials and military in North China with puppets of the Japanese military, postponed major war until 1937. Tensions had risen so high, however, that war would have broken out elsewhere if it had not at Marco Polo Bridge. As will be discussed below, Jiang Jieshi changed his focus from fighting the CCP to fighting Japanese aggressors after the Xi'an incident of December 1936. This both strengthened the Nationalists' resolve and made Japanese leaders resist negotiating with Jiang.

Major policy changes in Japan also made maintenance of the status quo in China impossible. Hirota Kōki (1878–1948), prime minister after the 2-26 Incident, enunciated the "Fundamental Principles of National Policy" that called for stabilizing Japan's position in China and strengthening defenses against the Soviet Union. Eventually, the Principles asserted, Japan would move southward, but not until the navy was assured that this would not provoke an unwinnable naval clash with the United States and Britain.

As a first step toward strengthening Japan's defenses against the USSR, Japan negotiated the Anti-Comintern Pact with Nazi Germany in September 1936, requiring both sides not to support the Soviets should war break out between the USSR and a signatory. Fascist Italy joined the Pact in 1937. By throwing in its lot with Germany and Italy, Japan was increasingly seen as a "pariah" by other Western nations. The Hirota government tried to persuade Jiang Jieshi to sign an anti-Communist pact in the fall of 1936, but the actions of the Japanese armies in the field belied any olive branches Hirota and his successor as prime minister, General Hayashi Senjūrō (1876–1943), may have extended.

The Second Sino-Japanese War started with Konoe Fumimaro as prime minister. His initial desire to localize the skirmishes soon gave way to plans to crush the Nationalist Chinese state. Japan's conquest of Shanghai in November 1937 led to his decision to take the war to the Nationalist capital at Nanjing. Relocating to Chongqing in the face of Japanese invasion, Jiang's government vowed to continue a war of resistance. Konoe, furious at Jiang's defiance, in January 1938 claimed he would "annihilate" the Nationalists. President Roosevelt made a stirring speech about "quarantining" Japanese aggression in October 1937, but only the Soviets offered material aid to the Chinese.

The battle for Nanjing ended in a few days. But the Japanese soldiers proceeded to brutalize the city's inhabitants for six weeks after its fall on December 13. The numbers of dead and injured will never be known, but estimates suggest that around 200,000 people, of whom just 20,000 were males of military age, were killed, and tens of thousands of women were raped. Japanese troops captured an additional 60,000 refugees outside the city limits, and many of them were killed or starved to death. Various explanations have been advanced to explain this massacre, including soldiers' reactions to the loss of their comrades, harsh hierarchical treatment of soldiers within the military itself, mob mentality, and the dehumanizing of the enemy that occurs in all wars. Knowing that this type of brutality is common in all wars does not excuse the "Rape of Nanjing."

Particularly heinous was the refusal of the Konoe government to stop the atrocities. Hoping to force Jiang to negotiate, Tokyo allowed the raping and killing to continue for six weeks. Clearly the Tokyo government knew the brutality in Nanjing was wrong. They even believed they could have controlled it, although they based their solution on faulty science. They blamed the atrocities, especially the rapes, on a medical notion of uncontrollable male sexuality. To control the incidence of rape in areas occupied by the Japanese military in the future, the military proceeded to set up a vast system of sex stations, called "comfort stations." The Japanese military recruited many of the sex slaves, euphemistically called "comfort women," as factory workers and duped them into serving as sex slaves. Others were simply kidnapped. Korean, Chinese, Japanese, Vietnamese, Dutch, Filipina, and other women made up this army of sex slaves. Historians and politicians dispute the numbers, which will never be known, but reasonable estimates suggest about 150,000–200,000 women served as sex slaves, about 80 percent of them Koreans. The "comfort women" continue today to be a critical issue in Japanese foreign relations, especially with North and South Korea.

YAMAMOTO ISOROKU

Yamamoto Isoroku as a young naval officer, c. 1918.

Admiral Yamamoto, commander-in-chief of Japan's Combined Fleet from 1939 to 1943, who planned and led Japan's attack on Pearl Harbor, epitomized the modern Japanese Imperial Navy. Soon after graduating from Japan's Naval Academy, he went to sea, where he was wounded at the Battle of Tsushima (1905) in the Russo-Japanese War (see p. 239). On a fast career track, he graduated from the prestigious Japanese Naval Staff College in 1916, studied at Harvard University from 1919 to 1921, and then joined the faculty at the Naval Staff College. In 1924, he received naval pilot training, an experience that changed his life. After two years as a naval attaché in the United States, he received command of his first aircraft carrier in 1928.

Made head of the technological division of the Naval Air Corps in 1929, Yamamoto was promoted to increasingly important commands. His international experience led to his appointment as a member of Japan's London Conference delegations in 1930 and 1935, and in 1936, as vice minister of the navy. In that capacity, he apologized to the US ambassador when Japanese naval aircraft bombed the USS *Panay* during the Battle of Nanjing in December 1937. This apology, coupled with his opposition to the Manchurian Incident (1931), the Second Sino-Japanese War (1937), and the Tripartite Pact (1940), made him a target of rightists. Appointed commander-in-chief of the Combined Fleet, Yamamoto again went safely to sea.

This placed Yamamoto in Japan's key naval post on the eve of Pearl Harbor. While other admirals believed Japan could fight the British and Dutch to gain access to oil without the United States joining the war, Yamamoto disagreed. He initially argued against engaging the United States but, in the fall of 1941, persuaded the emperor and cabinet that the only way to avoid a long, unwinnable war would be to

Against the background of their respective flags, German and Japanese officials celebrate the signing of the Tripartite Pact in 1940. Foreign Minister Matsuoka Yōsuke, third from right, raises a toast.

Japan had 600,000 troops in China by the fall of 1938, but it failed to defeat Jiang's ROC, and the war became a quagmire. Japan controlled cities and railroads and continued brutalizing people in the hinterlands. No plans had been made to govern the 300 million people in areas under the Japanese military—except for puppet administrations. The most notable was that of Wang Jingwei, former leader of the GMD left wing, who defected and established a puppet regime in March 1940 (see p. 291).

THE ROAD TO PEARL HARBOR

While becoming hopelessly bogged down in China, Japanese leaders expected to carry out the Hirota "principle" of strengthening defenses against the USSR by escalating border skirmishes into war. In July 1938, Japanese forces started a battle at the border of Korea, Manzhouguo, and Russia. Surprised by Soviet strength, they had to negotiate a peace settlement. In May 1939, the Kantōgun once again challenged Russia at Nomonhan on the border of Manzhouguo and Outer Mongolia. Soviet troops and tanks devastated the Japanese, who lost 20,000 of their 60,000 troops in a few months. This battle continued until Germany invaded Poland on September 1, 1939, setting off World War II in Europe. Neither Tokyo nor Moscow wished to be vulnerable, and they negotiated a ceasefire.

Konoe tried to end the China quagmire, soliciting American and British help, but neither would accept Japan's actions in China. Konoe resigned in January 1939, succeeded by a nationalistic bureaucrat and two military men. The bureaucrat, Hiranuma Kiichirō (1867–1952), tried to negotiate an alliance with Germany against the Soviet Union, the United States, and Britain. But Hitler violated the Anti-Comintern Pact by signing a non-aggression treaty with Stalin while the Soviets pounded the Japanese at Nomonhan.

Hiranuma quit in embarrassment, replaced by General Abe Nobuyuki (1875–1953) and then Admiral Yonai Mitsumasa (1880–1948). Both tried to improve relations with the United States, but Japan's actions in

destroy the American fleet at Pearl Harbor and hope the United States would then negotiate.

In the six months after Pearl Harbor, Yamamoto's plans earned Japan a string of victories. The tide of war turned, however, in June 1942 at the Battle of Midway. Concerned that the US Pacific fleet was still formidable, Yamamoto conceived a highly complex plan to take Midway Island, involving eight naval task forces. But American cryptographers had cracked the Japanese code, and the United States had advance notice of Yamamoto's plan. Instead of being drawn into a trap, the US navy destroyed four Japanese carriers, and the Combined Fleet retreated. No longer strong enough to disable the US navy, Yamamoto's forces were again defeated at Guadalcanal (February 1943). Nevertheless, the American military believed that Yamamoto was so brilliant that he had to be assassinated. Again decoding an encrypted message, Americans learned of his flight plans during an inspection tour of the Solomon Islands, and long-range P-38 fighters shot his transport plane down in April 1943. Japan mourned him as a fallen national hero.

China led FDR to abrogate the US–Japan Commercial Treaty in 1939, opening the door to potential American embargoes of strategic imports like steel and oil. The army forced Yonai to resign in July 1940 because he appeared too willing to work with the Americans, so Konoe returned to power and accelerated down the path to war with the United States and Britain.

That same month, Konoe got his cabinet to agree to a policy statement calling for education to eliminate people's "selfish thoughts," creating a new "rational" political and economic structure, settling the war with China, and building a "New Order" in East Asia. The cabinet also decided that Japan would move toward the oil-rich Dutch East Indies at the appropriate time, even though the United States and Britain would likely resist. In September, Konoe's foreign minister, Matsuoka Yōsuke (1880–1946)—who had walked out of the League of Nations in 1933—negotiated the Tripartite Pact with Germany and Italy. Under this pact, the three agreed to aid one another should they be attacked by a nation not yet at war, that is, the United States. Japan wasted no time advancing into northern Vietnam, with the agreement of the French colonial administration (very recently taken over by the Vichy government, a puppet of the Nazis), in the summer of 1940. The United States placed its first embargo—of iron and steel—on Japan, having moved its Pacific fleet to Hawaii's Pearl Harbor that spring.

In October, Konoe attempted to put his new political structure in place by establishing the Imperial Rule Assistance Association (IRAA). Diet members of the former political parties ran as IRAA candidates in elections—the IRAA supposedly replaced all the political parties—but everyone knew that these politicians represented their constituencies as before. The IRAA failed as a mass organization, and never functioned like the Fascist parties in Germany and Italy.

Independent labor and women's organizations likewise came under the control of mass state organizations. The government dissolved labor unions by 1940, requiring workers to become members of labor councils under the Federation for Patriotic Industrial Service, which 6 million employees had joined by 1942. Despite the undemocratic nature of the Federation, its wartime policies—seniority-based wages and the inclusion of both white- and blue-collar workers in the same union—became characteristic of labor–management relations in the postwar period. Women were encouraged to join national organizations that gave them a voice in politics, but many paid for that involvement after the war by being called collaborators with a wicked government.

Matsuoka's turn to be humiliated by the Germans came in 1941. Enamored of Hitler's policies, he was blindsided in June when the Germans invaded the Soviet Union. Matsuoka had just negotiated the Japan–Soviet Neutrality Pact in March. On July 2, at a cabinet meeting attended by the emperor—a rare occurrence indicating its importance—the government decided to march into southern Vietnam, understanding the possible repercussions on relations with the United States and Britain, and to establish a Greater East Asia Co-Prosperity Sphere.

The move into southern Vietnam triggered an American embargo of oil and freezing of Japanese assets in the United States in July 1941. Because 90 percent of Japan's oil came from the United States, intense negotiations to reopen the supply began immediately. The Americans demanded that Japan return to its 1931 position in East Asia and abrogate the Tripartite Pact, both of which Japan refused, so negotiations continued in the fall. Konoe resigned in October, replaced by General Tōjō Hideki (1884–1948), and the new cabinet agreed to go to war in early December if negotiations failed.

To gain access to the oil supplies in the Dutch East Indies—the nearest replacement for imports from the United States—the military planned to disable the American fleet at Pearl Harbor while moving southward, taking the Philippines (a US-dominated commonwealth), Singapore (a British colony), and all of the Dutch East Indies. This they did, starting on December 8 (December 7 in Hawaii). Admiral Yamamoto Isoroku (see pp. 288–89), who opposed the war against the United States as unwinnable, planned the attack on Pearl Harbor.

THE PACIFIC WAR ON THE BATTLEFIELD

Yamamoto had contended that Japan could win the first six months of a war but would begin to lose thereafter. Indeed, by the summer of 1942, the Japanese had driven the colonial powers from Singapore, the Philippines, the Dutch East Indies, Burma, and Guam and made an alliance with Thailand. Including the Micronesian

Islands, held under a League of Nations mandate, Japan now controlled territory that stretched thousands of miles. This vast empire depended on the Co-Prosperity Sphere, an autarkic (self-sufficient) economic bloc intended to supply the empire's needs.

Japanese planners designed the Co-Prosperity Sphere as a mutually supporting group of independent nations—Burma, Thailand, Manzhouguo, the Philippines, and China under Wang Jingwei—but in none of these "states" did the Japanese military permit local self-rule. In fact, cruelty followed the Japanese flag once the former colonies were set free from their European and American colonial masters. By the end of the war, the Co-Prosperity Sphere "members" bitterly opposed the Japanese, who conscripted them for labor and in some cases destroyed their food supplies.

Moreover, the Co-Prosperity Sphere concept depended on shipping. Before the Battle of Midway in June 1942, American cryptographers deciphered a Japanese code, giving them advanced knowledge of Japan's strategic plans. From then on, Japan lost every major naval battle and thus lost control of their shipping lanes to American submarines and carrier-based aircraft. By the end of the war, 88 percent of Japan's merchant shipping lay at the bottom of the sea.

The Americans undertook an "island-hopping" strategy until they came close enough to begin aerial bombardment of the Japanese homeland. Taking each island required brutal warfare, with enormous death tolls among soldiers and civilians. As one scholar put it, this was a "war without mercy." Tōjō was forced out as prime minister when Saipan fell. The Americans began bombing the home islands in the fall of 1944. In March 1945, American B-29s firebombed Tokyo—a city constructed largely of wood—killing 100,000 people and making 4 million homeless in one night. In August, President Truman, who took office when FDR died on April 12, ordered use of the newly invented atomic bomb against Hiroshima and Nagasaki—the first and only inhabited targets of nuclear warfare—killing hundreds of thousands more. The Greater East Asia Co-Prosperity Sphere and Japan's empire came to a dead end.

Japanese theaters of war, 1940–45

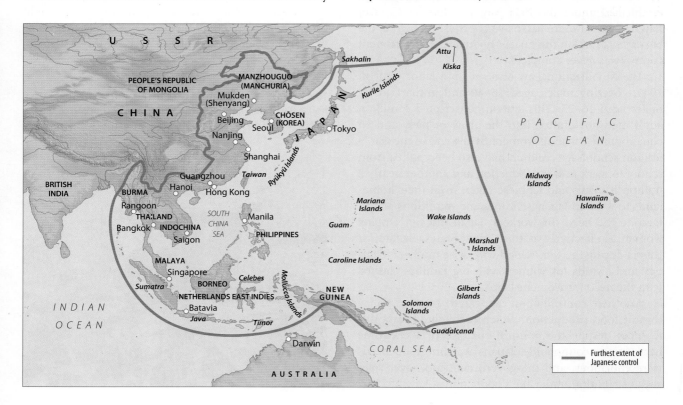

THE WAR AT HOME

Just as the Co-Prosperity Sphere was to be Japan's "New Order" in Asia, the "New Order" was to restructure Japanese society, economy, and politics at home. As noted above, the political component, the IRAA, replaced the parties, but unlike Germany's Nazi Party or Italy's Fascist Party, the IRAA had no political philosophy and little support. Its only real role involved the distribution of rice rations through the Neighborhood Associations under IRAA jurisdiction. Because everyone needed rice, everyone had contact with the IRAA. In the absence of men away at war, women played an important role in rice distribution and Neighborhood Association leadership. This experience served them after the war, when they gained political rights.

The 1938 National General Mobilization Law underlay all "New Order" programs. Konoe promised a wary Diet that he would not implement the law immediately, asking them to pass it for a "time of national emergency." Soon thereafter, however, Konoe declared a time of national emergency. The longstanding ambivalence toward big business in Japan led to the creation of Control Associations. These cartels resembled those established under the 1931 Major Industries Control Law, only with more extensive controls. As before, the big *zaibatsu* sat on the cartels' boards, and government control was never complete.

The Mobilization Law also set up a labor draft in 1941, covering males aged 16–40 and unmarried females aged 16–25. This system conscripted 1 million adult men not drafted into the army or navy and an equal number of adult women. By the end of the war, 3 million school-age children had also been pulled from school to work in war production and another nearly 2 million Koreans and Chinese taken from their homelands to work in Japanese mines and munitions plants. Despite the need for workers, Japan did not employ women as effectively as the United States, Britain, or Russia during the war. "Good wife, wise mother" ideology and awards for women with big families clashed with the need for women's labor.

Another contradiction appeared in the policy toward food production, which highlighted class differences despite the political rhetoric of a class-free harmonious countryside. Japan's wartime food needs were enormous, and the government took over sales and distribution under the Food Control Law of 1942.

To encourage greater productivity, by the end of the war the government paid rice producers (both independent and tenant farmers) five times as much as they paid landlords for rice grown by their tenants. The price landlords received failed to keep pace with inflation, so many sold their land to their tenants during the war. One of the key changes of the postwar American occupation was land reform—the elimination of landlordism—but the landlord system had already been undermined by wartime policy.

The New Order was also intended to purify people's thoughts. It forbade "decadent" American and British movies, attacked fancy clothing and permanent waves, targeted American jazz (very popular in Japan, then as now), and replaced English words, such as those used in Japan's national pastime, baseball, with Japanese terms. Even intellectuals jumped on the bandwagon, holding an important conference at Kyoto Imperial University in 1942 to discuss the meaning of the war in terms of "overcoming the modern" and rescuing the non-West from the cultural dominance of the West. Japan's great task lay in liberating Asia from individualism, hedonism, and modernity and forming an Asian cultural sphere under Japanese leadership. And yet, what could be more "modern" than the programs under the Mobilization Law, or the munitions used on the battlefield,

This Japanese family moved back to the spot where their house had stood before the August 9, 1945 dropping of the atomic bomb on Nagasaki.

or most horrendously, the "Unit 731" research team that used living Chinese subjects for inhuman biological experimentation?

Historians have debated whether to call Japan "fascist" from 1937 to 1945. The restrictions on freedoms enjoyed before the war, the government's attempts to structure industrial, political, and social controls, and the critique of modernity as decadent certainly had significant parallels with Japan's allies, Germany and Italy. But differences also abounded. Japan had no singular fascist party with an irreplaceable dictator, and big business never completely lost control of the economy to the state. In the end, the label is less important than understanding the details of Japanese militarism, Japan's horrendous war at home and in Asia, and the effects of wartime policy changes on the postwar era.

The last years of the war brutalized the Japanese people. Almost 3 million died: 1.7 million military men; 300,000 Manchurian settlers killed by the Soviets; and 500,000 civilians in air raids. Nine million people were left homeless. On average, Japanese lost 22 lb (10 kg) of weight during the war, a huge reduction for already thin people. By the end of the war, many were starving because fertilizer production had all been converted to explosives production. Most of Japan's dead perished in the last eight months of the war, long after the war was lost.

And yet, the government remained opposed to surrender. The Allies' Potsdam Declaration (July 26, 1945) demanded unconditional surrender, and some in the cabinet feared the possible loss of the emperor more than the death of the nation. Even the Soviet Union's long-dreaded entrance into the war on August 8, two days after the Americans dropped the first atomic bomb on Hiroshima and one day before Nagasaki, did not succeed in ending the war. Finally, the emperor broke the impasse, and on August 15 spoke to the Japanese people for the first time by radio broadcast, announcing Japan's surrender and asking them to "endure the unendurable."

CREATING TWO CHINAS

NATION-BUILDING IN THE NANJING DECADE

In 1927–28, the GMD (Nationalist) government under Jiang Jieshi had eliminated many of its rivals, driving the Communists into the hills and defeating, neutralizing,

or absorbing many of the regional warlords, but it nonetheless stood on shaky ground. The new government at Nanjing still formally recognized six provincial warlord centers as legitimate, so the national government had to maintain huge military forces. Demobilization of excess armies made sense, but the independent generals would not consent to having their forces trimmed as long as Jiang's central military remained intact, so the swollen armies continued to devour most government revenues.

Beginning in 1929, the unstable balance of power between Nanjing and the provincial generals stimulated a number of civil wars, which Jiang "won" by bribing or coercing some warlords to rejoin Nanjing. Often satirized as "silver bullet" wars because so much money changed hands, these conflicts nonetheless caused enormous damage. For example, a northern warlord coalition rebelled in July 1929, and the war cost 250,000 casualties before Jiang Jieshi persuaded (bribed) Manchurian general Zhang Xueliang to abandon his allies and recommit to the national center. Jiang's passive acquiescence in Japan's takeover of Manchuria frustrated many nationalists, so in late 1931, a coalition of civilian and military leaders from the south, led by Hu Hanmin, drove Jiang from office. Sun Fo (see p. 267) headed a short-lived national government, but Jiang's indispensable military leadership, despite his decision not to confront the Japanese, allowed "the Generalissimo" to return to power within a month.

From early 1932 until 1949, Jiang Jieshi *was* the Republic of China. The Huangpu-trained officers remained personally loyal to him, as did his foreign military advisers, primarily from Germany until the mid-1930s. Jiang commanded greater revenue resources than his rivals, for he controlled Shanghai, with its banks, industries, and lucrative underworld connections. Unlike the Qing's base in the land tax, Jiang's Nationalist government relied primarily on commercial and manufacturing taxes for its budget, as well as the sale of bonds and forced "loans" (rarely repaid) to the government.

The Nationalist state-building effort in the 1930s faced tremendous obstacles. Almost two decades of political disintegration had produced widespread disaffection from government, which always demanded more taxes, more conscripts, and more sacrifice, without providing anything in return. Regional and provincial sentiment continued to rival national loyalty. The economy had been badly damaged by warfare, foreign incursions, fragmented authority over currency, and the world Depression after 1929. Japan's conquest of Manchuria, with its rich mineral and agricultural resources, also weakened the economy and Nanjing's prestige. Endemic rural poverty, closely linked to high rates of tenancy in southern China, could only be improved by producing more food per farmer. Agronomic research made some headway, but without a national agricultural extension service, it had only limited impact on rural management. Industry also progressed, but in very limited areas and with considerable government involvement.

Like the late Qing before them and the Communists after, the Nationalists aimed to centralize power in the national capital, end the fragmenting effects of provincialism and warlordism, ensure domestic peace, modernize China's culture and society, defeat foreign invaders, and enhance government revenues by taxing agriculture and commerce more efficiently. That they failed in most of these efforts stemmed both from the GMD's internal weaknesses and from external circumstances such as imperial domination of the treaty ports, worldwide Depression, and Japan's implacable aggression. The GMD-dominated, Nanjing-based ROC had formal structures of government—legislative, judicial, executive, examination (personnel), and oversight (censorate) branches—but factionalism, cronyism, bureaucratic inertia, and the overwhelming dominance of the military prevented effective governance.

Jiang Jieshi recognized the GMD's shortcomings—in 1932 he lamented that "the revolution has failed"—but he continued to believe that only he could lead China to national power and prestige. Preferring to work without reference to formal structures of state, Jiang ensured that neither the GMD nor the government functioned efficiently. Bureaucrats went to the office, drafted proposals for procedure or reform, and sent them through channels toward the decision-makers,

Wedding photograph of Jiang Jieshi (Chiang Kai-shek) and Song Meiling (Soong Mei-ling), December 1, 1927.

but even if approved they only received funding and human resources if Jiang or one of his entourage personally backed them. Idealistic party members, optimistic about fulfilling the dreams of May Fourth through the GMD and the Nanjing government, grew disillusioned and disaffected.

Jiang had become a Christian in order to marry Song Meiling (1898–2003), the Wellesley-educated daughter of a wealthy publisher, but his speeches combined Confucian rectitude with ardent nationalism. He admired national unifiers and loyal ministers such as Zeng Guofan (see pp. 188–89) and restored worship of Confucius in government-sponsored temples. Like Lu Xun, he believed that China needed a spiritual rejuvenation—not through literature and the arts, but rather through a military culture with strong elements of Confucianism, such as he had observed in Japan, the only foreign country he really admired. Jiang thus embodied two related conflicts felt by many Chinese: ambivalence about Japan, whose modern society they respected while they loathed its imperialist actions; and mixed feelings about Chinese tradition, rejected by May Fourth iconoclasts but still a powerful component of personal and collective identities.

The New Life Movement, inaugurated in 1934, aimed to achieve the social goals of the GMD regime, articulated by Jiang himself:

…to militarize thoroughly the lives of the citizens of the entire nation so that they can cultivate courage and swiftness, the endurance of suffering and a tolerance for hard work, and especially the habit and ability of unified action, so that they will at any time sacrifice for the nation.[1]

Clearly these goals owe a great deal to the totalitarian political philosophies of Benito Mussolini and Adolf Hitler, which some GMD leaders esteemed, and to prewar Japan. The GMD created fascist-style organizations, such as the "Blue Shirt Society" youth corps, and one modern scholar called Jiang's regime "Confucian Fascism." But Jiang made no attempt to mobilize workers or the general citizenry, as Europe's fascists did.

Some Chinese consented to Jiang's centrality and regarded him as the Supreme Leader, the embodiment of China's virtues and its future. Many others did not, including those attracted to democracy. They founded "third-party" organizations to advocate "enlightened" May Fourth values, enlisting hundreds or thousands of well-educated urbanites, but none gained much national support in a wartime atmosphere. Among the foreign powers, Germany provided military advisers; Britain and the United States both maintained strong commercial, military, and missionary presence; but only the Soviet Union sent direct foreign aid. From 1931 onward, the struggle over "who controls China" had three key players: Japan, especially its military; Jiang Jieshi and the GMD, allied with the United States after 1937; and the CCP, pushed into peripheral hill country but still armed and dangerous, and to some extent responsive to the USSR.

COMMUNISTS IN POWER: THE JIANGXI SOVIET

Why did Jiang Jieshi and his national army not resist when Japan removed Manzhouguo from the Republic in 1931? The Generalissimo argued that the Japanese constituted a disease of the limbs, but the Communist affliction lay close to China's heart. This stand did not make him popular with ardent nationalists, but Jiang resolved to eliminate the CCP before confronting Japan, for he could not tolerate a second government and independent CCP army inside the Republic. Despite the Nationalists' overwhelming superiority in troops and modern weapons, this proved to be a more difficult and costly operation than Jiang predicted.

After 1927, the main leaders of the CCP remained underground in Shanghai and other cities, attempting to resurrect their movement under Soviet guidance, relying on labor organizing and armed uprisings. A new generation of leaders tried to imitate the USSR's revolutionary experience: Qu Qiubai (1899–1935), who replaced Chen Duxiu as Party leader during the 1927 debacle; Li Lisan, who had organized workers at the Anyuan coalmines; and Wang Ming (1904–1974), who spent several years in Moscow. None of them could devise successful strategies against Nanjing's domination of the cities, and by 1931 the leadership of the CCP shifted away from conventional Marxist focus on the working class toward China's overwhelmingly numerous peasantry. Communist organizers continued underground urban work, but the labor movement had been decisively coopted by the Guomindang, and violent, effective repression prevented any large-scale CCP successes in Nanjing-controlled areas.

Fleeing from the defeats of 1927 (see p. 267) with 1,000–2,000 poorly armed men, Mao Zedong and General Zhu De, a German-educated soldier from a Hakka family, rebuilt their forces and established a CCP rural "base area"—a region of effective military and political control—in the Jinggang Mountains. They allied with local bandits, who flourished in the peripheral zone between Hunan and Jiangxi provinces, and fought off several Nationalist army columns before being driven southward in 1929. CCP commander Peng Dehuai (1898–1974), later in charge of China's intervention in the Korean War, continued resistance in Jinggang until 1934.

In retreat, Mao and Zhu's army created a much larger base area, the Jiangxi Soviet, around the town of Ruijin, on the peripheries of Jiangxi and Fujian, where they held off attack after attack by Nanjing's national army for almost five years. Other CCP military leaders, including Zhang Guotao (1897–1979) and He Long (1896–1969), created more than two dozen base areas all over southern and central China, independent of and opposed to Nanjing. The base areas served as refuges for CCP forces and as staging areas for guerrilla warfare against national and local armies. Altogether, they constituted the "Chinese Soviet Republic" (CSR), the CCP's first opportunity to govern substantial territory and population, albeit under heavy military pressure. There Mao Zedong and his closest colleagues tested many of the policies that shaped the CCP's political evolution.

Because of constant military engagement, the base areas had to maintain and improve their military, which they called the Red Army, as their top priority. These peripheral regions were poor, mountainous, and thinly populated, so their recruits came entirely from the villages and local bandit gangs. Funds to purchase weapons, ammunition, and food for the troops had to be taken from the peasants as taxes; this meant Communist leaders immediately faced problems of political and social mobilization, which they solved using Marxist theory as they understood and adapted it. That is, they approached local society as being made up of *social classes* determined by "means and relations of production."

The German political economist Karl Marx (1818–1883) had theorized that *socioeconomic class* lies at the root of all human activity. Observing Western Europe, he found that some people, the capitalists or *bourgeoisie*, have capital (money) to purchase the "means of production"—urban factories or agricultural land—while others, the workers or *proletariat*, own only their own labor, which they sell for wages. Capitalists own the products created by the labor of the workers; that is, factory owners *exploit* the labor of others and enrich themselves by selling the products in markets. After investigating rural Hunan before and during the Northern Expedition (see pp. 266–67), Mao Zedong wrote "Analysis of the Classes in Chinese Society" (1927), one of his first important theoretical essays, to develop a workable Marxist methodology for differentiating social classes in the Chinese countryside. He concluded that "our friends" included those who experienced exploitation in their "relations of production," and "our enemies" were those who exploited others. Obvious in the case of capitalists and workers in urban industry, in the villages these relationships required more subtle explanation.

Mao theorized five classes of rural people, distinguished by their relationship to land, the most important rural "means of production." At the bottom, the "landless rural laborers," like urban workers, lived on nothing but their wages. "Poor peasants" owned land, but not enough to support themselves, so they rented more from a landlord and thus experienced exploitation. "Middle peasants" owned and cultivated sufficient land but did not exploit anyone else's labor. "Rich peasants" cultivated their own fields and also rented out surplus land, exploiting tenant labor by taking a portion of their crop and loaning them money at high interest. At the top of rural society, "landlords" owned land but did not cultivate it, earning their entire living from commerce, interest on loans, and the labor of tenants.

In order to gain the support of the poorest, most exploited classes (the majority of the population), the base area governments undertook "land reform,"

first analyzing every rural family and giving it a class label. The CCP's local officials thus used Mao's categories, clear in theory but difficult to apply in practice, to categorize the varied, complex society of the base areas. They then confiscated land and "factors of production" such as draft animals and tools from "exploiter" families—those labeled as landlords and rich peasants—distributing these resources to "exploited" families classified as poor peasants and rural workers. This labor-intensive process engaged the government with every person in a base area, and it later became a model for state penetration to the grassroots level, which the Qing, the warlords, and the GMD had not managed.

But the process was not smooth. CCP leaders fought viciously among themselves over matters such as "rich peasant policy"—what percentage of family income must be derived from exploitation in order to classify a family as rich peasants? Should the good land of rich peasants be confiscated, or their poor land? Zhang Guotao argued for strenuous confiscation of rich peasant property, while other leaders favored leniency in the interest of unity. Though local and small-scale, such decisions meant life or death to the CCP, which relied entirely on young rural males to fight in the Red Army. They needed rural families to support the base area governments with taxes, knowledge of local terrain, and military intelligence.

The "rich peasant problem" was made more complex by the importance of wealthier rural families in commercial networks, essential for distribution of indispensable commodities such as salt and grain. The CCP also needed to ally with powerful local families for smuggling weapons and other commodities not produced in their isolated border regions. These different imperatives required multiple classification movements, with serious consequences for rural families, who strove to change or conceal their actual economic conditions in order to be placed in a "good" (that is non-exploiting) category.

The land reform process often became violent—people did not usually give up their land and possessions peacefully—but did, in fact, gain many allies for the CCP. Even foreign missionaries hostile to "atheistic Communism" observed that the base area residents, numbering in the millions by the early 1930s, seemed to support the CCP wholeheartedly. The base areas' isolation from urban influence, and from Comintern guidance, may have given the Communist leadership time to develop local Marxist solutions rather than following Stalin's policy of expropriation and execution of rich peasants.

The base area governments did not rely on land reform alone to build local alliances. Social policy formed crucial links among party, army, and the villages. For example, the CCP—in principle favoring the "thorough emancipation of women"—initially decreed women's freedom of unilateral divorce, previously unknown in China. This regulation created considerable support for the CCP among younger women. But the enlightened ideal foundered on local social realities, because young rural men serving in the Red Army found their wives—mostly purchased in the traditional manner—suing them for divorce, leaving their mothers without the labor of their daughters-in-law. Soldiers and older women thus opposed the policy, so the base areas faced a contradiction between female emancipation and maintaining Red Army morale. Choosing the latter, in 1934 the Jiangxi Soviet issued revised marriage

regulations stipulating that a soldier's wife could only obtain a divorce with her husband's consent.

DEFEAT AND RETREAT

Land reform and revolutionary social ferment took place under attack from the Nanjing government. Jiang Jieshi continued to regard defeating the Communists as a higher priority than resisting Japan, so between late 1930 and 1934, the Nationalist army undertook five "encirclement and annihilation" campaigns against the Chinese Soviet Republic. GMD armies overran some small base areas in late 1932, forcing relocations, but the Jiangxi Soviet held out. Initially defeated by the Red Army's deceptive tactics and rapid troop movements, Jiang sought the advice of his German adviser, Hans von Seeckt (1866–1936), who designed a more effective strategy. Advancing slowly into the central Jiangxi Soviet area, Jiang's army constructed fortified blockhouses, more than one per mile, and foiled the Red Army's rapid mobility tactics. After losing many soldiers in futile attempts to storm the blockhouses without artillery, the CCP leadership had to retreat to more defensible base areas elsewhere.

Starting in October 1934, over 100,000 troops withdrew from the south and central China base areas of the Chinese Soviet Republic, heading first west and then north toward a destination that even Mao Zedong did not initially know. CCP historians have converted this retreat, which cost the Communists 90 percent of their soldiers and most of their rural constituency, into a heroic victory called "The Long March." Like other epic mass journeys in history—the Exodus of the Israelites or the *Voortrek* of the Boers—the Long March has become an emblem of unity and a proof of rectitude for the CCP. It also determined the party's leadership for more than 40 years.

Three main Red Army units made the Long March, along three somewhat different routes. The First Front Army, under Mao and Zhu, broke out of the besieged Jiangxi Soviet in October 1934, moving southwest. A few months later, under much less pressure, Zhang Guotao led the Fourth Front Army westward from northern Sichuan into the Tibetan foothills to meet Mao and Zhu. In November 1935, He Long's Second Front Army, based in Hunan, broke a determined siege to follow the First Front Army's route through Guizhou and Yunnan then northward.

The Long March, 1934–35

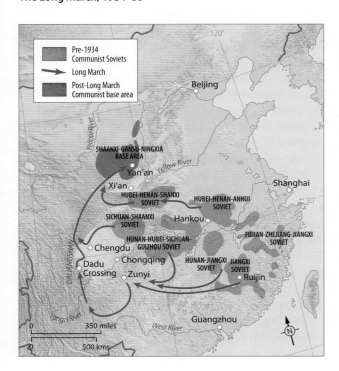

The CCP's leadership in northern Shaanxi after the Long March, 1936 (from left): Qin Bangxian (Bo Gu, 1907–1946), Zhou Enlai, Zhu De, Mao Zedong.

A series of CCP leadership conferences in 1935 examined the fate of the CSR and planned the CCP's next moves. Challenged by Zhang Guotao, Mao Zedong gathered support for his plan to take the Red Army to northern Shaanxi, where two small CCP base areas could constitute a new home for the party and army. Zhang Guotao, persuaded that the CSR had been a failure, favored a retreat farther west, to Gansu or even Xinjiang, to give the Red Army time to recuperate. Zhang recommended building an independent northwestern government, not socialist base areas, out of reach of national army attacks.

Mao rejected this policy change and took the more optimistic view: the CSR had been successful, and its construction should be repeated in northern Shaanxi. Both Zhang and Mao claimed CCP leadership and regarded one another as insubordinate, so the party briefly split. Zhang Guotao called a fourth conference, attended by his own followers, which confirmed his supremacy over Mao, but his Fourth Front Army met with military defeat at the hands of a Sichuanese warlord. Still heading for a safe haven in the far northwest, Zhang's troops crossed the Yellow River only to be routed by the cavalry of Gansu's Muslim warlords. With his

army in tatters, Zhang lost all stature in the CCP, leaving Mao and his allies in complete control.

YAN'AN, XI'AN, AND THE SECOND UNITED FRONT

Victorious in CCP infighting, firmly in control of both party and army, in late 1935 Mao and Zhu led their remnant, battle-hardened troops—less than 10,000 of them—to unite with local forces in northern Shaanxi, where they established a new base area and renewed their calls for a Second United Front against Japan. Since leaving Jiangxi, various CCP leaders had proposed Chinese unity against the external enemy. Some (such as Mao Zedong) excluded Jiang Jieshi and the GMD right wing from the theoretical alliance, while others included them. In August 1935, Wang Ming, a Soviet-oriented member of the CCP Central Committee, declared Japan rather than Jiang Jieshi to be the main enemy of the Chinese people and invited Jiang to call off his campaigns against the CCP and fight Japan. Mao, on the other hand, continued to revile Jiang as a "running dog" of imperialism while proposing an alliance of all *patriotic* Chinese against Japan.

To confirm its anti-Japanese intentions, in February 1936 the Red Army launched an eastward attack through Shanxi toward Japanese positions in Hebei and Rehe. Although defeated by Shanxi warlord Yan Xishan and Nationalist troops, this campaign enhanced the CCP's credentials and recruited thousands of new soldiers. It also persuaded many GMD generals that the Communists were Chinese patriots, not tools of the USSR as Jiang had claimed. In March, Mao Zedong declared the CCP's willingness to talk peace with Nanjing, but Jiang Jieshi responded with a military offensive against the northern Shaanxi base area.

Confident in China's rising nationalist sentiment, the CCP sent Zhou Enlai—former political commissar at Huangpu Military Academy, Long March veteran, and the CCP's most skillful negotiator—to Shanghai to discuss a new United Front with high GMD officials. The last half of 1936 found Jiang under increasing pressure to resist Japan, not only from the CCP but also from nationalistic students, leading intellectuals, and even his own party and generals.

Having driven the Communists into a remote northwestern refuge, Jiang refused to give up his goal of eliminating them. He ordered Zhang Xueliang ("the

Young Marshal"), with his Manchurian army, and Yang Hucheng, the GMD's northwestern commander, to surround and destroy the northern Shaanxi base area from their headquarters at Xi'an, the provincial capital. But Yang and Zhang had been impressed with the fighting qualities of the Red Army and with the CCP's stand against Japan. After all, the Japanese army had assassinated Zhang Xueliang's father, Zhang Zuolin (see p. 267), and Zhang's troops wanted to fight their way home to Manchuria, not to kill other Chinese. So they did not press their anti-Communist campaign with any enthusiasm; instead, they initiated contacts with the CCP to arrange a ceasefire.

Enraged by this insubordination, in early December Jiang flew to Xi'an, where discussions with Zhang and Yang took a dramatic turn. On December 12, Zhang Xueliang's personal guards surrounded Jiang Jieshi's guest-house at his headquarters outside the city, overpowered his bodyguards, and kidnapped their commander-in-chief. Never intending to kill Jiang, the mutineers demanded that he end civil conflict, release political prisoners, and include all responsible parties in a government of national salvation. Because of Jiang's international stature, the incident gathered immediate, worldwide attention—the *New York Times* headline read, "Chiang Kai-shek [Jiang Jieshi] Is Prisoner of Mutinous Shensi [Shaanxi] Troops, Demanding War on Japan."

For the next two weeks, China and the world watched tensely as negotiators gathered in Xi'an. Zhou Enlai and Ye Jianying (1897–1986) represented the CCP. Madame Jiang arrived from Nanjing with her brother Song Ziwen (T.V. Soong, 1894–1971), Jiang's Australian adviser W.H. Donald, and the dreaded chief of military intelligence, Dai Li (1897–1946), who headed the Blue Shirt Society. Some GMD factions favored a military strike on Xi'an to rescue Jiang and punish Zhang Xueliang. Radicals among the Manchurian troops wanted to execute Jiang for abandoning their homeland. The USSR, afraid that China without Jiang would

Jiang Jieshi (Chiang Kai-shek), right, and Young Marshal Zhang Xueliang in Nanjing before the Xi'an incident (1936).

immediately be overrun by Japan, directed the CCP to safeguard his life, and calmer heads, especially Zhang Xueliang's, prevailed.

Although Jiang swore that he made no concessions to his captors, he clearly did make a verbal promise to cease attacking the Communists and to resist Japan. So on Christmas Day, released by his "rebellious" troops, Jiang flew back to Nanjing amid national rejoicing, bearing the possibility of a new United Front. Zhang Xueliang returned with him and was placed under house arrest, where he remained for over 50 years.

Negotiations ensued immediately, reaching a comprehensive agreement in April, despite disagreements within the CCP. Some Communist leaders, including Wang Ming, believed that class struggle (such as land reform) should be set aside during the national crisis and that the CCP should return to the cities, giving up independent military forces in the name of national unity. Mao, on the other hand, mistrusted Jiang Jieshi and argued that the CCP should retain its rural base areas and an independent Red Army. Zhang Guotao had recommended defeating both the Japanese and Jiang, but Mao advocated a limited united front while continuing his guerrilla strategy of "encircle the cities from the countryside." Mao's view prevailed, and he and Zhu De retained independent command of the Red Army, reclassified as the "Eighth Route Army" of the combined national forces.

INVASION AND ALL-OUT WAR, 1937–38

As narrated above, the Kantōgun had been edging south and west from Manzhouguo for years, so the Marco Polo Bridge incident and full-scale war caught neither side unprepared. Within a month, Japan invaded China by two main routes, from Manzhouguo via Beiping and the North China plain and from the east through Shanghai. Jiang Jieshi, finally determined to resist the external enemy, threw his best armies—German-trained, officered by Huangpu and Central Military

Academy graduates—into the defense of Shanghai, a destructive battle that lasted over three months and cost both sides dearly.

Expecting light resistance from the "racially inferior" Chinese, Japanese troops at Shanghai needed wave after wave of reinforcements until they had over 300,000 men on the ground against nearly 600,000 Chinese. Jiang Jieshi demanded that his generals hold out at all costs, hoping for foreign intervention. He appealed to the League of Nations, and President Roosevelt recommended international action in his famous "Quarantine Speech" of October 5. But no aid ever materialized,

except small amounts from the USSR. By November, overwhelming Japanese firepower, including air and naval bombardment, had driven Jiang's forces from the city, reduced much of Shanghai to rubble, and killed almost 200,000 Chinese soldiers (and untold numbers of civilians), making Shanghai the bloodiest battle since World War I.

Defending Shanghai cost Jiang Jieshi his finest divisions—10,000 out of his 25,000 elite junior officers died there—and made him more dependent on his provincial allies for the remainder of the war. But the sight of national and provincial troops fighting the vaunted

FENG ZIKAI, BUDDHIST CARTOONIST

Feng Zikai's (1898–1975) hometown in Zhejiang had been sacked during the Taiping wars, so his family turned from scholarship to business. But Feng's free-spirited paternal grandmother, who loved wine, local opera, and opium—he often compared her to Chen Yun (see p. 108)—allowed her son to study for the official examinations, and he achieved the provincial degree in 1902, just in time for the system to be abolished. Deprived of his career path, Feng's father taught his son the Classics and quietly smoked and drank his days away, dying of tuberculosis in 1906. Attracted to the illustrations in his father's old books, Feng Zikai began to draw and paint, using both traditional art manuals and new European-style books published in Shanghai.

Skilled enough that neighbors and relatives asked him to paint funeral portraits, Feng also took great joy in prose and calligraphy. His teenage essays reveal early attention to Buddhist ideas: "When the heart gives birth to desire then defeat is hard to avoid."[2] Feng studied the new-style curriculum at the teacher's college in Hangzhou, where Lu Xun taught (see pp. 262–63). Academically successful, Feng was attracted to romantic, individualistic companions and teachers. When the Buddhist adept Li Shutong (1880–1942)

returned from art school in Tokyo to teach the school's painting classes, he redirected Feng's life toward art.

Through Li's instruction, Feng Zikai discovered that his hobby could be taken seriously, that his emotional reactions to line, form, color, and shading actually mattered: "It was as if the branches, leaves, flowers, and fruits of every plant were vying to tell me something."[3] Graduating in 1919 and already married to Xu Limin, an educated woman whom he adored, Feng went to Shanghai to teach. But even Shanghai could not provide deep understanding of Western art, so Feng left for Tokyo in 1921 to experience a Japan very different from that of his more politically minded compatriots. Besotted with the work of modern realist Takehisa Yumeji (1884–1934), he threw himself into the Japanese art world, in which traditional painting, poster-making, cartooning, calligraphy, and the humanistic philosophies of both East Asia and Europe could be combined.

With all of those skills honed, Feng Zikai returned to China to become one of the twentieth century's most loved artists. His paintings, book illustrations (including, memorably, Lu Xun's "Ah Q"), essays on theory, and especially his cartoons became unmistakable landmarks. He introduced the word

Japanese army to a standstill encouraged nationalist sentiment all over China and increased Jiang's domestic support. The loss of China's most important commercial city weakened Nanjing both economically and psychologically, but Chinese resistance impressed foreign observers, creating lasting images of "gutsy China."

The impact of the battle on the Japanese military has been widely debated. It delayed the invasion of the Yangzi valley and required the Japanese army to commit far greater resources than they had planned. Given prewar slogans predicting rapid victory, the Tokyo government suffered domestic embarrassment. Most

controversially, some scholars have argued that the unexpected, deadly Chinese resistance—Japan lost nearly 40,000 men at Shanghai—set the stage for the horrific results when the invading army reached its next major target, the Nationalist capital of Nanjing.

The story of Nanjing, described above, has become commonplace knowledge. After capturing Nanjing in December 1937 with relative ease, against ill-organized Nationalist resistance, the Japanese army massacred Chinese POWs and the undefended civilian inhabitants in a six-week bloodbath. Figures vary widely, ranging from a few hundred, proposed by Japanese

manhua (J. *manga*, K. *manhwa*) to China and excelled in its deceptively simple techniques. During the war, he took his family west to Guilin, where he continued his search for meaning in a chaotic world. His wartime cartoons illustrated war's horrors but also gently reminded his audience of humankind's fundamental goodness. Devoted to his wife and children, profound in his insights into the human condition, Feng Zikai remained a Buddhist and humanist, despite the brutality of war and Chinese politics, until his death in 1975.

BELOW Feng Zikai, *War and Music*, 1925.
LEFT Feng Zikai in his studio, 1975

massacre-deniers, to 300,000, with "over 200,000" as a scholarly consensus. The rape and murder of tens of thousands of women has drawn particular attention to this atrocity, as has the Tokyo government's unwillingness to order its troops to desist. Analysts have offered many explanations: a breakdown of discipline because of exhaustion and poor logistics; the poor quality and brutal training of Japanese recruits; deep anti-Chinese racism at all levels of the Japanese military; and a deliberate policy of slaughter undertaken by Japanese officers to discourage further Chinese resistance. Even the chaotic Nationalist withdrawal from Nanjing has been blamed for creating conditions in which atrocities might occur.

The Japanese army did perpetrate similar horrors elsewhere. During the lengthy battles around Xuzhou, for example, on the North China plain, in 1938, Japanese army units deliberately exterminated villagers and refugees, on one famous occasion burning hundreds of young men alive in a surrounded courtyard. On another, all of the monks at a Buddhist temple were killed for "harboring guerrillas," as were 200 civilians in a nearby town.

One useful explanation (certainly not an excuse) for this horrific behavior lies in the Japanese army's complete failure to prepare for postconquest administration of civilian populations. Even after almost a year of warfare, some Japanese armies operating in China had few or no Chinese speakers to communicate with the local people. Plans had been made only for conquest, and field commanders often found themselves victorious, surrounded by Chinese civilians, with no officials or police to restore or maintain order. In addition, fear of Chinese guerrilla fighters pervaded the Japanese military. Any Chinese *might* be an armed enemy, disguised as an ordinary person, so slaughter of civilians might have seemed a justifiable response.

Nor was the Japanese army the only cause of anguish. In June 1938, the Nationalist government, in an attempt to delay the motorized Japanese invasion of northern China, breached the dikes of the Yellow River and inundated a vast area. Nearly 1 million people perished in the flooding, at least 4 million were left homeless, and the Japanese advance was delayed by three months. This incalculable anguish and dislocation—remember that every individual, even in such huge numbers, suffered individually—repeated in many parts of China over the next seven years, created a culture bent on survival, one in which normal social relationships were destroyed or distorted by omnipresent fear of sudden death. Many Chinese still live with the memory or long-term effects of the "War of Resistance against Japan," as World War II is called in China, and feelings against Japan still run strong.

THE LONG WARS OF RESISTANCE, 1938–45

By the end of 1938, the Japanese army had driven the Nationalist forces out of Wuhan, past the formidable Yangzi gorges, to their wartime capital of Chongqing (Chungking). Hundreds of industries, dozens of universities, and several million refugees followed them upriver to establish "Free China" in Sichuan, Yunnan, and Guizhou provinces. Much of eastern China, however, remained beyond the control of the Japanese army, which defended cities and railroads, leaving its newly established puppet, the "Reformed Government" of Wang Jingwei, to administer the rest. Both the Japanese and their puppets faced formidable difficulties despite their armed strength. Both the GMD and the CCP, operating as a United Front but divided by suspicion, immediately organized guerrilla warfare behind Japanese lines.

Observers foreign and domestic described the differences between Chongqing, the GMD's capital, and Yan'an, headquarters of the CCP. Swollen, disease-ridden, corrupt, and dirty, Chongqing reflected the chaos of Jiang Jieshi's rule, dependent to some extent on shipments of foreign aid—American supplies began to arrive under the Lend-Lease program in 1940—and on the opium trade with Japanese-controlled areas.

In contrast, Yan'an seemed idealistic, open, clean (though poor), and dedicated to the war effort. The GMD army, dug in along a lengthy, immobile front, demanded unending recruits and treated them badly. Although abandoning land reform for the United Front, the CCP attracted volunteers through local mobilization, organizing and arming the peasantry for guerrilla warfare, often dispersing its forces behind Japanese lines to strike at local targets. This kind of warfare, fought at a low technological level but depending upon the local population for people and intelligence, marked the CCP as dedicated, courageous, concerned for ordinary folks, and closely connected to rural China, all very different from the prevailing images of the GMD.

But Yan'an was not paradise. In the interest of internal discipline, leaders of the rapidly expanding CCP declared that all members should undergo "rectification" during the war, a major campaign directed especially at intellectuals who joined the party but did not submit to its anti-individualist ethos. For two years, mass criticism meetings and small group self-criticism sessions began the long process of making diverse, quirky Chinese people into regimented cadres. Some did not survive, and many remembered the process as brutal. This rectification campaign set the style for years thereafter, culminating in the Cultural Revolution of the late 1960s.

When the United States joined the war after Pearl Harbor, President Roosevelt sent Joseph Stilwell (1883–1946)—a Chinese-speaking general eager to fight Japan—to head the US military mission in China. Stilwell and Jiang Jieshi hated one another, and their constant disagreement destabilized the alliance. Jiang preferred his American air adviser, General Claire Chennault (1893–1958), who advocated attacking Japan with bombers rather than using Jiang's ground troops. This suited the Generalissimo, who wished to preserve his forces to fight the Communists after Japan's defeat.

American air power did achieve some success against Japanese positions, but the GMD army could not defend its airbases. In 1944 the Japanese army initiated Operation Ichigo, throwing 400,000 men at GMD lines, most of which broke quickly and gave Japan dominion over even more Chinese territory, including the entire north–south railway system and the American airfields. Stilwell demanded that he be placed in supreme command over all Chinese armies, but Jiang arranged for Roosevelt to recall the feisty general and

Japanese troops celebrating a victory in China, 1937.

continued to hoard troops and supplies for the civil war to come.

The war cost 20 million Chinese lives, destroyed most of China's modern industries, and, despite the United Front, exacerbated the longlasting enmity between the two main political parties. When Japan surrendered in August 1945, over 1 million Japanese troops remained in China, with all of their equipment and skills. Had they been employed elsewhere, the course of the war might have been different, so both the GMD and CCP claim victory and a substantial role in defeating the Japanese empire. The United States and its allies, acknowledging China's sacrifice and contributions, ended the last of the unequal treaties, finally conceding China a place as an equal in the family of nations.

KOREA

COLONIAL DEVELOPMENT AND WAR MOBILIZATION

In the 15 years after the seizure of Manchuria in 1931, the power and reach of the Japanese empire reached its zenith then withered and dissipated in defeat at the hands of the Allied powers in August 1945. For its Korean colony this period was, particularly after 1937, marked by serious cultural, social, and economic trauma. Indeed, Japanese excesses during the harsh mobilization that accompanied the war in Asia largely determine the poisonous memory of colonialism in Korea that lingers today.

Moreover, the establishment of Manzhouguo altered Korea's position in the empire, particularly in economic terms. Korea became a geographical center with the addition of Manzhouguo to the Japanese *gaichi* (outer territory). As an older, more developed part of the empire, it took the lead in development and close linkage to Japan. The Government-General of Korea (GGK) thus shifted its economic policies away from the agriculture-first plans that dominated the 1920s toward a new investment strategy that placed key industries in northern Korea to utilize Manchurian raw materials and new hydroelectric investments on the Yalu, now truly a Japanese river. With this began an industrialization unprecedented in colonial history. Colonial powers generally take primary resources—minerals,

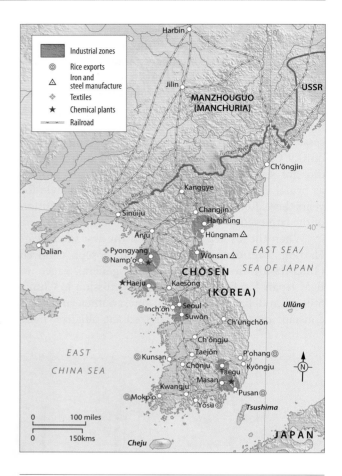

Transport and industrial development in colonial Korea, c. 1940

fuel, timber, fibers, food—from colonies and process them in the metropolitan center. In Korea after 1931, Japan reversed this pattern and made important manufacturing investments in the colony.

With this shift in economic policy caused by the external realignment of the empire came modification of domestic control and cultural policies. As Japan pulled Korea closer, it demanded of Koreans more active participation in and identification with the empire. This meant intensifying the previously mild campaigns to assimilate Korean subjects into the spiritual values, culture, and language of Japan. Before 1935 assimilation had been fundamental policy but not an active priority. After all, the Cultural Policy in the wake of the 1919 disturbances had placed the goal of assimilation behind that of mollifying Korean cultural sensibilities. But as Japan's involvement on the Asian mainland deepened after 1931, it began to demand more than passive compliance. To this end, the Governor-General (GG) inaugurated "forced" assimilation projects under the banner of the "Create Imperial Subjects Movement" in 1936. The mobilization of Korean resources and human capital to support the war in China and finally the horrors of "total war" mobilization after 1941 intensified these imperial projects.

MANCHURIA, KOREA, AND DEVELOPMENTAL COLONIALISM

The GGK watched the events in Manchuria with intense interest. Linked by rail to Korea's main lines, home to 1.45 million Korean emigrants, Manchuria's development would be the key to the Korean colony's economic future. A new GG arrived in 1931, Ugaki Kazushige, an ultranationalist with close ties to the Kantōgun. He believed the empire should be economically autonomous, entirely self-sufficient—that is, autarkic—and he shifted colonial policy to complement the economic development of Manchuria. As GG, he had many economic levers to pull. Indeed, the 1930s witnessed the emergence of what postwar development economists refer to as "state-guided capitalism" in Japan. The colonial state's Bank of Chōsen (the Japanese name for Korea, Chosŏn) acted as an informal central bank for development in the entire region, maintaining 20 branches

in Manzhouguo alone. Other semi-governmental institutions—including the Korean Industrial Bank and the Oriental Development Corporation—acted as funnels for capital and state guidance in the economy. The GGK maintained close ties with the enormous South Manchurian Railway Corporation, a key institution in the development of Northeast Asia, which controlled region-wide railroad building. After 1931, new lines connected the emerging industrial base in the Korean northeast with Manzhouguo, and tiny villages like Najin and Chŏngjin became major ports and export centers on the Japan Sea.

Japanese planners began to sketch out a vision of an autarkic economy that would integrate the home islands, Manzhouguo, Korea, Taiwan, and later, newly conquered territories in China and Southeast Asia. In the protectionist global trade climate of the Great Depression, Japan wanted to protect its supply lines and raw material sources as well as markets. Japanese businessmen and entrepreneurs worked closely with officials of the Japanese central government, Manzhouguo, and GGK, often using special subsidies, to accomplish the grand plan. Noguchi Jun's (1873–1944) "new" *zaibatsu*, Nippon Chisso, invested in hydroelectric capacity, an oil refinery in Wŏnsan, and the beginnings of what would become one of the largest chemical complexes in the world at Hŭngnam, all in northern Korea.

Korean entrepreneurs who had taken advantage of subsidies and close ties to colonial banks in the 1920s

also profited from the development of Manzhouguo. The most spectacular investment was Kim Sŏngsu's giant textile company, which opened a new plant, the Southern Manchurian Textile Corporation, in December 1939. By that time a core of Korean businessmen had fully integrated themselves into the empire's economy, so leaders like Kim Sŏngsu and Pak Hŭngsik (1903–1994) invested heavily in other companies in Manzhouguo. These two also joined forces with Japanese investors to manufacture airplanes toward the end of the war.

Bank of Chōsen, Seoul, 1930s.

The economic development of Korea during the 1930s had a profound effect on the Korean population. As industry expanded, hundreds of thousands of peasants found themselves in factory jobs. The factory workforce in Korea doubled in the 1930s and increased further after the outbreak of the Pacific War, from 99,400 in 1932 to 390,000 in 1943, a 392 percent increase. If we include the mining and transportation sectors, the increase was even more dramatic. Moreover, this does not count the tens of thousands of Koreans working in industrial plants in Manzhouguo by 1945.

The expansion of the manufacturing economy not only pulled peasants off the land and into the alien world of factory labor, it also displaced large numbers of Koreans from their home regions. Workers generally moved from the more populous south to the industrial north. Before 1937, private industry had to recruit its own labor, but the increasingly desperate situation in the Korean countryside simplified their task. With the outbreak of war in China, recruitment by the market alone could not meet industry's demands. After 1937, government labor conscription moved even larger numbers of Koreans all over the empire to fulfill the needs of war production.

GROWTH OF THE WORKING CLASS: 1933–43

Type of worker	1933 No. of workers	1943 No. of workers	1943 % workforce
Factory workers	99,400	390,000	22.3
Mine workers	70,700	280,000	16.0
Transportation workers	n/a	170,000	9.7
Construction workers	43,600	380,000	21.7
Miscellaneous workers	n/a	530,000	30.3

Statistics Source: 1933 Shokusan Bank Monthly Survey Report; 1943 Imperial Diet Summary Report; in Soon-Won Park (1999, p. 29). Table taken from: Michael Robinson (2007, p. 86).

The discriminatory nature of the colonial system guaranteed that Korean laborers worked in ethnically segregated workplaces and occupied the bottom of the labor hierarchy. Even on the shop floor, Koreans ranked lower than Japanese laborers and were paid accordingly. Before the war, only a small percentage of Koreans rose into leadership or technical roles, while Japanese dominated foreman positions as well as the skilled trades. The few Koreans who rose to management level occupied only middle levels of authority or clerical jobs. With the coming of the war and the draining away of Japanese personnel through military conscription, Koreans could advance to higher positions on the factory floor and in offices. Yet the trend came too late and produced too few Korean managers to make a difference in the postwar era.

THE GREAT DEPRESSION, TENANCY, AND RURAL MISERY

While government planners and Japanese and Korean businessmen anticipated the great possibilities of Manzhouguo's development, Korea's peasantry reeled from the effects of the global Depression after 1929. The 1920s had been relatively prosperous for rice farmers, even more so for landowners in the colony. Rice prices had slowly risen, and GGK programs to raise productivity levels succeeded in making more rice available for sale on the export market. Perversely, by the time of the Depression there was a glut of rice and a steep drop in prices that had already thrown the rural countryside into a recessionary spiral. This, and protectionist pressure from Japanese rice growers, exacerbated negative trends within the land-tenure system already apparent in the 1920s—rising rents, increased concentration of landownership, and higher rates of tenancy.

A rapid increase in the Korean population after 1920 combined with market forces to increase the rate of tenancy. Between 1910 and 1940 tenancy steadily rose, with a tremendous spike during the Great Depression and war years. Because of the intense pressure on available land resources, landowners raised rents almost at will, further increasing peasant distress. Large numbers of peasants were forced off the land in search of jobs as casual laborers, in the service sector, or in small urban factories. Motivated by economic need, this pool of labor became available for migration to the new industries in the north and opportunities in Manzhouguo.

Rural distress also generated a rise in the number of peasants engaged in slash-and-burn agriculture in Korea's numerous hills and mountains. In 1936, over 300,000 families lived by such marginal farming, a 300 percent increase from 1916. The GGK also recorded an increase in landowner–tenant disputes, from 667 in 1931 to 7,544 in 1934; a year later this number had tripled to 25,834. This forced the GGK to institute new tenancy and arbitration laws to provide relief for peasants caught in the spiral of rising rents.

In spite of the GGK's efforts to ameliorate the worsening conditions in the countryside, landownership concentration continued to increase, constituting one of Korea's worst problems after 1945. By the end of the war, the tenancy rate in Korea was 69.1 percent, but in some areas of the southwest Chŏlla provinces the rate approached 80 percent. With more absentee landownership, more peasants fell under the control of land agents whose income was linked to rent collection, a system that further depersonalized owner–tenant relations. Moreover, Japanese investment in land rose during the 1930s, swelling the numbers of large Japanese landowners. The majority of landlords, however, were Korean. As a class they were liable to the charge of collaboration, for they had done very well under colonialism.

NATIONALIST RESISTANCE

Nationalist resistance of both moderate and radical groups in Korea had continued sporadically during the late 1920s. The decade closed with two major demonstrations against Japanese power: the Kwangju Incident and the Wŏnsan General Strike of 1929. The Kwangju Incident started as a localized conflict between Korean and Japanese students in the provincial city of Kwangju. The local Sin'ganhoe (New Korea Society, see p. 276), aided by its national organization, stepped in to inspire a series of colony-wide demonstrations, and its role ultimately led to its demise in 1931. The Wŏnsan General Strike was the culmination of increasing labor unrest that had sputtered throughout the 1925–29 period. Again, the strike began as a local protest, this time against a brutal Japanese foreman at an English-owned oil company, but soon the Wŏnsan Federation of Labor had linked with other nationalist groups to create a general strike that gained material support from workers from all over Korea.

By the time of the Sin'ganhoe's demise in 1931, and coincidental with the seizure of Manchuria, Japanese policing in the colony had sharply reduced overt resistance. In the 1930s, the movement to resist Japanese rule by violence moved underground in the colony and in some cases connected with exiled nationalist and communist groups. In the early 1930s, Red Peasant Unions carried out a series of violent attacks against landlords and local police stations in the far northeastern Hamgyŏng province. Communist activists, who could easily infiltrate the northern villages from Manzhouguo, organized these unions clandestinely to generate some of the few instances of physical resistance in Korea during this period.

The exiled nationalist movement revived briefly after 1931. Japan's seizure of Manchuria made operations there more difficult, but Koreans both in Manzhouguo and in China Proper gained support from the Chinese Nationalist government and the CCP. Based in Shanghai, Kim Ku (1876–1949)—a conservative nationalist and, like Syngman Rhee (see p. 235), staunchly anti-communist—made a name for himself by staging a series of successful bombings and assassinations in China. Between 1930 and 1935, two leading nationalist parties emerged from among a number of Korean groups in Shanghai and Nanking. Cho Soang (1887–1958) and Kim Ku formed the Korean Independence Party (KIP), attempting to monopolize the legacy of the defunct Shanghai Provisional Government of a decade before. A more powerful group coalesced around the leftist Korean National Revolutionary Party headed by Kim Wŏnbong (1898–1958?). While these groups tried to unite, doctrinal and personal differences, exacerbated by fickle GMD support, led to failure.

By 1937, most Korean Communists working within the various nationalist parties in China had moved their operations to Yan'an and Manzhouguo. By then under direct attack by Japan, the Nanjing government had withdrawn most of its war effort to Sichuan and the west, so the CCP military forces in Manzhouguo and northern China provided the only organizations within which Korean activists could continue to fight against Japan.

The exiled nationalist movement continued in disarray through the wartime period. After 1937, Korean nationalists linked to the GMD solidified their position by reviving the Korean Independence Party, claiming to be the sole Korean government in exile, but their role in the larger war effort remained limited. In 1940, they received GMD support to build a Korean Restoration Army, which swelled to a force of 3,600 by 1943, but it languished in the GMD's "rear areas" and undertook only limited propaganda, intelligence, and guerrilla operations. Its main struggle was internal, its energies consumed by the effort to maintain a united front in the face of GMD demands for unity and allegiance. A fragmented alliance, the KIP National Council, reorganized in 1944, included leaders of the Korean National Revolutionary Party, the People's Liberation League, an anarchist, and others. Clearly opportunistic, and under pressure from the GMD, they never worked well together.

In the United States, several Korean independence organizations continued to provide support to long-standing activists like Syngman Rhee (Yi Sŭngman, 1875–1965) and An Ch'angho. The teenaged Syngman Rhee had been active in the Independence Club (1896–98) and had spent 35 years in exile. He had organized support groups in Hawaii and the mainland United States and in the 1920s had been named president of the first government in exile. In the mid- to late 1930s he continued a dogged campaign in Washington, DC, to obtain US State Department support for the Korean cause. After the attack at Pearl Harbor, Korean exile groups—mostly led by Syngman Rhee—increased pressure on the US government to grant American aid or recognition, but the war closed with no US commitment to support any Korean leader or organization.

THE ANTI-JAPANESE GUERRILLAS IN MANZHOUGUO, 1937–45

Manchuria had been a Korean problem for the Japanese long before they established Manzhouguo as a puppet regime. The geographical remoteness, rugged terrain, and large Korean community of the Korea–Manzhouguo frontier region made it a haven for anti-Japanese partisans. Consequently, the Japanese military found it difficult to control the rugged border along the Tumen River, with Hamgyŏng province in the far northeast being particularly vulnerable. Manchuria was also a stronghold of CCP guerrilla fighters, and during the early 1930s they brought most local Koreans under their party discipline. As economic conditions among the Chinese and Korean peasantry of Manzhouguo worsened in the 1930s, Communists made headway organizing at the village level to create mass organizations for popular education, cooperatives, and anti-Japanese resistance. The Japanese responded with programs that mirrored the new tenant–landlord arbitration regulations in Korea, and they organized a strategic hamlet system to isolate the peasantry from the active resistance fighters.

The CCP operations, however, were so effective that the Japanese had to organize a series of military encirclement campaigns (very similar to GMD tactics used against the Jiangxi Soviet in 1934) to destroy the guerrilla resistance. The Communists responded by centralizing military operations, folding 11 separate military units then operating in Manzhouguo into the Northeast Anti-Japanese United Army. Korean detachments within this army carried out a desperate and ultimately losing battle against the Japanese pacification campaigns.

One group, led by Kim Il Sung (1912–1994), the future "Great Leader" of North Korea, numbered between 50 and 300 men, and carried out a number of raids in Manchuria as well as Korea in the 1935–40 period. Kim's most publicized success was a raid on and occupation of the strategic town of Poch'ŏnbo in 1937. His partisans forced contributions from wealthy farmers, impressed peasants into the force, and endured the defection of leaders from the ranks. His successes singled him out as a special target for capture, and local Japanese forces enlisted defectors from Korean Communist ranks to help hunt him down. Ultimately, in early 1941, Kim crossed with his remaining followers into the Soviet Union and ended the war with other retreating Korean partisans in training camps in the Vladivostok area. There Kim's son, Kim Chong Il (Kim Jong Il, b. 1941)—North Korean leader after 1994—was born.

During the 1930s, the domestic nationalist movement was for the most part quiescent. The exiled nationalists in Nationalist China spent most of the decade squabbling over GMD financial support, and the propaganda activities in the United States were inconsequential. In this light the Manchurian guerrillas stand out, and it is upon this record of small but authentic successes against Japan that Kim Il Sung based his inflated claims to sole leadership of the anti-Japanese revolution. This became an important thread in the fabric of his personality cult after 1955.

COLONIAL MODERNITY, URBANIZATION, AND MASS CULTURE IN KOREA

The period between 1931 and the beginning of the China War was in some respects a high point for Japanese rule in Korea. They had firm political control, and the colony began to reap the economic benefits (for Japanese businessmen and selected Korean elites at least) of its new position within the empire. On the downside, political repression ruled the day, the situation in the countryside worsened, and the rural population suffered from landlessness and the beginning of what would be come the great labor migrations of the war years. In contrast, Korea's urban centers boomed. There, the swelling Japanese communities and new Korean middle class enjoyed the fruits of the modernization that could be traced to the precolonial era and the first penetration of global capitalism in the late nineteenth century. Seoul had begun to take on the trappings of a modern city—Western-style buildings, modern transportation, and a high-rise downtown. Both Seoul and, to a lesser extent, the great port city of Pusan in the south generated a modern, mass culture fueled by the consuming habits of the new middle class.

This modernity might properly be called colonial modernity. Having developed in tandem with imperialism and fixed within a colonial structure, it distributed the spoils and the privileges of modernity unevenly, on the basis of ethnic difference between colonizers and colonized. Japanese dominated the new modern sector of the economy. The large population of Japanese who lived and worked in Korea enhanced this split—by 1940 over 800,000 Japanese residents clustered in the urban centers—and the lifestyle of this large expatriate enclave defined modern living. Colonial bureaucrats, intellectuals, teachers, and businessmen, with their residential neighborhoods and the service economy that supported them, represented islands of Japanese modernity surrounded by a developing Korea. To enter Japanese enclaves was to enter a different cultural zone, making explicit colonial modernity's hybrid predicament. For socially and economically ambitious Koreans, working or playing in the modern sectors of Korea's new cities meant participating in a world dominated by Japanese culture. Colonial modernity privileged Japanese cultural and material influence in Korea and skewed its reception by Koreans as a consequence.

Modernity in Korea also contained elements of liberation within its cultural and intellectual matrix. Development created new occupations and introduced new avenues of mobility. Liberation from traditional ways did not necessarily make life easier, but movement to the cities, working in industrial settings, even leaving the country to seek employment in Manzhouguo or the metropole itself changed peoples' consciousness of life's possibilities. Even in colonial form, the expansion of the educational system brought literacy, new skills, and a widened consciousness to the hundreds of thousands of Koreans who had earlier had no access to even a rudimentary education.

MODERN WOMEN

Educating women was particularly revolutionary. The old taboo against women's learning had been broken at the turn of the century, and by the 1920s entire journals focused on the discourse of modern women. Educated young women challenged traditional roles by appearing in public wearing Western clothes and engaging in activities previously the monopoly of men. At least for middle-class women of the cities, the evolution of colonial modernity opened a new space, created new roles and styles, and defined rights for women. Finally, within the visual and aural representations of cinema and popular song, an entirely new dream world emerged that affected the imaginations of everyone from the poorest peasant to the scions of the wealthy new commercial class.

Modern Girls and Modern Boys, couples on an outing at the Ŭlmildae pavilion in Pyongyang, 1930.

NA HYESŎK

Na Hyesŏk. *Self-portrait*, c. 1920s

Na Hyesŏk (1896–1948) was one of Korea's first feminists. A tragic figure in modern Korean history, her life followed an arc from prominence as a brilliant example of talent and promise in artistic, literary, and political circles to end as an embarrassment to her family, ostracized from polite society, dying in anonymity and destitution in a mental asylum.

Born to a wealthy lineage whose ancestors included a number of high Chosŏn officials, Na had extraordinary educational opportunities because of her family's money and relative progressivism. After primary school, she attended the Chinmyŏng School, an institution prominent among girls' schools established after 1900. Graduating in 1915, she became one of the first women to study abroad, at the Tokyo Women's College of Arts. Her studies in Western oil painting became a sideline activity, for she joined the Bluestocking Society, led by Hiratsuka Raichō (see p. 222). In 1915 she fell in love and had an affair in Tokyo, earning her the ire of her family, who recalled her to Korea.

Eventually she returned to Tokyo, but her student career was eclipsed by her literary activity and her involvement with groups advocating women's rights. Her first publications had appeared in *Light of Korea* in 1913, and she became known for her fiction. Her short story "Kyŏnghŭi," published in *Women's World* (1918), is now cited as the first example of feminist fiction in the modern Korean literary canon. Na also joined the Korean independence movement. Along with major leaders in the Korean women's movement, Kim Maria and Pak Indŏk, she organized women to participate in the March First Movement, for which she was arrested and served a five-month prison term in 1920.

No moderate woman reformer, Na Hyesŏk lived according to her belief in freedom and agency for women in all affairs, so in both words and actions she frankly attacked the sexual double standard in Korea. Her family connections provided her with connections to the upper rungs of Korean society, but her personal behavior challenged the deep conservatism that lurked below the still superficial concessions to modern style and behavior in interwar Korea. Well married to a rising star within the colonial bureaucracy who ultimately served as consul in Manzhouguo, she had the extraordinary opportunity to accompany her husband on an extended tour of Europe and the United States.

In 1923, she broke off her travels to spend a year in Paris to further her art training. At this time she conducted a well-publicized and scandalous affair with a prominent moderate nationalist activist, Ch'oe Rin (1878–?). Divorced as a consequence and estranged from her children, who were taken by her husband's lineage, Na spent the balance of her active life as a freelance journalist and literary/art critic. Of her publications during this period, most notable was a powerful, self-revelatory, serialized article, "Confessions on My Divorce" (1934). In this "confession" she attacked male hypocrisy, named names, and generally excoriated the behavior of the Korean elite, for which she was ostracized from polite society.

In the last decade of her life, Na lived on the charity of a dwindling circle of friends and became involved with Buddhism. Tragically, she died anonymously in 1948 in a mental hospital. In recent decades, Na's career and literary oeuvre have been resurrected along with a new interest in the history of women's activism in Korea. Her story is emblematic of the struggles of women for a place in modern Korean society.

Perhaps no development was more emblematic of the changes wrought in Korea than the changing position of women in society. This phenomenon can be traced to the early nationalist reform movements of the 1890s. As in Meiji-period Japan and late Qing China, nationalists emphasized elevating the position of women. In Korea, the Christian churches brought men and women together for public worship; established schools for women; and encouraged the organization of women's groups devoted to practical reform issues.

Women had participated in the early nationalist movement, and their patriotic associations had been instrumental in the movement to repay the national debt and other nationalist projects at the end of the Chosŏn period. As in Japan and China (see pp. 220–22, 228–30, 253–55), the larger national struggle quickly absorbed these early women's activities, thus linking women's liberation with national liberation. Korean modernists made educating women a particularly important national goal, and by all measures it succeeded. Long before the 1930s, uniformed girls commuting to schools in Korean cities had become a common sight.

By the 1930s, the women's movement had split between a smaller, more radical feminist movement and the majority, who urged moderate reforms focused on education and enlightenment of Korea's women. The more radical feminism failed to take hold in part because the goals of the more conservative women's groups coincided with formal colonial programs to educate a new generation of wives and mothers in scientific methods of child rearing, hygiene, nutrition and food preparation, and other womanly arts. Women's education changed only the content and not the social role of women in Korean society. After all, colonial policy supported the raising of a new generation of strong and healthy *colonial subjects*. The less radical, mainstream women's movement aimed to create better mothers for Korea's children. This conformed to the role of modern women—urban middle-class women, at least—as the most important consumers in the expanding commodity markets. Women's journals and newspapers frequently published articles on managing the household budget and making the right consumption decisions.

But while a more radical idea of female liberation may have been subordinated to a reformist agenda within the mainstream women's movement, or, in the case of the socialist women's movement, taken a back seat to the goal of class liberation, women leaders in general promoted antitraditional life choices with their own behaviors. Many leaders in the women's movement chose to remain single, cut their hair short, refused to follow restrictive clothing traditions, and became public figures. In the 1920s and 1930s these radical choices drew social disapprobation, even ostracism. This happened to Na Hyesŏk (see box opposite), feminist, writer, and painter, who was much in the public eye in the 1920s. But as a very public figure, Na's unconventional lifestyle and outspoken commitment to female autonomy made her a target of the conventional press and an object of scorn and gossip.

Finally, the rise of women entertainers in the public spotlight of the new mass culture decisively changed perceptions about women's roles in society and broadened the spectrum of possible action and identity. During the 1920s and 1930s, the "Modern Girl" appeared, a reflection and further development of her Japanese counterpart. Cruising the streets of the modern city in the latest Western fashions, the Modern Girl became a symbol of change and an inspiration to young girls. And the popular press covered the phenomenon and milked it for its sensational and prurient content to boost circulation.

Of course, only a few women could afford such display, but to see and be seen in the new department stores, tearooms, or at the public cinema or theater challenged hundreds of years of custom that restricted women to the home precincts. The voices of women announcers on Korean radio, the songs of female entertainers (K. *kisaeng*) heretofore unheard in public, the images of Korean actresses in the cinema, and the pictures, records, and news stories of the first generation of Korean popular song stars all created a different world of images, roles, and imagined possibilities for Korean women. Nor did this happen only in Seoul. By the 1930s, Seoul participated in the burgeoning mass, modern culture that flourished in the great urban centers of Japan and the modern sectors of the great cities of China, such as Shanghai, Guangzhou, and Hong Kong.

FORCED ASSIMILATION AND WAR MOBILIZATION

The events of the last colonial decade, 1935–45, have dominated the postwar memory of colonialism in

Korea and in East Asia generally. Japan's new intrusion on the continent began with the seizure of Manchuria and extended to the war with China after 1937, ending with the catastrophic Pacific War. This memory still informs and complicates the relationships among Korea, China, and Japan. The unique blend of selective overdevelopment—industrialization of the colony—and worsening conditions in the countryside had already destabilized the Korean population. The war, however, accelerated the movement of people from the populous south to jobs in the north and factories in Manzhouguo and Japan. By war's end, fully 11 percent of the Korean population had been dislocated abroad or internally from the south to the industrialized areas of the north. Against this backdrop of instability, Japan intensified its campaigns to force Korean assimilation under the slogan, "Japan and Korea as One."

The increased emphasis on cultural assimilation might be dated from Governor-General Ugaki's order of January 1935 requiring Korean attendance at Shintō shrines on all occasions of national importance, a regulation including all school students and members of Japanese organizations (official and private). Such "forced worship" deeply offended all Koreans, but they precipitated a particular crisis within the large Korean Christian communities. Each church had to decide whether to obey or defy the order as a religious matter; some refused, others found ways to comply. The GGK only applied real pressure for compliance after the outbreak of war in 1937. Between 1935 and 1940, the Japanese closed 200 churches, revoked the charters of all Presbyterian schools, and arrested 2,000 Christians who continued to resist shrine attendance or other colonial duties on religious grounds.

The new GG, Minami Jirō (1874–1955), ordered recitation of the "Oath as Subjects of the Imperial Nation" at all public gatherings and at the beginning of each school day for students, inaugurating the formal Movement to Create Imperial Citizens in October 1937. A former commander of the Kantōgun, a major power within the Japanese high command, and

The Chōsen Shrine on Namsam in Seoul, 1930s.

a leading member of the dominant Control faction within the Japanese military, Minami brought a harder line to the colony. By 1937 Saitō's and Ugaki's relatively "soft" approach to assimilation was a memory, amid preparations for total war.

Language represented another important element of assimilation. Japanese had become the "national language" (J. *kokugo*) of the peninsula in 1910, but its spread remained tied to the public education system and voluntary use until the 1930s. Ambitious Koreans learned Japanese as a skill to gain entry to good jobs in the modern sector, and a high percentage of intellectuals were fluent in Japanese. In 1938, however, Japanese became the language of instruction for all subjects in the colonial schools, and Korean language study was formally removed from the curriculum in 1942. In the same year, the GGK arrested the entire leadership of the Korean Language Movement and seized the manuscript of the comprehensive Korean dictionary they had been preparing, then nearing completion.

Unlike Japan's language policies in Taiwan, formal Japanese outreach programs in Korea began only in 1938, and the movement to establish a registry of "National Language Families" that had been very successful in Taiwan failed in Korea. In 1944, even by the overly optimistic GGK estimates, barely 12 percent of the Korean population had functional Japanese. The corollary to forced use of Japanese was censorship of the printed word. Censorship of all Korean publications increased with the coming of the war; by 1940 the GGK had closed the independent Korean-run daily newspapers and many of the monthly journals.

Perhaps most galling, in November 1939 the GGK ordered all Korean names changed to Japanese names, a program formally called "changing family names." Ostensibly part of the reform of the Household Registration Law, the new regulations brought colonial practice in line with Japanese norms regarding head of household, registration of births and deaths, and family law in general. Within the six-month deadline established in February 1940, over 3.17 million households, or 75 percent of the population, had registered new names. This policy struck at the most personal and perhaps the most cherished source of Korean identity. The heartrending spectacle of family heads abandoning ancient names became a daily event at the local registry offices, and the memory of this policy lives on in novels, short stories, and memoirs.

Gradually the logic of assimilation worked to open the way for Korean participation, at first voluntary and later compulsory, in military service. From 1934 Korean volunteers had been selectively admitted to the military; the new Manchurian Military Academy (1937) trained imperial subjects for the officer corps. But with the outbreak of the Pacific War in 1941 standards were changed to receive more Koreans, and by 1943 the GGK instituted general conscription for the military and labor service. Most Korean conscripts ended up in non-combatant roles, over 200,000 in the army and 20,000 in the imperial navy.

Increasing demands for labor and military personnel anticipated the full-scale mobilization of the colony. No part of society was left untouched in the search for labor and resources—financial and otherwise—to support the war. In 1940, the Japanese organized the entire population into 350,000 Neighborhood Patriotic Associations, each consisting of ten mutually responsible households. These constituted the basic units for a variety of government programs for extracting labor, forced contributions in cash or materials (precious metals, etc.), rice "donations," internal security, and rationing. Professionals were mobilized into "All Korea Leagues" of artists, writers, journalists, filmmakers, actors, musicians—in short, centralized organizations of all identifiable occupational or interest groups. Cultural organizations sponsored patriotic contests of all sorts: song writing, short stories, art fairs, and poster art. Famous Korean writers, intellectuals, businessmen, and the socially prominent were cajoled or forced to give patriotic speeches urging Koreans to "give the ultimate sacrifice" in prosecution of the war.

COMFORT WOMEN AND THE END OF JAPANESE RULE

Of all the cruelties and injustices suffered during the wartime mobilization, perhaps none was more appalling than the systematic recruitment of Korean women to work in Japanese military sex stations (see p. 288). While the exact number will probably never be known, between 150,000 and 200,000 women, 80 percent of

An American soldier took this photograph in the Philippines in 1944. It is believed to show a group of Korean comfort women dressed in traditional Japanese costume in the third row. Comfort women, who were under strict orders not to speak their own language in public, were sometimes made to wear traditional Japanese costumes and sing Japanese songs for the soldiers.

them Korean, were recruited either by deception or force into units euphemistically termed the "comfort corps." These unfortunate women found themselves attached to garrisons in the far-flung Japanese military, from northern China to as far away as Indonesia, where they endured servicing the sexual needs of Japanese soldiers and officers. Under such horrible conditions many of the women died, some were disfigured and rendered infertile, and most were abandoned in their camps abroad after the war. Those who managed to return to Korea came home to lives forever altered by the experience.

In summary, the last years of Japanese rule were certainly horrific for Korea, distorted under the weight of the war mobilization and political repression. With almost any act defined as a crime against the state, from linguistic scholarship to sabotage, the prisons of the colony overflowed with political prisoners. By modest estimates, millions of Koreans had been uprooted from their homes and sent to work abroad or in the northern provinces. Households buried their rice to prevent its seizure, and families sent their sons into hiding in the countryside to avoid conscription. War-related shortages made life unbearable; the state rationed dwindling food supplies, melted down personal effects for war production, and apparently even destroyed every film print it could gather—the entire creative product of the early Korean film industry—to extract its silver. Korean-language publications all but disappeared.

Under these conditions, it came as no surprise that the announcement of the Japanese surrender on August 15, 1945 was greeted with public demonstrations of joy and relief. Unfortunately, things did not improve with the departure of the Japanese. Thirty-five years of colonialism left Korean society without leaders and riven with internal conflict and instability. And to compound this instability, Korea found itself occupied by the two future superpowers of the post-World War II era—hardly auspicious conditions in which to build a national future.

DIASPORAS

JAPAN

The "new paradise" of Manzhouguo lured some 380,000 Japanese farming immigrants between 1932

and 1945. Japan's agrarianist ideologues of the early 1930s proposed massive Japanese migration—5 million settlers—to Manzhouguo to relieve overpopulation at home. The Kantōgun joined the call for Japanese settlement to build the new state economically and strategically. Some scholars opposed migration, refuting the notion that Manchuria was unoccupied and asserting that Japanese farmers were unprepared for Manchurian conditions. They lost the debate, although the Kantōgun's dream of sending 5 million also never materialized.

Tales of migrants fighting bandits, overcoming natural disasters, and settling their families inspired poor Japanese. Village leaders used the "Community Emigration Program" to encourage families to migrate, praising the racial harmony (J. *minzoku kyōwa*) to be fostered among the Japanese, Chinese, and Koreans in Manzhouguo. In reality, the land settled by the Japanese was taken from its owners through forced sales at extortionate prices—hardly racially harmonious. When too few families migrated to Manzhouguo, colonial agencies began to promote Youth Brigades in 1938, recruiting young men, aged 13 to 16, to be settlers. But many youth became depressed and homesick and targeted their Chinese and Korean neighbors for violence. In 1939, Japan's colonial authorities began recruiting Japanese girls to be "continental brides" for these boys. The Youth Brigades and their brides accounted for a third of all Japanese migrants to Manzhouguo.

The military later conscripted both adult male migrants and Youth Brigade boys, leaving their women and children behind to be killed by the Soviets in August 1945. Kantōgun troops seized available transportation for themselves, abandoning women and children to rape, slaughter, and starvation. Despite the failure of Japanese settlers to promote "racial harmony," some 30,000 Japanese children survived because their mothers left them with kindly Chinese neighbors. Raised as Chinese, many attempted to find their Japanese families only after diplomatic relations resumed in the 1970s (see p. 379).

Japanese in North America also suffered tragically during the war. Executive Order 9066 (February 19, 1942) continued the United States' history of racial discrimination, placing 110,000 Japanese and Americans of Japanese ancestry in concentration camps until 1945–46. The US government also rounded up

2,264 Latin Americans (mostly Peruvians) of Japanese descent and shipped them to US camps. Canada incarcerated 22,000 Japanese Canadians. Both the US and Canadian governments apologized and granted reparations in 1988.

CHINA

Chinese men had come to the United States in the nineteenth century to work on railroads, in mines, and on farms. In 1880, only 22 percent of Chinese residents lived in US cities. By 1940, this had been reversed, and the census classified 91 percent of the Chinese as "urban." They worked overwhelmingly in restaurants, laundries, and retail shops. US law excluded Chinese women, and Chinese could not become citizens, so their communities remained sojourning bachelor establishments. One wrote, "If we were allowed [to become citizens]…I think many of us Chinese would not think so much of going back to China."[4] Racism kept them both physically and psychologically confined in Chinatowns. Any white person could call them "Chink!" or throw stones at them if they strayed beyond Chinatown's well-known borders.

By 1930, however, women had begun to trickle into Chinatowns, producing sons and daughters determined to become Americans. Their public schools pushed them to speak only English, to reject their "heathen, non-Christian" Chinese culture, while their parents sent them to Chinese school in the evenings and on Saturdays. Despite their parents' first-generation nostalgia, the second generation rarely became literate in Chinese—"After all, weren't we Americans?"[5]

Japanese aggression in China during the 1930s stimulated a strong nationalistic reaction from diasporic Chinese, who donated generously to the GMD and other homeland institutions. After Pearl Harbor, Chinese suddenly became "the good Asians," America's allies against "the Japs." Like Filipinos and Koreans in the United States, they discovered new wartime employment, finally escaping from the laundry and restaurant into the factory and office building. Over 13,000 Chinese men enlisted or were drafted into the US armed forces. In 1943, at FDR's request, Congress repealed the Chinese exclusion acts and allowed Chinese to become naturalized citizens.

In Malaya, the Japanese invasion of 1942 enabled an upper stratum of Malays to join the ranks of officialdom, which the British had not allowed. Many Malayan Chinese, in strong contrast, resisted Japanese colonialism with violence, joining the Communist-led "Malayan People's Anti-Japanese Army." Ong Boon Hwa (aka Chin Peng, b. 1922) received British decorations for successes against Japan, but became a tenacious opponent of British colonialism after the war.

KOREA'S POPULATION HEMORRHAGE

In the second half of the colonial period, Japan's advance into Asia and continuous warfare after 1937 uprooted much of Korea's population. Although some population movement was temporary, hundreds of thousands of Koreans pushed hither and yon by the migration of labor from south to north and from Korea to Manchuria, Japan, and beyond found themselves stranded or chose to stay elsewhere and make new lives in distant lands after 1945.

The pace of labor migration from the countryside to cities and new factories in the north accelerated in the 1930s, a movement spurred by rural distress as well as opportunities for jobs in the industrial northeast. Throughout this period, labor also migrated to Japan proper. Particularly after 1937, Japan's labor supply decreased because of the drain of manpower to the armed forces. Korean labor filled much of the shortfall, particularly at the low end of the labor hierarchy—mines, construction, and day labor. Of more than 400,000 laborers who migrated to Japan between 1921 and 1931, 90 percent came from agricultural households. This migration spilled over into Manzhouguo, boosting the Korean population there to 1.45 million by 1940. And within Korea, there was a net movement of people from the southern provinces to the north.

By 1944, almost 11 percent of all Koreans resided outside the homeland. This rough figure included 1.6 million Koreans in Manchuria, 1.8 million in Japan proper (1943), and smaller numbers in China, Mongolia, Central Asia, and Southeast Asia. This outflow of people reached its extreme during the 1940–45 period, and with the end of the war an enormous reverse migration ensued. However, not all Koreans returned home. Many died abroad, most notably thousands of forced sex slaves of the Japanese military and at least 30,000 who perished in the nuclear bombings of Hiroshima and Nagasaki. After 1945, more than half of the Koreans in Japan repatriated to either the northern or southern zone of occupation, but this still left 600,000 Koreans to form the largest minority population in Japan.

Many Koreans never returned home, stranded in Manzhouguo or China Proper. Some 50,000 Koreans who worked in the coalmines of Sakhalin remained in the Soviet-occupied portion of the island; they became permanent residents, their return home blocked by the Cold War. Perhaps the strangest "forced diaspora" of the 1931–45 period was the deportation of 75,000 Koreans from the Soviet Far East to Central Asia, where they became the core of flourishing Korean communities in Uzbekistan and Kazakhstan. In sum, the war violently churned the Korean population, resulting in considerable domestic instability after 1945 and the permanent resettlement of perhaps a million Koreans in Manchuria, the Soviet Union, and Japan.

CONNECTIONS

The Great Depression hit East Asians hard, especially people working in rural export sectors—silk, cotton, rice. Economic privation caused by international market forces encouraged many people to consider autarky, detaching their country and economy from events out of their control and becoming entirely self-sufficient. Some Japanese nationalists took the Depression as a call to return to traditional virtues, to an idealized rural harmony unperturbed by the schemes of foreigners or the chaotic modernity of cities. They wanted the emperor to take charge and the empire to supply all of Japan's needs. Taking over the territory and rich natural resources—coal, iron, hydroelectric power, rubber, cotton, and tungsten—of Korea, then Manchuria, then China and Southeast Asia, they wished to move toward self-sufficiency as an industrial power.

To hold the empire together, the Japanese navy and merchant marine had to transport armies and products over increasingly long and vulnerable sea-lanes. To protect its territories, the army needed trucks, tanks, and aircraft. But East Asia does not possess major reserves of petroleum, essential as fuel on both land and sea, so Japan continued to import most of its oil from the United States. In the late 1930s, allied with Nazi Germany and Fascist Italy, Japan tried to take on the land-based might of the USSR—the Red Army's tanks—and failed. Only by expanding southward, to the Dutch East Indies,

could the Japanese empire truly be self-sufficient, and that meant direct confrontation with the United States. A preemptive strike on the US fleet might, in the minds of some Japanese planners, have forced the United States to recognize Japan's predominant position in the western Pacific. That did not happen, and World War II destroyed the Japanese empire.

In another version of autarky, the CCP's rural bases, the headquarters at Yan'an and over a dozen more, fought the Japanese invaders through guerrilla warfare. Taking supplies and recruits from the local population, the Communist fighters earned a reputation for frugality, honesty, and courage that the GMD, stuck behind an immobile front in the far west, could not match. Connected to the USSR only tenuously, especially after Hitler's invasion (1940) kept Stalin completely occupied in the west, the CCP could claim the mantle of nationalism over the GMD, which remained dependent on the United States even for its printed currency.

Koreans fought on all sides in the wars of 1937–45. In Manzhouguo and North China, the CCP enlisted and trained Korean fighters, with some similar units (including Kim Il Sung's) supported by the USSR. In Chongqing, the GMD sustained and constrained the Korean Restoration Army, using its symbolic value but giving its fighters little to do. On the Korean peninsula itself, the GGK and Japanese military conscripted millions of Koreans—men for military or labor service, women for sexual slavery—during the war. Some Koreans became officers in the Imperial Army—Park Chung Hee (Pak Chŏnghŭi, 1917–1979), later president of South Korea, served as a second lieutenant in Manchuria after attending a prestigious military academy in Japan (see p. 385). As noted above, by the end of the war more than 11 percent of the Korean population lived outside Korea, forming crucial connections, both positive and negative, between their homeland and the rest of East Asia.

All of the wartime economies of East Asia, even those on opposite sides of the battle lines, remained closely linked through the opium trade that plagued China. In the 1930s, the Mitsubishi and Mitsui *zaibatsu* imported opium from Iran into Manzhouguo for distribution throughout North China. After 1938, Japan's occupation armies and puppet regimes encouraged local production, including heroin and morphine as well as opium paste. The Reformed Republican

Government, one of Japan's puppets, licensed a "traditional philanthropy," the Hongji Benevolent Society, to handle the drugs, dealing as far as Jiang Jieshi's capital of Chongqing. Koreans sometimes played crucial roles as transporters, brokers, or muscle for the drug trade. Many CCP cadres and soldiers, including General Zhu De, had been opium addicts, and even the CCP, which has maintained an opium-free image, engaged in the export of opium from Yan'an to GMD- and Japan-held areas.

The leaders of the Japanese empire, which reached its height between 1938 and 1942, tried to replace European and American colonialism with the Greater East Asia Co-Prosperity Sphere, asserting that its benevolent rule suited Asians better than that of the whites. Welcomed by some—Wang Jingwei and other Chinese fed up with Jiang Jieshi, Korean businessmen who welcomed order, Sukarno in Indonesia, anti-British Indian radical Subhas Chandra Bose—the war-oriented, exploitative Japanese occupations nonetheless served the metropole alone, alienating most conquered populations before 1945.

East Asians have produced an important discussion on the meaning of "collaboration"—to what extent may Koreans, Chinese, and other conquered people be blamed for cooperating with, or even working for, their conquerors? To what extent were "the Japanese people"—as distinguished from their leaders and the armies that fought in their name—responsible for the war? Postwar regimes, sometimes in formal tribunals, judged both Japanese leaders and some of their Korean and Chinese allies to hold primary responsibility for the war's horrors, but as we will see below, in all three countries those judgments did not end the story. World War II, Japanese colonialism, local collaboration, and leadership of the states that emerged after the war remain vibrant, living, painful issues for Chinese, Koreans, and Japanese.

All of East Asia experienced, to unimaginable levels, the suffering of ordinary people in wartime. From the millions killed or wounded in combat to villagers killed for being at home, from kidnapped sexual slaves called "comfort women" to women raped and murdered, from brutalized teenage soldiers to elderly victims of American bombing—World War II in East Asia was total war. Some people profited through smuggling, weapons production, or corruption, but far more found themselves impoverished, their land and crops devastated, their businesses bankrupt, their homes destroyed. With such dangers so close, most people thought only for themselves and their families, and society grew distorted and callous. Only rarely could anyone imagine the humanity of other peoples, much less the enemy—a constraint that continues to plague East Asia today.

CHAPTER TEN

OCCUPATIONS, SETTLEMENTS, AND DIVISIONS (1945–1953)

WORLD CONTEXT

Fractured by World War II, the world redivided with the coming of peace. In place of the Axis vs. the Allies, the Cold War pitted the Communist bloc led by the USSR against the "free world" (called capitalists, imperialists, and hegemonists by the Soviets), with the United States more or less in command. Some "non-aligned" nations tried to avoid taking sides, but they, too, often found themselves caught up in confrontational politics and proxy wars. Initially the sole atomic power, by the late 1940s the United States was locked into nuclear rivalry with the USSR.

To frustrate what he saw as Soviet expansionism, and to expand US influence, President Truman articulated the policy of *containment*, aiding friendly governments threatened by "communist subversion" (or domestic revolution) to surround the USSR with US allies. Under the European Recovery Program, called the Marshall Plan after General George Marshall (1880–1959), its originator, American economic assistance helped revive the economies and military capacities of Western Europe to prevent any further expansion of Soviet influence there.

To the same end, the United States founded the North Atlantic Treaty Organization (NATO) in 1949, a collective defense arrangement originally including 12 countries.[1] Its objectives, according to its first secretary-general (a British military officer), were: "to keep the Russians out, the Americans in, and the Germans down."

The containment doctrine, first proposed for Greece and Turkey, rapidly grew to include a circle of East and Southeast Asian countries surrounding the USSR on the east. Hoping that China would form part of that containment perimeter, the United States successfully argued that the Republic of China deserved a major power's permanent seat (and veto) on the Security Council of the newly established United Nations (1945–46). Cold War rivalry divided some countries into Soviet and American zones of influence, a fate that befell defeated Germany, liberated Korea, China, and Vietnam. Of those, only Germany escaped civil war, though it often threatened as West Germany joined NATO in 1952 and East Germany became a dependable, belligerent Soviet ally.

Since the nineteenth century, many forms of radical politics—communism, socialism, anarchism, trade unionism, and pacifism—had been repressed in the United States but persisted in institutions like the American Federation of Labor (1886), the Congress of Industrial Organizations (1932), and the Socialist Party of America. The Communist Party of the United States, founded in 1919, participated actively in racial and labor politics in the face of severe repression as an agent of foreign subversion.

With the Cold War, a new wave of anticommunism, sometimes called the Second Red Scare, swept the United States. The convictions of Klaus Fuchs, Ethel and Julius Rosenberg, and Alger Hiss as Soviet spies; the Soviet blockade of West Berlin (1948–49); CCP victory in China; and the beginning of the Korean War persuaded many Americans that their country was besieged,

infiltrated by enemy agents, and in danger of succumbing to Soviet power and "going communist." Riding this wave, anticommunist crusaders such as the House Committee on Un-American Activities (HUAC), Senator Joseph McCarthy, and J. Edgar Hoover (head of the FBI) accused numerous Americans of disloyalty, even treason. They especially targeted intellectuals, artists, Hollywood actors and filmmakers, African American leaders, and homosexuals. Tens of thousands of "suspected communists" lost their jobs, and hundreds were imprisoned in an atmosphere of hysterical, irrational paranoia. US policy in East Asia must be understood in light of this political condition.

East Asia, c. 1945–54

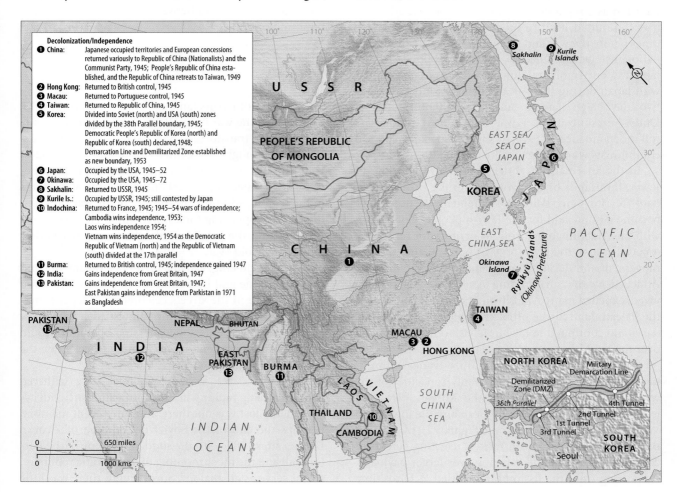

Decolonization/Independence

❶ China: Japanese occupied territories and European concessions returned variously to Republic of China (Nationalists) and the Communist Party, 1945; People's Republic of China established, and the Republic of China retreats to Taiwan, 1949

❷ Hong Kong: Returned to British control, 1945
❸ Macau: Returned to Portuguese control, 1945
❹ Taiwan: Returned to Republic of China, 1945
❺ Korea: Divided into Soviet (north) and USA (south) zones divided by the 38th Parallel boundary, 1945; Democratic People's Republic of Korea (north) and Republic of Korea (south) declared, 1948; Demarcation Line and Demilitarized Zone established as new boundary, 1953

❻ Japan: Occupied by the USA, 1945–52
❼ Okinawa: Occupied by the USA, 1945–72
❽ Sakhalin: Returned to USSR, 1945
❾ Kurile Is.: Occupied by USSR, 1945; still contested by Japan
❿ Indochina: Returned to France, 1945; 1945–54 wars of independence; Cambodia wins independence, 1953; Laos wins independence 1954; Vietnam wins independence, 1954 as the Democratic Republic of Vietnam (north) and the Republic of Vietnam (south) divided at the 17th parallel

⓫ Burma: Returned to British control, 1945; independence gained 1947
⓬ India: Gains independence from Great Britain, 1947
⓭ Pakistan: Gains independence from Great Britain, 1947; East Pakistan gains independence from Parkistan in 1971 as Bangladesh

Apart from the Cold War, World War II's aftermath included a fatal weakening of colonial empires and consequent independence for former colonies. The defeated Japanese and Germans lost their overseas dominions, but the victorious British, French, and Americans also came under increasing pressure—primarily from nationalists inside the colonies—to take their armies and administrations home. The French had to cope with uprisings in Madagascar, Algeria, and Southeast Asia, where communists and nationalists under Ho Chi Minh fought a successful eight-year war to force France out.

Led by Gandhi and his colleagues in the Indian National Congress, Indian nationalists undertook a campaign of non-violent resistance against the British that created an independent India by 1947, the triumph muted by the horrors of Partition and the emergence of Pakistan as a separate Muslim state. The United States had committed itself to independence for the Philippines before the war and granted it in 1946. Indonesian nationalist leader Sukarno, who had hoped for the Japanese ouster of the Dutch from Java, collaborated with Japan during the war and declared independence two days after Japan's surrender. Fighting against Dutch recolonization, a war that gained Indonesia's full independence in 1949, Sukarno also executed local communists who challenged his leadership.

In the aftermath of Hitler's slaughter of European Jewry, thousands of survivors fled to the British Mandate Territory in Palestine, intended eventually to become a homeland for the Jewish people. Competing with the Arab inhabitants of the territory for resources, especially land, the Jews forged a political and military movement and declared an independent state in 1948. Attacked by the surrounding Arab states, Israel survived, expelled many Arabs from its territory—creating the Palestinian refugee problem, which persists to this day—and continued to take in Jewish refugees from all over the world.

With so much warfare going on, advances in military technology increased the deadly capacities of the world's armies. Both sides in the Korean War used jet aircraft, first developed in Germany during World War II and capable of supersonic flight by 1947. Missiles continued to improve, with rockets reaching heights of 250 miles (402 km) and carrying ever-larger payloads. Advancing from the fission bombs used at Hiroshima and Nagasaki, first American and then Soviet scientists succeeded in creating fusion (hydrogen) bombs of far greater explosive power—a relatively small fusion bomb is equivalent to all of the conventional explosives used in World War II. Using American technology, Great Britain also succeeded in building an atomic bomb (1952).

In more peaceful innovation, electron microscopy (1949) enabled scientists to explore nanospace. Chemists and doctors built rapidly on the successes of interwar science to develop a wide array of new drugs, including antibiotics such as aureomycin (1948), cortisone (1949), meprobromate tranquilizers and antihistamines (1950), and chemical contraceptives (1952). Dr. Jonas Salk began vaccinating children against polio (1954), Edmund Hillary and Tenzing Norgay climbed Mount Everest (1953), and, for the first time, scientists reported a connection between lung cancer and cigarette smoking.

KOREA

The emperor of Japan's famous broadcast on August 15, 1945, ended the war in the Pacific and began a cascade of events that transformed East Asia in only a few years. War's end brought the United States into East Asia as victor and occupier, and over the next 50 years it became key arbiter of political and economic alignments in the region. Additionally, the end of the war presaged the clash of opposing forces that would cleave not just East Asia but the entire world—the forces that underpinned the Cold War.

At first rejoicing, Japan's surrender meant the end of colonial rule and liberation for Korea. By afternoon Koreans were in the streets celebrating independence, though probably few had the faintest idea what new political arrangements and leadership liberation would bring. For the moment, it was enough to celebrate the end of the colonial nightmare.

The formidable Japanese colonial state withered with surprising rapidity in the month after surrender—it suddenly just was not there. In more recent memory, perhaps the end of the Soviet domination of Eastern Europe after 1989, with the sudden toppling of the Berlin Wall and the mushrooming of democratic republics, might serve as an analogy. Surprisingly, there was little personal violence toward the former colonial masters. In a few months, almost 1 million Japanese residents were speedily, if chaotically, repatriated. Some Koreans who had been part of the colonial police force did suffer reprisals, and some of the Shintō shrines that dotted the landscape were burned and ransacked. But while the first months after liberation were relatively peaceful, they were only a lull before what would become a political hurricane.

This storm fed on a legacy of political, economic, and social problems resulting from 40 years of Japanese rule, which had created deep divisions within Korean society. Most notably, its support of the landed class and its economic policies had led to massive tenancy and, as a result, an explosive potential for rural class conflict awaited liberation. Active and passive complicity with the colonial state by many Koreans—especially educated urbanites—compromised as "collaborators" a significant portion of Korea's elites. The evaporation of the Japanese empire left a power vacuum in Korea, bitterly contested by numerous pretenders to national leadership.

Finally, the vast mobilization of Korean society for the Japanese war effort had churned the population and drawn millions of Koreans away from their homes: to factories and mines abroad, as conscripts for military and labor service in the far-flung Japanese army, or from the agricultural south to the newly industrial north. Politically mobilized by their extraordinary experiences abroad, many returned to find their land untilled or occupied by new tenants. Great numbers collected in the cities to seek casual employment or handouts at the soup kitchens organized to feed the homeless. This huge movement of people added greatly to the political and social instability of postwar Korea, particularly in the more densely populated south.

Korea lacked a unified nationalist movement or a clearly transcendent leader who might have unified the broad spectrum of contending political forces and negotiated with the defeated Japanese and victorious Allied powers. On the contrary, colonial rule had left a legacy of political factionalism. This opened the way for numerous segments of the nationalist movement, representing political views from extreme left to extreme right, to compete for leadership.

Members of the coalition nationalist government in exile—including the rightist Kim Ku and leftist Kim Wŏnbong—returned from China. Newly organized as the Korean Provisional Government (KPG), they were accompanied by elements of the Korean Restoration Army. Syngman Rhee (see p. 307) came home from the United States without a domestic political base, basing his legitimacy on name recognition and a 40-year record as exile leader. On the left, Pak Hŏnyŏng (?–1955), leader of the domestic Korean Communist Party, was one of 30,000 prisoners released after August 1945.

In the north, Kim Il Sung, who had led one of the Korean guerrilla groups based in Manzhouguo, returned sometime in September 1945. In the political middle, well-known nationalist figures such as Song Chinu (1889–1945), Yŏ Unhyŏng (1885–1947, see p. 322), and Cho Mansik (1883–1950) could have become leaders of a united Korean nation. In the first years after liberation these men contended for control of Korean politics in an atmosphere of brutal struggle, recrimination, and even assassination, their domestic conflict compounded by foreign occupation; the United States in the south and USSR in the north. Both Kim Ku and Yŏ Unhyŏng died from assassins' bullets, while Cho Mansik and Pak Hŏnyŏng disappeared in the north, purged after the Korean War.

JAPANESE SURRENDER, THE CPKI, AND THE KOREAN PEOPLE'S REPUBLIC

Governor-General Abe (Nobuyuki, see p. 289) had only a week's notice of the home government's decision to surrender. He immediately sought out moderate Korean leaders to act as conduits for the transfer of power. He first approached Song Chinu, a prominent moderate nationalist leader not compromised by collaboration. Fearing that working with the Japanese would damage his political future, Song refused. On the morning of August 15, Abe approached a moderate leftist, Yŏ Unhyŏng, who agreed to organize a coalition to accept the surrender and guarantee the safety of the Japanese population.

Yŏ had impeccable nationalist credentials, a long history of service to nationalist causes, and while sympathetic to Korean communists he had never joined the Communist Party. Yŏ demanded the immediate release of all political and economic prisoners, a three-month food supply, and assurance of non-interference with Korean political activity or organizing of workers and peasants. Having accepted responsibility for the welfare of the Japanese population and the maintenance of peace and order, Yŏ designed a provisional organization to undertake these activities.

To fill the vacuum left by Japan's surrender, Yŏ created the Committee for the Preparation of Korean Independence (CPKI). The CPKI began to organize prominent Koreans of all political persuasions into "People's Committees" to act as interim authorities at the provincial and county levels. By the end of August, every province and major city had a provincial committee, and three months later 145 committees covered all of Korea. The organizing extended downward to virtually every subcounty unit, and the committees linked with local youth and civic groups—peasant, worker, and tenant unions. From this base, on September 6, Yŏ convened a representative assembly of several

YŎ UNHYŎNG

Yŏ Unhyŏng, 1947

A major nationalist leader and postliberation statesman, Yŏ Unhyŏng (1885–1947)— often romanized as Lyuh Woon-hyung—was born in Yangpyŏng, Kyŏnggi province, to a low-status *yangban* lineage. He attended the progressive Paeje School and went to China in 1914, where he became embroiled in exile nationalist activity. A founding member of the Shanghai Provisional Government (SPG) (1921), he worked with nationalist leaders such as An Ch'angho, Kim Kyusik, and Sin Ch'aeho. Yŏ's career embodied his pragmatism and eclectic ideology. An activist, unusual for Korean politicians, he could work with groups of widely varying political stances, drawing ideological inspiration from Christianity, Marxism, and Wilsonian democratic thought. Throughout his early career, he focused on Korean independence rather than the triumph of an ideology.

Yŏ spent the bulk of the 1920s in China working for the SPG and Chinese nationalist groups. In 1921 he joined a 30-member delegation from the SPG that attended the Conference of the Toilers of the Far East in Moscow, where he met both Lenin and Trotsky. Japanese police arrested him in Shanghai in 1929, returning him to Korea to be convicted of sedition and eventually serve three years in prison. Upon leaving prison he stayed in Korea and began a career in journalism, ultimately becoming editor of the *Central Daily News*, constantly pressured by Japanese authorities to recant his opposition to imperial rule. The pressure increased after the outbreak of war with China (1937) and general mobilization in Korea, for the governor-general needed him to support the war and give speeches recruiting young men for the army. He never gave in, and his broad contacts across the political spectrum and high standing as a nationalist put him in a position of leadership at the end of the colonial period.

In August 1945, Governor-General Abe asked Yŏ to lead a Korean group to take responsibility for peace and order after the dissolution of the colonial government. Within a few weeks, he organized coalitions—the People's Committees—to carry out local government functions and created an interim national government, the KPR. Not recognized by the US occupation authorities, Yŏ's KPR continued to work to bridge the growing splits within Korean politics as the joint occupation deepened. His final effort to create a single, unified Korean government failed in the summer of 1947. On July 15, 1947, a 19-year-old gunman belonging to a right-wing group—with loose ties to Kim Ku as well as Syngman Rhee—assassinated Yŏ, whose death was widely mourned throughout the peninsula.

hundred delegates to announce the formation of a government, the Korean People's Republic (KPR), and plans for elections.

The KPR leadership attempted to bridge the divide between the right and left, but its first political program outlined a decidedly progressive agenda. Their 27-point platform guaranteed civil rights—speech, association, and religion—and equal rights for women. It proposed nationalization of major industries, communications, railways, and shipping. Furthermore, it provided for the confiscation of the lands of Japanese and "national traitors" (collaborators), to be distributed without payment to peasants who would cultivate them; and it limited agricultural rent to 30 percent of the crop.

Until the arrival of the US occupying force three weeks after Japan's surrender, the KPR continued to forge alliances with other groups in the cities. In the countryside, the People's Committees maintained the peace, guaranteed food stocks, oversaw the beginning of the fall harvest, and, most important, built mass organizations and mobilized the rural population. The KPR and People's Committees thus represented the beginning of a future Korean nation—a government connected to society—that was, unfortunately, stillborn. The arrival of US forces on September 8 under General John R. Hodge, commander of the XXIV Corps from Okinawa, began what became an occupation of Korea south of the 38th parallel of latitude and a new intrusion of foreign power into Korean affairs.

THE REOCCUPATION OF KOREA

The origins of the decision that the United States and USSR would jointly occupy Korea lay in discussions between England, China, and the United States during the Cairo Conference of December 1943. The conference established a principle of trusteeship for Japan's colonial possessions, the ultimate independence of which would be granted, in the now-famous diplomatic phrase, "in due course." Subsequent meetings of the Allied leaders, including Stalin, at Yalta and Potsdam in early 1945 reaffirmed the concept of trusteeship. This idea projected American power into the Pacific and forced a reevaluation of the United States low profile in Northeast Asia since Japan annexed Korea in 1910.

But not without a challenge. Manchuria and Korea held considerable strategic importance for the USSR, which shared borders with both, Korea lying perilously close to the Soviet Union's only major Pacific ports. Having entered the anti-Japanese struggle in Northeast Asia, Stalin was not willing simply to cede Japan's continental possessions to the United States.

By summer 1945, the United States had begun planning the invasion of the Japanese home islands, with much trepidation. The Pacific war had been won at enormous cost in American lives, fighting against only a portion of the Japanese Imperial Army. Major Japanese forces—over a million troops based in China and in Japan itself—had yet to be engaged. The prospect of invading Japan looked even bleaker after the protracted, bloody battle to seize Okinawa earlier that year. Consequently, US strategists negotiated in July to bring the USSR into the final battles with Japan, making the Soviets relevant to the disposition of Japan's territories after its defeat. At Yalta, the United States conceded occupation of Manchuria and Korea to Stalin. But after the atomic bombs and Japan's sudden, unanticipated surrender, US negotiators moved to limit Soviet involvement in Korea—what one historian calls America's "first act of containment."

On August 10–11, with Soviet troops already moving onto the peninsula, the Americans proposed a joint occupation, with the USSR occupying the north and the United States the south, the two zones divided by the 38th parallel. Here we find a rare historical moment—a single, identifiable decision spawned an aftermath of terrible import, in this case for the Korean people. During a meeting in the Executive Office Building in Washington, DC, Colonel Charles Bonesteel (1909–1977), commander of US forces in Korea in the late 1960s, and Major Dean Rusk (1909–1994), destined to be secretary of state in the Kennedy administration, were given an hour to create a boundary for the proposed US–USSR occupation. Using a small wall map, the two men settled on the 38th parallel, placing Seoul, along with most of Korea's light industry and agricultural production and two-thirds of its population, under US jurisdiction. This almost casual, hurried decision sowed the first seed of long-term division of the Korean peninsula. To the surprise of many American leaders, Stalin accepted the 38th parallel. Nothing could have stopped a complete Soviet takeover of Korea, and forward units of the Red Army had already reached the environs of Seoul, only to be recalled behind the newly created demarcation line.

From 1945 until 1948, we thus must recognize Korea's division into northern and southern zones of occupation. No Korean at the time imagined the sundering of the homeland into separate states, but with our 20/20 hindsight, we can see the beginnings of North and South Korea in those years. Only three weeks after liberation, the Koreans found themselves reoccupied by two foreign powers.

General Hodge arrived with a combat force untrained in civil governance, only later joined by military government teams. The occupation of Japan had originally been conceived as a military government, but General Douglas MacArthur (1880–1964), appointed by President Truman as Supreme Commander of the Allied Powers (SCAP), decided to work through a cleansed version of the existing Japanese administration. This left Hodge's USA Military Government in Korea (USAMGIK) the only such occupation government in the Pacific.

Hodge made several fateful, early decisions. Intending to create his own government, Hodge refused to recognize both the KPR and the People's Committees, and he staffed his government with Japanese and Korean colonial administrators, though Korean public outcry forced him to dismiss the Japanese officials almost immediately. This reversal of decolonization outraged many Koreans, especially members of the People's Committees. After all, establishing a US military government denied Koreans the political independence they assumed they would achieve from the moment of liberation.

Ousting the People's Committees from the countryside was no easy task. It took until late 1946 to eliminate them, the process often violent and including a strike of railway workers in Pusan that led to major riots in Taegu. For support, Hodge turned to conservative Korean elements in Seoul. With few interpreters, the Americans remained captives of English-speaking Koreans, who came primarily from conservative, wealthy backgrounds. Conservatives also organized themselves, one group called the Korean Democratic Party (KDP) emerging to offer Hodge support in the early months of occupation. KDP members, conservative landlords and businessmen, wanted to counter the left-leaning KPR and protect their own established interests. They need not have worried, for USAMGIK chose many KDP members as administrators. Cho Pyŏng'ok

(1894–1960), for example, became the hated head of the national police and an important figure in the suppression of the left in the following years.

The economic and social policies of USAMGIK reflected its reliance on conservative Koreans. While providing some tenant relief in the form of rent controls, it refused to consider comprehensive land reform in its first years. Because of the strong voice of landlords among USAMGIK's advisers, land reform came only in 1948, limited to land formerly held by Japanese—only about 20 percent of the total. While the rent control program proved very popular, USAMGIK's delayed and limited land reform created a strong contrast with the early, rapid, and comprehensive land reform undertaken in the north. This was a major mistake for an occupation government in desperate need of public support.

USAMGIK did create new labor laws, limiting the workweek to 60 hours and mandating time-and-a-half pay over 40 hours. It also issued strict child labor laws, banning employment of children under 14. However, other laws also limited labor unions, for Hodge and his advisers considered them hotbeds of communist agitation. In general, USAMGIK's social and economic reform measures, tepid and slow, failed to legitimize American occupation of the south and created active Korean antagonism.

We know less about the Soviet occupation in the north. Clearly, however, it evolved in stark contrast to the US zone. Taking an opposite approach, the Soviets worked through the People's Committees while staying in the background. They had much better intelligence about Korean conditions than the Americans, and also had the advantage of Korean communists accompanying them into Korea. After accepting the Japanese surrender, the Soviets never established a formal occupation government, allowing the People's Committees to dismantle the colonial state and institute de-Japanization. The USSR certainly gave guidance at the top and was sympathetic to the social revolutionary tenor of the moment.

Indeed, the policies of the KPR in the north were decidedly revolutionary, most notably a sweeping land reform. The authorities confiscated all Japanese-held land and that of more than 5,000 large Korean landlords, redistributing it to tenants. The KPR distinguished clearly between landlords considered collaborators and others, the latter allowed to keep a small portion of land if they promised to farm it themselves. This land reform directly attacked the inequitable distribution of wealth that had supported the ruling classes in Korea for centuries. Although it was not accomplished without violence and some tenant reprisals, the exodus of many landlords to the south contributed to a generally peaceful process.

The KPR also instituted social and economic reforms in other sectors. They nationalized large-scale industry, though small factories continued under private ownership. A new set of labor laws stipulated an eight-hour workday, set a minimum wage, prohibited child labor, and regulated working conditions. Reforms also included guarantees of women's equality and prohibitions against prostitution, concubinage, and female infanticide. This entire program resembled the original KPR reform proposals issued for the whole country, but, unlike the south, the political right in the north had to concede to (or flee from) the relatively moderate leftist program of the northern KPR.

In short, within several months of liberation, two very different occupations took shape on the peninsula. While the idea of trusteeship implied that a single, unified Korean government would ultimately emerge, the joint occupation structure created obstacles to this process from the very beginning.

THE EVOLUTION OF SEPARATE STATES

By the end of 1945, the elements had been put in place for the evolution of separate states on the peninsula. Koreans had never imagined this outcome, for it resulted from the growing animosity between the United States and USSR and a polarization of political forces around each occupier. The Soviet recognition of the People's Committees and their usurpation by the Korean communists, the thorough-going land reform, and the early progressive reform program had laid the groundwork for Korean communist dominance in the north. Hodge's decisions to abolish the People's Committees by force, not to recognize the KPR, and to establish a military government favorable to landed and business interests anticipated the emergence of a conservative Korean regime in the south. In the first six months, like strong magnets, the Korean leadership groups—encouraged and protected by increasingly antagonistic occupying powers—attracted like-minded supporters.

In fall 1945, Korean politicians of all stripes, in both occupation zones, struggled to establish their credentials and enter the ongoing negotiations over the future course of the nation. Outside Korea, the Allied governments also worked to resolve the Korean situation. The December 1945 Moscow Agreement between Great Britain, the United States, and the USSR attempted to create a roadmap for Korea's future and the withdrawal of occupation forces. This agreement established several principles: (1) creation of a provisional Korean democratic government; (2) establishment of a Joint Commission (composed of US and Soviet representatives) to aid in the formation of such a government; and (3) formalization of a five-year trusteeship over Korea by the United States, the USSR, Great Britain, and China.

Initially, Korean conservatives and communists alike denounced the agreement, particularly trusteeship. In time the communists embraced the plan, using the south's opposition as a pretext to maneuver them out of representative bodies in the north. The Joint Commission, a nice idea on paper, had little chance for success, given the rivalry between the occupiers. Through 1946 and 1947, the Joint Commission foundered on Soviet and US disagreement over a host of issues. During this impasse, both Syngman Rhee and his conservative allies in the south and Kim Il Sung and the Korean communists in the north continued their consolidation of political power. In doing so, they outmaneuvered other potential leaders such as Cho Mansik, Kim Ku, and Yŏ Unhyŏng, who strove for a broad coalition government.

As the Soviets tightened their grip on Eastern Europe in mid-1947, the United States moved toward global containment of communist expansion. The Cold War had begun, with Korea as one of its hotspots. By the summer of 1947, all the ingredients for a separate southern Korean government were in place. The military government created a Representative Democratic Council, with Syngman Rhee at its head. Rhee gradually squeezed moderates out and turned this body into a tool of the political right wing. He also controlled or dominated the National Police force and the beginnings of what would become the Republic of Korea's army. Eventually, USAMGIK inched toward the creation of a separate South Korean government by establishing an Interim Korean Representative Assembly.

With the Joint Commission at an impasse due to US–Soviet rivalry, the United States brought the Korea question to the new United Nations. In February 1948, the General Assembly of the UN, rejecting Soviet counterproposals, gave the United States a mandate to establish a United Nations Temporary Commission on Korea (UNTCOK) to conduct the election of a national assembly that could form a unified government and negotiate the withdrawal of all occupation forces. The Koreans in the north rejected the idea of elections, and moderates in the south, notably Kim Kyusik and Kim Ku, organized their own opposition to the elections, seeing them as a device to split the nation.

In spite of the valiant attempts to stop them, UNTCOK scheduled its election for May 10, 1948. The north refused UNTCOK access, so the election proceeded only in the south. The outcome established a National Assembly, which elected Syngman Rhee its chairman. The National Assembly adopted a new constitution establishing the Republic of Korea (ROK) with, not surprisingly, Rhee as its first president. In response, a Supreme People's Assembly met on September 3, 1948 in Pyongyang to ratify a constitution; it elected Kim Il Sung premier and Pak Hŏnyŏng vice premier of a new government, the Democratic People's Republic of Korea (DPRK). Thus the late summer of 1948 saw the establishment of two formal Korean states, the ROK in the south and the DPRK in the north, each claiming to be the legitimate political expression of all the Korean people.

THE ROAD TO CIVIL WAR

The two fledgling republics divided the Korean peninsula along the "temporary" line chosen by Colonel Bonesteel and Major Rusk, which was roughly at the 38th parallel. That line of convenience separating occupying powers had become a national border, dividing the territory of the Korean people. The peninsula—from the Yalu and Tumen rivers to the South Sea and Tsushima Straits—had been integrated as a cultural, linguistic, political, and economic unit since at least the beginning of the Chosŏn period in the late fourteenth century. To divide it along such an arbitrary line made no sense whatsoever.

As the border began to harden in the coming years, the disastrous consequences of the division for each republic became clear. The DPRK controlled a territory larger than that of the south, but with scarcely a third of the total population. The north, even more mountainous than the south, harbors the bulk of Korea's mineral wealth. Moreover, the north contained much of the heavy industry built by Japanese companies during the late colonial period and the bulk of the peninsula's hydroelectric potential—around the elections in summer 1948, the northern authorities simply cut off the south's electric supply.

The north's agricultural potential, however, was only a fraction of the south's. A short growing season and lack of arable land remain problems today for the DPRK. The south had most of the light industry, two-thirds of the population, the major rice-growing regions, and the traditional cultural, political, and economic center of Korea—Seoul, now the ROK's capital. The south also inherited the bulk of the political and social problems left over from the colonial period. Both republics, therefore, began the project of nation-building with less than half of Korea's potential and serious internal conflicts.

Syngman Rhee faced many difficulties in his first year in office, but he mobilized the resources of the National Police and rammed through a National Security Law (NSL) that gave him virtually unlimited power to consolidate his regime. The constitution provided the National Assembly and judiciary few checks on the chief executive's power. Problems began even before the formal declaration of the Republic. In the summer of 1948, demonstrations on Cheju Island, opposing the elections, turned into a full-scale insurrection led by guerrilla forces hiding in the island's mountainous interior. South Korean police and troops brutally suppressed what became known as the Cheju Rebellion in a village-by-village encirclement campaign. Within a year, the government had pacified the island at the price of 30,000 islanders' lives—10 percent of the population—and the destruction of half its villages.

In October, during the Cheju pacification campaign, troops waiting to be sent to the fighting mutinied in the southwestern port of Yŏsu, and this rebellion spread to the Sunchŏn area. The Yŏsu–Sunchŏn Rebellion represented a further challenge to the authority of the ROK state. The rebels, led by communists, gained the sympathy of the local peasantry, and the suppression of the rebellion—ROK forces killed 1,200 rebels—further alienated the local population. Both insurrections smoldered into 1949 and provided Rhee the opportunity to use his emergency powers against internal opposition.

Rhee's accession to power had necessitated an alliance with the conservative Korean Democratic Party (KDP), its southern landlords and businessmen providing the necessary base and electoral strength to win the election. Many of them, however, needed protection from charges of collaboration, since most of them had done well under Japanese colonialism. Having secured the presidency, Rhee used his personal patronage to create a fresh set of supporters solely loyal to him, so the KDP became an opposition party.

Rhee's control of the National Police, the growing ROK Army, and the provisions of the National Security Law allowed him to take autocratic measures. In the name of fighting communism, he turned these instruments against his opponents in the National Assembly who, while weak, had provided some semblance of an opposition and public criticism. Rhee's anticommunist campaigns arrested close to 60,000 people in the first year of his rule. By 1950, Rhee had firmly established himself and enjoyed the advantage of US support. The Truman administration did not particularly like Rhee, but his militant anticommunism served the United States evolving containment policy, so the United States provided the ROK with military training and economic assistance that further legitimated Rhee's harsh, unilateral rule.

The DPRK evolved with considerably less social unrest, smoothly putting many features of its future social and economic system in place. The land reform of 1946 redistributed land and eliminated the landlord class; after the Korean War, land would be centralized under cooperatives and state farms. The Soviet occupation authority had also nationalized large-scale industry as the beginning of what would become the socialization of the entire economy. Politically, the early DPRK consolidated control of the Korean Workers Party (KWP), created an army, and constructed a police and internal security apparatus. The Party purged itself and the nascent government of "bourgeois" elements and began the process of creating mass organizations to mobilize all sectors of society. The KWP carried out a massive "re-education" campaign in factories, schools, government offices, and villages. In those early years, "education" meant basic tutorials on the simple protocols of the meetings themselves, subjecting all members of society to rigorous public discipline.

The People's Interim Committee, the government during the Soviet occupation, gradually became a tool of the KWP and its leader, Kim Il Sung. In his early days as national leader, Kim had to maneuver moderate elements out of the government and deal with a number of small parties. In particular, he had to eliminate popular northern moderate leader Cho Mansik. Even after the formation of the DPRK, Kim still did not have total control of the KWP, for domestic communist leader Pak Hŏnyŏng commanded the loyalty of many communists who had fled from the south. The KWP's base, in contrast, lay in the northern Korean peasantry. It had originally opened its ranks to large numbers of ordinary peasants, but anticipating the need for leaders and experts, it also admitted intellectuals. Interestingly, one of the early KWP logos featured a crossed hammer and sickle—the conventional communist insignia—and an ink brush representing the intelligentsia.

From its beginning, the DPRK created a formidable internal security apparatus to gather intelligence on its own population and act as the state's main coercive instrument. It organized and classified all members of society, collecting and storing information on all citizens: name, address, class background, party affiliation, political attitudes, work record, and rating of political reliability. People belonging to categories with suspect loyalties, opinions, or backgrounds were placed under surveillance: remaining Christian leaders, former landlords, officials of the old colonial government, and people with relatives in the south. This intense surveillance and organizational apparatus, combined with early enthusiasm for the DPRK's redistributive social and economic programs, helped keep social disruption low. Compared to the ongoing insurgencies and domestic unrest in the ROK, the DPRK appeared socially at peace.

In their first years, both Korean republics gave special emphasis to military development. The ROK army grew from very modest beginnings with considerable US material aid and technical advice. Korean veterans of the Japanese Imperial Army held many important positions. ROK forces guarded the 38th parallel, coming into almost constant conflict with the DPRK's Korean People's Army. Kim Il Sung had fought the Japanese as a guerrilla leader, and his generals had either commanded guerrilla units or served with the CCP's armies in Manchuria and North China.

The North Korean army, officers and rank and file, had a considerable advantage over the South in experience of war. As many as 100,000 Koreans—residents of Manzhouguo and North Koreans—fought with the People's Liberation Army (PLA) during the Chinese civil war (see pp. 335–38). Kim sent troops at a critical moment in 1947 to aid in the war against the GMD. And the CCP returned the favor a thousand-fold before and during the Korean War. These veterans began returning to North Korea in late 1948; with the CCP's victory in 1949, even larger units returned in their entirety. By the spring of 1950, North Korea had a battle-trained, tested army. With the addition of modern equipment and heavy armor, it would become a formidable fighting force.

THE KOREAN WAR

Americans sometimes refer to the Korean War as "the forgotten war." Forgotten by some in the United States, perhaps, but for Koreans it was the defining event of the second half of the twentieth century, and its effects live on in the continued division of the peninsula. The origins of the war should by this point be clear. Perhaps it began with the establishment of the joint occupation, and it certainly appeared likely after the creation of two antagonistic states in 1948. Clearly, the war had both domestic and international causes.

The immediate domestic issue was the struggle for national leadership between two contenders with diametrically opposing views of the nation's social, political, and economic future. From an international perspective, the intrusion of the United States and USSR into the volatile mix of class contradictions, economic collapse, and polarized politics of the immediate post-liberation era fueled and sharpened this contradiction. The actual causes of the war were obscured, particularly from the United States' point of view, because Korea came to represent the larger Cold War conflict of Capitalism vs. Communism, not a domestic struggle between North and South Korea.

The Korean War embodied a number of "firsts." It was the first American war of containment. Indeed, it was the first use of American force to stop what many Americans believed to be the spread of Soviet-led international communism. It also became the first of

many wars of stalemate, "limited wars"—sometimes called "proxy wars"—fought during the Cold War. Necessity limited these conflicts, considering the catastrophic consequences of direct confrontation between the world's two nuclear superpowers. Moreover, the Korean War helped to refine euphemisms obscuring the reality of the terrible weapons and tactics being used. Calling the remobilization and engagement of the US army a "conflict" or a "police" action—not a "war"—blunted public anxiety and the political liability of actually declaring war. The war brought the concepts of "brainwashing," "surgical bombing," and "wind chill," into the English vocabulary, and it involved the first extensive use of jet aircraft.

Calling this war a "conflict" certainly obscured its scope and size. Over 53,000 Americans, hundreds of

Korea, 1950–53

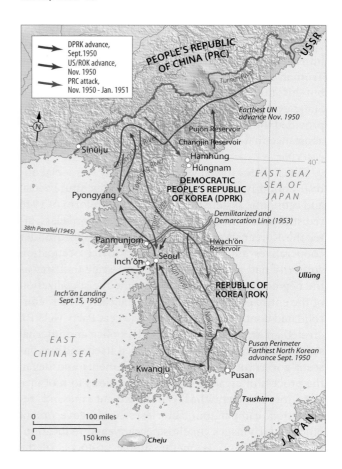

thousands of Korean and Chinese soldiers, and millions of civilians died in this "police action." Yet, if asked to compare the Vietnam and Korean wars, few Americans nowadays would have much sense of how big a war it was. This crucial memory gap conceals the fact that the general contours of East Asian security are still determined by the inconclusive truce that ended the war in 1953 and drew a hard line between the two Koreas.

By June 1950, North and South Korea had been engaged in a low-level border war for over a year, each attacking the other to improve their tactical advantage along the 38th parallel. We know that North Korea had been preparing for an attack for a number of months. Kim Il Sung traveled to Moscow and obtained Soviet material assistance—tanks, heavy artillery, and munitions. He also went to Beijing and received Mao's acquiescence to an armed reunification of the peninsula. So in the early morning hours of June 25, 1950, whether provoked or by design, the Korean People's Army (KPA) invaded the South in force.

The North Korean army overran Seoul in three days, forcing the ROK to retreat to the southern port city of Pusan. The North Korean blitzkrieg revealed the South Korean forces to be unprepared and ill equipped. Up to the invasion, many US advisers had considered the South's army superior to the North's, but it lacked armor, antitank weapons, heavy artillery, and, most important, combat experience. The battle-tested North Korean veterans of China's civil war proved unstoppable for several weeks. Disaster followed disaster for the South Koreans and the small American units hastily sent to their aid from Japan. This war tested the containment strategy, the linchpin of American Cold War foreign policy, and the test came at the worst possible moment for the United States. The American army, demobilized after 1945, was hard-pressed to find troops to send to the conflict. A war-weary American public doubted the wisdom of more fighting in East Asia to protect South Korea.

The inexorable North Korean advance continued, and in mid-July the KPA took the key railroad junction of Taejŏn near the Kŭm River, 100 miles (160 km) south of Seoul. In that battle, the North Koreans captured the commander of the US forces, Major General William F. Dean (1899–1981). Splitting its forces at this point, the KPA sent one army down the west coast into the Chŏlla provinces, ultimately wheeling east to confront the famous Pusan perimeter, the defensive line that the ROK established along the Naktong River north and west of Pusan. The main KPA force continued to drive the South Koreans and Americans to the southeast.

On June 27, the United States successfully petitioned the UN Security Council for a mandate to defend the ROK and roll back the invasion. In the summer of 1950, the Soviet delegation boycotted the Security Council over the continued representation of the Nationalist government (on Taiwan) rather than the People's Republic of China (PRC) in the "China" seat. With no Soviet veto to block the petition, the United States turned the Korean War into a "UN police action," with US General Douglas MacArthur—simultaneously commanding the occupation of Japan—appointed commander of UN forces in Korea.

When the North Korean advance stalled in August, it had occupied virtually all of South Korea save 50 square miles (129 sq km) in the southeast around Pusan. During the roughly 50-day occupation, the North Koreans replicated their northern revolution in the south, restoring the People's Committees. The DPRK had created a list of enemies, so they scoured the country, arresting and killing known collaborators with Japanese colonialism and prominent supporters of the ROK. They even began a land reform, hastily implemented and temporary, that created major tensions in the south after the North Korean retreat. By emptying the jails of political prisoners, they unleashed a political backlash, often violent, against the ROK's power structure.

The North Korean revolution in the south attracted many to its cause, exposing them to reprisals when the North Korean presence proved temporary. Confusion and violence convulsed South Korea in the scorching summer of 1950, with mass killings and arrests following on atrocities committed by the retreating ROK troops and their American allies. Survivors of this violence rallied to the advancing KPA. Military history's focus on battles and the movement of troops obscures the pervasive violence of this period. When ROK troops reoccupied their territory in September, they rounded up and sometimes shot those who had supported the KPA. For their part, the North Koreans either killed or abducted to the North thousands of prominent South Korean politicians and intellectuals.

On September 15, the course of the war shifted abruptly with a massive counterattack by US forces. Landing 40,000 troops on the treacherous tidal flats near Inch'ŏn, MacArthur drove behind North Korean lines to retake Seoul and strike the exposed KPA rear. Simultaneously, South Korean and US forces broke out of the Pusan perimeter, driving the KPA north in full retreat. Not content with restoring the 38th parallel border after recapturing Seoul, MacArthur received Washington's permission to "roll back" the line, march north and eliminate the KPA, though only in the absence of Chinese or Soviet intervention. Washington instructed that only Korean troops should be used as they approached the Chinese border. In late November, forward units of the UN forces reached the Yalu River in the northwest and captured the far northeastern port of Ch'ŏngjin. We now know that MacArthur ignored the presence of massive Chinese armies that had already moved into North Korea. Why did MacArthur put his army in danger? The issue is still debated, but MacArthur's conservative politics and desire to widen the war to engage the fledgling People's Republic of China (PRC) provide some of the answer.

MacArthur got his wish, but the conflict remained in Korea. On November 27, PRC armies struck along the entire northern front, cutting off thousands of US troops and forcing a rapid retreat. Chinese, American, and Korean troops fought some of the war's bloodiest battles in one of Korea's severest winters. By December 6, the Chinese People's Volunteer Army (PVA) and KPA had overrun Seoul for a second time. Eventually the communist counterattack fizzled; UN forces retook Seoul and reestablished a defensive line very close to the original line along the 38th parallel. Here the war stalemated, resulting in a bloody conflict of attrition that provided the backdrop to a two-year negotiation to end the conflict.

During the stalemate, the debate continued about rolling back the line or even using nuclear weapons against North Korea and the PRC. Contrary to US policy, MacArthur called publicly for use of Jiang Jieshi's ROC troops from Taiwan in Korea and a broader war with the PRC. Truman judged him insubordinate, removing him from command in April 1951. During the negotiations to end the war, the United States mounted a dreadful bombing campaign against the north. In two years, the US Air Force destroyed every North Korean city, its industrial capacity, and its railroad infrastructure, leveling the major dams and hydroelectric plants (resulting in catastrophic floods) and napalming villages suspected of harboring troops. By the end of their campaign, US bombers could find no meaningful targets anywhere in North Korea and were reduced to bombing footbridges or jettisoning their ordnance into the sea in order to land safely upon return. The memory of this devastation and carnage remains at the heart of North Korean enmity and distrust of the United States to this day.

In spite of the bombing, the truce talks made no headway, the main issue being the repatriation of prisoners of war. The DPRK insisted that prisoners be returned to their country of origin, while the UN insisted that individual prisoners be able to choose where to reside. When a truce was finally signed on July 27, 1953, the three years of fighting had resolved nothing.

Refugees flee the Chinese advance across the destroyed bridge over the Taedong River at Pyongyang, December 4, 1950.

A village in flames after American bombers unload napalm bombs on a communist supply depot near Hanchon in North Korea, May 10, 1951.

Signing the armistice at Panmunjon, July 27, 1953. The American General William K. Harrison, Jr. is seated at left and the North Korean General Nam Il is seated at right.

The border remained substantially where it had been in June 1950; Seoul had been reduced to rubble, having been fought through four times; the North lay in ruins from the American bombing; and hundreds of thousands of soldiers—Chinese, Korean, American, and UN—and millions of civilians had been killed or displaced. The first American war of containment had succeeded at a terrible cost, with tragic implications for the evolution of North and South Korea.

CHINA

CONDITIONS AT WAR'S END

When World War II ended, China had been at war for over 30 years. Cities lay in ruins, and warfare, heavy taxation, conscription, and confiscation had left hundreds of millions of rural people in dire poverty. Parties, armies, warlords, and puppet governments had broken the elite at all levels into contending factions, so society—local, provincial, national—had no unified leadership, only conflict.

Jiang Jieshi and his Nationalist government at Chongqing, internationally recognized and domestically legitimate, nonetheless constituted a "weak state," unable to enforce its will in most of the country. The CCP, based at peripheral Yan'an, had earned the loyalty of tens of millions of peasants, but it had neither the troops nor the political organization to seize national power. The atomic bombs and Japan's unexpected surrender required both Chongqing and Yan'an to act quickly, for they both sought the same goals—to receive the Japanese surrender, secure territory, and seize Japan's huge stockpiles of military equipment. Jiang Jieshi commanded the Japanese army to surrender only to his forces, and Japanese theater commander General Okamura Yasuji (1884–1966), a committed anticommunist, tried to comply.

Jiang also asked General Albert Wedemeyer (1897–1989), Stilwell's successor, for American assistance. US ships landed 50,000 American marines in key ports to await Nationalist forces, and US planes transported Nationalist troops all over the country. The Nationalist government thus regained control of most major cities, while CCP forces remained largely in the countryside. GMD officers used Japanese troops to supplement their own, so some Chinese associated the Nationalist government with both Japanese and American imperialism. The Soviets maintained working relationships with the CCP and GMD while seizing considerable Manchurian loot, especially industrial equipment. Not completely committed to supporting the CCP, the

USSR signed treaties with the GMD but also turned over captured Japanese arms to communist forces.

Less than two weeks after the Japanese emperor's surrender, Jiang Jieshi invited Mao Zedong to negotiate in Chongqing. Mao spent six weeks with Jiang and his ministers, both sides trying to appear reasonable and flexible without making any important concessions. Confident in his larger army and treaties with the United States and USSR, Jiang declined to share power with his weaker, dispersed communist foes. Mao, in response, refused to compromise the independence of the CCP's army. The talks continued into October, but the final documents included only vague generalities, not concrete progress toward peace.

THE MARSHALL MISSION AND PEACEMAKING

The Truman administration's China policy contained a fundamental contradiction: US policy-makers wanted a stable, well-governed China to balance the USSR, but could not afford to support the Nationalist government's military. Their best-case scenario lay in a coalition government including both Chinese parties. In a civil war, the United States could either back Jiang, investing billions of dollars and hundreds of thousands of American troops, or stand down and let the Chinese fight it out.

Many US diplomats and soldiers who had served in China, knowing the deficiencies of Jiang's ROC—corruption, brutal repression, and ineffective management—argued that the United States should not pour out more blood and treasure for so unsuitable an ally. Other Americans, however, claimed that Jiang's anticommunism made him China's ideal leader. Ambassador Patrick Hurley (1883–1963), General Albert Wedemeyer, former China missionary Representative Walter Judd (R-MN, 1898–1994), and China-born media mogul Henry Luce (1898–1967) led a movement in the United States—usually called "the China Lobby"—to support Jiang and the GMD to the hilt.

ZHANG JUNMAI, CONFUCIAN COSMOPOLITAN

Zhang Junmai, c. 1923

Younger than Lu Xun, older than Hu Shi, Zhang Junmai (1886–1969), who used the English name Carsun Chang, belonged to the first generation of Chinese intellectuals educated in both the Euro-American curriculum and the Chinese Classics. After Confucian training at home (Jiading, near Shanghai), Zhang studied English *and* passed the first-level Qing examination to become a *xiucai*. His new-style education and conservative upbringing led him to become a disciple of Liang Qichao (see p. 225) and the constitutionalists. After teaching English for several years, he entered Waseda University in Tokyo in 1906, majoring in law and political economy, participated in non-revolutionary Chinese political groups, then followed Liang Qichao into journalism, editing newspapers and magazines.

After Yuan Shikai seized power, Zhang spent years in Germany and England, where he studied philosophy, especially the European idealism that dovetailed with his personal Confucian principles. He attended the Versailles Conference as part of Liang Qichao's unofficial delegation. After returning to China, he wrote a famous essay on the "philosophy of life" (1923), attacking scientific materialism and advocating spiritual freedom, individual choice, and personal conscience as the core of humanity. Zhang's essay sparked months of debate, with Liang Qichao and Liang Shuming (1893–1988) defending Zhang and metaphysics, while the geologist Ding Wenjiang (1887–1936) and Hu Shi weighed in for science. This May Fourth-era discussion, published as a book that

In November, Ambassador Hurley resigned, charging that leftist diplomats in the State Department had undermined US policy by championing the CCP. In his place, President Truman sent General George C. Marshall to negotiate peace. FDR's former military adviser, Marshall had no China experience but a distinguished career as a problem-solver. President Truman hoped that Marshall's good sense could untangle "the China problem," allowing the United States to deal with higher-priority conflicts in Europe.

On December 15, President Truman announced that the United States aimed to create a "unified, democratic, and peaceful China" with a broadly based government, criticizing both Jiang's single-party regime and the CCP's separate military. CCP analysts correctly concluded that the United States would not fully support Jiang Jieshi in a civil war. Jiang and his closest advisers worried that Marshall could force them into another United Front, correctly asserting that China could never be stable with two contending governments and armies. The Americans nonetheless demanded a ceasefire and peaceful resolution.

In December 1945, Soviet troops remained in control of Manchuria. When they permitted Nationalist troops to move north, Jiang immediately committed 500,000 of his best soldiers—airlifted in US planes—to reoccupy Changchun, Shenyang (Mukden), and the railroads. Since the CCP already had armies there, large-scale combat seemed inevitable, but Marshall worked quickly. By January 10, 1946, the CCP and GMD agreed to an immediate ceasefire and the creation of an "Executive Headquarters" with three members—a Nationalist, a Communist, and an American—whose decisions had to be unanimous. Wherever CCP and GMD forces confronted one another, similarly composed military teams went into the field to supervise the ceasefire, their jeeps crisscrossing the battle zones.

same year, epitomized Chinese intellectuals' struggle somehow to be both Chinese (Confucian, humanist) and modern (Western, scientific) simultaneously.

In the 1930s, Zhang rejected both GMD and CCP autocracy and established a National Socialist Party (no relation to Nazism) as an alternative, nonetheless rallying to the GMD cause when Japan attacked in 1937. He spent the war years in Chongqing and Yunnan, often in trouble with GMD ideologues, and sponsored many united front organizations, including the China Democratic League (CDL). Despite Zhang's opposition status, Jiang Jieshi appointed him as a member of the ROC's delegation to the United Nations' founding conference in San Francisco in 1945. Unlike many CDL members, Zhang did not drift toward the CCP during the civil war but continued to argue for parliamentary democracy, state ownership of key industries, and constitutionalism. The CCP victory in 1949 drove him out of China, first to Macao, then India, then Hong Kong, and finally to the United States. His autobiography, *Third Force in China* (1952), damned all parties in the civil war—GMD, CCP, and the United States.

Zhang Junmai spent the rest of his life studying and writing about Neo-Confucianism. He belonged to a small group of intellectuals who attempted to make Confucianism relevant and potent in twentieth-century China. Despite May Fourth rejection of tradition, science's powerful call, and predictions (even announcements) of Confucianism's demise, they persisted in studying and adapting tradition to modern times. Now led by former Harvard professor Du Weiming (Wei-ming Tu, b. 1940), among others, this latest Confucian movement has created a living philosophy based on both ancient texts and contemporary realities.

Marshall's ceasefire coincided with the convening of a Political Consultative Conference (PCC) in Chongqing. Only 15 of the Conference's 38 delegates spoke for the GMD (8) and CCP (7); the rest represented "third-party" groups—the China Youth Party (5), the Democratic League (9)—and distinguished non-party civilians. By January 31, the delegates had undertaken heated debate, during which Zhou Enlai's CCP delegation avoided all "class struggle" arguments in favor of "united front" tactics. The PCC passed resolutions establishing a supreme state council; recognizing Jiang Jieshi as leader and Sun Yat-sen's Three Principles of the People as the guiding ideology; pledging democracy and unification of the armed forces; eliminating politics from the military; creating a constitutional revision commission; and planning a constitutional convention. The PCC resolutions seemed an epochal achievement, especially since they coincided with the Chinese New Year. People began their 1946 holiday dancing in the streets at the prospect of peace and coalition. Marshall's personal charisma seemed to have overcome decades of conflict.

Jiang Jieshi and Mao Zedong during negotiations at Chongqing, 1946.

But peace never came. The Soviet withdrawal from Manchuria that spring unintentionally sparked a civil war. With Marshall in the United States to arrange loans for China, GMD and CCP armies raced to fill the gap left by the USSR's departure. By April, fighting had spread throughout Manchuria. Although Marshall returned and arranged another ceasefire, by early June Jiang Jieshi had defied the PCC resolutions, the CCP had maneuvered to defend itself, and Marshall's mission had failed. Although he remained in China for another seven months, working tirelessly toward a ceasefire, neither side would compromise. Both the Nationalist government and the CCP thought they could win on the battlefield.

A coalition of Chinese moderates, a "third party" between CCP and GMD, also attempted to mediate the conflict. Exemplified by Zhang Junmai (Carsun Chang, 1886–1969, see pp. 332–33), these democracy-oriented elites appealed very much to Americans. Marshall called them "a splendid group of men," but they could not achieve national leadership in the polarized, militarized Chinese politics of the Republican period. They lacked popular organization, never developed any military capacity, and had no territorial base. Despite severe repression in GMD areas, the China Democratic League and its allies argued for ceasefires, negotiations, and peace. In October 1946, the third-party leaders succeeded briefly—Zhou Enlai met with Jiang Jieshi—but by mid-November that possibility had faded, and war recommenced in deadly earnest. As in Korea, the moderates compatible with American ideals could not establish a viable middle ground between Communists and Nationalists, and the US supported the Nationalists.

After recovering Japan-controlled areas, the GMD appointed civil officials to restore and maintain order, collect taxes, and establish local administration. In most jurisdictions, they assigned central government officials who had been in Chongqing during the war. Treating local dignitaries as collaborators with Japan (some of them were), these officials alienated local elites, whose support might have enabled the government to function. Many GMD officials indulged in spectacular corruption, and the government's legitimacy plummeted as they piled surtaxes upon taxes, delivering neither order nor services. The ROC thus came to be seen as predatory, alienated from business, and actively hostile to local urban elites.

Equally harmful, the Nationalist government, unable to raise sufficient revenues for its huge armies, printed large issues of unbacked currency, hoping to delay their budget crisis until they won the civil war. This plan failed completely, for inflation turned to hyperinflation, and prices skyrocketed through the late 1940s, on average 30 percent higher every month for three years. Knowing that their currency would be worth less tomorrow than today, people hoarded precious metals, jewelry, food, even matches and soap. By 1948, going to the market to buy rice required a wheelbarrow filled with paper money. This devastated the lives of businessmen and wage-earners, who saw their salaries buy fewer goods each week, giving them more reason to mistrust the government.

Nonetheless, in 1946 Jiang Jieshi had clear superiority in troops, weapons, and position. The United States had supplied him with billions of dollars in military aid, and the Nationalist high command confidently predicted victory, especially after seizing control of Manchuria's cities and railroads.

LARGE-SCALE CIVIL WAR

The Chinese civil war of 1946–49 was, and remains to this day, the largest military conflict after World War II. The People's Liberation Army (PLA) continued its guerrilla tactics, but also undertook positional battles engaging hundreds of thousands of soldiers. Tactical decisions—where to garrison and how to supply troops, where to place artillery, when and on what scale to engage the enemy—played an important part in determining victory or defeat. The CCP had a closely unified military leadership, with general policy set by Mao Zedong, Liu Shaoqi, Marxist theorist Ren Bishi (1904–1950), and the Central Committee of the Party's Political Bureau (Politburo). Their generals, including Lin Biao, Peng Dehuai, and Liu Bocheng (1892–1986), usually obeyed orders, their respect for Mao Zedong overcoming disagreements.

China, 1945–49

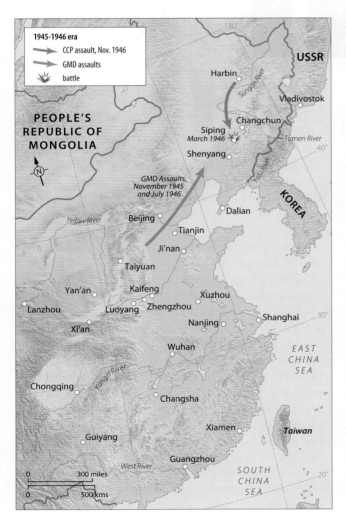

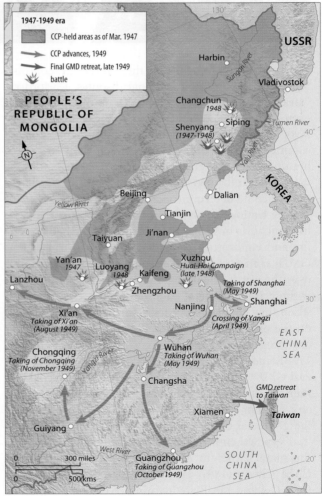

Mao Zedong, on horseback, moving with a unit of the newly named Chinese People's Liberation Army (PLA) during the civil war, 1947.

spies at GMD headquarters, reacted effectively, intending to cut the railroads connecting the Manchurian cities, thereby breaking the GMD forces into smaller units and destroying them separately. Lin and Mao combined this strategy with a political campaign to gather food supplies and recruits locally, undertaking limited land reform to win the Manchurian peasants to the CCP cause. Effective exchange with the USSR procured military equipment as well as engineers to repair and make use of captured railways.

As the bitter Manchurian winter began in late 1947, Lin's initial strikes succeeded. Probing the GMD lines around Shenyang (Mukden), PLA generals discovered weakness and attacked, routing an entire army, so Lin ordered a general assault south and eastward, not on Shenyang but toward the coast. His forces pushed the GMD into full retreat, leaving the large Shenyang garrison behind and reaching the sea, destroying several divisions on the way. In Shenyang when the PLA attacked, Jiang Jieshi personally witnessed the destruction of some of his best units. The PLA had reversed the GMD advantage in Manchuria, isolating GMD garrisons in Shenyang and Changchun.

Receiving dire accounts of Jiang's mismanagement from American observers, the Truman administration tried to prevent CCP victory, in their eyes tantamount to Soviet takeover. But their dilemma remained. Short of massive US intervention, neither politically feasible nor certain of success, the United States could not disengage from Jiang without strengthening the CCP. US media, especially Henry Luce's *Time* and *Life* magazines, had publicized the Generalissimo and his wife, Song Meiling, as international heroes during World War II. In the election year of 1948, with anticommunist fear on the rise, Truman could not be seen as abandoning a loyal Christian ally in the fight against international

The high command of the GMD, in contrast, remained fractured by factional disputes, warlord rivalries, and Jiang Jieshi's insistence on micromanaging even distant battles. Generals out of the Generalissimo's favor received fewer supplies and more dangerous assignments. These differences between the two armies became crucial when they engaged in huge battles, in which well-informed command decisions immediately obeyed could determine victory or defeat.

The Nationalists had successfully attacked the CCP in Manchuria in spring 1946, breaking Marshall's ceasefire and vindicating Mao's decision not to trust Jiang. GMD armies continued to take cities and towns all over the north, including Yan'an itself in March 1947, without inflicting fatal damage on the CCP. Attacking when they could achieve local surprise, the CCP went on the offensive in summer 1947. Liu Bocheng, Deng Xiaoping (1904–1997; China's supreme leader after 1978), and Chen Yi (1901–1972) outmaneuvered several GMD armies in North China, killing over 80,000 men. They made their headquarters between Nanjing and Wuhan, placing a powerful CCP army close to Jiang's capital.

Despite their threat, Jiang Jieshi still planned to fight the main battles in Manchuria, where he appointed Chen Cheng (1897–1965) to overall command. The CCP General Lin Biao, learning of Chen's plans from communism. Here another external circumstance impinged upon China: the accelerating hostility between the United States and USSR, simmering in divided Korea and Europe, came to the boil in China.

In summer 1948, Peng Dehuai and Liu Bocheng defeated substantial GMD forces, and CCP leaders began to hear of GMD generals eager to switch sides in hopes of backing a winner. Based on intelligence from well-placed spies, Mao urged an all-out offensive to drive the GMD from Manchuria. Jiang Jieshi once again flew to the scene to take personal charge, but to no avail. At Jinzhou, the PLA took 90,000 GMD prisoners then surrounded and destroyed a relief army from Shenyang, killing 25,000 and taking another 60,000 prisoners. The remaining GMD forces in Changchun defected and attacked their former comrades. Lin Biao took Shenyang in late October, and Manchuria, with its mineral and industrial riches and proximity to the USSR, became CCP territory.

In North China, the GMD still held cities and railway lines, but the intervening countryside belonged to the CCP, giving them greater mobility and more effective intelligence. The next decisive battle, the Huai-Hai campaign of late 1948, centered on the town of Xuzhou, where east–west and north–south railway lines meet in the center of the North China plain. Both sides moved their massed armies toward Xuzhou—almost 2 million troops along a 130-mile (209-km) front. The CCP developed an overall plan of attack, while the GMD general staff argued whether to make a stand or withdraw southward. The PLA struck first, capturing an entire army group. Jiang Jieshi, convinced of his own superiority as a tactician, commanded the GMD armies by telegraph and telephone from Nanjing, hundreds of miles away, creating fatal confusion for his generals.

Around Xuzhou, the PLA made good use of heavy artillery, mostly American or Japanese guns taken from GMD units. Pounding the core of the GMD formations, Chen Yi and Liu Bocheng trapped and destroyed the main GMD army. When the remaining Nationalist forces attempted to retreat southward, the PLA surrounded them. Starving and running out of ammunition, they surrendered on January 10, 1949.

The GMD had lost its best armies and huge stockpiles of weapons. That same week, a CCP assault on Tianjin took less than a day to persuade the GMD to surrender. On January 31, Lin Biao's troops moved into Beiping as GMD General Fu Zuoyi (1895–1974), his staff penetrated by CCP members (including his own daughter), surrendered without a fight. The Communists' infiltration of GMD headquarters, successful tactics, and GMD factionalism had given control over North China to the CCP.

The initiative had clearly shifted. Jiang Jieshi resigned as head of the ROC government and army, leaving Li Zongren (1890–1969), a weak leader, to negotiate with the CCP and buy time, hoping for an influx of US aid to prevent a communist victory. Li Zongren appealed to Mao to negotiate and to Washington and Moscow for mediation. Stalin, fearing direct US intervention, considered participating, but Mao urged him not to accept in light of the CCP's impending victory.

Eager to end the war and implement the social revolution that was his primary goal, Mao nonetheless agreed to talks in order to prevent American intervention and give the PLA a rest before assaulting the Yangzi River. On April 1, 1949, Zhou Enlai and Lin Biao met with a GMD delegation and demanded surrender, giving them two weeks to respond. Li Zongren requested last-minute assistance from the British, Australians, and Americans, but they turned him down, claiming "non-interference in China's internal affairs."

On April 21, the CCP armies crossed the Yangzi at many points, meeting only sporadic resistance as the GMD river navy defected en masse. GMD commanders, some obeying Li Zongren and others waiting for Jiang Jieshi, had no coordinated strategy. When his negotiating team in Beiping changed sides, Li Zongren evacuated Nanjing on the April 23, flying home to Guangxi to plan a stand against the PLA. The citizens of Nanjing pillaged the homes of Nationalist officials and GMD generals. Wealthy residents loaded their fortunes onto airplanes to flee, only to find that the pilots had defected to the CCP.

The American bailout that Jiang expected never arrived. A late 1948 visit to Washington by Madame Jiang (Song Meiling), enormously popular in the United States, failed to persuade the US government to provide further aid, though she had tea with President and Mrs. Truman. She remained in the United States for over a year, organizing support for the Nationalist cause and stimulating the China lobby to maintain the GMD government's legitimacy in American eyes, even as the civil war turned against them. Riding the rising tide of the Second Red Scare—the USSR tested its first atomic bomb in August 1949—her intervention helped to keep the United States on Jiang Jieshi's side until the late 1970s.

Jiang had promised to defend Shanghai to the bitter end, but the city's elite, including Green Gang chief Du Yuesheng, who later fled to Hong Kong, sent representatives to CCP headquarters, proposing a peaceful takeover. After a flurry of arrests and executions of the GMD's local opponents, Jiang left Shanghai for Taiwan in early May, and the PLA entered the city the following day without a battle.

Li Zongren's remnant GMD government fled from Guangzhou to Chongqing to Taiwan, and the civil war ended in complete victory for the PLA and CCP. On October 1, 1949, Mao Zedong and his comrades stood on Tiananmen, the Gate of Heavenly Peace in front of the Forbidden City in (newly renamed) Beijing, and announced the establishment of the People's Republic of China (PRC) as the sole legitimate government of China. He declared that the CCP and PRC represented "the will of the whole nation."

Did the CCP win the war, or did the GMD lose it? The CCP claimed to have been correct in its political and military strategy, courageous in battle, virtuous in opposition to GMD perfidy, and guided by the genius of Mao Zedong. The GMD, on the other hand, blamed the USSR for backing the CCP, the United States for abandoning its anticommunist ally, and the CCP for being an anti-Chinese tool of the Soviets. Needless to say, neither story conforms to the complex realities of the late 1940s. Although CCP claims of moral as well as military victory continue to underlie its legitimacy for many Chinese people, neither party was foreordained to win. Many causes—decisions by individuals at all levels of military and civil authority, social and political arrangements ("structures"), and luck—determined the outcome of the Chinese civil war.

PREPARING TAIWAN

Recovering Taiwan from the Japanese in 1945, after 50 years of colonial occupation, had been one of Jiang Jieshi's happiest achievements. Its post-1945 administration by the Nationalist government, however, consisted of authoritarian repression, hyperinflation, corruption, and military domination of civilian life. These led to discontent, particularly among

the "native Taiwanese," the vast majority of the island's 6 million people.

Jiang appointed Chen Yi (1883–1950; not the CCP general mentioned above), former governor of Fujian, as the first ROC governor of Taiwan. Chen discriminated against the local people, whom he regarded as collaborators, and employed only officials and troops from the mainland. Although fluent in Japanese, Chen Yi insisted that Taiwanese elites address him in Mandarin, which few of them knew, rather than Japanese or their native Taiwanese. Accustomed to efficient (though repressive) Japanese administration, the Taiwanese elites soon lost their initial enthusiasm for Nationalist rule in the face of Chen's arrogant mismanagement.

On February 28, 1947, a squabble between unlicensed cigarette vendors and government enforcers turned violent, troops fired on civilians, and weeks of civil unrest ensued. Chen Yi called for reinforcements to quell this "2/28 Incident" and took the opportunity to imprison or execute thousands of educated, politically active Taiwanese on charges of communism or communist sympathies. This response decimated local elites and alienated them from the government, entirely controlled by recently arrived "mainlanders." Some Taiwanese perceived themselves as being recolonized by the ROC.

In late 1948, with the military situation on the mainland deteriorating, Jiang Jieshi appointed General Chen Cheng as Taiwan governor. The GMD prepared the island as a refuge from which to organize a revival, evacuating the government's gold reserves, foreign exchange holdings, archives, art treasures (including much of the Qing imperial collection), and most remaining military equipment to Taiwan in 1949. After the GMD's defeat, over 2 million people—soldiers and officers, GMD officials, businessmen and intellectuals—crossed the Taiwan Straits to become the "mainlander" population of the island. The GMD established autocratic military-political rule over Taiwan, with Jiang at its center, mainlanders as its personnel, and very little role for the Taiwanese.

The GMD insisted that the Republic of China, not the PRC, constituted China's only legitimate government, creating a situation not unlike that in Korea, or in Vietnam after 1954. Two governments, one communist and allied with the USSR, the other anticommunist and allied with the United States, claimed sole sovereignty over what had been (briefly) one postwar country. As the Cold War heated up, Jiang Jieshi and his generals concluded correctly that the United States would not allow the PRC to invade Taiwan, and concentrated on making the island an "anticommunist bastion in the Pacific." When the Korean War began, the United States confirmed Jiang's judgment, sending the 7th fleet into the Taiwan Strait to protect the bastion.

THE PRC AND ITS FRONTIERS

Over the course of the Republican period (1912–49), the GMD and CCP had come to very similar conclusions about what "China" should be, in geographical terms. Both conceived China as a modern nation-state covering the entire territory of the Qing empire. That is, they saw Manchuria, Mongolia, Xinjiang, Tibet, and the Southeast Asian borderlands and their non-Chinese inhabitants as integral parts of the nation. Some communists argued for a federal form of government like the USSR's, even for frontier peoples' right to secede. But once in power, Mao and his party denied that possibility and firmly established New China's borders as encompassing all those culturally non-Chinese regions. The PRC, like the GMD before it, defined the indigenous peoples of the frontiers as members of "the Chinese people."

The USSR returned all of Manchuria to China in 1946. Mongolia, on the other hand, continued divided after 1949. Jiang Jieshi signed a treaty with the USSR agreeing to self-determination for Outer Mongolia. That large, sparsely inhabited region had declared itself the People's Republic of Mongolia in 1924, under Soviet "guidance," and remained a loyal, obedient satellite state until the dissolution of the USSR.

In 1944, the Eastern Turkestan Republic (ETR), based in northwestern Xinjiang, had claimed sovereignty and Soviet protection against the GMD provincial government.[2] Despite internal conflicts between secular (Soviet-oriented) and religious (Islamic modernist) factions, the ETR posed a significant challenge to Chinese dominion for five years. As the PLA planned its entry into Xinjiang in August 1949, GMD Governor Zhang Zhizhong (1895–1969) switched sides and negotiated with Burhan Shahidi (1894–1989), head of the ETR. After many of the ETR's most effective leaders died in a still mysterious airplane crash on the way

to talks in Beijing, the breakaway ETR declared allegiance to the PRC.

Many PLA units remained in Xinjiang as permanent garrisons. For the next three years, the CCP recruited women from China Proper to settle in Xinjiang and marry those mostly Han Chinese soldiers. This policy, similar to the frontier military garrisons of former dynasties, gave Xinjiang a core of Han Chinese settlement that has grown rapidly since then. In 2010, the formerly dominant Turkic-speaking Muslims (Uyghurs, Kazakhs, Kyrgyz, Uzbeks) represented less than half the province's population.

Tibet, de facto an independent state since the late Qing, presented even greater difficulties. The Tibetan parliament expelled all GMD officials from what they saw as their realm in July 1949 and a year later enthroned the 14th Dalai Lama (b. 1935), then 15 years old, as temporal ruler. Under heavy pressure, with few resources, in summer 1951 the Dalai Lama sent a delegation to Beijing to negotiate a Seventeen-Point Agreement recognizing PRC sovereignty—"the Tibetan people shall return to the big family of the motherland." In return, Beijing promised to protect freedom of religion; not interfere with the status, functions, and powers of the Dalai Lama; and incorporate the Tibetan army into the PLA. This document has been controversial since its signing, the PRC affirming its validity and Tibetan nationalists claiming both that it was signed under illegal duress and that the PRC has routinely violated it. The Dalai Lama has repudiated it.

Easily defeating the small Tibetan army in eastern Tibet, the PLA entered Lhasa in September 1951. For the next eight years, the Dalai Lama and the PRC coexisted uneasily, the Tibetan leader attended the National People's Congress, of which he was a vice-president, and once met Mao Zedong. With the absorption of Tibet, the PRC succeeded where the ROC had failed—all the recognized territory of the former Qing (except Outer Mongolia and Taiwan) had been unified as "China."

LAND REFORM

Since the Jiangxi Soviet, the CCP had been undertaking land reform to increase food supplies, recruit peasant allies, and overturn conventional authority in rural China. Ranging from rent reduction to outright redistribution, its methods had been refined and systematized. After 1949, Mao Zedong saw nationwide land reform as the nation's most important means to enlist the entire peasantry on the government's side; eliminate local power-holders opposed to the CCP; and increase agricultural production to support industrialization.

CCP work teams followed the PLA into all "liberated" areas, seeking local activists—usually poor peasants, often women—to encourage their neighbors to participate in land reform. Using these activists as leaders, CCP cadres then measured all agricultural land, determined its ownership, and registered all families in the five classes that Mao had described in 1927 (see p. 296). The cadres organized "struggle meetings" against landlords and rich peasants, often savagely beaten or executed, and confiscated their land, redistributing it to landless and poor peasants. Never simple, always contested, the 1950–52 land reform generated injustices at every stage, and at least 1 million people died. Nonetheless, over 100 million acres of farmland changed hands, and many "new middle peasants" rejoiced at finally possessing sufficient farmland.

INTERNATIONAL RELATIONS AND THE KOREAN WAR

From the outset, the PRC declared itself an ally of the USSR and opponent of "Western imperialism." The CCP had hoped for good relations with the United States, but after 1944, Mao and his colleagues saw the United States, supporting Jiang Jieshi with its escalating anticommunism, as an intransigent, reactionary enemy. Zhou Enlai and Mao agreed that the United States intended to invade China on three fronts: Taiwan, Vietnam, and Korea. Although Americans called it "containment" rather than "invasion," Zhou and Mao correctly predicted the three major Sino-American confrontations of the next two decades.

As tensions rose in divided Korea in 1948–49, the PLA reorganized to station substantial armies near the Korean border. The CCP's relations with Kim Il Sung and his colleagues had been ambivalent. Comrades in the struggle against Japan and imperialism, they clashed on issues of nationalism and independence.

A land reform team member (left), holding new land ownership certificates, helps local peasants redistribute land in Linping, a township about 18 miles (30 km) from Hangzhou, in Zhejiang province. This 1950 scene was played out in hundreds of thousands of villages during the land reform campaign, 1950–52.

Nonetheless, in 1949–50 the CCP sent tens of thousands of Korean veterans of the PLA back to Korea, with their weapons, at Kim's request.

When Kim came to Beijing in mid-May 1950, having obtained Stalin's approval for a war of reunification, Mao asked him how the United States would react to a military strike against South Korea and whether he needed direct Chinese aid. Kim responded that the war would only take two or three weeks, so the United States would not have time to react with troops, and the Koreans could handle it themselves. Mao concurred, because Kim's desire for war fit the PRC's strategy of confronting the United States, and he placed the expanded northeastern command on high alert. When MacArthur crossed the 38th parallel in September 1950, heading toward the Chinese border after the Inch'ŏn landing, Mao telegraphed Zhou Enlai:

> ...we unanimously believe that having our troops enter Korea is more advantageous...if we do not send troops, it will be most disadvantageous to Manchuria...the Northeastern border defenses will be absorbed, and South Manchurian electric power will be controlled [by the enemy].[3]

Chinese troops, commanded by General Peng Dehuai, entered North Korea in October and November, reversing the American northward drive, retaking Seoul, and reestablishing the division of the peninsula near the 38th parallel. The war cost the PLA over 500,000 casualties.

SOCIAL MOBILIZATION

When the Korean War began in June 1950, the CCP ordered a national campaign to "Resist America and Aid Korea." Apart from gathering concrete resources, Beijing mobilized political emotions all over China in favor of the PRC's alliance with the USSR and North Korea. From schoolchildren to soldiers to neighborhood committees, everyone had to do their part. Teachers who refused to organize children for the campaign were criticized then persuaded that patriotic movements and social mobilization transcended their intellectual tasks. This CCP "campaign style"—society-wide mobilization, meetings and social pressure, criticism and self-criticism—first tested in land reform and party rectification movements, became a hallmark

of the PRC and a major difference between China and the USSR.

Needing the expertise of China's businessmen and engineers for the crucial goal of industrialization, the CCP encouraged Chinese capitalists (called "national bourgeoisie") to remain on the mainland and continue operating their factories. Believing that the CCP would destroy capitalism, some fled to Taiwan, Hong Kong, or farther, but others stayed. The CCP initially treated them well, making them members of the Shanghai Political Consultative Committee, among other bodies, and their factories received government contracts as well as continuing private business.

The honeymoon lasted through China's entry into the Korean War and ended in early 1952, when the government attacked the capitalists directly in the Five-Anti campaign—directed against bribery, tax evasion, stealing state assets, fraudulent practices, and theft of government economic secrets. This campaign included mass demonstrations and denunciations, forced inspections of factories and account books, and public confessions by selected targets. Even those who had honestly committed themselves to the PRC suffered attacks, and industrial production fell sharply in 1952, so the party shortened and curtailed the campaign.

The CCP did not restrict its campaigns to capitalists. Having expanded very rapidly during and after the civil war, the CCP found that many new party members did not conform to its rigid discipline. The Three-Anti movement of 1951 targeted CCP cadres, especially former GMD members, accused of corruption, waste, and "bureaucratism," rigid application of rules without attention to goals. Discovering corruption and illicit private economic activity at every level of party and society, the Three-Anti campaign then extended outside the party to investigate and, in some cases, nationalize voluntary associations of every kind. Although not a mass movement, the Three-Anti alerted new party members that they were not immune to public exposure and punishment.

Eager to diminish the power of traditional patriarchal authority—which they called "feudal"—and to liberate the productive capacities of women, the new government returned to the issue of family reform, postponed since the Jiangxi Soviet (see pp. 295–97). In 1950, the PRC promulgated a new Marriage Law. Article 1 proclaimed its revolutionary purposes:

The feudal marriage system based on arbitrary and compulsory arrangements and the supremacy of man over woman, and in disregard of the interests of the children, is abolished. The new democratic marriage system, which is based on the free choice of partners, on monogamy, on equal rights for both sexes, and on the protection of the lawful interests of women and children, is put into effect.[4]

The law did not grant unilateral right to divorce, but either spouse could seek divorce through the courts, if mediation failed. Almost immediately, hundreds of thousands of women, most of them urban and thus exposed to media and able to draw on government protection, sought and obtained divorces. In rural areas, however, millions of recently recruited cadres refused to cooperate with marriage reform. Resistance came, as in Jiangxi, from men and from older women, who saw the new law threatening their authority over daughters-in-law. Busy with land reform, Korea, and the Three- and Five-Anti campaigns, the PRC did not mount a nationwide campaign for marriage reform until 1953.

Republican China had been plagued by many social ills, especially opium addiction and prostitution. Although the Republican government had pledged to eliminate both, they had failed. Reformist Chinese felt degraded by the national and "racial" weakness demonstrated by opium use and sexual servitude. By late 1951, urban administrators had more effective tools to eradicate social evils than their GMD predecessors.

To undertake a campaign against prostitution, local leaders needed space to house former prostitutes, educated caretakers to "reform" and teach them, money for salaries, medical treatment, food, and day care. Police arrested the women, initially in large-scale sweeps, and took them to "Women's Labor Training Institutes." To gain the women's trust, doctors treated their sexually transmitted diseases, drug addictions, and other health problems, persuading most of them that their lives had value in New China.

Then they began studying—literacy, politics, consciousness-raising, and perhaps a trade—to learn that they had been oppressed (a new concept) and that they should not return to their antisocial profession. The cadres brought the former madams to the Institutes and organized "struggle meetings" against them. The routines of life at the Institutes gave the inmates a sense of belonging and self-worth. After individual investigation and approval, the Institutes released the women to their natal families, husbands, factory jobs, or areas where men sought wives, such as Xinjiang. The women had to consent to their destination, and no coercion was permitted. Because the CCP controlled the countryside and had already developed nationwide networks of information and communication, Institute cadres could prepare the women's families before sending them home and monitor them afterwards. This campaign trained 7,000 women in Shanghai alone, so the national total must have been very large.

In contrast to the publicity accompanying the antiprostitution campaign, the PRC undertook the movement against opium in complete silence. Not wishing to encourage international rumors about China as a source of illegal drugs, the Ministry of Public Security used local officials to mobilize people through highly ritualized, emotional propaganda meetings and public trials involving an astonishing 75 million people. Police executed large-scale drug dealers in public, about 800 nationwide. Officials gave speeches describing the suffering inflicted on ordinary Chinese as a result of drugs, invariably blaming foreign imperialists (especially Great Britain and Japan) and Chinese drug traffickers. Information gathered in the Five-Anti campaign often pointed to drugs as an aspect of corruption, so local cadres could organize effective eradication campaigns by eliminating sources of supply. Addicts received treatment, assignment to labor camps, or, if old or infirm, monitored supplies of drugs.

By 1958, both prostitution and opium addiction had been successfully controlled, even eliminated in some places, and the PRC claimed, with some justification, to have freed China of social ills that their "reactionary" predecessors had allowed. After 1978, both reappeared along with free markets and private wealth (see p. 456).

THE OCCUPATION OF JAPAN

Emperor Hirohito's radio announcement on August 15, 1945—the first time the general Japanese population had ever heard an emperor's voice—that they must now "endure the unendurable and bear the unbearable" stunned its listeners. For most, surrender did not initiate

A group of people weep amidst the rubble of their homes while listening to Emperor Hirohito make his fateful broadcast announcing Japan's capitulation, August 15, 1945.

their suffering. They had long been enduring—especially the 9 million homeless, the untold millions whose loved ones and family breadwinners were among the 3 million dead, and the 7 million soldiers and civilians still scattered about the former empire who needed to return to Japan, often to destroyed homes or wiped-out families. Many thousands more would die of starvation or radiation disease in the months after August 1945.

Hirohito's words fell in a variety of ways on Japanese ears. Some people felt liberated, rejoicing in freedom from wartime oppression, but for most, liberation took the form of freedom from the daily threat of death from the sky or an anticipated Allied invasion. Some feared the future. Most were psychologically paralyzed in the weeks after Hirohito's broadcast. Even before war's end, Japanese psychologists noted that the population suffered from *kyōdatsu*, a clinical term for a patient's emotional collapse, now applied to the whole society to mean debilitating despondency and exhaustion. Together with hunger and physical disease, *kyōdatsu* could make Japan's recovery difficult. Even the American occupiers who arrived in September worried that despondent Japanese might not adapt well to the American reform policies.

Hirohito's words did establish the *meaning* of the war that dominated Japanese interpretations for several decades. He avoided terms like "surrender" or "defeat," noting, seemingly without irony, that the war "did not turn in Japan's favor." He stated that his country had entered the war against the United States to guarantee Japan's survival and the "stability of Asia" and had not intended to infringe on Asian countries' sovereignty. He expressed deep regrets to Asian countries that had cooperated with Japan for "the liberation of East Asia." Japan, he continued, had to abandon its war efforts to save humanity:

> *The enemy...for the first time used cruel bombs to kill and maim extremely large numbers of the innocent.... To continue the war further could lead in the end not only to the extermination of our race, but also to the destruction of all human civilization.*[5]

In addition, his statement that he suffered when considering the plight of the Japanese people allowed many listeners to believe that, rather than leading the country during the war, Hirohito had been surrounded and misrepresented by evil advisers. In this speech, then, Hirohito established key postwar themes about the war: Japan's victimhood due to the suffering of its people, the empire's noble efforts to liberate Asia from Western imperialism, and the emperor's essential distance from what would later be defined as war crimes committed by individual government and military officials. These have all been challenged in recent years.

Except for the notion of Japan's liberation of Asia, the emperor's statement paralleled key parts of US policy when the American occupation began, following the signing of the instruments of surrender on September 2, 1945. The occupation—with General Douglas Mac-Arthur as Supreme Commander for the Allied Powers (SCAP)—took as its primary goal the "democratization and demilitarization" of Japan. Hirohito had not articulated this theme, but democratization and demilitarization required rooting out and bringing to justice those who had led Japan astray.

After much debate, SCAP decided that the institution of the emperor was too politically valuable to jettison and defined Hirohito himself as an impotent victim of treacherous officials, an interpretation that some listeners had drawn from the emperor's August

15 speech. Although the US occupation could not accept the notion of Japan's victimhood, the American view, like Hirohito's stress on Japanese victimhood, essentially obliterated the suffering of other Asians. The American erasure of Asian suffering resulted from Americans' singular focus on the war after Pearl Harbor. In December 1945, American censors required Japanese writers to use the term "Pacific War" rather than "Great East Asia War" in an attempt to remove nationalistic connotations from the war's name. In effect, SCAP introduced a lasting shift in focus from Asia to the Pacific. Historian John Dower calls this a "maladroit rectification of names [that] facilitated the [Japanese] process of forgetting what they had done to their Asian neighbors."

THE WINTER OF 1945–46

For the first time in 75 years, China and Korea played no role in average Japanese people's lives. Japan's physical territory reverted to its 1870s boundaries; soldiers returned from the former empire; Korea and Taiwan were no longer colonies; and the former puppet states in Manchuria and North China no longer answered to the Japanese military. In the immediate aftermath of the war, former Japanese preoccupations lost their relevance. For example, the question of modernity became entirely moot—it did not matter whether present society was better, richer, more technologically sophisticated than the past or whether modernity was foreign and hedonistic, an obstacle to be overcome (see pp. 283–84). Food, shelter, and acquiring the means to pay for them quickly became most Japanese people's sole concerns. Into that barren landscape entered an unknown factor—an army of occupation.

The Japanese government anticipated the occupation's arrival with fears that the starving, kyōdatsu-afflicted population could not afford to indulge. Even before the occupation forces arrived, the Japanese government got to work on the tasks they thought most important—destroying wartime records and creating sex stations for the army of occupation. A pall of smoke hung over Tokyo for two weeks in late August as officials burned tons of documents. Planning for sex stations began on August 18, just three days after the emperor's radio address. The Home Ministry sent secret messages to local police chiefs asking them to set up "comfort stations." When the government learned that MacArthur opposed official stations, it shifted responsibility for prostitution to private entrepreneurs, guaranteeing them government loans and police protection.

Recruiting posters called on "new Japanese women" to "participate in the great task of comforting the occupation force." By August 27, 1,300 women in Tokyo had signed up as workers in the Recreation and Amusement Association (RAA). Most of these first postwar military "comfort women" were starving and had only shabby clothes; few had experience in sex work. Many were widows and orphans, and this job promised food. At the inauguration of the RAA on August 28, the women took an oath that stated they were "defend[ing] and nurtur[ing] the purity of our race," but they aimed only for personal survival.

The government urged other young women to go to the countryside and continue to wear their frumpiest wartime monpe (pantaloons) to avoid sexual assaults. The newly recruited sex workers would hold back the "raging waves" at Japan's shores. It may never be known if the RAA centers held back those waves, though they certainly did brisk business. Workers serviced between 15 and 60 US soldiers a day, earning 15 yen (about US$1 at the time) for each visit. Facilities were primitive, and many sexual acts took place in corridors.

SCAP asked the head of Tokyo's hygiene department to divide RAA workers into three groups to service different types of Americans: officers, white enlisted men, and black enlisted men. The centers were closed in January 1946 when SCAP discovered that 90 percent of the RAA workers and 70 percent of one unit of the US Eighth Army had syphilis. In addition, SCAP determined that the RAA centers violated women's rights. Sex work then moved to licensed brothels and the streets, where it continued to be a significant part of the survival efforts of women and their families.

Thousands of women became pan-pan (the term used for prostitutes during the occupation). Some felt compelled to do so to feed their families, while others made a more positive choice to earn good wages and have a degree of freedom to spend those wages that other women, unemployed or in poorly paid jobs, did not. Despite restrictions on "fraternization," many American soldiers formed longer-term, loving relationships with Japanese women, fathering children and, by the end of the occupation, being allowed to marry.

Japanese Christian feminist organizations, especially the YWCA and the WCTU, fought vigorously against prostitution. They also loudly protested SCAP's treatment of all Japanese women as prostitutes when SCAP officials began to grab women of all classes and ages from trains or the street to test them for syphilis.

The sexual nexus of Americans and Japanese was a significant part of the occupation, though, of course, only one part. It had both social and economic ramifications; the first US patents for penicillin were sold to Japanese companies in 1946 to combat sexually transmitted diseases. The ubiquity of sexuality constituted an important part of a larger phenomenon called "*kasutori* culture."[6] *Kasutori*, a cheap but powerful liquor associated with decadence and nihilism, was favored by artists living at the fringes of society, and it gave its name to an era when many people had little food and shelter and got by on semi-legal or illegal activities.

Ordinary Japanese received daily rations of 1,050 calories in the postwar months. Bad harvests, combined with wartime conversion of fertilizer to munitions, made food scarce just as millions returned from the empire. Many died; in October 1945, an estimated six people starved to death each day in Tokyo's Ueno railway station. Food shipments from the United States began to arrive in January 1946, but the winter of 1945–46 was brutal. No one could survive without bartering clothes for food and buying supplies at the thousands of illegal black markets. The culture of illegality and living for the moment, lubricated by wine and drugs to ease the despondency and exhaustion of a senseless, losing war, permeated early postwar Japanese society. Even children's games reflected the ways adults learned to make do—kids played "*pan-pan* and customer."

THE AMERICAN OCCUPATION

The occupation was, in theory, a multinational effort, with the 11 member states of the Far Eastern Commission in charge of setting policies for SCAP.[7] In early 1946, a more streamlined Allied Council for Japan with four members—the British Commonwealth, the United States, USSR, and China—was set up to advise MacArthur. MacArthur paid little attention to either body and took orders only from Washington, so historians correctly consider it an American occupation.

Occupation officers began to arrive in September 1945. By early 1946, 1,500 civilian and military officers occupied many of the unbombed buildings in central Tokyo; their numbers reached 3,200 two years later. This relatively small number confirms SCAP's intention for the Japanese to administer their own government. While generally using the Japanese government, SCAP retained certain tasks for themselves as part of democratization and demilitarization.

These tasks included immediately disbanding the Japanese army and navy and beginning repatriation of 3.7 million troops to Japan—the armed forces were officially terminated on November 30, 1945. SCAP also purged about 220,000 men and 8 women from government and business implicated in the Japanese war effort. SCAP eliminated government institutions it believed had fostered repression at home, disestablishing State Shintō as the official religion of the state; dismantling the Home Ministry, starting with the Special Higher Police ("thought police") in October; and freeing political prisoners, including communists, from jail. Believing wartime censorship to have been repressive, SCAP (ironically) substituted its own form of censorship of books, newspapers, and artistic production. During and immediately after war, the occupation conducted trials of 6,000 people for war crimes—of whom 930 were executed—in addition to carrying out the International Military Tribunal for the Far East (1946–48), commonly called the Tokyo Trial.

For the Japanese government to administer the country, it needed bureaucrats and elected officials. SCAP "guided" (that is, directed) the Japanese government through "suggestions," but Japanese officials passed laws and implemented policies. The use of "suggestions"—as close to orders as possible without actually being orders—strongly resembled Japan's "administrative guidance" (see p. 372), later considered by American critics to be based in Japanese culture. Shidehara Kijūrō, the multilateralist foreign minister in the 1920s, became prime minister in October, and called the first postwar Diet elections in April 1946. The former Seiyūkai ran as the new Liberal Party, and the Minseitō as the Progressive Party, later changing its name to the Democratic Party. Together, these two parties won about 50 percent of the vote in 1946, with the Japan Socialist Party gaining about 18 percent. The Japan Communist Party, now legal, won 3 percent of the vote. Women voted for the first time, and 39 women won seats in the Diet.

The Liberal party won a plurality in 1946, but before its head, Hatoyama Ichirō (1883–1959), could become prime minister, SCAP purged him, so Yoshida Shigeru (1878–1967), former ambassador to Great Britain, assumed the prime ministership. In the next election, called after the adoption in 1947 of the new constitution, the Japan Socialist Party won the largest number of seats. Its head, Katayama Tetsu (1887–1978), formed a government, but discord within the JSP led Katayama to resign after less than a year in office. There would not be another Socialist prime minister for almost 50 years, though the Socialists remained in coalition with the Democratic Party (under Prime Minister Ashida Hitoshi [1887–1959]) for another year. Thereafter, Yoshida returned and remained prime minister from October 1948 to December 1954. In many ways, a coalition of Yoshida Shigeru and SCAP governed Japan's postwar years.

SCAP announced policies in the fall of 1945 that ultimately had to be codified in Japanese law; hence the need for a Japanese government. These included freedoms of speech, press, and assembly; women's political and social rights; the right to form unions; redistribution of farmland from landlords to tenants; dissolution

KUROSAWA AKIRA, FILMMAKER

Kurosawa Akira filming on location, 1970.

The youngest of eight children, Kurosawa (1910–1998) first studied painting, switching to filmmaking in 1936. His early films reflected the age, as they had to pass the critical eyes of wartime and occupation censors. During the war, he directed two films about a judo practitioner (*Sanshirō Sugata* I, 1943, and *Sanshirō Sugata* II, 1945) and one honoring women factory workers (*The Most Beautiful*, 1944).

Shortly after releasing *The Most Beautiful*, Kurosawa unromantically proposed to its leading lady, Yaguchi Yōko (1921–1985), stating that since everyone might die in Japan's anticipated last stand against the Allies, they may as well experience the marital state. Yōko continued acting after their marriage. The couple had two children: a daughter, costume designer Kazuko, and a son, movie producer Hisao. Even in his autobiography, Kurosawa wrote little about his family, claiming that he spent most of his time thinking about films. Despite its odd beginning, their marriage lasted until Yōko's death.

SCAP rejected his first postwar film, based on a medieval play, as "feudalistic," because it portrayed a samurai and his loyal servant. The next, *No Regrets for Our Youth* (1946), featured a young woman, Yukie, who dutifully served the parents of her leftist lover after his death in jail for opposing the war. While of the *zaibatsu*; and amendment of the Meiji Constitution. The question of the emperor did not appear in the reforms announced in the fall of 1945. In fact, when MacArthur became SCAP, he was informed that his authority superseded that of the emperor and the Japanese government.

SCAP implemented its policies by using the legal authority of the Japanese government. Basic civil and civic rights were guaranteed in the 1947 Constitution; farmland was redistributed under the Farm Land Reform Law, passed by the Diet in 1946; and some *zaibatsu* were broken up under the Law for the Elimination of Excessive Concentration of Economic Power, passed in 1947. The Women's Suffrage League (see pp. 254–55) reconstituted itself ten days after surrender and persuaded the Japanese cabinet to grant women the vote. Japanese feminists finally succeeded, after decades of struggle, to gain the vote, and were disappointed when MacArthur received credit for granting Japanese women's civil rights.

Of the two major economic reforms, land reform lasted longer. The transfer of land had already begun before the war. In the 1920s, some absentee landlords, tired of dealing with tenant unions, sold some of their

criticizing Japan's militaristic wartime leadership—Kurosawa especially hated the censors who stifled his creative work—he did not question the heroine's dedicating herself as a "wifely" servant to her "in-laws." Gender relations did not concern Kurosawa, even when the protagonist was a woman; rather, he concentrated on Yukie's search for life's meaning in a confusing world.

The following year, *One Wonderful Sunday* depicted a young couple trying to enjoy life against a realistic backdrop of poverty in Tokyo. *Drunken Angel* (1948), a gangster film, focused on *kasutori*-culture era issues of health, prostitution, and the black market—though censors deleted a burned-out building as being critical of the Americans. Kurosawa wished to force viewers to abandon their complacency in the face of postwar dislocation and poverty just as his elder brother had forced him, at 13, to confront the death and destruction of the 1923 Tokyo earthquake, an event that profoundly affected his life and artistic work.

His breakthrough film in the West, *Rashōmon*, won the Honorary Academy Award for best foreign language film in 1951. Adapted from a story by Akutagawa Ryūnosuke (1892–1927), the film tells of a rape and murder from the contradictory perspectives of four living people and the ghost of the murdered samurai, questioning the singular, objective existence of truth in descriptions of human experience. His last two occupation-era films were *The Idiot* (1951), based on the Dostoevsky novel, and *Ikiru* (*To Live*, 1952), which some consider his finest. *Ikiru*'s protagonist, Watanabe, a middle-aged man with a boring bureaucratic job and a selfish son and daughter-in-law, turns to drink when diagnosed with stomach cancer. A woman toymaker reverses his outlook on life; energized, he dedicates his last year to cutting through red tape to build a playground. Like the protagonist in *No Regrets*, Watanabe finds his life's meaning in the context of postwar society.

After the occupation, Kurosawa made numerous period films that inspired world cinema, including *The Seven Samurai* (1954), *The Hidden Fortress* (1958), *Yojimbo* (1961), and *Kagemusha* (1980). Several adapted works by Shakespeare, Gorky, Natsume Sōseki, and Dostoevsky, while others commented on social injustice. Altogether, Kurosawa made 30 movies. One of the most influential filmmakers of the twentieth century, he won an Academy Award for Lifetime Achievement in 1989.

holdings. More important, the government paid different prices during the war for rice sold by its growers and by landlords who collected it as rent. This led additional landlords to sell their acreage. Nevertheless, 45 percent of cultivated land was still rented to tenants at the end of the war. The veterans of FDR's New Deal who served in the US occupation wished to eliminate rural inequality and pushed to abolish landlordism altogether. SCAP did not realize how easy their task would be. Farmers often rented plots *from* neighbors while renting other plots *to* neighbors, thus serving as both landlord and tenant. Only 2,000 landlords nationwide owned 100 acres or more, and most farmers had just 10 acres.

The Farm Land Reform Law prohibited all absentee landlordism and limited ownership by farmers who lived in the village to 10 acres (the amount many already held), of which no more than 2.5 acres could be rented out. The government bought excess land and sold it to farmers who had less than the maximum. With rampant inflation, land had become exceedingly cheap—some said a family's plot of land could be had for the price of a carton of cigarettes. By 1950, only 5 percent of farmers were still fully tenants. This resulted, in the postwar decades, in a politically conservative rural sector without the tenant–landlord strife of the 1920s and 1930s.

The other economic reform, *zaibatsu* dissolution, was less thorough-going than land reform. The SCAP commission set up under the Law for the Elimination of Excessive Concentration of Economic Power initially targeted 1,200 companies. Pressure from US business leaders and government officials, who called that plan detrimental to Japan's recovery, stifled it. As the Cold War intensified—with the CCP's increasing success and worsening tensions between the USSR and United States—concern for Japan's recovery took precedence over the economic ideals of SCAP's New Dealers. In the end, they dismantled just 83 *zaibatsu*, and 5,000 other companies had to reorganize. The commission separated Mitsui and Mitsubishi into over 200 individual companies.

They also carried out other economic changes to shatter the power of the *zaibatsu*—forced divestment of rich families' shareholdings and the breakup of cartels and trusts. Divestment of shareholdings helped build the modern Tokyo stock-exchange system. When the occupation ended in 1952, many of the former *zaibatsu* reestablished links among the companies forced apart in the late 1940s. But the window of opportunity for companies independent of the old *zaibatsu* during this period encouraged the growth of companies that later served as export leaders: Sony, Honda, Toyota, and Panasonic, among others.

SCAP believed that democratization also required education reform. Elementary schools had instilled allegiance to the emperor since the 1890 Imperial Rescript on Education, and postelementary schools, segregated by sex, offered inferior education to girls. SCAP targeted both of these problems. Pedagogy was changed from a rote-learning system to greater encouragement of independent thought. Until new textbooks could be published, existing textbooks had to be used, so, as in the repressive days of wartime censorship, American censors deleted line after line of forbidden words.

SCAP set up local school boards to run schools on the American model. Boys and girls attended the same schools, and mandatory schooling was extended to nine years. (In 2009, 93 percent of Japanese graduated from high school, as compared to 72 percent in the United States.) Access to college education was enhanced by the 1949 upgrading of some former technical schools to university status. Because some new universities continued to have poor reputations, however, competition for admission to the prewar elite universities intensified.

In another key social reform, SCAP encouraged labor unions. The Trade Union Law of December 1945 legitimized labor organizing, and by the end of 1946, union membership had grown to 5 million. But as workers and their families enthusiastically took to the streets to demonstrate for their political viewpoints and for food, SCAP became scared. MacArthur issued a statement in May 1946 condemning "excesses by disorderly minorities," the same language used in repressive prewar laws recently struck down by the occupation. When a large cross-section of unions, both communist-influenced and moderate, planned a general strike of 3 million workers for February 1, 1947, SCAP outlawed it. Three years later, the Japanese government, encouraged by SCAP, initiated a Red Purge, firing 13,000 public- and private-sector employees for allegedly impeding the occupation's goals through communist activities.

The shift in SCAP's policy toward labor unions coincided with the relaxing of the *zaibatsu*-dissolution program. This shift, called the "reverse course," has remained controversial among historians since 1947. Some consider it an abandonment of SCAP's early goals of democratization, while others see it as a pragmatic response to changing global conditions. In any case, SCAP never reversed some of the central reforms of the occupation, most significantly the 1947 constitution.

The Meiji Constitution had vested sovereignty in the emperor, allowed the military to act independently of the elected government, and limited civil rights. MacArthur believed constitutional revision to be an essential part of the democratization project and asked the Japanese government to make appropriate amendments. The cabinet dragged its feet and appointed a committee only when convinced that MacArthur was serious, stacking the committee with conservatives. They handed MacArthur a revised draft that contained none of the changes he demanded. MacArthur, who strongly wished to retain the institution of the emperor while diminishing its powers, threatened the Japanese constitutional committee with elimination of the imperial institution if the requested changes were not made. In fact, MacArthur feared that the Far

Eastern Commission, whom he otherwise ignored, would press both for the elimination of the imperial institution and for the trial of Hirohito as a war criminal. He strongly suggested to the Japanese government that he, MacArthur, was the emperor's best hope.

While ostensibly awaiting the Japanese committee's next draft, in February 1946 MacArthur secretly appointed a committee of 24 Americans (16 officers and 8 civilians), of whom 4 were women, to write a constitutional draft for Japan. The key figures were lawyers: General Courtney Whitney (1897–1969) and Lieutenant Colonel Charles Kades (1906–1996), as well as Beate Sirota (b. 1923), a 22-year-old woman who had grown up in Japan, one of just a few in the occupation's staff fluent in Japanese. When the Japanese committee met with General Whitney to discuss their second draft, Whitney handed them the US committee's draft, suggesting that nothing less than the contents of that draft would be acceptable to SCAP. In early March, the Americans and Japanese undertook a harrowing 30-hour translation session, with the Americans trying to make sure their intent was preserved, and the Japanese trying to use words that would retain some of the meaning of the Meiji Constitution.

On March 6, Prime Minister Shidehara introduced the translation as the government's own, Hirohito issued an imperial rescript calling on the Japanese government to accept the new constitution, and MacArthur issued his approval of the "decision of the Emperor and the Government of Japan to submit to the Japanese people a new and enlightened constitution." After lengthy debate, the Diet approved the document as an expression of the "will of the Japanese people"—a requirement under the Potsdam Declaration of July 1945. The new constitution went into effect in May 1947.

The 1947 constitution contained many crucial changes from the Meiji Constitution.

- Sovereignty resided in the people, not the Emperor, who was now the "symbol of the State and unity of the people."
- The cabinet was responsible to the Diet, not appointed by oligarchs.
- The Diet consisted of two houses, the House of Representatives and the House of Councillors, which replaced the House of Peers.

A woman running for political office addresses a neighborhood crowd, January 1949.

- The people were granted absolute rights of speech, press, assembly, social welfare, public health, and labor organizing and collective bargaining.
- Women and men were made equal before the law, and husbands and wives were granted equal rights.
- The judiciary was to be independent, and the Supreme Court was given the right of judicial review.
- Japan renounced war forever as a sovereign right of the nation (Article 9).

The "reverse course" did not overturn the progressive new constitution. The entry of the United States into the Korean War in June 1950 did, however, induce SCAP to press for a Japanese National Police Reserve of 75,000 men to take the place of the American soldiers who left Japan for Korea, and many Japanese felt this undermined the "No-War" clause, Article 9. (Article 9 continues to play an important and controversial role in Japanese politics.) Some of the other human rights, especially those of women, have taken years to implement, but as we shall see in later chapters, the constitutional guarantee of equality has aided women's quest for equal rights in the postwar decades.

The new constitution articulated the revised role of the emperor, a policy linked to another important component of the occupation, the Tokyo Trial. Even before the end of hostilities, some American planners of the occupation had begun to advocate driving a wedge between evil advisers and government officials, on the one hand, and the emperor and his devoted subjects, on the other. These Americans believed the best way to ensure the cooperation of the Japanese people would be to use their loyalty to the emperor who, saved by SCAP, would rededicate himself to peace.

Surveys done by the occupation in the fall of 1945 showed that MacArthur and others might have overestimated the loyalty of the Japanese people to the emperor. Most did not care whether he was retained or not, and many laughed at jokes at his expense. Hirohito's New Year's Rescript, drafted by the occupation, clearly renounced his divinity in the English-language version—the Japanese version left this ambiguous—but food and shelter continued to be more important to most Japanese than whether they had an emperor or whether he was descended from the Sun Goddess.

Nevertheless, SCAP believed that uprisings might occur if the emperor were removed. If Hirohito were

The defendants' dock at the Tokyo War Crimes Trial, c. April 1946.

guilty of war crimes, however, the pressure to bring him to trial and eliminate the imperial institution, which SCAP tried to avoid, would be too great to ignore. As a result, Hirohito had to be divided from all other wartime leaders subject to the Tokyo Trial. Testimony from other defendants placed Hirohito in the room when key military decisions were made, but this testimony was not used in the trial.

The eleven justices of the Tokyo Trial, formally the International Military Tribunal for the Far East, represented 11 countries—including the British colony of India, not independent until August 1947, and the American commonwealth of the Philippines, not free until July 1946—that had suffered at the hands of the Japanese empire. Originally, only nine justices were to be on the panel, eight white men and one Chinese, until the Indians and Filipinos protested. Tellingly, Korea, which had been Japan's colony, was not one of the 11; nor were Vietnam and the Dutch East Indies, still under European colonial control. Indeed,

Justice Radhabinod Pal of India noted that some of the charges against the Japanese defendants had precedents in other imperialist nations' actions. He condemned the Japanese perpetrators, but asserted that they were not unique.

Twenty-eight men, four of them former prime ministers, were tried as Class A war criminals between May 1946 and April 1948. Seven of the Class A defendants received death sentences for waging aggressive war and carrying out crimes against humanity. Sixteen were sentenced to life imprisonment, two received shorter prison terms, two died during the trial, and one had a mental breakdown. The imprisoned men were all released in the next decade. Thousands of others were tried as Class B and Class C criminals, lesser categories of crimes. In the end, about 930 men were executed for war crimes.

In return for turning their data over to US authorities, the evil doctors of Unit 731, who undertook bacteriological experimentation and vivisection on live human beings, mostly Chinese, were not brought to justice at the Tokyo Trial. A number of American officials believed that many of those convicted had not been the most heinous brutes of the war, but rather men who made terrible policy with horrific outcomes. They did not, however, publicly express this unpopular view at the time.

THE END OF THE OCCUPATION AND THE BEGINNING OF RECOVERY

Large stockpiles of war matériel left over at the end of the war disappeared quickly into the black market. Before anyone could notice, military officials siphoned off government funds to pay contractors and provide severance pay to demobilized troops. In addition, the Japanese government paid the expenses of the US occupation. About half the annual Japanese budget went to these "war termination costs," leaving the government with few resources. Some funding went to businesses to stimulate production, but many of those simply bought raw materials and resold them on the black market—a quick, though illegal, way to profit. As we have seen, millions of Japanese were homeless, and three years after the end of the war, a quarter of all families still did not have proper housing. The end of the war left the food-distribution system in chaos. Industrial production in the first year after the war sank to 10 percent of its prewar level. High inflation—though not the hyperinflation of China—drove the consumer price index to 240 times its prewar level by 1949.

Although some consumer industries had begun to recover—including those that catered to the occupation, such as Canon and Nikon cameras and construction companies—most industry could obtain neither materials nor financing. Finally, in 1947, the government initiated a Priority Production program giving preference to industries it deemed critical. Steel manufacturers received priority for coal, for instance. Modeled on wartime allocation programs and paralleling the "integrated approach across the entire economy" proposed by MacArthur, this government economic regulation helped stimulate the economy to a limited but noticeable degree. This type of planning continued in the postwar period as "administrative guidance."

In spite of the Priority Production program, inflation exploded, and industry did not take off. Something had to make Japan the "bulwark against communism" in Asia, as the US secretary of the army expressed it. In February 1949, the US government sent Detroit banker Joseph Dodge to Tokyo to advise SCAP on recovery policies. He called for harsh measures—a balanced budget, the end to loans and business stimulus subsidies, and the fixing of the yen exchange rate at 360 yen to the dollar. By the following year, Dodge had almost killed the already stumbling Japanese economy.

But another form of American stimulus—the beginning of the Korean War in June 1950—set Japan on the road to recovery. Between 1950 and 1953, the United States requisitioned US$2.3 billion in vehicles, aircraft, napalm, and tanks from Japan, as well as housing and recreational facilities for Americans, a larger sum than all the economic aid, in every form, received from 1945 to 1951. Key industries recalled many long-unemployed workers as production doubled. Prime Minister Yoshida, tactlessly, called the war a "gift from the gods." Some businessmen, like the president of Toyota, whose production increased 40 percent, later noted how guilty he felt rejoicing over Korea's war. Producing supplies for America's war in Korea, Japanese businesses acquired new technologies from the United States and began Japan's postwar industrial rebirth.

By 1950, SCAP's objectives had clearly been achieved, so a peace treaty could be forged. Forty-eight nations met at San Francisco, but not all signed the treaty formally ending the war. Neither the ROC (Taiwan) nor the People's Republic of China (Beijing) was invited, but Asian countries were urged to negotiate their own treaties and reparations with Japan later. The United States forced Japan to sign a bilateral peace agreement with the ROC (on Taiwan) as a condition of ending the occupation.

The Soviets and East Europeans walked out of the San Francisco meetings because the United States planned to maintain a large military presence in Japan and retain Okinawa as a military possession. In bilateral talks, the Soviets and Japanese could not settle the issue of the Kurile Islands north of Japan. Within two hours of the signing of the San Francisco Peace Treaty, diplomats formalized the US–Japan Security Treaty. The Japanese public viewed this very negatively—in fact, some considered it a repeat of the nineteenth-century unequal treaties—and it was revised in 1960. Despite all the turmoil and the issues left unsolved, the occupation ended on April 28, 1952.

The policies developed during the occupation underscore the importance of viewing the war and occupation as part of a transwar continuum. The economic planning of the prewar cartels, rationalization, and the wartime Munitions Ministry all continued in the Priority Production program and SCAP planning. "Administrative guidance" of the postwar era—essentially government orders to business—replicated SCAP's "suggestions." The occupation's land reform program had its start in the wartime preferential treatment of producers over landlords. Occupation censorship repeated wartime censorship, with roots as far back as the Meiji era. As we will see in Chapter 11, the roles of women during the war allowed them to gain a greater presence in Japanese society in the 1950s and later. The preferential treatment for conservatives over socialists in the late occupation era allowed the former to blossom into a political movement that has held power for all but a few years since the end of the occupation. And the migration of large number of Koreans, either voluntarily or by force, before and during the war, has a postwar legacy; 540,000 Koreans remained in Japan after the war.

Much also changed during the occupation. The 1947 constitution is unmistakably a progressive document, as the Meiji Constitution was not. The occupation reforms radically opened up education, and a meritocratic hierarchy has emerged, replacing the economic class and gender inequality of the prewar period. Although SCAP plans had little to do with the economic rebuilding of Japan, American orders for munitions and other matériel for the Korean War certainly did set Japan on the road to recovery. And, as we shall see later, Japan reembarked on its long-time quest for modernity.

DIASPORAS

KOREA

The period from liberation through the Korean War entailed tremendous movement and instability for Koreans. From January through August 1945, Koreans began returning from Japanese and Manchurian factories, the coalmines of Kyūshū and Sakhalin, and military/labor/sexual service throughout Asia. According to Japanese colonial figures, as many as 500,000 Koreans reentered the colony during the months before the surrender. After September 1945 and before establishment of formal repatriation facilities in October, another 555,000 returned. The official repatriation office in South Korea recorded the following numbers for returnees between October 1945 and December 1947: 859,930 from North Korea; 304,391 from Manchuria; 1,110,972 from Japan; 71,611 from China; and 33,917 others for a total of 2,380,820. This means that over 3 million people came back to Korea in three years.

The division of the peninsula, first into two occupation zones and then into two contending states, compounded the problems of movement and reunion among Koreans. The early land reform in North Korea drove many middle class and landed people south just as the growing anticommunism in the south pushed leftists north. During the Korean War, no place was safe for the civilian population. Modest estimates claim that the Korean War and division of the peninsula separated 10 million people from their families. Before the armistice, as many as 1 million Koreans left the north to find safety in the south. South Koreans who trace their origins to the north experienced (and still experience) subtle discrimination. This caused many northerners to move to the United States after the legalization of Asian immigration in 1965.

The war also left over 300,000 widows and 100,000 orphans. Korean social custom inhibits adoption of non-kin, so thousands of orphans were stranded in a shattered society. A number of foreign organizations, most notably the Holt Adoption Agency, have addressed the orphan problem in Korea. Social dislocation, poverty, and lack of government resources in the immediate aftermath of the Korean War explain the large numbers of adoptions. South Korea remains one of the top five nations of origin for adoptions into the United States, with 37 percent of the total (1,794 adoptees) as recently as 2001.

CHINA

After the war, as local Southeast Asian nationalisms arose to demand independence, Chinese came to be seen as interlopers and aliens. Especially with the CCP victory in 1949, people perceived the threat of Chinese economic domination combined with the communist threat of political subversion. Over the ensuing decades, this double characterization gave rise to violence, sometimes on a wide scale, in Malaya, Indonesia, the Philippines, Vietnam, Cambodia, and Burma. Mobs, often incited or tolerated by army and police, burned Chinatowns, murdered Chinese, and forced the survivors into camps or out of the country.

Some overseas Chinese were communists, but most were not. The GMD, particularly after the retreat to Taiwan, paid assiduous and expensive attention to overseas communities—naturally enough since the party's foundations had been laid in diaspora (see p. 277). The Six Companies in San Francisco, for example, representing the conservative, established business interests of the community, stood foursquare behind the GMD and built organizations to raise money and make propaganda for its cause. Organizations such as the Anti-Communist Committee for Free China and the All-American Overseas Chinese Anti-Communist League mobilized Chinese-American resources and demonstrated to non-Chinese Americans that Chinese could be reliable allies in the fight against communism. The China lobby (see p. 332) made good use of their visibility and passion in advocating continued US support for the ROC on Taiwan.

After 1949, and especially after the beginning of the Korean War, the association of "Chinese" with "Communist" had been firmly fixed in American minds. When the McCarran Act of 1950 allowed internment of communists, Chinese-Americans concluded that they, like the wartime Japanese-Americans, might be herded into camps. At the same time, however, the United States could not entirely exclude its anticommunist allies. Thousands of Chinese fled the mainland in 1949 to North America as political refugees and displaced persons, including 7,000 war brides and 5,000 professionals and students already in the country. This wave of Chinese immigration—elite, well educated, and Mandarin-speaking—contrasted sharply with the working class, Cantonese sojourners of the nineteenth century and changed the place of Chinese-Americans in US society.

JAPAN

SCAP allowed few Japanese to leave the country before 1950; as in Korea, people returned to Japan from the former empire. Most had come home by late 1948, but at least half a million disappeared entirely. The Soviets took as many as 1,700,000 Japanese from Northeast Asia as forced labor. They repatriated about 625,000 by the end of 1947, and another 294,000 escaped from the Soviet zone in northern Korea, returning to Japan from the American zone in the south. Hundreds of thousands died of cold, hunger, and overwork.

While their experience was less horrific than that of Japanese in Northeast Asia, Japanese-Americans also experienced a painful postwar transition. Although most of the 110,000 people of Japanese descent in US concentration camps entered quietly—half were children—some sued, unsuccessfully, to end internment. Others protested denial of rights or resisted military conscription and were sent to Tule Lake, a camp for "disloyal" internees. Religious organizations, notably the Quakers, found ways—e.g., enrolling students in eastern and midwestern colleges—to release some people from the camps. Many young men left by joining the all Japanese-American 442nd Regimental Combat Team, the most decorated unit in the US military, activated on February 1, 1943.

On December 17, 1944, the US government announced it would begin closing the camps. Up and down the west coast, anti-Japanese organizations (Japanese Exclusion League, Native Sons of the Golden West, and others) sprang into action. Some unions and farmers' organizations joined the clamor for permanent banishment, more fearful of having to relinquish economic gains made at the expense of Japanese-Americans—such as taking over their property—than of their military threat. Indeed, no Japanese-American was ever convicted of espionage. Most interned Japanese-Americans had lost everything. Strangers occupied their houses, and they faced racist threats everywhere, from graffiti to letters to the editor. Some politicians proposed using them as forced labor.

Other Americans publicly supported the Japanese-Americans' return. University presidents encouraged former internees to attend their institutions, and the Council of Churches offered to help resettle them. But thousands of former internees left the west coast for the east and midwest, abandoning their former homes and farms. The government shut down most of the camps by the end of 1945, and Tule Lake closed in March 1946.

CONNECTIONS

The United States became the crucial connective tissue of East Asia after World War II, occupying Japan and South Korea, confronting the communists in the Korean War, materially aiding Jiang Jieshi in China's civil war, then protecting the defeated ROC on Taiwan. Although each of those states, and many distinct classes and factions within them, had its own interests and goals, all had to adapt to the presence not only of the United States but also of its nuclear power rivalry with the USSR, which evolved into the Cold War. In one enduring legacy of this period, the United States built military bases in a ring around the PRC; in the early twenty-first century, key garrisons remain in South Korea and Japan—60,000 soldiers and 10,000 sailors at the end of 2007.

Both Korea and China ended World War II as singular entities, and their elites aimed at unity as a high national goal. Divided by ideological, institutional, and historical contingencies, each had split into two warring states by 1949, a situation that persists into the twenty-first century. The United States and USSR stepped into the Chinese and Korean civil wars, the outcome of which could not have been predicted, and prevented one side from eliminating the other. Most Chinese and Koreans have found this division unnatural, blaming their domestic and foreign enemies—communists or anticommunists—for causing it.

Defeated Japan faced a very different, ironically more peaceful, postwar. American occupation brought a respite from warfare and immediate inclusion in the anticommunist bloc. The new constitution and American influences liberalized the state in many ways—meritocracy, universal suffrage, a symbolic and human emperor, a discourse of citizens' rights. Land reform created a longlasting constituency for conservative politics, while Yoshida Shigeru's tenure as prime minister consolidated the institutions of power for business and alliance with the United States. Rather than fighting a civil war, Japan began to rebuild its shattered families, cities, and economy, providing supplies to the United States and its allies in the Korean War. Without the domestic conflict suffered by both Korea and China, Japan proceeded more directly toward revived economic development than either of its neighbors.

Hundreds of thousands of Japanese who had been living in the Korean colony went home; so did most of the Koreans who had been living in Japan, but they left behind a substantial Korean diaspora that remains a contentious minority to this day. The more unfortunate Japanese in Manzhouguo, swept up by the Soviet invasion in August 1945, spent years in Siberia as forced labor, with many lives lost.

The Japanese troops who remained in China entered the initial stages of the Chinese civil war as allies of the GMD, as garrisons and, occasionally, as colleagues fighting the CCP. Captured or surrendered Japanese weapons formed an important component of the military hardware used in the Chinese civil war. Tens of thousands of Koreans who had been fighting the Japanese from bases in Manzhouguo and the USSR joined the PLA after Japan's surrender. Their return to North Korea after the CCP victory gave Kim Il Sung the battle-hardened core of his army and confidence that he could defeat South Korea in 1950.

Most dramatically, Peng Dehuai led more than 2 million Chinese troops—the Chinese People's Volunteer Army—onto the peninsula to stop MacArthur's drive toward the Yalu River. That war, which did not eliminate either contender for legitimacy in Korea, cemented the PRC's relationship with North Korea, where Chinese troops remained until 1958. It also created deep enmity between the PRC and United States, which began to ease only in the 1970s. The Korean War also provided Japan with vital economic stimulus, as the United States ordered supplies and munitions from Japanese firms and prepared for its Korean battles at bases in Japan.

The ROC, having retreated to Taiwan, wanted to express its continuing importance and volunteered 33,000 troops to the UN for the Korean War, to balance the PRC's aid to North Korea. MacArthur, an anticommunist crusader, argued for accepting the offer, hoping to embroil the PRC in a wider war and prepare the way for a United States-supported ROC invasion of the mainland. Truman and Secretary of State Dean Acheson disagreed, hoping to dissociate the United States from the ROC and build a long-term, stable relationship with the PRC. MacArthur made numerous public statements in favor of a US–ROC military alliance, contributing to Truman's sense of the general's unwillingness to support administration policies. After a Republican congressman publicly read MacArthur's recommendation of use of ROC troops in Korea, the president dismissed MacArthur from command.

All three East Asian countries had to deal with the problem of *collaboration*. Should those who had created the Japanese empire be punished for doing so? What crime(s) had they committed? What about Koreans and Chinese who had worked for and with them? What kinds of courts or authorities would be competent to make such judgments and mete out penalties? Using the model of the Nuremberg trials in Europe, the Allies established the Tokyo Trial to try the leaders of wartime Japan for various "crimes against humanity," a category invented *post facto* to describe some Ottoman atrocities 30 years earlier. Some historians call this "victor's justice," a process with no legal jurisdiction, while others justify it on grounds of the brutality of Japanese imperialism in Asia.

North and South Korea undertook very different processes to deal with collaboration. The communists made as clean a sweep as they could, purging Koreans who had held authority under the colonial state from all positions of power. In the South, in contrast, many of the conservative nationalist leaders had worked for the Japanese empire. Despite popular sentiments against collaboration, no comprehensive investigations ever took place, many records were destroyed, and former officials of the Japanese empire served at every level of the state.

Both GMD and CCP did punish some Chinese collaborators in their own territories. The ROC, for example, arrested Liang Hongzhi—head of the first puppet Reformed Government—tried him for treason and shot him in 1946, along with Wang Jingwei's minister of industry, Mei Siping. On the other hand, the Nationalists also employed numerous collaborators, some at fairly high rank, such as General Li Shouxin, appointed to command the Tenth Route Army, and Li Xianliang, chosen to be mayor of Qingdao. Unwilling thoroughly to investigate and punish collaborators—preferring in some cases to blackmail them—GMD officials suffered the cynical public's perception that they were more interested in profit than justice. The CCP, like North Korea, tended to be much more systematic in excluding collaborators from its ranks, but when puppet troops were rejected by the GMD immediately following Japan's surrender, they enlisted with the communists *en masse* and served in the PLA.

CHAPTER ELEVEN

RECONSTRUCTION AND DIVERGENT DEVELOPMENT (1953–LATE 1970s)

WORLD CONTEXT

The 1950s, 1960s, and 1970s saw momentous changes on every continent. Decolonization created dozens of new countries in Africa, Asia, and the Caribbean, many of them unstable and dependent on their former colonizers. In Cuba, revolutionaries under Fidel Castro and Che Guevara created a pro-USSR communist regime 90 miles (144 km) from the United States (1959). Hundreds of thousands of Cubans fled to Florida, becoming a powerful ethnic enclave committed to an anti-Castro boycott. After a United States-backed invasion failed in 1961, the USSR attempted to place nuclear-armed medium-range ballistic missiles (MRBMs) in Cuba but desisted in exchange for US promises not to invade the island and to remove American MRBMs from bases in Turkey.

The march of science took a dramatic leap with the USSR's launch of the first manmade satellite, Sputnik I (1957). Reacting with Cold War competitiveness, the United States inaugurated a "Space War" that put American astronauts on the moon in 1969. With unforeseeable long-term consequences, engineers rapidly improved the huge, unwieldy vacuum-tube computing machines of the 1950s by developing microchip technology—the printing of electrical microcircuits on tiny bits of silicon. Constant innovation enabled a single chip to hold tens of thousands of transistors by the mid-1970s, leading the way to the computer revolution of the 1980s and beyond (see p. 393).

A list of scientific advances during this period would be as long as this chapter. A top ten might include: invention of the birth control pill, lasers, artificial hearts and lungs, synthetic DNA and genes, antiviral drugs, and the neutron bomb; and discovery of dozens of subatomic particles, humanoid origins going back millions of years, damage to the earth's ozone layer from accumulated aerosol spray gases, and the cause of multiple sclerosis. Space exploration continued with direct investigations of the planets and the sun's magnetic field.

International politics, too, changed dramatically. Israel fought two wars against its neighbors (1967, 1973), undertaking the ongoing occupation of Gaza and the West Bank. Beginning with the 1957 Treaty of

Rome, Europeans created transnational institutions—the Common Market, the European Atomic Energy Community—that would lead to the European Union of the twenty-first century. With many long-term results, United States-backed military coups overthrew the popular governments of Mohammed Mosaddeq in Iran (1953) and Salvador Allende in Chile (1973). The map of Africa grew increasingly complex as colonial empires withdrew, leaving local elites with few economic resources to build nation-states out of ethnically diverse, often contentious populations. India and Pakistan fought large-scale wars in 1965 and 1971, the latter splitting Pakistan in two and creating Bangladesh, the world's seventh most populous country.

In American popular imagery, the 1950s represented a time when families (mom, dad, and two kids) lived happily on one male's income. Television shows such as *Ozzie and Harriet* portrayed the "typical" American family—always white, always middle-class, always stable—as good-natured and amusing. World politics appeared as a cowboy movie, with white hats (us) and black hats (them), and the hero always won the final showdown. The United States supported the "good guys" overseas, and the lower classes (including women) knew their place.

That fantasy still has power, despite being, as one scholar put it, "the way we never were." In the 1950s, racial discrimination, sexism and patriarchy, corporate greed, and heavy-handed international intervention continued to be as much a part of American life as hamburgers and baseball. Less optimistic images included African American victims of lynching, DDT-poisoned migrant farm workers, "The Man in the Grey Flannel Suit"—the stressed-out, conformist, "successful" executive—and depressed, isolated suburban housewives.

Resistance to the established order took many forms. The civil rights movement gained momentum after the US Supreme Court ruled segregated public schools to be unconstitutional in *Brown v. Board of Education* (1954). Rosa Parks refused to move to the back of the bus in Montgomery, AL, sparking a victorious, 381-day bus boycott by black workers (1956). The "beatniks"—Jack Kerouac, Lawrence Ferlinghetti, and Allen Ginsberg—mocked conformist society and condemned it as a prison. The American Federation of Labor (AFL) and the Congress of Industrial Organizations (CIO) merged in 1955, unifying and expanding the labor movement. Journalist Betty Friedan's research on American women's lives led to the publication of *The Feminine Mystique* (1963), a core text of late twentieth-century feminism.

The popular culture of the 1950s did not remain comfortably unquestioning, either. Chuck Berry, Bo Diddley, and Little Richard merged a variety of styles—blues, country, gospel—into "rock and roll," soon joined by "rockabilly" singers Elvis Presley and Jerry Lee Lewis. This sexy, danceable music, condemned by the White Citizens' Council as satanic and degenerate, attracted both black and white "teenagers," a new demographic category created by advertisers capitalizing on postwar prosperity. Jazz, too, continued to evolve. "Bebop" performers John Coltrane, Miles Davis, and Thelonius Monk rebelled against convention with discordant, polyrhythmic compositions drawing on influences as diverse as African call-and-response and Igor Stravinsky.

In the mid-1950s, Vietnamese revolutionaries decisively defeated French colonialism, but US interventions, beginning with President Eisenhower in 1954, prevented the establishment of a communist Vietnam. Instead, a Geneva convention divided the country in two, a communist north and non-communist republic (led by Roman Catholics) in the south, eerily reflecting the divisions of China and Korea. That division led inexorably to war, for the United States—beginning with President Kennedy—sent advisers, then troops, and finally an enormous army to support its South Vietnamese allies.

The Vietnam War stimulated confrontations ranging from street violence to the worldwide cultural revolution now called "The Sixties." American bombing reduced most of North Vietnam (and parts of Cambodia and Laos) to rubble; over 50,000 Americans and over 4 million Southeast Asians died. American society, and many others, split painfully into pro- and antiwar factions, resulting in a youth revolution of international antiwar demonstrations (1968). Politically and racially motivated assassins took the lives of President John Kennedy, Senator Robert Kennedy, and civil rights leader Reverend Martin Luther King, Jr. Richard Nixon's decisive second presidential victory (1972) demonstrated the strength of the pro-war political forces, but his resignation in the wake of the Watergate scandal (1974) presaged American military defeat and withdrawal (1975) and the reunification of Vietnam under communist leadership (1976).

Over all of these changes loomed the Cold War, the daily threat of universal annihilation marketed as "deterrence." With thousands of thermonuclear warheads aimed at one another from land-based silos and nuclear-powered submarines, the superpowers could not afford to fight directly. So the United States–USSR confrontation, painted as Good vs. Evil on both sides, erupted in proxy wars from Cuba to Afghanistan to Vietnam. China and Korea remained divided into communist and anticommunist states, so East Asians participated fully in this worldwide conflict.

CHINA

HUKOU, DANWEI, AND MASS MOBILIZATION

To control its vast population, the PRC brought Party and government directly into its citizens' lives. The household registration system (c. *hukou*) fixed every person's residence and social services—rural or urban—forming an unyielding system of social control rather than a traditional device for census, taxation, or conscription. Efficiently enforced, the *hukou* system prevented most physical mobility. Urban police made periodic sweeps, demanding *hukou* identification and shipping illegal rural migrants back to their villages. Urban *hukou* carried social benefits—health insurance, education, grain rations, housing—but holders of rural *hukou* had to provide their own food and shelter and received no guarantees of health care or education. The *hukou* system thus reinforced a two-tiered society, a deep divide between rural and urban Chinese.

Since the new government encouraged (and sometimes forced) both men and women to work outside the home—in Marxist theory, women could only be liberated by participation in production—almost everyone belonged to a work-unit (c. *danwei*). The *danwei* became the primary identification outside the family, its cadres mediating access to housing, ration coupons, health care, and contraception. As organizers of participation in mass campaigns, work-units could also label people as misfits or even criminals, subjecting them to public humiliation and punishment.

Paralleling *hukou* and *danwei*, the PRC also created mass organizations to lead the campaigns. The

CCP had over 10 million members by the mid-1950s, and the youth league, women's federation, and national trade union enrolled millions more. All demanded participation in movements such as "Resist America, Aid Korea," the Five-Anti campaign (see p. 341), and meetings to criticize local and national political targets.

SOCIALIST ECONOMIC TRANSFORMATION

In 1951, following the Soviet example, Chinese economists began designing a first Five-Year Plan (FYP), taking heavy industry as the core of development and aiming to double factory output by 1957. With central control over the production and distribution of key commodities, such as coal and steel, planners hoped to achieve greater efficiency than a capitalist economy. The government took over heavy industry, mining, and public utilities, leaving entrepreneurs—those who weathered the Five-Anti campaign—as managers of small- and middle-sized factories. In 1956, the state nationalized all industrial facilities under a system of "joint state-private ownership," which removed capitalists from managerial functions, leaving them only dividend payments.

By 1953, rapid reduction of the amount of paper money in circulation and banning of foreign currencies had brought inflation under control, and the government stabilized its revenues with production, sales, and income taxes. An innovative wage system, the "commodity basket," calculated workers' weekly wages on the basis of the prices of everyday items such as flour and cotton cloth. As prices rose and fell, so did wages, protecting workers to some extent from inflation and price fluctuation, which had devastated so many lives during the previous decades. Although applied only to industrial and office workers, the "commodity basket" increased popular support for the government.

Under the First FYP, over half of the state's capital investment went to industry. The USSR provided thousands of advisers in every field, from designing steel mills to physical education. According to official statistics, the First FYP exceeded its goals with spectacular increases, especially in 1956, when industrial output, stimulated by a burst of government spending and the elimination of private ownership, rose by 25 percent. Production surpassed state targets in steel, coal, machine tools, and trucks, crucial for further industrial development.

In the rural areas, where the vast majority of Chinese lived, land reform had distributed over 100 million acres to cultivator families, who responded with increased production. Experience with "class analysis" and attacks on formerly powerful individuals had changed how peasants viewed their neighbors and their world. Rather than belonging just to families, lineages, villages, and market areas, they began to understand society as made up of classes—landless, poor, middle, and rich peasants, and landlords—and to regard the former rich peasants and landlords among them as "class enemies," not just neighbors, patrons, or fortunate relatives.

Eager for enhanced tax revenues and the efficiencies anticipated from rural mechanization and management above the level of the household, the PRC encouraged farmers to begin forming mutual-aid teams as a precursor to collectivization. In theory, large fields worked by teams using tractors and other machinery had to be more productive than small, non-mechanized family farms. Rather than force farmers into cooperatives, however, until 1955 the CCP allowed wide variation. Some families shared labor in small groups at planting and harvest seasons. Others, regarded as more advanced, pooled labor, tools, and sometimes draft animals while retaining family ownership of their land.

In 1955, however, an impatient Mao Zedong challenged the Chinese people to choose between socialism, meaning collective or state ownership of the means of production, and capitalism, meaning private ownership and management. Hindsight tells us that he also intended to identify his friends and enemies in the CCP leadership by their attitudes toward socialist development. In a July 1955 speech, Mao called for rapid collectivization of agriculture, arguing that industrial success depended on agricultural growth and the expansion of domestic markets. Some scholars see this rural push as Mao's reaction to covert Sino–Soviet tensions, which burst into the open a few years later. Rejecting the Soviet model, the CCP would rely, as in the wartime Jiangxi and Yan'an base areas, on the peasants' revolutionary energy.

Mao ordered local cadres to organize agricultural producers' cooperatives (APCs), in which the collective unit owned the land. Having distributed land to peasant households during land reform, Mao's faction in the CCP wanted to remove it from household management into larger, supposedly more efficient, collective units. In a lower-level APC, households put in their land, tools, and animals, with returns based on the family's contributed resources. More radical upper-level APCs required households to give their property to the collective in exchange for wages paid on the basis of labor, making peasants into workers rather than free-holding farmers.

Many CCP planners and economists thought Mao's ambition excessive and his timing unrealistic, but this demand from the supreme leader produced a rush toward communal ownership. When Mao demanded collectivization in July 1955, about 15 percent of China's peasants belonged to lower-level APCs. Only six months later, 80 percent of the peasants had been enrolled, and by late 1956, 88 percent belonged to upper-level APCs. In this campaign, the CCP contradicted its own rural experience by not building long-term, stable social units. Organizing farmers into larger and larger *danwei*, the collectivization drive of the mid-1950s took decision-making away from rural households and gave it to village-level cadres. Usually farmers themselves, the cadres had to manage the work and welfare of their neighbors, a task for which many were ill prepared.

Each upper-level APC sold a quota of grain to the state—at an artificially low price—then issued surplus grain and other products to member families in proportion to their contributed labor. Credit cooperatives offered loans of cash or seed to APCs, making peasants even more dependent on collective organizations. Mao called this a "socialist upsurge" and believed it would mobilize the enthusiasm of the farmers. In some places it did, but the planning of supply, farming, processing, and distribution for an upper-level APC resembled running a small corporation, beyond the skills of many local cadres. The resulting waste, mismanagement, and corruption generated poor harvests and bad feelings. Despite Mao's rhetoric of rapid development and enthusiastic participation, hasty collectivization without adequate preparation or voluntarism did not invariably increase production.

"IDENTIFYING" CHINA'S ETHNIC GROUPS

Since the early 1950s, the National People's Congress (NPC) has functioned as the PRC's rubber-stamp legislature. The Election Law of 1953 specified that every *minzu*, "ethnic or national group" (к. *minjok*, ɪ. *minzoku*) in China must be represented by at least one NPC delegate, but no one knew how many such groups existed or how large they might be. A preparatory study in Yunnan—China's most diverse province—found over 250 ethnic names, and a national investigation collected over 400. Beijing required that this impossible number be reduced to less than 60 and assigned a team of social scientists to "identify" and count the various *minzu* of Yunnan.

Relying on *language* as the most important ethnic marker, the team interviewed a few "representative" people claiming each ethnic name and "identified" 20 *minzu* as official "minority nationalities," folding most other ethnic claims into them. In the next few years, projects in each province produced a nationwide total of 56 *minzu*, including the enormous and variegated Han Chinese majority (itself a mélange of ethnicities), as the members of China's "great *minzu* family." Despite the hasty and often arbitrary process that produced it, and the prearranged final result (under 60), that

number has become "factual" knowledge about China, cloaked in scientific language and repeated endlessly for over 50 years.

A HUNDRED FLOWERS

Mao's "rectification" campaign in Yan'an (1942–44) had set a pattern for the CCP's relationship with China's intellectuals. Recognizing the importance of educated people for China's development, the Party nonetheless demanded that they work for public rather than personal goals. Famously hostile to individualism, Mao found intellectuals self-seeking and unreceptive to party discipline. Hu Feng (1902–1985), a Japan-trained novelist and literary theorist, had worked with Lu Xun (see pp. 262–63) and after 1949 became director of the Chinese Writers' Association. Because he stressed the creative individual in literature, he disagreed with Mao's view that all intellectual work must serve "the Party and the masses."

YUE DAIYUN, AMBIVALENT MAOIST

For a citizen of the PRC, Yue Daiyun (b. 1931) lived very well. A Beida graduate and CCP member, in 1952 she had been selected as a Beida instructor in Chinese literature and married the university vice-president's son. Sent as a student representative to the USSR and Czechoslovakia, she rose to be Party branch secretary in her department. Active, intelligent, and well connected, she seemed sure of a successful career. When the Anti-Rightist Movement began in summer 1957, she worked diligently to find "rightists" in her *danwei* and participated in the accusation of a number of colleagues. When Yue Daiyun's second child, a boy, was born in December, rejoicing filled their comfortable campus home.

In January 1958, Yue Daiyun's department—desperate to meet their "quota" of "rightist" victims, arbitrarily set at 5 percent by Mao—convened a series of struggle meetings at which *they* accused *her* of being an enemy of the Party. Big-character posters

on campus called her a "big traitor" and demanded punishment for her as a corrupter of China's youth. By February she had been dismissed from the Party, forced to confess to counterrevolutionary crimes, and sentenced to labor in the countryside. There she spent most of the Great Leap Forward separated from her husband and children, allowed only one three-week visit to Beijing in two years. Initially "utterly lost, a stranger in my own land," she nonetheless came to see her rural exile as a positive phase, for she experienced the hardship of physical labor and the hunger and kindness of peasants, so different from the intellectual urbanites of her professional world.

For 20 years, Yue Daiyun struggled to regain her respect and self-confidence. In subsequent campaigns, she returned to rural exile three more times, for terms of a few weeks to 18 months. Red Guards destroyed her family's books and forced them into much smaller, less "bourgeois" quarters. Her

Under scrutiny for "bourgeois idealism" in 1954, Hu and several colleagues wrote a lengthy memo to the CCP Central Committee, claiming that Party control over art resulted in unimaginative work that alienated its audience. This "300,000 Word Report" became a hot topic, engaging Zhou Enlai, Deng Xiaoping, Liu Shaoqi, and Mao himself with the role of culture under socialism. They declared a campaign of mass demonstrations culminating in Hu Feng's arrest and imprisonment, serving notice that independent thinking would have serious negative consequences.

But China's progress required intellectuals' active participation. Mass literacy could only be achieved by millions of teachers, and only scientists could propel China's economic and technological advancement. So in late 1956, Mao Zedong invited criticism of the Party, raising the slogan, "Let a hundred flowers bloom, let a hundred schools of thought contend," which echoed the "Hundred Schools" of ancient China.

The campaign began slowly, as fearful intellectuals balked at criticizing the Party, but in May and June 1957, finally persuaded that their leaders wanted their views, they created a storm of prose. Scientists complained that political activities interfered with their research. Journalists called the CCP a privileged, exploiting class and Mao a high-living hypocrite. Flowers bloomed among non-intellectuals, too. In Shanghai, workers organized strikes, slowdowns, and demonstrations affecting over 500 enterprises. Causes ranged from oppressive CCP cadres to reduction of benefits under "joint state-private ownership," but most labor actions focused on workplace grievances, so workers rarely linked their protests to those of intellectuals.

Historians still debate whether Mao intended the Hundred Flowers campaign to stimulate discussion (commonly believed outside of China) or to unmask hidden enemies (the consensus inside China). Whatever the initial motivation, the CCP struck back against

husband joined the "Two Schools" group, Mao's wife Jiang Qing's personal propaganda staff during the campaign to "Criticize Lin Biao and Confucius," and his star rose quickly. With Jiang's arrest in 1976, however, he became the object of severe struggle meetings at Beida and spent two years in confinement before being allowed to teach philosophy again in 1979.

Yue Daiyun's children were both sent to the countryside as "educated youth." Both passed the university entrance exams in 1977, but could not be admitted because of their parents' dubious political status. For two years, Yue Daiyun poured out time, energy, connections, and valuable gifts to obtain university admission for them, finally succeeding in 1979. The Party offered Yue Daiyun "rehabilitation"—a return to full membership—in 1978. Despite her years of suffering and exclusion and the near destruction of her family, she continued to believe that only the CCP could develop China, and she accepted.

Yue Daiyun (center) with her peasant hosts during her first involuntary sojourn in rural China, 1960. Decades later, writing her autobiography, she remembered their generosity and kindness toward an urban intellectual unaccustomed to physical labor.

critics in July 1957 with a nationwide "Anti-Rightist Movement." By year's end, over 300,000 "rightists" had been "identified," including feminist writer Ding Ling (1904–1986) and engineer-economist Zhu Rongji (b. 1928), later the PRC's fifth premier, who had called Mao's high-growth policies irrational. Punishments ranged from dismissal to "reeducation in the country-side" to death. Most regained their status as citizens, a process called "rehabilitation," only after 1976, often posthumously (see p. 395).

THE GREAT LEAP FORWARD

To be less dependent on the USSR, Mao intensified his calls for a "great leap" economic strategy, dramatic mobilization of the "boundless energy" of the work-ers and peasants. He opposed CCP leaders, especially Liu Shaoqi and Deng Xiaoping, who recommended step-by-step progress toward socialism, rational eco-nomic planning, and gradual accumulation of capital. In ideological terms, Mao conceptualized this as a con-tradiction between "red" and "expert," between "left" and "right," between reliance on the whole Chinese people and reliance on a small technocratic elite.

After forcing rapid collectivization of peasants into upper-level APCs, Mao announced the "Great Leap Forward" (GLF) in 1958, proposing that China catch up with industrialized Great Britain in 15 years. In the countryside, this meant combining upper-level APCs into huge *danwei* called "People's Communes," each including numerous villages and thousands of house-holds. The communes abolished all private property, even family vegetable plots and draft animals, in a rush toward communism. Since family meals interfered with collective life, each commune established dining halls, theoretically liberating the labor power of women and directly attacking family autonomy and intimacy. Com-munal nurseries took the care of small children away from grandparents, and communes encouraged par-ents to send even kindergarteners to boarding school to liberate adult labor.

The language of the GLF recalled military life. Communes were divided into brigades, companies, and platoons; red flags waved to mark worksites and encampments; bugles blared; and propaganda work-ers urged people into the battle for China's growth. Most dramatically, in summer 1958 Beijing mandated that rural Chinese participate in industry as well as agriculture. To increase steel production—the heart of industrialization—the Party initiated widespread construction of "backyard furnaces" made of clay and bricks. Rural workers felled whole forests to stoke the fires, and families gave up their cooking pots and door hinges to the smelters. The effort and resources went to waste, for despite enthusiastic sacrifices, the backyard furnaces produced mostly brittle, useless pig iron, not industrial steel.

The communes did have a powerful impact on women's lives. Rural women generally labored within households, the value of their work accruing to the family. In the late 1950s, the communes made peasants more like workers, paying individuals not in cash but in *work-points*, which accumulated over a year in the bookkeeper's ledger. At harvest time, the bookkeeper calculated the total number of work-points earned by brigade members and distributed grain, surplus cash, and other products on that basis. In this system, wom-en received independent wages (though not as many work-points as men), part of the transformation of gen-der relations in rural China.

A brickwork "backyard steel furnace" built by villagers during the Great Leap Forward, 1958.

MANMADE FAMINE

Rapid collectivization and mass participation in militarized production departed radically from Soviet experience. Chinese diplomats began to claim that Mao Zedong rather than the USSR should delineate the road to socialism for underdeveloped countries. Beijing, meanwhile, described Nikita S. Khrushchev's (1894–1971) doctrine of "peaceful coexistence" with the capitalist powers as a betrayal of Marxism. When Khrushchev met with President Eisenhower in 1959, Chinese leaders worried that the PRC might become their target. After heated arguments in June 1960, the USSR withdrew its support for China's development. Aid payments and loans ceased, and thousands of Soviet advisers departed, taking their blueprints and technical manuals with them, leaving hundreds of projects unfinished.

This Sino–Soviet split could not have happened at a worse time. The GLF's reliance on "red" enthusiasm had stifled negative reports from any sector of the economy. If production did not meet projections, leaders must have failed to mobilize the masses' energy, so cadres falsified statistics at every level. Relying on spurious data, central planners demanded unreachable quantities of grain and other products from the communes. At the same time, commune officials, ignorant of village-level conditions (because the communes were so huge) and under pressure to achieve great things, called upon the farmers to engage in "deep plowing and close planting" to extract vast output from limited land.

"Deep plowing and close planting," reported as wildly successful in a few test sites, required that farmers plow as much as 10 feet (3 m) deep and plant enormous quantities of seed in extravagantly fertilized fields. Central planners mindlessly ordered all communes to follow this model regardless of local conditions. Similarly, a campaign to kill sparrows and other birds—believed to spread disease—resulted in increased insect populations, with predictable consequences for crops. The GLF thus drastically reduced food production, just as state procurement rose and nature delivered catastrophes—droughts in some places, typhoons and severe flooding in others.

Following its own spectacularly inaccurate estimates of food production, the state took excessive grain from the communes to feed the cities, leaving the farmers with little or nothing to eat. Between 1959 and 1962, as many as 30 million Chinese people, mostly rural, starved to death in one of history's most devastating famines. Although nature had not cooperated, this tragedy must be seen as primarily manmade, the result of unrealistic policy goals, inappropriate methods, cadres unwilling to tell the truth about local conditions, and a supreme leader with unlimited self-confidence.

Mao tolerated no opposition. In 1957, he fired Deng Tuo (1912–1966), editor of the Party newspaper *People's Daily* and an ally of Liu Shaoqi, for editorials opposing "impetuosity." When Defense Minister Peng Dehuai, China's most successful general, wrote Mao a letter criticizing the GLF in 1959, Mao turned on him viciously at a leadership conference, purged him from all of his posts, and reemphasized the utopian goals of the GLF.

But the GLF's failures could not be hidden from the Party's leadership, which had begun to split as early as the mid-1950s over the timing of China's march to socialism. PRC President Liu Shaoqi and Party leader Deng Xiaoping opposed rapid collectivization and the GLF. Heading the central bureaucracy in Beijing, they argued for deliberate, carefully planned steps toward socialism. Mao and his faction, including General Lin Biao (who replaced Peng Dehuai as defense minister) and the diplomatic Zhou Enlai, urged continuous revolutionary enthusiasm. Once the extent of the famine became known, Mao sent out trusted investigation teams, and even they joined Liu and Deng in recommending that some agricultural production be returned to individual households.

A FRONTIER DEBACLE: THE TIBETAN UPRISING

The Seventeen-Point Agreement of 1951 had spared the Tibetan heartland from land reform, collectivization, and the GLF, but the Tibetan parts of several other provinces had been socialized and collectivized. By 1956, some Tibetan leaders had organized a resistance army, fantasizing elimination of PRC authority from Tibetan areas. Supported by CIA covert operations, the rebels' influence spread westward to Lhasa, Tibet's political and cultural capital.

On March 1, 1959, the Dalai Lama received an invitation to attend a musical performance at a PLA base. In Lhasa's tense conditions, rumors spread that he would be detained, and crowds of Tibetans—estimates range from 30,000 to 300,000—surrounded his palaces to prevent

The Sino-Indian War, 1962

him from going. Rather than risk violent confrontation, he cancelled his acceptance and spent the next week consulting human advisers and divine oracles; all advised him to flee. On March 17, the Dalai Lama and his entourage left Tibet and crossed the formidable Himalayas to exile in India. Lhasa exploded in violence, the PLA shelled the Dalai Lama's palaces and the three great Lhasa monasteries, and tens of thousands of Tibetans died. The Indian government, nervous about offending China but unwilling to turn away so prestigious a refugee, allowed the exiled Tibetans to build a community at Dharamsala, in northern India.

India's grant of asylum to the Dalai Lama and mutual intransigence about locating the border between the two countries brought China and India to war in 1962. In a month-long conflict fought in very difficult terrain, Chinese troops advanced at both the eastern and western ends of the Himalayas, driving as much as 30 miles (48 km) into Indian territory. Although neither country deployed its air force nor expanded the conflict outside the immediate region of border conflict—almost all of it over 14,000 ft (4,267 m) in altitude—both armies

suffered numerous casualties. China declared a unilateral ceasefire and withdrew from any territory it had not originally claimed, but relations between the two countries remained strained and difficult for decades. Although the CIA gave up direct support in the 1970s, the Dalai Lama and his Tibetan government in exile in India remain a source of irritation and tension for the twenty-first-century PRC, which maligns him as a feudal despot and imperialist tool while negotiating with his representatives.

MAO ON THE MARGINS

When Mao's responsibility for the disasters of the GLF could no longer be denied, Liu Shaoqi, Deng Xiaoping, and their colleagues in Beijing edged the Chairman out of daily government business. He went voluntarily into semi-retirement to concentrate on "theoretical work" as the economy gradually recovered in the early 1960s. But Mao could not tolerate remaining on the margins, nor forgive his former comrades for opposing his socialist vision. During those years he developed a doctrine of "permanent revolution," claiming the necessity of class struggle even after the revolution destroyed the old ruling class. In this conception of history, the "capitalist road" endured in an unending series of contradictions between elites and the masses. Whenever a new elite arose, like the CCP leaders who had criticized the GLF, Mao proposed that revolutionaries oppose them through class struggle.

Liu and Deng's officials disagreed. Stressing pragmatism and collective decision-making, in contrast to Mao's autocracy, they focused on economic recovery, social order, and education. Reversing the GLF investment strategy, they put government money into agriculture first, so food supplies improved and remained in the villages. Party directives moved agricultural accounting, management, and daily operations from the commune level—too large and distant for effective feedback and decision-making—to the production teams and brigades, village-sized units within which people knew one another. This did not guarantee concord, of course, but planning tended to have some relationship to local reality.

Historians call 1962–66 the years of "two-line struggle." Mao's allies, especially Defense Minister Lin Biao and public security chief Kang Sheng (1898–1975), proclaimed "Mao Zedong Thought" to be the highest

Marxist truth, while Liu and Deng worked to rationalize China's economy and government along Soviet lines. The clash at the highest level between these two versions of communism—called "leftist" (radical) and "rightist" (conservative) in Chinese documents—played out in the press, in secret meetings, and in social movements.

Because Liu and Deng controlled Beijing, Mao rarely lived there, preferring to stay in luxurious guesthouses around the country. He found close allies in Shanghai's intellectual and labor circles, in the army, and among radical students recruited in part by his wife, Jiang Qing (1914–1991). A former film actor and self-proclaimed arbiter of culture, she used her invulnerable position as Mao's wife to organize against "revisionism," a code word for Soviet and Chinese communists who promoted gradual progress. In such uneasy times, everyone had to read the newspapers and Party directives with extreme care to discover "which way the wind is blowing." The Maoist "left" demanded permanent revolution and class struggle against "bourgeois revisionists," while the Party "right" emphasized the economy and disciplined obedience.

When Mao proclaimed a "Socialist Education Movement" in 1962, designed to purify politics, economy, organization, and ideology (the "Four Cleanups"), his opponents prevented significant changes. Hoping to defuse urban conflict, the CCP bureaucracy began sending educated urban youth to the countryside to bridge the rural–urban divide and end the distinction between mental and manual labor. These "sent-down youth" became a significant presence in many villages, especially after 1969.

On the radical side, Lin Biao created a brief booklet of Mao's revolutionary slogans and aphorisms, *Quotations from Chairman Mao Zedong*, usually called the "Little Red Book." Memorized by millions, including illiterates who learned it by hearing it recited, the *Quotations* became an authoritative source of truth for a decade. With the highest leadership so divided, its factions imbedded in leadership at every level, and the cult of Mao deepening among young people, open conflict could not be avoided for long.

One early confrontation occurred in the fall of 1965, when Mao's literary allies in Shanghai criticized the vice-mayor of Beijing, an ally of Deng Xiaoping, for a play he had written in 1960, *Hai Rui Dismissed from Office* (see pp. 38–39). Correctly perceiving praise for

that Ming dynasty official as covert approval of Peng Dehuai's critique of Mao in 1959, radical essayists demanded that the playwright be censured. They called his boss, Beijing Mayor Peng Zhen (1902–1997), part of a "Black Gang" opposed to socialism.

THE GREAT PROLETARIAN CULTURAL REVOLUTION

In May 1966, a philosophy instructor at Beida pasted a "big-character poster" on a university wall. Denouncing the university administration as a "sinister anti-Party, antisocialist gang," she demanded that the university end its paternalism and elitism, unleashing the revolutionary energy of the "broad masses." Mao and Kang Sheng had her poster broadcast nationwide, and student groups calling themselves "Red Guards" began to form in high schools and colleges throughout China to promote Mao's vision and attack his opponents.

The Red Guards attacked authority with wall posters and demonstrations, focusing on people with "bad class backgrounds," CCP officials, school administrators, and intellectuals. From the outset, they used shocking, offensive language. They called their targets "cow-devils and snake-spirits," "sons of turtles," and "dog's heads," maligning perceived enemies' writings as "poisonous weeds" and their wives as "counterrevolutionary whores." This vulgar language became commonplace, as did military metaphors for the Red Guards' own behavior; they staged offensives along the front lines, sounding the signal to charge. Mao Zedong, their 72-year-old Great Helmsman, swam in the Yangzi River that July to prove his fitness and revolutionary enthusiasm.

Liu and Deng's Party leadership, especially strong in Beijing, struck back by sending work-teams to campuses to quell student unrest. In August, after Lin Biao and the PLA had secured Beijing and neutralized Liu and Deng's adherents, Mao responded with his own wall poster, "Bombard the Headquarters," calling the Party itself reactionary and bourgeois and authorizing attacks on the CCP leadership: "They have stood facts on their heads, juggled black and white, encircled and suppressed revolutionaries, stifled opinions differing from their own…How poisonous!" Thus began the Great Proletarian Cultural Revolution (GPCR), a period of chaos unprecedented even in China. From rural villages to the Central Committee, people battled

Red Guards march with their "Little Red Books" in a Tiananmen Square rally at the beginning of the Cultural Revolution, 1966.

to prove themselves most revolutionary, most loyal to Chairman Mao.

Three days after Mao's poster, the Central Committee, reformed by Mao's loyal allies, called on the people to carry out the GPCR by writing wall posters and engaging in a great national debate over the direction of the revolution: "Our objective is to struggle against and crush those persons in authority who are taking the capitalist road." Aimed clearly at Liu Shaoqi, Deng Xiaoping, and their faction, this directive opened the door for attacks against "enemies" everywhere, some of them motivated by principle, some by opportunism, many by personal animus and desire for revenge. Red Guards converged on Beijing to attend giant rallies in homage to Chairman Mao, then fanned out across the country—taking advantage of free railroad transportation granted by the Central Committee—to "exchange experience" with their counterparts elsewhere.

In a vast, bewildering three-year series of blows and counterblows, ideological pronouncements and personal slander, struggle meetings and violence, *danwei* all over China exploded in conflict. High-school students humiliated and physically beat their teachers and principals and dismissed them for authoritarianism and elitism. Then, in the absence of effective authority, the students attacked one another with homemade weapons and high-volume slogans, killing and maiming in Mao's name. Middle-aged professors, wearing four-foot-tall dunce caps, their "crimes" enumerated in signs glued to their backs, stood for hours before

struggle meetings in the agonizing "airplane position," backs bent and arms widespread, as their own students screamed indictments. After such experiences, many committed suicide.

Nor did the Red Guards restrict themselves to their schools and colleges. Armed with their belt buckles and pure righteousness, they entered homes and apartments to search and confiscate, attacking people regardless of age or gender to "eradicate the Four Olds"—old customs, culture, habits, and ideas. Foreign connections, such as an American education or a Mozart recording, led to summary punishment as a GMD spy or CIA agent. In the public realm, they destroyed ancient sites, historical buildings, libraries, and museums in order to purge China of its "feudal" heritage and clear the way for revolutionary purity.

Scenes like these, played out hundreds of thousands of times, deadened their viewers and forced people to protect themselves against apparently random and vicious attacks, even at the cost of principle and integrity. Although cadres generally succeeded in preserving agricultural production, even rural people were exhausted by the pressure of constant struggle meetings, Maoism study meetings, meetings to learn of new structures of authority. Everyone had to participate; inaction constituted counterrevolutionary apathy, itself an object of attack. Schools closed, college entrance examinations ceased, and Party branches shut down. Red Guards raided offices and stole personnel files, raided arsenals and armed themselves, raided people's homes and took whatever they pleased. "Bad class background" became hereditary, and the descendants of class enemies suffered for the sins of their ancestors. No one knows how many people died in GPCR violence, but estimates run as high as 1 million.

The GPCR did bring down the "capitalist roaders" from Party power, beginning with Peng Zhen in the spring of 1966. In 1967, Liu Shaoqi and his wife disappeared into house arrest. In 1968, the CCP dismissed him, and in 1969 the Ninth Party Congress denounced him as an enemy agent. He died that year, under horrible conditions, and was not rehabilitated and granted a state funeral until 1980. Deng Xiaoping, whom Mao saw as essential for the rebuilding of the Party center, was sent to a rural tractor factory to be "reeducated through labor." He survived to become China's supreme leader after Mao's death (see p. 369). His son Deng

Pufang (b. 1944), attacked by Red Guards as the "spawn of a capitalist-roader," jumped (or was pushed) from an upper-story window and broke his back. Wheelchair-bound since then, he later won awards as an advocate for the disabled and served as Executive Director of the Organizing Committee for the 2008 Beijing Olympics.

GPCR violence escalated in waves through 1967 until Chairman Mao, who had authorized the violence in the first place, called out the army to restore order and protect production. The PLA suppressed many Red Guards, siding with one faction (deemed more "revolutionary") against another. Local administration had been thoroughly disrupted by radical attacks, including outright "seizures of power" by Red Guards or workers, so Beijing mandated "revolutionary committees" as the new form of political leadership. "Revolutionary rebels," whether workers or Red Guards, joined with CCP cadres and PLA officers in a three-way alliance. Many danwei experienced difficulty finding CCP cadres to participate—they had been purged, imprisoned, or sent to labor reform—but the PLA wielded effective military control, and by late 1968 revolutionary committees governed almost everywhere. In the following year, Party committees regained their former power, keeping the PLA on board for muscle and the "revolutionary rebels" for show.

In 1969–70, with the violence sharply diminished and the Party back in charge, the problem of "intellectual youth" had to be solved without educational institutions. The People's Daily announced a program of sending educated youth to the countryside to be educated in rural poverty. Around 15 million young people found themselves strangers in the villages, ignorant of physical labor or agriculture, expected to "learn from the peasants," produce their own food, and serve the community. Those able to pull strings or pay bribes quickly found their way home, but millions remained in villages until 1980 or even later. Some are still there. Beginning in 1968, hundreds of thousands of CCP cadres shared this experience. Sent to rural "May 7th Cadre Schools," they spent months or even years at hard labor and study of Mao's works.

Many people who lived through the GPCR, remembering the pain and injury inflicted on colleagues, neighbors, even relatives, wondered, "How could we have come to that? What caused us to lose our moral compass so completely?" Answers have ranged from

some genetic flaw in the Chinese people to the personal evil of Mao Zedong, Jiang Qing, and their factional allies. Chinese writers and artists have produced "scar literature" to catalogue and describe the Cultural Revolution's damage. Scholars have isolated numerous causes, among them people's willingness to obey the god-like Chairman Mao as a modern version of traditional obedience to authority. By 1968, everyone had learned to perform the "loyalty dance" and to confess sins to Mao's portrait. With Marxism–Leninism as its guiding philosophy, the PRC made class rather than common humanity the crucial moral category. Mao and the CCP had mandated mass campaigns and struggle meetings as the proper forums for moral judgment, and mob violence became social justice.

In contrast, other GPCR participants, even some victims, claim that the chaos and destruction of central authority created a sense of democracy, common purpose, and egalitarianism. Although many suffered, they say, politics became the property of all Chinese people, not just Party members, and they compare the GPCR favorably to the materialism and cynicism of today's China. Deng Pufang, Deng Xiaoping's paraplegic son, wrote that the GPCR generation had grown tougher, more thoughtful, and more able to take initiatives. Movement of intellectuals to the countryside also brought education and rudimentary health care—the paramedics called "barefoot doctors"—to the villages, providing previously unknown services to peasants. Mao had said, "Women hold up half the sky," and many women's lives had been substantially altered by the movement's egalitarianism. Women had filled formerly male occupations and status, modeling themselves on "Iron Girl" brigades of tough female laborers.

DÉTENTE AND CHANGING THE GUARD

In September 1971, conflicts within the Chinese leadership again broke into the open. According to unverifiable Chinese sources, Lin Biao, Mao's "close comrade-in-arms" and chosen successor, plotted to assassinate the Chairman. When the plan failed, he fled with his family and allies, but their plane crashed with no survivors in the People's Republic of Mongolia. This bizarre incident, called the "571 Project," resulted in the purge of much of the PLA's high command. Jiang Qing, taking advantage of Lin's fall, started a campaign to "Criticize Lin Biao and Confucius," attacking not only the ancient sage and late general but also Zhou Enlai, whom she hated. Lin Biao's sudden fall from "Chairman Mao's chosen successor and closest comrade-in-arms" to "renegade and traitor" caused many Chinese to reconsider their confidence in their government's personnel and pronouncements.

Since 1949, the United States had maintained the Republic of China government (Taiwan) in China's seat at the United Nations, including permanent membership and veto power in the Security Council. In 1971, the staunchly anticommunist President Richard Nixon and his national security adviser, Henry Kissinger, moved to balance Soviet power through US–PRC relations and to use China's influence to end the Vietnam War. They found a willing counterpart in Zhou Enlai, who wanted to secure UN membership and international legitimacy for the PRC. That October, the General Assembly voted to replace the ROC (Taiwan) with the PRC in the UN.

After an American table-tennis team visited the PRC ("ping-pong diplomacy"), Kissinger and Zhou secretly arranged a dramatic journey to China by President Nixon in February 1972, including a meeting with an ailing Chairman Mao. Although the surprise visit angered some US allies, including Japan, it changed the international balance of power in East Asia permanently. The PRC gradually established diplomatic relations with any country that would agree to break relations with the ROC (Taiwan).

US President Richard Nixon's meeting with Mao Zedong, February 21, 1972. From left to right, Zhou Enlai, the interpreter Tang Wensheng, Mao Zedong, Richard Nixon, and Henry Kissinger.

Afflicted with ALS ("Lou Gehrig's disease"), Mao could only walk and speak with difficulty after 1972. Zhou Enlai, the international face of the PRC, was dying of cancer. To prevent Jiang Qing and her faction from monopolizing the PRC government—Mao and Jiang's relationship had deteriorated considerably—in 1973 Mao recalled Deng Xiaoping from his rural tractor factory to rebuild the CCP's central bureaucracy, preparing him to assume greater power as Mao and Zhou grew weaker.

When Zhou Enlai died in January 1976, people placed wreaths and poems on the obelisk in Tiananmen Square, a spontaneous outpouring of grief for the popular premier. Huge demonstrations in April against removal of the memorials met with swift repression, and Mao had to decide how to balance Deng Xiaoping, said to have allowed the people's outbursts, and Jiang Qing, who ordered their suppression. In a final attempt at compromise, Mao again demoted Deng Xiaoping and appointed new Premier Hua Guofeng (1921–2008)—a former public security minister from Hunan—as his successor, supposedly saying, "With you in charge, I can rest easy."

Zhu De, the founder and commander of the Red Army, died that July. In the same month a devastating earthquake destroyed the city of Tangshan, east of Beijing, killing 250,000 people. For many Chinese, so much catastrophe and turmoil within eight months predicted great changes, and they were right. On September 9, 1976 Mao Zedong died, leaving the CCP and government partially disabled by a decade of civil conflict and political instability. Hua Guofeng immediately arrested Jiang Qing and her closest allies, Yao

Wenyuan (1931–2005), Zhang Chunqiao (1917–2005), and Wang Hongwen (1935–1992)—called "the Gang of Four"—and announced that the PRC would return to Soviet-style central planning.

For the next two years, amid factional wrangling, Deng Xiaoping carefully arranged his own return to central power, ousting Hua Guofeng by 1980. Setting a new precedent, Deng did not dispose of Hua but instead gradually limited him to insignificant government posts and then to retirement. Experienced in political battle, well connected throughout the state apparatus, and opposed to radical policies, Deng Xiaoping finally had his chance to lead China. He and his allies wasted no time.

THE OTHER CHINA

While the Great Leap Forward and Cultural Revolution brought chaos to the PRC, the ROC on Taiwan took a very different developmental path. Authoritarian and centralized like the CCP, the GMD under Jiang Jieshi undertook land reform, compensating landowners with stock in state-owned industries. The ROC established mainlanders and the military in government power and planned Taiwan's economic growth, with the state controlling key industries. Reliant on US aid and military presence, the ROC claimed to be the sole legitimate government of China, trumpeting a future counterattack on the mainland but digging in for defense. When Jiang Jieshi died in 1975, 18 months before Mao, he ruled over a flourishing economy and a divided society. Taiwan's development will be covered in Chapter 12.

JAPAN: THE ERA OF DOUBLE-DIGIT GROWTH

Looking back to the years immediately after the American occupation ended in 1952, a Japanese observer in the mid-1970s could be excused if she saw little that seemed familiar. Japan's US$500 billion Gross National Product (GNP) in 1975, the world's third largest after the United States and USSR, dwarfed 1951's US$14 billion. Little more than 1 percent of Japan's roads had been paved right after the war, but by 1975 Japanese could travel from city to city on the world's first high-speed rail lines—the *Shinkansen*, nicknamed "bullet trains" in English, inaugurated in time for the 1964 Tokyo Olympics.

The bombing of Japan's cities in 1945 had led to a mass exodus of urban residents to the countryside, where they lived with relatives on farms their parents and grandparents had left. Although many had moved back to the cities by the end of the occupation, in 1950 only 38 percent of the nation's population lived in cities; by 1975 that percentage had reached 75 percent. While half of the labor force worked in the primary sector—farming, fishing, forestry—in 1950, only about 10 percent did so in the 1970s. A huge baby boom accompanied the post-surrender return of Japanese soldiers and civilians from the continent—Japan gained 20 million souls between 1945 and 1955, a 30 percent increase—and those children came of age in the mid-1970s, contributing to the "demographic dividend" that fueled Japan's rapidly growing economy. A demographic dividend occurs when the working-age population grows faster than other age groups.

The productive conditions of 1975 seemed to bear little resemblance to the economic doldrums of the years right after the occupation, when the Korean War armistice ended the economic stimulus produced by American munitions purchases. In addition to enormous quantitative differences in the quarter-century before 1975, qualitative changes presented striking contrasts with the 1950s. Daily life had revolved around one's family and neighborhood in the early 1950s; by 1975, a shared national culture replaced the local with the national and even global. In the 1950s, there was widespread poverty—Japanese lucky enough to have houses often occupied tiny wooden buildings with a few electric bulbs, a radio, and a telephone, but no flush toilet. Home-prepared food and local festivals and entertainment at neighborhood shrines and temples kept most Japanese at home and in their neighborhoods.

By 1975, public and private railroad companies mounted lively advertising campaigns to encourage frequent travel to a countryside no longer depicted as a site of backbreaking work and social conflict but rather of picturesque villages—the urban residents' *furusato* (old home village) painted in nostalgic hues. Domestic travel brought Japanese of all areas closer together, as did television, inaugurated in 1953 by NHK (J. *Nippon Hōsō Kyōkai*, Japan Broadcasting Corporation). Commercial stations quickly joined the national network. Regional accents that had made understanding Japanese from other areas difficult were increasingly superseded by the Tokyo accent that predominated on TV; commercials often employed regionalisms for their quaintness. Newspapers (24 million copies per day) and magazines (11.5 million per week) blanketed the country. TV and print media shrank the cultural distance between cities and farms.

In the decades after the occupation, neighborhoods of wooden houses gave way to over 1 million apartments in huge public housing complexes and millions of single-family, middle-class homes extending for miles along the commuter rail lines surrounding Japan's cities. In 1955, almost 60 percent of Japanese had reported to pollsters that they were "lower class," but by 1975, public surveys indicated that 75 percent to 90 percent identified themselves as middle-class. Most Japanese had come to use commercial venues, similar throughout the country, for family events like weddings and funerals that had been performed at home or at neighborhood temples or shrines in the 1950s.

Japanese people increasingly shared life experiences and practices. Hospitals welcomed most babies into the world by 1975; home births fell from 82 percent in 1955 to 1.2 percent in 1975. Social diversity defined by level of schooling had been very evident in the early 1950s. While educational and gender differences continued to track young people into different career paths in 1975, the specific patterns shifted significantly. In 1955, about half of all boys and girls graduated from middle school and then went to work in blue-collar jobs, and only about one-third graduated from high school. Male high-school graduates often entered skilled jobs with the possibility of rising in their companies, while their sisters could become secretaries. Male college graduates could enter management- or government-training positions. University-educated women had few professional opportunities other than teaching and nursing in 1955, and this was still the case in 1975. Education and gender defined career paths, but the levels required for job entry changed within less than a generation. A high-school education replaced a middle-school education as the basic blue-collar requirement; management trainees increasingly needed college.

Although widespread poverty, the focus on neighborhood and home, and pronounced regional and economic diversity made the 1950s appear quite distinct

An early version of the Shinkansen ("bullet train") flies past a Buddhist temple in 1966.

from 1975, some important features continued. As in the 1950s, many Japanese protested social inequalities in the 1970s. As the postwar political parties rebuilt themselves, the diversity of experiences in the 1950s generated political differences. Movements of students, women, laborers, minorities, and peace activists created a volatile cultural and social landscape. Rapid economic growth in the 1960s, both at the national and at the family level, moderated some of that volatility. Japanese people sensed that their experiences were more shared than divisive and came to desire reconnection with their Asian neighbors and the rest of the world.

But by the end of the 1960s and into the 1970s, Japanese people realized that they did not all benefit equally from the period of "income doubling" in the 1960s. Many questioned Japan's foreign policy, the roles and status of women, the destruction of the environment through industrial pollution, and the failure of government to deliver social services and promote the welfare of all its citizens, even as it stimulated big business.

CREATION OF THE "1955 SYSTEM"

As we saw in Chapter 10, governance under the US occupation blended American and Japanese initiatives. Yoshida Shigeru, prime minister for most of the period, faced challenges from both the left and the right. Leftists, students, union members, and progressives resented Yoshida's passage of legislation to stifle activism, demonstrating and rioting against these measures on May 1, 1952. Yoshida had agreed, under American pressure, to permit American military bases to continue in Japan; establish the Defense Agency; and transform the already controversial national police force into the Ground, Maritime, and Air Self-Defense Forces. All of these angered many Japanese. Critics claimed they violated Article 9—the no-war clause of the new constitution—but Yoshida argued that Article 9 did not prohibit self-defense.

Meanwhile, the right also criticized Yoshida. Like the left, they decried his subservience to the Americans. But unlike the left, who wanted a neutral, non-militarized Japan, the right advocated ending occupation-era policies—especially Article 9—that they identified with Yoshida. A de-purged Hatoyama Ichirō reemerged as the loudest anti-Yoshida voice. By 1954, Hatoyama joined forces with the Progressive Party, formed a new Democratic Party, and forced Yoshida out with a vote of no confidence in December 1954. Hatoyama became prime minister.

Warring internal left and right factions hampered the Socialists. The Socialist left opposed the US–Japan Security Treaty as well as the San Francisco Peace Treaty because it excluded the PRC and USSR, while the Socialist right accepted the Peace Treaty but opposed the Security Treaty. Despite these differences, the Socialist factions laid down their swords and reunited in 1955. Fearful of the unified Socialist Party, business leaders pressed the Liberal and Democratic parties to do likewise, which they did, creating the Liberal Democratic Party (LDP). Ruling until 1993, the LDP and its staunch supporters in business and the bureaucracy—nicknamed the Iron Triangle—formed what came to be called the "1955 System."

Hatoyama did not last long as prime minister. During his two years—ill health forced him to step down in 1956—he pushed for a foreign policy more independent of the United States and for revision of the constitution to allow rearmament and the elevation of the emperor's position to "head of state." He had partial success with the former, but failed with the latter. Hatoyama normalized relations with the Soviets—without settling the dispute over islands claimed by both sides—but was unable to do the same with the PRC, with which full normalization of relations would have to wait until the 1970s.

Before stepping down, Hatoyama set up a commission to study constitutional revision, which the Socialists boycotted. Kishi Nobusuke (1896–1987),

prime minister from 1957 to 1960, continued the commission's meetings, but nothing came of their work. Kishi, released from prison after being charged (but not tried) as a Class A war criminal, was best known for forcing the Diet to accept his revised US–Japan Security Treaty, without popular support and after using the police to eject opponents from the Diet. The decade of the 1950s did not end peacefully, partially due to Kishi's tactics. His successor had to restore tranquility and rebuild the Japanese people's confidence in their government.

All Japanese had to find their way in a political and social environment that had new rules in the 1950s—new laws, a new constitution, and new promises of democracy. As we have seen, even the mainstream political parties differed greatly over how best to rebuild Japan at home and in the world. Small wonder that members of Japan's civil society—public interest groups, women, unions, students, minorities—made their voices heard.

THE CLIMATE FOR RECOVERY

The international climate that formed the backdrop for popular movements was changing quickly, as global economic conditions helped Japan to rebuild its economy. The United States recognized that expanded trade would permit the rapid recovery of Europe and Asia's war-torn economies, simultaneously opening new markets for United States' products. In 1947, the United States thus spearheaded the creation of the General Agreement on Trade and Tariffs (GATT), a regulatory organization for international trade. The Americans persuaded the other members to admit Japan; when Great Britain, the strongest holdout, agreed after years of resistance, Japan joined GATT in 1955. Oil was extremely cheap in the 1950s, and Japan gained access to global oil markets just as its coalmines began to play out. In addition, the United States pegged the yen at 360 to the dollar at the end of the occupation to curb the massive inflation that hindered economic recovery (see p. 351). When its economy recovered, this rate turned out to be so low that Japanese exports entered the world market attractively underpriced, an enormous benefit that later triggered a backlash among its trading partners.

Citizens' behavior also helped recovery. Before the enactment of a secure safety net of social security and improved national health care, individual families eagerly followed the government's exhortation to save money for a rainy day. By 1960, personal savings rates reached 15 percent of disposable income. Banks, therefore, had capital that could be used by industrial investors to build their companies—Japanese firms relied much more on debt than did firms in other capitalist countries during these years. Because they saved so frugally, average citizens had money to spend on durable consumer goods after paying for food, housing, and other necessities. Indeed, families rushed with cash in hand to purchase washing machines, TVs, refrigerators, electric rice cookers, and sewing machines as they became available.

The postwar economy also relied on "administrative guidance," the practice of government bureaucracies nurturing favored industries by helpful interventions. Government actions included approving requests to convert yen to dollars to purchase raw materials for production and licenses for new technologies; offering tax breaks, building permits, and loans on favorable terms; and guiding firms in industries with too much capacity through a managed process of cutbacks so competition would not undercut them. Administrative guidance, a crucial part of Japan's postwar industrial policy, had its roots in the prewar and wartime eras. As noted in Chapters 9 and 10, the Japanese government set up cartels to "rationalize" business in the prewar era, and the American occupation continued some of these practices.

While the Finance, Construction, and other ministries as well as the Economic Planning Agency played roles in administrative guidance, the most important actor was the Ministry of International Trade and Industry (MITI), newly renamed in 1949. By the 1970s however, Japanese companies no longer needed government guidance to succeed in world markets, and foreign pressure made it difficult for MITI to control Japanese firms. Some important innovators, most notably Sony and Matsushita (Panasonic), resisted MITI's advice and developed on their own. MITI's power declined starting in the 1970s, and in 2001, it was replaced with the much less powerful Ministry of Economy, Trade, and Industry (METI). But in the 1950s, MITI played a powerful role in guiding the economy. Japanese entrepreneurs and average citizens sometimes praised it and sometimes resisted its "guidance."

Japanese foreign policy in the 1950s developed in the context of the US–Japan Security Treaty. Hampered by US policies, Hatoyama's attempts to improve relations with the USSR and the PRC succeeded only partially, but the alliance with the United States helped Japan in other diplomatic areas. As we have seen, the United States facilitated Japan's entry into GATT and in 1956 promoted Japan's membership in the United Nations, a significant arena for Japanese diplomacy.

At the same time, many Japanese, especially those concerned about American nuclear policy, resisted continuation of strong ties with the United States. Atmospheric nuclear bomb testing, though discontinued by the United States in the 1960s, had been common in the 1950s. A 1954 American bomb test over Bikini Island in the Pacific dropped fallout on a Japanese fishing boat. Having experienced nuclear bombing, with many thousands of survivors of Hiroshima and Nagasaki still suffering from its effects, Japanese were acutely sensitive to nuclear fallout. Following the Bikini Island incident, over 30 million people signed antinuclear petitions.

Many others objected to the continuing presence of American military bases in Japan. Not only did they fear that they would invite attacks by the USSR, they also resented the daily pain of prostitution and crime around the bases. From 1952 to the end of the 1970s, 100,000 crimes involving off-duty US military personnel—including 500 deaths due to accidents or assaults—occurred but could not be tried under Japanese law, a stark reminder of nineteenth-century extraterritoriality. Okinawa, occupied by the United States until it reverted to Japan in 1972, had (and continues to have) an overwhelming US military presence, leading to Okinawan anger at Tokyo for concentrating US bases in their prefecture (see p. 432).

DIVERSE AND CONFLICTING VOICES IN THE 1950s

Women played major roles in the peace and anti-Security Treaty movements of the 1950s. As we have seen, Japanese feminist organizations had worked to gain political and civil rights for women since the Meiji period. Ten days after the surrender, feminists established a Women's Committee on Postwar Policy, calling for suffrage and civil equality, and the New Japan Women's League, later renamed the League of Women Voters, in November 1945. Occupation officials encouraged the Women's Democratic Club, formed in March 1946, but later criticized it because it had some left-leaning women among its leaders. Although their leaders differed on some issues, these groups shared goals of peace and equal rights. In 1948, the Housewives Association was established to promote housewives' rights through consumer economics. Although it viewed women in a more essentialized way than the political rights groups, the Housewives Association—founded by Oku Mumeo, an originator of the New Woman's Association in 1919—advocated improving the lives of women and their families.

Women also played active parts in the reconstituted labor unions of the postwar period. The All Japan Federation of Labor Unions, linked to the socialists, came together in fall 1945, followed shortly by the communists' National Congress of Industrial Unions. After 1948, the Socialist Party affiliated with the General Council of Trade Unions of Japan. Women's divisions of these and other unions marched under their own banners in the first postwar May Day marches in 1946, calling for jobs, food, and workplace protections. Women's ability to voice protest increased as their legal status changed after the war. They received the vote in December 1945, and the new constitution granted sexual equality and freedom of choice in marriage and domicile.

The revised constitution, in turn, required changes to the Civil Code and Labor Standards Law. Although it intended to conform to the new constitution, not all the provisions of the 1947 Civil Code improved the status of women, especially laws concerning family/household registration, marital name, and nationality. The household registration system required all members of a family to register as one unit with one family name. Each unit had a head, usually the senior male. Although the single family name could be either the wife's or the husband's, in most cases a woman assumed her husband's surname upon marriage. Professional women, especially academics, soon found their inability to retain their premarital name a burden in the workplace and sought to overturn the single-marital-name provision through the courts. When that failed, they continued their struggle through legislation, still under consideration.

The nationality issue also created problems for women. Under the new Civil Code, only Japanese males could pass their Japanese citizenship to their children. Japanese mothers lost that right upon marriage to a foreign national. The courts overturned this provision in

1984 and granted equal nationality rights to Japanese mothers with foreign husbands.

The Labor Standards Law of 1947 required equal pay for equal work and provided several types of gendered "protections": maternity leave, nursing leave, menstruation leave, and prohibition of female labor in dangerous places or at night. Unionized women demanded other rights—such as the right to work after marriage and identical ages of retirement for women and men—which they legally gained in the early 1960s. In practice, however, companies continued to discriminate. Protections and discrimination lay at the heart of the feminist debates over workplace equality in the 1980s.

Just as the issue of gendered workplace protection suggested difference between women and men, so, too, did the Mothers' Convention established in June 1955. In 1960, 13,000 women gathered in Tokyo for the annual meeting, and thousands more met in regional meetings. These women believed that women, as mothers, had unique ability to work for peace and democracy. Women of all ages and classes, from radical college students to middle-aged housewives, played key roles in the demonstrations against the revision and renewal of the US–Japan Security Treaty.

Women addressed two other significant issues in the period before 1960, both concerning sexuality: reproduction and prostitution. The birth control movement of the prewar period had been suppressed under the wartime ideology of producing more soldiers for the empire. After the war, feminists' desire for reproductive freedom joined with the government's need to control the enormous postwar baby boom that threatened to undermine economic recovery. Although feminists wished to advocate contraception, the government focused on abortion, which involved more direct medical intervention. By the 1950s, Japanese doctors performed a million abortions annually, and not until 1955 did pregnancy prevention begin to take hold.

In that same year, the New Life Movement was founded—promoted by the government and big businesses to persuade women to stay at home, taking care of their husbands so the men could give more energy to their companies. In addition to encouraging a housewifely ideal that harked back to the Meiji period ("good wife, wise mother"), the New Life Movement also promoted birth control. The movement distributed condoms to workers' wives, not to the male workers themselves. Women participated in birth control distribution as one of the New Life Movement's civic activities before taking up peace, environmental, and other forms of activism—often in opposition to the government or corporations.

Regarding prostitution, feminists had struggled for over half a century to eradicate licensed brothels and finally succeeded in 1956. This did not eliminate prostitution itself but rather government licensing of the industry. The 1956 law became controversial, however, as impoverished sex workers organized a union and protested the loss of their livelihoods.

The 1960 movement against the revision and renewal of the US–Japan Security Treaty brought together many otherwise unconnected Japanese. In that huge movement, millions of women committed to antinuclear and pro-peace positions joined students, labor union members, Socialist party politicians, and even some members of the LDP. The students were members of the All-Japan Federation of Student Self-Governing Associations, founded in 1948 and fairly quiescent until the mid-1950s, when the antinuclear movement gave it a burst of energy.

The Security Treaty issue unfolded over many months. Kishi Nobusuke made revision of the treaty a major priority when he became prime minister in 1957, as both the right and the left desired change. By January 1960, the United States and Japan had agreed to a revised treaty, from which Japan actually gained—the United States was obliged to protect Japan, not required under the old treaty, in return for occupying bases paid for by Japan. The Americans also had to consult with Japan before stationing nuclear weapons there. The new treaty had a time limit—the original one did not—of ten years, after which it could continue until one or both parties wished to abrogate it.

Despite these improvements, millions of Japanese wanted no part of any security treaty. Massive demonstrations filled Tokyo's streets beginning in April 1960. Kishi rammed the revised treaty through the Diet on May 19, as police removed Socialists and others who opposed ratification from blocking the progress of the speaker of the lower house to the podium. The treaty passed, with many members absent. Demonstrations continued, and US President Dwight Eisenhower had to cancel a planned trip to Japan when demonstrators attacked his press secretary's car, requiring a helicopter

Demonstrators marching in front of the American embassy in Tokyo protesting against the revised Security Treaty, June 4, 1960. Numbering some 30,000, they carried banners with slogans reading "Demand the immediate resignation of Kishi and dissolution of the Diet" and "Don't come Ike" (in reference to US President Eisenhower).

rescue. In a later demonstration, a woman university student was killed, but the treaty went into effect, and the demonstrations subsided.

Kishi resigned, replaced by Ikeda Hayato (1899–1965), who promised to calm the waters. In September, he announced his plan to double Japan's GNP by 1970. The plan—including active administrative guidance, government setting of investment priorities, lowering of taxes and interest rates, and cutting competition by corporate mergers—came as a breath of fresh air to strife-weary Japanese. To be sure, the plan called for doubling the *national* income, not that of *individuals*, but average citizens interpreted the new policy as helpful to themselves.

Before Ikeda could calm Japan's social unrest, however, a few remaining issues remained, the most important the long strike at Mitsui Corporation's Miike coalmine. Miike management had determined to install new machinery to raise productivity in the face of competition from oil. This required firing some 2,000 workers, and Miike decided to break the union at the same time by firing union leaders. The union went on strike in January 1960. Opposing their own union, about 3,000 of the miners formed a new pro-company union. When the anti-Security Treaty demonstrations ended in Tokyo, some of those involved in that movement traveled to the mine in Kyūshū to show their support for the striking miners. The strike went on for 313 days, until the Ikeda government mediated a settlement, a critical step in the development of pro-company unions in Japan. In another 1960 trauma, the head of the Japan Socialist Party was assassinated while speaking at a televised election debate. Horrified by this act of terror, Japanese people yearned for whatever peace Ikeda could bring.

THE 1960s AND INCOME DOUBLING

The Japanese family envisioned in the 1950s by the New Life Movement became the norm during the 1960s. Men and women, married and unmarried, had different daily lives, and company leaders believed these divisions helped to grow their firms and the economy as a whole. Educational requirements had shifted from the 1950s, when middle-school graduates had been able to find work as laborers. By the 1960s, a high-school diploma increasingly became the entry ticket to factory

A station porter pushes passengers onto a packed commuter train during rush hour in Tokyo, 1967. Rapid growth was accompanied by urban overcrowding.

jobs, and companies expected white-collar workers to have college degrees. They recruited white-collar males straight from school, and most expected to spend their entire career with the same firm. Living in company dorms until marriage, they developed company loyalty and became the *sarariman* ("salary men") who epitomized the male life pattern.

Although farmers, blue-collar workers, small shop owners, and other men—that is, three out of four workers—were not *sarariman,* popular discourse in Japan and overseas suggested that the "typical Japanese" worked as a *sarariman.* Like *Ozzie and Harriet* in the United States, television sitcoms and dramas beamed throughout Japan presented the middle-class *sarariman* family as the model for emulation. The stereotypical *sarariman* left for work at dawn, after his wife had helped him dress, and did not return home until late at night, following a long day of work and then drinking with coworkers. Often exhausting rather than enjoyable, drinking sessions might occur several nights a week. Because companies viewed evening "recreation" as building *esprit de corps,* employees felt compelled to attend.

At home, their wives were expected to take care of the children and monetary matters. Mom assisted the children's education, as did after-school examination preparation academies. The stereotypical wife budgeted her husband's income, giving him a weekly allowance, and made many major economic decisions. The husband focused on the company and the wife on the family. Although the reality was never quite so stark, the *sarariman* model did influence behavior. During the 1960s and early 1970s, employment rates for women in their childbearing years dropped significantly from earlier decades, following the powerful norm of the stay-at-home "education mama." This pattern changed later.

Hardworking Japanese families had much to celebrate in the 1960s. Tokyo staged a brilliant Summer Olympics in 1964, showcasing Japan's recovery from the war to TV audiences around the world. The government built roads, subways, and the bullet trains, and inspirational architecture housed the Olympic events and thousands of athletes from 94 countries. When Japan's women's volleyball team took the gold medal, they became national heroes. The 1970 World's Fair in Osaka and the 1972 Winter Olympics in Sapporo continued Japan's streak of international success and pride.

375

Ikeda remained in office until ill health forced him out in 1964, to be followed by Satō Eisaku (1901–1975), who remained prime minister until 1972, the longest term in Japanese history. Satō normalized Japan's relations with South Korea, signing the Treaty on Basic Relations on June 22, 1965. In 2005, the South Korean government released documents from the treaty negotiations, and the process has since then become controversial. As part of the agreement, the Japanese government paid the Korean government reparations for conscripted workers as well as death and injury costs to those forced to work for Japan from 1910 to 1945. Instead of distributing those funds to survivors, Park Chung Hee's government used them for national construction projects (see p. 386).

In subsequent discussions about reparations, particularly with North Korea, the Japanese government contended that all reparations must be paid on a government-to-government basis, and yet these documents indicate that the Japanese government intended to give reparations to individuals. This may complicate diplomatic relations in the future. In 1965, however, Japanese people viewed the settlement with South Korea positively, and it accelerated the development of active international trade.

Japan's economic and cultural relations with the PRC began to improve slightly at the same time, despite Japan's inability to modify their political relations because of its Cold War tie with the United States. In 1962, the PRC and Japan concluded a commercial agreement, but as late as 1971 Japan continued to vote with the United States against seating the PRC in the United Nations.

The LDP worked hard to build a political power structure to last for decades, and it succeeded until 1993. In addition to placating the average citizen with its plan to double GNP by 1970—it reached that goal three years early, in 1967—the LDP constructed electoral alliances with farmers. The government mandated price supports and import restrictions for rice as well as shielding gerrymandered rural areas from electoral redistricting for as long as possible. The LDP also courted small shop owners, passing a law preventing large department stores from constructing branches outside downtown areas. It even tried to improve labor relations—Ikeda invited the head of the General Council of Trade Unions to discuss wages

for public-sector workers. Other, less militant, unions agreed to accept new technologies in exchange for higher wages and job protection.

At the same time, the Japan Socialist Party weakened in 1960 when its right wing bolted to form the Democratic Socialist Party. A new Buddhist religion, the Sōka Gakkai (Value Creation Society), also formed a political party, the Clean Government Party in 1969. Established in 1930, Sōka Gakkai stressed ritual chanting and active proselytizing. The Clean Government Party positioned itself in the political center, although it often supported the Socialists. Since 1993, its members have rearranged themselves in a variety of political factions tending to ally with the LDP.

THE ATTAINMENT OF WEALTH AND THE RISE OF DISCONTENT

At the end of the 1960s, Japanese people could take pride in the fact that their country's GNP was surpassed only by those of the United States and the USSR. Yet wealth had come at a high price, and prosperity had not yet spread evenly across Japanese society. Tokyo children had to stay indoors much of the summer of 1970 due to air pollution, and people elsewhere suffered pain and disease from foul air and poisoned water. Women tired of playing second fiddle to men at work, and men tired of being absent fathers to their children. Many people again opposed the Security Treaty when it came up for renewal in 1970. And Japan's minorities, Koreans and *burakumin* (see p. 251), Ainu and Okinawans, began to demand better treatment. In the late 1960s and early 1970s, at the height of Japan's prosperity before the 1973 oil crisis, middle-class Japanese questioned prosperity's costs.

The most militant form of questioning, which attracted most media attention, was the student movement beginning in 1968. Part of an international movement that included universities in Europe, Central and South America, elsewhere in Asia, and the United States, student activists in Japan closed Tokyo University and other schools for a period in 1969. Opposition to America's war in Vietnam fueled the global protests, and each country had its own local issues as well. For Japan, the renewal of the Security Treaty in 1970 brought almost 800,000 people to the streets of Tokyo in a massive demonstration in June. Despite the opposition, the treaty was renewed. Many of the students went on to protest the building of Tokyo's new Narita Airport, joining farmers who refused to give up their land. They, too, eventually lost.

Other protests succeeded. Bitter anger at deadly pollution coalesced in several stunning cases: dumping of mercury-laden effluents into the sea in Minamata and Niigata caused death and paralysis for those who ate local fish; cadmium poisoning brought on the *itai itai* ("it hurts, it hurts") disease in central Japan; and foul air produced debilitating asthma in many urban industrial areas. Corporate polluters hid evidence and physically attacked university researchers trying to discover the causes of these strange diseases. Local and national political leaders ignored citizens' complaints in the headlong rush to industrialize.

Finally public pressure, including sit-down strikes and boycotts by middle-class housewives and others, forced the government to listen. Victims won in court, and the LDP government altered its environmental policy overnight, passing numerous environmental laws in 1972–73, dubbed the "First Year of the Welfare State." Victims of environmental poisoning received reparation through the Pollution Related Disease Compensation Law. Companies had to cut back on pollution, so they turned this to their economic advantage by the end of the 1970s, pioneering and profiting from new antipollution technology. At the same time, average Japanese also benefited from other welfare measures. Since the 1920s, Japanese citizens had received partial health care insurance from the government, and this improved incrementally every decade or so. In 1972, senior citizens received completely free health coverage, and benefits expanded for younger families.

Other protests emerged in the same period. Hundreds of thousands of Koreans remained in Japan after the war, required to be "resident aliens," rather than citizens. They rarely intermarried with Japanese; most earned considerably less than other residents of Japan; and they were barred from government jobs. These forms of discrimination continued long after 1975. Continuing movements to improve their status will be discussed below. Among the minorities, *burakumin* organized most effectively.

- Sites of Industrial Pollution

N

EAST SEA/
SEA OF JAPAN

HOKKAIDŌ

Niigata Minamata Disease,
Niigata (1965)

Sendai

Itai-itai Disease,
Toyama (1950)

HONSHŪ

Tokyo

Kyoto
Nagoya

Hiroshima
Osaka

Fukuoka
SHIKOKU
KYŪSHŪ

Yokkaichi Asthma,
Yokkaichi (1961)

PACIFIC
OCEAN

Nagasaki

Minamata Disease,
Minamata (1956)

0   250 miles
0   400 kms

Sites of serious industrial pollution in Japan, 1950–70

After decades of social and economic discrimination—illegal lists of people with *burakumin* ancestry circulated in the business world—the *Buraku* Liberation League won some court and legislative battles. The 1969 *Buraku* Special Measures Law provided generous funds to *burakumin* communities. Although they advanced economically as a group, the status of individual *burakumin* remained low in succeeding decades.

IENAGA SABURŌ, CRUSADING HISTORIAN

Ienaga Saburō speaking to reporters in Tokyo after winning his third lawsuit against government censorship, August 29, 1997. Ienaga had discussed a number of topics in a textbook on Japanese history, including the medical atrocities of Unit 731's research during World War II, which the government had tried to excise from the text. In the third ruling on this lawsuit the Japanese Supreme Court judged such censorship was "unlawful" and ordered the government to pay Ienaga compensation.

Historian Ienaga Saburō (1913–2002) fought against government censorship for three decades. Author of modern history textbooks, he contested the power of the Ministry of Education to censor his descriptions of the Nanjing Massacre (see p. 287) and the atrocities of Unit 731 (see pp. 293, 351). The courts repeatedly ruled that the Ministry *could* censor his textbooks before approving them for classroom use. Only in 1997 did he receive a favorable verdict: although the Ministry of Education could require changes to textbooks, Ienaga's accurate descriptions of wartime atrocities should not have been censored. Nominated twice for the Nobel Peace Prize, Ienaga tenaciously continued suing the Japanese government.

A frail child with lung disease and terrible eyesight, Ienaga came from a poor family—his father was an underpaid military officer who received no pension and his mother was sickly. His poor health made him physically unfit for military service during World War II. In middle school, little Saburō loved history and believed in "Japan's beautiful national character."

In the mid-1930s, however, he began to question his own nationalistic attitude. At Tokyo University, he decided to study the history of seventh-century Buddhism, far removed from nationalistic modern history. Following graduation in 1937, he worked as a historical researcher, then became a college professor in Niigata prefecture and, after 1944, at Tokyo University of Education. Despite his personal opposition to the war, he said nothing at the time. As he wrote in his autobiography, guilt about his wartime silence inspired him to write critical books and fight against censorship.

Fortunately, Ienaga survived the March 10, 1945 firebombing of Tokyo. His students had been sent to work in an aircraft factory in 1944, and he accompanied them, so he was away from home when it was destroyed. He had married in 1944, so after the firebombing, he moved in with his wife Miyoko's family in Sendai. Immediately after the war, Ienaga joined a team producing a new Japanese history book, *Progress of the Country* (1946) under the direction of the American occupation. Ienaga considered this an unsatisfactory book and began work on his first singly authored Japanese history textbook in the late occupation years. When he finished in 1952, he had to submit it to the Ministry of Education. They required significant changes, which Ienaga made, and subsequent editions in the 1950s also underwent censorship. By 1965, he could no longer bear the Ministry's restrictions and the psychological damage they caused him and began the first of many court cases. Ienaga's lawsuits made him a hero in the movement against censorship, both in Japan and abroad.

The "second wave" of the women's movement washed over Japan in the early 1970s, including non-militant but widespread citizens' groups of housewives. Many focused on food purity, consumerism, childcare, and other issues that affected the daily lives of women and their families. Their "housewife feminism" merged with other political organizations and helped bring reformist and progressive mayors and governors to power in the 1970s.

A more spectacular wave—unfairly ridiculed by the media—was the *uuman ribu* ("women's lib") movement that began in 1970. This movement focused on liberation of the body and sexuality, critiquing men for violating women both in Japan and abroad. Feminist intellectuals and activists formed groups with names like Fighting Women, and magazines like *Feminisuto* ("Feminist") popularized the idea of "flying women" who could break through social barriers. The United Nations International Women's Year in 1975 brought together first-wave feminists like Ichikawa Fusae and second-wave feminists in a nationwide movement.

THE END OF AN ERA

Two decades of double-digit growth came to an end in 1974. The previous year, OPEC cut off oil exports to countries that had supported Israel in the 1973 war, including Japan. After an overnight policy shift —Japan distanced itself from Israel—OPEC resumed oil shipments, but petroleum prices skyrocketed, plunging Japan into a condition of "stagflation": GNP dropped while prices jumped 25 percent in one year. Government told citizens to conserve energy, and rumors of shortages led to panic buying of consumer goods like toilet paper. Unions demanded pay increases, and a large, illegal strike of public-sector employees took place in November 1975. When it failed to gain its objective—the legal right to strike—unions weakened further. Despite these difficulties in the mid-1970s, the economy turned around more quickly than it would after later recessions. Japanese planners turned to alternative energy sources—wind, waves, solar, and nuclear—and lessened their dependency on Middle Eastern petroleum.

Another seemingly overnight policy shift—long desired by the Japanese government and people—was Japan's diplomatic recognition of the PRC, part of Japan's reorientation toward Asia and expanding global interests. Japan's new directions chipped away at the tightly bilateral relationship with the United States that had circumscribed its foreign policy since the end of World War II. President Richard Nixon's 1971 announcement, without prior notification to his Japanese counterpart, of his planned visit to Beijing stunned Prime Minister Satō, who had been conducting close negotiations with the United States to return Okinawa to Japan (1972). Until that moment, Japan had followed the US lead in diplomatic relations with China. Just two months later, in August 1971, Nixon announced that the United States would allow the dollar to float against other currencies. Previously undervalued at 360 yen to the dollar, Japan's currency suddenly jumped in value, making Japanese products significantly more expensive overseas.

The Japanese dubbed these two actions the "Nixon shocks." Japan's next prime minister, Tanaka Kakuei (1918–1993; see p. 421), quickly visited China himself and signed an agreement to normalize relations with the PRC in 1972. China's insistence that a formal treaty with Japan include a "non-hegemony clause" directed against the Soviet Union slowed diplomatic progress, but the PRC later modified that demand, allowing Japan and the PRC to conclude a treaty of peace and friendship in 1978. As it did with the United States, Taiwan ended formal diplomatic relations when Japan recognized the PRC, but maintained an economic and cultural relationship under an agreement signed in 1973.

Japan experienced conditions of modernity similar to those throughout the world in the postwar quarter-century—the growth of women's, student, and environmental movements; adjustments of the relationships of citizens with the state; responses to the global economy; and creation of shared national experiences. Chapter 12 will discuss how these were addressed in the arts as well as the transition to the globally interconnected high-technology world.

NATION-BUILDING IN THE KOREAS

The truce signed on July 27, 1953 ended the Korean War. With the guns silent, the final battle lines evolved into an impenetrable barrier between North and South Korea. More than 50 years later, these lines still form the contours of the Demilitarized Zone (DMZ), a 155-mile (250-km) long, heavily fortified no-man's land, averaging two and a half miles (4 km) in width, cutting across the entire peninsula. The line hardened immediately after the war as North and South Korea hunkered down behind the fortifications and minefields of what has become the most militarized strip of land in the world.

On each side of the DMZ, the Koreas followed separate, divergent developmental paths. North Korea, led by the Korean Workers Party (KWP) with Kim Il Sung at the helm, emerged as a rigorously centralized and regimented socialist state and society. Nominally a constitutional republic, South Korea's political system became increasingly authoritarian and closed as its first president, Syngman Rhee, used wartime emergency measures and martial law to create a de facto dictatorship. We shall trace the political and economic evolution of the Koreas in parallel.

AUTHORITARIAN PATTERNS IN SOUTH KOREA: SYNGMAN RHEE'S FIRST REPUBLIC

During the war, the South Korean state under Syngman Rhee augmented its control through "emergency measures," which expanded presidential powers even beyond the draconian National Security Law (NSL) of 1948. Rhee took advantage of the "national emergency" to intimidate opposition and ram through a constitutional amendment mandating direct popular election of the president, not an indirect election by the National Assembly. To do this, Rhee used the National Police to round up the boycotting opposition Assembly members, locked them into the Assembly chamber to create a quorum, and then used his majority to pass the amendment.

Rhee won the first popular presidential election in 1952, during the war, and in the 1954 National Assembly election his reorganized Liberal Party gained a two-thirds majority. Rhee used this majority to amend the constitution and remove the two-term presidential limit—allowing him to run for a third term in 1956. In this election, however,

The first President of Korea, Syngman Rhee seated with US General Douglas MacArthur, during the ceremony in Seoul inaugurating the new Republic of Korea, August 14, 1948.

he won only because his opponent, Sin Ikhŭi (1894–1956), suddenly died. The opposition Democratic Party candidate, Chang Myŏn (1899–1966), won the vice-presidential election.

Beyond manipulation of the constitutional system, Rhee based his power on several extra-legal factors. He controlled the National Police and the vastly expanded ROK Army and its security services, using them for political purposes. He also exploited the enormous opportunities for patronage from his position at the top of this highly personalized system. American officials working in the ROK found Rhee grasping and difficult, but they valued his staunch anticommunism and uncompromising enmity toward North Korea as an important pillar of US containment policy in East Asia. Dispensing political patronage and economic rewards, Rhee gained almost total control of the central bureaucracy as well as solid support in the ROK business community. Enormous amounts of US economic aid kept South Korea's faltering economy afloat and built up its military. Rhee's government, rife with corruption, squandered aid money and defeated the often well-designed programs and policies of the First Republic.

Due in part to his administration's corruption, Rhee's popularity declined steadily in the late 1950s. In the 1958 National Assembly elections, his party lost its majority to Chang Myŏn's rising Democratic Party. Given widespread public disapproval, it appeared that Rhee's power was waning as the presidential elections of 1960 approached. Nonetheless, Rhee won the March election by a landslide, helped again by the coincidental death of opposition candidate Cho Pyŏng'ok at Walter Reed Medical Center in January.

Reports of massive election fraud galvanized public protests, led by university and high-school students in Seoul. The protests spread nationwide, and the National Police responded violently. At the height of the demonstrations, a dead student was pulled from Masan Bay with a tear-gas canister embedded in one eye, setting off an enormous public outrage and violent clashes between

Students commandeer a tank during the 1960 Student Revolution that toppled President Rhee.

students and police on April 19. Bloody suppression brought university professors and the general public into the streets.

At this critical point, the ROK army refused to intervene, and the United States pressured Rhee to step down. As a result of what is now known as the "April 19 Student Revolution," Rhee resigned on April 26 and left Korea for exile in Hawaii, where he died five years later at 94. A caretaker government under Foreign Minister Hŏ Chŏng took control, charged to create a new constitution and prepare for immediate elections. The new constitution altered the pattern of power by creating a parliamentary system with a premier responsible to the National Assembly. It also featured more protections for speech and the press in a public sphere that began to flourish in the post-Rhee climate, bringing heightened expectations for more open and pluralistic governance. In November elections, the Democratic Party won a majority and selected former Vice-President Chang Myŏn as premier. This election and the creation of the new constitution ushered in a short-lived Second Republic.

POLITICAL CONSOLIDATION IN NORTH KOREA

Kim Il Sung had become North Korea's leader with Soviet backing, but not without challenges to his leadership.

Distinct groups emerged among the communists: a domestic faction led by Pak Hŏnyŏng (1900–1955); the Yan'an faction of Kim Tubong (1886–1957?), formed by Korean communists active in China's civil war; a pro-Soviet faction; and Kim Il Sung's own Kapsan faction of former Manchurian guerrillas. Before and during the Korean War, Kim Il Sung commanded the allegiance of all in order to consolidate the DPRK and attack the South.

The destruction of the KPA after MacArthur's counterattack, however, spelled potential disaster for Kim. Some rivals assigned him direct responsibility for the army's failure, but he maneuvered adroitly and successfully blamed them in return. In 1954, Kim used the pretext of "war difficulties" to purge Pak Hŏnyŏng and members of his faction, many with colonial era ties to the South. Two years later came another showdown, and Kim managed to purge Kim Tubong from the party. Kim Il Sung's consolidation of power continued into the late 1960s, a process still obscure to outside viewers. By 1972 and the promulgation of an amended constitution, Kim entirely controlled both the party and government.

The DPRK rigorously centralized North Korean society. Commanding the top tier of the Korean Workers Party (KWP) and the DPRK government, Kim Il Sung stood at the apex of two huge bureaucratic pyramids, linked by a series of concurrent titles—top leaders occupied party and government positions simultaneously. The Korean People's Army (KPA) constituted a third hierarchy. As in China, other mass organizations—for women, youth, farmers, artists, etc.—also reported to the top leader. By the mid-1960s, Kim Il Sung wore many hats: leader of the party, head of state, commander-in-chief of the KPA, and so forth. Systematically purging potential challengers, he had become the all-powerful boss, with the sobriquet "Great Leader" welded to his name, harbinger of the all-encompassing cult of personality spun around him thereafter.

North Korea had begun its revolution before the Korean War, and most of its organizational features had been created before 1950. The central organ of society, the KWP, organized all aspects of economic, social, and political life. By 1949, it had swollen to over 3 million members, 12 percent of the population (a much higher percentage than the CCP in China). Party authority emanated downward from Kim Il Sung and his core supporters in the Standing Committee and the larger Political Bureau (Politburo). The lower levels of government mimicked the organization of the center, down to neighborhood, factory, school, or communal farm committees.

As individuals, all party members belonged to a basic cell, the lowest level of organization, which educated its members in party doctrine and socialized them as good communists, so they could provide examples for the population at large. At the beginning, "pure class origins," meaning working-class background, constituted the main qualification for membership, so the party admitted many uneducated working-class members. This became a problem later, when the Party needed more sophisticated leaders.

The KWP and society's work-units (similar to the PRC's *danwei*) vigorously organized all North Koreans under the broad surveillance of the Ministry of People's Security. The state built—and still maintains—a political classification system dividing the population into three groups: the "core class" of workers, poor peasants, soldiers, and revolutionary fighters; the "wavering class" of people with relatives in the South, rich farmers, service workers, or immigrants from South Korea, China, or Japan; and the "hostile class" of former Japanese collaborators and their descendants, Buddhists, Confucian scholars, Christians, or anyone known to be unfriendly to the regime. The state provided rations, job placement, and other privileges on a descending scale, with the hostile class often receiving less. Members of the wavering class were assumed to be redeemable and eligible for KPW membership after proper reeducation, but members of the hostile class could never hope to join the Party. The DPRK maintains to this day a large system of prisons and, more notoriously, work camps. North Korea watchers in the 1990s estimated that this penal system might hold as many as 200,000 people. Large though this appears, it still represents a lower percentage of the population than in the twenty-first-century United States.

Whatever might be said about the North Korean political system and its stultifying regimentation, we must remember that the North underwent a social revolution after 1945. As in China before 1978, the centralized party and government structure served as the planning agencies for the command economy (see pp. 358–59) and broad social welfare programs. Also resembling the PRC, it redistributed land to the tillers, creating the

basis for reorganizing rural areas into communal and state farms. The revolution established the primacy of collective life over the individual; by surrendering individual agency, individuals received entitlements in the socialist program. Education, health care, and employment became collective and state matters.

REBUILDING AND NORTH KOREA'S COMMAND ECONOMY (1953–72)

In the first 15 years after the war, North Korea surged forward in reconstruction and laid the basis of an impressive socialist economy. Aided by the state's mobilization of people's energy and the initial enthusiasm of the population, North Korea built, at the very least, a society in great contrast to the misery and poverty of the colonial past and the bitter war years—even if it was not the "worker's paradise" trumpeted in its propaganda.

Two years of intensive bombing had laid waste to North Korea's cities, industrial infrastructure, communications systems, and physical plant, including homes and offices. The USSR helped with major grants—2 billion rubles, only a fraction of US aid to South Korea—and hundreds of Russian technical advisers. The Chinese PLA provided labor for rebuilding until its final withdrawal in 1956. Despite the war's devastation, the North rebuilt its factories, created new housing, and revived its communications infrastructure with surprising speed. Beyond aid and foreign labor, the North was reviving a previously existing industrial base rather than starting from scratch, for much of the Japanese colonial investment in heavy industry had been located in the North. Moreover, strong organizational skills and early enthusiasm for the regime motivated and mobilized the population for this effort. Finally, the North did not have to contend with the political instability that plagued the South.

North Korea's command economy used multiyear plans, familiar from the USSR and PRC, to create goals and implementation processes. The Three-Year Plan (1954–57) emphasized rebuilding and production of basic necessities. The subsequent Five-Year Plan (1957–61), like China's First FYP in the 1950s, focused on heavy industry as well as completion of the collectivization of agriculture. During this plan, the DPRK introduced mass mobilization—for example the 1958 "Flying Horse" campaign—to exhort workers to greater efforts.

These campaigns became a standard feature of North Korean life, a pervasive culture of exhortation. The Great Leader himself tirelessly visited factories and farms to give "on-the-spot guidance." Two crucial elements of North Korean ideology came from these visits, one from Kim's visit to a communal farm, Chŏngsan-ni, and another from Taehan Electrical Appliance factory. These two work-units gave their names to work systems and decision-making techniques, one for agriculture, the other in industry. Their model directed managers to "go to the people," bring their feedback to the leadership for formulation of policy, and then return it to the masses as directives. The so-called Chŏngsan and Taehan systems strongly resemble "mass line" politics in other socialist states.

More than likely, the North Korean leadership considered "mass line" feedback loops as an antidote to the bureaucratism and inertia that they saw in other command economies. The North Korean economy did in fact expand rapidly in the 1950s and 1960s, with the "mass line" as part of the mix of policies that led to success. Another motivating strategy ultimately became the linchpin of all North Korean ideology. *Chuch'e* (*juche* in North Korea), meaning self-reliance (see pp. 236–37), struck a nationalist chord in the population, after almost a century of meddling by outsiders. By the end of the Five-Year Plan, all core elements of the North Korean economic policy had been put in place: self-reliance in all matters, a Stalinist emphasis on heavy industry, and the use of mass-mobilization campaigns—all with Soviet and Chinese aid and technical assistance in the background.

A more ambitious Seven-Year Plan (1961–67) followed the FYP's successes, aiming to triple national income with continued emphasis on heavy industry. By 1967, national income had increased 8.6 times, with an average annual growth rate of 16.6 percent. Since the DPRK started from complete destruction, the annual growth rate of industry in the first decade after the war was an astonishing 41.7 percent—the envy of American and Korean planners in the South. Indeed, through the 1960s, North Korea's economic expansion outpaced the South—a fact little noted today, now that the situation has been decisively reversed.

Under the Seven-Year Plan in the 1960s, North Korea's economy began to falter. Soviet aid ended—the DPRK supported the PRC in the Sino–Soviet split—goals were not met, and the plan had to be extended for three more years. North Korea had exhausted its indigenous resources and capital. Its technology base remained rooted in 1950s-vintage Soviet technology transfers. By 1970, North Korea began to shop tentatively in the international market for loans to buy turnkey plants. This saddled its economy with an unsustainable US$2–3 billion debt burden, and defaults on loans from Japanese and European banks hindered the acquisition of more capital. In spite of all the problems and the slowing of growth, North Korea's per capita income equaled or exceeded South Korea's until 1976.

IMPORT SUBSTITUTION IN SOUTH KOREA, 1953–60

While the Korean War had devastated Seoul, South Korea as a whole suffered less damage to its infrastructure and housing stock than did the North, but the South's larger population, political instability, and poor leadership complicated the process of rebuilding.

POPULATION OF NORTH AND SOUTH KOREA: 1945–2000

Year	South Korea	North Korea	Seoul
1950	20,845,771	9,471,140	648,432 (1951)
1960	24,784,140	10,391,902	2,445,402
1970	32,241,000	13,911,902	5,537,000
1980	38,124,000	17,113,626	5,433,198
1990	42,869,000	20,018,546	8,364,379
2000	47,351,083	21,647,682	10,627,790

Sources: North/South population: US Census Bureau, Population Division, International Programs Center. Seoul: Seoul Metropolitan Government; In Michael Robinson (2007, p. 124).

Colonial development had left South Korea only light industry (mostly textiles), but it had been Korea's rice basket. The South suffered from insufficient electric generation capacity, lack of raw materials for export, and severe population pressure requiring massive food imports, covered through the 1950s by US bulk grain. South Korea became almost immediately dependent upon US aid to run its government and provide capital for economic growth. Scholars estimate that between 1953 and 1961, US aid financed fully 70 percent of South Korea's imports and 80 percent of its capital formation, mainly in transportation, manufacturing, and electric power. The United States provided about US$12.6 billion in economic aid to South Korea between 1945 and 1971.

During the Rhee years, South Korea used import substitution as its guiding economic philosophy. They invested scarce capital to build basic industries, gradually substituting for and eliminating imports of essential commodities. This industrialization laid the foundation for the core of the economy and eventually provided exports with which to earn foreign exchange.

For this strategy to work, the Rhee government needed to enforce discipline by investing in appropriate industries and capacities, something it was never able to do. Instead, Rhee provided capital to his cronies for their pet projects and constantly intervened in the economic planning process to skew projects in favor of key political supporters. The corrupt bureaucracy could not provide leadership in the economy, either. With US bulk grain shipments making up for food shortfalls, there was little incentive to increase agricultural production. By the end of the Rhee years, the South Korean economy had become the poster child of failed US postwar foreign aid programs. To the bafflement of US economic advisers and aid officials, nothing seemed to generate the positive growth that would provide a better tax base for government or savings for capital formation.

Despite lackluster economic performance, the Rhee administration did invest heavily and successfully in mass education. In 1948, South Korea made six years of elementary education compulsory for both sexes, and opportunities for middle- and high-school education expanded widely. By 1960, South Korea's literacy rate reached 70 percent, a four-fold increase since 1945. Post-secondary education expanded to meet a long suppressed demand left over from the educational discrimination of the colonial era. A new national post-secondary system placed public universities in all eight provinces, with its centerpiece at colonial Keijō Imperial University, remade as Seoul National University. Expanding literacy widened the public sphere fed by newspapers, magazines, and other publishing. Private universities clustered in Seoul, and by 1960 perhaps two-thirds of South Korea's 92,934 college students lived in the capital. This army of activist, politically conscious college students became a major political force; their "April 19 Student Revolution," described above, toppled the Rhee regime in April 1960.

THE SECOND REPUBLIC AND THE 1961 MILITARY COUP

Chang Myŏn's Second Republic represented an opening for the ROK political system. The newly empowered National Assembly established the possibility of real competition between parties. Unfortunately for Premier Chang, splits within his own Democratic Party hobbled his efforts to mount a reform movement and continue the improvements. With a split governing party and the emergence of more contenders for power, the government lapsed into deadlock. Concurrently, students continued to rally in the streets to demand change. The Second Republic saw a reemergence of press freedoms, and numerous new publications sprang up to feed the hunger for information and free political speech.

On the political left, labor leaders and members of long-repressed progressive groups joined the students. The National Teacher's Union, a new and powerful progressive force, formed in May 1960 and joined the fray. Political discourse, long suppressed by Rhee's censorship, now swung in the opposite direction. Students called for direct meetings with their counterparts in the North to solve the problem of national division. Labor and student organizers demanded punishment of those responsible for death and injury during the April 1960 student revolution. Other demands included withdrawal of all foreign troops, political and cultural exchanges with the North, and permanent political neutrality for a future united Korea. The public clamor caught Premier Chang between the students and activists in the streets, his own divided party, and conservative, anticommunist groups, including the powerful ROK army.

By the early 1960s, the ROK army had become the most modern and dynamic institution in South Korea. The early creation of the Korean Military Academy and the heavy involvement of US military advisers had transformed the army, but "politicized" generals—all Rhee appointees—continued to block the advancement of younger, more professional mid-level commanders. When Rhee fell, a group of lieutenant-colonels, all members of the 1949 class of the Korean Military Academy, mounted a movement to purify the Army's upper leadership. For this some were punished, others demoted.

As the Chang government continued to waffle over the rising tide of public discourse, the young colonels watched the growing radicalization of the student demonstrations with alarm. Finally in the winter of 1961, a group of about 250 mid-level officers led by Colonel Kim Jong Pil (Kim Chŏngp'il, b. 1926) and Major General Park Chung Hee (Pak Chŏnghŭi, 1917–1979) mounted a military coup. In the pre-dawn of May 16, 1961, 1,600 marines occupied key points in Seoul while the bulk of the army remained in barracks, and the leaders announced that a Military Revolutionary Committee now controlled the government. Premier Chang Myŏn fled briefly into religious sanctuary, then retired and lived quietly in Seoul until his death in 1966.

With General Park at its head, the Military Revolutionary Committee promulgated a six-point plan to stabilize ROK politics, based on the new military leaders' unflinching anticommunism. It promised to maintain diplomatic ties, uphold the UN Charter, open a campaign to eliminate corruption, attack poverty, and build national strength through economic development and a strong military. The coup represented a second major course correction in Korean politics, returned power to the center, and began a 31-year military intrusion into politics. In the next two years, under a new name—the Supreme Council for National Reconstruction (SCNR)—Park Chung Hee led a restructuring of South Korean political, economic, and foreign policy.

Born in a poor family in North Kyŏngsang province, near the city of Taegu, Park worked as a primary school teacher after graduating from normal school, then in 1937 he joined the Japanese Army and eventually graduated from the Manchurian Military Academy. His experience as an officer in the Japanese military had profound effects, evident in his predilection for mass mobilization and Japanese military-style organization. Park shared with Syngman Rhee a virulent anticommunism, but he also had a strong vision of national wealth and power through economic development. He aimed to strengthen the economy for wealth formation, but even more importantly as a means toward independence in military and foreign affairs. Economic development also stood as a key method to legitimate his power. As his leadership continued—he ruled South Korea in one capacity or another for the next 18 years—he repeatedly invoked national wealth (economic development) and power (national security) as the twin pillars justifying his authoritarian rule; policy goals reminiscent of Meiji Japan's "rich country, strong army."

The SCNR mounted a purification campaign to remove corruption from the bureaucracy and punish those who had enriched themselves at the expense of the people. Very quickly, however, domestic and US pressure forced him to promise a return to civilian rule. In preparation he set in motion another transformation of the political order—through a new constitution reverting to a president-dominated system. He created his own political party, the Democratic Republican Party (DRP), and used martial law to repress any opposition. Park's colleague, Kim Jong Pil, created the Korean Central Intelligence Agency (KCIA), an internal security force used for rounding up suspected communists and purging the universities of radical professors. In the 1963 elections, inaugurating the Third Republic, Park was elected to the presidency and his party to a dominant position in the General Assembly.

THE ECONOMIC TRANSFORMATION OF SOUTH KOREA

In contrast to the Rhee government's inability to follow any economic plan, Park used his authoritarianism to stimulate economic development. Not personally, politically, or socially connected to South Korea's political and economic elites, the new military leaders stayed free of debts or obligations that could compromise planning. Park began with a plan for export-led development, which had been developed under Rhee but never implemented. It was wildly successful. The estimated per capita income in the ROK rose from US$100 in 1963 to US$6,614 in 1990, then more than doubled to US$13,980 by 2004. This dramatic expansion of wealth changed Korea's world image—from 1950s aid junkie and economic basket case to middle-class global trading power and high-tech, postindustrial society.

The mechanics of this phenomenal rise are now well known. South Korea's rapid growth combined a good plan; an inexpensive, disciplined labor force; entrepreneurial talent; and historical and cultural factors such as colonial development and a culture emphasizing education. Furthermore, South Korea was lucky. The 1960s saw global markets relatively open, and world events such as the Vietnam War, the OPEC oil shocks, and an international construction boom contributed to ROK success. The reorganized, authoritarian state under Park Chung Hee orchestrated the planning process, sometimes with considerable coercion, to ensure that investment was channeled effectively and foreign exchange earnings not frittered away in unproductive ventures. As a result, the

South Korean GDP increased by an annual average of 8.2 percent between 1962 and the early 1980s—an impressive growth rate by any standard.

Park created a new economic ministry (Economic Planning Board, EPB) to coordinate the development plans. The state borrowed capital from global banks (and used US loans and grants), distributing the funds to entrepreneurs who agreed to invest according to government five-year plans. The plans required investment in a graded set of priorities. South Korea possessed abundant, educated, and trainable labor, so the first five-year plan emphasized labor-intensive manufactures for export. With foreign exchange earnings from exports, subsequent five-year plans moved to invest in more capital-intensive industries. Along the way, the government required entrepreneurs who gained access to capital to develop basic industries as well.

This state-guided capitalism concentrated economic activity in a relatively small number of businesses. Since the government gave successful exporters access to more capital, eventually a small number of enormous business combines emerged to dominate the South Korean economy. Called *chaebŏl*—the Korean pronunciation of the Japanese *zaibatsu*—companies such as Samsung (Samsŏng), Hyundai (Hyŏndae), Daewoo (Taeu), and Lucky Goldstar (LG) have become familiar global corporations.

Important positive incentives for businessmen included access to capital, tax benefits, and rewards for reaching goals. The state also used considerable coercion, for South Korea's rapid economic growth required much from its labor force—willingness to train and retrain, work incredibly long hours, and accept (for a time) very low wages. By the early 1970s, however, labor began to chafe at government constraints and the use of National Police to repress strikes, for part of the devil's bargain that allowed the *chaebŏl* to flourish lay in the government's repression of labor unions, thus guaranteeing low labor costs. The economy continued to expand, but workers felt they were denied the benefits of their dedicated efforts. In 1970, a textile worker named Chŏn T'aeil immolated himself in the East Gate Market of Seoul to protest the treatment of women in the textile sweatshops in the area. His example began a slow crescendo of labor militancy that over the next 15 years generated constant conflict in both economy and society.

The exodus from rural areas to the cities and a lag in agricultural development spawned by industry-centered government programs became obvious by the late 1960s. To counter criticism that the government was ignoring poverty in rural Korea, Park created a program of mass mobilization known as the New Village Movement. This movement provided materials and expertise to villages and enjoined them to revitalize the countryside's infrastructure. New Village activists mobilized farmers to replace thatched roofs with steel roofing supplied by the government. They provided free cement for new bridges and road improvement. In the end, the New Village Movement had only mixed success in stemming the exodus from the countryside, but it did provide Park with a political lift and created support for his policies among the farming poor.

The Vietnam War also helped South Korea on its developmental path, playing a role similar to what the Korean War had done for Japan. The United States provided enormous amounts of money for Korean troops (two divisions served in Vietnam), their equipment and weapons, and for lucrative construction contracts to build airports, seaports, and roads for the US military. Having gained expertise in overseas contracting in Vietnam, Korean businesses then took advantage of the building boom in the Middle East and new supertanker orders—Hyundai created its own shipbuilding industry in response to international demand—to offset the precipitous rises in oil prices of 1972 and 1979. All of these factors, including the government's economic policies, led to two decades of economic boom that transformed South Korea's economy, resulting in the wholesale industrial transformation of society, with all its attendant benefits and miseries.

THE NEW HERMIT KINGDOM AND THE CULT OF THE LEADER

In the 1970s, North Korea became more and more closed to the view of the outside world. Its economy solidly tied to the communist bloc, it nonetheless never joined ECONCOM, the international trade association of socialist states. Into the 1960s, North Korea still intended to reunify Korea by any means necessary. In 1968, North Korea marked the height of hostilities by staging a commando raid across the DMZ to assassinate President Park—it came within a few miles of penetrating the presidential mansion, the Blue House. That same year, North Korea seized a US military surveillance ship, the USS *Pueblo*, and in 1969 downed a US communications plane. Eventually, such overt hostility waned in direct proportion to economic development in the South and stagnation in the North.

In the 1970s, the DPRK elevated Kim Il Sung's aura as the Great Leader into an elaborate personality cult, even more extravagant than that of Stalin in the USSR or Mao Zedong in China. No part of North Korean society was untouched by Kim, and his eyes stared everywhere from portraits in the workplace, homes, classrooms, and on billboards. By this time, even Marxist-Leninism took a back seat to the thought of the Great Leader. Propaganda spun corporal metaphors around him—in their imagery, Kim was the "great brain" of society, the KWP the nervous system, and the people the muscle and sinew.

The concept of *juche* (*chuch'e*), first mentioned in speeches in 1955, expanded to be the single integrating principle of life in North Korea. Reflecting Kim Il Sung's unifying great idea, all thoughts, all actions, indeed every person's core subjectivity itself, must be infused with *juche*. In spite of increasing economic difficulties, the DPRK spent enormous sums on monuments to Kim. From the early 1970s, he began to prepare for his son, Kim Jong Il, to succeed him. The younger Kim's rise in rank in the party, bureaucracy, and army prefigured the succession, and soon father and son merged into one in ideology and propaganda. By the Sixth Party Congress in 1980, Kim Jong Il had apparently taken up the day-to-day management of the country. He thus oversaw a gradual weakening of the North Korean economy and its further isolation in global politics following the collapse of the socialist world after 1989.

Monumental bronze sculpture of Kim Il Sung erected in the center of Pyongyang in celebration of his 60th birthday, 1972.

THE YUSIN CONSTITUTION AND THE FOURTH REPUBLIC

In the South, national security and successful economic growth helped Park Chung Hee legitimate his presidency, despite his manipulation of the political system and heavy-handed use of the KCIA and emergency powers against opponents. Nevertheless, opposition to Park grew until he could no longer be assured of electoral victory. A revitalized New Democratic Party (NDP), led by the young and charismatic Kim Dae Jung (Kim Taejung, 1925–2009, p. 446) and Kim Young Sam (Kim Yŏngsam, b. 1927), challenged him in the Assembly. His narrow victory over Kim Dae Jung in the 1971 presidential elections convinced Park to reshuffle the political deck and stack it in his own favor.

So in 1972 Park carried out an internal coup, dissolved the government, and announced "Revitalization Reforms." Using emergency decrees, he rounded up his opponents, stifled the press, and repressed student protest. A national referendum validated a new constitution in November 1972, ushering in the Fourth Republic. In this Yusin (J. *isshin*, C. *weixin*, "restoration") constitutional system, a National Conference for Reunification with 2,359 members elected the president. Since Park directly appointed one-third of them, this virtually assured his continuing reelection for life.

In the next five years, Park faced increasing hostility from students, labor, and elements of the middle class, for successful economic development had wrought demographic and social changes that fed the opposition. For 20 years, an exodus from the countryside had swollen South Korea's cities, especially Seoul, to include nearly 80 percent of the population. Korean city-dwellers struggled for jobs and housing while watching the growing wealth of a new upper-middle class. Expanding white-collar labor created a highly educated, urban middle class that did not accept Park's "security and growth" excuses for closed political rule and the abridgement of human rights. Park became increasingly isolated; an assassination attempt in 1974 missed the president but killed his popular wife, Yuk Yŏngsu (1925–1974). Thereafter, Park retreated to the Blue House and made fewer public appearances.

An economic downturn in 1979 added to this tension, with an increase in strikes (all illegal) by workers throughout the country. In one instance, women workers of the YH Trading Company—protesting the fraudulent takeover of their union by the company—staged a sit-in at the headquarters of the opposition New Democratic Party. Police broke the sit-in with extreme violence, killing one worker and injuring many others. This case galvanized labor protests throughout the country, and intellectuals, churches, and students joined them to rally against the government. In October, huge demonstrations at the factory complexes in the southern port town of Masan threatened to spark even wider protests. Since Park was unsure how to pacify the demonstrations, a split developed among his top advisers. Kim Jae Kyu (Kim Chaegyu, 1926–1980), the

KIM CHI HA, DISSIDENT POET

Kim Chi Ha, 1972.

Kim Chi Ha (Kim Chiha; b. 1941) is one of South Korea's best-known poets, as well as a novelist and social activist. Born in the southern port of Mokp'o during the Pacific War and raised during the Korean War and its aftermath, he studied Fine Arts at Seoul National University in the early 1960s and there began his career as a poet. Perhaps the first Korean poet to be known outside of Korea, his international reputation derives more from his identity as an activist and dissident than as a purely literary figure.

Kim Chi Ha became famous for satirical poems attacking political and intellectual repression during Park Chung Hee's administration. His biting satire of the rich and politically powerful caused the government considerable trouble and delighted the public in the first years of the Yusin (1972) system. The ROK arrested him many times—for his poems, his activist defense of political prisoners, and his uncompromising resistance. Many of his poems circulated in underground form while he hid from the police.

Park used emergency measures, particularly the hated and abused Emergency Measure Nine, to imprison his critics, often charging them with conspiracy and communist plots linked to North Korea. The dreaded KCIA tortured confessions from innocent citizens, and even recantation of these confessions in open trial could not save them from prison. Kim Chi Ha, arrested and charged with treason in connection with one of these conspiracies, was sentenced to death in 1974, but an international movement helped commute the sentence to life imprisonment. Jailed for six years, he wrote one of his most famous works—"Declaration of Conscience"—on toilet paper and had it smuggled from prison.

In an earlier poem, "Cry of the People," Kim mocked the totalitarian society created by the Yusin system:

> The Yushin signboard advertisement
> Is merely to deceive the people;
> On democratic constitution's tomb
> Dictatorship has been established;
> Human rights went up in smoke;
> Now sheer survival is at stake.
> The people's leaders thrown in prison
> For espousing democratic rights.
> For their deep belief in freedom
> Students and Christians are labeled "traitors;"
> Rule by fear and violence
> Shows total desperation.[1]

In well-known poems such as "The Story of a Sound," Kim Chi Ha adapted the oral *p'ansori* narrative style, popular for its satire of traditional social and political norms. Scholars believe that Kim's poetry influenced both the substance and the articulation of student movement ideology of the 1980s. Kim remains an important activist and public intellectual in twenty-first-century South Korea.

head of the KCIA, argued restraint, while others, notably Cha Chich'ŏl, head of Park's personal security force, wanted to use paratroops against protesters.

To settle this argument, Kim Jae Kyu assassinated Park and Cha at a private dinner party on October 26, 1979. ROK Army security arrested Kim, and Prime Minister Choi Kyu Ha (Ch'oe Kyuha, 1919–2006) took control of an interim government. The Yusin machinery elected Choi as president, and he began to maneuver among all the competing political forces to make major changes. He rescinded the hated Emergency Measure Nine, which prohibited any criticism of the president or the Yusin Constitution, and released hundreds of political prisoners, including Kim Dae Jung, under house arrest since 1978.

Park's death generated complicated feelings among South Koreans. Many citizens revered Park as the architect of the economic miracle, sure that he had made Korea safe in a dangerous international system. Nonetheless, his political methods and strict repression of human rights had caused great suffering. As 1979 came to end, cautious optimism grew, a sense that Korea had finally turned an important political corner, and people looked forward to the evolution of a new openness, pluralism, and freedom in the political sphere.

DIASPORAS

CHINA

In the 1960s, immigration reform allowed hundreds of thousands of East and South Asians to enter the United States. Unlike their predecessors, predominantly rural and uneducated Cantonese, the new wave of Chinese immigrants came largely from upwardly mobile families who had left China for Hong Kong or Taiwan after 1949. By the end of the 1970s, over half of the international students in the United States came from Asia. When they finished their degrees, they received certification as skilled worker immigrants and began to bring their families to the United States under the "family reunification" rules of the new law. The post-1965 wave included as many women as men and a high percentage of professionals, especially engineers and scientists. They came not as sojourners but to find opportunities in the burgeoning multinational economy of the United States. Some of their children and grandchildren went

to Harvard and Berkeley, not into the laundry or restaurant businesses.

Throughout Southeast Asia, the commercial classes continued to be dominated by Chinese. Anti-Chinese legislation and discrimination in the new postcolonial states resulted in violence—tragic, bloody race riots (1969) in Malaysia, for example—and in anti-Chinese quota systems for education, government jobs and contracts, even for corporate stockholding. So Chinese businessmen developed transnational networks to distribute their families' assets and minimize risk. Whether from Malaysia, Indonesia, Thailand, or the Philippines, they found a convenient, profitable entrepôt in the majority-Chinese city-state of Singapore, expelled from Malaysia in 1965.

In the 1960s and 1970s, Singapore's President Lee Kuan Yew (MANDARIN, Li Guangyao) encouraged the population—two-thirds Chinese by ethnicity—to learn English, to dissociate themselves from their native-place loyalties and become internationalists, loyal to Singapore and at home throughout the world. In a 1967 speech, he said, "I am no more a Chinese than President Kennedy was an Irishman." His authoritarian, elitist political style—he takes great pride in his "two firsts and a star for distinction" from Cambridge—left little room for dissent, but Singapore's strategic location and well-educated workforce have attracted huge foreign investment. At one time, this tiny country was the world's third largest oil-refining site.

JAPAN

The McCarran-Walter Act of 1952 allowed a small number of Japanese to emigrate to the United States; the 1965 Immigration and Nationality Act finally ended nationality-based quotas. But after World War II, foreign wives of American servicemen had an alternate route to citizenship. The War Brides Act (1945) and the Soldier Brides Acts (1946 and 1947) allowed almost 46,000 Japanese women to enter the United States between 1947 and 1964. Added to the 130,000 Japanese-Americans already in the United States, these women made Japanese-Americans the largest group of Asian Americans by 1970, though Chinese and Vietnamese immigrants surpassed them by 1990. Several thousand families also migrated to Canada, Latin America, and Australia, but "war brides" in the United States were the heart of the postwar Japanese diaspora.

Americans' reception of Japanese wives of US citizens changed in the 1950s, reflecting US–Japan relations as well as America's racial history. In the first postwar decade, the image of America as the strong leader/teacher and Japan as the grateful follower pervaded the US–Japan relationship. War brides and their American husbands were a good example of this paradigm. Nevertheless, interracial relationships troubled many Americans. At first, middle-class white Americans, fearing Japanese settlement throughout the country, did not accept Japanese war brides, especially at a time of difficulty in resettling previously interned Japanese-Americans. Many Americans also held racist fears of children of mixed ethnicity.

The shift in Americans' images of Japanese brides parallels the differences between James Michener's 1953 novel, *Sayonara*, and its 1957 movie version. The book portrayed two American soldiers and their Japanese fiancées. Unable to marry, one couple committed suicide while the other was forced to break up by the soldier's commanding officer. In the movie, the second couple resisted the officer's pressure. By 1957, Japanese war brides had been reconceived as ideal middle-class American wives and as "model minorities" against the backdrop of white Americans' fear of African Americans' demands for civil rights. More than convenient political stereotypes, however, these war brides were real women who helped create a vibrant interest in Japanese culture in the United States.

KOREA

The US Immigration and Nationality Act of 1965 reopened immigration, making large-scale entry of Asians possible for the first time since the Chinese Exclusion Act of 1895. Koreans made up a large proportion of this new "Asian Wave." Korean immigration was spurred by conditions in South Korea as well as a positive ROK emigration policy. Although the economy improved in South Korea between 1965 and 1980, urban crowding, tight job markets, and patterns of discrimination caused many South Koreans to look for opportunity in the United States. After 1970, South Korea filled its 35,000-person quota for immigrant visas to the United States every year. Because of the new "family reunification" mechanism built into the new law, once a newcomer became a landed immigrant, s/he had the right to obtain visas for immediate family members.

These visas could be given "over quota" and became the engine swelling the numbers of Korean-Americans over the next 20 years.

In 1960, there were approximately 65,000 people of Korean ancestry living in the United States, mostly the descendents of early twentieth-century migrant agricultural laborers. By 1980, that number exceeded 500,000, and by the 2000 census 1,076,822 Koreans lived in the United States, with 257,975 of them concentrated in greater Los Angeles. The newcomers overwhelmed the second and third generation Korean-Americans, particularly in urban settings like Los Angeles, New York, and Chicago, fostering the growth of Korean commercial and entertainment centers, "Koreatowns." This migration slowed in the 1980s, as South Korea emerged as an economic powerhouse able to provide more opportunities and a better material life to its citizens.

The demographic characteristics of the Korean immigrants contrasted strongly with the first generations of East Asians in the United States. By and large, the new immigrants had good educations, often college degrees, and came from urban backgrounds. Many were Christians. A significant proportion of the new immigrants came from North Korea and thus had already been displaced once by the Korean War. With no extended family connections in the South and a government suspicious of their political loyalty, many chose emigration. Koreans now occupy a significant place among Asian Americans. They have a strong propensity to seek higher education—34 percent of Koreans over 25 hold college degrees, as compared to 20 percent for the US population as a whole. Their drive for social mobility and economic success includes them in the United States' long history of dynamic immigrant groups that have contributed to growth and development. Indeed, the United States' gain has been South Korea's loss.

CONNECTIONS

From the 1950s through the 1970s, two different models of state engagement with the national and international economy competed in East Asia. The PRC and North Korea (DPRK) chose the command model developed in the USSR—central government agencies planned both agricultural and industrial production, from sourcing raw materials to distributing finished products, and all enterprises belonged to the state. Japan, South Korea, and Taiwan, calling themselves "capitalist" economies, left most productive enterprises in the hands of private entrepreneurs, but all three, in different ways, limited capitalism with government "guidance." Initially, neither model prevailed. North Korea's industrial growth exceeded the South's until the 1970s, when Park Chung Hee's export-led development policies began to bear fruit. The PRC, despite the traumas of the Great Leap and Cultural Revolution, did enlarge its GNP, while Taiwan became a supplier of inexpensive consumer goods to the United States and Europe.

In the 1960s and 1970s, Japan became the first East Asian economy to experience an extended period of rapid growth. In the 1950s, "Made in Japan" meant cheap knick-knacks. By the 1970s, Japanese industrial and technological innovation, the US defense umbrella, "administrative guidance" from the government, high rates of savings from consumers, and rapidly increasing international demand brought Japanese products to the top of world markets. Toyota, Honda, and others took on Detroit, produced world-class automobiles, and won ever-increasing market shares. Sony, Panasonic, and other electronics firms went head-to-head with General Electric and Westinghouse.

That pattern of export-driven growth, repeated later by Taiwan, South Korea, Singapore, and finally China (see pp. 389, 404, 451), required not only astute capitalists and hardworking, low-paid workers but also coordination and occasional overt control from government—what one scholar has called "getting the prices wrong." Even capitalist South Korea had five-year plans, during which the central state obtained foreign capital, distributed it to selected firms, and "guided" the growth and direction of industrial production. In the agricultural sector, too, the "free-market" economies of Japan, South Korea, and Taiwan all required state intervention—land reform, protective tariffs, and investment—to stimulate food production, protect domestic products, and mechanize the countryside.

In this period, the "capitalist" and "socialist" versions of East Asian development resembled one another more closely than they do now, when only North Korea remains as a failed example of Stalinist planning. The Cold War reinforced the division of Korea and China into warring camps; the PRC and DPRK allied with the USSR, while the ROK, ROC-Taiwan, and Japan remained in the US orbit. After the Sino–Soviet split, however, neither the PRC (until 1978) nor the DPRK (until now) had access to the global flows of capital and the export markets that enabled the "capitalist" economies to expand so rapidly.

All the East Asian states and their elites made use of nationalism and racialized identity to encourage unity and discourage dissent. Post-occupation Japan experienced widespread social mobilization and linkage to international influences: feminism, pacifism, anti-Vietnam War movements, and environmental activism, among others. In Japan, a national culture emerged that embraced modernity at the expense of local cultures. That modernity failed, however, to erase the continuing marginalization of and discrimination against ethnic minorities.

Similar uses of both traditional and modern aspects of collective identity arose in China and Korea, visible in the personality cults of Mao Zedong, Jiang Jieshi, and Kim Il Sung, even in anti-American movements in South Korea. *We* must unite behind our government to stand strong against our enemies—the other Koreans, the Americans, the imperialists, the Communists or Nationalists, the Soviets—however *they* might be defined. Only in Japan, constrained by Article 9 and defended by the United States, did the military not play a crucial role in politics.

Building on the experience of trade, diplomacy, and war of the previous century, East Asians in this period became important players in global politics and economics. Previously perceived as marginal to the Eurocentric world system, or at least less important than Europe and North America, the region came to be seen as an arena of world-shaking development, production, and conflict. Led by Japan, then by the "mini-dragons" (South Korea, Taiwan, Hong Kong, and Singapore), by the late 1970s East Asia was poised to become a center of the "Pacific Century." Dramatic developments in China after 1978 brought that promise to fulfillment.

CHAPTER TWELVE

SOCIAL TRANSFORMATIONS AND ECONOMIC GROWTH (MID-1970S–EARLY 1990S)

WORLD CONTEXT

The Cold War dragged on through the 1970s and 1980s. Although engaged in arms limitation talks and détente, the United States and USSR continued to support proxy states around the world. In eventful 1979, domestic rebels ousted pro-United States regimes in Iran and Nicaragua, creating an Islamic Republic in the Middle East and a Marxist government in Central America. That same year, the USSR invaded Afghanistan, supporting a Marxist Afghan state against Islamist guerrilla warriors (*mujahideen*). Called "the Soviets' Vietnam," this ten-year war cost the USSR dearly and created the core of the Taliban movement, supported by the United States. After prolonged negotiations, the USSR withdrew by 1989, with 15,000 dead, its army's morale at low ebb, and Afghanistan on the brink of a civil war, which the Taliban won.

The 1979 Iranian Revolution sparked fear in neighboring Iraq, ruled by the secularist Ba'ath Party of Saddam Hussein. Saddam invaded Iran in 1980, initiating a brutal, costly (over half a million dead), and inconclusive eight-year war, the first in which both sides used ballistic missiles as battlefield weapons. The United States, Britain, and France supported secular Iraq against Islamist Iran, providing Saddam with financial and military aid. Using US-generated intelligence, Saddam's army attacked Iranian troop concentrations with poison gas. When Iranian bombers damaged Iraq's experimental nuclear reactor in 1980, French technicians repaired it, then Israeli warplanes destroyed it in 1981.

With historians' hindsight, we can see the deep irony in these wars. The Taliban and Saddam Hussein—both US targets after 9/11—received considerable US aid in the 1980s. The Reagan administration backed the *mujahideen* against the USSR and Saddam Hussein against the nascent Islamic Republic of Iran. Donald Rumsfeld, later architect of the 2003 US overthrow of

Saddam Hussein, served as President Reagan's personal emissary to Saddam.

The Reagan administration then linked Middle East policy to its actions in Central America. Still blockading Fidel Castro's Cuba, the United States could not tolerate the presence of a communist government in Nicaragua. But in 1982, the US Congress had banned funding for the rebels (called "Contras") against the Nicaraguan regime. At the same time, the United States wanted to free hostages held by Hezbollah, a Lebanon-based ally of Iran. In a convoluted plan that became a major scandal in 1986, the Reagan administration sold weapons—Hawk and TOW missiles—through Israeli intermediaries to Iran, our Iraqi ally's enemy, in order to purchase the Hezbollah hostages' release and to obtain a secret fund of cash to funnel to the Nicaraguan Contras. A number of high-level US officials were tried and convicted for the Iran–Contra affair, but none ever went to prison. The Nicaraguan leftist government survived the Contra insurgency, reintegrated its opponents into the political process, and was voted out of office in 1990.

Although the United States had been driven from Vietnam in 1975, Southeast Asia remained unstable, marked by Sino–Soviet rivalry, Vietnamese belligerence, communist victories in Cambodia and Laos in 1975, and a lengthy transition from military to democratic government in Thailand. Cambodia suffered particular horrors as the rural-based Khmer Rouge, allied with the PRC, took advantage of social dislocation—in part caused by indiscriminate US bombing in the early 1970s—to organize a spectacularly brutal revolution. Transferring millions of people to rural labor camps, the radicals under Pol Pot unleashed terror against intellectuals and businesspeople and forced urbanites to work 12-hour days in the fields. Famine and mass starvation followed. Although calculations differ, scholars agree that between 1.5 and 2 million Cambodians died in the "killing fields" of the late 1970s, about half of them executed. A Vietnamese invasion brought down the Khmer Rouge in 1979, beginning a ten-year civil war that crushed the already desperate Cambodian economy and populace.

In contrast to these deadly conflicts, science moved rapidly forward in this period. Astronomers expanded human understanding of the cosmos by exploration of the solar system with camera-bearing probes, detection of solar systems around distant stars, and the discovery of a giant black hole at the center of our galaxy. The United States successfully built reusable space shuttles, though an explosion killed seven astronauts aboard the *Challenger* (1986).

Finding that emissions from aerosol cans were destroying the earth's essential atmospheric ozone layer, scientists successfully advocated multinational controls on such dangerous conveniences. With the discovery that lead-bearing automobile emissions caused severe environmental and human damage, countries began to require catalytic converters on cars, allowing use of lead-free fuels. Acid rain, created by coal-burning installations, caused so much environmental destruction that "alternative energy" began to appear attractive to alleviate pollution. Most familiar to the contemporary public, scientists recognized patterns of climate change—"global warming"—with potentially catastrophic consequences for the entire planet. The year 1989 was the warmest yet recorded, stimulating debate over both causation and remedies.

Electronic computing continued its meteoric development. IBM introduced the "personal computer" (PC) in 1981, and British engineers created the first portable computer (1987) and "parallel information processing technology" (1985) that led to the development of Windows software. Microchips grew steadily more powerful. The first consciously constructed computer virus (1988), created by a US student, jammed 6,000 military computers and gave birth to an entire industry—electronic information security. In 1989, Tim Berners-Lee (b. 1955) proposed the "worldwide web," the basis of the internet, which has altered politics, communications, and human identities in ways unforeseen in the 1980s.

In medicine, the World Health Organization (WHO) announced that smallpox had been eliminated as a threat to humankind (1980), but the deadly human immunodeficiency virus (HIV), which caused acquired immune deficiency syndrome (AIDS), was identified in 1984, as the disease rapidly spread worldwide. DNA analysis became a forensic tool, and courts began to accept genetic evidence to identify perpetrators. Genome studies also led scientists to the conclusion that human beings and chimpanzees differ in only 1 percent of their genetic material.

The United Nations proclaimed 1975–85 the International Decade of Women, passed the Convention on the Elimination of All Forms of Discrimination Against Women (CEDAW) in 1979, and ushered in a global recognition of women's rights as human rights. Since then, the status of women around the world has gradually improved. Global reductions in birth rates also began in this period.

CHINA AND TAIWAN

THE BEGINNINGS OF REFORM

In the last year of his life, Mao Zedong had failed to balance the two factions contending in the central government—the Cultural Revolution radicals led by Jiang Qing and her allies (dubbed the "Gang of Four"), and the pragmatists (sometimes called "conservatives") led by Deng Xiaoping. In the spring of 1976, when the radicals suppressed public mourning for Zhou Enlai in Tiananmen Square as a "counterrevolutionary incident," Deng went into hiding. Protected by allies in the military, he stayed underground for six months and awaited Mao's death.

After Chairman Mao died (September 9, 1976), Deng allowed his appointed successor, Hua Guofeng, to take the lead in dismantling the Cultural Revolution, which was publicly declared the work of the Gang of Four. Hua announced his unequivocal Maoist adherence in the Two Whatevers: "Resolutely defend whatever policy Chairman Mao decided; steadfastly obey whatever directives Chairman Mao issued." Not yet returned to power, Deng Xiaoping nonetheless refused to endorse this doctrine, since Mao had twice ordered his dismissal.

By the summer of 1977, Deng's political alliances enabled him to regain all of his lost offices. He then directly challenged Hua Guofeng's leadership. Deng proclaimed a principle contrary to the Two

Deng Xiaoping dons a cowboy hat at a Houston rodeo, February 2, 1979. The Chinese leader made his first US trip into a public relations triumph.

Whatevers—"Seek truth from facts"—and attributed it to Mao, though it refuted the ideology of Mao's last years. Taken from an eighteenth-century "practical learning" text (see pp. 101, 137), this goal favored the "expert" of technical expertise over the "red" of ideological purity.

But China's "facts" did not look promising. With millions of young people returning from the countryside, urban unemployment skyrocketed. Severe problems plagued society—inefficient industrial organization, tyranny by local officials, absenteeism throughout the economy, low military morale, and ineffective agricultural administration. Even before Mao's death, Deng had proposed Zhou Enlai's Four Modernizations—agriculture, industry, national defense, and science and technology—as the essential remedy. After 1977, he and his allies acted to free the productive energy of Chinese people from stifling controls without relinquishing the CCP's exclusive hold on political power.

To carry out his "economics in command" ambitions, Deng brought two of his own protégés to the Party leadership. Hu Yaobang (1915–1989) and Zhao Ziyang (1919–2005) had risen through the ranks of the CCP and survived the Cultural Revolution. Hu replaced Hua Guofeng as Party general secretary in 1981, and Zhao took Zhou Enlai's old role as premier, the head of government. Deng Xiaoping continued as vice-premier and kept his crucial position as head of the Central Military Commission. A veteran commander himself, he retained lasting ties with important army leaders.

INTERNATIONAL RELATIONS AND WAR

The PRC established formal diplomatic relations with the United States on January 1, 1979. The United States agreed to terminate its formal relationship with the Republic of China, retaining the right to continue long-term economic and military ties with Taiwan. On his first visit to the United States, only 28 days later, Deng Xiaoping agreed to "permit the present system on Taiwan and its way of life to remain unchanged." He also wore a cowboy hat at a Texas rodeo, watched the Harlem Globetrotters play basketball, and told Congress that the USSR could not be trusted. No one could mistake the anti-Soviet tone of his visit and of Sino-American détente.

After 1975, the Vietnamese Communists, fearing dependence on China and increasingly hostile toward their own large population of Chinese descent (see pp. 426–27), had turned sharply toward the Soviet Union. PRC strategists found the Vietnam–USSR "Treaty of Friendship and Mutual Defense" (1978) to be a serious threat, surrounding China with hostile regimes. When Vietnam sent a powerful force into Cambodia in December 1978 to overthrow the radical Khmer Rouge government of Pol Pot—a PRC ally—the Chinese leadership decided to act. A week after Deng's US trip, the PLA invaded Vietnam with a quarter million troops supported by armor, artillery, and air power.

With Vietnam's best troops in Cambodia, the Chinese leadership hoped for a lightning victory like that over India in 1962, but the battle-hardened Vietnamese generals tied up the PLA in costly sieges. After less than three weeks and only local victories, China called for a ceasefire and soon withdrew behind the border. Although statistics are disputed, leaked sources attest that the PLA lost 7,000 men, with twice that number wounded, and that Vietnamese casualties were much higher. Both sides claimed victory. The PLA failed to humiliate Vietnam and could not save the Khmer Rouge, confirming Deng Xiaoping's claim that China's military needed modernization.

HANDLING MAO'S LEGACY

Healing a painful wound, Deng rehabilitated the reputation of his late comrade Liu Shaoqi. Labeled by Mao as an arch-traitor and "the number one person in Party power taking the capitalist road," Liu had died in agony in 1969. Many in the Party hierarchy believed that his case, the core of Mao's triumph over the CCP "headquarters," should be left alone. But Deng Xiaoping aimed to reverse the Cultural Revolution and forced the Central Committee to nullify all the charges against Liu. In May 1981, after a state funeral at which Deng spoke, Liu's ashes were returned to his wife, who received a permanent government appointment.

Since Mao Zedong had been enshrined as the revolution's greatest leader, the late Chairman could not be blamed directly for the excesses of the Cultural Revolution, but his allies could. China put the Gang of Four on trial in 1980. Only Jiang Qing defended herself, claiming that she had only obeyed Mao. Nonetheless, she and Zhang Chunqiao received death sentences, commuted to life in prison; Wang Hongwen and Yao Wenyuan served lengthy prison terms. Jiang Qing committed suicide in 1991, Wang died in 1992, Zhang and Yao in 2005. Most of the tragedies of the Cultural Revolution are still publicly blamed on the Gang of Four.

The new administration handled Mao's legacy in a series of delicately phrased Party history documents, drafted and redrafted until they caught precisely the right balance. Hu Yaobang presented the Party's judgment:

> Comrade Mao was a great Marxist, a great proletarian revolutionary, theorist, strategist and the greatest national hero in Chinese history....[But] Comrade Mao...was not free from shortcomings and mistakes.... He separated himself from the collective leadership of the party, often rejecting or even suppressing the correct views of others....Of course, we must admit that neither before nor after the outbreak of the 'Great Cultural Revolution' was the party able to prevent and

The Sino-Vietnamese War, 1979

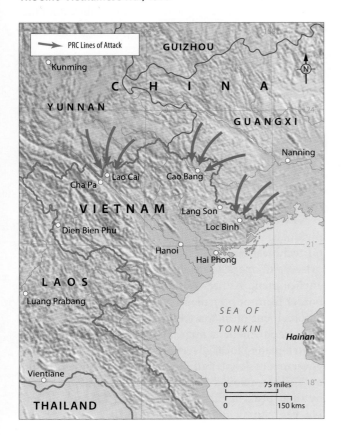

turn Comrade Mao from his mistakes....We who are long-time comrades-in-arms with Comrade Mao... must realize deeply our own responsibility...[1]

Chen Yun (1905–1995), the PRC's senior economist, took a more pithy and direct view of Mao's role as he prepared to rebuild China's economy in 1978:

> *Had Chairman Mao died in 1956, there would have been no doubt that he was a great leader of the Chinese people....Had he died in 1966, his meritorious achievements would have been somewhat tarnished. However, his achievements were still very good. Since he actually died in 1976, there is nothing we can do about it.*[2]

Thus did Mao's old comrade, and many ordinary Chinese people, judge the man who had led their revolution first in triumph and then in wasteful, fatal directions.

ECONOMIC LIBERALIZATION

Determined to turn the country toward prosperity and international stature, Deng Xiaoping started with China's villages. He broke up the communes, creating the "household responsibility system," which returned everyday agricultural decision-making to peasant families. Although ownership of the land remained with the state, farmers signed contracts for farmland, committing them to sell a fixed quantity of produce to the state and retain any surplus to use as they saw fit. That surplus could be sold in private markets or to the government at negotiated prices, higher than the fixed contract price. Stimulated by the prospect of greater income and the guarantees in the price contracts, farmers rapidly increased production, generating both supply and demand for previously forbidden rural markets. By 1985, China's villages had over 40,000 free markets.

In the first decade after 1978, annual grain production increased by almost 100 million tons (90 million metric tons), ensuring food supplies even for a growing population. Some collectives remained intact, retaining large farms suitable for mechanized agriculture. Others contracted grain land to small groups of families, leaving the rest of the village free to pursue profitable "sidelines"—vegetables, industrial cash crops, and local wage labor. Both the quantity and the variety of local products expanded.

The industrial equivalent of "household responsibility" was "profit retention," in which state-owned enterprises could keep a portion of their profits—presuming they made any—for reinvestment in capital projects, employee benefits, and management bonuses. They remitted the rest of their profits to the state. Within four years, enterprises had gained the power to set prices (within limits) and to fire employees, smashing the "iron rice bowl" of permanent employment and opening the door to price fluctuation. These changes approximated the conditions of capitalism: employers could add or eliminate workers, employees could seek jobs with multiple employers, and many (but not all) commodity prices could move with supply and demand.

In 1983, a new set of enterprise income taxes replaced profit remission, but nevertheless 30 percent of state-owned enterprises continued to lose money. The state gradually allowed unprofitable factories to fail, throwing hundreds of thousands, then millions of workers into the free labor market. To make use of all that labor, millions of private businesses started up—ranging from a single taxicab to a substantial factory—making multiple employers available to workers as in a capitalist economy.

Some of these new firms succeeded, some failed, but "old-fashioned" pre-1949 Chinese entrepreneurship had clearly not died under Mao. To use surplus rural labor, local governments and collectives contracted with ambitious people to operate "township and village enterprises" (TVEs), many of which had been commune enterprises. They mostly manufactured goods for local consumption, but some gradually engaged with the international markets opened to Chinese firms for the first time in decades.

Owned by collectives but managed by private individuals, the TVEs initially used local labor, drew on technical expertise from failed state-owned enterprises, and operated flexibly in the changing economic environment. As they expanded, they began to hire laborers from poorer places who took advantage of lax enforcement of *hukou* (residence registration) laws to seek employment as migrants. Taxation of TVE profits contributed to local government revenues as the central government's contributions dropped. In some provinces, TVEs employed 30 percent of the rural workforce; by their peak in the 1990s, they had 135 million employees nationwide.

ABOVE Shenzhen in August 1980, just after its designation as a Special Economic Zone; BELOW Shenzhen only 25 years later, in 2005, one of East Asia's largest cities.

To participate in international commodity and capital markets without exposing the domestic economy to foreign intervention, the PRC created "Special Economic Zones" (SEZs), beginning in 1980. Located along the coast, these specially governed areas followed rules designed to encourage export and foreign investment, whether capitalized as joint ventures, partnerships, or wholly owned foreign companies. As Taiwan had done earlier (see p. 404), the PRC provided tax incentives and deregulation, attracting business with an inexpensive, relatively well-educated labor force and ensuring low wages by prohibiting unions. Only one labor union exists in China—the All-China Federation of Trade Unions—and all other union organizing remains illegal.

The success of the SEZs may be measured by Shenzhen, near Hong Kong. A small town in 1980, in 2010 Shenzhen has a population of at least 14 million and boasts a major stock exchange, tens of thousands of enterprises, and dozens of skyscrapers. Despite its geographically marginal position in the deep south, it lies at the heart of the ultramodern China often seen in the media.

INFLATION AND PLANNED INEQUALITY

After the experience of hyperinflation in the late 1940s, China's consumers had welcomed state price controls and innovative wage strategies such as the "commodity basket" of the 1950s (see p. 358). The reforms of the late 1970s, however, eroded the state's ability to control commodity prices, especially for food products sold in free markets and everyday items such as cigarettes, paper, and watches. Consumer prices rose by 7.5 percent in 1980, driven by the cost of new agricultural inputs (chemical fertilizers, pesticides, etc.), the pent-up demand of decades without many products, and the new availability of domestically produced appliances.

Zhao Ziyang stressed the importance of allowing prices to fluctuate according to supply and demand, but he also insisted that ownership of large and medium-sized enterprises should remain with the state or the collective. By eliminating price controls gradually, Beijing kept inflation fairly low in the early 1980s, but it rose sharply again in 1985 and thereafter, with significant economic and political consequences.

Following more than 30 years of slow, egalitarian, centrally planned development, Deng Xiaoping and his colleagues concluded that rapid expansion of China's economy required *inequality*. Some regions would move faster, some enterprises would succeed sooner, and some people would get rich quicker. In order to maintain the legitimacy of the Chinese Communist Party's leadership, Beijing insisted that the reforms—including those that resembled capitalism—constituted "socialism with Chinese characteristics." As Deng told some Japanese visitors in 1984, "Marxism attaches utmost importance to developing the productive forces.... As they develop, the people's material and cultural life will constantly improve....Socialism means eliminating poverty. Pauperism is not socialism...." Although he may never have said it, people often credit Deng with a pithier version of this principle: "To get rich is glorious." What a change from the austere Maoism of previous decades!

The areas best able to take advantage of this new system lay along major transportation routes (railroads, rivers, paved roads, canals) and near the sea. Villages close to cities could produce vegetables for the burgeoning urban free markets, making more money than grain producers. Well-situated TVEs supplied consumer goods more efficiently than cumbersome state-owned enterprises. The reforms thus enabled *uneven development* in China, a condition that continues to this day, skewed toward the coast and the major river valleys. In the 1980s, Beijing encouraged this trend, only in the 1990s applying central government investment to develop the less developed western half of the country (see p. 454).

Since the reforms began, foreign observers and some Chinese intellectuals have predicted that economic reform would inevitably lead to large-scale discontent, forcing the CCP to institute political reforms as well. Incorrectly asserting that "free markets," "capitalism," and "democracy" constitute a single set of intertwined forms—or even that political liberalization must precede economic liberalization (as attempted in post-communist Eastern Europe)—these writers forecast the CCP's imminent downfall and a disastrous collapse of economic reform. Without "true" capitalism (private ownership) and "true" democracy (without CCP autocracy), they claimed, China's economic success would prove a short-term, anomalous accident.

These predicted disasters did not materialize in the 1980s, and China's economy grew at the same rate as Japan, Taiwan, and South Korea had grown in their rapid industrialization phases. Capitalized by foreign investors and domestic savings, as well as considerable state investment in SEZs, TVEs, and industrial zones around urban centers, Chinese business boomed. According to the World Bank, China's GDP grew at annual rates ranging from 5.2 percent (1981) to an astonishing 15.2 percent (1984), including both primary products and manufactured goods. Between 1978 and 1987, coal production increased by 50 percent, and electric power nearly doubled, as did finished steel.

THE "ONE CHILD" POLICY

Mao Zedong had advocated increasing the size of China's population—more people, more production—but even in the early 1970s, Chinese social scientists had sounded warnings about rapid population growth. State-mandated public health measures, plus rural health care, meant that people lived much longer than before 1949. Unregulated family size would demand that food production increase while expanding cities decreased the amount of farmland. In 1978, the PRC announced a "policy of birth planning." Urban Chinese couples could have only one child; rural Chinese could have a second if the first were a girl; and "minority nationalities" could have one more than their Chinese counterparts. Under this formula, about one-third of the PRC's families had to restrict themselves to a single child.

According to its administrators, this plan has prevented around 250 million births in the past 30+ years, even as China's population has grown beyond 1.4 billion. The policy's social effects, however, have been deeply troubling. Because many Chinese families continue to desire a son, female infanticide returned, skewing the ratio of boys to girls in some areas of China to 5:4, or even 4:3. In those regions, as many as 30 percent of males could not marry, so underworld gangs sprang up to kidnap 8–14-year-old girls to be sold as brides to these "bare sticks" (unmarried adult males). As advanced medical techniques became more available, couples used amniocentesis or ultrasound to determine the sex of a fetus, and selective abortion began to affect sex ratios.

State enforcement of birth control became heavy-handed in some places. Women were subjected to forced abortions and sterilizations. Even worse, families whose daughters-in-law bore only girls might find utility in divorcing the young woman, driving her to suicide, or even killing her, in order to get a substitute to produce a male descendant. Although not common, these cases occurred often enough to cause critics to question the policy. It may be good for the country at large, they wrote, but it cannot be good for China's women. Resistance to the birth-control policy ranged from open defiance to covert departure of young women to relatives, from whence they returned with an "adopted" child. This policy has been one of China's most controversial; feminists as well as religious groups continue to denounce it as immoral, unfair, and misogynist. The PRC defends it as necessary to the country's continued prosperity.

ATTACKING "BOURGEOIS LIBERALIZATION"

Many Chinese adapted to the transformed environment by focusing solely on making money, desiring only freedom from the political campaigns, disorder, and violence that had erupted since the 1950s. This uncompromising materialism led to ubiquitous corruption, conspicuous consumption, and rejection of political engagement. Some intellectuals, however, decided to record their experiences of the Cultural Revolution and produced an outpouring of "literature of the wounded." How, they asked themselves and their readers, could we have been so cruel to one another? What faults must we find in our culture to explain our people's suffering? Answers ranged from racial genetics to Confucianism to the personal responsibility of the Gang of Four. They left a textual legacy of witness and memory that still reverberates in China.

Others saw Deng's economic liberalization and opening to the outside world as implicit permission to speak out against CCP autocracy and repression of dissidents. As soon as Deng proclaimed, "Seek truth from facts," some Beijingers began to write "big-character posters" and post them on "Democracy Wall," near the highest leaders' compound in central Beijing. Publicly encouraged only to criticize the Gang of Four and the failed Cultural Revolution, these activists rapidly expanded their targets to include the CCP and China's political system.

Wei Jingsheng, a 28-year-old ex-Red Guard working as an electrician, had been born in a high-level CCP family and attended the best Party schools. On December 5, 1978, this "revolutionary successor" pasted up a poster, "The Fifth Modernization," arguing that only democracy and personal freedom would make the other Four Modernizations possible and meaningful. Courageously affixing his name and address, Wei continued to advocate political reform until his arrest in March 1979. Incongruously charged with espionage—he allegedly corresponded with foreigners about the Sino-Vietnamese War—he spent the rest of the 1980s in prison. Police shut down Democracy Wall by year's end, clearly demonstrating the state's continuing constraints on political speech. Deng Xiaoping announced "four cardinal principles" that could not be questioned—the socialist path, democratic dictatorship, the Party's leadership, and Marxism-Leninism-Mao Zedong thought.

Almost anything else could be discussed, and dissent resurfaced in forms ranging from political treatises to village theater to pornography. Even Beijing bureaucrats forsook their Mao jackets and wore Western-style clothes and mustaches. Fearing social chaos, in late 1983 the state struck back. Zhao Ziyang revived his Mao jacket, police raided an X-rated theater opened by a Fujian commune, and a campaign against "spiritual pollution" ran for a month or two, with solemn front-page articles and exemplary punishments. Philosopher-journalist Wang Ruoshui (1926–2002), of the *People's Daily*, lost his job for writing an article arguing that "alienation," associated solely with capitalism by Chinese Marxists, might also occur under socialism (see p. 400).

INTELLECTUALS UNDER REFORM

Indeed, "alienation" had taken hold among China's intellectuals, some of whom felt purposeless and depressed when radical materialism followed the Cultural Revolution's radical anti-intellectualism. After decades of believing that the state would respect their critique, some realized that the intellectual's historical duty of "worrying for the state, worrying for the people" had only brought them sorrow and misfortune. What then should intellectuals do in the face of the "four cardinal principles"? Should they "jump into the sea" of business? Should they become officials and collect "red envelopes" (bribes)? Should they risk their jobs and their futures by dissenting openly? Should they participate in the Party-state and try to reform it from within? Some made each of these choices, so we cannot conclude that "the intellectuals" took any one path.

Some did continue to advocate democracy, openly or covertly, in part because Hu Yaobang and his allies in the CCP encouraged them. A few academics, such as physicist Fang Lizhi (b. 1936), began to discuss human rights publicly, claiming that rights are not granted by the state but inherent in individual people—a potentially subversive idea. In 1986, professors and students again took to the streets. Like the May Fourth generation of 1919, they had been inundated with new ideas; translations of foreign works, from the Talmud to Foucault, crowded the bookstores. Still attracted by "science and democracy," these Chinese intellectuals searched for a *Chinese* modernity, a way to participate in global culture while remaining themselves. They engaged in a nationwide "cultural fever," ranging from Freud to Euro-socialism to post-structuralism.

Some of them also organized demonstrations against inflation (which had peaked in 1985), the rapidly widening gap between rich and poor, and their own lack of individual freedom and security. But Vice-Premier Li Peng (b. 1928), Chen Yun's protégé in charge of education, ordered the demonstrations suppressed as expressions of "bourgeois liberalism," the infiltration of

WANG RUOSHUI, LIBERAL MARXIST HUMANIST

Wang Ruoshui in the 1980s, after the start of Deng Xiaoping's reforms.

Born in Hunan (like Mao Zedong and Hua Guofeng), Wang Ruoshui (1926–2002) won admission to Beida and graduated in 1948 in philosophy. Intellectually attracted to Marxism, he joined the CCP and became a journalist, editing the Marxist theory page of the official *People's Daily*. Mao trusted his judgment and often phoned him, requesting attacks on intellectuals about to be purged in campaigns (see pp. 360–62). Enthusiastic about the Hundred Flowers movement of 1957, Wang praised it, then suffered a period of exile in the countryside during the antirightist campaign.

According to Wang's account, Mao Zedong's thought stimulated him to deeper analysis of Marxist philosophy, but, like so many others, he fell into the trap of Mao's personality cult. Despite initial doubts, he became a true believer and survived the Cultural Revolution by participating in the purges of his patron, Deng Tuo, and others. Almost immediately after Mao's death, however, Wang turned away from dogmatic Maoism—Hua Guofeng's Two Whatevers—to articulate an alternative vision of Marxism. His post-1976 essays criticized the Mao cult as "modern superstition," and he argued that the human liberation intended by Marx had been subverted by dogmatism and bureaucracy.

In the early 1960s, Wang had first been exposed to Marxist humanism, which argued that far from requiring Leninist or statist thought controls, Marx saw the liberation of the individual mind as a central feature of socialist development. On this principle, Wang Ruoshui argued that "alienation" could be characteristic not only of capitalism but also of socialism. That is, even after the establishment of socialism, "the people's servants [the Communist Party] sometimes made indiscriminate use of the power conferred on them by the people, and turned into their masters." In a popular 1983 essay, he wrote: "[Humanism] means firmly abandoning the 'total dictatorship' and...the cult of personality....It means opposing bureaucratism...and extreme individualism that benefits oneself at the expense of others."

After 1980, intellectuals associated with Deng Xiaoping's faction attacked Wang and his colleagues as "bourgeois liberals," and in 1983 the label stuck. As part of the CCP's brief campaign against "spiritual pollution," Wang lost his job at the *People's Daily* for claiming that bureaucratic privilege and the cult of personality had dehumanized Chinese society—that is, the Cultural Revolution and its aftermath had produced socialist alienation. Although he lived the rest of his life in the *People's Daily* compound, Wang Ruoshui never again worked at the paper or published in China. The CCP expelled him in 1987, along with others associated with Hu Yaobang. His essays have been widely available outside of China, and he has become a hero to the PRC's "liberal Marxists." He died of lung cancer in 2002 while visiting his wife, who had a journalism fellowship at Harvard.

socialist society by corrupt foreign values. Deng Xiaoping agreed with him.

Hu Yaobang's enemies in the Central Committee blamed him personally for the student protests and forced him to resign in January 1987. Zhao Ziyang became head of the Party and was replaced as premier by Li Peng. Like Mao, Deng Xiaoping tried to balance contending forces within the Party-state—Zhao Ziyang's faction favoring wide-ranging reform and Li Peng's adherents who opposed political liberalization. To unify both party and state, Deng permitted Hu Yaobang's removal and recommended that outspoken critics, including Fang Lizhi, be expelled from the CCP.

Repression did not end the cultural ferment. Some intellectuals prescribed a renovated Confucianism to solve the dilemmas of Chinese modernity, while others (like their May Fourth predecessors) saw tradition as the main obstacle to progress. Critical iconoclasm found its most spectacular expression in a six-hour television documentary, *River Elegy* (1988), shown twice on national television before being banned. Using the Yellow River, "70 percent mud," as a metaphor for China, the film contrasted its stagnation and backwardness with the open, blue sea of Europe, North America, and Japan. The film also characterized other symbols of China—Great Wall, peasant village, and dragon—as cruel and constraining, explicitly recommending a merger of the Yellow River's silt into the ever-changing, refreshing ocean.

Zhao Ziyang openly supported *River Elegy*, but his opponents denounced it as another expression of "bourgeois liberalism." Urging resistance to globalization in all its aspects—cultural, political, economic—Premier Li Peng and his faction strove to limit the effects of China's opening. They failed, and all the variety of the world's goods—from Gucci handbags to Michael Jordan's sneakers—appeared in China, advertised with shockingly "Western" images. Non-representational painting, imagistic poetry, avant-garde photography, and installation art, all forbidden under the former rule of "socialist realism," appeared in Beijing and Shanghai. When the first exhibition of oil paintings representing the nude human body opened in Shanghai, ticket queues stretched nearly a mile. The stage was set for another confrontation within the leadership—how much change, diversity, and individual expression should be allowed?

THE ROAD TO TIANANMEN

As it had in the 1940s, inflation lit the fire. Prices increased steadily through 1988, and real incomes fell. The leadership divided over how to combat this dangerous trend—Zhao Ziyang and Li Peng agreed that price controls should be lifted only slowly, but Deng Xiaoping insisted on allowing markets to determine prices and ordered Zhao to make the announcement (cutting into Zhao's public popularity). Commodity hoarding and panic buying resulted, reminding older people of the last days of the Guomindang, though the inflation was not nearly as dire.

In the spring of 1989, dissatisfaction permeated Chinese society. Intellectuals wanted more freedom, students wanted a brighter future, and consumers wanted a stable currency and low prices. State-sector workers feared for their jobs and resented the higher incomes of private employees. Grain-growing farmers envied those who earned more money working in sidelines. Everyone complained about the corruption of powerful people, from the arrogant sons and daughters of high officials to the "local emperors" who dominated everyday life in many villages. Even CCP politicians worried, as communism tottered in Eastern Europe and the USSR, where Mikhail Gorbachev (b. 1931) had proclaimed economic and political reform and openness as new policy goals.

Having served as chief of the US Liaison Office in China in the mid-1970s, President George H.W. Bush returned to Beijing in February 1989. Planning a state dinner, he invited leading Chinese dissidents, including Fang Lizhi, to underline US support for political reform. Li Peng and President Yang Shangkun (1907–1998) refused to attend the dinner if Bush planned to acknowledge the dissidents' presence, but accepted as long as the president offered no toast to Fang. Even this compromise broke down, and security officers prevented Fang Lizhi and his wife from reaching the event.

Learning of Fang's humiliation, some Beijing student leaders determined to restart the public protests that had been suppressed in 1986. When Hu Yaobang, purged in 1987 for supporting the students, died suddenly of a heart attack on April 15, 1989, the dissidents moved quickly. They put up posters praising Hu and attacking nepotism, corruption, restrictions on speech and the press, and poor working conditions in universities. On April 22, as Party leaders attended Hu

Yaobang's memorial meeting in the Great Hall of the People, 100,000 students staged a well-organized demonstration outside the Hall in Tiananmen Square, the heart of political Beijing. Zhao Ziyang's praise for Hu Yaobang confirmed that they had an ally at the top, and they decided to continue their protests in the Square, including a hunger strike, which began on May 13. Their colleagues in more than 20 other cities followed suit, and the movement received enormous press coverage outside China.

As in 1976 and 1986, the CCP's leadership split over whether to suppress the demonstrations. Zhao Ziyang, leading the CCP "reformist" faction, wanted to negotiate with the students, encouraging their public spirit. The antistudent faction, led by Premier Li Peng and President Yang Shangkun, called "conservatives" by the international press, seized the initiative with a revival of editorials and slogans opposing "bourgeois liberalization." They intended to end the demonstrations and to blunt Zhao's power in the Central Committee. Citing pro-reform press coverage and the students' intemperate demands, by April 25 they had won Deng Xiaoping—always the key vote—to their side against Zhao. The government officially branded the student movement "antipatriotic," blaming the students for causing "turmoil."

Mikhail Gorbachev, General Secretary of the Communist Party of the Soviet Union, had been leading his country toward reform since 1985. Increasingly public demands for radical change in Eastern Europe, especially Poland and Czechoslovakia, brought new urgency to stalled talks between Chinese and Russian diplomats, anxious to end Sino–Soviet hostility. Gorbachev arrived in Beijing on May 15, 1989 after accepting China's demands that the USSR cease supporting Vietnam's occupation of Cambodia, remove its troops from Mongolia, and demarcate the Sino–Soviet border. In exchange, both countries stood down from wasteful militarization of their long frontier and declared an end to 30 years of hostility.

What promised to be Deng Xiaoping's greatest diplomatic triumph—peace with the USSR at last—brought the international media to Beijing in droves, but their cameras focused on the hundreds of thousands of students in Tiananmen Square and the gaunt, determined faces of the hunger strikers. Embarrassed by the PRC's inability to control even the streets of its capital, Deng

leaned toward Li Peng and his allies. In their view, the students' antisocial turmoil stemmed from Hu Yaobang and Zhao Ziyang's tolerance of bourgeois liberalization, capitalism, and domestic dissidence.

A council of senior CCP leaders denounced Zhao, and Deng Xiaoping enlisted support from the military. On May 20, at 4:00am, an exhausted Zhao Ziyang visited the students in Tiananmen Square and urged them to end their militant demonstrations, especially the hunger strike. He had, he said, done all he could for them. Later that day, the government declared martial law. Zhao Ziyang, in charge for a decade, never appeared in public again, enduring house arrest until his death in 2005.

Tension escalated in Beijing. Over a million people gathered in Tiananmen Square as sympathy for the students spread widely through the city. Factory workers, clerks, and shop owners supported the students "as their own children," while rumors flew that the army would soon suppress them. Discouraged and afraid, many of the students left the Square, but over 10,000 stayed on. To bolster the students' spirits, sculptors from the Fine Arts Academy carved a styrofoam statue, "Goddess of Democracy," and erected it in the Square, where it became the symbol of resistance. The remaining students maintained their 24-hour vigil, the CCP leaders tried to find military units willing to enter Beijing, citizens built barricades at key intersections, and the world watched.

Paramedics caring for hunger strikers from Beijing University in Tiananmen Square, May 17, 1989, the fifth day of the hunger strike, which lasted until most of the demonstrators left on the night of June 4.

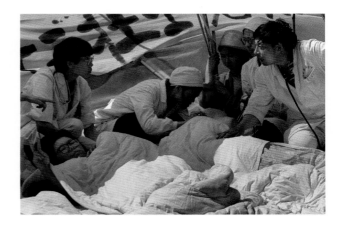

An ordinary citizen blocking a line of tanks heading east on Chang'an Blvd on June 5, 1989, the day after the army killed citizens in Beijing's streets and ended student demonstrations in Tiananmen Square. He tried to climb aboard the lead tank, but bystanders pulled him away, and the tanks continued. To this day, no one knows his identity.

On the night of Sunday, June 4, heavily armed PLA troops moved toward the city center, using tanks to clear away barricades, meeting bricks and stones thrown by residents. Firing live ammunition, not rubber bullets as had been forecast, they killed hundreds, perhaps thousands, of people along the way. In revenge, angry crowds seized soldiers amid the chaos and beat them to death. With the sound of gunfire approaching Tiananmen, student leaders negotiated with PLA officers, and before dawn almost all of the demonstrators left the Square. Tanks crushed the Goddess statue and the empty tent village of the hunger strikers. Reports of spectacular slaughter in the Square proved false; "eyewitness accounts" of "the Tiananmen massacre" did not conform to reality. No massacre took place in Tiananmen Square, but injured and dying citizens and soldiers filled the hospitals from the fighting along the city's streets. No reliable figure exists for the numbers of dead and wounded.

Deng Xiaoping and his allies emerged bloodstained but victorious from June 4. Zhao Ziyang, consigned to oblivion, could no longer advocate political reform. The student movement went back underground. Sino–Russian relations improved, even after Gorbachev's ouster and the fall of the Soviet Union. The army returned to barracks. Despite universal international condemnation, economic sanctions, and massive protests in Hong Kong, by 1992 the PRC was reestablished as a responsible member of the world community. The moral failure represented by the "People's Liberation Army" killing ordinary Chinese people, which many predicted would fatally injure the government, had few long-term consequences. Now the memory of June 4 looms large only for intellectuals, imprisoned demonstrators, and those who fled into permanent exile.

Only six months after Tiananmen, defying Chinese protests, the Dalai Lama received the Nobel Peace Prize in December 1989. Giving credit to Mahatma Gandhi and non-violence in his acceptance speech, the Dalai Lama praised the Beijing students and their supporters. He also expressed his belief that science and religion, rightly understood, never contradict one another, for both "tell us of the fundamental unity of all things."

TAIWAN UNDER THE GUOMINDANG

After 50 years as part of Japan's empire, the February 28 (1947) brutality, and the 1949 arrival of nearly 2 million "mainlanders"—most of them Guomindang military personnel and officials—Taiwan did not seem a promising place for the revitalization of the Republic of China or the building of a strong economy. Unlike Korea, the island had not been a major site of Japanese industrial development. The colonizers had created a modern infrastructure of railroads, electrical grids, and roads and trained a Japanese-speaking intellectual and business elite, but agriculture remained the island's most important sector, and the people remained poor.

Denouncing the PRC as a "bandit" regime and claiming sole legitimacy, the Nationalists occupied China's seat in the UN and maintained diplomatic relations with most non-communist countries, including the United States. The Cold War cemented the confrontation across the Taiwan Strait, generating a number of small battles over offshore islands. The

United States provided advanced weapons to the Republic of China in exchange for numerous bases and other military services.

Regarding the communists' violent land reform as a travesty, the Nationalists nonetheless required increased food production, both to feed the population (suddenly expanded by 30 percent or more) and to provide the capital for industrialization. Like South Korea, the ROC initiated rent control as a first step in alleviating tenants' burdens, then confiscated and sold to farmers all land that had been owned by Japanese nationals or corporations. Finally, in 1953, the ROC purchased all "surplus" (more than 7.5 acres) land from landlords—though obliged to sell, landowners did receive a price close to market value—and sold it to tenant farmers, with payments fixed no higher than their former rent. By creating a large class of owner-farmers, the government stimulated food production and reduced class conflict in the countryside.

Like the PRC on the mainland, the ROC fixed a low state purchase price for rice—around 70 percent of market value. Following earlier Japanese practice, they created a network of extension services to improve agricultural techniques, sometimes using police to enforce innovations. The Nationalists also required farmers to purchase high-priced fertilizers and pesticides, stimulating industrial production and bringing the farmers into the cash economy. Cash-poor after the flight from the mainland, the ROC government compensated landlords with government bonds or with shares in government-owned enterprises, drawing them closer to the state and into investment and entrepreneurship.

International demand for Taiwan's sugar and rice, and the savings of rural families, enabled early investment in export-oriented light industry. The villages provided a pool of labor no longer needed on the farms, mostly young and female, as well as capital to purchase technology from abroad. The Guomindang state established a public education system to enhance the skills of the labor force and gradually persuaded the suspicious rural population that sending their boys *and* girls to school made sense. Taiwan now has one of the best-educated populations in the world.

Jiang Jingguo, President of the Republic of China, 1978.

In addition to domestic savings and entrepreneurship, Taiwan received considerable investment from abroad. Like Japan and South Korea, the ROC constituted an important link in the United States-led "containment" of the PRC, so both military bases and defense contracts accelerated the island's economic growth. During the Vietnam War, for example, Taiwan supplied war matériel and became a popular "R & R" destination for free-spending American troops.

The ROC also benefited from continuing economic engagement with the Chinese diaspora, especially in Singapore, Hong Kong, Southeast Asia, and North America. Beginning in the 1960s, the Nationalists established Export Processing Zones with simplified regulations to encourage export-oriented foreign companies, a model similar to the SEZs created by the PRC after 1978. Like South Korea and (later) the PRC, the incentives included a well-educated, relatively inexpensive, and politically controlled workforce. With many students going abroad for advanced study and a rapidly developing domestic university system, by the 1980s Taiwan also possessed a corps of highly trained, English- and Japanese-speaking technical personnel.

Focusing on electronics, chemicals, and textiles, numerous Japanese and US firms brought both capital and technical expertise to this attractive destination, enabling Taiwan to become one of the "mini-dragons" of East Asia. By the 1980s, the ROC held one of the world's largest supplies of foreign exchange and had achieved as rapid a growth rate as that of South Korea under Park Chung Hee. Taiwan demonstrated conclusively that Chinese workers and entrepreneurs could, despite nineteenth-century predictions to the contrary, succeed in industrial and even postindustrial economic activity.

As long as Jiang Jieshi lived, the Guomindang remained doggedly committed to retaking the mainland by force, to martial law, the mainlander elite in control, and suppression of all dissident political activity, especially by Taiwanese. Former leftists, advocates of Taiwan independence, and activists hoping to form opposition parties were jailed or even executed. As in South Korea, anticommunism became a reflexive ideological tenet, closely linked to the United States and conservative organizations in the Chinese diaspora.

Jiang Jingguo (1910–1988), Jiang Jieshi's son with his first wife, had been educated in the USSR in the 1930s. After his return to China, he tried to control war profiteering in Chongqing but ran afoul of his stepmother's influential, corrupt family—he and Song Meiling never resolved their quarrel and remained on bad terms. Fluent in Russian and competent in English, Jiang Jingguo moved to Taiwan as head of the much-feared secret police. After a stint as administrator of Taiwan's highways, he rose to defense minister, vice premier, and finally premier.

After Jiang Jieshi's death in April 1975—Mao triumphantly outlived him by 17 months—his successors in the Guomindang recognized that without broadening their party to include more Taiwanese, the mainlander elite would be increasingly isolated from the local majority. Selected as party leader, Jiang Jingguo launched ambitious, successful economic projects that brought him considerable popularity, then handpicked a Taiwanese, Cornell-educated agronomist Li Denghui (Lee Teng-hui, b. 1923), to be his successor.

As the government eased its controls, civil society in Taiwan reacted by increasing the pressure for reform. During the last years of his life, Jiang Jingguo ended martial law and allowed the formation of an opposition political party, despite considerable resistance within the GMD. Jiang Jingguo is now remembered much more fondly than his dour, authoritarian father and credited—along with many dissenters and activists—with laying the foundation for democracy in the Republic of China (see p. 459). By the late 1980s, the Republic of China was poised to revive the long-postponed vision of Sun Yat-sen and Song Jiaoren: a *democratic* China, on the small scale of the island of Taiwan.

A WATERSHED DECADE FOR THE KOREAS

The assassination of President Park ended the 1970s on a surprisingly hopeful note. In 1980, Prime Minister Choi Kyu Ha's interim government made gestures to open the political system, and the press sensed that major changes were in the offing. Unfortunately, the hope for a "Seoul Spring" proved short-lived when General Chun Doo Hwan (Chŏn Tuhwan, b. 1931), head of the Defense Security Command as well as the KCIA, declared martial law in May and in the next ten months brutally maneuvered himself into power as president of a Fifth Republic, inaugurated in February 1981. As we will see, Chun's rise caused many Korean military and civilian deaths. While he managed to gain power equivalent to Park's at the height of Yusin, he never achieved legitimacy or respect.

The rapid development of South Korea had brought expansion of the middle class, an educational revolution, increasing militancy among labor, and a growing sense of security. That is, a thorough social and economic transformation had occurred. Ordinary people were no longer willing to accept authoritarian rule, with its repression of civil liberties and cowed public sphere, in the name of national development or military security. Chun Doo Hwan discovered that Pandora could not be put back in her box, no matter what force or appeasements he used. By the end of the 1980s, "people power" brought a new era of democratization.

Meanwhile, North Korea stagnated economically as the South forged ahead in economic wealth, technological prowess, and military preparedness. During the 1980s, Kim Il Sung laid the groundwork for the succession of his son, Kim Jong Il, to power. The younger Kim presided over a futile competition with the South in the court of global opinion, squandering billions staging world festivals and building obscenely expensive monuments to his father.

THE VIOLENT ORIGINS OF THE FIFTH REPUBLIC

In the aftermath of Park's assassination, internal strife rocked the ROK armed forces. Chun Doo Hwan, head of Military Security and responsible for the investigation of Park's murder, emerged as a new power within the high command. Chun plotted with Roh Tae Woo (No T'aeu, b. 1932) and other graduates of the Korean Military Academy's 11th class (1955) and gradually seized control of the government.

The first step was a bloody coup within the military itself. On December 12, 1979 Chun arrested Army Chief of Staff Chŏng Sŭnghwa (b. 1926) as a suspect in Park's assassination. Simultaneously, Roh Tae Woo's elite Ninth Division and other units loyal to Chun,

6,000 troops in all, occupied key areas of Seoul and began a bloody shootout with the forces defending Army Headquarters and the neighboring Ministry of Defense. When the fighting ended seven hours later, Chun and his group controlled the army. Both sides suffered considerable losses, and Chun's willingness to order the deaths of Korean soldiers to consolidate his power foreshadowed worse things to come.

In the first months of 1980, Choi Kyu Ha's interim government still sought ways to open the Korean political system. He restored political rights to politicians, Kim Dae Jung among them, and reinstated some dismissed university professors. But spring destroyed any hopes for a new departure in politics. Bitter struggles divided the opposition as Kim Dae Jung and Kim Young Sam split the New Democratic Party. The Democratic Republic Party (DRP) also divided between groups loyal to Lee Hu Rak (1924–2009), former head of the KCIA, and Kim Jong Pil (Kim Chŏngp'il), Park Chung Hee's old ally.

In the background, students, labor groups, and other radical organizations continued to demonstrate in the streets. In April, Chun Doo Hwan illegally took charge of the KCIA, a move that touched off militant demonstrations, which increased in intensity, augmented by labor strife in March and April. Public unrest peaked on May 15 with an enormous mass demonstration that involved 30 universities and as many as 100,000 students, setting the stage for Chun to seize complete control of the government.

A woman grieves at the Kwangju morgue, May 1980.

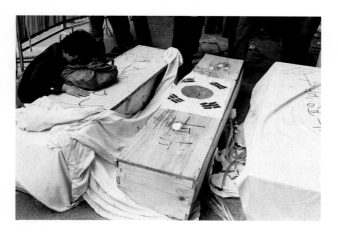

THE KWANGJU INCIDENT

Working through institutions of the Choi government, Chun declared Martial Law Decree Number Ten on May 17, dissolved the Assembly, closed all universities and colleges, and prohibited all political activity and labor actions. He followed this with the wholesale arrest of opposition political leaders. The next day, a small group of students staged a demonstration in the South Chŏlla provincial capital of Kwangju, demanding the release of Kim Dae Jung, a native son of the province. Special Forces Commander Chŏng Hoyong sent paratroopers to deal with them. The elite military unit began indiscriminately to bludgeon, beat, and even bayonet not only the demonstrating students but onlookers as well.

The brutality shocked and enraged Kwangju citizens, who retaliated violently. After two days of pitched battles, the citizens drove the Special Forces out of the city on May 21, starting a full-scale insurrection. With a citizens' council in charge, six days of negotiations ensued as the army cordoned off the city, isolating it from the rest of the country. The citizens unsuccessfully sought US intercession, and talks with the ROK army failed.

Finally, on May 27, units from the ROK Twentieth Division entered the city and reimposed martial law. The occupation turned violent, for some students and citizens had armed themselves and vowed to fight to the death. Meeting stiff resistance, the army slaughtered students and civilians at redoubts around the city, finally taking their last stronghold, the provincial capitol building.

In the following decade, the Kwangju uprising came to occupy a pivotal place in postwar Korean history, becoming a watershed event almost as important as liberation in 1945. Perhaps it may be more appropriately compared to the March First Movement of 1919. After Kwangju, South Korean politics were never the same. The rebellion came to symbolize the collective yearning of the Korean people for justice and democracy. It was also a turning point in people's attitude toward the United States. Despite American denials, many suspected that the United States—as leaders of the Joint UN Command—had approved the movement of troops to the Kwangju slaughter. President Reagan's reception of Chun Doo Hwan as the first foreign guest of his new administration cemented a growing anti-American sentiment in South Korea.

The counting of the dead and injured became a war of statistics between the Chun government and the opposition. The government claimed about 200 dead, while the opposition asserted that over 2,000 people died during the rebellion. Only after decades could the numbers be fixed precisely: 2,710 injured, 284 dead (154 citizens who died in the fighting, and 83 subsequent deaths, with 47 missing). More important for the political future, the tragedy of Kwangju attached itself to Chun Doo Hwan. He bore the stain of both the bloody military coup of December 12, 1979 and the Kwangju rebellion throughout his subsequent presidency (1981–88).

THE FIFTH REPUBLIC AND GROWING OPPOSITION

In the immediate aftermath of Kwangju, Chun Doo Hwan completed his seizure of power. He established a military-civilian Committee for National Security Measures chaired by Choi Kyu Ha. Behind this façade, Generals Chun and Roh Tae Woo, and Special Forces Commander Chŏng Hoyong, smoothed the way for Chun to be elected president by the National Council for Reunification and for the promulgation of a new constitution, creating the Fifth Republic in February 1981.

Chun began his rule by copying the tactics of Park Chung Hee 20 years before. He announced a movement to purify the bureaucracy and promised a new era of growth and justice. He also moved against his political enemies by banning a large number of people from political life. Kim Dae Jung was charged with sedition and responsibility for Kwangju, tried, and sentenced to death—soon commuted to life in prison, later reduced to 20 years. Moreover, Chun forced thousands of labor organizers, students, journalists, and civil servants, including teachers, into reeducation camps designed to dissuade political deviants from continued opposition. Chun clearly intended to use the Yusin system, its easily manipulated electoral college, and the power of a reorganized Democratic Justice Party (DJP) to cow the elected Assembly. Although he possessed all these instruments of power, Chun never successfully legitimated his government.

That is, even while invoking the necessity of political discipline for economic development and national security, Chun failed to justify the continuation of harsh, autocratic rule. The South Korean public now associated prosperity with the late president Park, and a new generation of Koreans had grown up without the chilling memory of the Korean War. South Korea had emerged from the 1979 recession, and its export-led economy continued to expand. Obvious economic prosperity contrasted directly with the impoverishment of political and intellectual life, as Chun's regime marginalized its political opposition and intimidated and controlled the press. He could repress demonstrations by force and jail his opponents, but he remained the most unpopular leader in postwar history.

Throughout his presidency, Chun promulgated a number of highly visible social reforms in order to blunt criticism of his regime and "liberalize" life in South Korea. He removed the nightly curfew left over from the Korean War, eliminated the military-style uniforms and hairstyles for middle- and high-school students—holdovers from colonial times—and built a number of new public museums and parks. But Chun's personal grandiosity and love of ceremony and public spectacle contrasted greatly with late President Park's much-admired reputation for sober asceticism. In addition, financial scandals plagued Chun's wife and family, widely viewed as venal and grasping in stark contrast to Park's popular, martyred wife, Yuk Yŏngsu.

Even with main opposition leaders in exile—Kim Dae Jung was allowed to go to the United States in 1982—or banned from politics, and the press cowed by censorship, opposition to Chun continued to build. In the wake of the changed political perceptions after Kwangju and the rise of the Fifth Republic came a transformation of the opposition. New ideas brought together formerly disparate movements. What had been principally a movement for democracy, led by students and intellectuals, began to merge with the grassroots labor movement that had arisen during the 1970s.

Kwangju and a subsequent wave of anti-Americanism radicalized the student movement, and the emergence of "professional" full-time activists, drawn from a cadre of expelled or jailed students from the 1970s, solidified this trend. The widely held belief that the United States was complicit in the Kwangju massacre and creation of the Fifth Republic allowed students to accept formulations delegitimating the Chun government as a puppet of American neo-imperialism.

THE *MINJUNG* MOVEMENT

A censorship thaw in the mid-1980s allowed formerly banned books to become commercially available—books on liberation theology, Marxism, neo-Marxist writing on dependency theory, world systems, and revisionist history of the Korean War. Many radical ideas blended in Korean intellectual life at this time, but a homegrown ideology brought together labor activists, students, and dissident intellectuals to forge a movement that would ultimately topple the Fifth Republic.

Minjung (J. *minshū*, C. *minzhong*), the concept that galvanized the opposition, may be translated as "the masses" or "the people." In its Korean use at this time, it connoted the peasant masses as a repository of true Korean identity. Not a divisive class term, ultimately it broadened to encompass all oppositional forces in society, which could include intellectuals and urban, middle-class students. *Minjung* ideology also stressed the concept of *han*, a Korean idea of the accumulated resentment and suffering of the oppressed.

By the 1980s the "*minjung* movement" had become at once a social, political, and cultural movement that advocated distributive equity, promoted democracy, and emphasized Korean cultural identity. *Minjung* historians recast modern Korean history as a narrative of the oppression and struggle of the *minjung*. *Minjung* political ideology attacked the oppressive structures of capitalism and neo-colonialism. *Minjung* cultural theorists called for recapturing a *minjung* identity obscured by the race to modernize society.

Indeed, the university students of the 1980s were thoroughly modern, middle class, and urbanized Koreans—South Korea was 80 percent urban by this time—and they felt that their very urbanity had cut them off from what it *truly* meant to be Korean. Eerily reminiscent of the "sent-down" students of the Cultural Revolution in the PRC, they went to the countryside to learn from farmers how to be themselves, to obtain a *minjung* consciousness. This perplexed the farmers, who wondered what they could possibly teach these privileged students, who already had every social advantage.

The *minjung* movement saturated Korean society of the 1980s. Folk forms such as farmers' music troupes, masked dance clubs, drumming groups, and *p'ansori* performances flourished on campuses. These attractions also appeared at labor actions; there was hardly a strike or sit-in without drumming or a theater performance.

Masked dance in particular became symbolically powerful because, in its original form, peasants had used it to satirize their *yangban* landlords. Students and labor leaders thus easily pilloried the government or company management with their adapted plays.

Traditional wine shops, folk crafts, *taekwando* (martial arts) exercise parlors for suburban housewives, and a full array of folk symbols and pictorial representations in advertising flooded the popular culture as well. Life in Seoul was chaotic by the mid-1980s. The city had been torn apart by huge public-works projects and the building of five subway lines in anticipation of the 1988 Olympic Games. Labor strikes and student demonstrations added to the confusion.

By late 1986, the stage had been set for confrontation between the government and this *minjung*-oriented civil society. There had been serious demonstrations in the fall and some highly visible student suicides. Moreover, in January 1987, the death of Seoul National University student Pak Chongch'ŏl during interrogation by police provoked further public outrage. Chun's single term in office was in its last years; he had earlier vowed not to seek another term.

But a new constitution and direct presidential elections had become the opposition's core demands. Chun opened a dialogue to amend the election law, but in the spring of 1987 he abruptly shut it down. This touched off widespread demonstrations led by students and the reorganized opposition party, now called the New Korean Democratic Party (NKDP). On June 10, Chun's DRP announced that his right-hand man, General Roh Tae Woo, would be its candidate for the upcoming presidential election, and this was the last straw. Demonstrations broke out all over Korea, and ordinary citizens from all walks of life joined the students in the streets. For the next two weeks, the most violent demonstrations since 1979 drew hundreds of thousands of people, in every Korean city.

In contrast to 1979–80, this time the United States did intercede. President Reagan sent Undersecretary of State Gaston Sigur (1925–1995) to Seoul to warn Chun of dire consequences for United States–ROK relations if he used his military against the citizenry. On June 29, in a surprise move, Chun's erstwhile successor Roh Tae Woo issued a "Declaration of Democratization and Reforms," consisting of eight points. The most important of these conceded to almost every opposition demand:

a new election law and direct elections, press freedom, local elections of county and provincial heads, and restoration of civil rights for Kim Dae Jung and others banned from politics.

Two days later, Chun accepted the declaration, the crisis passed, and a period of frenetic political activity followed. The National Assembly drafted a new constitution with a new election law that was ratified in a national referendum on October 27, 1987, and a presidential election was scheduled for December 16. Roh Tae Woo, who had seized the upper hand with his June declaration, ran as the Democratic Justice Party candidate. By taking the lead in negotiations over the new constitution and election law, Roh asserted considerable influence on the ultimate shape of the reform. The opposition party leaders sat at the table with him, not the students, labor leaders, or ordinary citizens who had precipitated the government capitulation.

Thus, contrary to overwhelming public opinion, the negotiations upheld presidential authority without restructuring government toward a parliamentary system. To the bitter disappointment of many, Kim Dae Jung (Party for Peace and Democracy) and his long-time rival Kim Young Sam (Reunification Democracy Party) both ran, splitting the opposition vote. When the dust settled, Kim and Kim divided 55 percent of the popular vote and Roh claimed victory with a bare plurality of 37 percent. But people's power had forced the end of the Fifth Republic and placed the ROK on a path of democratization.

MARKING TIME IN 1980s NORTH KOREA

By the beginning of the 1980s, economic growth in North Korea had stagnated for many reasons: lack of access to capital for investment, an increasingly outmoded technology base, heavy military expenditures (25 percent of annual GDP), flagging enthusiasm of workers, and above all the failure of centralized command economics itself. At early stages of economic growth, centralized planning can be feasible, even desirable, but as the North Korean economy expanded, planning became more difficult.

Moreover, DPRK command economics often placed political calculations and sometimes wishful thinking ahead of common sense, and—reminiscent of the Great Leap Forward in the PRC—the system produced misleading or even falsified information that frustrated

Students confronting riot police in front of Yonsei University, June 1, 1987. Mass demonstrations in June 1987 in Seoul led to the capitulation of the government and the creation of a new election law.

good planning. Growth began to falter, and inefficiencies and bottlenecks compromised the economy. North Korea was still a formidable problem for the South, but in this decade the balance of power on the peninsula shifted in the South's favor.

Throughout the 1970s, Kim Il Sung paved the way for his son to succeed him as Great Leader. At the Sixth Party Congress in 1980, Kim Jong Il assumed high-ranking positions in the Party Secretariat, the Standing Committee of the Politburo, and the Military Commission. Since he was poised to assume control, outside observers conclude that his father began to withdraw from active management of the government at this time. The process was obscured from the world's view, and we can only guess at the machinations within the Party and military that attended these political changes.

In the early 1980s, the North mounted several major terrorist attacks on the South, the most spectacular the attempted assassination of Chun Doo Hwan in Burma in October 1983. A bomb placed in a reviewing platform missed the president but killed 21 people, including three ROK cabinet ministers. In 1987, North Korean agents blew up a Korean Air flight over the Indian Ocean. Both incidents generated debates among Pyongyang watchers as to whether they indicated splits within the DPRK leadership.

The changing international climate of the 1980s also caused great difficulties for North Korea. In particular,

Deng Xiaoping's Four Modernizations (1978), which paved the way for the PRC to open to the global economy, placed North Korea in an awkward position. Beginning in 1979, China's rapid rapprochement with the North's sworn enemy—the United States—complicated the DPRK's relationship with its most important political ally and economic benefactor. The second Seven-Year Plan ended ambiguously in 1984, and the next plan was significantly delayed until 1987.

This period of "adjustment" indicated serious problems in the economy. North Korea began experimenting with new options by passing a Foreign Investment Law in 1984. But given its aging infrastructure and other logistical problems, few foreign firms seriously considered the DPRK as a site for investment, especially in contrast with the emerging PRC. A more serious attempt to capture foreign capital came in 1991, when the DPRK, emulating the successful SEZs in southeast China, opened the Najin-Sŏnbong free trade zone on its remote northeastern coast.

In the early 1980s, North Korea began an all-out competition with South Korea in the arena of world opinion. When, in 1981, the International Olympic Committee awarded the 1988 Olympic Games to Seoul, North Korea immediately lobbied that the games be held jointly, but the ROK refused these overtures. Trying to match the frenetic construction in preparation for the Seoul Olympics, North Korea went on a construction offensive by building expensive monuments. In 1982, the DPRK government completed the 490-foot (150-m)tall Tower of the *Juche* Idea, the world's tallest granite spire, to commemorate Kim Il Sung's 70th birthday. The construction of the 105,000-seat May Day stadium, housing for their

The 105-story Ryugyong Hotel in Pyongyang, planned as the tallest building in Asia. Begun in 1990, it stood uncompleted for 15 years, until a foreign contractor completed it in the late 2000s.

own International Youth Festival (1989), and more expensive public-works projects continued through the decade. One project, the 105-story, 7,665-room Ryugyong Hotel, trumpeted as the tallest building in Asia at the time, remained uncompleted until a foreign contractor resumed construction in 2008. Throughout the 1990s, its vacant concrete shell loomed over Pyongyang like the elephant in the living room, a testament to the waste and hubris of the North Korean leadership.

With the collapse of the USSR and the socialist system after 1989, North Korea's isolation from the world community deepened. DPRK trade relied almost exclusively on other socialist economies. With the Chinese opening to market economics and the disappearance overnight of the socialist trading bloc, North Korea found itself without trade partners. In 1990, North Korea's international trade peaked at US$4.7 billion, but it plunged to US$2.7 billion in 1991, according to the ROK's Korean Traders Association.

The DPRK could still trade, but the rules of the game had changed decisively. Even before its collapse in 1991, the Soviet Union had begun to demand market prices and foreign exchange for oil and other exports that had formerly been handled by barter or with special terms. This exposed North Korea's inability to earn foreign exchange in trade with the global capitalist economy. Now North Korea needed capital to finance basic needs, in particular oil, food, and technology transfers to improve its crumbling infrastructure.

By the early 1990s, cracks had appeared in the North's normally intransigent isolationism. Forced to respond to Roh Tae Woo's policy of *Nordpolitik* (see p. 414) that established diplomatic relations between the ROK, the PRC, and Russia, North Korea began a tentative program of opening. The DPRK hosted Korean emigrant groups from the United States on family re-unification visits, invited NGO consultants from the United States and Europe, and discussed normalization of relations with Japan. Hopeful beginnings, unfortunately, were not sustained, and in the next decade North Korean society would face its greatest crisis since the Korean War in the great famine of 1995–96.

DEMOCRATIZATION OF SOUTH KOREAN SOCIETY

The outcome of the December 1987 presidential ballot under the new election law—a narrow plurality for Roh Tae Woo—was a crushing disappointment to many who had struggled so long to break the grip of authoritarian politics on Korean society. In hindsight we can see why the opposition could not unite, even though they knew that a unified candidacy almost ensured a victory. Roh Tae Woo and the government party coopted the reform process in the summer of 1987, and though the opposition did obtain a new election law, this did not mean that the political system itself had been reformed.

The president would be elected directly, but even with the National Assembly strengthened and opposition parties stronger, the president's office still had enormous power. The personalization of politics resulted in part from the very narrow range of ideological difference tolerated in the post–World War II climate of anticommunism. Until the reforms for local autonomy could be worked out, the party in power could appoint provincial governors and county heads and had many other opportunities for patronage. The opposition aimed primarily at gaining power, rarely representing programs or policies significantly different from those of the government.

Politics thus remained a zero sum game. Party politics had always centered on personalities, not programs or policy positions. The fierce loyalties of followers to party leaders made unifying around a reformist program or idea very difficult. In 1987, with the chance to gain real power for the first time in over 20 years, neither Kim Dae Jung nor Kim Young Sam could resist the demands of their followers to grasp this opportunity and its potential for patronage jobs and local authority.

The elections revealed a crucial South Korean political pattern. Voting results demonstrated remarkable continuity between the candidates' home regions and the popular vote. The main candidates garnered in excess of 80 percent of the vote in their home provinces, and Kim Dae Jung captured 84 percent of the vote from the Chŏlla provinces. This preference for "our local candidate" highlighted the consistent economic and political discrimination that had characterized the authoritarian period. Since 1961, politicians and military men from the southeast Kyŏngsang provinces had dominated the government. Infrastructure investment, placement of factories, and other benefits of development thus flowed along the Seoul-to-Pusan corridor, leaving the southwest out in the cold. This discrimination had strengthened local political loyalties and identity for both the winners and losers.

The Roh Tae Woo presidency did not depart from business as usual in Korean politics, though some signs of change appeared. The National Assembly gained power vis-à-vis the executive branch of government, and the governing party lost its legislative majority in the elections of 1988. With the opposition and government party more or less in balance, all parties became more vulnerable to public displeasure.

The women's movement emerged as one of the early beneficiaries of the increased attention to public opinion. Since the beginning of the ROK, women had chafed under an inequitable family law that privileged patriarchal authority in household headship, inheritance, and custody. The revision of family law after 1945 had consciously attempted to erase Japanese family laws imposed during the colonial period, reestablishing Korean traditions that, in this case, strengthened patriarchy.

Under Roh's divided government, women's groups took advantage of their electoral power to pressure lawmakers to revise the family law. In 1989, they pushed through a major reform that provided them equal rights in inheritance and custody of children. With more equal protection for women, divorce rates skyrocketed, demonstrating that it was women's weak legal position in traditional society, not some inherent cultural virtue, that lay behind Korea's traditionally low divorce rate. The next legal step—removing the prohibition on women becoming "head of household"—would have to wait until the revision of 2005.

Roh's Sixth Republic also provided a new beginning for journalism and publishing in the ROK, as a new press law eliminated government censorship. Although the National Security Law (NSL) still restricted some political speech, new newspapers and periodicals

IM KWON-TAEK, AWARD-WINNING DIRECTOR

Im Kwon-Taek (Im Kwŏntaek; b. 1936), South Korea's best-known film director, was born in a small town in South Chŏlla province. He bracketed the 1980s with two of the most important films in South Korean movie history. *Mandala* (1981) was the first South Korean film to win international recognition (Grand Prix, Hawaiian Film Festival), and *Sopyonje* (1993) the first to draw over a million viewers. These movies led to a renaissance in popular cinema in South Korea and anticipated the Korean New Wave cinema of the 1990s. Along with Park Gwang-su (Pak Kwangsu, b. 1955) and Jang Seon-woo (Chang Sŏnu, b. 1952), Im has been recognized as one of the founding figures of the movement that gained international and critical recognition for Korean cinema.

Im did not start as an auteur or avant-garde filmmaker. Beginning in 1962, he directed numerous low-budget genre films, averaging five films a year, cranking out melodramas, action films, and historical dramas. At that time, the South Korean government demanded quotas of indigenous films from the Korean film industry. If a company met its quota of "Korean-made" films, no matter how awful, it could get a permit to import a Hollywood product as a real moneymaker. Im felt degraded by the process of producing disposable, cheap, "local" movies in a market dominated by American films, so in the late 1970s he successfully bargained with his producers for the latitude to make serious art films. *Mandala*, one of Im's first major feature films, focused on Buddhist monks and differing views on the attainment of enlightenment, a very different subject from his trivial earlier work.

The release of *Sopyonje* (its title refers to a "Western" style of *p'ansori* singing) in 1993 marked the beginning of a new career for Im as well as a turn within the marketplace for Korean cinema. *Sopyonje* showed that Korean films could be financially as well as critically successful. Thereafter, Im and other directors could command resources to mount

large-budget blockbusters and quality features to compete with Hollywood imports. Korean cinematic exports now make up a large portion of what has been termed the Korean Wave, the outpouring of Korean popular culture in response to demand in East and Southeast Asia. Im Kwon-Taek recently received his profession's highest honor, the Best Director Award at the Cannes film festival, for the film *Chihwaseon* (*Painted Fire*, 2002).

Im Kwon-Taek accepting an award in Cannes for the direction of his film *Chihwaseon*, May 26, 2002.

Still from the film *Chihwaseon* (2002).

flourished. One outstanding example was *The People's News*, which followed a progressive agenda and maintained strict independence from any party affiliation, loyal to neither government nor opposition. After its founding in 1988, its reportage criticized both sides, both government policy and the opposition's excessive machinations and demagoguery in the streets.

With new freedom of the press, hundreds of formerly banned publications reemerged. Even more significantly, the government cancelled and abandoned lists of banned writers going as far back as the colonial period, including many pre-liberation writers who had gone north after 1945. Many important voices in modern Korean writing—such as those of the Proletarian Literature movement of the 1920s—and other previously illegal works could now be read, evaluated, and included in the canon of modern literature. This climate of freedom encouraged a major renaissance in the public sphere, manifested in freer political discourse, as well as an outburst of creative expression in the arts, literature, theater, and cinema (see pp. 408, 412).

LABOR ACTIVISM AND POLITICS

Perhaps the most immediate impact of democratization lay in the realm of labor activism and organization. In 1987 began what was called "the great labor offensive," lasting for the next two years. The labor movement had grown in fits and starts since the early 1970s. Driven initially by women textile and garment workers at the lowest rungs of the labor hierarchy, the movement had gained strength during the tumultuous 1980s. The *minjung* movement gave labor a new vocabulary of resistance as well as a new identification of workers as an important component of society.

Clearly students drove the struggle for democratization of society in the 1980s, with labor as a supportive but mostly latent force constrained by strict laws and police control. But the dramatic events of the summer of 1987 stimulated the evolving labor movement into conscious, assertive action for higher wages and better working conditions at all levels of the workforce. The formerly less-engaged, elite, and predominantly male workers in heavy industry (auto manufacturing, shipbuilding, steel production, etc.) initiated the offensive once it was clear that the government would not intervene between labor and management. Moreover, the labor organizing and strikes begun by Hyundai workers

in Ulsan in the summer of 1987 arose spontaneously from the workers themselves without links to students or intellectuals.

The "great labor offensive" earned its name from the eruption of strikes and other labor actions beginning in 1987 and continuing through 1988 and 1989. This unprecedented level of activism revealed an enormous pent-up demand for economic equity. Notoriously authoritarian in their relations with labor, management of the large *chaebŏl* had managed, with government support, to delay wage increases throughout the development period. In 1986, only 276 labor disputes had occurred in all of South Korea. The numbers jumped to 3,749 and 1,873 respectively for 1987 and 1988.

Wages were the principal issue during these strikes, but prominent labor demands also included working conditions, reduction of hours, and more generous bonuses. Labor organizations also made ubiquitous demands for humane treatment of workers and democratic relations between labor and management. Clearly, one of the major complaints of laboring people in Korea was the perpetuation by white-collar workers and upper management of traditional, disparaging attitudes toward manual labor. Thus, among the plethora of issues placed on the table, labor included elimination of status distinctions between white-collar and blue-collar workers, abolition of arbitrary evaluations by foremen, improvement of workplace food, and an end to dress and hair codes for workers.

After two years, the number of labor actions returned to pre-1987 levels. Surprisingly, during the great offensive, management actually gave workers the majority of their demands. Workers in many of the bigger firms obtained wage increases between 20 percent and 30 percent, an indication of the enormous gap between labor productivity and an equitable wage. The fact that large firms could buy their way out of labor trouble showed just how large a surplus had been generated for the firms by the inequitable wage structure. Middle- and small-sized firms could not afford to pay such enormous wage hikes, but in general all of labor profited from the gains.

The great offensive ended Korea's vaunted comparative advantage in labor costs and began a process in which all exporting firms had to recalculate production inputs. Moreover, development and export success had infused contemporary Korean national identity so

413

strongly that any social action that undermined it could be labeled as "against the nation." Labor's threat to Korea's export advantage thus almost immediately came under fire as "unpatriotic" from conservative politicians and members of the vastly expanded and often conservative middle class.

INTERNATIONAL RELATIONS

Roh Tae Woo also made considerable effort to realign the ROK's international relations, reviving and intensifying Chun Doo Hwan's *Nordpolitik* policy, a broad program of engagement with the nations of the former Soviet bloc. South Korea established diplomatic relations with the PRC in 1991—by necessity breaking relations with Taiwan at the same time—and in 1992 Roh's initiative culminated in formal ties with the Russian Federation.

In addition, Roh opened a dialogue with North Korea on nuclear issues, joint trade zones on the DMZ, and the establishment of more permanent cultural exchanges, including family reunions. These talks resulted in the signing of two unprecedented agreements in February 1992: the "Agreement on Reconciliation, Non-aggression, and Exchanges and Cooperation" and the "Joint Declaration on the Denuclearization of the Korean Peninsula"—the most significant North–South accords since the 1972 Red Cross talks that had established the first "hot line" between the two Koreas.

THE 1992 PRESIDENTIAL ELECTION

The constitutional revisions in 1988 created a single five-year term limit for the presidency. In his first two years in office, Roh confronted a fractious Assembly in which his government party had to broker complicated coalitions with three opposition parties to accomplish anything. As a result, Roh resorted to reforms he could accomplish by presidential fiat. Still connected to the army himself, he began the process of reforming and ensuring civilian control over the military, leaving a more thorough purge to the next administration. His party regained a slim majority in the 1990 Assembly elections, and this emboldened him partially to stifle continuing labor strife, to the relief of the business lobby. After 1990, the number of political arrests under the NSL also rose noticeably.

Still, Roh faced the problem of how to maintain power in the face of the new term limit, finding a solution in a brilliant but extremely complicated political maneuver. He enticed long-time opposition leader Kim Young Sam to bring his Reunification Democratic Party (RDP), along with Kim Jong Pil's National Democratic Republican Party (NDRP), into a coalition with his own Democratic Justice Party (DJP). This coalition party, named the Democratic Liberal Party (DLP), represented an attempt to create a broad, stable, and enduring government party similar to Japan's Liberal Democratic Party. In any election, this coalition could overpower Kim Dae Jung's much smaller party.

This was a move of stunning cynicism and calculation on the part of Kim Young Sam, who had been in the opposition his entire political career. He calculated that if he remained outside the government and fought for power, competing with Kim Dae Jung, he would likely fail repeatedly. Therefore, he concluded that it was better to compromise with the government party, gain power, and work within the system.

The creation of the grand coalition party, an adroit move by Roh, enabled him to sustain the power of his governing party and arrange a controlled transfer of power. While a new leader would take over in his stead, any radicalism would be tempered by obligations to the coalition and its diversity. Kim Young Sam's political gamble paid off. He won the 1992 election, gaining 41.4 percent of the vote for the coalition and defeating his old rival, Kim Dae Jung. His ascension marked the first presidency of a civilian without former military ties since 1961, over 30 years. In spite of the opportunism obvious in Kim's political machinations, the public was optimistic, and he enjoyed a 92 percent approval rating at the beginning of his term. The stage was set for significant reforms and the possibility of a breakthrough to a new era in South Korean politics.

THE RISE OF JAPAN'S BUBBLE ECONOMY

The double-digit annual growth of the postwar reconstruction period, called Japan's "economic miracle," came to an end in the mid-1970s with oil crises, economic stagnation, and high inflation. But Japan soon returned to the path of economic growth, causing scholars and pundits alike to proclaim that Japan would soon surpass the United States as "Number One."

That growth took different forms from the immediate postwar decades, however. Japan's economic and cultural roles in East Asia expanded. In 1965, Japan's balance of trade with the United States went from negative—importing more from the United States than exporting to the United States—to positive. Growing trade imbalances with the United States led Japan's government to try to ease tensions through fiscal and economic policies.

Those policies, together with lax oversight of banks and risky loans, produced an enormous real-estate and stock-market bubble. In one notorious case, the Industrial Bank of Japan gave US$2 billion in loans, based on forged collateral, to an Osaka restaurant owner who held séances to decide how to invest that money in stock-market speculation. By the late 1980s, the nominal real-estate value of the city of Tokyo alone surpassed that of the entire United States. The bubble burst between 1989 and 1992, destroying US$10–20 trillion in assets, about half the world's GDP at the time. By the early 1990s, Japan could no longer be touted as "Number One." Although Japan's per capita GDP was the world's highest in the mid-1990s, the last decade of the twentieth century came to be dubbed "Japan's Lost Decade."

The early 1990s was a watershed era in politics, as well. Emperor Hirohito, whose long reign spanned Japan's rise to great power status, imperialism in East Asia, defeat in World War II, and rebirth as the world's second largest economic power, died in 1989. In stark contrast to the outpouring of grief when the Meiji Emperor died in 1912, few Japanese bothered to watch his funeral on television, preferring to rent videos, and even fewer lined the streets to view the funeral cortège. The Liberal Democratic Party, which had controlled the government as part of the "1955 System"—the coalition of the LDP, bureaucracy, and big business—suffered electoral losses that ended its rule in 1993 after 48 years of dominance.

JAPAN IN ASIA

Japan returned to Asia in the 1970s and 1980s. Japan and South Korea had normalized diplomatic relations in 1965, and trade and diplomatic ties with most other Asian countries had gradually been built before the 1970s. The "Nixon shocks" of 1971 ushered in a dramatic shift from Japan's focus on the United States to an expanding role in East Asia. Richard Nixon stunned Japan with the sudden announcement that the United States would allow the dollar's value to float against the world's currencies. This produced an abrupt appreciation of the yen that, together with a 10 percent US surcharge on imports, made Japanese imports much more expensive in the American market. President Nixon shifted US policy toward the PRC in 1971 without prior consultation with Japan, which the United States had long proclaimed its closest ally in the region. These blows led the Japanese to believe that the United States did not, in fact, view Japan as an equal partner.

In the early 1960s, Japan had tried to maintain trade relations with both the Republic of China (Taiwan) and the PRC. Nixon's plans to visit China prompted Beijing and Tokyo to accelerate discussions to improve their relations, leading to formalized diplomatic ties in September 1972. They still did not have a peace treaty—Japan and the Republic of China on Taiwan had signed a peace treaty in 1952—but finally agreed to terms of peace in October 1978, after settling disputes over some uninhabited islands and China's insistence that Japan accept language condemning the USSR.

As expected, Taiwan cut its diplomatic relations with Japan but continued trade and cultural relations through non-governmental organizations. As late as 1995, Taiwan surpassed the PRC in purchases of Japanese exports—Taiwan bought 6.5 percent and the PRC 5 percent of Japanese exports—though the figures for imports were reversed. Products from the PRC constituted 10.7 percent and from Taiwan 4.3 percent of Japan's imports that year.

In general, after 1972 economic interests characterized Sino–Japanese relations. After the peace treaty, Japanese investors built a steel mill in Shanghai and drilled for oil off China's coast. Hundreds of Japanese companies set up offices in China, and Chinese "paramount leader" Deng Xiaoping visited Japan in 1987. Imports and exports grew exponentially—in 2010, the PRC is Japan's largest trading partner.

Despite successful trade relations, Chinese government officials, and Chinese people through street demonstrations, continued to protest against Japanese politicians' statements minimizing Japan's wartime aggression in China. In 1982 and subsequently, the PRC government disputed the Japanese Ministry of Education's changing the word "invasion" to "incursion" in textbooks to describe Japanese actions in North China in 1937 (see p. 378). Words mattered; Japanese cabinet ministers and other politicians failed to learn that incendiary comments, such as downplaying the scope of Japanese wartime atrocities, would lead to Chinese protests and eventually the offending politician's resignation.

Actions mattered, too. Japanese political leaders, including prime ministers, had visited the Yasukuni shrine to Japan's war dead since 1975. But the 1978 enshrinement of the souls of 14 men convicted of war crimes, followed by Prime Minister Nakasone Yasuhiro's declaration that he was making an "official" visit to pray at the shrine in 1985, infuriated Chinese, South Koreans, and many Japanese as well.

South Koreans were even more upset by the insensitivity of Japanese government leaders to events of the recent past. Koreans, like Chinese, protested against Japan's textbook revisions. But they had additional causes for resentment in 35 years of colonialism, continuing unequal treatment of Koreans living in Japan, and Japan's failure to resolve the "comfort women" issue with official reparations to the surviving victims. Apologies like the emperor's "sincere regret for the unfortunate past" did not satisfy Korean sentiment.

The Japanese also had cause to be angry at Korea, both North and South, during these decades. In 1973, KCIA agents, acting on orders from the authoritarian regime of Park Chung Hee, kidnapped pro-democracy opposition leader Kim Dae Jung (see p. 446) from a Tokyo hotel. Japan protested this violation of Japanese sovereignty, though South Korean democratization and Kim's eventual election as president of South Korea have erased those bad memories. While legacies of the twentieth century hang over South Korea–Japan relations, they have not affected commercial relations—South Korea became Japan's third largest trading partner in 1990. Relations with North Korea are another story. North Korea's kidnapping of 16 Japanese nationals between 1978 and 1983 continues to impede bilateral relations and affects Japan's role in the Six-Party negotiations including Japan, PRC, North and South Korea, Russia, and the United States (see pp. 435–36).

Japan's relations with Southeast Asia expanded rapidly after the late 1970s. Despite Japan's reparations to several Southeast Asian countries in the 1950s, Southeast Asians continued to express bitter feelings toward Japan over wartime atrocities. Japanese Prime Minister Tanaka Kakuei's visits to Thailand and Indonesia in 1974 met with angry protests. Several years later, the Japanese government decided to meet regularly with ASEAN (Association of Southeast Asian Nations) and increase direct investments and foreign aid in Southeast Asia.

Because of the increase in Official Development Assistance (ODA) in the region, which accounted for 60 percent of Japan's global ODA, Japan passed the United States as the world's largest ODA donor in 1991. Anti-Japanese sentiments did not completely abate with all this aid, however. In fact, some Southeast Asians claimed that Japan's aid and investment in the 1980s and 1990s created, through non-military means, the economic domination Japan had sought during World War II.

TRADE TENSIONS WITH THE UNITED STATES

The United States supported Japan's economic growth in the decades following the occupation. Tensions in the relationship had been more political than economic. Many Japanese citizens had objected to the use of US bases in Japan to launch military operations in Southeast Asia and to Japan's serving as an "R & R" location for American military personnel. So the end of the United States' Vietnam War removed a major source of political friction. President Nixon's 1969 agreement to restore Okinawa prefecture to Japanese sovereignty by 1972 also eased ill feeling, though the continuing presence of American bases in that prefecture still plays a role in Japan's domestic and foreign affairs.

Economic tensions replaced political tensions in the 1970s. Japan's positive balance of trade with the United States, which first appeared in 1965, became the largest source of contention in the next few decades. The imbalance first affected textiles. Nixon had made a campaign promise to America's southern states, where the textile industry was concentrated, to negotiate import restrictions. Japanese exports to the United States decreased drastically after the textile agreement in 1971, but pressuring Japan to limit exports failed to save the declining American industry. In fact, the Japanese clothing industry, except for high-end fashions, was itself shrinking, as cheaper imports replaced Japanese products at home.

In the 1970s and 1980s, American businesses pressed the US government to act against Japan in a variety of areas. Accusing Japanese manufacturers of unfair practices such as selling products in the United States below cost to gain market share ("dumping"), American producers persuaded the government to force Japan to "voluntarily" limit exports. These limits had to be characterized as "voluntary" because they otherwise would have challenged the spirit of free trade, for they required the Japanese government to stipulate which companies were allowed to export their products and in what quantities. MITI exercised "administrative guidance" (see p. 351) until the 1980s, but new startup companies often resisted government guidelines, and foreign governments ironically criticized Japan's "guidance" as a violation of free trade.

In the end, the United States restricted a succession of Japanese imports: steel, color televisions, autos, consumer electronics, machine tools, and semi-conductors. Restrictions against Japan did not save these American manufactured goods in the long run, for both Japan and the United States eventually faced stronger competitors, paying lower wages, in South Korea, Taiwan, China, and other countries.

At the same time, Japan also erected barriers to protect agricultural products, especially rice, beef, and citrus fruits, making it impossible for Japan to wave the banner of free trade. Japanese farmers could not compete with American agribusiness; Japanese rice cost six times as much to produce as American rice. But urban Japanese nostalgia for the vanishing farm as well as farmers' loyalty to the LDP made it politically impossible to lift import limits on those food products until the 1990s. Despite continuing import restrictions and the negative image they produced, Japan was, in reality, a huge consumer of American agricultural goods. In 1990, more than a fifth of all US agricultural exports, including over half of American beef exports and almost two-thirds of American pork exports, went to Japan. Two-thirds of all grain products consumed in Japan in 1995 came from the United States.

In a pattern later followed by Taiwan, South Korea, and the PRC, Japan's growing reserves of dollars allowed it to play a more active role in the US economy. Japanese direct investment in the United States increased greatly in the 1980s, though few Americans realized that it remained less than Canadian and European investment, and that those investments produced American jobs. In addition, Japanese banks bought up large sums of US Treasury bills—that is, they purchased American debt—allowing the American government to sustain the Reagan administration's huge deficits.

These shifts in economic circumstances, with Japan's transformation from a debtor to a creditor, gave rise to American anger. In a profoundly disturbing case, two Detroit autoworkers received very light sentences for the brutal 1982 murder of a young Chinese-American man whom they believed to be Japanese. Some US pundits, resurrecting early twentieth-century "yellow peril" rants, even claimed that Japan's economic success was part of a long-term, sinister plot to take over the world.

Not all US reactions were violent or racist. More thoughtful people sought to find cultural explanations for the trade imbalance. The two governments negotiated the Structural Impediments Initiative in 1989–90. This initiative contained many recommendations, many of them politically impossible. For example, it urged the Japanese government to repeal laws that protected small businesses by outlawing department stores in residential neighborhoods—the negotiators assumed that department stores were more likely to sell imported goods than small shops. On the other side of the Pacific, the initiative encouraged the American government to cut the federal deficit and argued that individual Americans should save more of their income.

Despite continuing trade tensions with the United States and diplomatic tensions with East Asia, more positive networks of cooperation have been growing throughout the region. In 1989, responding to an Australian initiative, 12 countries launched the Asia-Pacific Economic Cooperation (APEC) forum, which now represents 21 member economies bordering the Pacific. APEC uses the term "member economies," as "Chinese Taipei" (Taiwan) and Hong Kong attend in addition to the PRC. Members extend from Russia and Canada in the north to New Zealand and Chile in the south, and most are on the Asian side of the Pacific.

STOCK-MARKET AND REAL-ESTATE BUBBLES

The Japanese Ministry of Finance responded to American anger in the mid-1980s by agreeing through the "Plaza Accord"—named for New York's Plaza Hotel, where the finance ministers of the G-5 (United States, Great Britain, France, Germany, and Japan) met in 1985—to take actions to reduce exports and encourage domestic consumption. They made low interest rates, combined with grants to local governments to build libraries, museums, roads, and bridges, key elements of the Finance Ministry's plan to improve Japanese lifestyles while cutting exports. In addition, the G-5 ministers agreed to devalue the US dollar significantly to help the United States cut its trade deficit. The dollar dropped 51 percent against the yen between 1985 and 1987. Unfortunately, Japanese exports did not decline, and the revaluation of the yen meant Japanese investors now had much more cash, calculated in dollars. This allowed them to make highly visible purchases of American trophy properties, including Rockefeller Center in 1989 and Pebble Beach golf course in 1990. These have long since been sold.

The Plaza Accord not only failed to rectify the trade imbalance, it also set in motion a wild escalation of Japanese stock-market and real-estate prices. The Finance Ministry tried to deflate the "asset price bubble" gently by raising interest rates in 1989, but this led the Tokyo stock market's Nikkei Index to plunge by half from December 1989 to October 1990. The bursting of the stock-market bubble was followed in the next two years by the crash of the real-estate market. Both stock-market and real-estate speculation had been supported by the same unsecured loans. Banks became skittish, and their refusal to lend to solvent companies dragged the economy into recession. The weak US dollar in the 1990s kept the value of the yen high, so exports could not lead the Japanese economy out of the doldrums. The Japanese government was reluctant to bail out the banks, so economic recovery was slow. By the middle of the decade, a weak recovery began, only to be shut down when the government increased the consumption tax in 1997.

THE ERA OF NATIONAL CONFIDENCE

Having weathered the economic setbacks of the early 1970s and, of course, with no premonition of the far worse troubles to come in the 1990s, many Japanese in the late 1970s and 1980s shook off their long-held sense of national inferiority and gained a feeling of self-confidence. International praise for the "Japanese management system" led commentators to develop a common understanding of that system, including "permanent employment," Quality Circles, and the just-in-time inventory system, all believed to be uniquely Japanese and to spring from the unique Japanese culture.

Companies granting permanent employment assumed that employees would abandon union militancy in exchange for a guaranteed lifetime of work and a voice in company decisions. Unions indeed increasingly muted their demands in the late 1970s and 1980s, and workers did participate in company decision-making to an extent uncommon in Western countries. But most of Japan's workers never had permanent employment. Until the passage of the Equal Employment Opportunity Law in 1985, no women—and few even after that law was passed—enjoyed that guarantee. Nor did men working for small businesses, at least 50 percent of the male workforce, have the benefit of lifetime employment enjoyed by male employees of large corporations. Many of the privileged men who had had lifetime employment lost that benefit in the Lost Decade of the 1990s.

Quality Circles, another pillar of the Japanese management system, allowed workers to have a voice in the workplace. Although not inherently Japanese—American W. Edwards Deming had introduced the QC principles in 1950—they came to be seen as a major Japanese contribution to management practices around the world. Each QC included about a dozen white-collar, blue-collar, and pink-collar employees, tasked with using statistical methods to study workplace efficiency and propose improvements. Some QCs came up with ideas to make their jobs safer or easier, but others worried that statistical studies might also show ways in which they were not as productive as they should be. Employees had mixed feelings about QCs—some saw them as exciting, while others found them stressful.

The just-in-time (JIT) inventory strategy was developed in Japan and emulated by businesses around the world. Rather than holding vast stores of parts and materials on-site, manufacturers requested that needed supplies be delivered just when they needed them. Although weather, transportation strikes, or changes in suppliers' products could snag the delivery system, many managers viewed JIT as increasing the efficiency of production.

Japan's transformation from a country with an inferiority complex engendered much theorizing about its identity. All nations examine their identity and eagerly consume writings about themselves. Just as Frenchman Alexis de Tocqueville's *Democracy in America* (1835) still resonates in the United States, Ezra Vogel's *Japan as Number One* impressed many Japanese when it was published in 1979. But as in the United States, domestic writers have produced most of the discussion of Japanese identity.

Some of that writing, lumped together in a genre called *Nihonjinron* (discourse on Japaneseness) has been thoughtful; much has been silly. In the latter category, some books argued for short-term goals like import restrictions based on supposed "Japanese" characteristics. For example, one author claimed that because Japanese people's intestines were shorter than Western intestines, Japan should not be forced to import Western beef. Other *Nihonjinron* commentators resurrected inane notions introduced during World War II by American and British anthropologists asserting that Japanese culture was deeply influenced by patterns of toilet training. We know from more recent research that the notions of "Japanese" toilet training on which they based their theorizing were themselves incorrect.

An influential collection of essays, *The Japan That Can Say "No"* (J. *"No" to ieru Nihon*, 1989), by former novelist and right-wing LDP politician (later governor of Tokyo) Ishihara Shintarō (b. 1933), with Sony founder Morita Akio (1921–1991), expressed both confidence and anger. Both authors called on Japanese to recognize Japan's technological advances, wealth, and educational excellence and to stop wallowing in insecurity toward the United States. Morita outlined ways in which Japanese business practices were more efficient and profitable than American practices. Both noted that it was time for Japan to act independently of the United States (to say "no") when necessary and to say "yes" when appropriate. Morita argued that Japan should increase its foreign aid and role in international decision-making, consistent with its enormous economy. These were obvious and reasonable ideas.

But Ishihara went much farther, asserting that the United States dropped atomic bombs on Japan and not Germany for racist reasons (an argument also made by some US scholars), that Japan's former colonies were thriving while America's were not, and that Japan's national character was better than America's. Needless to say, what might have been an important statement of the maturation of postwar Japan turned into a nationalistic screed, angering Americans and East Asians alike.

Ishihara added fuel to the fire over the following decades. In 1990, he claimed that the Nanjing Massacre of 1937 never occurred. In 2000, he used a racist epithet formerly used to denigrate Koreans to refer to all foreigners. In 2001, he stated that women who lived beyond the age of reproduction were useless. Finally, in 2009, he assailed a Japanese journalist as "un-Japanese" when he questioned Ishihara's environmental policies. With all of these pronouncements, Ishihara epitomized the thoughtless jingoism, racism, and sexism sometimes embedded in *Nihonjinron*.

Although Ishihara continued to have a bully pulpit as governor of Tokyo in the first decade of the twenty-first century, the heyday of *Nihonjinron* publications ended around 1990. The bursting of the economic bubble deflated the confidence that supported *Nihonjinron* and rendered many of its predictions groundless. This did not prevent Ishihara from claiming in 2000 that "foreigners"—immigrant workers in Japan—committed most domestic crimes. By then, however, public opinion condemned Ishihara's comment, though some Japanese did agree with him. By that time, artists, filmmakers, and writers had developed many more thoughtful ideas about Japanese national identity.

SOCIAL CHANGE AND CONTINUING NATIONAL CONCERNS

Japan's competitors considered unfair trade practices the reason for Japanese economic success in the 1980s, while scholars on both sides of the Pacific attributed that success to Japanese business efficiencies and culture. All of them neglected the most significant factor: Japan's demographic dividend (see p. 369). A baby boom right after World War II produced a huge number of young adults in the most productive years of their lives from the 1960s to the 1980s. By the late 1950s, Japan's fertility rate had turned around and was rapidly declining. Those baby boomers had smaller families when they matured, so more women could spend more years working outside the home.

Thus, before the 1980s, a large number of both men and women contributed to the economy, supporting a relatively small number of children and retirees. This demographic dividend ended, however, as Japan attained the world's longest life expectancy in 1977. The rising percentage of non-working retirees in the population led to a new problem—too few working-age adults paying into the retirement system to support too many retirees.

This imbalance will only increase in the future. Japan's fertility rate fell below replacement level (2.1 children per woman) by the 1980s, and at 1.21 in 2010 is now one of the world's lowest. Other developed East Asian countries now share Japan's low fertility rate: South Korea at 1.21, Taiwan at 1.14, and Singapore at 1.09. These other countries have not yet reached a crisis, as the initial decline in their fertility rates occurred two decades later than in Japan, but they will soon face a similar "graying" of the population.

The government contemplated how to increase the size and quality of the workforce to address the rise in the number of retirees. Many younger Japanese did not share their parents' commitment to the workplace or to building families, preferring to focus on their own lives. Commentators labeled such young people a "new species" because of their quest for self-fulfillment, very different from their overworked, "company man" elders. For the latter, the Ministry of Labor recognized "death by overwork" as a condition for which surviving family members could be compensated. Several dozen families received compensation for the death of middle-aged husbands and fathers in the late 1980s.

In contrast, an increasing number of young people have postponed marriage, traveled, and worked at short-term jobs before settling into their own families or long-term jobs. Until the 1990s recession, young men often preferred short-term jobs in new technology sectors, with plentiful freelancing opportunities. In 1990, the average marriage age for Japanese men reached 28.4; even in their early 30s, 43 percent had not yet married. Women's average marriage age reached 26, and in big cities like Tokyo, a third of all women remained unmarried in their early 30s. Age of marriage correlated directly with fertility rate, as unmarried women rarely had children. In 1990, only 1 percent of Japanese babies were born to unmarried women; at that time in the United States the rate was 28 percent, and reached 41 percent in 2007. So the fact that women postponed marriage to travel—women took 40 percent of the 10

Young couple, c. 2000, typical of the "new species," who prefer traveling to settling down.

million overseas trips taken by Japanese in 1991—and enjoyed themselves in other ways had demographic as well as personal consequences.

With a plummeting birth rate, growth in the number of retirees, and insufficient workers, Japan needed to entice more people into the workforce. One obvious way would be to encourage women to take well-compensated, skilled jobs. Employers resisted this, however. Japan's government had agreed to sign the United Nations' Convention on the Elimination of All Forms of Discrimination against Women, and therefore increased its efforts to pass an Equal Employment Opportunity Law (EEOL) so it could ratify that Convention in 1985.

Business leaders, accustomed to a sex- and age-segregated labor market with men in skilled positions, young women in temporary office jobs, and older women in factory work, fought against any change in the law.

A weak EEOL passed in 1985 asked only that companies "endeavor" to hire women. Despite its lack of teeth, the law did have some effect. Responding to the strong demand for labor in the late 1980s, many companies hired a small number of women into promotion-track positions, and the idea that women could be professionals slowly began to take hold. But many women were reluctant to take formerly all-male jobs that demanded excessive overtime, frequent company travel, and socializing at bars with mostly male coworkers. Women with children and elderly parents to care for could not work on such arduous schedules. A dual-track employment system, not officially but in practice divided by gender, reemerged.

Subsequent legislation improved conditions for women in the workplace. New laws included the 1992 Child-Care Leave Law; though it applied to both fathers and mothers, few mothers and almost no fathers initially took child-care leave for fear of losing their jobs. In 1997, the government strengthened sanctions in the EEOL against hiring discrimination. The Gender Equality Law of 2007 stipulated penalties for discrimination against both women and men in hiring and workplace conditions. Despite legislation intended to improve women's workplace status, income inequality and women's access to management positions continue to be much worse in Japan than in all but a handful of industrialized countries. Japanese women's incomes still average about 68 percent of male wages, compared to about 78 percent in the United States and 90 percent in most European countries.

Reluctant to hire women to alleviate labor shortages, employers turned to immigrant workers. They employed both legal and undocumented workers from South Asia and Southeast Asia in "three k" jobs: *kitsui*—difficult; *kitanai*—dirty; and *kiken*—dangerous. A new group of immigrants arrived after 1990 when changes in immigration law permitted foreigners of Japanese ancestry (J. *Nikkeijin*) to stay indefinitely. Japanese-Brazilians and other South Americans of Japanese descent found these laws particularly inviting. In 2009, following the 2008 economic downturn, the government offered *Nikkeijin* payments to return to their countries of origin, but most have remained (see p. 425).

POLITICS IN THE ERA OF NATIONAL CONFIDENCE

In the exuberant economic climate of the late 1970s and 1980s, the Liberal Democratic Party enjoyed continuing electoral success. They stole some of the Socialist Party's appeal by enacting environmental legislation and greatly expanding medical coverage for all Japanese. In the prosperous 1980s, the LDP returned to more conservative policies, privatizing the national railroads and telecommunications system and charging seniors a small fee for medical care.

The power broker behind the LDP juggernaut was Tanaka Kakuei. He served as prime minister for just two years (1972–74), but members of his LDP faction dominated that office until the old boss died. Tanaka used his construction-business fortune to build his faction, which had links to the criminal underworld. In 1976, a witness in a US Senate inquiry testified that Tanaka had taken huge bribes in 1972 from America's Lockheed Corporation in exchange for Japanese government purchases of Lockheed aircraft. Although convicted in 1983, Tanaka never served a day in jail. He continued to play a powerful role in politics, and his friends continued as government leaders.

Following the 1976 Lockheed incident, in 1988 Prime Minister Nakasone Yasuhiro (1918–1987) and

Equal employment opportunities were extended to women in 1986, but in the 2000s men still outnumbered women.

other politicians were caught illegally trading shares of the Recruit Company. This continuing pattern of corruption angered many voters. In addition, just as the House of Councillors stood for election in the summer of 1989, LDP Prime Minister Uno Sōsuke's (1922–1999) sexual infidelities came to light, upsetting women voters already peeved by the increase in the consumption tax and the Recruit scandal.

Doi Takako (see pp. 422–23), the first woman chair of a major Japanese party (Japan Socialist Party, 1986–91), encouraged a large number of women to run in 1989. Her so-called "Madonna strategy" brought 22 new women into the Diet, resulting in the largest number of women members since 1946. Although Doi was unable to continue her winning streak in the 1991 elections, corruption scandals had weakened the LDP, which lost the prime ministership in 1993 for the first time since 1955. Doi became Japan's first woman speaker of the House of Representatives, a post she held until 1996.

JAPANESE ARTS ON THE GLOBAL STAGE

Japanese writers, film directors, and designers assumed global stature by the 1980s for works initially created for domestic audiences. With far more nuance and artistry than the *Nihonjinron* writers noted above, artists examined Japanese identity for a Japanese audience. By the 1980s, their audience had become global and their influence transnational.

Several leading writers in the decade after the war mined their experiences as soldiers or prisoners-of-war in novels and non-fiction that probed the meaning of Japan's war. Ōoka Shōhei's (1909–1988) *A Prisoner's Record* (1948) recounted his experience as a POW in the Philippines. Unlike most of the other war tales of his day, which blamed Japan's leadership for forcing Japan into a disastrous war, Ōoka critiqued the people of Japan, including himself, for failing to question the politicians' march toward war. His most famous novel, *Fires on the Plain* (1951), made into a film in 1959, exposed the senselessness of the war by depicting soldiers committing extreme acts like cannibalism to survive.

Noma Hiroshi's (1915–1991) *Zone of Emptiness* (1952), also made into a film, showed Japanese military life as meaningless, with one of the protagonists languishing in a military prison, a victim of factional rivalry in his regiment, for a crime he did not commit. Other postwar works, many written by women,

focused on the inhumanity of mindless patriotism. Tsuboi Sakae's (1899–1967) *Twenty-Four Eyes* (1952), made by director Kinoshita Keisuke (1912–1999) into one of the most revered antiwar films in 1954, showed a kind-hearted teacher who lost her boy students to the war and her girl students to poverty.

The devastation of the war caused many Japanese artists to question Japanese identity. Most of these antiwar works examined what the Japanese had done to themselves or allowed their leaders to do to them. Few in the 1940s and 1950s extended this questioning of Japanese identity to confront what Japan had done to other Asians. The suffering experienced by every family in Japan sufficed to condemn their country in the war years. Gomikawa Junpei's *The Human Condition* stood out for its depiction of the Japanese as aggressive victimizers of Chinese and Koreans as well as of Japanese who resisted the brutalization of other Asians. A bestseller when published in 1958, it was made into

DOI TAKAKO, POLITICAL LEADER

Japan's first female head of a major political party (Japan Socialist Party chair, 1986–91; Social Democratic Party chair, 1996–2003) and first female Speaker of the House of Representatives (1993–96), Doi (b. 1928) has been a role model for women politicians and a champion of world peace and gender equality. The lively and athletic child of a middle-class professional family in Kobe, she first developed a commitment to peace during World War II. She and her classmates, sent to work in munitions production, narrowly escaped death in the firebombing of Kobe in March 1945.

Doi graduated from Doshisha Law School in Kyoto, one of just two women students in the school. Her graduate studies in constitutional law led to an academic career. Known for her commitment to pacifism and opposition to LDP proposals to revise the antiwar Article 9 of Japan's Constitution, she won a Diet seat in 1969 as a member of the Japan Socialist

Party (JSP). Feisty and self-confident, she accepted the JSP's nomination to disprove the prediction of the deputy mayor of Kobe, who told her that she would certainly lose the election. In the legislature, Doi became a leader on many issues: foreign affairs, aid to African famine victims, revision of the Nationality Law to permit women married to non-Japanese to pass their Japanese citizenship on to their children (a right only men in international marriages had until 1984), elimination of girls-only home economics requirements in schools, and passage of the international Convention on the Elimination of All Forms of Discrimination Against Women (CEDAW).

After the JSP's poor showing in the 1985 election, the party chose Doi as its new chair. Under her leadership, the JSP gained popularity and financial support, rejecting their formerly Marxist ideology. Unwavering in her conviction that Japan must retain its constitutional renunciation of war, Doi remained a a three-part movie in 1959–60 (directed by Kobayashi Masaki, 1916–1996) and reproduced as a *manga*—a book in graphic or cartoon form—in 1971.

More than the war itself, the legacy of the war, especially the continuing discrimination against the victims of the atomic bombings, was replayed in Japanese classrooms even as *Nihonjinron* drew the attention of jingoistic politicians and pundits in the 1980s. Works like Ibuse Masuji's (1898–1993) *Black Rain* (1966) painted atomic-bomb survivors as victimized first by Japanese militarism and later by discrimination within their own communities. Teachers used both the book and the later film to criticize social discrimination.

Another post-atomic bomb work, *Barefoot Gen*, began as a *manga* by Nakazawa Keiji (b. 1939) in 1977 and was made into a major *anime* (animated film) in 1983. In that story, Gen's antiwar father and his siblings die in the Hiroshima bombing. The collapse of the Japanese authority system—which Gen's father had resisted

before his death—permeates the tale. Left alone with his mother, Gen struggles to survive in a bleak environment. The film probes the renewal of Japanese society after cataclysmic destruction.

Not all postwar writers who addressed the war years condemned those times. Mishima Yukio (1925–1970), a friend of Ishihara Shintarō and one of Japan's most prolific writers, longed for a return to the patriotism and emperor-worship of the war years. Mishima failed his draft physical during World War II and tried to atone for that for the rest of his life. He worshipped the male physique and vigorously practiced bodybuilding. Disgusted with postwar Japan, he formed a private militia of young men who shared his views about politics and physical fitness.

In 1970, leading four of his devotees, Mishima forced his way onto a balcony at the Self-Defense Forces headquarters in Tokyo and called for a military coup to restore the emperor to power. When the soldiers

pragmatist, gradually softening her opposition to the US–Japan Mutual Security Treaty. She steered the JSP to big electoral gains in 1989 and 1990, especially by urging women to run for office, but stepped down as JSP chair after failing to repeat her success in 1991.

Following three years' service as Speaker of the House, Doi once again took charge to save the party in 1996, when it began to collapse and lose its role in the governing coalition. She changed its name to the Social Democratic Party (SDP) to broaden its appeal to the political center, but the SDP nonetheless continued to decline. When it became clear in 2003 that North Korea had abducted Japanese citizens in the 1970s and 1980s, Doi's political opponents broadcast videos of her showing support for the DPRK and ignoring the plight of the abductees' families. As a result, she stepped down as party head in 2003, and lost her Diet seat in 2005.

Doi Takako celebrates her election as head of the Japan Socialist Party in September 1986.

gathered below mocked him, he committed suicide. Considered one of Japan's finest novelists and esteemed outside Japan for works such as *Confessions of a Mask* (1948), *Temple of the Golden Pavilion* (1956), *The Sailor who Fell from Grace with the Sea* (1963), and *Sea of Fertility* (1970), Mishima was nominated several times for the Nobel Prize in Literature.

Kawabata Yasunari (1899–1972) had introduced Mishima to Japan's literary circles in 1946. Kawabata had won Japan's first Nobel Prize in Literature (1968). The Nobel committee cited three of Kawabata's works as having particularly universal meaning. All three—*Snow Country* (1947), *A Thousand Cranes* (1952), and *Sound of the Mountain* (1954)—deal with impossible love affairs, vaguely suggestive of incest, as well as the tension between Western-style modernity and traditional Japan. In his Nobel acceptance speech, Kawabata defined Japanese identity as linked to nature, beauty, and the simplicity of medieval Zen poetry.

Ōe Kenzaburō (b. 1935), Japan's second Nobel Prize winner in Literature (1994), referred to Kawabata's speech in his own Nobel speech, but focused on Japan's need to remember the war and prevent a revival of militarism. Expressing delight that the world had come to accept Japanese literature, Ōe continued to develop more universal themes such as father–son relationships, coming to terms with disability in the family, and opposition to war. Like other recent writers, Ōe has built global appeal while redefining Japanese identity in the modern world (see pp. 436–37).

Modernity and the individual, especially during an era of changing gender expectations, concerned a number of Japanese writers from the 1960s through the 1980s. Numerous women writers, such as Tsushima Yūko (b. 1947; *Child Of Fortune*, 1978 and "The Silent Traders," 1982), Enchi Fumiko (1905–1986; *The Waiting Years*, 1949–57), and Ariyoshi Sawako (1931–1984; *The Doctor's Wife*, 1966), gained both a devoted following and critical esteem in Japan. They wrote of stalwart women, dysfunctional families, single motherhood, and weak or absent father figures.

Abe Kōbō (1924–1993) also dealt with individuals' struggle with modernity, his characters often alienated and lonely. Critics claimed that Abe's avant-garde, surrealistic style was not particularly "Japanese," and yet many of his characters' struggles can best be interpreted in the context of shifting postwar identities.

For example, Abe's best-known novel outside Japan, the existential work *Woman in the Dunes* (1962), made into a film in 1964, concerns a man, locked in an apparently meaningless sand pit, trying to reclaim his masculinity in a world in which women have begun to gain power.

Japanese cinema emerged into a golden age in the 1950s and 1960s. Film directors of the first postwar decades, like writers of that era, examined Japanese identity. In addition to antiwar films, Japanese movies addressing the ambiguities of postwar cultural identities found wide audiences at home and abroad. During his long career, Kurosawa Akira (see pp. 346–47) created masterpieces that probed Japanese identity, war, justice, and humanity. Mizoguchi Kenji (1898–1956) and Ozu Yasujirō (1903–1963) both focused on women characters. In *Life of Oharu* (1952), Mizoguchi created a sympathetic woman surviving despite the sexist attitudes of her day. Ozu's *Tokyo Story* (1954) highlighted a noble young war widow living in fast-paced modern Tokyo, who rose above the pettiness of her brother-in-law and sister-in-law and treated her rural parents-in-law with kindness.

The leading director in the 1980s, Itami Jūzō (1933–1997), satirized Japanese cows both sacred and profane: the funeral business, *yakuza* gangsters (for which one gang tried to murder him), foodie snobbery, tax evasion, modern business practices, even sex and money in politics. Itami's body of work comically and decisively challenged *Nihonjinron*'s claims of Japanese exceptionalism and superiority. While his characters were quirky local people, they had transnational appeal.

Japanese fashion also became international, with designers setting up shops in cities on every continent and showing their work in Paris, New York, London, and Milan as well as Tokyo. Although the low-end textile industry declined rapidly in the 1970s, high-fashion designers flourished, claiming not only a Japanese following but also a global market. Mori Hanae (b. 1926) pioneered Japanese fashion at the international level. After her first foreign show in 1965 in New York, in 1977 she was elected the first Japanese member of the Chambre Syndicale de la Haute Couture, the governing body of French fashion. Her transnational designs incorporate *kanji* characters and kimono-like sleeves into evening gowns. Mori paved the way for a wave of younger designers. Takada Kenzō (b. 1939), whose design house is known simply as "Kenzo," had his first Paris show in 1970. His "big silhouette" designs, reminiscent of kimonos, have won international awards and been on display in museums.

DIASPORAS

In this period, as advanced industrial societies, both South Korea and Japan had to cope with the presence of diasporic foreigners—including immigrant workers—in what they had regarded as their ethnically and culturally homogeneous nations.

JAPAN

Beginning in the 1990s, Toyota, Sony, and other large manufacturers recruited South Americans of Japanese ancestry, mostly from Brazil (300,000) and Peru (55,000), to work in skilled production jobs. Their immigration status is overwhelmingly legal. Japanese emigrants had poured into South America, especially Brazil, until the 1960s, when Japan's economy took off. By the early 1980s, the direction of migration was reversed as hyperinflation ravaged Brazil's economy. Initially, some first-generation migrants returned to Japan.

Japanese-Brazilians living in Japan celebrate the Asakusa Samba festival, Tokyo, August 2007. Although few had taken part in Carnival festivals in their native Brazil, they embraced Brazilian culture after moving to Japan.

Some of these returnees, having established connections with major Japanese manufacturers needing workers, went back to South America as recruiters. In the late 1980s, the Japanese government allowed the second generation, children of Japanese citizens, to "return."

In 1990, the Diet changed Japan's immigration law to allow foreigners of Japanese ancestry (J. *Nikkeijin*) up to the *third* generation—grandchildren of emigrants—to receive permanent resident status. As blue-collar workers in Japan they could earn five to ten times their middle-class Brazilian salaries. The change in the law did not simply bring in workers but was also historically linked to imperialism. Colonial-era Korean migrants to Japan and their descendents gained "special permanent resident" status under a new Japan–South Korea agreement. In the 1980s, some Japanese children left in Manchuria after World War II and raised by Chinese families returned to Japan with their children and grandchildren, also as "special permanent residents." The Japanese government applied these precedents to all *Nikkeijin* up to the third generation.

Believing culture to be embedded in ethnicity (that is, in "blood"), employers reluctant to hire "foreigners" saw Japanese-Brazilians as "culturally Japanese" and thus easier to integrate into the workforce. Treated as exotic outsiders in Brazil, Japanese-Brazilians also expected an easy integration, but Japanese also viewed the South American *Nikkeijin* as exotic foreigners. Some faced discrimination. At their factories, Brazilians usually ate lunch and socialized separately. School districts scrambled to set up Japanese-as-a-second-language classes for their children. Although Japanese-Brazilians were virtually all middle class and well educated in Brazil, 50 percent of their children dropped out of high school in Japan.

Some effectively celebrated their transnational status by embracing their distinctiveness. Few took part in samba festivals in Brazil, but in Japan, most do. Brazilian-style "Carnival" has become a major celebration in several Japanese cities, and Japanese-Brazilians dance in "exotic" (Brazilian) costumes to the delight of large crowds.

KOREA

The remarkable economic growth of South Korea between 1965 and 1990 transformed the country in a number of ways. As incomes rose, Koreans moved up and away from the low end of the labor hierarchy, the so-called three D's, the dirty, dangerous, and difficult jobs (similar to Japan's "three k's"), following the pattern of Japan's development in the 1960s and 1970s. After the great labor offensive of 1987–88 that raised wages roughly 20 percent, many small and medium-sized companies began actively to recruit foreign labor. Even the lowest wage rates in Korea became attractive to laborers in the developing world.

One obvious source of labor lay in China, with its large population of ethnic Korean-Chinese in northeastern Manchuria, but they also looked in Vietnam, the Philippines, Bangladesh, Mongolia, Indonesia, and Sri Lanka. The number of foreign workers living in South Korea mushroomed after 1988:

1989	7,410		1996	210,494
1990	14,610		1997	245,899
1991	45,449		1998	157,689
1992	73,668		1999	217,884
1993	66,668		2000	258,866
1994	77,546		2001	314,086
1995	142,405		2002	336,955

In 2009, this number reached 551,133; about half of the total foreign population of South Korea.

At the outset, South Korea established an "Industrial Labor Training" program. The government set quotas, and recruiters contracted laborers for "training" in South Korea. They received wages set at 60 percent of the open market rate and three-year visas. This poorly disguised labor recruitment system immediately caused problems. Laborers quit and moved to better-paying jobs on the open market, then overstayed their visas. By the mid-1990s, over 50 percent of the foreign workers had become illegal sojourners. Better registration, more lenient work permits, and more effective enforcement have lowered the number of illegal migrants, but the influx continues. South Korea has been slow to apply the national labor laws and provide protections for foreign workers.

Because rural Korean men cannot attract young Korean women to leave the cities for marriage, many imported wives from abroad. By 2008, South Korea had registered 167,000 marriages between Korean men and foreign women, with over 30,000 children of school age. This number will continue to rise, forcing Koreans—faced with the children of these mixed marriages—to redefine their sense of what constitutes a "native" Korean. The presence of a large, semi-permanent non-Korean population challenges Korean attitudes about ethnicity and race. Long used to taking pride in the homogeneity of their population, Koreans now must learn to live at home with people of different ethnic and racial backgrounds.

CHINA

As soon as the PRC began its "opening to the world" under Deng Xiaoping, a wave of students left China. Like those who fled from the civil war and via Taiwan, they tended to be better-educated and more upwardly mobile than nineteenth- and early twentieth-century migrants. Many of them stayed where they studied—Australia, Europe, Canada, and the United States—and never lived in Chinatown, instead establishing a strong Chinese presence in academe, business, and the professions. In the United States, they and their children, born in the 1970s and 1980s, became part of the category, "Asian American," a complex and heterogeneous group often referred to as the "model minority." That stereotype masks both the effects of racism and many individuals and communities in need.

Most of Southeast Asia, with its large Chinese populations, experienced less violent conflict but continuing tension and debate over the place of the Chinese as a minority. The late 1970s, however, proved catastrophic for the 1.3 million Hoa people, Vietnamese of Chinese descent, who lived primarily in and around Saigon, doing business. After reunifying the country in 1975, the Vietnamese government attacked capitalism and the bourgeoisie, targeting Hoa by banning private commerce, confiscating property, and forcing people to the countryside.

This pressure increased after China invaded (see p. 395). Around 200,000 Hoa fled directly into the PRC, but a much larger number—estimates range as high as 800,000—escaped Vietnam in small boats, unsuitable for ocean voyages. More than half of them perished at sea. The surviving "boat people" became a cause of great tension between Vietnam and its neighbors, who either unwillingly absorbed them or sent them onward to final destinations in Europe and North America. In China, they lived (and many still live) in refugee camps and remain without citizenship rights. Chinatowns from Paris to Houston to Sydney gained more of a Vietnamese flavor, and the Gulf oil spill (2010) destroyed the livelihood of many Louisiana-based Hoa fishing people.

CONNECTIONS

In this period, a deep connection emerged among the East Asian countries. With the exception of North Korea, all became rapidly growing, export-driven, industrial economies. Although some analysts claimed that the legacy of "Confucian civilization" produced this result, both the timing and the disjuncture between "tradition" and "modernity" have led most scholars to look for other causes. Japan, South Korea, Taiwan (ROC), and the PRC all succeeded in part due to massive flows of international capital, a dramatic rise in demand for consumer goods in North America and Europe, the transportation revolution embodied in container shipping (see p. 451), and the rapid development of the electronics industry and information technology.

All four had also utilized not only private entrepreneurship but also central government authority—whether called "guidance" or "planning"—as crucial actors in economic development. Japan's postwar MITI, Park Chung Hee's Yusin system, Taiwan's government control over capital, and the PRC's "socialism with Chinese characteristics" all enabled the state to direct industrial growth, to varying degrees at different moments, toward a government-defined "national interest." All four focused on macroeconomic growth, repression of union organizing to keep wages low, public education to raise the "quality" of the workforce, and flexible response to the demands of the international market through "guided" research and development. All allowed for a fairly high level of corruption—mostly payments by business to government officials—to link business success to state authority. By the end of the 1980s, Japan, South Korea, and Taiwan had democratized political systems, but, like the PRC, those states retained a powerful role in the economy.

Culture did, of course, have something to do with this success. Analysts have isolated "traditional" factors such as family solidarity, emphasis on education, obedience to authority, and "collective mentality" to explain why East Asia, rather than other parts of the world, has succeeded in this way. Some have even fallen back on genetics—East Asians congenitally work harder, have greater stamina, and are willing to suffer more than other people (especially Europeans). None of these explanations has yet become widely accepted, and the debate will continue, as both East Asian and foreign scholars try to understand why the late twentieth century brought such rapid growth to these countries.

Other connections lie in the opposite direction. Except under the DPRK's extremely repressive government, the East Asian countries have developed flourishing opposition movements. In Japan, Doi Takako represented a vocal, persistent antiestablishment segment of the population, often centered on Christians, leftists, feminists, and pacifists. In South Korea, in the face of the KCIA and the army, the *minjung* movement, student activism, and labor actions pushed the military regimes toward democracy. In Taiwan, violent repression could not stifle a deep resentment of the mainlander-centered Guomindang's monopoly on political power, and the mid-1980s saw the formation of a maverick opposition political party. In the PRC, anger at the CCP's corruption, nepotism, and authoritarianism broke out in student demonstrations and overwhelming support for the Tiananmen demonstrations from the ordinary citizens of Beijing.

By the early 1990s, the East Asian countries had developed strong mutual trading relationships. Even Taiwan–PRC trade, non-existent before 1979, began to grow after 1985, when Taiwan announced the principle of "Non-Interference with Indirect Exports to the Mainland." Thereafter, Taiwanese products and capital flowed into the PRC through Hong Kong, reaching US\$3.9 billion in 1989. By the mid-1990s, the PRC would be Taiwan's third largest trading partner, after Japan and the United States.

Taiwanese, Japanese, and South Korean companies are also welcome in the coastal SEZs, drawn by the same incentives as North American and European capital. Again with the exception of the DPRK, the East Asian economies have become increasingly interdependent, making violent conflict among them less likely. The DPRK, which refused to join the export-driven boom, has fallen sharply behind, its drive for autarky foiled by inadequate arable land, the collapse of the socialist bloc, resource poverty, and the inefficiencies of its planned, heavy industry-oriented economy.

CHAPTER THIRTEEN

GLOBALIZATION WITH EAST ASIAN CHARACTERISTICS (EARLY 1990s–2010)

WORLD CONTEXT

High drama and stunningly rapid change marked this period in world history. Eastern Europe's socialist regimes fell one by one; the Soviet Union and Yugoslavia disintegrated in 1991; and the remaining socialist countries—the PRC, Cuba, Vietnam, and North Korea—all had to adapt to a world with only one superpower. The Cold War's end, with its hopes for peace and international integration, resulted instead in new polarizations focused on the Muslim world. Iraq's invasion of Kuwait (1990) brought heavy sanctions, UN condemnation, and finally a massive international military assault (1991) led by the United States.

Post-Soviet Russia, shorn of its Central Asian, Ukrainian, and Eastern European republics, remained unstable for several years. Newly elected president Boris Yeltsin (1931–2007), determined to implement privatization of the former Soviet economy—similar to that attempted in Poland in the late 1980s—had to send tanks to do battle with parliament in 1993. His victory paved the way for a dismantling of Soviet resources and the disappearance of its vast wealth into private hands,

many of them belonging to former communist officials and their friends. Shortly thereafter, the republic of Chechnya declared independence, and Yeltsin sent 40,000 troops to prevent its secession, the first in an ongoing series of brutal wars in that region.

Post-communist Yugoslavia suffered bitterly. Fragmented by demagogues into "ethno-religious" republics divided by "primordial" differences—Serbia, Croatia, Bosnia, Montenegro, and Kosovo—southeastern Europe exploded in a horror of war and "ethnic cleansing." Actively fought between 1991 and 1995, then resuming in Kosovo in 1998–99, these conflicts brought international intervention—including an air war against Serbia by NATO (1999)—and are still the subject of war crimes trials. Casualty estimates run between 100,00 and 200,000, mostly civilians slaughtered for their ethnicity. The legacy of hatred, fear, and dislocation remains powerful.

In 1997, following the collapse of Thailand's currency, a massive financial crisis hit much of East and Southeast Asia, causing severe recession in many regional economies. The devaluation of currencies brought inflation and sharp rises in prices. Indonesians, particularly hard hit by their currency's weakness, rioted and drove President Suharto from power (1998) after nearly 30 years of autocratic rule. Although the PRC, Taiwan, and Singapore did not suffer as severely, their export-oriented economies declined in the face of sharply reduced regional demand.

South Korea looked to the International Monetary Fund (IMF) for currency stabilization in the face of huge foreign debt. Several nations experienced reduction in GDP of as much as 33 percent. Japan, the PRC, and South Korea decided to build up large foreign exchange reserves as cushions against future crises. The expanding economies of Brazil, Russia, and India

joined them in buying enormous quantities of US debt, abetting the US stock-market bubble of the late 1990s and the housing bubble, which burst in 2008.

The coming of the millennium brought not only the predictable prophecies of apocalypse and doom but also a new kind of international crisis. Computer systems, by this point essential parts of every military, economic, political, and academic control apparatus, contain automatic dating devices, with the dates generally expressed as two digit numbers—97 for 1997, 98 for 1998, and so on. What sorts of failures would occur when 99 turned into 00, reversing the ascending order of chronology? Some analysts predicted widespread chaos, so countries, international bodies, corporations, and individuals worldwide spent an estimated US$300 billion fixing this "Y2K bug," which some called a hoax. In the event, few breakdowns occurred on January 1, 2000.

East Asia, c. 2010

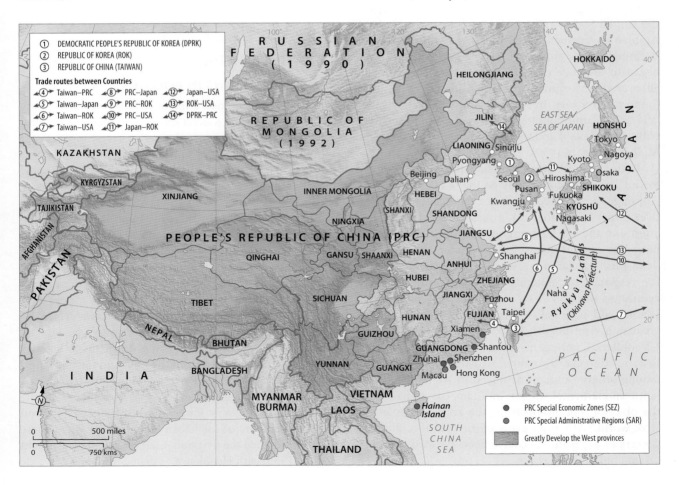

On the morning of September 11, 2001, 19 Arab men—15 from Saudi Arabia, 1 from Egypt, 2 from the United Arab Emirates, and 1 from Lebanon—hijacked four already airborne US commercial aircraft. Two of them flew into the twin towers of New York's World Trade Center and one into the Pentagon in Washington. The fourth, which targeted the US Capitol Building, crashed in Pennsylvania after passengers attempted to overpower the hijackers. The suicide mission destroyed the World Trade Center, damaged the Pentagon, and killed 2,995 people.

Subsequent investigations revealed that the operation had been planned and carried out by a shadowy transnational Muslim network called al-Qaeda, led by Osama bin Laden (b. 1957), a Saudi ideologue from a wealthy business family. Bin Laden's Sunni Islam, in contrast to other versions of that faith, emphasizes Shari'a law, strict personal morality, and violent action (jihad) against Islam's enemies—heretics, Shi'ites, the United States, and Israel. He broke with the Saudi Arabian government when it allowed US troops to be stationed on its soil (1990), sacred to Muslims, and began to organize radical opposition to governments all over the Muslim world. Bin Laden and his allies found a safe haven in Afghanistan, which they called "the only Islamic country in the world," after the Soviet withdrawal (1989) and the Taliban's rise to power under Mullah Omar (b. 1959).

Both US and German intelligence quickly pointed to Bin Laden and al-Qaeda as the 9/11 perpetrators. Although no connection has ever been proved between the September 11 attack and Iraq, by that afternoon the US government had decided to invade both Iraq and Afghanistan. On September 16, President Bush declared a "war on terrorism," shifting the response to September 11 from criminal prosecution to warfare. That "war on terror," embodied in Islamic and nationalist "insurgents" in Iraq and Afghanistan, continues in 2010, engaging nearly 200,000 US soldiers. Contingents from other countries—Great Britain, Canada, Romania, Australia, and Poland, among others—remain deployed in Afghanistan. "Islamic fundamentalism" or "militant Islam" has taken the place of "communism" as the great enemy of the "free world." Although many of the planners and supporters of September 11 have been arrested or killed, Osama bin Laden has not.

Rapid developments in computer software have been intimately tied to the growth of transnational organizations and every kind of human communication since 1990. The internet, a global network of linked computer networks, became commercially available in the mid-1990s and since then has revolutionized both transmission and accessible storage of information worldwide. Using linkages such as the internet and email, people in every country can now communicate with one another, search information stored in billions of websites in microseconds, and find and read documents from all over the planet. Universities, libraries, and corporations—most notably, Google—have developed plans to digitize and electronically store every existing book in machine-searchable format. From al-Qaeda's jihadist sermons to Red Cross disaster relief plans to World Cup soccer matches, internet technology now enables instant connections and information retrieval unimaginable even in the 1990s.

GLOBAL JAPAN

NEW DIRECTIONS IN POLITICS

Japanese politics took a major turn in 1993. The aging LDP boss, Tanaka Kakuei (see p. 421), became increasingly frail and was succeeded by an even more corrupt politician, Kanemaru Shin (1914–1996). Party boss Kanemaru served as an intermediary between some LDP politicians and the Sagawa Express Company, which had bribed them for favorable legislation and hired gangsters to threaten the opposition. Searching Kanemaru's home, police found 220 lb (100 kg) of gold bars. The opposition parties in the Diet called for legislation to clean up the political mess, but LDP Prime Minister Miyazawa Kiichi (1919–2007) ignored them. So they called for a vote of no confidence.

A leading member of the LDP, Ozawa Ichirō (b. 1942), joined the opposition and brought enough of his followers with him to bring down the Miyazawa cabinet. Ozawa bolted from the LDP and formed a new party (Japan Renewal Party), as did Hosokawa Morihiro (b. 1938, Japan New Party). Together with the Democratic Socialist Party, some Socialists (JSP), and some members of the Clean Government Party, these parties formed the first non-LDP coalition government since 1955, with Hosokawa as prime minister.

Although he remained in office for only nine months, Hosokawa initiated a significant change in the structure of government, focusing on the way in which Diet members were elected. He hoped to move toward a two-party system to prevent a resurgence of LDP dominance. From 1947 until 1993, the members of the House of Representatives had been elected from multimember districts, making it advisable for parties to run just the right number of candidates to maximize electoral success in each district. This benefited the LDP, as it encouraged many small parties that could win a seat or two but never win enough votes to form a government.

Hosokawa's new coalition government replaced the old electoral system with a larger House of Representatives with 480 members, 300 of them directly elected from single-member districts and the other 180 selected from party lists in proportion to the votes gained by each party. This "parallel system" required voters to vote for a candidate *and* a party. The House of Councillors was similarly reconstructed, with 242 members.

Hosokawa resigned in April 1994, and Hata Tsutomu (b. 1935) came in. But Hata only lasted as prime minister till June, when the LDP negotiated with its long-time opponent, the Japan Socialist Party, to form a different coalition government. This brought the LDP back into the ruling circle, but with a socialist, Murayama Tomiichi (b. 1924), as prime minister. Despite their formal opposition, the LDP and the JSP had been increasingly working together on social legislation, and their foreign policy differences had diminished as the Cold War came to a close.

But the coalition rubbed many liberals in Japan the wrong way. Liberals had long resisted the LDP's cozy ties with business and its desire to amend Article 9 of the constitution to allow Japan to play a greater military role in the world. They believed the JSP went too far in forming a coalition with the LDP. On the other hand, Murayama did assert himself on a particularly contentious foreign policy issue. In 1995, on the 50th anniversary of Japan's surrender, he made a strong apology to Asians for Japan's wartime atrocities, including the sensitive issue of sexual slavery (the "comfort women"), something no LDP prime minister would have done.

Soon the LDP maneuvered to get Murayama out of the prime ministership by forming a different coalition government. The JSP, renamed the Social Democratic Party in 1996, stayed on in government as the junior partner, having lost support from disgruntled liberals. Another small new party joined the coalition—New Party Sakigake (NPS), headed by Kan Naoto (b. 1946), now head of the Democratic Party of Japan (DPJ) and prime minister since June 2010. Kan had begun as a student protester against the Vietnam War, then entered formal politics as a member of the campaign staff of feminist politician Ichikawa Fusae. Kan's support of LDP Prime Minister Hashimoto Ryūtarō (1937–2006) earned him a position in the cabinet as minister of welfare. In that office, he catapulted to national attention by exposing the Ministry's culpability for failing to protect the nation's blood supply from the HIV virus.

Kan's New Party Sakigake, Doi's Social Democrats, and Hosokawa's New Party worked together in the elections of 1996, hoping to become a major second party to the LDP. But they failed, and the LDP formed a cabinet. Ozawa's new party then fell apart, and he and some of his followers joined the LDP coalition. It looked like the old ruling party was back in the saddle, but the LDP, without a parliamentary majority, remained relatively weak, and LDP prime ministers did not stay long in office. All told, six prime ministers served between 1993 and April 2001. At that point, Koizumi Junichirō (b. 1942) became LDP prime minister, a position he held until September 2006. During the Lost Decade, when Japan most needed consistent and effective leadership, the government—built of brief, fragile coalitions—could accomplish very little.

THE TRAUMATIC 1990s

Even before the parliamentary turmoil of 1993, Japan faced resistance to its foreign policy decisions, both at home and abroad. The disastrous situation of the country's economy, severely weakened by the bursting of the stock-market and real-estate bubbles (see pp. 417–18) had ironically provided a silver lining in foreign relations by reducing Japan's trade imbalance. Trade tensions gradually declined by the end of the century, but military issues again caused problems in the 1990s.

The United States pressed Japan to join its coalition against Iraq in the first Gulf War in 1991. Japan refused to send troops, citing the no-war clause of the constitution. Japan eventually gave the US$13 billion toward the costs of the war, but the Japanese public was

Over 90,000 Okinawans rally to protest at the relocation of a US marine base within the prefecture, April 25, 2010.

angered by Japan's financial involvement in the war. Many Americans, however, resented both that Japan did not participate militarily and that the US$13 billion took a long time to arrive. The Gulf War thus opened up a major debate in the Japanese government about the role of the Self-Defense Forces. Most citizens did not wish to reinterpret the constitution to permit sending troops overseas, but an influential segment of the LDP advocated expanding Japan's military, either by reinterpreting or revising the constitution. The United States continued to pressure Japan to increase its military involvement in United Nations peacekeeping missions and its financial support for US ("international") military initiatives.

The debate over expansion of the military occurred simultaneously with Okinawans' growing resentment of the US presence there. The island prefecture had more than its share of US military operations—three-quarters of all US service personnel in Japan were stationed in Okinawa, and bases covered 20 percent of the island. The presence of the bases promoted prostitution, accidents, and crime. The final straw for many locals was the kidnapping and rape of a 12-year-old child in 1995 by three American servicemen. Okinawans directed their anger as much at Tokyo as at the United States, because the Japanese government had failed to move some of the bases' operations to other parts of the country.

The Okinawa base question had powerful resonances in Japanese politics. In 2009, the Democratic Party of Japan won a landslide victory over the LDP. During the campaign, new Prime Minister Hatoyama Yukio (b. 1947) promised to negotiate with the United States when the bases agreement came up for renewal in 2010, proposing that the United States move some of the operations of the Futenma Air Station to another part of Japan or even to Guam. Hatoyama failed in these negotiations, and he resigned in June 2010. With an overwhelming parliamentary majority, the DPJ remained in power but needed a new prime minister. They selected the veteran reformer Kan Naoto, minister of finance and deputy prime minister in the Hatoyama cabinet. Kan was the popular former minister of welfare who had exposed the tainted blood supply scandal in the 1990s (see p. 431). Immediately after he became prime minister, T-shirts with Kan's image and the slogan "Yes, We Kan" hit the market. The Okinawa base issue has not, however, disappeared, and Kan has not changed Hatoyama's agreement with the United States.

Japanese liberals wish to keep the Japanese military small *and* reduce the US military presence in Japan, and American policy-makers share the latter position, hoping to have Japan assume a larger burden of its own defense. But many East and Southeast Asians, remembering the Japanese empire and World War II, still worry about expansion of the Japanese military. American bases in Japan, they figure, prevent the reemergence of Japanese militarism.

Japan's military role has evolved and increased since the first Gulf War, despite domestic opposition and neighbors' concerns. The Japanese government did reinterpret Article 9—the antiwar clause of the constitution—to allow Japanese involvement in United Nations peacekeeping operations, though not in combat roles. Japanese troops served under the UN as truce observers or election supervisors in Cambodia (1992), Mozambique (1993–95), El Salvador (1994), the Golan Heights (Israel/Syria, 1996), East Timor (2002, 2007), and Nepal (2007).

Over considerable domestic objection, the Japanese government agreed to "New Guidelines" for military cooperation with the United States in 1998. These guidelines allowed the Japanese to take part in expanded maritime operations. After 9/11, the government passed an Anti-Terrorism Law that allowed Japan to participate in US operations in Afghanistan in a logistical support capacity. In addition, the Self-Defense Agency was restructured as the Ministry of Defense and gained a cabinet seat for the first time in 2007.

Other traumatic events rattled the Japanese people in the 1990s. On January 17, 1995, the Kobe earthquake killed 6,400 people and left 300,000 homeless. The government responded to the massive earthquake—which measured 6.8 on the Moment Magnitude Scale—with agonizing slowness, and people lost faith in the government's ability to respond to a natural disaster. Fortunately, college students and others rushed to Kobe to help, convincing many observers that the young people whom older folks had disparagingly called a "new species" (see p. 420) actually could be unselfish and civic-minded.

Just two months later, members of the Aum Shinrikyō religious cult, guided by their leader Asahara Shōkō (b. 1955), released highly toxic sarin gas in the Tokyo subway at rush hour, killing 12 and injuring 5,500. The previous year, this fringe group had killed eight people with the same gas while attacking the homes of judges presiding over a lawsuit affecting the cult. The first attack had never been successfully linked to Aum Shinrikyō, but the second resulted in numerous arrests, including Asahara. The subway attack persuaded the government to strengthen laws to monitor groups like Aum Shinrikyō, shifting policy away from protecting religion from state control toward protecting citizens from abuses committed by religious groups. In 2010, Asahara, convicted of multiple murders, awaits execution.

The news media in the 1990s were also filled with stories of schoolyard bullies, teenagers committing violent crimes, and schoolgirls "dating" older men in exchange

A street in Kobe following the earthquake of January 1995.

for designer clothes or money. Although the murder rate in Japan remains very low (about one-tenth the US rate), shocking cases like a 14-year-old boy's decapitation of an 11-year-old stunned the nation. Horrified parents read sensational articles about students selling sex at a prestigious Christian girls' school. Some critics blamed the schools; perhaps children had to work too hard or received insufficient moral guidance.

But students' lives in the 1990s were not necessarily harder than those of earlier generations. In fact, the decline in the number of high-school-aged students made college more accessible to larger numbers, and by the turn of the century, the Japanese school week had been cut from six to five days. Assuming laxness in the schools' moral guidance, in 2006 the government amended the Fundamental Law of Education of 1947. Over some teachers' objections that this revision was reminiscent of wartime ideology, Japan added the goals of maintaining tradition and fostering "love of country and community" to the postwar law's original purpose of teaching peace and democracy.

The most powerful trauma of the 1990s, affecting the largest number of people, was economic stagnation. The bursting of the stock-market and real-estate bubble in the early 1990s dragged Japan into recession. Major banks faced insolvency. The government responded only with a weak public-works stimulus plan. The economy began a slow recovery by 1994 but needed more action. In that year, the government initiated a much more vigorous stimulus package, lowered interest rates to encourage private investment, and worked with the United States to lower the value of the yen against the dollar (1995).

The economy responded with significant rates of growth in 1995 and 1996. But private companies still feared new hiring, so unemployment continued despite macroeconomic growth, and joblessness depressed consumer purchases. In 1997, fearing the deficits produced by the stimulus package, the government raised the consumption tax, abruptly cutting off recovery. Japan's economy plunged into a very deep recession in 1997 and 1998.

Japan finally addressed the problem of insolvent banks—created by the end of the bubble—in 1998. The government set up a Financial Reconstruction Commission to restructure the entire banking system, and banks began to write off bad debts. At the fiscal level, the government continued to invest in the economy despite continuing high deficits. By 2000, these actions had finally turned the Japanese economy around, and the 2000s saw steady growth until the global recession of 2008. New industries such as biotechnology played major roles in the recovery, as Japanese exports rebounded, especially to other Asian countries. The PRC became Japan's largest trading partner in 2004.

THE KOIZUMI YEARS AND BEYOND

Known for his "maverick" positions in the LDP, Koizumi had held a number of ministerial posts before being elected as an "outsider" as the LDP party president in 2001. He put together a coalition cabinet, remaining prime minister until the end of his term in 2006, something no prime minister had been able to accomplish since the 1960s. Not a stereotypical "faceless" Japanese politician, Koizumi was divorced, a big Elvis Presley fan, and unafraid of alienating devoted constituencies in the LDP and public opinion in the rest of Asia. He wore a "big hair" style, unusual for a man of his generation, and appointed women to a quarter of his cabinet posts.

Koizumi entered office vowing to improve the economy by eliminating support for declining sectors, getting rid of factional politicking within the LDP, and privatizing the postal savings system. He gained popularity by supporting banks' clearing away of bad debts and serving as prime minister while the stock market rebounded. By 2004, Japan's GDP growth rate had returned to being the strongest among industrialized countries. At the same time, Koizumi was willing to risk alienating supporters—the LDP's longstanding rural base—by cutting public funds for infrastructure development in rural areas.

Post offices in Japan had offered savings accounts and life insurance since 1875, giving access to these financial services to people in villages, towns, and urban neighborhoods. Government agencies used the Japan Post Office's huge reserves of savings for all sorts of investments, unmonitored by the Diet. Koizumi believed that private banks would use Japanese savings more efficiently and made privatizing the postal savings system a key element of his administration. He ran into rural voters' fear that they would lose access to banking services in remote areas if the post office could no longer function as their bank. When a number of LDP Diet members refused to go along with Koizumi's plan, he dissolved the Diet and called for new elections in 2005, packing the candidate lists with supporters of his postal savings reform. In the end, urban voters approved of his bold and controversial action, giving him a landslide victory. It certainly appeared that the LDP had reemerged from the doldrums of the 1990s.

Koizumi remained a controversial prime minister throughout his term in office. Japanese voters strongly opposed his support for President George W. Bush's policies in Afghanistan and Iraq as well as his bill to upgrade the Self-Defense Agency to a cabinet post. His actions surrounding the Yasukuni shrine and his minister of education's approval of a textbook that downplayed wartime atrocities soured relations with South Korea and China.

Prime Minister Koizumi visited Yasukuni shrine every year around August 15, the date of Japan's surrender in World War II. Since the shrine honored the souls and sacrifices of Japan's war dead, every visit by a sitting prime minister elicited a protest from China and South Korea. Chinese and South Korean leaders refused to hold bilateral meetings with Koizumi either in Japan or in their own countries, though they met on several occasions in multinational meetings, such as APEC conferences and the Six-Party Talks (about North Korea) that began in 2003. On the 60th anniversary of war's end in 2005, Koizumi expressed his remorse for the suffering Japan had caused, but his Yasukuni shrine visits overshadowed this statement.

Textbooks had long been a controversial issue in Japan's relations with China and South Korea, but they reached a fever pitch in the first decade of the twenty-first century. While politically tone-deaf politicians had periodically made comments that denied Japan's actions in the war, others apologized. Although Japan's neighbors usually found these apologies insufficient and sought compensation instead, apologies—especially by prime ministers like Miyazawa and Murayama—produced domestic reactions among right-wing pundits and revisionist historians in Japan. They resented and reviled books and comments that might diminish people's nationalistic pride in Japan.

The Association to Write New Textbooks, a revisionist group, sent a textbook to the Ministry of Education in 2001 that took a nationalistic approach. The Ministry forced the Association to remove errors and incendiary rhetoric and approved a modified version for sales

to schools. Very few schools bought the book—historians and school districts, (as well as the Chinese and South Korean governments) condemned it—but anger remained high overseas. When the Ministry—renamed the Ministry of Education, Culture, Sports, Science, and Technology in 2001—approved a revised edition in 2005, riots broke out in China, targeting Japanese businesses, consulates, and individuals. The Japanese government protested that the Chinese government had fueled public anger; whether they did or not, the textbook issue continues to be an incendiary reminder of past bitterness.

South Koreans also protested the 2005 textbook changes, though less violently. Two other relatively small diplomatic issues, both concerning geography, generated more heat in Japan–Korean relations. The sea between Japan and Korea is called Sea of Japan in Japanese and the East Sea in Korean, producing controversy about the "official" name to be used in international documents. Moreover, both countries claim some tiny islands in that sea. Currently administered by South Korea, the islands—called Dokto in Korea, Takeshima in Japan, and Liancourt Rocks in English—have an area of only 45 acres (about 0.18 square km). When Shimane prefecture, which views the rocks as part of its territory, celebrated "Takeshima Day" in 2005, protests broke out in Korea. These protests have not, however, overshadowed the growing cultural, political, and economic links between the two countries.

Prime Minister Koizumi attempted to improve Japan's relations with the DPRK. Japan had been engaged with North Korea for years. During the deadly famines in North Korea in the 1990s, Japan joined South Korea in providing food aid. In 1994, Japan (and South Korea) also agreed to help North Korea build nuclear power plants incapable of producing weapons-grade nuclear fuel. In exchange for these new plants, the United States had persuaded North Korea to promise to stop using nuclear facilities that could produce enriched fissile materials. Japan and South Korea hoped this assistance would lead to normalized relations with North Korea. But economic problems in South Korea and Japan as well as President Clinton's impeachment and trial in the United States put these construction plans on hold.

In 2002, North Korea, in desperate need of financial aid, tried to reopen talks with Japan. The plight of the kidnapped Japanese in North Korea (see p. 416) threatened to doom the negotiations, but then Prime Minister Koizumi unexpectedly announced that he would go to North Korea for direct discussions. Even more unexpected, DPRK leader Kim Jong Il apologized to the visiting Koizumi for the abduction of 13 young Japanese people—the Japanese government believes there were 17—and claimed 8 had died. The Japanese public did not believe Kim Jong Il's report of the deaths, and the abduction issue continues adversely to affect DPRK–Japan relations. While Japan's bilateral relations with North Korea have not been normalized, Japan has continued to meet with them at the Six-Party Talks, multilateral negotiations aimed at resolving the issue of North Korea's nuclear capability.

THE END OF LPD GOVERNMENT?

Abe Shinzō (b. 1954) succeeded Koizumi as prime minister. Abe had advocated greater Japanese naval involvement in the Indian Ocean and supported the right-wing versions of wartime history written by the Association to Write New Textbooks. He and his two LDP successors each lasted only one year in the job. Despite the succession of these three short-term LDP leaders, Japanese politics entered a new phase in 2007, when the Democratic Party of Japan won 109 of 242 seats in the House of Councillors. The LDP won just 83 seats and smaller parties won the rest, but their plurality in the House of Representatives allowed the LDP to continue in the prime minister's office for another two years.

Continuing voter disgust with political scandals in the LDP finally kicked that party out of power in 2009. The Democratic Party of Japan won a landslide of 308 (out of 480) seats in the House of Representatives. Hatoyama Yukio (b. 1947), nicknamed "ET, the Alien" for his quirky hairstyle, formed a non-LDP cabinet that

ŌE KENZABURŌ, NOBEL LAUREATE

Ōe Kenzaburō, 2004.

Born in a small hamlet in the deep forests of Shikoku, Ōe Kenzaburō (b. 1935) was raised by a mother and grandmother who educated him in the values that would sustain his life and art. Ōe's grandmother, a skilled storyteller, transmitted tales of history and nature. She taught him the ways in which the "nation" conflicted with village traditions, a stance that challenged the hyper-patriotism of the war years. She died in 1944, and shortly thereafter, his father died in the war. Ōe's mother took over his education, introducing him to books like *The Adventures of Huckleberry Finn*.

Ōe took off for Tokyo, abandoning his beloved forests, in search of what he came to love even more—democracy. His professors at Tokyo University introduced him to humanism and French literature. By 1957, Ōe had begun to write, blending ideas from university with his grandmother's rural tales. Some early works dealt with the traumas of urban life under the shadow of the US occupation. One of his first published stories won the 1958 Akutagawa Prize for the best short story by a young author.

In 1960, Ōe married Itami Yukari, sister of filmmaker Itami Jūzō (see p. 424). His life seemed charmed; he traveled to China and met Mao, and to Europe, where he met Jean-Paul Sartre, and wrote a number of well-received works. Then, in 1963, his first son, Hikari, was born with severe brain damage.

promised reform, political transparency, and a foreign policy more independent of the United States. The DPJ's lack of a majority in the House of Councillors, however, meant it needed to form a coalition. The Social Democratic Party, a party to the left of the DPJ, agreed. SDP party head Fukushima Mizuho joined the cabinet as Minister for Consumer Affairs and Food Safety, Social Affairs, and Gender Equality. But when Hatoyama failed to reduce the US military presence in Okinawa in 2010, Minister Fukushima resigned her position, and Hatoyama had to step down. The Diet elected Kan Naoto as prime minister in June 2010.

Kan aimed at reducing Japan's massive deficits and balancing the budget, while at the same time enhancing social welfare policies. In addition, he planned to build the economy by developing more environmental initiatives and drastically reducing carbon emissions. His support for consumers over bureaucrats and for public participation in government furthered the decline of the centralized developmental state that had characterized LDP rule in the postwar decades.

The DPJ sought to enhance Japan's links with Asia, especially trying to improve relations with China and South Korea that had cooled in the last years of LDP government. The DPJ foreign policy statement on the party website—"Toward Realization of Enlightened National Interest: Living Harmoniously with Asia and the World"—noted that:

The Japanese must bear in mind that the offended will not easily forget the pain and humiliation, while the offenders are liable to amnesia. It is absolutely undeniable, as recorded in Prime Minister Murayama's remark of August 15, 1995, that Japan's invasion and occupation brought tremendous loss and pain to our neighboring countries. After honestly and

---

This had a profound effect on Ōe's career. As his son grew up, Ōe wrote several novels dealing with father–son relations and with disability, including *A Personal Matter* (1964), *Teach Us to Outgrow our Madness* (1969), and *Rouse Up, O Young Men of the New Age* (1983). In *The Silent Cry* (1967), Ōe linked his grandmother's tales, the village, and the complexities of modern life.

While contemplating the pain of his own son's limitations, Ōe thought deeply about the suffering of victims of the atomic bombing. This led to his essay *Hiroshima Notes* (1965). He next examined another victimized population, Okinawans forced to suicide by the Japanese military at the end of the war, resulting in *Okinawa Notes* (1970). For the next 35 years, Ōe published numerous and varied works—fiction and non-fiction—receiving virtually every literary prize in Japan and the 1994 Nobel Prize in Literature.

In 2005, his work came to an abrupt halt, as he dedicated himself to defense against right-wing attacks. A Japanese military veteran and the relatives of another man mentioned in his *Okinawa Notes* sued him for defamation. Right-wing historians used this lawsuit as a test case. For almost three years, Ōe read books of dubious historical truth to prepare his defense. "Nothing," he claimed, "could have been as boring and painful as reading those books." At the same time, Prime Minister Abe Shinzō was supporting historians who wanted to censor references to the military's role in the forced suicides of Okinawans—precisely what Ōe had exposed in 1970. Okinawans strongly protested Abe's policy, with 110,000 people joining one demonstration, and the government backed down. In 2008, the judge rejected the defamation lawsuit.

humbly reflecting on our past conduct, we must work determinedly to build a future-oriented relationship with our Asian neighbors.

While affirming that the basis of Japan's foreign policy would continue to be its relationship with the United States, the DPJ policy statement stressed the goal of taking global actions in accord with United Nations initiatives.

The summer of 2010 also saw a shift away from a narrowly nationalist idea of who should have a voice in Japanese public life. As his Minister for Administrative Reform, Kan appointed a woman born as a Taiwanese citizen. Renhō (b. 1967 as Xie Lianfang), who goes professionally by one name, has a Japanese mother and Taiwanese father. She was not considered a Japanese citizen until 1985, following 1984 legislation allowing mothers to pass their citizenship to their children. The DPJ also claimed the only naturalized citizen in parliament; Tsurunen Marutei—born in Finland in 1940 as Martii Turunen—serves in the House of Councillors.

While political representation may be emerging from the grip of old ideas and practices, a few areas of Japanese life—that of the imperial family, for example—remain old-fashioned and seemingly out of step with Japan's cosmopolitan new directions. Marriage has a very different meaning for the emperor's sons than for his daughters. The 1947 constitution, in almost every other way more progressive than the 1889 Meiji Constitution, forced imperial daughters who married commoners—inevitable unless they married their first cousins—to leave the imperial family and assume commoner status. Sons were not similarly treated. In 1993, Crown Prince Naruhito (b. 1960) finally persuaded his sweetheart, Owada Masako (b. 1963), to marry him. Having been educated at Harvard and Oxford, she gave up her position in the Japanese foreign service to marry the Prince, and feminists publicly rued the end of a brilliant career. Upon marriage, Owada, a commoner, became Princess Masako.

Unfortunately for Masako, the royal couple's one child was a girl, Aiko, born in 2001. The imperial succession law (1890) required male succession, but no boy had been born to the imperial family in decades. Japanese politicians almost changed the law in 2006, but Naruhito's brother and sister-in-law—who already had two girls and seemed to be past their child-bearing

Crown Prince and Princess Naruhito and Masako, with their daughter Aiko, 2006. Aiko's gender led to controversy about the exclusive right of males to ascend the throne.

years—suddenly announced that they were expecting. The question of female succession became moot when they gave birth to a boy. Masako suffered from depression for several years, and Princess Aiko refused to go to school for a while in 2010 when boys in her class bullied her. Even the "fairy-tale life" of the imperial family cannot escape entirely from social reality.

JAPANESE ARTS AND CULTURE ON A GLOBAL STAGE

The creative arts and the artists who produce them increasingly belong to a *global* cultural scene, with multidirectional (sometimes even contradictory) trends. South Korean television dramas draw a huge Japanese audience—and an even larger audience in the PRC, where over half of the foreign programs aired are South Korean. The romantic and historical tales that predominate in Korean dramas resonate with audiences all over East Asia and have gained a foothold in Latin America and the United States. Their influence in Japan runs deep, for they have spawned a love of all types of Korean arts called the "Korean Wave" (к. *Hallyu*, с. *Hanliu*, ј. *Kanryū*). Thousands of young Japanese women have signed up for matchmaking services to find a Korean husband, and millions of Asian women have taken vacations in Korea. Although Beijing journalists coined the term "Korean Wave," it applies equally to Japanese appreciation of Korean culture, which has helped the younger generations to diminish the legacy of the war and anger about Japanese politicians' insensitive statements.

Recent popular music also crosses many boundaries. Japanese artists have such a huge fan base in Japan and East Asia that many do not seek markets for singles or albums in the United States or Europe. Some artists draw 200,000 people to concerts and sell 7 million copies of albums in Japan alone. In "J-pop," a style of singing popular since 1990, the singers pronounce Japanese vowels like speakers of English. Even without marketing, and sometimes without their Western listeners knowing their names, "J-pop" performers have reached large audiences in the West through the soundtracks of widely disseminated anime movies and cartoon shows. American action movies often use "J-pop" music. In addition, "J-pop" singers like Hamasaki Ayumi (b. 1978) and Utada Hikaru (b. 1983) sing the background music—produced by studios in Japan and the United States—for video games by Sony and Nintendo. The sound of Japanese pop music has global appeal.

The Japanese culture of *kawaii*—cuteness—has also saturated the world. The Sanrio Company observed Japanese teenage girls' passion for cuteness in the 1970s and, wishing to develop a market for toys, they created "Hello Kitty" in 1974. Thousands of versions of the exceedingly cute kitty may now be seen and purchased throughout the world. A big Hello Kitty balloon floats in the Macy's Thanksgiving Day parade; she has her own cartoon show; and items from paper to pens to personal hygiene products bear her likeness. Nor is Hello Kitty alone. Puffy and adorable cartoon characters adorn aircraft—All Nippon Airways planes have Pokemon characters painted on them—as well as serving as mascots for police stations and prefectural offices. Cute anime cartoon characters appear on Self-Defense Forces' military recruiting posters. The *kawaii* culture, most striking in Japan, has international appeal, particularly in the PRC, South Korea, and Taiwan.

Cuteness found a natural home in Japanese manga, comic books or print cartoons. To be sure, most manga did not strive for cuteness, but a significant subset, manga for girls, usually produced by women writers and cartoonists, did. Manga have a long history in Japan, dating from the cartoon-like artistic sketches of the Tokugawa period. They developed in their modern form, often with satirical meaning, in the Meiji period and became extraordinarily popular with children and adults after World War II. *Astro-Boy* first appeared in 1952 and has been translated into a number of languages and made into anime and video games. *Sazae-san*, the story of an average housewife and her family, has been published continuously since 1946.

Manga for boys focus on science fiction, robots, sports, and space travel. The relaxation of censorship laws in the 1990s led to more violent and sexually explicit manga directed at older teenage boys and adult men, many of them quite creepy and misogynist. The manga market in Japan grew rapidly, selling over US$3 billion of cartoon books per year at the turn of the twenty-first century. Japanese-style manga studios cropped up throughout East Asia, where the style has become a dominant form, as well as in Europe and the United States (producing *Amerimanga*). Since the late 1990s, video games—themselves an amalgam of "global" characters like Nintendo's Super Mario Brothers—and cellphone applications have taken away some of the appeal and market of manga.

Many manga have been made into a newer genre of Japanese art, the anime film. An abbreviation of the English-derived Japanese word *animēshon*, the term suggests a connection with Western animated movies. The first Japanese anime was made in 1917 and the first feature-length anime produced for the Japanese Navy during World War II. Anime had a large following after the war, with versions of comics like *Astro-Boy* produced for television, but really took off in the 1980s and 1990s. By 1990, half of all Japanese studio releases were anime. Miyazaki Hayao (b. 1941) wrote and produced some of the most sophisticated anime, including *Princess Mononoke* (1997), the first anime to win the top movie award in Japan; *Spirited Away* (2001), the first to win an Academy Award in the United States; and *Howl's Moving Castle* (2004).

Miyazaki often sets his anime in mythical worlds best described as historical fiction. For example, *Princess Mononoke*, set in what appears to be fourteenth-century Japan, incorporates social critiques that feel modern to Japanese and Western audiences. The heroes struggle with the clash between the modern world and the world of nature, fast being destroyed by industrial greed. And yet, Miyazaki makes his antinature "villain" a complex woman who aids the poor and dispossessed in the world, displaying a modern, feminist consciousness. Some of Miyazaki's films have also been situated in a mythical European past, blending elements of Japanese culture with a European setting.

The work of contemporary Japanese architects has also combined western and Japanese elements in the most global of all contemporary Japanese arts. Japanese architects have helped to shape the environment in which we all live. Winner of the competition to design the Hiroshima Peace Memorial (1955), Tange Kenzō (1913–2005) went on to design the Tokyo Olympic arenas (1964). He also developed large-scale projects, such as the masterplan for rebuilding earthquake-shattered Skopje, Yugoslavia (1966) and the federal capital of Nigeria (1982), as well as signature buildings in Europe, Asia, the Middle East, and the United States. In 1987, Tange won architecture's highest honor, the Pritzker Prize. One of Tange's students, Isozaki Arata (b. 1931), is internationally known for his bold, inventive shapes. The designer of many significant public buildings, Isozaki, like his mentor, has a global reach, with landmark buildings on every continent. His buildings include the Museum of Contemporary Art in Los Angeles (1986) and arenas for the Barcelona (1992) and Turin (2006) Olympics. Sejima Kazuyo (b. 1956) and her partner Nishizawa Ryue (b. 1966) are one of the leading teams in Japanese and world architecture. Sejima and Nishizawa have designed dozens of houses and living spaces in Japan and China, as well as the new Museum of Contemporary Art in New York (2007). Sejima is only the second woman to win the Pritzker Prize (2010).

Contemporary writers Murakami Haruki (b. 1949) and Yoshimoto Banana (b. 1964) have huge global audiences and view their writing as part of a global rather than a narrowly Japanese body of work. Murakami's works have been translated into over 40 languages, and filmmakers and playwrights in the United States, England, Germany, Vietnam, and elsewhere have adapted his works to their media. A number of his novels and short stories borrow their titles from Western (now "global") music, including Rossini and Mozart operas and Beatles songs ("Norwegian Wood"). Winner of the Czech Republic's Kafka Prize, Israel's Jerusalem Prize, several major Japanese prizes, and honorary degrees from Princeton University and the University of Liège (Belgium), Murakami is one of the world's truly transnational writers. His use of surrealism and wit to express the alienation of the postwar generation has struck a chord with millions of readers around the world.

Yoshimoto Banana's audience is also global. Like Murakami, she claims non-Japanese writers as her primary influences. Her 12 novels (including *Kitchen* and *Amrita*) have sold over 6 million copies worldwide and been made into movies both inside and outside Japan. She has won prizes in Japan and Italy. Although some critics view her work as light, her legions of global fans consider her works an accurate reflection of the lives, loves, and frustrations of young people around the world.

KOREA AT CENTURY'S END: NEW BEGINNINGS

Kim Young Sam's election as president of the Sixth Republic in 1992 marked a major shift in the political history of South Korea. After 1961, a succession of military men dominated the executive, so Kim's election as the first civilian president in almost 30 years was noteworthy in itself. Although Kim headed the Democratic Liberal Party (DLP), with strong ties to the Fifth Republic, historians date the process of democratization from this point.

Democratization required settling a number of outstanding grievances left over from the period of authoritarian rule. It also came to mean the gradual devolution of power to the cities and provinces, as mayors and governors gained their positions through election, not appointment from Seoul. Voters gained power, and political parties had to pay more attention to public opinion. After the advent of the new Press Law in 1988, censorship no longer stifled the public sphere, and in the 1990s South Korea experienced a burst of publishing and creative expression in the arts. An affluent, developed consumer society, the country had more resources available to support a new Korean cinema, theaters, and government investment in culture. People had organized their lives around authoritarian politics and the pall of repression for so long that they felt disoriented by society's new freedoms. The big project—to realize democracy—had seemingly been successful, leaving a void in public life thereafter.

Cast adrift after the fall of the Soviet Union and the socialist states of Eastern Europe, North Korea in contrast had to contend with the consequences of economic and diplomatic isolation. Compounding its economic problems, a series of natural disasters and the collapse of agricultural production in the 1990s led to a catastrophic famine, the effects of which have lasted into the twenty-first century. This decade also marked the passing of Kim Il Sung (1994) and the emergence of his son, Kim Jong Il, as the new supreme leader.

The DPRK's isolation and economic woes generated a new "military first" policy as well as its decision to become a nuclear power. Since 1994, a series of crises on the peninsula has focused on the North's drive to develop nuclear weapons. They accelerated their program after 2002 and by the end of the decade had developed a nuclear bomb, destabilizing security arrangements throughout the region. Economic collapse and famine also spurred some reforms, and the 2000s saw the DPRK experimenting with market principles and "free trade" zones as solutions to the food crisis and economic stagnation.

SETTLING ACCOUNTS AND DEMOCRATIZATION

In spite of Kim Young Sam's alliance with his former political enemies as head of the DLP—often referred to as the "grand coalition party"—he won the presidency in 1992 with a 92 percent approval rating. Given this strong mandate, expectations ran high, and his first moves rewarded this confidence. He removed members of the so-called TK group from sensitive positions in the administration that they had dominated in the previous decade. Many of these officials belonged to the Unity Society that had included Chun Doo Hwan and Roh Tae Woo. Many were ex-military, and all came from the Kyŏngsang region in the southeast. "TK" stood for Taegu City, their hometown.

Kim not only broke the power monopoly of ex-military men in government, he also eroded the political domination of southeasterners, making way for former dissidents and intellectuals to take office. The new administration restored the civil rights of thousands of dissenters, expanding the limited amnesty granted during Chun's presidency. Moreover, Kim Young Sam

reorganized and defanged the hated KCIA. These early initiatives in 1993 and 1994 all enhanced his popularity and foreshadowed more ambitious policies to come.

In a surprising innovation during those same years, the promulgation of a Real Name Verification System (Law) required citizens to use their real names on all financial transactions. This forced businessmen and, more importantly, politicians to declare their assets. The Real Name System formed a crucial part of a general anticorruption campaign at the beginning of the Kim presidency. For years it had been possible to hold accounts under pseudonyms, which greatly facilitated corruption, tax evasion, and the manipulation of illegal slush funds in politics. After a grace period, the new law demanded full disclosure of all assets under a single legal name. Politicians and government bureaucrats were threatened with exposure. Many powerful people abandoned their secret accounts, and new prosecutors indicted and tried many ex-politicians, bureaucrats, and businessmen.

More spectacularly, Kim's efforts to reckon with the abuses of the authoritarian period led him to appropriate for the government the very memory of the Kwangju Rebellion. In a formal statement in 1993, he asserted that the democratizing government constituted an extension of the Kwangju Democratization Movement, heretofore carried out only by victims of the incident and dissidents in general. His early attempts at national reconciliation earned little response; so in an effort to regain flagging public support, in 1995 Kim announced a special prosecution law to "right the wrongs of the past."

This led directly to the indictment of former presidents Chun Doo Hwan and Roh Tae Woo for treason, based on their roles in the military coup of 1979 and the subsequent Kwangju massacre. Their spectacular 1996 trial held the nation rapt as the secrets of the Fifth Republic emerged, most dramatically the revelation of hundreds of millions of dollars in secret slush funds under the control of each former president. In the end, the court found both Chun and Roh guilty, sentencing Chun to death (later commuted to life in prison) and Roh to 22½ years for mutiny, treason, and corruption in office.

During the Kim Young Sam years, South Korea's economic growth rates became more modest, ending the heady years of 8–10 percent annual GDP increases.

Moreover, management of the economy became more difficult, because the government had to be more responsive to competing economic interests. Businessmen lobbied for new controls over labor and favorable central bank policies, while the public demanded more social spending.

This marked a painful transition away from the singular national goal of expanding the GDP through ever-increasing exports. As a middle-class industrial power, South Korea had to compete for market share with emergent Chinese, Indian, and Southeast Asian exporters. Just as labor had demanded its fair share during the Roh years, the public now focused on social safety nets. Roh Tae Woo had created the beginnings of a social security system in 1988, but it had remained poorly funded. Kim's administration now met increased demands to fund this program fully, along with cries for further government sponsorship of environmental protections and programs for the disabled. In the end, Kim made little headway on these issues.

By the end of Kim's second year in office, the public enthusiasm and optimism that had greeted his presidency had evaporated. The public blamed the deadlock between the executive and Assembly on what was perceived to be Kim's "imperial style." Moreover, Kim used heavy-handed tactics to force the passage of a controversial Labor Law in 1996, further eroding public goodwill. In the end, however, Kim's administration foundered on the one issue he had sworn to tackle—corruption in high places. A financial scandal surrounding the collapse of the Hanbo Steel Corporation and other companies in the Hanbo group implicated key administration advisers. An embarrassed Kim reshuffled his cabinet and named yet another prime minister, the fifth in four years.

The collapse of Hanbo in early 1997 anticipated even greater problems later that year, brought by the Asian financial crisis. A number of undercapitalized banks failed, bringing down several large, overly leveraged *chaebŏl* and plunging South Korea into the worst recession in its postwar history. Worse yet, the public learned that Kim Young Sam's son, Kim Hyun Chul (b. 1960), had been a major player in the Hanbo disaster, having solicited political funds from the corporation. By the election year of 1997, Kim's approval rating had fallen to 4 percent, opening the field for the presidential contest that fall.

THE GREAT TRANSFORMATION: SOUTH KOREAN SOCIETY IN THE 1990s

By the 1990s, the demographic distribution of the South Korean population had been completely reversed. In 1950, the population was 21.4 percent urban and 78.6 percent rural; in 1990 it was 80.8 percent urban, and only 19.2 percent of the population remained in the countryside. Much of this migration went to the Seoul–Inch'ŏn–Suwŏn megalopolis, which had swollen to over 20 million people. This vast movement to the cities meant changing lifestyles, the growth of an industrial laboring class, expansion of the white-collar middle class, and the formation of an enormous service sector. The rapidity of this demographic transition brought social turmoil. Social dislocation of peasants new to city life, substandard and crowded housing, political strife, severe pollution, and (by the 1970s) frequent street demonstrations had all become ordinary in South Korea's cities.

The South Korean economy had expanded at a similarly rapid rate, and incomes rose rapidly and relatively evenly, particularly in the 1960–80 period. As domestic consumption played a more important role, the economy shifted away from being predominately driven by exports. Indeed, Korea's new middle class redefined itself every decade as personal incomes increased, fueling conspicuous consumption and status-based competition. In the 1960s, televisions had been the "must-have" consumer item for middle-class status, by the end of the 1980s replaced by ownership of a new apartment in the right neighborhood and a private car. Consumers could choose from a cornucopia of products and styles, buying the latest fashions, technological gadgets, more expensive automobiles, lavish weddings, and jewelry.

The rapid increase in private automobile ownership illustrates how consumption drove change. Korea's export drive had led to the development of overcapacity in the Korean auto industry. A downturn in auto sales abroad during the early 1980s left only the domestic market to absorb the excess capacity. In 1971, Seoul had 26,806 registered private autos. By 1989, this had increased 32 times to 883,415, and it continued to soar exponentially in the 1990s. Soon cars overwhelmed the roads, tunnels, and bridges built in the 1960s and 1970s, requiring enormous public expenditures and ultimately the creation of an extensive metropolitan Seoul subway system—nine lines—by 2000. The same drama plays out in the PRC today, as it did in Taiwan in the 1980s and in Japan in the 1970s. Private automobiles expressed the new lifestyle of status-consumption and required major construction of new roads and bridges to accommodate their use.

The more affluent society's new patterns of behavior and consumption did not go unchallenged. Indeed, the new consumerism directly repudiated decades of constant government injunctions to save money and live modestly. Throughout the period of rapid development, government campaigns had urged people to defer consumption as a patriotic duty to help the nation develop. These values paralleled "traditional Confucian" frugality, ascetic values that many believed were being challenged by the rapid pace of modernization.

In the early 1990s, conservative editorialists and citizen movements, one led by the leaders of the Korean YMCA, challenged the new consumerism and sought to "abolish excessive consumption." Conference panels, public speakers, and editorialists condemned selected examples: the obscene sums paid for entertainment in swank nightclubs, competition among the young for the latest and most expensive designer fashions, obsession with luxury imports, and rivalry among the upper middle class to stage the most extravagant weddings, along with new and novel additions to conventional wedding gift exchanges.

To its critics, conspicuous consumption was socially, morally, and politically offensive. Did Korea's youth not understand the sacrifices and travails of the Korean War and aftermath that shaped their grandparents' lives? Had they no commitment to the struggle to save and work hard for the sake of national (as contrasted to personal) development and wealth? Finally, had this new "me" generation lost any understanding of the importance of collective life and the value of intergenerational relationships and solidarity? These questions plagued South Korean society in the midst of the consumer boom of the 1990s. They accompanied a general sense of lost purpose in the aftermath of the long struggle for democracy and economic security.

ISOLATION, ECONOMIC FAILURE, AND NUCLEAR POLITICS IN NORTH KOREA

The collapse of the Eastern European socialist bloc followed by the Soviet Union in the early 1990s severed the North Korean economy's only important international trade relations. These momentous events came in the middle of the North's Third Seven-Year Plan (1987–93)—its middle year, 1990, marked the first year of *decrease* in GDP. By 1993 the government had acknowledged the failure of the Seven-Year Plan and extended it to 1995.

The DPRK continued to trumpet its *juche* rhetoric of self-reliant economics, but it also quietly inaugurated

Rush hour traffic on Yulgok Street in central Seoul, 1993. An explosion of private car ownership had overwhelmed Seoul's infrastructure by 1990.

new policies calculated to reduce its isolation. In 1991 it established a Foreign Trade Zone on the remote northeastern coast at Najin-Sŏnbong. The Najin-Sŏnbong zone echoed the PRC's successful SEZs of the 1980s but was placed in a very remote area—at the confluence of the Chinese, Russian, and North Korean borders—so as to minimize the corrupting influences of foreign firms operating there. The DPRK planners need not have worried, because so remote a zone, with such poor infrastructure, tempted very few foreign firms to invest. The DPRK followed the Najin-Sŏnbong zone with another on the northwest border with China, at Sinŭiju, with similar results. Only a decade later did they achieve modest success with the DPRK–ROK joint free manufacturing zone at Kaesŏng, just north of the DMZ near Panmunjom (see p. 450).

Kim Il Sung and Jimmy Carter, June 17, 1994. The former US president's private diplomacy helped to defuse the nuclear crisis of that year.

The DPRK followed these economic experiments with a brief opening to foreign visitors and a diplomatic offensive. Perhaps as a counter to President Roh's successful establishment of ties with the PRC and the Soviet Union, North Korea loosened travel restrictions, invited delegations from the United States, and opened a program for expatriated Koreans to visit family members in the North. Given DPRK demands for US troop withdrawal from the south and outstanding reparations issues with Japan, normalizing relations with either country could not be considered. But relations with South Korea softened at this time and, relying on Red Cross contacts, led to the creation of a limited visitation program between relatives separated by the North–South division. The thaw culminated in talks and the 1991 South–North Basic Agreement that acknowledged reunification as the goal of each government. A Declaration of Denuclearization of the Korean Peninsula in 1992 followed shortly after.

Events over the next two years, however, led to renewed tensions as well as US–DPRK conflict. The new openness ended abruptly in what has become a seemingly intractable multilateral conflict over the rise of North Korea's nuclear program. The 1992 accords with the South had obligated the DPRK to submit to the International Atomic Energy Agency (IAEA) inspection regime. Pyongyang had signed on to the international Treaty on the Non-Proliferation of Nuclear Weapons the same year.

In February 1993, however, the DPRK suddenly began denying access to IAEA inspectors while simultaneously hinting that it would pull out of the Non-Proliferation regime. This led to renewed talks with the South and indirectly with the United States over fears that North Korea would reprocess its considerable stock of spent nuclear reactor fuel into weapons-grade plutonium. Censored by the IAEA for refusing its inspectors access, the North announced it would consider further sanctions an "act of war," which escalated the issue to the point that the US military prepared contingency plans to destroy the DPRK fuel stocks.

Cooler heads prevailed, and former US President Jimmy Carter's eleventh-hour mission to Pyongyang (June 1994) broke the standoff by bringing the United States and North Korea to discuss the issue in Geneva. These talks led to a United States–DPRK rapprochement and the signing of a protocol known as The Agreed Framework that structured relations for the balance of the decade. The Agreed Framework called for the North not to reprocess its spent fuel rods and to freeze its nuclear program in exchange for energy assistance (bunker oil) and the construction of two non-plutonium-producing nuclear reactors.

The oil and reactors were ostensibly to replace energy-producing capacity lost through closing existing nuclear plants. Many observers believed that the North manufactured the crisis with the intention of bargaining away their nukes in exchange for assistance. True or not, for the remainder of the Clinton administration, the United States found itself supporting the DPRK with direct aid in kind and brokering financing among a consortium of parties—Japan and South Korea—to provide the promised reactors.

The 1994 nuclear crisis occurred at a pivotal moment for North Korea. The Great Leader, Kim Il Sung, died on July 8, 1994, at the age of 84. Kim had ruled North Korea since its inception in 1948, and his person had become coterminous with the nation itself because of his elaborate cult of personality and the pervasiveness of his *juche* ideology. The entire nation mourned his death in a cataclysm of grief. He was named "eternal president," and many of his other titles were retired permanently. His son Kim Jong Il had assumed day-to-day management of the country during the 1980s, and no effort had been spared to create a seamless transition from father to son within the leadership cult.

Nonetheless, the elder Kim's death, combined with the rapidly deteriorating economic situation, created a frenzy of speculation. Could the younger Kim hold onto the reins of power without the legitimating presence of his charismatic father? In the end, Kim Jong Il weathered the transition in complete control of the Party and military, successfully steered the nation through the first nuclear crisis, and created a new *modus vivendi* with the United States and South Korea.

THE GREAT FAMINE

Disaster, however, lurked in the near future. The steadily worsening economic situation left the DPRK to its own resources for production of basic commodities. The Soviet Union and the East European socialist countries could no longer serve as outlets for trade or sources of cheap energy and food imports. In 1995–96, North Korea faced a perfect storm of failed policies, lack of inputs, and antiquated technology combined with a series of natural disasters—especially floods during the growing season—that produced a catastrophic collapse of its agriculture.

The same factors that had led to increased food production in the 1970s contributed to the collapse. The electric pumps (rather than gravity) that moved water in the irrigation systems now suffered power failures as the price of oil imports rose. Interruption in trade relations led to shortages of chemical fertilizers. And the decision to clear-cut steep hillsides to expand upland acreage left slopes vulnerable to erosion in heavy rain and floods. The water destroyed the upland crops, then silting ruined tens of thousands of acres of vital downstream paddy fields.

At the height of grain production in the mid-1980s, North Korea produced 8 million tons of grains every year. By the early 1990s, this had fallen to 4.5 million tons, and in 1995, the DPRK harvested only 2.5 million tons. The rationing system broke down, and the government left the population to forage for themselves. The resulting famine hit the northeast Hamgyŏng provinces the hardest, but every locale outside of the capital suffered. Word of the disaster leaked to the world by late 1996, but the North Korean government was slow to ask for international aid.

In retrospect, the lack of government response to this catastrophe seems appalling. How could the leadership stand by while as many as 1 million people perished in the famine? Incompetence, extreme paranoia, ideological rigidity, or sheer callousness have all been offered as explanations. The state's delayed response certainly made things worse, and even after soliciting international food aid, the suspicious government limited access of NGO workers to the hardest hit areas. Only after the UN World Food Program and other private relief organizations threatened to pull out were they given direct access to the affected areas.

In the end, the PRC, South Korea, and Japan provided direct food aid, and the United States became a major donor through the UN. The collapse of agriculture for the remainder of the 1990s and shortages since have traumatized an entire generation of North Koreans, who had already endured malnutrition and a failed rationing system even before the great famine. These conditions have stunted the physical stature of the population, and their effect on the cognitive and psychological development of millions of children cannot be calculated.

The famine altered the political and social landscape of the DPRK. The economic downturn had already required a "Military First" policy, under which the Korean People's Army gained first call on the dwindling resources of the state. In addition, the government moved to recognize informal private markets that had grown up to replace the defunct rationing system. Like the limited experiments with export zones, however, piecemeal economic reforms presaged no comprehensive reordering of economic policy.

KIM DAE JUNG, FROM PRISON TO PRESIDENCY

Kim Dae Jung (1925–2009)—the eighth president of the ROK and the first Korean to win the Nobel Peace Prize—had a long and distinguished career as a leader of the democratic movement in Korea and champion of civil rights. Remembered for his courage and tenacity, he confronted horrendous treatment by a succession of authoritarian South Korea regimes. He also brought his country out of the worst economic crisis of the postwar era. His legacy includes the inauguration of a ten-year period of positive relations with North Korea, the "Sunshine Policy," marked by reconciliation and mutual engagement.

Born to a middle-class farming family in rural Chŏlla province (southwestern Korea), Kim Dae Jung graduated from commercial high school in Mokp'o, a port city on the southern coast. At 36, he interrupted a very successful business career to enter politics, earning a seat in the National Assembly in 1963 and 1967. A fierce critic of Park Chung Hee, beginning with the military coup of 1961, he persisted during Park's 18 years as president. Running against Park as the opposition candidate in the presidential elections of 1971, he gained 46 percent of the vote, nearly enough to win. His performance in this election created his national reputation as a charismatic orator and major figure in South Korean politics.

Kim became a target of Park's government because of his vociferous criticism of the 1972 Yusin "reforms" that made the Korean presidency a virtual lifetime dictatorship. In 1973, while in Japan, Kim was abducted by the KCIA and avoided assassination only through last-minute intervention by the US government. For the next decade, Kim suffered detentions—both in prison and under house arrest—including beatings that scarred his health for life. Only after Park's assassination in 1979 was he released and his civil rights restored.

After the Kwangju insurrection of 1980 and Chun Doo Hwan's seizure of power, the South Korean government again arrested Kim Dae Jung and

Kim Dae Jung at a rally in Seoul in 1989.

charged him with treason. President Chun commuted his initial death sentence to 20 years in prison, but US government intervention enabled him to go into exile in the United States from 1982 to 1985.

Back in Korea in 1985 to participate in the Democracy Movement, Kim was once again placed under house arrest, but after the successful movement to restore direct elections and civil rights in 1987, he reentered politics. After two failed bids (1987 and 1992), Kim Dae Jung was finally elected the eighth president of the ROK in 1997. Immediately faced with the worst economic crisis of the postwar era, he cut subsidies to *chaebŏl* corporations and called for greater transparency, successfully brokering reforms to restructure the economy after the 1998 IMF bailout. Most dramatically, he initiated a shift in ROK–DPRK relations toward engagement, reconciliation, and exchange. Based on this "Sunshine Policy" toward the North and his lifetime work for democratic rights in South Korea, Kim received the 2000 Nobel Peace Prize.

Even when the DPRK conducted an underground nuclear test in 2006, the still-feisty former president defended the Sunshine Policy, arguing that North Korea developed nuclear weapons because the United States imposed near-fatal economic sanctions and refused to engage in dialogue. Kim Dae Jung died in 2009, at the age of 85, having survived more beatings and torture than most heads of state.

At century's end, North Korea fragmented into four separate economies. The military ran its own factories and cultivated fields for part of its food resources. The Korean Workers Party and state elite—perhaps 1.5 million people—had next priority on state resources after the military. The old and dysfunctional planned economy continued to exist on paper, including the useless food rationing system. Finally, the rest of the population lived by necessity through the black market. The famine also caused an exodus of North Koreans into Manchuria.

Since the famine, extensive smuggling, abetted by corrupt border authorities, has challenged North Korea's control of their northern frontier. Moreover, the porous border with the PRC and multiple crossings in both directions have led to a flow of information into the North, breaking a 40-year moratorium on knowledge of the outside world. The rise of cellphone technology—including phone videos—has also enhanced cross-border connections.

THE ASIAN FINANCIAL CRISIS AND ITS AFTERMATH

As North Korea reeled from its collapsing economic fortunes in the 1990s, South Korea had to endure its own economic crisis, in the form of the 1997 Asian financial shock, which tipped the South Korean economy into a severe recession and stimulated a number of changes in economic policy. The crisis began in Southeast Asia with a run on the Thai currency (baht) that burst the price bubble that had emerged in currency and asset prices throughout the region.

Soon the contagion spread to South Korea, the world's 11th largest economy. It was widely believed that a South Korean default on its extensive international debt obligations would imperil the entire international monetary system. Ironically, this crisis came at a high point of Korean economic confidence and pride, for the ROK had just been admitted to the Organization for Economic Cooperation and Development (OECD) in the winter of 1996. Thus, the crisis and resulting economic downturn created a trauma of the first order for South Koreans. Cascading loan defaults led to bankruptcies of some of the largest Korean firms, exposing the financial precariousness of many overleveraged companies.

The South Korean government responded slowly, and labor refused to give up hard-won wage gains.

Throughout late 1997, the Korean currency (wŏn) continued to fall in value, reaching an all-time low of 1,640 to the dollar in January 1998. In December 1997, unemployment reached 9 percent, and the next year brought 20,000 more bankruptcies. Most dramatically, Korea's GDP growth rate, a perennial public and governmental obsession, fell precipitously to –5.8 percent in 1998.

The ROK had to appeal for help from the International Monetary Fund (IMF) in order to avoid defaulting on billions of dollars in government debt. The IMF ultimately provided US$57 billion, but the aid came attached to mandatory economic and fiscal reforms. The Korean public viewed the rescue as a humiliation, generating a passionate nationalist reaction to the IMF-dictated reforms as an intrusion on Korean sovereignty. The IMF required the ROK to reform its banking and accounting practices, reorient anachronistic government growth policies around market principles, and restructure industry, downsizing the giant *chaebŏl*. Patriotic feelings notwithstanding, the real pain came in the form of layoffs of millions of workers, including for the first time tens of thousands of middle-class managers and office workers.

The crisis hit during an election year, with Kim Young Sam's party and administration in disarray, haunted by corruption scandals within his inner circle. The economic crisis delivered the final blow, and leadership of the crippled party went to a newcomer, former Supreme Court judge Lee Hoi Chang (Yi Hoech'ang; b. 1935). The fall election produced another three-way race. Lee Hoi Chang ran against another newcomer, Rhee In Je (b. 1948) of the New Party for the People, and a reinvigorated Kim Dae Jung, who had formed the National Congress for New Politics.

Many analysts expected Lee Hoi Chang to win in spite of his weakened party base, because his opposition would once again split the anti-incumbent vote. However, revelations that Lee's two sons had avoided compulsory military service—deliberately losing unhealthy amounts of weight before their physical exams—doomed his candidacy, and Kim Dae Jung eked out a victory on December 18, 1997 with 39.7 percent of the vote against Lee's 38.2 percent and Rhee's 18.9 percent. Kim's victory represented the first peaceful transfer of power to an opposition party in ROK history.

Given his almost permanent status as a political outsider, many doubted that Kim Dae Jung, already over 70, could manage the executive, much less the extensive IMF reforms, which included downsizing the powerful *chaebŏl*. To meet the economic restructuring goals, Kim would also have to alter practices in the labor market, facing determined union opposition. The general financial reform required layoffs; the acquisition and recapitalization of large firms and banks by foreign investors would demand that they be able to shed workers.

Kim Dae Jung established a presidential advisory group (The Tripartite Commission) and charged it with creating a plan to confront the crisis. The resulting plan came as a package deal. Labor had to concede job security in return for strengthened rights and welfare programs for discharged workers, and the *chaebŏl* would submit to downsizing. Finally, the government would disengage itself from the financial markets.

This plan forced Kim Dae Jung, populist and long-term champion of labor, to oversee what was in effect a neo-liberal downsizing that would ask much of the long-suffering Korean workers. Yet this grand compromise addressed the crucial issues. Employers would be able to lay off workers, unions gained the right to engage in political activity, the *chaebŏl* would have to reform their reckless financial practices, and banks would hold businesses to higher standards of financial probity. While not perfect, these reforms provided a way out of the mess, and by the turn of the millennium the Korean economy once again stood on a firm footing.

Not just an economic crisis, this region-wide financial collapse became a social crisis that disrupted the lives of millions of Koreans. The 9 percent unemployment rate meant close to 2 million people out of work in a society accustomed to full employment and decades of consistent growth. What had been a constantly increasing middle class actually began to shrink in the years following the crisis. One survey estimated a drop in overall income of 20 percent between 1997 and 1999, a decrease affecting over 90 percent of the population. The poverty rate—annual income under US$500—rose to 12 percent, according to the Korean Development Corporation.

The crisis was psychologically traumatic as well. Few Koreans, particularly middle-class managers and white-collar workers, had anticipated unemployment. Cut loose from their jobs, people fell back on family networks, straining both relationships and savings. At the height of the crisis, the divorce rate climbed to 34 percent, with a 38 percent increase in suicides among middle-aged males. The government expanded social spending, but as in previous crises, the Korean extended family provided loans, housing, day care, role switching, and, most importantly, psychological succor to see relatives through hard times.

THE "SUNSHINE POLICY" AND RAPPROCHEMENT WITH NORTH KOREA

Battling the economic downturn did not stop the Kim Dae Jung administration from launching a series of diplomatic overtures to the North in 1998, under the banner of the Sunshine Policy. Kim had promised such an overture during the election campaign, building on Roh Tae Woo's 1991 *Nordpolitik*, which had created stable relations with the PRC and the former Soviet Union. Kim's stance had long been more favorable to the North than the conservative and hawkish authoritarian governments up to 1987. But changed times meant a general shift in public attitudes toward the North after the famine in 1996.

Kim Dae Jung opened inconclusive state-to-state talks in April 1998, but they required a private initiative to break the deadlock. The Chairman of the Hyundai Corporation, Chung Ju-Yung (Chŏng Chuyŏng; 1915–2001), himself a displaced northerner, proposed a joint tourism project to open the famous and scenic Kŭmgang (Diamond) Mountains in North Korea to strictly controlled tours from the South. Hyundai paid the North over US$330 million between 1998 and 2001 for the rights and never made a profit on the tours. But the venture established that the North was interested in new relationships, particularly if they could obtain much-needed foreign exchange.

The Sunshine Policy revolved around an open-ended engagement with the North, setting no agenda or timetable for reunification, declaring it an issue for future generations. Instead, it emphasized fundamental principles of non-aggression, cooperation, and exchange. Conservatives charged that this policy only rewarded "bad behavior" by the North. But the Sunshine Policy prevailed, bringing ROK engagement with the North in line with the US–DPRK Agreed Framework (see p. 444).

Just before the National Assembly elections of 2000, Kim Dae Jung abruptly announced his intention to

Kim Jong Il warmly greets ROK president Kim Dae Jung at the first North–South Summit Meeting, June 13, 2000. The North Korean leader's polite deference to the older South Korean president impressed viewers in the South.

meet with North Korean leader Kim Jong Il face to face. The announcement caused a political uproar, as his opponents charged him with using foreign policy to curry favor with the electorate. As it turned out, Kim's party did poorly, and the opposition Grand National Party fell only a few seats short of the majority. This meant trouble for Kim's legislative agenda for the rest of his term, but it did not derail the June 13, 2000 summit meeting in Pyongyang.

In the run-up to the summit, the press had speculated widely on how the reclusive Kim Jong Il would handle the meeting's public rituals. After all, for decades rumor and innuendo had circulated about the DPRK leader's villainy, dissipation, and depravity. In the event, Kim Jong Il personally greeted Kim Dae Jung and guided him on an inspection of a Korean People's Army contingent in full parade dress. In keeping with traditional respect for elders, the younger Kim Jong Il made a spectacular show of good manners and deference to his older counterpart from the South. This made for sensational video coverage that played to an entire population glued to their TV sets throughout the three-day Summit.

The elder Kim Dae Jung reciprocated the warmth, and the images of the smiling leaders seemingly melted decades of bitterness and enmity and augured the

possibility of a new future. The imagery and symbolism of the Summit might have been its most important achievement, but it also produced a Joint Declaration on areas of common agreement. The two sides agreed to accomplish reunification independently, recognize common points in their respective reunification formulae, encourage humanitarian reunification of separated relatives, and undertake joint development. As with all previous North–South agreements, once the document had been signed, the proof and difficulty remained in the doing.

Although Kim Dae Jung received the 2000 Nobel Peace Prize, the high point of his presidency, his five-year term ended amid political controversy and personal humiliation. He could not bring many of his reform proposals to fruition, and scandal involving his sons' influence-peddling scarred his reputation in his last year in office. Corruption at the top and overly personalized politics continued to plague a democratizing South Korea.

From the early 1990s on, the ROK army remained on the sidelines, helping to routinize the lawful transfer of power between administrations. Many of the dysfunctional features of the political process awaited reform, but new voices emerged in all areas of public life. While political parties continued to operate with narrow social bases, a flourishing NGO movement emerged in the 1990s to lobby the government on specific issues or to solve independently the myriad problems of social welfare, environmental quality, gender equality, governmental transparency, distributive justice, labor reform—in short all the problems faced by any modern society.

THE TWO KOREAS IN THE NEW MILLENNIUM

As our narrative moves closer to the present, events become more vivid and immediate—we can all remember them—but without the passage of time and the historian's detachment, we cannot be as certain about their causes and interconnections. If we closed the story of modern Korea with the 2000 North–South Summit, it would end on a hopeful note of impending reconciliation, the possible resolution of more than 50 years of division, war, and turbulent politics.

But final solutions to the division remain elusive, and the story of the two modern Koreas remains fraught with instability and unresolved conflict. Throughout the 2000s, North Korea has played a dangerous game of nuclear politics on the global stage while simultaneously (until 2008) opening new forms of relationship with the South. For its part, the South continues to develop and has become one of the most technologically sophisticated and globalized societies in the world. But a recently elected (2008) conservative government finds itself moving away from reconciliation with the North.

The sorry end to the Kim Dae Jung administration left the way open for conservative forces to regain the presidency. But the election of 2002 turned on a late wave of anti-Americanism. The death of two schoolgirls run over by a US tank moving through a suburban neighborhood became the core of a unique email campaign by incensed young voters. Under rights negotiated in the Status of Forces Agreement, the US army refused to hand over the tank crew to Korean authorities, further infuriating the Korean public.

The progressive candidate, human rights lawyer Roh Moo Hyun (No Muhyŏn; 1946–2009), aligned himself with this public anger and eked out a victory in the fall election. Roh's administration (2003–8) continued the Sunshine Policy and made strides in opening a new joint-manufacturing zone in Kaesŏng, inside North Korea just a few miles north of the Joint Security Area on the DMZ. Roh's stance toward the North was increasingly at odds with that of the United States under President George W. Bush, indicating a new independence for ROK foreign relations after years following the American lead.

While Roh's administration failed to initiate any new social legislation, it did deepen the government's commitment to Korean-style globalization, a movement that strives to connect with the world while promoting Korean culture abroad. It also expanded educational requirements to meet the challenges of an interconnected globe, upgrading public schools' technological resources and mandating English language education in the elementary grades.

Indeed, during the first decade of the 2000s, South Korea's reputation as a high-tech society deepened. Now an industrialized power, its GDP ranking 15th in the world, the ROK had long since graduated to capital intensive manufacturing of high-value-added goods: computers, microchips, LCDs, and advanced machine tools. The products of corporations like Samsung were now famous for low price and high value and consumed globally; South Korean automobiles ranked in quality with the best Japanese, American, and European products. Even more impressive, broadband connections among South Korean households compare favorably to even the most developed nations. In 2010, 77.3 percent of South Koreans regularly use the internet, ranking seventh in the world. In terms of broadband subscriptions, South Korea ranks fifth (2009), with 15,938,529 subscriptions out of a population of 48.6 million, making it one of the most widely connected countries.

Equally important, South Korea has become a trendsetter in popular culture. The so-called "Korean Wave" of cultural products such as film, TV dramas, and audio recordings has spread worldwide, with exceptional popularity in East Asia. In 2002, the television series *Winter Sonata* began a craze in Japan centered on its male lead, Bae Yong Joon (Pae Yongchun; b. 1972). The popular series spawned "cultural tours" of the story's principal settings, patronized by middle-aged Japanese women enamored of "Yon-sama," as he became known in Japan.

Since the early 2000s, the Korean government has aggressively promoted cultural exports as a part of its globalization (K. *syegyehwa*, J. *sekaika*, C. *shijiehua*) strategy, embodied in the slogan "the world to Korea, Korea to the world." This brings South Korea a long way from its earlier reputation as either "hermit kingdom" or imitator and cultural follower. Indeed, South Korea has long since shed its negative identity as an aid junkie or, alternatively, as a development miracle. It now has multidimensional relationships with the rest of East Asia—economic, political, and cultural—and has decisively altered its relationship with the United States and the world beyond.

In sharp contrast, in the last decade North Korea has clung to its hermit status in an increasingly interconnected globe. Regime survival appears to remain the font of all policy. While no longer facing the extreme crisis of the famine years, it has made only incremental changes in its *juche*-centered strategy of self-reliance and economic autarky. And for now, at least, the DPRK has found a way to maintain its huge, but aging military deterrent. It has made nuclear weapons development a key part of its survival strategy, continuing to destabilize the region and threaten the global nuclear non-proliferation regime.

A newly assertive PRC addressed this crisis by leading the regional powers—Japan, Russia, both Koreas, and the United States—in the Six-Party Talks on North Korea's nuclear program in the summer of 2003. The Chinese lead marked a significant change in the regional politics of the Korean division, one of a number of Chinese foreign policy initiatives that signaled its rise to stronger leadership, not only regionally but in global politics as well. The talks initially brought North Korea back into compliance with its obligations as signer of the Non-Proliferation Treaty, but again and again the North obstructed progress to a final agreement. During a lapse in the discussions, the North surprised the world by testing a nuclear weapon in 2006 and has since declared itself to be a member of the nuclear club. The situation remains in flux at the end of the decade, and the seemingly intractable problem of North Korea and the divided peninsula remains.

Amid international disagreements—especially with Japan and the United States—the 2008 elections in South Korea brought a conservative politician, former businessman and Seoul mayor Lee Myung Bak (Yi Myŏngbak, b. 1941), to the presidency. He immediately reversed the decade-long Sunshine Policy of engagement with the North just as the new Obama administration was moderating the previous hardline US attitude.

With South Korea developing a clearly independent foreign policy, the growing economic power and global political influence of China, and a weakened yet less dependent Japan, a new era has opened in East Asia. Gone are the days when the United States could dictate policy to its allies in the region. On the Korean peninsula, only the South seems ready to embrace the new era and its possibilities. The continuing political division of the peninsula and the existence of a politically intransigent, nuclear-armed North Korea thwart the emergence of political stability upon which to build a peaceful, better integrated future.

THE REEMERGENCE OF CHINA AND TAIWAN

POST-TIANANMEN FOREIGN RELATIONS AND TRADE

Many nations reacted swiftly and punitively to the 1989 Tiananmen crackdown. The US Congress legislated sanctions prohibiting some US exports to the PRC—defense, nuclear, crime control, and satellite technologies, among others—and suspending some types of project financing. Canada, Australia, and the EU also imposed sanctions. Even Japan, reluctant to punish the PRC after years of strong bilateral trade relations, froze aid payments and openly criticized the PRC government.

But some of China's neighbors did not. In 1990–91, the PRC established full diplomatic relations with Indonesia, Singapore, and Brunei, all strongly anticommunist Association of Southeast Asian Nations (ASEAN) members. The PRC bowed to Singapore's desire to continue military training in Taiwan, insisting only on changes of titles for Singapore's various representatives to the ROC. Vietnam undertook secret talks with Beijing aimed toward normalizing relations after years of tension.

The Tiananmen sanctions did not deeply affect China's economic progress, for Japan and the EU restored most trade and aid by 1992. Although US politicians continued to criticize China's human rights record, business interests triumphed, and even in 1990 the PRC received its annual designation as one of the United States "most favored nation" trading partners.

Most of the world's economies benefited from access to China's expanding exports. The development of standardized shipping container technology (in the 1970s) drastically reduced transportation costs for most goods, enabling China's entry into every world market. By the early twenty-first century, 25 percent of all sea-borne loaded containers originated from ports in the PRC, demonstrating the extraordinary impact that China has had on the production and consumption of a vast range of products.

Warned by the collapse of the USSR, China's leaders paid increasing attention to frontier affairs, especially the economic and political integration of Tibet, Xinjiang, and Mongolia. The Dalai Lama in India, the Taliban in Afghanistan, instability in Pakistan, Russia, or the newly independent states of Central Asia—any of these might threaten China's domestic order by supporting separatist movements, destabilizing frontier zones, encouraging smuggling, or providing a safe haven for dissidents.

Both to protect its frontiers and to integrate the region's economies, in 1996 China invited Russia, Kazakhstan, Kyrgyzstan, and Tajikistan to a Shanghai conference, where they signed a "Treaty on Deepening Military Trust in Border Regions." The agenda focused on mutual security but also included economic and cultural cooperation. The Shanghai Five met annually thereafter and signed a frontier military reduction treaty in Moscow in 1997.

Adding Uzbekistan in 2001, the renamed "Shanghai Cooperation Organization" (SCO) promoted both multilateral and bilateral relations. Russia and China signed a "good neighbor" treaty (2001), and the SCO has undertaken projects in transportation, energy (including oil and gas pipelines), and telecommunications. In 2005, the SCO invited nearby countries—India, Iran, Mongolia, and Pakistan—to attend as observers, so its meetings now represent over half of humankind.

Thus far, SCO diplomacy has prevented any of China's western neighbors (except Afghanistan before 9/11) from supporting dissident Xinjiang Muslims. Slow improvement in China–India relations has eroded China's resentment of the Dalai Lama's presence in northern India. China protested India's development of nuclear weapons, but they regularly exchange high-level visits and have reopened several roads over the Himalayas. They also meet at the occasional summit meetings of BRIC—Brazil, Russia, India, China—the world's largest emerging economies.

The PRC has effectively used nationalism and mistrust of foreigners' motives to create strong domestic support for its international policies. This patriotic defensiveness appears most vividly at moments of crisis—when India tested its first nuclear weapon (1998), when an American warplane accidentally bombed the PRC Embassy in Belgrade (1999), when Japanese government officials denied the Nanjing Massacre (2007), when Tibetan dissidents rioted in the run-up to the 2008 Olympics. The PRC can produce overwhelming demonstrations of domestic unity and also count on tens of millions of ethnic Chinese living outside the PRC to confront those branded as China's adversaries.

DENG'S LAST YEARS

Already 85 years old in 1989, Deng Xiaoping decided to phase himself out of everyday political life, so he resigned as chair of the Central Military Commission. Ensuring orderly succession to his role as "paramount leader," he chose Jiang Zemin (b. 1926) to replace Zhao Ziyang as Party general secretary. Trained as

an engineer, Jiang had worked in China's infant automobile industry before beginning a steady rise within the CCP. Minister of electronic industries in the early 1980s, he then became both mayor and Party secretary of Shanghai, China's largest and most advanced city.

Shanghai thrived under the 1980s reforms, and Jiang developed a reputation for being both cosmopolitan—he could converse in Russian and English and often sang foreign songs—and a tough opponent of political reform. During the Tiananmen crisis, he kept order in Shanghai, shutting down a newspaper sympathetic to the students, and Beijing noticed. Jiang was appointed over Premier Li Peng, another engineer, known to prefer Chen Yun's more centralized, less "reformed" economic vision. Jiang Zemin immediately replaced Deng as chair of the Central Military Commission and took Yang Shangkun's office as president in 1993.

Deng Xiaoping had resigned but remained the most influential man in Beijing, standing behind Jiang Zemin. Li Peng, with Chen Yun's backing, continued to criticize China's market reforms and advocated retention of central economic planning, with substantial approval from Party leaders. To protect "socialism with Chinese characteristics," in early 1992 Deng went on the offensive in a manner that would have pleased the Qianlong Emperor. He undertook a "southern tour" (using the Qing term for an "imperial journey"), visiting Wuhan, the

Zhuo Lin and Deng Xiaoping in the Taihang Mountains shortly after their marriage in Yan'an, 1939.

Zhuo Lin laying flowers on Deng Xiaoping's coffin, February 1997.

Guangzhou area, Shanghai, and two SEZs—Shenzhen, near Hong Kong, and Zhuhai, near Macao.

Only months later did the *People's Daily* report four important speeches he gave on the tour, which we now know indicated conflict at the Party center. The Hong Kong newspapers, however, widely publicized his arguments for continuing economic reform, allegiance to the "four cardinal principles" of Party dictatorship, and further "seeking truth from facts." The positive popular response, especially in the south, ensured at least a temporary victory over Chen Yun.

The 1992 rivalry between Party elders—Deng Xiaoping (now 88) and Chen Yun (only a year younger)—demonstrated Jiang Zemin and Li Peng's dependence on their patrons. The army gained ground as a mediator, and the 14th Party Congress (October 1992) elected a Central Committee with 25 percent military membership. The military men continued to press for a stronger stand against the United States, especially regarding Tibet and Taiwan. Deng finally conceded that "hegemonism" (a code word for US power) still constituted a threat to the PRC's unity and sovereignty. The Congress gave Deng Xiaoping, who made a brief appearance, a heartfelt ovation of gratitude.

Deng Xiaoping died of Parkinson's disease on February 19, 1997. In his funeral eulogy, Jiang Zemin equated Deng's contribution to China's progress with Mao's and assured the 10,000 guests that the Party would persist in the directions Deng had pioneered: socialism with Chinese characteristics, maintenance of the Party's dictatorial power, fervent nationalism, and opening to the world. The years since 1997 have seen China's leaders attempting to achieve all of Deng's goals, which some analysts find mutually incompatible, in a world both promising for and threatening to CCP rule.

THE PRC AT THE MILLENNIUM: GLOBALIZATION AND DOMESTIC CONTROL

Like the leaders of the Soviet Union after Khrushchev, most of China's recent top-level leaders have been university-trained engineers, a profession both prestigious and patriotic in rapidly industrializing economies. Deng Xiaoping, the last "old revolutionary," passed the status of "paramount leader" to Jiang Zemin, succeeded by Hu Jintao (b. 1942), both of whom simultaneously served as general secretary of the CCP, president of the PRC, and chairman of the Central Military Commission.

As in any centralized state, whether autocratic or democratic, the character and connections of the top politicians matter a great deal (compare the US president or British prime minister). Jiang Zemin and his colleagues—many of them from Shanghai—had to work both with and against the military, which had its own factional infighting, and rival civilian factions, such as those led by Premier Li Peng and his successors, Zhu Rongji (b. 1928) and Wen Jiabao (b. 1942). Far from being obscure or faceless bureaucrats, these men occupy the highest-profile offices in China. Their decisions, personalities, lifestyles, and relationships with one another constitute part of the daily business of Chinese life, especially in Beijing. Like any capital city, Beijing thrives on political gossip. Officials and cabdrivers, shopkeepers and customers speculate on the latest scandal or intra-Party scuffle, just as they did under the Empress Dowager or Yuan Shikai.

Jiang Zemin's presidency saw the PRC's economy continue to grow at a rapid, some say overheated, rate. During the 1990s, the PRC pegged its currency, the yuan (also called renminbi, "the people's currency"), to the US dollar, which kept prices for Chinese goods low in the US market. This policy, about which many Americans complained because it damaged US employment, was revised in 2005. After the yuan appreciated gradually for several years, the world economic crisis of 2008 forced the PRC to reconnect the yuan to the US dollar and shelter the PRC from some of the economic shocks of 2008–10. But in 2010 some American economists and politicians again called for the PRC to revalue the yuan, raising the prices of Chinese exports and making US goods more affordable in China.

China's economic growth has accelerated and broadened rapidly since 2001, when the PRC joined the World Trade Organization (WTO), the international body that provides regulation, negotiation, and conflict resolution for international trade. In its initial application, the PRC requested classification as a developing country, citing its low per capita GDP and huge population below the poverty line. But the WTO took the enormous size of its economy, the continuing power of central planning, and the economic boom of the 1980s as evidence that China should not be treated as an ordinary developing country.

As a result of WTO pressure, the PRC agreed to liberalize aspects of its domestic market and to open its economic processes to greater international transparency. WTO rules also require China to develop its legal system quickly, a process already begun in commercial and civil law. The PRC has thus far resisted international demands for political reform, but greater exposure to the world market will certainly generate many unintended consequences. The WTO is one of few international organizations to which the PRC and the ROC (Taiwan) both belong.

The bare statistics of China's economic growth since 1989 look impossible. Per capita GDP has multiplied more than ten times in less than 20 years, at rates of 7–14 percent per year. China now produces 44 percent of the world's cement and has become the world's second-largest energy producer. About 65 percent of that energy comes from burning coal, and in 2007 the PRC opened two new coal-fired generator plants *per week*. By 2010 the PRC, a developing economy in 1989, held the world's largest foreign exchange reserves, over US$2.4 trillion.

In 2009, China produced more than twice as many automobiles as the United States, 13.8 million, almost all for the domestic market, an increase of more than 15 times since 1989. That places the PRC in structural competition with other petroleum-consuming countries, affecting relations with oil producers (such as Iran and Nigeria) and oil consumers (such as Japan, the EU, and the United States). Not coincidentally, China is also the world's largest producer of renewable energy, wind turbines, and solar panels. The PRC's leaders recognize

that neither petroleum nor coal can constitute the sole basis for a twenty-first-century economy.

The Three Gorges Dam, the world's largest electricity-generating plant, was first proposed by Sun Yat-sen in 1919. Completed in 2008 and fully operational by 2011, it has displaced over a million people, created a reservoir over 400 miles (643 km) long, and caused significant environmental changes such as landslides and erosion. Scholars, journalists, and engineers continue to argue: Is it an engineering triumph and enduring source of renewable energy, as its builders claim, or a grandiose and dangerous experiment, threatening hundreds of millions of people living downstream?

China's coal-dependent energy industry has produced some of the world's worst air pollution, and its water has been fouled by every manner of organic and inorganic waste. Local politicians make both money and prestige by protecting polluting industries. Even in the highly centralized party-state, locals usually win the conflict against central regulators, who lack both personnel and incentives to overcome local money and power networks. A prohibition on retailers using plastic bags has resulted in a 10 percent drop in usage, but 700 million rural Chinese lack access to clean water, and most urban groundwater is contaminated.

The effects of China's rapid economic growth on its citizens have varied widely. Some have become enormously wealthy, while others remain mired in poverty. Some have traveled the world for business, education, or pleasure. Some have relocated from villages to towns and cities, working long hours for low wages. Some have stayed home on the farm. New cities, new professions, new economic forms, and new opportunities have enabled some Chinese to live very different lives from their parents, but this transformation has required many other Chinese to stay poor, or even get poorer.

Still acknowledging the necessity for uneven development, in 1999 the PRC began to use state investment to stimulate the country's less populated, more isolated western half under the slogan, "Greatly Develop the West!" Headed by Premier Zhu Rongji, this ambitious plan has invested trillions of yuan in infrastructure, education, environmental protection, and pipelines. Despite this huge outlay, eastern China continues to outstrip the west in growth. Minority peoples, in particular, have not received proportionate shares of jobs or subsidies. Some dissident leaders claim that even educational benefits have gone primarily to Chinese migrants rather than indigenous peoples, and some frontier peoples resent the influx of settlers brought by new highways and railroads into what they see as their homelands.

Uneven development continues to create striking gaps in privilege and lifestyle between PRC citizens, clearly visible in a well-studied single-lineage village in Guangdong province. In the mid-1960s, this impoverished rice-growing village could not even find wives for its sons. Urban youth sent there during the Cultural Revolution reported widespread illiteracy, tiny incomes, and hard scrambling for basic food and shelter. But the village lay close enough to Hong Kong for discontented peasants to flee to the British colony, swimming for many hours in search of better pay.

In the early 1980s, Hong Kong capital began to make its way into China to fuel the economic boom, with astonishing effects. In 2010, the village has *no agricultural land at all*, only row upon row of factory buildings and dormitories for migrant workers. The hills behind the village have been leveled, the dirt trucked to the sea for landfill, and the new flatland rapidly paved and built up. Restaurants and strip malls line the "village" streets.

Villagers can reach Hong Kong by light rail, and almost all the ex-farmers from the original lineage have become real-estate developers. The 1,000+ members of that core lineage now share their "village" with more than *50,000* migrants who work in the factories, many for less than US$100 per month. Mostly from other provinces, they have no legal right to be there, no social services, and no stake in the success of the village. The members of the Communist Party committee that serves as the village government—formerly the "local emperors" who dominated village politics—receive annual bonuses of 200,000 yuan (US$30,000) each.[1]

Begun in 1994 and completed in 2008, the Three Gorges Dam is 7,661 feet (2,335 m) long and contains a reservoir covering 403 square miles (1045 square km).

That one village's story reveals a transformative, complex, and problematic fact: huge numbers of rural residents have moved to towns and cities, creating a giant and unstable class of migrant laborers, as many as 150 million people. Constrained by the PRC's household registration (C. *hukou*) system until 1978, rural people now leave the villages for wage-paying jobs. The TVEs, SEZs, and new factories all over China could not function without them. The state regards them as temporary residents and does not provide them with any urban social benefits. They thus constitute a second-class citizenry, often despised by city-dwellers, unprotected from exploitative conditions in the workplace or on the street. Many urbanites fear migrants as sources of crime, disease, and potential disorder, and they worry about the implications of this huge underclass.

Predictably, the rapid increase in the size of the Chinese economy, added to the CCP's monopoly on political power, has generated a culture of corruption at every level of government. Businesses making huge profits bribe low-paid officials to circumvent antipollution regulations, obtain licenses to monopolize markets, and construct substandard buildings. Officials with power to approve or block business expansion find themselves wined, dined, and gifted, even hosted by in-house corporate brothels. Although some officials—such as former premier Zhu Rongji—maintain positive reputations, ordinary Chinese citizens complain that *all* government cadres demand illegal money for their official functions and informal influence.

Nor is corruption the only crime flourishing in the PRC. Smuggling, tax evasion, kidnapping of young girls (see p. 398), extortion, and protection rackets have appeared throughout the country. Prostitution and the illicit drug trade, effectively shut down during the Maoist period, have reemerged. Opium smuggling, from producers in Southeast Asia and Afghanistan, makes some frontiers unstable and dangerous. Prostitutes, from high-class call girls with cellphones and limo service to streetwalkers serving migrant laborers, may be found in every city and town.

Critical intellectuals, still "worrying for the country and the people," have debated how China can reform its society and culture, even its soul. Far from concluding unanimously that, "democracy is the only way to fix China," they have created a bedlam of theories, explanations, and solutions for their country's problems.

Contemporary Chinese intellectuals have considerable latitude to speak publicly, as long as they do not violate the "four cardinal principles" of CCP dominance. The existence of a well-organized, effective state makes the contemporary scene very different from that of the May Fourth era. Like earlier iconoclasts, however, twenty-first-century Chinese intellectuals recommend a hodge-podge of solutions, from socialism to capitalism, Confucianism to Buddhism, eugenic engineering to "improving the quality of the people." No single voice or system of ideas has prevailed among the regime's critics, so Party authority remains publicly unchallenged, if not unquestioned in private.

The PRC permits many kinds of public demonstrations, from obviously pro-government gatherings vilifying Tibetan rioters to rallies against unsafe working conditions or corrupt local officials. This type of resistance tends to be "single-issue," focused on *local* environmental, economic, or political problems. Sometimes work-teams of officials mediate such disputes, while others result in legal penalties.

Although labor organizing outside the All-China Federation of Labor Unions remains illegal, strikes and other labor actions have been taking place in China for years. In 2010, for example, international media reported a violent strike at a Honda plant in Shenzhen, resolved with a 24 percent wage hike. A Taiwan-owned electronics firm making iPhone and iPad components offered workers a 66 percent raise after ten young migrant workers killed themselves, apparently to obtain large compensation packages for their families.

China is one of only a few countries where more women than men commit suicide. Based on incomplete statistics, scholars have concluded that young rural women help to create this anomaly. Some kill themselves to escape dreadful conditions—kidnapped and sold to bride-less families, blamed and abused for not producing a son—in a time-honored form of social resistance. The birth control rules have made them more vulnerable. "Causing a person to commit suicide" carries a social stigma and may even be prosecuted as a crime, so a young woman, otherwise helpless in the control of her husband's family, may take this route to end her own suffering *and* attack those who torment her.

The birth control regulations have also created skewed sex ratios in some parts of China as ultrasound testing makes selective abortion possible. Recent scholarship has shown, however, that many Chinese families want very much to have a daughter, though they continue to *need* a son, and that adoption of girls inside China has become a desirable option. The PRC, however, allows domestic adoption only under specific circumstances—both parents over 35 years of age and childless, in some provinces. Thus, many families cannot achieve what is widely regarded as the ideal household, one son *and* one daughter.

RELIGION AND FALUN GONG

The post-Mao reforms have allowed a multifaceted and widespread revival of religion in China. From Buddhist and Daoist adepts to Christians of every kind to Islamic revivalists, believers have disagreed with their officially atheist government. Although "freedom of religion" is constitutionally guaranteed, the state takes a very narrow view of what constitutes "religion." "Illegal religious activity" remains a serious crime, to be prosecuted selectively but brutally if religion intersects with politics.

Hundreds of millions of Chinese practice some form or other of *qigong*. Meaning "breath exercise" or "energy cultivation," *qigong* originated in ancient physical and spiritual practices designed to foster health and longevity (even immortality). Containing elements of athletics, healing, philosophy, psychology, and religion, *qigong* has spread widely to all regions and levels of Chinese society. In 1992, during a *qigong* boom, Li Hongzhi (b. 1951 or 1952) introduced a new *qigong* system, derived from Buddhist, Daoist, and folk religious practice (all legal in China), calling it *Falun Gong*, "the *Qigong* of the Dharma Wheel." Li and his disciples taught physical exercises and Buddhist-Daoist-Confucian values, rejecting materialism and science in favor of miracles, millennial prophecies, and conservative social behavior. The movement soon claimed tens of millions of adherents, including many CCP members.

Noting Falun Gong's immense popularity, and Li Hongzhi's departure for residence overseas (1998), the PRC government began to crack down. When Tianjin police arrested several dozen adherents (1999), the movement planned and carried out an audacious response. Over 10,000 Falun Gong members appeared without warning, silent and orderly, directly outside the gates of the highest leadership's compound in Beijing.

No one in authority had known what was coming, and that deeply worried Party leaders, accustomed to effective intelligence and control.

The PRC banned Falun Gong that summer, calling it "heterodox teaching" (translated as "evil cult"), the same criminal label that the Qing attached to the Taipings. Since then, numerous adherents have been jailed, tortured, and executed, countered by international protests and high-profile awards to Li Hongzhi, who lives in the United States. From the PRC's perspective, some forms of *qigong* may be socially positive and patriotic, but the political will to confront the state must be the mark of an "evil cult."

THE GREAT FIREWALL AND TRANSNATIONAL DISEASES

Within China's peculiar pattern of opening to the world—economic globalization without political reform—the PRC has tried to prevent "bourgeois liberalization" by controlling information flows and content. But the sheer volume of communication and contact between its citizens and the rest of the world, whether direct (through travel) or written (electronic and printed), has challenged the party-state's resources and resolve.

With its hundreds of millions of computers, rapidly expanding middle class, and high-tech industries, China is a major growth market for search engines such as Google and Yahoo. But the PRC government, allowing only its own version of events (and reality) to be disseminated within its borders, has created a "Great Firewall of China." Officially called the "Golden Shield Project," this sophisticated censorship apparatus foils many citizens' attempts to obtain information the PRC judges to be subversive, destabilizing, or illegal. This includes not only pornography but also images of Tiananmen such as the "tank man" (see p. 403) and names of Chinese dissidents such as Fang Lizhi (see p. 399).

In early 2006, Google launched a Chinese-language version of its search engine—google.cn—announcing that it would comply with the internal censorship regime of the PRC. This compromise of free information flow grew controversial, as Google discovered that the PRC government not only censored but also utilized Google systems to spy on human rights activists, obtain valuable source codes for software, and hack into "secure" corporate databases.

The confrontation became public in early 2010. US Secretary of State Hillary Clinton criticized China's internet censorship, and Chinese commentators characterized Google as a component of US worldwide hegemony based on "Western values." On March 22, 2010, Google redirected all China-based searches to google.com.hk, its Hong Kong site. A week later, the PRC government briefly banned searches on *all* Google sites, regardless of their location, and PRC media continue to blast Google as anti-China. Analysts estimate that about 10 percent of internet users in China can circumvent the Great Firewall and the other 90 percent see no need to do so. Google's market share has fallen steadily with the rise of Baidu, a Chinese search engine that now holds nearly two-thirds of the market and complies unquestioningly with state censorship.

Post-reform China has opened not only to information but also to microbes. As tens of millions of people move in and out of China every year—tourists, students, scholars, businesspeople—so do diseases. Scientists found HIV/AIDS in China in 1984, and by 1998 cases had been reported in all provinces, spread primarily through tainted blood products and blood banks. In Henan, a huge network of commercial blood purchasing stations, using contaminated needles and processes, infected tens of thousands of donors. Prostitution and illegal drug use have recently become more common HIV transmitters, especially in the southwestern province of Yunnan, where domestic sex tourism has grown rapidly and opiates easily cross the border from "the Golden Triangle" of Southeast Asia. Of China's HIV-infected citizens—estimates range from 650,000 to 1.5 million—25 percent live in Yunnan.

The PRC government has been criticized for its slow and inconsistent response to the HIV/AIDS epidemic. Although sexual issues remain on the fringes of public discourse in China, schools in high-risk areas such as Yunnan have begun establishing educational programs about sex and HIV. The government has created treatment centers and non-discrimination regulations, but the police still sometimes arrest activists and harass NGOs—still anomalous in state-centered China—engaged in HIV/AIDS work. And state-owned corporations often fire HIV-infected employees rather than be burdened with continuing their health insurance coverage. But on World AIDS day in 2003, Premier Wen Jiabao went to a hospital to talk and publicly shake hands with AIDS patients, raising national consciousness and gaining media attention.

Diseases have moved out from China as well. Beginning in late 2002, severe acute respiratory syndrome (SARS) spread with terrifying speed from Guangdong province, via businesspeople and tourists, to 37 countries, killing almost 1,000 people. The PRC government, though aware of the potentially fatal disease and queried by the World Health Organization, did not begin to issue comprehensive information until thousands had been affected and hundreds had died. Even then, the PRC only reluctantly allowed international health officials to investigate Chinese hospitals. But China rapidly increased its capacity for effective response. When an influenza virus peculiar to birds—usually called "avian flu"—fatally infected two Chinese in 2009, the PRC reacted much more quickly and openly, resulting in a lower death toll (262 people in 12 countries), despite the danger of a worldwide pandemic.

9/11 AND THE SCO

The 9/11 attacks allowed the PRC greater latitude to suppress domestic dissent involving Muslims but also brought US military power to China's doorstep. In 2002, the Bush administration listed the East Turkestan Islamic Movement (ETIM), a small Uyghur separatist group, as an international terrorist organization. The PRC responded with a variety of operations against any public expression by Uyghur nationalists, accusing them of "separatism," "illegal religious activity," and "terrorism." One suspected ETIM leader was killed by the Pakistani military during an antiterrorism operation in 2003.

For a number of years, the United States held several dozen Uyghurs from Xinjiang, citizens of the PRC identified as Taliban or al-Qaeda supporters, at Guantanamo. Deciding that none of them constituted a threat, US authorities refused to repatriate them to China (as the PRC requested), citing China's poor human rights record. After complex legal battles, the Uyghur detainees were resettled in Albania, Palau, Bermuda, and Switzerland.

In 2001, the United States leased airbases in Uzbekistan and Kyrgyzstan to support the war in Afghanistan. The SCO, led by Russia and China, demanded that the United States set a timeline for withdrawal but was refused. Under Russian pressure, Uzbekistan ended the lease in 2005, and Kyrgyzstan did the same four years later, but in 2010 US troops remain at both bases and continue their support functions. China views the presence of major US troop concentrations in Afghanistan, Pakistan, and Iraq as regionally destabilizing and hopes to press for their withdrawal through consensus in the SCO. At the same time, PRC and US intelligence agencies have been sharing information about Islamist groups throughout the region.

HONG KONG

The Qing government ceded Hong Kong island and the neighboring Kowloon peninsula to Great Britain in the mid-nineteenth century. Britain took a 99-year lease on a larger area abutting Kowloon—the New Territories—in 1898. Since World War II, the colony of Hong Kong has become a major financial and industrial center. When much of Shanghai's business community moved there in 1949, and refugees flowed in from neighboring Guangdong province, Hong Kong's population leaped from less than a million in 1945 to 2.2 million in 1950. With over 7 million residents in 2010, it has become one of the world's most densely populated cities, dedicated almost entirely to commerce.

Great Britain's lease on the New Territories was due to expire in 1997. So in 1979, at the very beginning of the PRC's reform period, the British governor of the colony raised the issue of continuing British sovereignty in talks with Deng Xiaoping, who flatly rejected anything but return of the colony to Chinese sovereignty. Five years of complex, contentious negotiations produced the Sino–British Joint Declaration, formalized in 1984, in which the two sides agreed that the PRC would "resume the exercise of sovereignty" over the colony on July 1, 1997. For 50 years thereafter, the PRC promised, Hong Kong's capitalist economy and limited democracy would continue in a Special Administrative Region, governed by a Basic Law granting constitutional authority to the government in Beijing. Conservative politicians and pundits have criticized this "one country, two systems" compromise as a sell-out of Hong Kong's people to the PRC.

In the decade preceding its "return to the motherland," Hong Kong lost about 1 million people, emigrants who had no desire to live under the PRC. They and their companies scattered around the world, to sites of enormous new Chinatowns in Canada—especially Vancouver, BC—Australia, and the United States. Larger companies, hedging their bets, opened new offices in Vancouver or London *and* in Shanghai and Beijing, fueling the construction boom in those cities and adding more capital to the PRC's foreign direct investment. The emigrant flood increased after 1989, for Hong Kong reacted to the Tiananmen crackdown with massive demonstrations against the PRC.

The last British governor of Hong Kong, Conservative Party politician Chris Patten (b. 1944), enlarged the colony's electorate, giving its Legislative Council more power and its citizenry a greater say in governing their about-to-be ex-colony, reforms that the Joint Declaration guaranteed after retrocession. The PRC government reacted angrily to these changes, calling them imperialist tricks, but could do nothing. The 1997 ceremonies went smoothly, and Hong Kong became an odd new hybrid, an independent economy within a state. The schools still teach English, along with Cantonese and Mandarin, but the Queen's picture has been removed from the currency and postage stamps. Cars still drive on the left, but the ex-colony's chief executive must be approved by Beijing. Although conflicts with Beijing can still bring people into the streets, Hong Kong remains one of the world's great commercial centers.

TAIWAN AND THE POLITICS OF REUNIFICATION

GMD Chairman Jiang Jingguo had allowed (still illegal) opposition political parties to form in the mid-1980s, opening the door to democratic reforms and an end to single-party rule. Jiang's successor, Li Denghui—from a Hakka family, like Deng Xiaoping and Singapore's Lee Kuan Yew—appointed a majority of native Taiwanese to the Party's Central Committee. A 1990 pro-democracy student movement coincided with Li's selection as president—by an internal GMD process—and drew 300,000 people to Taipei's main square. Choosing a very different path from Beijing's in 1989, Li welcomed student representatives to his office and promised to begin reforms immediately. He also told them that the end of his six-year term would see a democratic election to choose Taiwan's next leader.

As planning went forward for the historic vote—the first in China since the flawed, limited election of 1913 nullified by Yuan Shikai's autocracy—the PRC reacted

ZHANG RUIMIN, LEGENDARY ENTREPRENEUR

Zhang Ruimin (b. 1949) became one of China's most famous businessmen by destroying his own factory's products. A high-school graduate from a working-class Shandong family—the Cultural Revolution prevented college—he had climbed from line worker to general manager in one of Qingdao's city-owned plants, taking business courses during his off-hours. His division, in deep financial trouble when he took over, manufactured refrigerators for the local market, relying on technical expertise from a German partner. During a visit to Germany, Zhang had learned how poorly his products compared to theirs. He returned to China determined to prove that Chinese products could be world-class.

When a customer returned a faulty refrigerator, Zhang found 20 percent of the warehouse stock defective and decided to conduct a dramatic presentation for his workers. He had over 70 faulty units brought onto the shop floor, distributed sledgehammers to the workers, and told them to smash the refrigerators they had made. Quality and productivity quickly turned around, the sledgehammer story gained them recognition, and their products sold better.

Taking advantage of the 1980s reforms and the newly granted power to hire, evaluate, and fire his workers, Zhang linked workers' wages to sales and instituted systematic customer feedback. In an incident almost as famous as the sledgehammers, he responded to customer demand by reengineering the company's washing machines, so rural people could use them to wash not only clothes but also vegetables. The division's sales increased so rapidly that Qingdao's city government asked him to run the microwave oven, air conditioner, and freezer factories as well. Zhang earned his MBA in 1994, by which time he was CEO of the Haier Group, formed from the municipal enterprises he headed. A CCP member, he took advantage of Party connections to run his "worker-owned collective" like a private enterprise.

Zhang Ruimin analyzing a technical index with staff in an air conditioner assembly workshop in Qingdao, September 25, 1997.

Zhang expanded into international markets, beginning with Europe (through its German connection), then the Middle East, Africa, and Southeast Asia. In the United States, he found untapped demand for low-price mini-refrigerators for college dormitories and, as US wine sales rose steadily, electric wine coolers. By 2000, Haier manufactured over half of the wine coolers sold in North America, and in 2002 they bought the Roman-style Greenwich Bank Building—now the Haier Building—in Manhattan. With factories all over the world, in 2010 Haier employs over 50,000 people and has become a leader in technical innovation and business strategy, listed as number one among China's global brands.

At 61, Zhang Ruimin still runs Haier, still belongs to the Chinese Communist Party, and still does not drink alcohol. To many Chinese and foreign observers, he represents the best of the new generation of Chinese entrepreneurs, demonstrating conclusively that Chinese people can and do run world-class businesses. He keeps one of the original sledgehammers on display in company headquarters.

with vitriolic rhetoric and military preparations, calling Li Denghui's reforms an attempt to "split the motherland." In 1995, Li gave a speech on democratization at Cornell, which further inflamed the conflict with the PRC. The United States had previously refused him a visa (the United States and Taiwan did not have diplomatic relations), and Beijing claimed that welcoming Li Denghui created a deep rift in United States–China relations. The PRC began to conduct missile tests in the Taiwan Straits, and the United States sent powerful navy battle groups into the area to demonstrate its commitment to Taiwan's defense.

This "Third Taiwan Straits Crisis" lasted through the March 1996 elections, with PRC missiles landing less than 30 miles (48 km) from Taiwan's main harbors and large PLA amphibious exercises off the coast of Fujian. A majority of Taiwan's voters reacted to the PRC's belligerence with support for Li Denghui, who gained a four-year term as Taiwan's first popularly elected president. In 2000 he stepped down, and the opposition Democratic Progressive Party (DPP) candidate Chen Shuibian (also a Hakka) won a three-way election. Chen's election ushered in the Republic of China's first democratic transfer of power, ending over 70 years of GMD domination. During his eight years in office, President Chen deemphasized Jiang Jieshi's status, closing monuments and "Taiwanizing" the island's history.

Having openly advocated Taiwan independence before the election, Chen Shuibian did challenge the "One China" orthodoxy, but without triggering war with the PRC. Stating that the ROC and PRC are two separate countries, he left the question of reunification up to the popular will of Taiwan's people. The PRC reacted with predictable fury but also protected the huge flow of capital from Taiwan to the mainland and the economic interdependence built over two decades. The PRC has become Taiwan's largest trading partner, and economists estimate Taiwanese investment on the mainland at US$150–300 billion. The United States, among other countries, continues to insist that only one China exists and that reunification must be an explicit goal.

Amid charges of corruption and abuse of authority, the DPP lost the 2008 elections to GMD candidate Ma Ying-jeou (Ma Yingjiu, b. 1950), who immediately instituted investigations into Chen Shui-bian's financial dealings in office. Convicted on a number of charges,

ex-president Chen remains in prison in the summer of 2010. His supporters charge the GMD with politically motivated prosecution.

Both Li Denghui and Chen Shuibian attempted to walk the thin line between declaring Taiwan's independence and appearing too weak in the face of Beijing's belligerence. Ma Ying-jeou's version of this policy—"no reunification, no independence, no war"—has been more effective in cross-strait relations than either Li or Chen. Direct air, sea, and mail links between Taiwan and the mainland resumed in 2008 after a 60-year hiatus. The opposition DPP has criticized Ma Ying-jeou's détente with the PRC, so the PRC openly supports the GMD against its more "independence-minded" opponents. The old enemies—CCP and GMD—have thus become allies, of a sort, in changed conditions.

THE 2008 BEIJING OLYMPICS

On July 13, 2001, the International Olympic Committee awarded the 2008 Summer Olympic Games to Beijing. Having lost narrowly to Sydney for the 2000 Games, Beijingers and Chinese all over the world celebrated in triumph. Like Tokyo in 1964 and Seoul in 1988, this international recognition symbolically affirmed the PRC as a world player, and both citizens and state exerted themselves energetically to make the games a success. The PRC invested somewhere between US$15 and US$40 billion (sources disagree), mandated factory closings to improve air quality, focused on training athletes for virtually every Olympic event, and mobilized the country's most famous entertainers and impresarios to stage the Olympic ceremonies.

After prolonged and delicate negotiations, Taiwan participated in the Beijing games as "Chinese Taipei," sending 80 athletes under a specially designed flag. Other political controversies marked the run-up to the games, most notably severe rioting by Tibetans in several provinces and at Chinese embassies in Europe, North America, and other parts of Asia. Even the privileged Tibetan students at the Nationalities University in Beijing staged a silent sit-in to demonstrate their solidarity with the rioters. Dozens, perhaps hundreds, of people were killed or wounded, and the PRC executed at least four Tibetans in the aftermath. Chinese authorities accused the Dalai Lama of masterminding the international protests, but diplomatic meetings between

The opening ceremony of the 2008 Beijing Olympic Games, August 8, 2008. Beijing National Stadium, known as the "Bird's Nest," was designed by Swiss architects and built with 110,000 tons (100,000 metric tons) of steel, all of it made in China.

representatives of the PRC and the Tibetan government in exile continued less than two months later.

The opening ceremony, one of the most elaborate ever staged, involved 15,000 artists, including 2,008 masters of *taiji* (*t'ai-chi*) performing in perfect unison and a duet by British singer Sarah Brightman and Chinese superstar Liu Huan. As they had in previous Olympics (beginning in 1984), PRC athletes competed successfully, especially in diving, gymnastics, weightlifting, table tennis, and badminton. The PRC won 51 gold medals, more than any other country, stimulating both worldwide Chinese nationalistic joy and accusations of cheating (especially regarding apparently under-age female gymnasts).

International media proclaimed the 2008 Olympics as "China's coming-out party." But as we have seen, China has been an important world actor for a very long time. We must see the "rise" of China proclaimed in recent years as a *reemergence*, for China has been a major economic center, a powerful state, and a cultural innovator for most of the past millennium. Relatively weak, invaded, and divided against itself for 200 years, China—including both the PRC and Taiwan—has once again become a source of everyday and luxury products, a player in international politics, and a vital wellspring of invention and human creativity. Enormous problems and conflicts remain, but China must be seen as a center, not a periphery, of the twenty-first-century human community, sharing in its triumphs and dangers.

DIASPORAS

JAPAN

The Japanese diaspora, from the late nineteenth century until the mid-1960s, had been a story of poor but hopeful people traveling to Northeast and Southeast Asia, and across the Pacific, for economic opportunities. Farm families went to Manchuria, Brazil, and North America. Shopkeepers traveled to the far-flung Pacific Islands, and sex workers were indentured throughout the Pacific Rim and in Korea and Manchuria. A smaller number sojourned as students in Europe and America. Most hoped to return home, but many stayed abroad and created new identities.

Since the 1960s, a new type of overseas Japanese has emerged—expatriates. Initially mostly men who worked for Japanese multinational corporations, they left their families at home so their children would not miss out on Japanese schooling. All expected to return home, and most did, unlike their predecessors. But as Japan recovered from the Lost Decade and East Asia pulled out of the Asian financial crisis of the late 1990s, Japanese expatriates made their way into cities around the world. According to the Japanese Foreign Ministry, over one-third of the 911,000 Japanese working overseas in 2003 resided in the United States, with New York City alone claiming over 62,000. China had the second highest number—almost 80,000—with 25,000 in Hong Kong and 24,000 in Shanghai. Not surprisingly, Brazil had the third largest number of Japanese expatriates (about 71,000), an interesting counterpoint to the large number of Brazilian *Nikkeijin* working in Japan (see p. 425).

The most significant change in the early twenty-first century was in the expatriates' gender; more than 51 percent of Japanese living overseas on a long-term basis (more than three months) were women. While many worked for overseas offices of Japanese firms, others sought work in local companies. In surveys, many indicated that they appreciated what they believed, perhaps over-optimistically, to be more meritocratic work environments than Japan's, where gender, age, or marital status did not prevent their advancement. The *Nihon Keizai Shinbun*, Japan's leading economic newspaper, reported as early as 1993 that Japanese women, frustrated with unequal treatment in Japanese workplaces, ventured abroad to "test themselves," "develop their language skills," and "search for new meaning in life." This trend grew rapidly in the next decade, as women sought not economic survival but self-fulfillment in overseas employment.

NORTH KOREAN REFUGEES

One of the singular tragedies of Korea's division has been the forced movement of people out of North Korea over the last 60 years. The majority of displacement occurred during the period between 1945 and the end of the Korean War in 1953. Estimates of the migration from the northern occupation zone, later the DPRK, range from 1.5 to 2.5 million refugees.

This created a large pool of northern refugees in the South, a displaced population cut off from their hometowns, ancestral graves, and most destructively from their extended family networks. As the division line hardened into an impenetrable border, these refugees had to settle in the South. There they faced social discrimination and were considered politically unreliable by a ROK government whose internal security agencies maintained lists of northerners. Many of these northerners eventually emigrated, making up a high percentage of Koreans entering the United States after 1970.

Since the mid-1990s, the situation has changed radically. The dire economic situation in the DPRK began a movement of economic refugees. They fled from the frontier provinces into Manchuria, joining a population of 2 million ethnic Koreans already there. This flow became a flood during the great famine of 1995–98; at its height as many as 150,000 North Korean refugees lived illegally in China. Since then there has been considerable back-and-forth movement along the Chinese–North Korean border, abetted by corruption in the North Korean border security service.

From Manchuria, some refugees have made their way to South Korea. In 2004, 1,894 refugees from North Korea entered the ROK. In 2010, approximately 18,000 North Korean refugees lived in the South. They have a 50 percent unemployment rate, and 80 percent of those with jobs make less than US$900 a month, half the average income in the South. Although co-ethnics, they find life in the ROK bewildering and receive little support from the population. The plight of these refugees, both as cheap labor in Manchuria and as unwelcome "guests" in the ROK, reminds us again of the human costs of the peninsula's political division.

CHINA

In 2010, over 40 million people of Chinese descent live outside of the PRC and Taiwan, more than 75 percent of them in Asia. A majority in Singapore, they form significant minorities in Indonesia, Malaysia, Thailand, the Philippines, and Japan. Among cities, Kuala Lumpur and Penang—both in Malaysia—have over 600,000 Chinese residents each, as does the New York metropolitan area. The San Francisco Bay area, Vancouver, and Toronto all have over 400,000. Recent targets for emigration have included Africa, where Chinese now constitute an important commercial minority; the Caribbean, especially its ex-British colonies; and the eastern provinces of Russia. Over 200,000 ethnic Chinese live in South Africa, and estimates of the generally illegal Chinese population of Russia range from 200,000 to 2 million.

In short, the Chinese may be found everywhere. As varied as China itself, the diaspora includes university professors and laborers, trinket-sellers and artists, Christian ministers and gangsters. The restaurant business occupies many of them, and so does trade in China's vast array of consumer products. Companies owned by Chinese people around the world produce their own goods for sale, from fortune cookies to software.

Hong Kong has historically been the hub of the diaspora and its gateway to the homeland. It has produced much of the "overseas Chinese" culture—kung fu movies, business networks, popular songs, and intellectual journals—that unites this otherwise wildly diverse population. Partly because it remained outside both GMD and CCP control, the British colony provided neutral ground on which Chinese of all persuasions and professions could meet.

Especially since 1989, Chinese people living outside China have built a transnational network of political advocacy. Some of them, especially the 1989 exiles, have organized an oppositional movement to urge democracy on their homeland. On the other hand, many overseas Chinese respond with nationalistic energy whenever China is disparaged. The governments of both Taiwan and the PRC, like Kang Youwei and Sun Yat-sen at the turn of the twentieth century, can still call upon the ethnic and national identification of the diaspora. The 2008 Tibetan riots, for example, generated a storm of anti-Chinese demonstrations worldwide, to which many Chinese communities responded with counterprotests and accusations of anti-Chinese racism. We can no more homogenize or essentialize the Chinese diaspora than we can China itself. Many Chinese have become deeply patriotic citizens of their new countries, entirely unconcerned with the PRC or Taiwan, but many Chinese around the world remain deeply attached to their ancestral homeland.

CONNECTIONS

POLITICS

The clearest East Asian connections in the past decades have been diplomatic. The Six-Party Talks on North Korea's nuclear program have brought the DPRK, ROK, PRC, Japan, Russia, and the United States to the table regularly since 2003. But in the spring of 2009, North Korea withdrew from the talks, expelled all international nuclear inspectors and, on May 25, detonated its second underground nuclear explosion. In a second confrontational incident, in March 2010 a South Korean naval vessel was torpedoed and sunk near the North Korean border. South Korean and international investigators concluded that a North Korean torpedo had done the damage, killing 46 sailors and further derailing North–South relations. Doubts about Kim Jong Il's successor and the South Koreans' election of a conservative government have ended the Sunshine Policy of the 1990s and returned the peninsula to tension and angry rhetoric.

In contrast, the PRC and Taiwan, despite angry words before each ROC election, have been getting along well. Billions in trade and investment, constant official exchange at every level, direct air and postal service, cross-strait family visits, and tourism have alleviated tension. Although no closer to reunification, the two Chinas share more interest in stability and peace than at any time since 1949.

Since the end of exclusive LDP government in the mid-1990s, Japanese politicians have exerted themselves to improve relations with the rest of East Asia. Prime ministers and the emperor have expressed apologies and regrets for their neighbors' and colonies' wartime suffering. But nationalist sentiment often intervenes—in the form of racist or historically "insensitive" (that is, inaccurate) assertions by right-wing Japanese politicians or journalists—to keep anti-Japan public opinion alive in the PRC, Taiwan, both Koreas, and elsewhere. For those countries' politicians, Japan-bashing represents a foolproof method to whip up domestic nationalist sentiment.

Anti-Americanism has also proved politically useful throughout the region. Although roundly condemning the 9/11 attacks, for example, East Asian governments and public opinion have been less than enthusiastic about the ongoing wars in Iraq and Afghanistan. In the PRC, closest to the combat zones, both military forces and diplomatic initiatives (the SCO) have been deployed to counter the US presence in Central Asia.

Specific incidents can create temporary fury—including the US bombing of the PRC embassy in Belgrade (1999), the collision of a US spy plane with a PRC fighter jet (2001), the killing of two schoolgirls by a US tank in Seoul (2002), anti-China pro-Tibet protests in the United States (2008). More chronically, the presence of US military bases—especially in Okinawa (where they occupy 25 percent of the island's territory) and South Korea—provides constant irritation in the forms of crime, prostitution, racism, and a strong sense of "national violation" maintained by local media.

ECONOMICS

As noted in Chapter 12, regional interdependence has progressed rapidly since the 1970s. Taiwan, South Korea, and the PRC have followed Japan's example in creating export-driven economies and accumulating vast stores of foreign exchange, especially dollars and euros. They buy from and sell to one another at an accelerating pace. Only the DPRK, with its failed but persistent efforts at self-sufficiency (κ. *juche*), has kept itself aloof from rampaging prosperity. The other four East Asian societies share rapid urbanization, a growing middle class (except Japan, where the population is decreasing), consumerism, media saturation, and high-tech products galore. South Korean *chaebŏl* conglomerates strongly resemble Japanese *zaibatsu*. Although the corporate structures of Japan, Taiwan, South Korea, and the PRC do show national differences, all rely on close connections with government "guidance" or "planning" to define the national interest, ensure capital flows, and regulate competition.

CULTURE

Increasing media connectivity and the rise of the internet have generated a truly regional cultural complex. Anime and manga, originally Japanese, have developed as indigenous arts in China (including Taiwan) and Korea. Chinese kung fu movies and novels, led by Hong Kong products, have been widely appreciated and imitated. Korean television dramas (soap operas), especially those featuring attractive and sensitive male stars such as Bae Yong Joon (Yon-sama), have become sensational hits throughout East Asia.

Popular music—songs and accompanying videos—easily crosses cultural and linguistic borders to achieve regional fame. "Mandopop" (Mandarin pop music), centered in Taiwan, has joined Japanese boy bands ("J-pop"), Korean Wave "K-pop," and Hong Kong-based "Cantopop" (sung in Cantonese) to create a regional network of mutual influences and non-threatening music. Even the culturally conservative PRC has generated its own rock scene, pioneered by Sino-Korean Cui Jian (b. 1961), who performed with the Rolling Stones in Shanghai and Public Enemy in Beijing. Rock—especially heavy metal and punk—has not caught on in the PRC like the milder, more "innocent" Mandopop, but a devoted subculture, including music, drugs, and alienation, has evolved since the 1990s.

REGIONAL CONNECTIVITY

East Asians have connected with one another since the 1990s through cellphone technology, the internet, greater media openness (underground in the DPRK), and expanding travel for business, family, tourism, and nostalgia. Their interactions, not mediated by influences from elsewhere in the world (but connected to them), will be crucial in the region's future. Will traveling to one another's countries lessen or enhance the sense of ethnic difference and cultural barriers strengthened by twentieth-century conflicts? Will anti-Japanese sentiment in China and Korea gradually dissolve in a generation that loves anime? Will Japanese condescension toward Koreans disappear in national affection for Yon-sama and Korean soap operas? Will Mandopop, Cantopop, J-pop, and K-pop mediate a new mutuality among East Asians?

These questions will be answered in the ultramodern cities of East Asia—Hong Kong, Seoul, Shanghai, Tokyo, Taipei, Beijing—and their hinterlands. Mutual investment has already motivated four of the East Asian states to improve their international relations. Mutual tourism and diasporas—Koreans in Japan and China, Japanese in China and Hong Kong, Chinese everywhere in the region—may provide both information and impetus for deeper cooperation and understanding.

NOTES

CHAPTER 1

1   And Vietnam, whose culture ascribed the same quality of canonical truth to those texts.
2   Only northern Chinese would pronounce it *liangban*. A Cantonese would pronounce it *leungban*, and a Hokkien speaker would say *nengban*, but the characters and meaning would always be the same.

CHAPTER 2

1   Gary Nash, Charlotte Crabtree, and Ross Dunn. *History on Trial: Culture Wars and the Teaching of the Past*. New York: A.A. Knopf, 1997, p. 47.
2   Daniel Gardner. *Chu Hsi and the Ta-hsüeh: neo-Confucian Reflection on the Confucian Canon*. Cambridge: Harvard University Council on East Asian Studies, 1986. pp. 91–92. Here "principle" means the fundamental form or *pattern* of reality.
3   Lin. *My Country and My People*. p. 337.
4   Berry. *Hideyoshi*. pp. 207–208.
5   Hideyoshi edict, cited in Berry. *Hideyoshi*. p. 102.

CHAPTER 3

1   Chun-shu Chang and Shelley Hsüeh-lun Chang. *Crisis and Transformation in Seventeenth-Century China: Society, Culture, and Modernity in Li Yü's World*. Ann Arbor: University of Michigan Press, 1992. p. 329.
2   Kai-wing Chow. *The Rise of Confucian Ritualism in Late Imperial China: Ethics, Classics, and Lineage Discourse*. Stanford: Stanford University Press, 1994. p. 223.
3   Spence. *Emperor of China*. p. 29.
4   Ch'oe. *Sources of Korean Tradition*. vol. 2, p. 79.
5   Kumazawa Banzan, cited in Totman. *Early Modern Japan*. p. 147.
6   Hayashi Razan, cited in Totman. *Early Modern Japan*. p. 166.
7   Cited in Harold G. Henderson, *An Introduction to Haiku*. New York: Doubleday, 1958. p. 18.
8   Cited in Keene. *Anthology of Japanese Literature*. p. 384.
9   Cited in Keene. *Anthology of Japanese Literature*. p. 384.
10 Lynn Pan. *Sons of the Yellow Emperor: A History of the Chinese Diaspora*. Boston: Little Brown, 1990. p. 26.

CHAPTER 4

1   James Hevia. *Cherishing Men from Afar: Qing Guest Ritual and the Macartney Embassy of 1793*. Durham: Duke University Press, 1995. p. 30.
2   Spence, *Emperor of China*, p. 131.
3   Cited in Ching Young Choe. *The Rule of the Taewong'gun*. Cambridge: Harvard University Press, 1972. p. 22.
4   Cited in Saikō. *Breeze through Bamboo*. p. 50.
5   Cited in Totman. *Early Modern Japan*. p. 438.

CHAPTER 5

1   James Millward. *Beyond the Pass: Economy, Ethnicity, and Empire in Qing Central Asia, 1759-1864*. Stanford: Stanford University Press, 1998. pp. 243-44.
2   Lydia Liu. *The Clash of Empires: The Invention of China in Modern World Making*. Cambridge: Harvard University Press, 2004. pp. 233.
3   Cited in Chai-sik Chung. *A Korean Confucian Encounter with the Modern World: Yi Hang-No and the West*. Berkeley: Center for Korean Studies, University of California, Berkeley, 1995. p. 41.
4   Donald Keene. *The Japanese Discovery of Europe, 1720–1830*. Stanford: Stanford University Press, 1969. pp. 75–76.
5   H. Paske-Smith. *Western Barbarians in Japan and Formosa in Tokugawa Days, 1603–1868*. New York: Paragon, 1968. p. 131.
6   Bob Tadashi Wakabayashi. *Anti-Foreignism and Western Learning in Early Modern Japan*. Cambridge, MA: Harvard University Press, 1986. p. 169.
7   Richard T. Chang. *From Prejudice to Tolerance*. Tokyo: Sophia University Press, 1970. p. 55.
8   Chang. *From Prejudice to Tolerance*. pp. 150–151.
9   DeBary, et al. *Sources of Japanese Tradition*. vol. 2, p. 512.

CHAPTER 6

1   Basil Hall Chamberlain. *Things Japanese*. London: K. Paul, Trench, Trubner & Co, Ltd., 1891. p. 1.
2   Yamagata Aritomo, cited in Steven Vlastos. "Opposition Movements in Early Meiji," in *The Cambridge History of Japan*, vol. 5, ed. Marius Jansen. Cambridge: Cambridge University Press, 1989. p. 411.
3   The whole short story, "The Beefeater," is in Donald Keene, ed. *Modern Japanese Literature*. New York: Grove Press, 1956. pp. 31–34.
4   Natsume Sōseki. *Kokoro*. New York: Regnery, 1958. p. 30.
5   DeBary, et al. *Sources of Chinese Tradition*. vol. 2, pp. 235-37.
6   Cited in Catherine Yeh. "Creating a Shanghai Identity," in Tao Tao Liu and David Faure eds. *Unity and Diversity: Local Cultures and Identity in China*. Hong Kong University Press, 1996. p. 114.
7   Cohen. *Between Tradition and Modernity*. pp. 106–7.
8   DeBary, et al. *Sources of Chinese Tradition*. vol. 2, pp. 239.
9   Cited in Eric Goldman, *The Crucial Decade—and After: America, 1945-1960*. New York: Vintage, 1960. p. 116.
10 Examples are taken from Pan. *Sons of the Yellow Emperor*. Chapter 8.

CHAPTER 7

1   E. Patricia Tsurumi. *Factory Girls: Women in the Thread Mills of Meiji Japan*. Princeton: Princeton University Press, 1990. p. 93.
2   Yosano Akiko. "Do Not Give Up your Life for the Emperor," cited in Vera Mackie. *Creating Socialist Women in Japan: Gender, Labour and Activism, 1900–1937*. Cambridge: Cambridge University Press, 1997. p. 60.
3   Paula Harrell. *Sowing the Seeds of Change: Chinese Students, Japanese Teachers, 1895-1905*. Stanford: Stanford University Press, 1992. p. 26.
4   DeBary, et al. *Sources of Chinese Tradition*. vol. 2, pp. 259–60.
5   DeBary, et al. *Sources of Chinese Tradition*. vol. 2, pp. 312.
6   Kang had written biographies of Peter the Great of Russia and the Meiji Emperor of Japan, both modernizers, and forwarded them to the Guangxu Emperor, who read them eagerly and, according to some accounts, aimed to copy their achievements.
7   Cited in Immanuel Hsü, *The Rise of Modern China*, 6th edition. New York: Oxford University Press, 2000. p. 372.
8   Joseph Esherick. *Origins of the Boxer Uprising*. Berkeley: University of California Press, 1987. p. 225.
9   Reynolds. *China, 1898-1912*. p. 114.
10 Cited in Mary Wright. *China in Revolution: The First Phase, 1900-1913*. New Haven: Yale University Press, 1968. p. 30.
11 This club, like some Chinese study societies, modeled itself to some extent on Fukuzawa Yukichi's famous Meiji Six Society—see p. 183.

CHAPTER 8

1 Translation revised from Tse-tsung Chow. *The May Fourth Movement: Intellectual Revolution in Modern China*. Cambridge: Harvard University Press, 1960. pp. 106-107.
2 Chow. *The May Fourth Movement*. p. 173.
3 Lu Xun. *The Diary of a Madman*. pp. 23–24.

CHAPTER 9

1 Cited in Eastman. *The Nationalist Era in China*. p. 31.
2 Cited in Barmé. *An Artistic Exile*. p. 26.
3 Cited in Barmé. *An Artistic Exile*. p. 36.
4 Cited in Ronald Takaki. *Strangers from a Different Shore: A History of Asian Americans*, rev. ed. Boston: Little Brown, 1998. p. 244.
5 Cited in Takaki. *Strangers from a Different Shore: A History of Asian Americans*. p. 258.

CHAPTER 10

1 The original members of NATO were Belgium, Canada, Denmark, France, Iceland, Italy, Luxembourg, the Netherlands, Norway, Portugal, Great Britain, and the United States.
2 Chinese sources do not use the term "Eastern Turkestan" except to call it a political error, preferring to call this movement "The Three Districts Uprising."
3 Atwill and Atwill. *Sources in Chinese History*. p. 255.
4 Johnson. *Women, the Family, and Peasant Revolution*. p. 235.
5 Cited in Dower. *Embracing Defeat*. p. 36.
6 Dower. *Embracing Defeat*. p. 107.
7 The original eleven members were Australia, Canada, China, France, India, Netherlands, New Zealand, Philippines, Great Britain, United States, and USSR. Burma and Pakistan were added later.

CHAPTER 11

1 Cited in John Lie. *Han Unbound: The Political Economy of South Korea*. Stanford: Stanford University Press, 1998. p. 114.

CHAPTER 12

1 Cited in Hsü. *Rise of Modern China*. pp. 827–28.
2 Cited in Richard Evans. *Deng Xiaoping and the Making of Modern China*. New York: Viking, 1994. p. 249.

CHAPTER 13

1 Chan, et al. *Chen Village: Revolution to Globalization*, p. 344.

GLOSSARY

TERMS USED IN CHINESE, JAPANESE, AND KOREAN

hanzi (K. **hanja**, J. **kanji**): Mandarin Chinese term for Chinese characters, the non-phonetic writing system used throughout East Asia in pre-modern times. It remains the main writing system in China, part of ordinary writing in Japan, and is still occasionally used in Korea.

isshin (K. **yusin**, C. **weixin**): Japanese term for "restoration" or "revitalization," from the ancient Chinese *weixin*; in modern times in East Asia it has been used for the elimination of the shogunate, adopted back into Chinese for the Qing "self-strengthening" movement, and into Korean for the 1972 constitutional reforms augmenting presidential power under Park Chung Hee.

jiapu/zupu: (K. **chokpo**, J. **kafu**) Mandarin Chinese term for genealogical records, which were originally kept to preserve hereditary status, and later to demonstrate upward mobility and clan status.

kokka (C. **guojia**, K. **kukka**): Japanese term for "state" or "country" (lit. "state-family"), a neologism of the Meiji period intended to encompass shared ethnicity and community, including men and women.

kuksu (J. **kokusui**; C. **guocui**): Korean term for "national essence" or "spirit," often invoked to define "us" as a people.

li (J. **ri**, K. **i**): Mandarin Chiense term for "principle," the fundamental abstract forms or patterns for all reality in Neo-Confucian philosophy; it is usually paired with **qi**.

minzoku (K. **minjok**, C. **minzu**): Japanese term for "a people", a term with many meanings including race, nation, the people, and the citizenry.

minjung (J. **minshū**, C. **minzhong**): Korean term for the "oppressed masses;" in Korea it came to refer to the core of Korean identity and to all oppressed Koreans—including peasants, workers, intellectuals, and students—in opposition to the authoritarian government .

qi (K. **ki**, J. **ki**): Mandarin Chinese term for "material existence;" that is the material from which all things are made—"psychophysical stuff." It is usually paired with **li**.

segyehwa (J. s**ekaika**, C. **shijiehua**): Korean term for "globalization."

shixue (K. **silhak**, J. **jitsugaku**): Mandarin Chinese term for "practical learning," a strand of Confucianism concerned with issues of practical statecraft and reform that emerged throughout seventeenth and eighteenth century East Asia.

tianxia (K. **chŏnha**, J. **tenka**): Mandarin Chinese term for "All Under Heaven;" originally it was used in reference specifically to the entire cosmos ruled by the **huangdi**, but later it was reduced in meaning to "the realm" of Qing, Chosŏn, or the Tokugawa shogunate.

xiao (K. **hyo**, J. **ko**): Mandarin Chinese term embracing filial piety and ritual and behavioral devotion to parents, grandparents, and ancestors; it is a concept central to East Asian family ideology.

zen (C. **chan**, K. **chon**): Japanese term for the Buddhist sect that in its practice emphasizes self-denial, meditation, and sudden enlightenment.

zhonghua (K. **chunghwa**, J. **chūka**): Mandarin Chinese term for the "central civilization," used at times to designate China and Chinese culture itself, but also used in in Korea and Japan to mean "our" (civilized) culture.

CHINESE TERMS

Unless otherwise indicated all terms are in Mandarin Chinese.

cohong (MANDARIN **gonghang**): Cantonese term for merchant houses officially appointed by the Qing to deal with foreign commerce.

dao: the "Way"; any systematic "path" to self-cultivation or enlightenment, such as can be found in Buddhism, Neo-Confucianism, or Daoism.

fangyan: "local speech"; the (often mutually unintelligible) versions of Chinese speech.

fengshui: geomancy, lit. "wind and water;" a system for locating the beneficial flow of *yin-yang* energy in human surroundings.

huangdi: "Supreme Divine Ruler;" usually translated into English as "emperor."

jinshi: "presented scholar;" one who has passed the highest level civil service examination.

kaozheng: "evidential research;" a meticulous and evidence-based style of scholarship popular during the Qing period.

kongsi (MANDARIN *gongsi*): Cantonese term for a Chinese merchant corporation or company, usually in southeast Asia.

sancong: "three obediences;" the ideological tenet demanding that women obey their fathers in youth, their husbands in maturity, and their sons in old age.

yin-yang: complementary qualities (cold-hot, female-male, etc.) inherent in all reality that act together in dynamic tension to produce energy and action.

JAPANESE TERMS

bunjin: a person who has mastered the elite cultural arts (*yūgei*).

bunmei kaika: "civilization and enlightenment;" a slogan referring to Westernization.

bunraku: puppet plays.

burakumin: "hamlet people," the modern name for Japan's hereditary degraded status group.

daimyō: feudal lords; fief-holders under the Tokugawa and previous warrior regimes, the highest group within the samurai status system.

eejanaika!: "isn't it great!" or "what the hell!" A popular chant during *yonaoshi* celebrations.

fudai: the loyal *daimyō* comprising Tokugawa Ieyasu's inner circle and those descended from them.

fukoku kyōhei: "rich country, strong army;" an ancient Chinese slogan (*fuguo qiangbing*) adopted by anti-

Tokugawa rebels, and later the Meiji political elite, to express their goals.

furusato: "old home village;" a nostalgic term like "my home town."

haiku: a poem of a single 17-syllable stanza, with lines of 5-7-5 syllables.

itai itai disease: "it hurts, it hurts," a name describing the effects of environmental cadmium poisoning.

kabuki: a style of drama; originally performed by women, but after 1629 only by males.

kana: the phonetic syllabaries of written Japanese, originally evolved from Chinese characters .

kyōdatsu: emotional collapse, debilitating despondency and exhaustion; used to characterize Japanese people at the end of World War II.

nikkeijin: foreigners ("non-citizens of Japan") of Japanese ancestry.

pan-pan: prostitutes, especially during the US occupation.

rangaku: "Dutch learning;" eighteenth- and nineteenth-century European knowledge (especially medicine and other sciences) brought by Dutch merchants trading in Nagasaki.

shingaku: "heart learning;" an eighteenth-century religion combining Buddhist, Shinto, and Confucian elements to stress the equal worth of all people.

shinkansen: "bullet train;" the world's first high-speed railroad line.

shinpan: a group of *daimyō* who were direct descendants of Tokugawa Ieyasu's sons, and whose families could, if necessary, provide a legitimate heir to the Tokugawa shogun.

shishi: "men of high purpose;" used in reference to the often violent, radical anti-shogunate activists of the late Tokugawa period.

tozama: descendants of *daimyō* who had opposed Tokugawa Ieyasu at the Battle of Sekigahara in 1600; their fiefs are usually located at the outer edges of the Tokugawa realm.

ukiyo: "floating world;" a Buddhist conception of the transience of life which

came to be used to refer to the urban pleasure quarters of Tokugawa Japan.

yonaoshi: "healing the world;" a goal of religious and popular movements that arose during hard times in Japan.

yūgei: "polite elite arts;" these include poetry, painting, tea ceremony, music, and calligraphy, as practiced by *bunjin*.

zaibatsu: "financial group;" industrial conglomerates such as Mitsui and Mitsubishi (same as the Korean *chaebŏl*).

KOREAN TERMS

chaebŏl: "financial group;" identical to the Japanese *zaibatsu* and used in reference to huge industrial conglomerate corporations such as Hyundai and Samsung.

ch'ŏndogyo: "religion of Heaven's *Dao*;" the established "church" of the *tonghak* religion.

chuch'e (in North Korea *juche*): "autonomy," "independence," "self-reliance;" the linchpin of North Korean ideology.

chung'in: "middle people," a Chosŏn status group of government technicians intermediate between commoner and *yangban*.

han'gŭl: the Korean alphabet, invented in 1446 under the fourth Chosŏn monarch, Sejong the Great.

kong'in: "tribute men;" government-designated merchants who obtained supplies for the court.

mudang: "shamans," often female.

p'ansori: traditional narratives set to music; revived in the 1970s and associated with the deep suffering of the *minjung*.

sadae, sadaejuŭi, sadaeŭisik: "to serve the great;" term for servitude and servile consciousness. It has been used in modern times as a pejorative description of Chosŏn's ritually subordinate relationship with Ming and Qing.

sŏhak: "Western learning;" originally meaning all European knowledge, but later referring primarily to Roman Catholicism.

sŏwŏn: rural academies devoted to Confucian learning; by the eighteenth century they had become gathering places for elite political factions.

Taewŏn'gun: "royal regent;" referring to Yi Haung, father of King Kojong, who played a major role in Chosŏn politics in the nineteenth century.

tonghak: "Eastern learning;" originally "East Asian teachings" in opposition to **sŏhak**. It later became the name of a mid-nineteenth-century syncretic religion, which since the early twentieth century has been called **ch'ŏndogyo**.

ŭibyŏng: "righteous armies;" initially the irregulars who resisted Hideyoshi's invasions, then the guerrilla bands opposing Japanese colonialism from 1905 to 1912.

yangban: status group claiming hereditary elite status and privileges; the "ruling class" until the end of the nineteenth century.

BIBLIOGRAPHY

CHAPTER 1

GENERAL HISTORIES

Cumings, Bruce. *Korea's Place in the Sun*. New York: Norton, 1997.

Gordon, Andrew. *Korea, Tradition and Transformation: A History of the Korean People*. Elizabeth, NJ: Hallym, 1988.

Pratt, Keith. *Everlasting Flower: A History of Korea*. London: Reaktion, 2006.

Robinson, Michael. *Korea's 20th Century Odyssey: A Short History*. Honolulu: University of Hawaii Press, 2007.

Seth, Michael J. *A Concise History of Korea: From the Neolithic to the Nineteenth Century*. Lanham, MD: Rowman and Littlefield, 2006.

SOURCEBOOKS

Atwill, David and Yurong Atwill (eds.), *Sources in Chinese History: Diverse Perspectives from 1644 to the Present*. New York: Prentice-Hall, 2009.

Ch'oe, Yongho, Peter H. Lee, and Wm. Theodore DeBary (eds.), *Sources of Korean Tradition*, vol. 2. New York: Columbia University Press, 2000.

DeBary, Wm. Theodore and Richard Lufrano (eds.), *Sources of Chinese Tradition*, vol. 2. New York: Columbia University Press, 2001.

DeBary, Wm. Theodore, Carol Gluck, and Arthur Tiedemann, eds. *Sources of Japanese Tradition*, vol. 2. 1600-2000. New York: Columbia University Press, 2005.

Ebrey, Patricia B. (ed.), *Chinese Civilization: A Sourcebook*, 2nd edition. Free Press, 1993.

Keene, Donald. *Anthology of Japanese Literature: From the Earliest Era to the Mid-Nineteenth Century*. New York: Grove, 1994.

CHAPTER 2

Berry, Mary Elizabeth. *Hideyoshi*. Cambridge: Harvard University Press, 1982.

Deuchler, Martina. *The Confucian Transformation of Korea: A Study of Society and Ideology*. Cambridge: Harvard University Press, 1992.

Brook, Timothy. *The Confusions of Pleasure: Commerce and Culture in Ming China*. Berkeley: University of California Press, 1998.

Duncan, John. *The Origins of the Chosŏn Dynasty*. Seattle: University of Washington Press, 2000.

Farris, William Wayne. *Japan's Medieval Population*. Honolulu: University of Hawaii Press, 2006.

Gardner, Daniel. *The Four Books: The Basic Teachings of the Later Confucian Tradition*. Indianapolis: Hackett, 2007.

Jansen, Marius, ed. *Warrior Rule in Japan*. Cambridge, UK: Cambridge University Press, 2008.

Lin, Yutang. *My Country and My People*. New York: Reynal & Hitchcock, 1935.

Yi, Ki-baek (Edward Wagner, trans.; Edward Shultz, contributor). *A New History of Korea*. Cambridge: Harvard University Press, 1984.

CHAPTER 3

Crossley, Pamela K. *The Manchus*. Cambridge: Blackwell, 1997.

Eckert, Carter, et al. *Korea Old and New*. Seoul: Ilchogak (distributed by Harvard University Press), 1991.

Palais, James. *Confucian Statecraft and Korean Institutions: Yu Hyŏngwŏn and the Late Chosŏn Dynasty*. Seattle: University of Washington Press, 1996.

Spence, Jonathan. *Emperor of China: Self-Portrait of K'ang-hsi*. New York: Vintage, 1974.

Struve, Lynn, ed. *The Qing Formation in World-Historical Time*. Cambridge: Harvard University Asia Center, 2004.

Totman, Conrad. *Early Modern Japan*. Berkeley: University of California Press, 1995.

CHAPTER 4

Crossley, Pamela K., Helen Siu, and Donald Sutton, eds. *Empire at the Margins: Culture, Ethnicity, and Frontier in Early Modern China*. Berkeley: University of California Press, 2006.

Elliott, Mark. *Emperor Qianlong: Son of Heaven, Man of the World*. New York: Longman, 2009.

Haboush, JaHyun Kim. *A Heritage of Kings: One Man's Monarchy in the Confucian World*. New York: Columbia University Press, 1988.

Haboush, JaHyun Kim and Martina Deuchler, eds. *Culture and the State in Late Chosŏn Korea*. Cambridge: Harvard-Hallym Series on Korean Studies, 1999.

Hall, John W., ed. *Cambridge History of Japan*, vol. 4: *Early Modern Japan*. Cambridge, UK: Cambridge University Press, 1991.

Sato, Hiroaki. *Breeze through Bamboo: Kanshi of Ema Saikō*. New York: Columbia University Press, 1998.

Setton, Mark. *Chŏng Yagyong: Korea's Challenge to Orthodox Neo-Confucianism*. Albany: State University of New York Press, 1997.

Shen, Fu. *Six Records of a Floating Life*. Harmondsworth: Penguin, 1983.

Smith, Thomas C. *Native Sources of Japanese Industrialization*. Berkeley: University of California Press, 1988.

CHAPTER 5

Brook, Timothy, and Bob Tadashi Wakabayashi, eds. *Opium Regimes: China, Britain, and Japan, 1839-1952*. Berkeley: University of California Press, 2000.

Craig, Albert M. *Chōshū in the Meiji Restoration*. Cambridge: Harvard University Press, 1961.

Kim, Sun Joo. *Marginality and Subversion in Korea: The Hong Kyŏngnae Rebellion of 1812*. Seattle: University of Washington Press, 2007.

Mann, Susan. *The Talented Women of the Zhang Family*. Berkeley: University of California Press, 2007.

Naquin, Susan. *Millenarian Rebellion in China: The Eight Trigrams Uprising of 1813*. New Haven: Yale University Press, 1976.

Palais, James. *Politics and Policy in Traditional Korea*. Cambridge: Harvard University Press, 1975.

Vlastos, Stephen. *Peasant Protests and Uprisings in Tokugawa Japan.* Berkeley: University of California Press, 1990.

Walthall, Anne. *The Weak Body of a Useless Woman: Matsuo Taseko and the Meiji Restoration.* Chicago: University of Chicago Press, 1998.

CHAPTER 6

Cohen, Paul. *Between Tradition and Modernity: Wang T'ao and Reform in Late Ch'ing China.* Cambridge: Harvard University Council on East Asian Studies, 1974.

Deuchler, Martina. *Confucian Gentlemen and Barbarian Envoys: The Opening of Korea, 1875-1885.* Seattle: University of Washington Press, 1977.

Gluck, Carol. *Japan's Modern Myths: Ideology in the Late Meiji Period.* Princeton: Princeton University Press, 1985.

Kim, Key-Hiuk. *The Last Phase of the East Asian World Order: Korea, Japan, and the Chinese Empire, 1860-1882.* Berkeley: University of California Press, 1980.

Kim, Kyu Hyun. *The Age of Visions and Arguments: Parliamentarianism and the National Public Sphere in Early Meiji Japan.* Cambridge: Harvard University Asia Center, 2007.

Millward, James. *Eurasian Crossroads: A History of Xinjiang.* London: Hurst, 2007.

Molony, Barbara and Kathleen Uno, eds. *Gendering Modern Japanese History.* Cambridge: Harvard University Asia Center, 2005.

Spence, Jonathan. *God's Chinese Son: The Taiping Heavenly Kingdom of Hong Xiuquan.* New York: Norton, 1996.

CHAPTER 7

Cohen, Paul. *History in Three Keys: The Boxers as Event, Experience, and Myth.* New York: Columbia University Press, 1997.

Daniels, Roger. *The Politics of Prejudice: The Anti-Japanese Movement in California and the Struggle for Japanese Exclusion.* Berkeley: University of California Press, 1977.

Duus, Peter. *The Abacus and the Sword: The Japanese Penetration of Korea, 1895-1910.* Berkeley: University of California Press, 1996.

Hunter, Janet. *Women and the Labour Market in Japan's Industrialising Economy: The Textile Industry before the Pacific War.* London: RoutledgeCurzon, 2003.

Larsen, Kirk W. *Tradition, Treaties, and Trade: Qing Imperialism and Chosŏn Korea, 1850-1910.* Cambridge: Harvard University Asia Center, 2008.

Ning, Lao-t'ai-t'ai, and Ida Pruitt. *A Daughter of Han: The Autobiography of a Chinese Working Woman.* Stanford: Stanford University Press, 1945.

Reynolds, Douglas R. *China, 1898-1912: The Xinzheng Revolution and Japan.* Cambridge: Harvard University Council on East Asian Studies, 1993.

Schmid, Andre. *Korea Between Empires 1895-1919.* New York: Columbia University Press, 2002.

Shimazu, Naoko. *Japanese Society at War: Death, Memory and the Russo-Japanese War.* Cambridge, UK: Cambridge University Press, 2009.

CHAPTER 8

Bergere, Marie-Claire. *The Golden Age of the Chinese Bourgeoisie, 1911-1937.* Cambridge, UK: Cambridge University Press, 1989.

Eckert, Carter. *Offspring of Empire: The Koch'ang Kims and the Colonial Origins of Korean Capitalism, 1876-1945.* Seattle: University of Washington Press, 1991.

Garon, Sheldon. *Molding Japanese Minds: The State in Everyday Life.* Princeton: Princeton University Press, 1997.

Lu, Xun (William A. Lyell, trans.). *Diary of a Madman and Other Stories.* Honolulu: University of Hawaii Press, 1990.

Mackie, Vera. *Feminism in Modern Japan: Citizenship, Embodiment and Sexuality.* Cambridge, UK: Cambridge University Press, 2003.

Robinson, Michael. *Cultural Nationalism in Colonial Korea 1910-1925.* Seattle: University of Washington Press, 1988.

Schwarcz, Vera. *The Chinese Enlightenment: Intellectuals and the Legacy of the May Fourth Movement of 1919.* Berkeley: University of California Press, 1986.

Shin, Gi-Wook. *Peasant Protest and Social Change in Colonial Korea.* Seattle: University of Washington Press, 1996.

Silverberg, Miriam. *Erotic, Grotesque Nonsense: The Mass Culture of Japanese Modern Times.* Berkeley: University of California Press, 2009.

CHAPTER 9

Barmé, Geremie. *An Artistic Exile: A Life of Feng Zikai (1898-1975).* Berkeley: University of California Press, 2002.

Clark, Donald. *Living Dangerously in Korea: The Western Experience 1900-1950.* Norwalk: Eastbridge, 2003.

Cook, Haruko Taya and Theodore Cook. *Japan at War: An Oral History.* New York: The New Press, 1992.

Dower, John. *War Without Mercy: Race and Power in the Pacific War.* New York: Pantheon, 1986.

Eastman, Lloyd, ed. *The Nationalist Era in China, 1927-1949.* Cambridge, UK: Cambridge University Press, 1991.

Park, Soon-Won. *Colonial Industrialization and Labor in Korea: The Onoda Cement Factory.* Cambridge: Harvard-Hallym Series on Korean Studies, 1999.

Soh, C. Sarah. *The Comfort Women: Sexual Violence and Postcolonial Memory in Korea and Japan.* Chicago: University of Chicago Press, 2008.

Snow, Edgar. *Red Star over China.* New York: Random House, 1938.

Young, Louise. *Japan's Total Empire: Manchuria and the Culture of Wartime Imperialism.* Berkeley: University of California Press, 1999.

CHAPTER 10

Chen, Jian. *China's Road to the Korean War: The Making of the Sino-American Confrontation.* New York: Columbia University Press, 1994.

Cumings, Bruce. *The Origins of the Korean War,* 2 vols. Princeton: Princeton University Press, 1981 and 1990.

Dower, John. *Embracing Defeat: Japan in the Wake of World War II.* New York: Norton, 1999.

Gordon, Andrew, ed. *Postwar Japan as History.* Berkeley: University of California Press, 1993.

Kurosawa, Akira. *Something like an Autobiography.* New York: Vintage, 1983.

Johnson, Kay Ann. *Women, the Family, and Peasant Revolution in China.* Chicago: University of Chicago Press, 1983.

Matray, James Irving. *The Reluctant Crusade: American Foreign Policy in Korea, 1941-1950.* Honolulu: University of Hawaii Press, 1985

Westad, Odd Arne. *Decisive Encounters: The Chinese Civil War, 1946-1950.* Stanford: Stanford University Press, 2003.

CHAPTER 11

George, Timothy. *Minamata: Pollution and the Struggle for Democracy in Postwar Japan*. Cambridge: Harvard University Asia Center, 2000.

Han, Sung-ju. *The Failure of Democracy in South Korea*. Berkeley: University of California Press, 1975.

LeBlanc, Robin. *Bicycle Citizens: The Political World of the Japanese Housewife*. Berkeley: University of California Press, 1999.

MacFarquhar, Roderick, and Michael Schoenhals. *Mao's Last Revolution*. Cambridge: Balknap Press of Harvard University Press, 2006.

Sasaki-Uemura, Wesley. *Organizing the Spontaneous: Citizen Protest in Postwar Japan*. Honolulu: University of Hawaii Press, 2001.

Vogel, Ezra. *Canton under Communism: Programs and Politics in a Provincial Capital, 1949-1968*. New York: Harper & Row, 1969.

Woo, Jung-en. *Race to the Swift: State and Finance in Korean Industrialization*. New York: Columbia University Press, 1991.

Yue, Daiyun, and Carolyn Wakeman. *To the Storm: The Odyssey of a Revolutionary Chinese Woman*. Berkeley: University of California Press, 1985.

CHAPTER 12

Chen, Calvin. *Some Assembly Required: Work, Community, and Politics in China's Rural Enterprises*. Cambridge: Harvard University Asia Center, 2008.

Field, Norma. In *the Realm of a Dying Emperor: A Portrait of Japan at Century's End*. New York: Pantheon, 1991.

Kendall, Laurel, ed. *Under Construction: The Gendering of Modernity, Class, and Consumption in the Republic of Korea*. Honolulu: University of Hawaii Press, 2002.

Lee, Namhee. *The Making of Minjung: Democracy and the Politics of Representation in the Republic of South Korea*. Ithaca: Cornell University Press, 2009.

Link, Perry. *Evening Chats in Beijing: Probing China's Predicament*. New York: Norton, 1992.

Nelson, Laura C. *Measured Excess: Status, Gender, and Consumer Nationalism in South Korea*. New York: Columbia University Press, 2000.

Perry, Elizabeth, and Mark Selden, eds. *Chinese Society: Change, Conflict, and Resistance*. London: Routledge, 2000.

Robertson, Jennifer. *A Companion to the Anthropology of Japan*. Malden: Blackwell, 2006.

Vogel, Ezra. *Japan as Number One: Lesson for America*. Cambridge: Harvard University Press, 1979.

CHAPTER 13

Abelmann, Nancy. *The Melodrama of Mobility: Women, Talk, and Class in Contemporary South Korea*. Honolulu: University of Hawaii Press, 2003.

Chan, Anita, Richard Madsen, and Jonathan Unger. *Chen Village: Revolution to Globalization*. Berkeley: University of California Press, 2009.

Economy, Elizabeth. *The River Runs Black: The Environmental Challenge to China's Future*. Ithaca: Cornell University Press, 2004.

Oh, Katie and Ralph Hassig. *North Korea: Through the Looking Glass*. Washington D.C.: Brookings Institution Press, 2000.

Moon, Seungsook. *Militarized Modernity and Gendered Citizenship in South Korea*. Durham: Duke University Press, 2005.

Napier, Susan J. *Anime from Akira to Howl's Moving Castle, Updated Edition: Experiencing Contemporary Japanese Animation*. New York: Palgrave MacMillan, 2005.

Saxonhouse, Gary, and Robert Stern, eds, *Japan's Lost Decade: Origins, Consequences and Prospects for Recovery*. Malden: Wiley-Blackwell, 2004.

Seraphim, Franziska. *War Memory and Social Politics in Japan, 1945-2005*. Cambridge: Harvard University Asia Center, 2006.

Wang, Chaohua, ed. *One China, Many Paths*. London: Verso, 2003.

INDEX

PICTURE CREDITS

Laurence King Publishing Ltd, the authors, and the picture researcher wish to thank the institutions and individuals who have kindly provided photographic material for use in this book. Sources for illustrations, additional information, and copyright credits are given below. Numbers are picture numbers unless otherwise indicated.

T = top, **B** = bottom, **L** = left, **R** = right, **C** = centre